Counterpoints

Counterpoints

TWENTY-FIVE YEARS OF

The New Criterion

ON CULTURE AND THE ARTS

Edited with an Introduction by
Roger Kimball *&* Hilton Kramer

Ivan R. Dee
Chicago 2007

Library of Congress Cataloging-in-Publication Data:
Counterpoints : twenty-five years of the New criterion on culture and the arts / edited with an introduction by Roger Kimball & Hilton Kramer.
    p. cm.
   Includes index.
  ISBN-13: 978-1-56663-706-0 (cloth : alk. paper)
  ISBN-10: 1-56663-706-6 (cloth : alk. paper)
  I. Arts, American. 2. Arts. 3. New criterion (New York, N.Y.)
  I. Kimball, Roger, 1953– II. Kramer, Hilton. III. New criterion (New York, N.Y.)
NX503.N484 2007
700.973—dc22

2006100485

Contents

III. Recuperations

Introduction

LOOKING BACK in the 1940s to the creation of his magazine *The Criterion* in 1922, T. S. Eliot wrote that he and his colleagues had intended it to be partly a means of fostering "common concern for the highest standards of both thought and expression" and partly a means of discharging "our common responsibility . . . to preserve our common culture uncontaminated by political influences." That comes close to describing our abiding ambition with *The New Criterion*. In the editorial note introducing our first issue in September 1982, we wrote that

> Today . . . the prevailing modes of criticism have not only failed to come to grips with such tasks, they have actually come to constitute an obstacle to their pursuit. A multitude of journals of every size and periodicity—quarterlies, monthlies, fortnightlies, weeklies, and even the daily papers to the extent that they concern themselves with matters of the mind—lavishes upon the life of culture a vast amount of attention. Yet most of what is written in these journals is either hopelessly ignorant, deliberately obscurantist, commercially compromised, or politically motivated. Especially where the fine arts and the disciplines of high culture are concerned, criticism at every level—from the daily newspaper review of a concert or a novel to the disquisitions of critics and scholars in learned journals—has almost everywhere degenerated into one or another form of ideology or publicity or some pernicious combination of the two. As a result, the very notion of an independent high culture and the distinctions that separate it from popular culture and commercial entertainment have been radically eroded.

A lot has changed in the quarter century since we wrote those words, but the fundamental threats to our culture that we identified have only become more entrenched and insinuating. With *Counterpoints*, we offer a generous sampling of *The New Criterion*'s response to the cultural challenges and opportunities of our times, a response that we have organized under the rubrics "Determinations," "Contentions," "Recuperations," and "Discriminations." Taken together, the essays in this volume aspire to live up to Eliot's definition of the vocation of criticism as "the common pursuit of true judgment."

In his poem "At the Grave of Henry James," W. H. Auden spoke of the "Resentful muttering Mass," its "ruminant hatred of all that cannot/ Be simplified or stolen" and "its lust/ To vilify the landscape of Distinction." James dedicated his career to opposing that hatred of complexity and lust for leveling. From the beginning, *The New Criterion* has understood its vocation in similar terms. "All will be judged," Auden declaimed in the last stanza of his elegy for that master of discrimination. For us, the imperative of judgment, of criticism, has revolved primarily around two tasks.

The first was the negative task of forthright critical discrimination. To a large extent, that meant the gritty job of intellectual and cultural trash collector. In that note to our inaugural issue, we spoke of applying "a new criterion to the discussion of our cultural life—a criterion of truth." The truth was, and is, that much of what presents itself as art today can scarcely be distinguished from political sermonizing, on the one hand, or the pathetic recapitulation of Dadaist pathologies, on the other. Mastery of the artifice of art is mostly a forgotten, often an actively disparaged, goal. At such a time, simply telling the truth is bound to be regarded as an unwelcome provocation.

In the university and other institutions entrusted with preserving and transmitting the cultural capital of our civilization, kindred deformations are at work. Pseudo-scholarship propagated by a barbarous reader-proof prose and underwritten by adolescent political animus is the order of the day. *The New Criterion* sallied forth onto this cluttered battlefield determined not simply to call attention to the emperor's new clothes, but to do so with wit, clarity, and literary panache. We acknowledge that these have been hard times for the arts of satire and parody. With increasingly velocity, today's reality has a way of outstripping yesterday's satirical exaggeration. Nevertheless, *The New Criterion* has always been distinguished by its effective deployment of satire, denunciation, and ridicule—all the astringent resources in the armory of polemic—and that is one of the things that enabled the magazine to live up to Horace's injunction to delight as well as instruct.

But *The New Criterion* is not only about polemics. An equally important part of criticism revolves around the task of battling cultural amnesia. From our first issue nearly a quarter century ago, we have labored in the vast storehouse of cultural achievement to introduce, or reintroduce, readers to some of the salient figures whose works helped weave the great unfolding tapestry of our civilization. Writers and artists, philosophers and musicians, scientists, historians, controversialists, explorers, and politicians: *The New Criterion* has specialized in resuscitating important figures whose voices have been drowned out by the demotic inanities of pop culture or embalmed by the dead hand of the academy.

It is worth noting that our interest in these matters has never been merely aesthetic. At the beginning of *The Republic*, Socrates reminds his young interlocutor, Glaucon, that their discussion concerns not trifling questions but "the right conduct of life." We echo that sentiment. *The New Criterion* is not, we hope, a somber publication; but it is a serious one. We look to the past for enlightenment and to art for that humanizing education and ordering of the emotions that distinguish the man of culture from the barbarian.

Allan Bloom once observed that a liberal education consists in knowing and thinking about the alternative answers to life's perennial questions. Today, when some of history's less savory alternatives are once again on the march, the claims of culture—and criticism, which keeps culture vital—are particularly exigent.

Five years ago, in a note introducing our twentieth-anniversary issue, we quoted two passages from Evelyn Waugh. The first, written near the end of Waugh's life, concerned Rudyard Kipling's conservative view of culture. Kipling, Waugh wrote, "believed civilization to be something laboriously achieved which was only precariously defended. He wanted to see the defenses fully manned and he hated the liberals because he thought them gullible and feeble, believing in the easy perfectibility of man and ready to abandon the work of centuries for sentimental qualms."

In the second passage, written three decades earlier, Waugh dilates more fully on this theme. "Barbarism," he wrote in 1938,

> is never finally defeated; given propitious circumstances, men and women who seem quite orderly will commit every conceivable atrocity. The danger does not come merely from habitual hooligans; we are all potential recruits for anarchy. Unremitting effort is needed to keep men living together at peace; there is only a margin of energy left over for experiment however beneficent. Once the prisons of the mind have been opened, the orgy is on. . . . The work of preserving society is sometimes onerous, sometimes almost effortless. The more elaborate the society, the more

vulnerable it is to attack, and the more complete its collapse in case of defeat. At a time like the present it is notably precarious. If it falls we shall see not merely the dissolution of a few joint-stock corporations, but of the spiritual and material achievements of our history.

We wrote this only a few weeks before the terrorist attacks of 9/11. In the years since, we have often returned to Waugh's prescient observations. "Conservative": that means wanting to conserve what is worth preserving from the ravages of time and ideology, evil and stupidity. In some plump eras, as Waugh says, the task is so easy we can almost forget how necessary it is. At other times, the enemies of civilization transform the task of preserving culture into a battle for survival. That, we believe, is where we are today. And that is one reason that *The New Criterion*'s effort to tell the truth about culture is as important today as it was in 1982. *Counterpoints* is a wide-ranging record of *The New Criterion*'s contribution to this imperative task.

FROM ITS BEGINNING, *The New Criterion* has been a collaborative enterprise, not least a collaboration between editors and writers. We have been particularly fortunate in attracting some of the most vital critical talent of our time, and we are pleased to have this opportunity to acknowledge our gratitude to the many writers who, for meager recompense, have provided so much insightful and gracefully written commentary. We wish also to acknowledge our gratitude to the staff of *The New Criterion*, past and present, who over the years have made this dream a reality. Jeremy Axelrod, our intern in the summer of 2006, and Andrew Cusack, our new Assistant Editor, were particularly helpful in putting together *Counterpoints*. David Yezzi, our Executive Editor, James Panero, our Managing Editor, and Stefan Beck, our former Associate Editor, were indispensable in helping to shape the book and oversee its production. Finally, we would like to acknowledge our gratitude to the many individuals and institutions that, for a quarter century, have underwritten our efforts and made *The New Criterion* possible. We wish in particular to thank The Lynde and Harry Bradley Foundation, The John M. Olin Foundation, the Sarah Scaife Foundation, and Donald Kahn. Without their stalwart support, neither *The New Criterion* nor *Counterpoints* would exist.

RK

HK

January 2007

I. Determinations

The Fortunes of Permanence

Roger Kimball

*Do not be proud of the fact that your grandmother was shocked at something
which you are accustomed to seeing or hearing without being shocked. . . . It may
be that your grandmother was an extremely lively and vital animal, and that you
are a paralytic.*
—G. K. Chesterton, *As I Was Saying*

*How but in custom and in ceremony
Are innocence and beauty born?
Ceremony's a name for the rich horn,
And custom the spreading laurel tree.*
—W. B. Yeats, "A Prayer For My Daughter"

"Seven and a half hours of mild, unexhausting labour, and then the soma *ration
and games and unrestricted copulation and the feelies. What more can they ask
for?"*
—Mustapha Mond in Huxley's *Brave New World*

I REMEMBER THE first time I noticed the legend "cultural instructions"
on the brochure that accompanied some seedlings. "How quaint," I
thought, as I pursued the advisory: this much water and that much sun,
certain tips about fertilizer, soil, and drainage. Planting one sort of flower
nearby keeps the bugs away but proximity to another sort makes bad things
happen. Young shoots might need stakes, and watch out for beetles, weeds,
and unseasonable frosts . . .

The more I pondered it, the less quaint, the more profound, those cultural instructions seemed. I suppose I had once known that the word "cul-

ture" comes from the capacious Latin verb "*colo*," which means everything from "live, dwell, inhabit," to "observe a religious rite" (whence our word "cult"), "care, tend, nurture," and "promote the growth or advancement of." I never thought much about it.

I should have. There is a lot of wisdom in etymology. The noun "*cultura*" (which derives from *colo*) means first of all "the tilling or cultivation of land" and "the care or cultivation of plants." But it, too, has ambitious tentacles: "the observance of a religious rite," "well groomed" (of hair), "smart" (of someone's appearance), "chic, polished, sophisticated" (of a literary or intellectual style).

It was Cicero, in a famous passage of the *Tusculan Disputations*, who gave currency to the metaphor of culture as a specifically intellectual pursuit. "Just as a field, however good the ground, cannot be productive without cultivation, so the soul cannot be productive without education." Philosophy, he said, is a sort of "*cultura animi*," a cultivation of the mind or spirit: "it pulls out vices by the roots," "makes souls fit for the reception of seed," and sows in order to bring forth "the richest fruit." But even the best care, he warned, does not inevitably bring good results: the influence of education, of *cultura animi*, "cannot be the same for all: its effect is great when it has secured a hold upon a character suited to it." The results of cultivation depend not only on the quality of the care but the inherent nature of the thing being cultivated. How much of what Cicero said do we still understand?

In current parlance, "culture" (in addition to its use as a biological term) has both a descriptive and an evaluative meaning. In its anthropological sense, "culture" is neutral. It describes the habits and customs of a particular population: what its members do, not what they should do. Its task is to inventory, to docket, not judge.

But we also speak of "high culture," meaning not just social practices but a world of artistic, intellectual, and moral endeavor in which the notion of hierarchy, of a rank-ordering of accomplishment, is integral. (More etymology: "hierarchy" derives from words meaning "sacred order." Egalitarians are opposed to hierarchies in principle; what does that tell us about egalitarianism?) Culture in the evaluative sense does not merely admit, it requires judgment as a kind of coefficient or auxiliary: comparison, discrimination, evaluation are its lifeblood. "We never really get near a book," Henry James remarked in an essay on American letters, "save on the question of its being good or bad, of its really treating, that is, or not treating, its subject." It was for the sake of culture in this sense that Matthew Arnold extolled criticism as "the disinterested endeavour to learn and propagate the best that is known and thought in the world."

It is of course culture in the Arnoldian sense that we have primarily in view when we speak of "the survival of culture." And it is the fate of culture in this sense that I will be chiefly concerned with in this essay. But it would be foolish to draw too firm a distinction between the realms of culture. There is much confluence and interchange between them. Ultimately, they exist symbiotically, nurturing, supplementing, contending with each other. The manners, habits, rituals, institutions, and patterns of behavior that define culture for the anthropologist provide the sediment, the ground out of which culture in the Arnoldian sense takes root—or fails to take root. Failure or degradation in one area instigates failure or degradation in the other. (Some people regard the astonishing collapse of manners and civility in our society as a superficial event. They are wrong. The fate of decorum expresses the fate of a culture's dignity, its attitude toward its animating values.)

THE PROBLEM with metaphors is not that they are false but that they do not tell the whole truth. The organic image of culture we have inherited from Cicero is illuminating. Among other things, it reminds us that we do not exist as self-sufficient atoms but have our place in a continuum that stretches before and after us in time. Like other metaphors, however, it can be elevated into an absurdity if it is pushed too far. Oswald Spengler's sprawling, two-volume lament, *The Decline of the West*, is a good illustration of what happens when genius is captivated by a metaphor. Spengler's book, published in the immediate aftermath of World War I, epitomized the end-of-everything mood of the times and was hailed as the brilliant key to understanding—well, just about everything. And Spengler really is brilliant. For example, his remarks about how the triumph of scepticism breeds a "second religiousness" in which "men dispense with proof, desire only to believe and not to dissect," have great pertinence to an age, like ours, that is awash in new-age spiritual counterfeits. Nevertheless, Spengler's deterministic allegiance to the analogy between civilizations and organisms ultimately infuses his discussion with an air of unreality. One is reminded, reading Spengler, of T. S. Eliot's definition of a heretic: "a person who seizes upon a truth and pushes it to the point at which it becomes a falsehood."

That said, for anyone who is concerned about the survival of culture, there are some important lessons in the armory of cultural instructions accompanying a humble tomato plant. Perhaps the chief lesson has to do with time and continuity, the evolving permanence that *cultura animi* no less than agricultural cultivation requires if it is to be successful. All those tips, habits, prohibitions, and necessities that have been accumulated from time out of mind and passed down, generation after generation: How much in our society militates against such antidotes to anarchy and decay!

Culture survives and develops under the aegis of permanence. And yet instantaneity—the enemy of permanence—is one of the chief imperatives of our time. It renders anything lasting, anything inherited, suspicious by definition. As Kenneth Minogue observed in "The New Epicureans" (*The New Criterion*, September 2001), "The idea is that one not only lives for the present, but also *ought* to live thus." We want what is faster, newer, less encumbered by the past. If we also cultivate a nostalgia for a simpler, slower time, that just shows the extent to which we are separated from what, in our efforts to decorate our lives, we long for. Nostalgia (Greek for "homesickness") is a version of sentimentality—a predilection, that is to say, to distort rather than acknowledge reality.

The political philosopher Hannah Arendt dilated on one essential aspect of the problem when she argued against taking an instrumental, "self-help" approach to culture. "What is at stake here," Arendt observed in "The Crisis in Culture,"

> is the objective status of the cultural world, which, insofar as it contains tangible things—books and paintings, statues, buildings, and music—comprehends, and gives testimony to, the entire recorded past of countries, nations, and ultimately mankind. As such, the only nonsocial and authentic criterion for judging these specifically cultural things is their relative permanence and even eventual immortality. Only what will last through the centuries can ultimately claim to be a cultural object. The point of the matter is that, as soon as the immortal works of the past became the object of social and individual refinement and the status accorded to it, they lost their most important and elemental quality, which is to grasp and move the reader or the spectator over the centuries.

The "objective status" of the cultural world to which Arendt appeals is precisely the aspect of culture we find hardest to accommodate. If there is a "nonsocial and authentic criterion" for judging cultural achievements, then what happens to the ideology of equivalence that has become such a powerful force in Western societies? Are we not committed to the proposition that *all* values are social? Isn't this part of what social constructionists like Richard Rorty mean when they say language goes "all the way down"? That there is no self, no value, no achievement, no criteria independent of the twitterings of fashion, which in turn are ultimately the twitterings of social power?

The attack on permanence comes in many guises. When trendy literary critics declare that "there is no such thing as intrinsic meaning," they are denying permanent values that transcend the prerogatives of their lucubrations. When a deconstructionist tells us that truth is relative to language, or to power, or to certain social arrangements, he seeks to trump the unanswerable claims of permanent realities with the vacillations of his ingenuity. When the multiculturalist celebrates the fundamental equality of all cultures—excepting, of course, the culture of the West, which he reflexively disparages—he substitutes ephemeral political passions for the recognition of objective cultural achievement. "A pair of boots," a nineteenth-century Russian slogan tells us, "is worth more than Shakespeare." We have here a process of leveling that turns out to be a revolution in values. The implication, as the French philosopher Alain Finkielkraut observed, is that

> the footballer and the choreographer, the painter and the couturier, the writer and the ad-man, the musician and the rock-and-roller, are all the same: creators. We must scrap the prejudice which restricts that title to certain people and regards others as sub-cultural.

But what seems at first to be an effort to establish cultural parity turns out to be a campaign for cultural reversal. When Sir Elton John is put on the same level as Bach, the effect is not cultural equality but cultural insurrection. (If it seems farfetched to compare Elton John and Bach, recall the literary critic Richard Poirier's remark, in *Partisan Review* in 1967, that "sometimes [the Beatles] are like Monteverdi and sometimes their songs are even better than Schumann's.") It might also be worth asking what had to happen in English society for there to be such a thing as "Sir Elton John." What does *that* tell us about the survival of culture? But some subjects are too painful. Let us draw a veil . . .

"The history of philosophy," Jean-François Revel observed in *The Flight from Truth* (1991), "can be divided into two different periods. During the first, philosophers sought the truth; during the second, they fought against it." That fight has escaped from the parlors of professional sceptics and has increasingly become the moral coin of the realm. As Anthony Daniels wrote in "The Felicific Calculus of Modern Medicine" (*The New Criterion*, November 2001), it is now routine for academics and intellectuals to use "all the instruments of an exaggerated scepticism . . . not to find truth but to destroy traditions, customs, institutions, and confidence in the worth of civilization itself." The most basic suppositions and distinctions suddenly crumble, like the acidic pages of a poorly made book, eaten away from within. "*A rebours*" becomes the rallying cry of the anticultural cultural elite. Culture degenerates from being a *cultura animi* to a *corruptio animi*.

ALDOUS HUXLEY's *Brave New World* may be a second-rate novel—its characters wooden, its narrative overly didactic—but it has turned out to have been first-rate prognostication. Published in 1932, it touches everywhere on twenty-first-century anxieties. Perhaps the aspect of Huxley's dystopian—what to call it: fable? prophecy? admonition?—that is most frequently adduced is its vision of a society that has perfected what we have come to call genetic engineering. Among other things, it is a world in which reproduction has been entirely handed over to the experts. The word "parents" no longer describes a loving moral commitment but only an attenuated biological datum. Babies are not born but designed according to exacting specifications and "decanted" at sanitary depots like The Central London Hatchery and Conditioning Centre with which the book opens.

As with all efforts to picture future technology, Huxley's description of the equipment and procedures employed at the hatchery seems almost charmingly antiquated, like a space ship imagined by Jules Verne. But Huxley's portrait of the human toll of human ingenuity is very up-to-date. Indeed, we have not—not quite, not yet—caught up with the situation he describes. We do not—not quite, not yet—inhabit a world where "mother" and "monogamy" are blasphemous terms from which people have been conditioned to recoil in visceral revulsion. Maybe it will never come to that. (Though monogamy, of course, has long been high on the social and sexual revolutionary's list of hated institutions.) Still, it is a nice question whether developments in reproductive technology will not soon make other aspects of Huxley's fantasy a reality. Thinkers as different as Michel Foucault and Francis Fukuyama have pondered the advent of a "posthuman" future, eagerly or with dismay, as the case may be. Scientists busily manipulating DNA may give substance to their speculations. It is often suggested that what is most disturbing about *Brave New World* is its portrait of eugenics in action: its vision of humanity deliberately divided into genetically ordered castes, a few super-smart Alpha-pluses down through a multitude of drone-like Epsilons who do the heavy lifting. Such deliberately instituted inequality offends our democratic sensibilities.

What is sometimes overlooked or downplayed is the possibility that the most disturbing aspect of the future Huxley pictured has less to do with eugenics than genetics. That is to say, perhaps what is centrally repellent about Huxley's hatcheries is not that they codify inequality—nature already does that effectively—but that they exist at all. Are they not a textbook example of Promethean hubris in action? It is worth stepping back to ponder that possibility.

In the seventeenth century, Descartes predicted that his scientific method would make man "the master and possessor of nature": are we not fast closing in on the technology that proves him right? And this raises another question. Is there a point at which scientific development can no longer be described, humanly, as progress? We know the benisons of technology. Consider only electricity, the automobile, modern medicine. They have transformed the world and underscored the old observation that art, that *techne*, is man's nature. Nevertheless, the question remains whether, after two hundred years of breathtaking progress, we are about to become more closely acquainted with the depredations of technology. It would take a brave man, or a rash one, to venture a confident prediction either way. For example, if, as in *Brave New World*, we manage to bypass the "inconvenience" of human pregnancy altogether, should we do it? If—or rather when—that is possible, will it also be desirable? Well, why not? Why should a woman go through the discomfort and danger of pregnancy if a fetus could be safely incubated, or cloned, elsewhere? Wouldn't motherhood by proxy be a good thing—the ultimate labor-saving device? Most readers will hesitate about saying yes. What does that tell us? Some readers will have no hesitation about saying yes; what does *that* tell us? (A recent article in *The Wall Street Journal* reported on the new popularity of using continuous birth-control pills or other methods to suppress women's menstrual cycles. The article quoted one obstetrician-gynecologist who, noting that most women in primitive societies had many more pregnancies than women today, argued that stopping monthly periods "gets women to a more natural state." Really?)

As Huxley saw, a world in which reproduction was "rationalized" and emancipated from love was also a world in which culture in the Arnoldian sense was not only otiose but dangerous. This is also a sub-theme of that other great dystopian novel, George Orwell's *1984*, which ends with the work of "various writers, such as Shakespeare, Milton, Swift, Byron, Dickens," being vandalized by being translated into Newspeak. When that laborious propaganda effort is finally complete, the "original writings, with all else that survived of the literature of the past, would be destroyed." The point is that culture has roots. It limns the future through its implications with the past. Moving the reader or spectator over the centuries, in Arendt's phrase, the monuments of culture transcend the local imperatives of the present. They escape the obsolescence that fashion demands, the predictability that planning requires. They speak of love and hatred, honor and shame, beauty and courage and cowardice—permanent realities of the human situation insofar as it remains human.

The denizens of Huxley's brave new world are designed and educated—perhaps his word, "conditioned," is more accurate—to be rootless, without culture. When a relic of the old order of civilization—a savage who had been born, not decanted—is brought from a reservation into the brave new world, he is surprised to discover that the literary past is forbidden to most of the population.

> "But why is it prohibited?" asked the Savage. In the excitement of meeting a man who had read Shakespeare he had momentarily forgotten everything else.
>
> The Controller shrugged his shoulders. "Because it's old; that's the chief reason. We haven't any use for old things here."
>
> "Even when they're beautiful?"
>
> "Particularly when they're beautiful. Beauty's attractive, and we don't want people to be attracted by old things. We want them to like the new ones."

Huxley's brave new world is above all a superficial world. People are encouraged to like what is new, to live in the moment, because that makes them less complicated and more pliable. Emotional commitments are even more strictly rationed than Shakespeare. (The same, again, is true of *1984*.) In the place of emotional commitments, sensations—thrilling, mind-numbing sensations—are available on demand through drugs and motion pictures that neurologically stimulate viewers to experience certain emotions and feelings. The fact that they are artificially produced is not a drawback but their very point. Which is to say that the brave new world is a virtual world: experience is increasingly vivid but decreasingly real. The question of meaning is deliberately short-circuited. "You've got to choose," the Resident World Controller for Western Europe patiently explains to the Savage,

> "between happiness and what people used to call high art. We've sacrificed the high art. We have the feelies and the scent organ instead."
>
> "But they don't mean anything."
>
> "They mean themselves; they mean a lot of agreeable sensations to the audience."

If this seems like a prescription for arrested development, that, too, is part of the point: "It is their duty to be infantile," the Controller explains, "even against their inclination." Promiscuity is encouraged because it is a prophylactic against emotional depth. The question of meaning is never pursued beyond the instrumental question of what produces the most pleasure. Socrates told us that the unexamined life is not worth living. Huxley (yet again like Orwell) pictures a world in which the unexamined life is the only one available.

Huxley's imagination failed him in one area. He understood that in a world in which reproduction was emancipated from the body, sexual congress would degenerate into a purely recreational activity, an amusement not inherently different from one's *soma* ration or the tactile movies. He pictured a world of casual, indeed mandatory, promiscuity. But he thought it would develop along completely conventional lines. He ought to have known that the quest for "agreeable sensations" would issue in a pansexual carnival. In this area, anyway, we seem to have proceeded a good deal further than the characters who inhabit Huxley's dystopia.

In part, the attack on permanence is an attack on the idea that anything possesses inherent value. Absolute fungibility—the substitution of anything for anything—is the ideal. In one sense, this is a product of what the philosopher Michael Oakeshott criticized as "rationalism." "To the Rationalist," Oakeshott wrote in the late 1940s, "nothing is of value merely because it exists (and certainly not because it has existed for many generations), familiarity has no worth and nothing is to be left standing for want of scrutiny." The realm of sexuality is one area where the effects of such rationalism are dramatically evident. It was not so long ago that the description from Genesis—"male and female created he them"—was taken as a basic existential fact. True, the obstinacy of sexual difference has always been a thorn in the side of utopian rationalism. But it is only in recent decades that the engines of judicial meddlesomeness, on the one hand, and surgical know-how, on the other, have effectively assaulted that once permanent-seeming reality.

For an illustration of how sexual politics has been enlisted in the attack on permanence, consider the recently acquired habit of using the term "gender" when we mean "sex." This may seem an innocent, nearly a euphemistic, innovation. But it is not innocent. It issues not from any residual sense of modesty about sexual matters but from a hubristic effort to reduce sex to gender. The term "gender" has its home in grammar: it names a certain linguistic convention. Sex describes a basic biological division. As the columnist George Will noted recently, the substitution of "gender" for "sex" is so widespread because it suggests that sexual differences are themselves a matter of convention—"socially constructed" and therefore susceptible to social deconstruction: susceptible to being "erased by sufficiently determined social engineers." A powerful legal tool in the campaign to substitute gender for sex is Title IX, which celebrated its thirtieth anniversary in May 2002. Written to prohibit discrimination on the basis of sex, it has, in the hands of what Will calls "Title IX fanatics," become a legal bludgeon that is wielded to deny the reality of sexual differences. It has already been used to gut the athletic programs of hundreds of schools and colleges across the country; the next target, Will suggests, will be the curriculum: if a college has an engineering department, it must also have proportional representation of the sexes—sorry, the genders—in that department. Anything less would be an insult to the ideal of equality.

A more florid example of sexual fungibility at work is the explosion of interest in—indeed, the incipient normalization of—"gender reassignment surgery" and other adventures in sexual plasticity. A glance at the personal ads of any "alternative" newspaper—to say nothing of Internet sex sites—will reveal a burgeoning sexual demi-monde where the "transsexual," "pansexual," and "virtually sexual" heartily compete with more traditional promiscuities.

Nor are such phenomena confined to such "help wanted" venues. Headline from a California newspaper last summer: "San Francisco is about to embark on another first in the nation: providing health care benefits for city workers undergoing sex-change procedures." "Oh, well," you say: "It's California, what do you expect?" Here's another headline: "Britain's free health care service should provide sex-change operations for transsexuals because they suffer from a legitimate illness, a court has ruled." Not to be left behind, *The New York Times Magazine* recently ran a long and sympathetic cover story about a "transgendered" thirteen-year-old who, though born as a girl, has lived for the last several years as a boy.

Real-life transsexuals are what we might call the objective correlative of an increasingly prominent strand in our culture's fantasy life. Consider, to take just one example, the British artists Dinos and Jake Chapman. Their signature works are pubescent female mannequins studded with erect penises, vaginas, and anuses, fused together in various postures of sexual congress. The thing to notice is not how outrageous but how common such items are. The Chapman brothers are not a back-alley, plain-brown-wrapper phenomenon. Their works are exhibited in major, once staid, galleries like the Royal Academy in London and the Brooklyn Museum in New York. They are "transgressive," all right. But the point is that the transgressions they announce have been to a large extent domesticated and welcomed into the mainstream. It would be bootless to multiply examples—readers will doubtless have lists of their own. Hardly anyone is shocked anymore, but that is a testament not to public enlightenment but to widespread moral anaesthesia. (The question of aesthetics, of distinctively artistic achievement, does not even enter the calculation: what does that tell us?)

What we are seeing in sexual life is the fulfillment, in some segments of society, of the radical emancipatory vision enunciated in the 1960s by such gurus as Herbert Marcuse and Norman O. Brown. In *Eros and Civilization*

Marcuse looked forward to the establishment of a "non-repressive reality principle" in which "the body in its entirety would become . . . an instrument of pleasure." The sexual liberation Marcuse hailed was not a fecund liberation. As in *Brave New World*, children do not enter into the equation. The issue is pleasure, not progeny. Marcuse speaks glowingly of "a resurgence of pregenital polymorphous sexuality" that "protests against the repressive order of procreative sexuality." A look at the alarmingly low birth rates of most affluent nations today suggests that the protest has been effective. When Tocqueville warned about the peculiar form of despotism that threatened democracy, he noted that instead of tyrannizing men, as past despotisms had done, it tended to infantilize them, keeping "them fixed irrevocably in childhood." What Tocqueville warned about, Marcuse celebrated, extolling the benefits of returning to a state of "primary narcissism" in which one will find "the redemption of pleasure, the halt of time, the absorption of death; silence, sleep, night, paradise—the Nirvana principle not as death but as life." What Marcuse encouraged, in other words, is solipsism, not as a philosophical principle but as a moral indulgence, a way of life.

It is often said that we are entering the "information age." There is doubtless some truth in that. But what does it mean? The shocking bulletins appear with clocklike regularity: students seem to know less and less history, less and less mathematics, less and less literature, less and less geography. In May 2002, Diane Ravitch bemoaned the "truly abysmal scores" high-school seniors made in an American history examination: only one in ten did well enough to be considered proficient in the subject. The week before, some other report had bad news about other students and some other subject. A look in the papers today will reveal yet another depressing finding about the failure of education.

Welcome to the information age. Data, data everywhere, but no one knows a thing. In the West, at least, practically everybody has instant access to huge databases and news-retrieval services, to say nothing of television and other media. With a few clicks of the mouse we can bring up every line of Shakespeare that contains the word "darkling" or the complete texts of Aeschylus in Greek or in translation. Information about contract law in ancient Rome or yesterday's developments in microchip technology in Japan is at our fingertips. If we are traveling to Paris, we can book our airline ticket and hotel reservation online, check the local weather, and find out the best place to have dinner near the Place des Vosges. We can correspond and exchange documents with friends on the other side of the globe in the twinkling of an eye. Our command of information is staggering.

And yet with that command comes a great temptation. Partly, it is the temptation to confuse an excellent means of communication with communications that are excellent. We confuse, that is to say, process with product. What Eric Ormsby observed about contemporary librarians in "Victor Hugo: the ghost in the pantheon" (*The New Criterion*, October 2002) goes for the rest of us: our fascination with means has led us "to ignore and neglect the ends."

That is not the only confusion. There is also a tendency to confuse propinquity with possession. The fact that some text is available online or on CD-ROM does not mean that one has read and absorbed its contents. When I was in graduate school, there were always students who tended to suppose that by making a Xerox copy of some document they had also read, or half-read, or at least looked into it. Today that same tendency is exacerbated by high-speed Internet access. We can download a veritable library of material to our computer in a few minutes; that does not mean we have mastered its riches. Information is not synonymous with knowledge, let alone wisdom.

This is not a new insight. At the end of the *Phaedrus*, Plato has Socrates tell the story of the god Theuth, who, legend has it, invented the art of writing. When Theuth presented his new invention to the king of Egypt, he promised the king that it would make his people "wiser and improve their memories." But the king disagreed, claiming that the habit of writing, far from improving memories, would "implant forgetfulness" by encouraging people to rely on external marks rather than "the living speech graven in the soul."

Well, none of us would wish to do without writing—or computers, come to that. Nor, I think, would Plato have wanted us to. (Though he would probably have been severe about television. That bane of intelligence could have been ordered up specially to illustrate Plato's idea that most people inhabit a kind of existential "cave" in which they mistake flickering images for realities.) Plato's indirect comments—through the mouth of Socrates recounting an old story he picked up somewhere—have less to do with writing (an art, after all, in which Plato excelled) than with the priority of immediate experience: the "living speech graven in the soul." Plato may have been an idealist. But here as elsewhere he appears as an apostle of vital, first-hand experience: a realist in the deepest sense of the term.

The problem with computers is not the worlds they give us instant access to but the world they encourage us to neglect. Everyone knows about the studies showing the bad effects on children and teenagers of too much time in cyberspace (or, indeed, in front of the television set). It cuts them off from their family and friends, fosters asocial behavior, disrupts their ability to concentrate, and makes it harder for them to distinguish between fantasy and reality. I suspect, however, that the real problem is not so much the sorry cases that make headlines but a more generally disseminated attitude toward the world.

When I entered the phrase "virtual reality," the Google search engine (at last count, 2,073,418,204 pages indexed) returned 1,260,000 hits in .12 seconds. There are many, many organizations like the Virtual Reality Society, "an international society dedicated to the discussion and advancement of virtual reality and synthetic environments." Computer simulations, video games, special effects: in some areas of life, virtual reality seems to be crowding out the other variety. It gives a whole new significance to Villiers de L'Isle-Adam's world-weary mot: "*Vivre? Les serviteurs feront cela pour nous.*"

The issue is not, or not only, the digital revolution—the sudden explosion of computers and e-mail and the Internet. It is rather the effect of such developments on our moral and imaginative life, and even our cognitive life. Why bother to get Shakespeare by heart when you can look it up in a nonce on the Internet? One reason, of course, is that a passage memorized is a passage internalized: it becomes part of the mental sustenance of the soul. It's the difference between a living limb and a crutch.

It used to be said that in dreams begin responsibilities. What responsibilities does a virtual world inspire? Virtual responsibilities, perhaps: responsibilities undertaken on spec, as it were. A virtual world is a world that can be created, manipulated, and dissolved at will. It is a world whose reverberations are subject to endless revision. The Delete key is always available. Whatever is done can be undone. Whatever is undone can be redone.

Of course, as the meditations of Huxley in the 1930s and Marcuse in the 1960s suggest, computers and the Internet do not create the temptations of virtual reality; they merely exacerbate those temptations. They magnify a perennial human possibility. Human beings do not need cyberspace to book a vacation from reality. The problem is not computers or indeed any particular technology but rather our disposition toward the common world that culture defines. When we ask about the survival of culture and the fortunes of permanence, we are asking about the fate of that common world. In many respects it is a political question—or, more precisely, a question regarding the limits of politics. When Susan Sontag, in the mid-1960s, championed the "new sensibility" she saw erupting across American society, she rightly observed that its representatives "have broken, whether they know it or not, with the Matthew Arnold notion of culture, finding it historically and humanly obsolescent."

What exactly is the "Matthew Arnold notion of culture" that Sontag and her cadre of hip intellectuals rejected as outmoded and irrelevant? For one thing, as we have seen, it is culture understood as a repository of mankind's noblest spiritual and intellectual aspirations: "the best," as Arnold put it, "that has been thought and said in the world." The "Matthew Arnold notion of culture" is thus a hierarchical idea of culture—a vision of culture as a "sacred order" whose majesty depends on its relevance to our deepest cares and concerns.

A second feature of the "Matthew Arnold notion of culture" is its independence—what Arnold summed up in the term "disinterestedness." Criticism achieves disinterestedness, Arnold said,

> by keeping aloof from what is called "the practical view of things"; by resolutely following the law of its own nature, which is to be a free play of the mind on all subjects which it touches. By steadily refusing to lend itself to any of those ulterior, political, practical considerations about ideas . . .

Understood in one way, Arnold's ideal of disinterestedness—with its emphasis on "a free play of the mind on all subjects"—might seem to be a prescription for moral quietism or frivolous aestheticism. What rescues it from that fundamental unseriousness is Arnold's unwavering commitment to truth and honesty. The business of criticism, he said, is to know and propagate the best, to "create a current of true and fresh ideas," and "to do this with inflexible honesty." It tells us a great deal about the state of culture that Arnold's demanding ideal of disinterestedness is not merely neglected but actively repudiated by many influential academics and intellectuals today.

A third feature of the "Matthew Arnold notion of culture" is its immediacy, its emphasis not on virtual but on first-hand experience. "Here," Arnold noted, "the great safeguard is never to let oneself become abstract, always to retain an intimate and lively consciousness of the truth of what one is saying, and, the moment this fails us, to be sure that something is wrong." The "Matthew Arnold notion of culture," then, comes armed with a sixth sense against the seductions of the spurious, the attractions of the ersatz.

Ultimately, what Sontag had against Arnold's view of culture was its earnestness, its seriousness. When she celebrated the Camp sensibility, she did so largely because in Camp she found a nimble ally in her effort "to dethrone the serious." Her praise of pop culture, pornography, and the pullulating ephemera of the counterculture must be understood as part of her battle against seriousness as traditionally defined. We have here that curious compact of moral levity and grim self-absorption that has characterized so many partisans of "advanced" opinion from Oscar Wilde on down to our own time. Redacted by the political passions of the 1960s, that strange compact resulted in the vertiginous relativisms that have overpopulated the academy, the art world, and other bastions of elite culture throughout Western society.

Part of what makes those relativisms vertiginous is their inconsistency. What we see in contemporary culture is relativism with a vengeance. It is a *directed*, activist relativism, forgiving and nonjudgmental about anything hostile to the perpetuation of traditional Western culture, full of self-righteous retribution when it comes to individuals and institutions friendly to the West. It incubates what Mark Steyn once described as "the slyer virus": "the vague sense that the West's success must somehow be responsible for the rest's failure." It is in effect a sort of secularized Jansenism: we are always in the wrong, not in the eyes of God but in the eyes of the exotic Other as imagined by us.

IT HAS LONG BEEN OBVIOUS that "multiculturalism" is an ornate synonym for "anti-Americanism." It is anti-Americanism on a peculiar moralistic jag. Its effect has been to pervert institutions hitherto entrusted with the preservation and transmission of our spiritual, political, and intellectual heritage. The institutions persist, but their purpose is stymied. Wherever we look—at our schools and colleges, at our churches, museums, courts, and legislatures—we see well underway a process of abdication: a process whereby institutions created to protect certain values have been "deconstructed" and turned against the very things they were meant to preserve.

Consider what has happened to the judiciary. In any society that enjoys the rule of law, courts are a custodian of permanence. The task of judges is to uphold the laws that have been passed down to them, not make new ones. But as Robert Bork has shown—and as we see all around us—the American judiciary has to an extraordinary extent become the "enemy of traditional culture." On issues from free speech and religion to sexuality, feminism, education, and race, the courts have acted less as defenders of the law than as an avant-garde establishing new beachheads to promulgate the gospel of left-liberal enlightenment. The recent attempt by the Ninth Circuit Court of Appeals in California to declare the Pledge of Allegiance unconstitutional because it includes the phrase "under God" is one of the more risible efforts in this campaign. The overall effect has been to inure society to rule by diktat, a situation in this country that is as novel as it is ominous. "It would," Judge Bork observes, "have been unthinkable until recently that so many areas of our national life would be controlled by judges." One again recalls Tocqueville's warning about democratic despotism. Only now it is not the sovereign but the judiciary that

> extends its arms over society as a whole; it covers its surface with a network of small, complicated, painstaking, uniform rules through which the most original minds and the most vigorous souls cannot clear a way to surpass the crowd; it does not break wills, but it softens them, bends them, and directs them; it rarely forces one to act, but it constantly opposes itself to one's acting; it does not destroy, it prevents things from being born; it does not tyrannize, it hinders, compromises, enervates, extinguishes, dazes, and finally reduces each nation to being nothing more than a herd of timid and industrious animals of which the government is the shepherd.

The attack on permanence is a failure of principle that results in moral paralysis. Chesterton once defined madness as "using mental activity so as to reach mental helplessness." That is an apt description of a process we see at work in many segments of our social and intellectual life. It is not so much a version of Hamlet's disease—being sicklied o'er with the pale cast of thought—as an example of what happens when conscience is no longer animated by principle and belief.

Item: Friday, May 17, 2002: "Hamas Founder Says Suicide Attacks Will Continue." Really? And what about us: what do we have to say about that abomination? Mostly, we wring our hands and mumble about restarting the "peace process." In a recent column, Linda Chavez reported on an episode of National Public Radio's "All Things Considered" in which a group of second- and third-generation Palestinian-Americans living in Northern Virginia were interviewed. If you had been thinking of taking a holiday there, you may wish to reconsider, or at least be sure that your life insurance premiums are paid up. As Ms. Chavez noted, the sentiments expressed could have come from Hamas. "It doesn't matter who dies," said one young boy who idolizes the suicide bombers, "just as long as they're Israeli." His mother blames Israel: "They've made him violent and hate them." His father swells with paternal pride: "If his time has come, he will die, regardless of where he is. But at least he will die for a cause. I will live the rest of my life being proud of him." What about the rule of law? Forget it. American democratic values? Don't make me laugh. What we have here, Ms. Chavez observes, is "a reflection of our new multicultural America, where young people are taught that one's allegiance to one's ethnic group takes precedence over allegiance to the United States or adherence to democratic values." Thus it is, as David Pryce-Jones observes in "A malign legacy" (*The New Criterion*, December 2001), that "contempt for democratic institutions was translated into contempt for the moral values that had underpinned those institutions."

When immigrants become American citizens, they take an oath of allegiance. Among other things, they must "absolutely and entirely renounce and abjure all allegiance and fidelity to any foreign prince, potentate, state, or sovereignty of whom or which [they] have heretofore been a subject or citizen." But such promises are only so many words to a population cut adrift from the permanent values enshrined in America's political principles. The fault lies with the elites who no longer respect and stand up for those principles. "No taxation without representation" is a splendid demand. But so is "no immigration without assimilation." Where is the simple imperative that one live up to one's oaths or face the consequences? If one becomes an American citizen, then one must become an American citizen, with the rights *and duties* pertaining thereto. If that proves too onerous, perhaps citizenship should be revoked and a one-way ticket to elsewhere provided. Such drastic measures would not be a sign of excessive rigor but an example of beneficence in action. It is kindness to stymie the forces of anarchy. By supporting the permanent values that undergird society, such enforcement would be a vote for civilization against chaos.

Since September 11, questions about the survival of culture have naturally taken on a new urgency. The focus suddenly shifted away from the airier purlieus of cultural endeavor to survival in the most visceral sense. The murderous fanatics who destroyed the World Trade Center, smashed into the Pentagon, and killed thousands of innocent civilians took the issue of multiculturalism out of the fetid atmosphere of the graduate seminar and into the streets. Or, rather, they dramatized the fact that multiculturalism was never a merely academic matter. In a sense, the actions of those terrorists were less an attack on the United States than part of what Binyamin Netanyahu called "a war to reverse the triumph of the West." We are very far from being in a position to assess the full significance of September 11 for the simple reason that the detonations that began that day continue to reverberate and destroy. A battle of wills, a contest of values, was initiated or at least openly acknowledged on September 11. It is much too early to predict the course of that conflict.

September 11 precipitated a crisis the end of which we cannot see. Part of the task that faces us now is to acknowledge the depth of barbarism that challenges the survival of culture. And part of that acknowledgment lies in reaffirming the core values that are under attack. Ultimately, victory in the conflict that besieges us will be determined not by smart weapons but by smart heads. That is to say, the conflict is not so much—not only—a military conflict as a conflict of worldviews. It is convenient to command the carrier battle groups and cruise missiles; it is essential to possess the will to use them and the faith that our cause, the cause of culture, is the best hope for mankind. Mark Steyn put it well: "If we are as ashamed as we insist we are—of ourselves, our culture and our history—then inevitably we will invite our own destruction." The horrifying slaughter of September 11 tempts us to draw a line around that day and treat it and its immediate consequences as an exceptional case. There is a deep sense, however, in which the terrorist attacks underscore not the fragility of normality but the normality of fragility. This is a point that C. S. Lewis made with great eloquence in a sermon he preached at Oxford in 1939. "I think it important," he said,

> to try to see the present calamity in a true perspective. The war creates no absolutely new situation: it simply aggravates the permanent human situation so that we can no longer ignore it. Human life has always been lived on the edge of a precipice. Human culture has always had to exist under the shadow of something infinitely more important than itself. If men had postponed the search for knowledge and beauty until they were secure, the search would never have begun.
>
> We are mistaken when we compare war with "normal life." Life has never been normal. Even those periods which we think most tranquil, like the nineteenth century, turn out, on closer inspection, to be full of crises, alarms, difficulties, emergencies. Plausible reasons have never been lacking for putting off all merely cultural activities until some imminent danger has been averted or some crying injustice put right. But humanity long ago chose to neglect those plausible reasons. They wanted knowledge and beauty now, and would not wait for the suitable moment that never comes. Periclean Athens leaves us not only the Parthenon but, significantly, the Funeral Oration. The insects have chosen a different line: they have sought first the material welfare and security of the hive, and presumably they have their reward.
>
> Men are different. They propound mathematical theorems in beleaguered cities, conduct metaphysical arguments in condemned cells, make jokes on scaffolds, discuss the latest new poem while advancing to the walls of Quebec, and comb their hair at Thermopylae. This is not panache: it is our nature.

Lewis's meditation is by turns cheering and sobering. On the one hand, it testifies to the heartiness of culture, which is the heartiness of the human spirit. Sonnets in Siberia, mathematical formulae in the besieged fortress. There is no time when cultural instructions are not pertinent. On the other hand, Lewis's meditation reminds us that culture, and the humanity that defines it, is constantly under threat. No achievement may be taken for granted; yesterday's gain may be tomorrow's loss; permanent values require permanent vigilance and permanent renewal.

What lessons may we draw from these Janus-faced conclusions? One is that it is always later than you think. Another is that it is never too late to start anew. Our French friends have lately taken to disparaging the *"simplisme"* of America's foreign policy. In their subtlety they ignore the fact that most important truths are—I use the adverb advisedly—terribly simple. Our complexity is much more likely to lead us astray than any simplicity we may follow.

In *Notes Towards the Definition of Culture*, T. S. Eliot observed that "If any definite conclusions emerge from this study, one of them surely is this, that culture is the one thing that we cannot deliberately aim at. It is the product of a variety of more or less harmonious activities, each pursued for its own sake." "For its own sake." That is one simple idea that is everywhere imperiled today. When we plant a garden, it is bootless to strive directly for camellias. They are the natural product of our care, nurture, and time. We can manage that when it comes to agriculture. When we turn our hands to *cultura animi*, we seem to be considerably less successful. The historian John Lukacs has just published a gloomy book called *At the End of an Age*. He argues that "we in the West are living near the end of an entire age," that the Modern Age, which began with the Renaissance, is jerking, crumbling irretrievably to its end. I believe Lukacs is precipitate. After all, prophecies of the end have been with us since the beginning. It seems especially odd that an historian of Lukacs's delicacy and insight would indulge in what amounts to a reprise of Spengler's thesis about the "decline of the West." How many times must historical "inevitabilities" be confounded before they lose their hold on our imaginations?

Where Lukacs is on to something, however, is in his meditations on the ideology of progress. Science does not deserve the scare quotes with which Lukacs adorns it, far from it. But it is true that much that we have taken for progress looks with the passage of time more and more dubious. Our stupendous power has accustomed us to say "yes" to every innovation, in manners and morals as well as the laboratory. We have yet to learn—even now, even at this late date—that promises of liberation often turn out to conceal new enchantments and novel forms of bondage. Our prejudice against prejudice tempts us to neglect the deep wisdom of tradition and time-sanctioned answers to the human predicament. The survival of culture is never a sure thing. No more is its defeat. Our acknowledgment of those twin facts, to the extent that we manage it, is one important sign of our strength.

June 2002

It's the Demography, Stupid

Mark Steyn

M OST PEOPLE READING this have strong stomachs, so let me lay it out as baldly as I can: Much of what we loosely call the Western world will survive this century, and much of it will effectively disappear within our lifetimes, including many if not most Western European countries. There'll probably still be a geographical area on the map marked as Italy or the Netherlands—*probably*—just as in Istanbul there's still a building called the Cathedral of St. Sophia. But it's not a cathedral; it's merely a designation for a piece of real estate. Likewise, Italy and the Netherlands will merely be designations for real estate. The challenge for those who reckon Western civilization is on balance better than the alternatives is to figure out a way to save at least some parts of the West.

One obstacle to doing that is the fact that, in the typical election campaign in your advanced industrial democracy, the political platforms of at least one party in the United States and pretty much all parties in the rest of the West are largely about what one would call the secondary impulses of society—government health care, government day care (which Canada's thinking of introducing), government paternity leave (which Britain's just introduced). We've prioritized the secondary impulse over the primary ones: national defense, family, faith, and, most basic of all, reproductive activity—"Go forth and multiply," because if you don't you won't be able to afford all those secondary-impulse issues, like cradle-to-grave welfare. Americans sometimes don't understand how far gone most of the rest of the developed world is down this path: In the Canadian and most Continental cabinets, the defense ministry is somewhere an ambitious politician passes through on his way up to important jobs like the health department. I don't think Don Rumsfeld would regard it as a promotion if he were moved to Health & Human Services.

The design flaw of the secular social-democratic state is that it requires a religious-society birthrate to sustain it. Post-Christian hyper-rationalism is, in the objective sense, a lot less rational than Catholicism or Mormonism. Indeed, in its reliance on immigration to ensure its future, the European Union has adopted a twenty-first-century variation on the strategy of the Shakers, who were forbidden from reproducing and thus could only increase their numbers by conversion. The problem is that secondary-impulse societies mistake their weaknesses for strengths—or, at any rate, virtues—and that's why they're proving so feeble at dealing with a primal force like Islam.

Speaking of which, if we are at war—and half the American people and significantly higher percentages in Britain, Canada, and Europe don't accept that proposition—than what exactly is the war about?

We know it's not really a "war on terror." Nor is it, at heart, a war against Islam, or even "radical Islam." The Muslim faith, whatever its merits for the believers, is a problematic business for the rest of us. There are many trouble spots around the world, but as a general rule, it's easy to make an educated guess at one of the participants: Muslims vs. Jews in "Palestine," Muslims vs. Hindus in Kashmir, Muslims vs. Christians in Africa, Muslims vs. Buddhists in Thailand, Muslims vs. Russians in the Caucasus, Muslims vs. backpacking tourists in Bali. Like the environmentalists, these guys think globally but act locally.

Yet while Islamism is the enemy, it's not what this thing's about. Radical Islam is an opportunist infection, like AIDS: it's not the HIV that kills you, it's the pneumonia you get when your body's too weak to fight it off. When the jihadists engage with the U.S. military, they lose—as they did in Afghanistan and Iraq. If this were like World War I with those fellows in one trench and us in ours facing them over some boggy piece of terrain, it would be over very quickly. Which the smarter Islamists have figured out. They know they can never win on the battlefield, but they figure there's an excellent chance they can drag things out until Western civilization collapses in on itself and Islam inherits by default.

That's what the war's about: our lack of civilizational confidence. As a famous Arnold Toynbee quote puts it: "Civilizations die from suicide, not murder"—as can be seen throughout much of "the Western world" right now. The progressive agenda—lavish social welfare, abortion, secularism, multiculturalism—is collectively the real suicide bomb. Take multiculturalism: the great thing about multiculturalism is that it doesn't involve knowing anything about other cultures—the capital of Bhutan, the principal exports of Malawi, who cares? All it requires is feeling good about other cultures. It's fundamentally a fraud, and I would argue was subliminally accepted on that basis. Most adherents to the idea that all cultures are equal don't want to live in anything but an advanced Western society: Multiculturalism means your kid has to learn some wretched native dirge for the school holiday concert instead of getting to sing "Rudolph the Red-Nosed Reindeer" or that your holistic masseuse uses techniques developed from Native American spirituality, but not that you or anyone you care about should have to live in an African or Native-American society. It's a quintessential piece of progressive humbug.

Then September 11 happened. And bizarrely the reaction of just about every prominent Western leader was to visit a mosque: President Bush did, the Prince of Wales did, the Prime Minister of the United Kingdom did, the Prime Minister of Canada did. . . . The Premier of Ontario didn't, and so twenty Muslim community leaders had a big summit to denounce him for failing to visit a mosque. I don't know why he didn't. Maybe there was a big backlog, it was mosque drivetime, prime ministers in gridlock up and down the freeway trying to get to the Sword of the Infidel-Slayer Mosque on Elm Street. But for whatever reason he couldn't fit it into his hectic schedule. Ontario's Citizenship Minister did show up at a mosque, but the imams took that as a great insult, like the Queen sending Fergie to open the Commonwealth Games. So the Premier of Ontario had to hold a big meeting with the aggrieved imams to apologize for not going to a mosque and, as *The Toronto Star*'s reported it, "to provide them with reassurance that the provincial government does not see them as the enemy."

Anyway, the get-me-to-the-mosque-on-time fever died down, but it set the tone for our general approach to these atrocities. The old definition of a nanosecond was the gap between the traffic light changing in New York and the first honk from a car behind. The new definition is the gap between a terrorist bombing and the press release from an Islamic lobby group warning of a backlash against Muslims. In most circumstances, it would be considered appallingly bad taste to deflect attention from an actual "hate crime" by scaremongering about a purely hypothetical one. Needless to say, there is no campaign of Islamophobic hate crimes. If anything, the West is awash in an epidemic of self-hate crimes. A commenter on Tim Blair's website in Australia summed it up in a note-perfect parody of a *Guardian* headline: "Muslim Community Leaders Warn of Backlash from Tomorrow Morning's Terrorist Attack." Those community leaders have the measure of us.

Radical Islam is what multiculturalism has been waiting for all along. In *The Survival of Culture*, I quoted the eminent British barrister Helena Kennedy, QC. Shortly after September 11, Baroness Kennedy argued on a BBC show that it was too easy to disparage "Islamic fundamentalists." "We as Western liberals too often are fundamentalist ourselves," she complained. "We don't look at our own fundamentalisms."

Well, said the interviewer, what exactly would those Western liberal fundamentalisms be? "One of the things that we are too ready to insist upon is that we are the tolerant people and that the intolerance is something that belongs to other countries like Islam. And I'm not sure that's true."

Hmm. Lady Kennedy was arguing that our tolerance of our own tolerance is making us intolerant of other people's intolerance, which is intolerable. And, unlikely as it sounds, this has now become the highest, most rarefied form of multiculturalism. So you're nice to gays and the Inuit? Big deal. Anyone can be tolerant of fellows like that, but tolerance of intolerance gives an even more intense frisson of pleasure to the multiculti masochists. In other words, just as the AIDS pandemic greatly facilitated societal surrender to the gay agenda, so 9/11 is greatly facilitating our surrender to the most extreme aspects of the multicultural agenda.

For example, one day in 2004, a couple of Canadians returned home, to Lester B. Pearson International Airport in Toronto. They were the son and widow of a fellow called Ahmed Said Khadr, who back on the Pakistani-Afghan frontier was known as "al-Kanadi." Why? Because he was the highest-ranking Canadian in al Qaeda—plenty of other Canucks in al Qaeda but he was the Numero Uno. In fact, one could argue that the Khadr family is Canada's principal contribution to the war on terror. Granted they're on the wrong side (if you'll forgive me being judgmental) but no can argue that they aren't in the thick of things. One of Mr. Khadr's sons was captured in Afghanistan after killing a U.S. Special Forces medic. Another was captured and held at Guantanamo. A third blew himself up while killing a Canadian soldier in Kabul. Pa Khadr himself died in an al Qaeda shoot-out with Pakistani forces in early 2004. And they say we Canadians aren't doing our bit in this war!

In the course of the fatal shoot-out of al-Kanadi, his youngest son was paralyzed. And, not unreasonably, Junior didn't fancy a prison hospital in Peshawar. So Mrs. Khadr and her boy returned to Toronto so he could enjoy the benefits of Ontario government healthcare. "I'm Canadian, and I'm not begging for my rights," declared the widow Khadr. "I'm demanding my rights."

As they always say, treason's hard to prove in court, but given the circumstances of Mr. Khadr's death it seems clear that not only was he providing "aid and comfort to the Queen's enemies" but that he was, in fact, the Queen's enemy. The Princess Patricia's Canadian Light Infantry, the Royal 22nd Regiment, and other Canucks have been participating in

Afghanistan, on one side of the conflict, and the Khadr family had been over there participating on the other side. Nonetheless, the Prime Minister of Canada thought Boy Khadr's claims on the public health system was an excellent opportunity to demonstrate his own deep personal commitment to "diversity." Asked about the Khadrs' return to Toronto, he said, "I believe that once you are a Canadian citizen, you have the right to your own views and to disagree."

That's the wonderful thing about multiculturalism: you can choose which side of the war you want to fight on. When the draft card arrives, just tick "home team" or "enemy," according to taste. The Canadian Prime Minister is a typical late-stage Western politician: He could have said, well, these are contemptible people and I know many of us are disgusted at the idea of our tax dollars being used to provide health care for a man whose Canadian citizenship is no more than a flag of convenience, but unfortunately that's the law and, while we can try to tighten it, it looks like this lowlife's got away with it. Instead, his reflex instinct was to proclaim this as a wholehearted demonstration of the virtues of the multicultural state. Like many enlightened Western leaders, the Canadian Prime Minister will be congratulating himself on his boundless tolerance even as the forces of intolerance consume him.

That, by the way, is the one point of similarity between the jihad and conventional terrorist movements like the IRA or ETA. Terror groups persist because of a lack of confidence on the part of their targets: the IRA, for example, calculated correctly that the British had the capability to smash them totally but not the will. So they knew that while they could never win militarily, they also could never be defeated. The Islamists have figured similarly. The only difference is that most terrorist wars are highly localized. We now have the first truly global terrorist insurgency because the Islamists view the whole world the way the IRA view the bogs of Fermanagh: they want it and they've calculated that our entire civilization lacks the will to see them off.

We spend a lot of time at *The New Criterion* attacking the elites and we're right to do so. The commanding heights of the culture have behaved disgracefully for the last several decades. But, if it were just a problem with the elites, it wouldn't be that serious: the mob could rise up and hang 'em from lampposts—a scenario that's not unlikely in certain Continental countries. But the problem now goes way beyond the ruling establishment. The annexation by government of most of the key responsibilities of life— child-raising, taking care of your elderly parents—has profoundly changed the relationship between the citizen and the state. At some point—I would say socialized health care is a good marker—you cross a line, and it's very hard then to persuade a citizenry enjoying that much government largesse to cross back. In *National Review* recently, I took issue with that line Gerald Ford always uses to ingratiate himself with conservative audiences: "A government big enough to give you everything you want is big enough to take away everything you have." Actually, you run into trouble long before that point: A government big enough to give you everything you want still isn't big enough to get you to give anything back. That's what the French and German political classes are discovering.

Go back to that list of local conflicts I mentioned. The jihad has held out a long time against very tough enemies. If you're not shy about taking on the Israelis, the Russians, the Indians, and the Nigerians, why wouldn't you fancy your chances against the Belgians and Danes and New Zealanders?

So the jihadists are for the most part doing no more than giving us a prod in the rear as we sleepwalk to the cliff. When I say "sleepwalk," it's not because we're a blasé culture. On the contrary, one of the clearest signs of our decline is the way we expend so much energy worrying about the wrong things. If you've read Jared Diamond's bestselling book *Collapse: How Societies Choose to Fail or Succeed*, you'll know it goes into a lot of detail about Easter Island going belly up because they chopped down all their trees. Apparently that's why they're not a G8 member or on the UN Security Council. Same with the Greenlanders and the Mayans and Diamond's other curious choices of "societies." Indeed, as the author sees it, pretty much every society collapses because it chops down its trees.

Poor old Diamond can't see the forest because of his obsession with the trees. (Russia's collapsing even as it's undergoing reforestation.) One way "societies choose to fail or succeed" is by choosing what to worry about. The Western world has delivered more wealth and more comfort to more of its citizens than any other civilization in history, and in return we've developed a great cult of worrying. You know the classics of the genre: In 1968, in his bestselling book *The Population Bomb*, the eminent scientist Paul Ehrlich declared: "In the 1970s the world will undergo famines—hundreds of millions of people are going to starve to death." In 1972, in their landmark study *The Limits to Growth*, the Club of Rome announced that the world would run out of gold by 1981, of mercury by 1985, tin by 1987, zinc by 1990, petroleum by 1992, and copper, lead, and gas by 1993.

None of these things happened. In fact, quite the opposite is happening. We're pretty much awash in resources, but we're running out of people—the one truly indispensable resource, without which none of the others matter. Russia's the most obvious example: it's the largest country on earth, it's full of natural resources, and yet it's dying—its population is falling calamitously.

The default mode of our elites is that anything that happens—from terrorism to tsunamis—can be understood only as deriving from the perniciousness of Western civilization. As Jean-François Revel wrote, "Clearly, a civilization that feels guilty for everything it is and does will lack the energy and conviction to defend itself."

And even though none of the prognostications of the eco-doom blockbusters of the 1970s came to pass, all that means is that thirty years on, the end of the world has to be rescheduled. The amended estimated time of arrival is now 2032. That's to say, in 2002, the United Nations Global Environmental Outlook predicted "the destruction of 70 percent of the natural world in thirty years, mass extinction of species. . . . More than half the world will be afflicted by water shortages, with 95 percent of people in the Middle East with severe problems . . . 25 percent of all species of mammals and 10 percent of birds will be extinct . . ."

Etc., etc., for 450 pages. Or to cut to the chase, as *The Guardian* headlined it, "Unless We Change Our Ways, The World Faces Disaster."

Well, here's my prediction for 2032: unless we change our ways the world faces a future . . . where the environment will look pretty darn good. If you're a tree or a rock, you'll be living in clover. It's the Italians and the Swedes who'll be facing extinction and the loss of their natural habitat.

There will be no environmental doomsday. Oil, carbon dioxide emissions, deforestation: none of these things is worth worrying about. What's worrying is that we spend so much time worrying about things that aren't worth worrying about that we don't worry about the things we should be worrying about. For thirty years, we've had endless wake-up calls for things that aren't worth waking up for. But for the very real, remorseless shifts in our society—the ones truly jeopardizing our future—we're sound asleep. The world is changing dramatically right now and hysterical experts twitter about a hypothetical decrease in the Antarctic krill that might conceivably possibly happen so far down the road there's unlikely to be any Italian or Japanese enviro-worriers left alive to be devastated by it.

In a globalized economy, the environmentalists want us to worry about First World capitalism imposing its ways on bucolic, pastoral, primitive Third World backwaters. Yet, insofar as "globalization" is a threat, the real danger is precisely the opposite—that the peculiarities of the backwaters can leap instantly to the First World. Pigs are valued assets and sleep in the living room in rural China—and next thing you know an unknown respiratory disease is killing people in Toronto, just because someone got on a plane. That's the way to look at Islamism: we fret about McDonald's and Disney, but the big globalization success story is the way the Saudis have taken what was eighty years ago a severe but obscure and unimportant strain of Islam practiced by Bedouins of no fixed abode and successfully exported it to the heart of Copenhagen, Rotterdam, Manchester, Buffalo . . .

What's the better bet? A globalization that exports cheeseburgers and pop songs or a globalization that exports the fiercest aspects of its culture? When it comes to forecasting the future, the birthrate is the nearest thing to hard numbers. If only a million babies are born in 2006, it's hard to have two million adults enter the workforce in 2026 (or 2033, or 2037, or whenever they get around to finishing their Anger Management and Queer Studies degrees). And the hard data on babies around the Western world is that they're running out a lot faster than the oil is. "Replacement" fertility rate—i.e., the number you need for merely a stable population, not getting any bigger, not getting any smaller—is 2.1 babies per woman. Some countries are well above that: the global fertility leader, Somalia, is 6.91, Niger 6.83, Afghanistan 6.78, Yemen 6.75. Notice what those nations have in common?

Scroll way down to the bottom of the Hot One Hundred top breeders and you'll eventually find the United States, hovering just at replacement rate with 2.07 births per woman. Ireland is 1.87, New Zealand 1.79, Australia 1.76. But Canada's fertility rate is down to 1.5, well below replacement rate; Germany and Austria are at 1.3, the brink of the death spiral; Russia and Italy are at 1.2; Spain 1.1, about half replacement rate. That's to say, Spain's population is halving every generation. By 2050, Italy's population will have fallen by 22 percent, Bulgaria's by 36 percent, Estonia's by 52 percent. In America, demographic trends suggest that the blue states ought to apply for honorary membership of the EU: in the 2004 election, John Kerry won the sixteen with the lowest birth rates; George W. Bush took twenty-five of the twenty-six states with the highest. By 2050, there will be 100 million fewer Europeans, 100 million more Americans—and mostly red-state Americans.

As fertility shrivels, societies get older—and Japan and much of Europe are set to get older than any functioning societies have ever been. And we know what comes after old age. These countries are going out of business—unless they can find the will to change their ways. Is that likely? I don't think so. If you look at European election results—most recently in Germany—it's hard not to conclude that, while voters are unhappy with their political establishments, they're unhappy mainly because they resent being asked to reconsider their government benefits and, no matter how unaffordable they may be a generation down the road, they have no intention of seriously reconsidering them. The Scottish executive recently backed down from a proposal to raise the retirement age of Scottish public workers. It's presently sixty, which is nice but unaffordable. But the reaction of the average Scots worker is that that's somebody else's problem. The average German worker now puts in 22 percent fewer hours per year than his American counterpart, and no politician who wishes to remain electorally viable will propose closing the gap in any meaningful way.

This isn't a deep-rooted cultural difference between the Old World and the New. It dates back all the way to, oh, the 1970s. If one wanted to allocate blame, one could argue that it's a product of the U.S. military presence, the American security guarantee that liberated European budgets: instead of having to spend money on guns, they could concentrate on butter, and buttering up the voters. If Washington's problem with Europe is that these are not serious allies, well, whose fault is that? Who, in the years after the Second World War, created NATO as a post-modern military alliance? The "free world," as the Americans called it, was a free ride for everyone else. And having been absolved from the primal responsibilities of nationhood, it's hardly surprising that European nations have little wish to re-shoulder them. In essence, the lavish levels of public health care on the Continent are subsidized by the American taxpayer. And this long-term softening of large sections of the West makes them ill-suited to resisting a primal force like Islam.

There is no "population bomb." There never was. Birthrates are declining all over the world—eventually every couple on the planet may decide to opt for the Western yuppie model of one designer baby at the age of thirty-nine. But demographics is a game of last man standing. The groups that succumb to demographic apathy last will have a huge advantage. Even in 1968 Paul Ehrlich and his ilk should have understood that their so-called population explosion was really a massive population adjustment. Of the increase in global population between 1970 and 2000, the developed world accounted for under 9 percent of it, while the Muslim world accounted for 26 percent of the increase. Between 1970 and 2000, the developed world declined from just under 30 percent of the world's population to just over 20 percent, the Muslim nations increased from about 15 percent to 20 percent.

1970 doesn't seem that long ago. If you're the age many of the chaps running the Western world today are wont to be, your pants are narrower than they were back then and your hair's less groovy, but the landscape of your life—the look of your house, the lay-out of your car, the shape of your kitchen appliances, the brand names of the stuff in the fridge—isn't significantly different. Aside from the Internet and the cellphone and the CD, everything in your world seems pretty much the same but slightly modified.

And yet the world is utterly altered. Just to recap those bald statistics: In 1970, the developed world had twice as big a share of the global population as the Muslim world: 30 percent to 15 percent. By 2000, they were the same: each had about 20 percent.

And by 2020?

So the world's people are a lot more Islamic than they were back then and a lot less "Western." Europe is significantly more Islamic, having taken in during that period some 20 million Muslims (officially)—or the equivalents of the populations of four European Union countries (Ireland, Belgium, Denmark, and Estonia). Islam is the fastest-growing religion in the West: in the UK, more Muslims than Christians attend religious services each week.

Can these trends continue for another thirty years without having consequences? Europe by the end of this century will be a continent after the neutron bomb: the grand buildings will still be standing but the people who built them will be gone. We are living through a remarkable period: the self-extinction of the races who, for good or ill, shaped the modern world.

What will Europe be like at the end of this process? Who knows? On the one hand, there's something to be said for the notion that America will find an Islamified Europe more straightforward to deal with than Monsieur Chirac, Herr Schröder, and Co. On the other hand, given Europe's track record, getting there could be very bloody. But either way this is the real battlefield. The al Qaeda nutters can never find enough suicidal pilots to fly enough planes into enough skyscrapers to topple America. But, unlike us, the Islamists think long term, and, given their demographic advantage in Europe and the tone of the emerging Muslim lobby groups there, much of what they're flying planes into buildings for they're likely to wind up with just by waiting a few more years. The skyscrapers will be theirs; why knock 'em over?

The latter half of the decline and fall of great civilizations follows a familiar pattern: affluence, softness, decadence, extinction. You don't notice yourself slipping through those stages because usually there's a seductive pol on hand to provide the age with a sly, self-deluding slogan—like Bill Clinton's "It's about the future of all our children." We on the right spent the 1990s gleefully mocking Clinton's tedious invocation, drizzled like syrup over everything from the Kosovo war to highway appropriations. But most of the rest of the West can't even steal his lame bromides: A society that has no children has no future.

Permanence is the illusion of every age. In 1913, no one thought the Russian, Austrian, German, and Turkish empires would be gone within half a decade. Seventy years on, all those fellows who dismissed Reagan as an "amiable dunce" (in Clark Clifford's phrase) assured us the Soviet Union was likewise here to stay. The CIA analysts' position was that East Germany was the ninth biggest economic power in the world. In 1987 there was no rash of experts predicting the imminent fall of the Berlin Wall, the Warsaw Pact, and the USSR itself.

Yet, even by the minimal standards of these wretched precedents, so-called post-Christian civilizations—as a prominent EU official described his continent to me—are more prone than traditional societies to mistake the present tense for a permanent feature. Religious cultures have a much greater sense of both past and future, as we did a century ago, when we spoke of death as joining "the great majority" in "the unseen world." But if secularism's starting point is that this is all there is, it's no surprise that, consciously or not, they invest the here and now with far greater powers of endurance than it's ever had. The idea that progressive Euro-welfarism is the permanent resting place of human development was always foolish; we now know that it's suicidally so.

To avoid collapse, European nations will need to take in immigrants at a rate no stable society has ever attempted. The CIA is predicting the EU will collapse by 2020. Given that the CIA's got pretty much everything wrong for half a century, that would suggest the EU is a shoo-in to be the colossus of the new millennium. But even a flop spook is right twice a generation. If anything, the date of EU collapse is rather a cautious estimate. It seems more likely that within the next couple of European election cycles, the internal contradictions of the EU will manifest themselves in the usual way, and that by 2010 we'll be watching burning buildings, street riots, and as-sassinations on American network news every night. Even if they avoid that, the idea of a childless Europe ever rivaling America militarily or economically is laughable. Sometime this century there will be 500 million Americans, and what's left in Europe will either be very old or very Muslim. Japan faces the same problem: its population is already in absolute decline, the first gentle slope of a death spiral it will be unlikely ever to climb out of. Will Japan be an economic powerhouse if it's populated by Koreans and Filipinos? Very possibly. Will Germany if it's populated by Algerians? That's a trickier proposition. Best-case scenario? The Continent winds up as Vienna with Swedish tax rates. Worst-case scenario: Sharia, circa 2040; semi-Sharia, a lot sooner—and we're already seeing a drift in that direction.

In July 2003, speaking to the United States Congress, Tony Blair remarked: "As Britain knows, all predominant power seems for a time in-vincible but, in fact, it is transient. The question is: What do you leave be-hind?"

Excellent question. Britannia will never again wield the unrivalled power she enjoyed at her imperial apogee, but the Britannic inheritance endures, to one degree or another, in many of the key regional players in the world today—Australia, India, South Africa—and in dozens of island statelets from the Caribbean to the Pacific. If China ever takes its place as an advanced nation, it will be because the People's Republic learns more from British Hong Kong than Hong Kong learns from the Little Red Book. And of course the dominant power of our time derives its political character from eighteenth-century British subjects who took English ideas a little further than the mother country was willing to go.

A decade and a half after victory in the Cold War and end-of-history triumphalism, the "what do you leave behind?" question is more urgent than most of us expected. "The West," as a concept, is dead, and the West, as a matter of demographic fact, is dying.

What will London—or Paris, or Amsterdam—be like in the mid-Thirties? If European politicians make no serious attempt this decade to wean the populace off their unsustainable thirty-five-hour weeks, retirement at sixty, etc., then to keep the present level of pensions and health benefits the EU will need to import so many workers from North Africa and the Middle East that it will be well on its way to majority Muslim by 2035. As things stand, Muslims are already the primary source of population growth in English cities. Can a society become increasingly Islamic in its demographic character without becoming increasingly Islamic in its political character?

This ought to be the left's issue. I'm a conservative—I'm not entirely on board with the Islamist program when it comes to beheading sodomites and so on, but I agree Britney Spears dresses like a slut: I'm with Mullah Omar on that one. Why then, if your big thing is feminism or abortion or gay marriage, are you so certain that the cult of tolerance will prevail once the biggest demographic in your society is cheerfully intolerant? Who, after all, are going to be the first victims of the west's collapsed birthrates? Even if one were to take the optimistic view that Europe will be able to resist the creeping imposition of Sharia currently engulfing Nigeria, it remains the case that the Muslim world is not notable for setting much store by "a woman's right to choose," in any sense. I watched that big abortion rally in Washington last year, where Ashley Judd and Gloria Steinem were cheered by women waving "Keep your Bush off my bush" placards, and I thought it was the equivalent of a White Russian tea party in 1917. By prioritizing a "woman's right to choose," Western women are delivering their societies into the hands of fellows far more patriarchal than a 1950s sitcom dad. If any of those women marching for their "reproductive rights" still have babies, they might like to ponder demographic realities: A little girl born today will be unlikely, at the age of forty, to be free to prance around demonstrations in Eurabian Paris or Amsterdam chanting "Hands off my bush!"

Just before the 2004 election, that eminent political analyst Cameron Diaz appeared on the Oprah Winfrey show to explain what was at stake:

"Women have so much to lose. I mean, we could lose the right to our bodies. . . . If you think that rape should be legal, then don't vote. But if you think that you have a right to your body," she advised Oprah's viewers, "then you should vote."

Poor Cameron. A couple of weeks later, the scary people won. She lost all rights to her body. Unlike Alec Baldwin, she couldn't even move to France. Her body was grounded in Terminal D.

But, after framing the 2004 presidential election as a referendum on the right to rape, Miss Diaz might be interested to know that men enjoy that right under many Islamic legal codes around the world. In his book *The Empty Cradle*, Philip Longman asks: "So where will the children of the future come from? Increasingly they will come from people who are at odds with the modern world. Such a trend, if sustained, could drive human culture off its current market-driven, individualistic, modernist course, gradually creating an anti-market culture dominated by fundamentalism—a new Dark Ages."

Bottom line for Cameron Diaz: There are worse things than John Ashcroft out there.

Longman's point is well-taken. The refined antennae of Western liberals mean that, whenever one raises the question of whether there will be any Italians living in the geographical zone marked as Italy a generation or three hence, they cry, "Racism!" To fret about what proportion of the population is "white" is grotesque and inappropriate. But it's not about race, it's about culture. If 100 percent of your population believes in liberal pluralist democracy, it doesn't matter whether 70 percent of them are "white" or only 5 percent are. But, if one part of your population believes in liberal pluralist democracy and the other doesn't, then it becomes a matter of great importance whether the part that does is 9 percent of the population or only 60, 50, 45 percent.

Since the President unveiled the so-called Bush Doctrine—the plan to promote liberty throughout the Arab world—innumerable "progressives" have routinely asserted that there's no evidence Muslims want liberty and, indeed, Islam is incompatible with democracy. If that's true, it's a problem not for the Middle East today but for Europe the day after tomorrow. According to a poll taken in 2004, over 60 percent of British Muslims want to live under Sharia—in the United Kingdom. If a population "at odds with the modern world" is the fastest-breeding group on the planet—if there are more Muslim nations, more fundamentalist Muslims within those nations, more and more Muslims within non-Muslim nations, and more and more

Muslims represented in more and more transnational institutions—how safe a bet is the survival of the "modern world"?

Not good.

"What do you leave behind?" asked Tony Blair. There will only be very few and very old ethnic Germans and French and Italians by the midpoint of this century. What will they leave behind? Territories that happen to bear their names and keep up some of the old buildings? Or will the dying European races understand that the only legacy that matters is whether the peoples who will live in those lands after them are reconciled to pluralist, liberal democracy? It's the demography, stupid. And, if they can't muster the will to change course, then "what do you leave behind?" is the only question that matters.

January 2006

Enoch Powell: Should He Have Spoken?

Roger Scruton

IN 1968 THE products of the postwar baby boom decided to seize the European future and to jettison the European past. In that same year Enoch Powell delivered to the Birmingham Conservatives the speech known forever after as "Rivers of Blood": a speech that cost him his political career, and which, on one plausible interpretation, made the issue of immigration undiscussable in British politics for close to forty years. It is a speech that raises in its acutest form the question of truth: What place is there for truth in public life, and what should a politician do when comfortable falsehoods have settled down in government, and their uncomfortable negations seek forlornly for a voice?

"Human kind cannot bear very much reality," said T. S. Eliot. It is not one of his best lines, but he used it twice—in *Murder in the Cathedral* and in *Four Quartets*—and in both places its prosaic rhythmlessness reinforces its sense, reminding us that our exaltations are invented things, and that we prefer inspiring fantasies to sobering facts. Enoch Powell was no different, and his inspiring fantasy of England caused him to address his countrymen as though they still enjoyed the benefits of a classical education and an imperial culture. How absurd, in retrospect, to end a speech warning against the effects of uncontrolled immigration with a concealed quotation from Virgil. "As I look ahead," Powell said, "I am filled with foreboding. Like the Roman, I seem to see 'the River Tiber foaming with much blood.'" These words were addressed to an England that had forgotten the story of the *Aeneid*, along with every other story woven into its former identity as the "sweet, just, boyish master" of the world—to borrow Santayana's luminous phrase. It is hardly surprising that Powell's words were instantly converted to "rivers of blood," and their speaker dismissed as a dangerous madman.

It is, in fact, the Cumaean Sybil who utters that prophecy in Book VI of the *Aeneid*, and although she is foreseeing the troubles that come from immigration, it is to the troubles suffered by an immigrant that she refers. The immigrant in question—Aeneas—travels to Italy at the head of a determined retinue, carrying his household gods and a divine right of residence. His intention to settle is not to be brooked, and if this means "wars, horrid wars," so be it. Modern immigrants don't, on the whole, behave so badly. They don't need to. They come as the heads of families, and even if the family might comprise four wives and twenty children, it arrives to a red carpet of legal privileges, eagerly unrolled by publicly funded lawyers, and to a welcome trough of welfare benefits that few indigenous citizens can claim, however much they have contributed to the common fund.

Yet, like Aeneas, our immigrants come carrying their household gods. Like Aeneas, they come with an unbrookable intention to make a home for themselves. And if their gods dislike the indigenous rivals, they will soon make this fact known. Such predictions as Powell made in his speech, concerning the tipping of the demographic balance, the ghettoization of the industrial cities, and the growth of resentment among the indigenous working class have been fulfilled. Only the sibylline prophecy has fallen short of the mark. Even so, the Madrid and London bombings and the murder of Theo van Gogh are viewed by many Europeans as a foretaste of things to come. It is now evident to everyone that, in the debate over immigration, in those last remaining days when it could still have made a difference, Enoch Powell was far nearer the truth than those who instantly drove him from office, and who ensured that the issue was henceforth to be discussed, if at all, only by way of condemning the "racism" and "xenophobia" of those who thought like Powell. As for the racism and xenophobia of the incomers, it was indiscernible to the liberal conscience, which has never been able to understand that liberalism is an *unusual state of mind*.

Liberalism emerges from a long-standing rule of law, shaped by the Enlightenment view of citizenship, and dependent upon the shared customs, shared language, and shared culture of a people who have lived together in a common home and acquired the habit of defending it. But it is virtually unknown among people who are seeking territory, and who have conscripted their gods to fight for it. The book of Joshua tells the story of such a people, and it contains in its bloodthirsty pages not a single liberal sentiment. The one gesture of kindness that the book records toward the indigenous people is bestowed on those who had betrayed their native city to its foes. This reward offered for the basest form of treachery indicates how far the Israelites were, in their need, from any liberal view of the human condition.

At the time when Powell made his speech, British politicians were schooled in the Bible and the Greek and Roman classics; they could dispute the factual basis for Powell's prophecy only by putting out of mind what they had every reason to know, namely that many of the newcomers to Britain would be strangers to liberal values, attached to their own communities, suspicious toward the host culture, and anxious to insulate themselves and their children from its influence. In the face of those manifest truths our political class had recourse to Doublethink. Like the White Queen in *Through the Looking Glass*, they practiced the art of believing six impossible propositions before breakfast, including the proposition that pious Muslims from the hinterlands of Asia would produce children loyal to a secular European state.

This flight from reality is not a new feature of political life. It is always easier to bequeath a problem to your successors than to face it yourself, and when the problem is intractable, Doublethink will soon erase it, as Hitler was erased from the thoughts of the appeasers, and the Gulag from the political map of the peaceniks. Nor are American presidents any more realistic than the rest of us. When the embassy in Tehran was invaded and United States citizens taken hostage, President Carter chose not to notice what was, certainly *de facto* and probably *de jure*, a declaration of war. That may prove to have been the costliest mistake made by America in the Middle East. Likewise, the silencing of Enoch Powell has proved more costly than any other postwar domestic policy in Britain, since it has ensured that immigration can be discussed only now, when it is too late to do anything about it or to confine it to those who come in a spirit of obedience toward the indigenous law.

As I implied, Powell was also in flight from reality—the reality of British society as it was in 1968. The British people had lost their imperial identity without gaining a national identity with which to replace it. There were Scottish nationalists, Welsh nationalists, and Irish nationalists, but no English nationalists and therefore—since England was the core of Britain, the seat of government, and the central fact of our history—no British nationalists either. Powell's invocation of Virgil fell on deaf ears—or rather on ears that pricked up only at the sound of "blood." And his punctilious syntax, resounding with the rhythms of the Book of Common Prayer and rich in allusions to a history that was publicly remembered, if at all, only as an object of ridicule, created the impression of a *paterfamilias* in some Edwardian play, strutting at the front of the stage while his disobedient daughter flirts unnoticed in the background.

Moreover, Powell's fantasy vision of Britain was absolutely necessary to him. The truths that he wished to put across were uttered in defense of Old

England, and it was unthinkable to him that he might be speaking into the void. Powell's England was a place made sacred by Chaucer and Shakespeare, by the Anglican settlement and the anointed monarch, by the common law and the Great Offices of State. It was the very same England that Churchill had invoked in his wartime speeches: a country whose past was lost in Arthurian mists, whose title was as God-given as that of the Israelites and whose patriotism outshone that of Rome. Those who silenced Powell therefore believed that it was not he but they who were on the side of truth. They were introducing realism and sobriety in the place of dangerous romantic dreams. Not for nothing, they said, did Powell refer to authorities who wrote in dead languages and believed forgotten myths; not for nothing did he choose, when invited onto BBC radio's "Desert Island Discs," only episodes from the *Ring of the Nibelung* of Richard Wagner. The man was clearly living in Cloud Cuckoo Land. And Powell accepted the expression with a wry smile: After all, it comes from Aristophanes.

Truth, Plato believed, is the business of philosophy, but it is rhetoric, not philosophy, that moves the crowd. So how can we protect people from fatal errors, such as those that tempted Athens into conflict with Sparta, or those which, much later, led the Germans, mesmerized by Hitler, into an equally suicidal war? Plato did not believe that philosophers would be listened to: Their words would sound strange and ambiguous, and their eyes would be turned from present and time-bound emergencies toward the stratosphere of eternal truths. Nevertheless among the rhetorical devices of politicians, it is still possible to distinguish the noble lies from their ignoble negations. The noble lie is the untruth that conveys a truth, the myth that maps reality. It is thus that Plato justified the stories of the gods and their origins which inspire people to live as though nearer to the source of things, and to discover in themselves the virtues that exist only when we find our way to believing in them.

In the Platonic scheme of things, Powell's vision of England might be seen as a noble lie. He was exhorting his countrymen to *live up to* something, and that thing was an ideal image of their country, shaped by myth in the style of Hesiod. The England of Powell's dream was fashioned from heroic deeds and immemorial customs, from sacred rites and solemn offices whose meaning was inscrutable from any point outside the social context that defined them. By fixing their sights on this vision, the British people would be in some way perfecting themselves, and establishing their right to their ancestral territory. In place of this noble vision, however, they were also being offered an ignoble lie. The emerging multicultural community would make no place for a common obedience, a common loyalty, or a shared history: It would inevitably deprive the British people of their geographical, cultural, and political inheritance. And yet they were being told that it would not harm them, that they would even be improved by it, since it would inject energy, variety, and youth into a tired old way of life.

The problem with Plato's theory of the noble lie is that noble lies have to be believed by the one who utters them. Otherwise people will see through the deception and withdraw their support. And a lie that is believed is not really a lie. It was impossible to discern, in Powell's steely manner, ancestor-laden syntax, and fixed, expressionless gaze, whether he really believed in the nation that he described with his toneless incantations. He was invoking England in the way that a Professor of Classics (which once he was) invokes Greece—as an idea whose roots are buried deep in the archaeology of consciousness.

Plato's theory of the noble lie was a first shot at describing the role of myth in human thinking. Myths are not falsehoods, nor are they scientific theories: They are attempts to capture difficult truths in symbols. Myths also arm us against realities that are otherwise too fateful or disturbing to bear contemplation. Powell's deep attachment to Wagner went hand in hand with his own desire for a national myth of England. The composer of *The Ring of the Nibelung* was adamant that the work possessed "the ring of truth." Myth, for Wagner, was the opposite of fantasy: It was a truth-directed, rather than an illusion-directed, device. He made this observation in connection with the old myths of Greek tragedy, and saw the tragedians as disinterring from those myths the "concealed deep truths" about the human condition that they symbolized. In the same spirit Wagner wished to use the old myths of the Germanic peoples to explore truths about the modern psyche. His success in this is of less importance than the attempt. Thanks to Wagner, mythmaking became a deliberate enterprise, rather than the work of the collective unconscious.

But conscious myth—the noble lie—is a different thing altogether from the myths that emerge from the unconscious fears and longings of a people. Unconscious myth conveys truth because it is the residue of life and the afterimage of suffering. Conscious myths, however, are the instruments of human purpose. In the work of a great artist like Wagner they may point toward the truth. Released into the stream of political life, however, they can be directed as easily toward falsehood. Many blame Wagner for that exercise in collective mythopeia which brought the Nazi Party to power in Germany and extinguished the light of civilization across the continent. And many, looking back on Powell's vision of England, believe that it showed the same dangerous tendency—not toward the truth of the modern condition, but toward a fantasy. Once released from the educated mind in which it was first conceived, this fantasy would run riot in the feelings of ignorant people and there fully justify the charge of "racism" that was wrongly but understandably directed at Powell.

Such is the controversy as we see it now, forty years on: an ignoble lie against a dangerous myth. Whichever way you look at it, truth was the victim, and while the truth can now be cautiously acknowledged, it is acknowledged too late. Decisions can still be taken, but only in the hope of limiting the damage. And even now, when opinion across Europe is unanimous that immigration must be controlled, and that Muslims must be integrated into the secular culture, liberal politicians are refusing to admit to a problem or to confess that they are the cause of it. They still preach "multiculturalism" as the sign of our "vibrant" future; they still condemn "racism and xenophobia" as the enemy; they still try to state and solve the problem by the promiscuous multiplication of "human rights." Their Enlightenment creed makes it all but impossible for them to acknowledge the fundamental truth, which is that indigenous communities have legitimate expectations which take precedence over the demands of strangers. True, indigenous communities may also have duties of charity toward those strangers—or toward some of them. But charity is a gift, and there is no right to receive it, still less to force it from those reluctant to give.

The destructive effects of liberalism are not usually felt by the liberals themselves—not immediately, at least. The first victim of liberal immigration policies is the indigenous working class. When the welfare state was first conceived, it was in order to provide insurance for poorer members of the indigenous community, by taxing their income in exchange for the benefits which they may one day need. The rights involved were quasi-contractual: a right of the state to levy contributions in exchange for a right of the citizen to receive support. The very term used to describe the deal in Britain—"national insurance"—expresses the old understanding, that the welfare system is part of being together as a nation, of belonging with one's neighbors, as mutual beneficiaries of an ancestral right. The liberal view of rights, as universal possessions which make no reference to history, community, or obedience, has changed all that. Indigenous people can claim no precedence, not even in this matter in which they have sacrificed a lifetime of income for the sake of their own future security. Immigrants are given welfare benefits as of right, and on the basis of their need, whether or not they have paid or ever will pay taxes. And since their need is invariably great—why else have they come here?—they take precedence over existing residents in the grant of housing and income support. Those with a handful of wives are even more fortunate, since only one of their marriages is recognized in European systems of law: the remaining wives are "single mothers," with all the fiscal advantages which attach to that label. All this has entailed that the stock of "social housing" once reserved for the indigenous poor is now almost entirely occupied by people whose language, customs, and culture mark them out as foreigners.

It is not "racist" to draw attention to this kind of fact. Nor is it racist to argue that indigenous people must take precedence over newcomers, who have to earn their right of residence and cannot be allowed to appropriate the savings of their hosts. But it is easier for me to write about these matters in an American intellectual journal than in an English newspaper, and if I tried to write about these things in a Belgian newspaper, I could be in serious trouble with the courts. The iron curtain of censorship that came down in the wake of Powell's speech has not lifted everywhere; on the contrary, if the EU has its way, it will be enshrined in the criminal code, with "racism and xenophobia"—defined as vaguely as is required to silence unwanted opinion—made into an extraditable offense throughout the Union.

The problem with censorship, as John Stuart Mill pointed out a century and half ago, is that it makes it impossible for those who impose it to discover that they are wrong. The error persists, preventing the discussion that might produce a remedy, and ensuring that the problem will grow. Yet when truth cannot make itself known in words, it will make itself known in deeds. The truth about Hitler burst on the world in 1939, notwithstanding all the pious words of the appeasers. And the truth about immigration is beginning to show itself in Europe, notwithstanding all the liberal efforts to conceal it. It is not an agreeable truth; nor can we, in the face of it, take refuge in the noble lies of Enoch Powell. The fact is that the people of Europe are losing their homelands, and therefore losing their place in the world. I don't envisage the Tiber one day foaming with much blood, nor do I see it blushing as the voice of the muezzin sounds from the former cathedral of St. Peter. But the city through which the Tiber flows will one day cease to be Italian, and all the expectations of its former residents, whether political, social, cultural, or personal, will suffer a violent upheaval, with results every bit as interesting as those that Powell prophesied.

September 2006

"Christophobia" and the West

Kenneth Minogue

P UBLIC POLICY in a democracy rests upon public opinion, which in turn rests on public feeling. The feelings people have toward remote and abstract objects such as states and categories are normally pretty stable, but when they do change, they resemble earthquakes in the political world. Shelby Steele has recently been writing of the revolution in public feeling that took place in America in the 1960s, when white racism was replaced by white guilt. Whole new social and moral structures have been thrown up. The appearance of anti-Americanism in Europe in the wake of 9/11 is less fundamental, but is also in many respects a revolution of feeling. Israel has found itself buffeted by this change. My concern is with another shift in recent sentiment, less dramatic but in my view no less significant. It is the rising hatred of Christianity among Western peoples, which I shall call "Christophobia."

I am not, of course, talking of secularism. Scepticism about Christianity largely began in the eighteenth century and increased steadily throughout the twentieth. It is hardly surprising that a revelation couched in the idiom of a remote past and purporting to reveal the transcendental aspects of the human condition could not survive the coming of what we may call "the scientific worldview," in which truth is tested by empirical confirmation. Much of Christianity has responded to this development by retreating into a modernist accommodation with what it takes to be science. It has generated the ecumenical movement, a kind of deism (if I understand it rightly) in which all religions are treated as variant responses to the one divine creation.

Secularism, then, is not at all puzzling. It leads one to expect that Christianity would slowly fade away, leaving Christians to their services and secularists to long Sabbath mornings with the Sunday papers. There are indeed exceptions to this general picture of accommodation mitigating decline. Christianity remains a cause of violent conflict in places like Northern Ireland. In the United States, there is trouble at the interface where evangelicals and Roman Catholics encounter feminism and abortion clinics. The Catholic Church remains resistant to the march of modernity in some striking respects, but it too has long been on the defensive, and liberation theology leaves ecumenism panting behind. In Africa and South America, Christians are prospering mightily, but the zeal to persecute heretics which periodically characterized Christian churches from the late middle ages into the early modern period has largely faded away. And this is why the problem arises. Why should significant numbers of Westerners, especially among the educated, increasingly exhibit a quite visceral hatred of this apparently declining set of beliefs?

I first noticed this sentiment in the case of the brothers Hitchens, celebrated journalists, one on each side of the Atlantic. Christopher is a "left-wing maverick" and recently visited his native Britain. He and his brother Peter, a patriotic Conservative in London, aren't very close. Why not, asked an interviewer in *The Times*. Is it because you are so far apart politically? Not at all, replied Christopher. What I can't stand is that Peter is a practicing Christian. Hitchens takes the view of the English publisher who once defined a religious fanatic as anyone who believed in God. But that was a joke, and Christopher isn't joking. Again, in November last year in Britain, an award for Christian athletes was dropped because of a reluctance among the athletes to be "outed" as Christians. The work of people like Richard Dawkins in Oxford breathes the passions of the long gone Rationalist Press Association for whose readers Christianity was a repressive power against which every form of free expression from science to free love was struggling to breathe. Meanwhile, Philip Pullman, whose best-selling trilogy for children promises to become, as it were, the new Narnia, is an atheist who has revived an old Gnostic doctrine to the effect that the temptation in the Garden of Eden was that of enlightenment rather than an invitation to evil disobedience. In another part of the forest, one might remember that some years ago in Lebanon a set of Christians began distributing pamphlets apologizing for the Crusades to the understandably bemused inhabitants of Beirut.

If we move from these straws in the wind to the wind itself, we might cite the results of recent polling in the United States by the American National Election Study which attempts to measure intergroup attitudes by "feeling thermometers" quantifying how one group regards another. Mutual hostility between religious groups such as Jews, Catholics, and Evangelicals appears in these results to have diminished, while secularists, who belong in the typology of "culture wars" as progressives rather than as orthodox in the moral and religious spectrum, have become increasingly hostile to the "religious right." Since the 1972 Democratic Convention, they have increasingly dominated the Democratic Party.

Why should intellectuals waste their shot and shell pounding a target which has largely faded from view (and indeed where the moral and logical issues are confused)? And what might this tell us about the internal cohesion of European or Western civilization? A more directly political question would take off from the contrast between the extraordinary solicitude for Islamic sensibilities in Western states since 9/11 and the insouciant clobbering of Christian totems by artists and writers. But before I suggest an explanation of this phenomenon, I need to explore its wider significance.

In the Middle Ages, Christianity was, like Judaism and Islam, a law to which its followers were subject: in other words, an identity. With the coming of the modern world, Christianity became, or perhaps was maneuvered into becoming, a set of beliefs purporting to answer the same questions as those asked by scientists, a role in which it was notably incompetent, and from which it has steadily withdrawn. Also, from the sixteenth century, the encompassing Church of the medieval respublica Christiana succumbed to the public-relations disaster of breaking up into a number of quarrelling versions. By the time of Voltaire in the eighteenth century, Christian churches had adopted a set of attitudes that has kept them on the defensive ever since. For one thing, Christianity was associated with orthodoxy and authority as against reason. For another, its language belonged to a posture of consolation and supplication at odds with the apparently realistic attitudes of the sceptic and the atheist who no longer hoped for an afterlife. *Epater les chrétiens* was no less amusing a sport than *épater les bourgeois*—indeed the two were often indistinguishable. The essence of the conflict between "science" and "religion" came to rest on the killer question: "Do you believe in God?" meaning by "God" a ubiquitous patriarch with the power to punish and reward. Nietzsche's crisp declaration that God is dead was widely accepted, though fewer people accepted the corollary that (as Dostoyevsky put it) everything is permitted.

It is important to observe that most of these battles were between science and "religion" rather than science and Christianity. Marx wrote that religion was the opium of the people, not Christianity specifically. The issue in those days was about the grounds of belief, of faith versus reason, and in principle all religious propositions were equally likely to be regarded as superstitious, as potential grounds of non-negotiable bigotry, or perhaps as "nonsense" in the technical sense affirmed by logical positivists. This was, significantly, the position of the Bolshevik regime, in which atheism was the basic religious doctrine taught in schools. Today, however, a significant change has occurred in progressive opinion: in a multicultural context, religious beliefs are taken to be part of "culture" and hence off-limits to criticism, unless they are Christian, and more recently also, Jewish.

We may call this sentiment "Christophobia," and its simplest version is the legend people got from Voltaire and others, namely, that mankind had hitherto been dominated by all kinds of strange prejudices and superstitions but that now at last (in the eighteenth century) a dawn of reason was rising in which human beings would abandon these divisive absurdities and recognize themselves as sharing a human essence with a right to happiness and the power actually to bring this about. Such was the core of belief found in Jacobinism, socialism, rationalisms of various kinds (including that of the American founders), logical positivism, and all other versions of what the nineteenth century espoused as progress and the twentieth century came to call "the Enlightenment Project." And it is very important to observe that all other civilizations and peoples were to be incorporated within this projected earthly salvation. It was a global project.

Voltaire's legend is, of course, simple-minded because it can give no account of why this dawn of reason should turn up in Europe, or indeed why it should turn up at all. The reason is that it is a political program unwilling to recognize its debt to a past which it is busily repudiating. It is averse to recognizing Christianity as a historical phenomenon rather than as a mere mistake. Let me merely point to one or two obvious ways in which the modern world has emerged out of Christianity, not by repudiation but by a continuous evolution.

Consider the crucial issue of the nature of human beings. The Greeks believed that man was a rational animal, which implied that being human was a function of being rational. Women and slaves being defective in rationality were also less human. Christianity replaced this with the idea that each person was an immortal soul equally valuable to God and constituted of a set of affections, which had been deranged by the Fall. It thus counterposed against the hierarchical structures of society a theological egalitarianism which periodically erupted in trouble for holders of high office, bishops in particular. In the course of developing this complex idea of what it is to be a human being, Christian thinkers evolved the organ called "conscience" which could be incorporated within the new forms of urban life to generate the mode of moral experience we call "individualism." Without this long development, the idea of human rights would be meaningless, as it largely is in other civilizations. The abolition of slavery was a major step in the advance of the progressive project, and it was, of course, almost entirely a Christian achievement.

The essential point may well be that Christianity as a religion was constituted by faith in Jesus as the redeemer. Faith is different from knowledge, and hence Christianity was hardly born before the philosophers were on board working hard to preserve some coherence in a doctrine that was never secure because of the human propensity to get things wrong (or indeed perhaps to get them inconveniently right). One of the earliest of the distinctions necessary to make sense of the world in terms of Christianity was, indeed, that between the secular and the sacred on which secularism itself depends. Another given in the gospels is the distinction between the civil and the sacred powers, between church and state. These are indispensable constituents of the pluralism at the heart of Western civilization. The relation between theology and science is much too complicated to be dealt with here, but one might point out that the emergence of experimental science (which allowed the modern world so greatly to surpass the Greeks) depended upon the proposition that man could only understand what man had made himself. Since nature had been made by God, our only way of learning about it was not by speculation but by "putting it to the torture" as Bacon put it.

These considerations are perhaps enough for our limited purpose: namely, to make it clear that the question "Do you believe in God?" is a very bad indicator of where anyone might conceivably stand on the relation between our Christian inheritance on the one hand and our modern sophistication on the other. They are also sufficient, I think, to indicate that the common identification of Christianity as a repressive force by invoking the Crusades, the Inquisition, and the trial of Galileo is merely a tedious misunderstanding of history. What human institution, one may ask, doesn't have its ups and downs? But before moving on to make sense of the curious Christophobia of the modern West, I need to indicate why this is, in civilizational terms, so strange a phenomenon.

The minimal account of religion as a human phenomenon must be that it is a set of stories and beliefs human beings tell themselves to account for what lies behind the manageable world (to the extent that it is manageable) in which we live. In other words, a religion is a response to the mystery of the human condition. The going secularist account of human life is that we are part of an evolving organic life that happened to develop on the edge of a minor planet in a universe of unimaginable vastness. Beyond this, questions of meaning and significance are in scientific terms unanswerable, and we tend to follow Wittgenstein: Whereof we cannot speak, thereof we must be silent. We have blocked off religious questions altogether, because they are empirically unanswerable, and people respond in a variety of ways. Some drop the questions and get on with life, others shop for a more exotic set of stories and rituals with which to respond, and many, of course, remain Christian to one degree or another. On the face of it, however, we have a culture which very largely carries on without seriously considering ultimates. We have abandoned the cathedral, and are content to scurry in and out of skyscrapers. So perhaps we are pioneering a new civilizational form in which the issues of human meaning have been recognized as essentially unsolvable, and left to one side. Or, alternatively, we may have transferred the passions appropriate to religion onto beliefs of some other kind.

Philosophers turn everything into preliminaries, and before I get to the main argument, I should perhaps declare my own position here. I am a simple child of secular times, and a sceptic, but one impressed by the grandeur and complexity of Christian intellectuality. The Voltairian and the village atheist, seen from this perspective, look a little shallow. In the vast rambling mansion of our civilization, the cobwebbed gothic wing containing our religious imagination is less frequented than previously, but it certainly remains a haunting presence.

And, of course, we have bought into substitutes. In secular terms, their basic feature must be that they look more like science than religion. Let me suggest that educated Europeans are today united in terms of a project we characterize as the perfecting of the human condition by the power of reason. Devotion to this perfection leads us to scan the news each day in search of signs of the times: we focus on the fate of rights and how they are violated round the world, at the poverty which signals the imperfection of inequality, at peace processes leading us forward and violence and bigotry dragging us backward. The aim is to foster the happiness of mankind, and we are buoyed up when the signs are good and cast down when they are bad. We seek, if we respond to this new form of devotion, to harness human power to control human folly, inspired by our past successes in triumphing over the vagaries of nature. There are many internal disagreements over what this perfection might mean, though currently there is a large measure of agreement that the central problem is war and other forms of human conflict. All of this can be subsumed under the famous slogan that mankind must take its destiny into its own hands.

We can, I think, distinguish three stages, or more exactly variants, in the development of this project. The first is the entirely familiar idea of progress. Nineteenth-century Europeans in contact with technologically incapable people not only brought them the benefits of Christian salvation but also clean water, railways, and industry. The whole package was understood as a god-like increase in human power controlling human circumstance. This was profoundly disruptive in other cultures because they had long been accustomed to a different idea of the balance between what could be changed and what must be endured. Here from the West came a set of aliens teaching that nasty things that had long seemed inevitable could be remedied. But the actual situation of these interesting aliens was that they were missionaries not only to other cultures, but also to the mass of people in their own culture as well. Technologists, administrators, and intellectuals had to become, as Ernest Gellner has called them, "the Westernizers of the West." The great figures of the movement to improve the lives of the heathen often happened to be Christian missionaries like Schweitzer and Mother Teresa, but in Europe itself, and in America and other Western parts, they were rulers and social reformers.

Christians might be believers in progress, but progressives were likely to find Christianity an optional extra, if not an actual impediment to the advance of reason. Christians were therefore often suspicious of progress. "To become a popular religion," wrote W. R. Inge, "it is only necessary for a superstition to enslave a philosophy. The Superstition of Progress had the singular good fortune to enslave at least three philosophies—those of Hegel, of Comte, and of Darwin." Beyond European civilization the demand was indeed for philosophies of one kind or another, not for religions, which many of them already had in abundance. Gunpowder, clean water, and vaccines were the thing, not routes to salvation. For most of the beneficiaries of Western enlightenment abroad, Christianity was for understandable reasons increasingly understood as an optional extra. The crucial thing was that scientists seemed to have a method of coming to agreement about what was true and what worked, whereas Christians and exponents of other religions seemed locked into endless irresolvable disputes. Hence the initial response of Indians, Chinese, and others was likely to be admiration for the technical skills of Europeans, and contempt for their beliefs and manners.

The smart thing to do seemed to be to copy Western technology and throw the rest away. Like most versions of smart cherry picking, this one turned out not to work. The baffling thing was that in often mysterious ways, the generation of railways, medical surgery, military science, and so on seemed to be inseparable from Western institutions and ideas. Foreigners are always detestable, and superior foreigners even more so. The horrible possibility loomed that in order to cut themselves in on this Western power, non-Europeans might have actually to become Europeans themselves. Even outsiders as culturally close to Europe as the Russians developed strong countercurrents to Western influence, as with the Slavophiles. The same was true in Eastern Europe. Even Germany before the First World War conceived of itself as a spiritually superior nation quite different from the shallow technology of the French and the British.

Progress was a development that sought to bring reason and betterment both to the poor in Western countries, and to the downtrodden in the rest of the world. It was a movement of benevolence, but benevolence at this level of human relations is not easy to distinguish from power. The West, it seemed, was bent on taking over the world. The result would be to turn everyone into imitation Europeans, and foreign cultures rebelled. It made no difference that their rebellion against the benevolence of the West could only be articulated in ideas and institutions (nationalism, self-determination, parliaments, etc.) borrowed from the arrogant West itself. Outsiders used whatever instruments were to hand and demanded for themselves the political freedoms the West claimed to champion.

This repudiation of progress hardly stopped the project in its tracks. Western ingenuity was more than equal to the task of creating more assimilable forms of Westernization. The trick was to combine some version of Westernization, or perhaps we should say modernization, that was both a recipe for "joining the modern world" and also the expression of a powerful hostility to the West itself. Such a package would allow resentful Chinese and Indians to absorb the West while at the same time rejecting it. Reason and passion might thus both be accommodated. This was the achievement, though not indeed quite the intention, of Marx and other socialists for whom Westernizing the West was no less central a project than spreading enlightenment to the rest of the world.

What I am treating as the "stages" of the Enlightenment Project are not, indeed, successive. There is a good deal of overlap. The Marxist version of progress was communism, and the term may stand for all forms of collectivism which took off from the view that bourgeois individualism had merely been one phase in the emergence of modernity, and one that was imminently to be superseded by higher communal forms of association. In its beginnings, communism counted itself as the real inheritor of progress. Whereas the enlightened looked to reason, communists looked to revolution as the way of blasting a path through reaction to the promised land of technology and equality, or soviets plus electricity. The Marxist version of human perfectionism had an irresistible appeal during most of the twentieth century, partly because it offered the promise not only of catching up with the West, but also of skipping a stage and jumping to the head of the progressive convoy.

The great drama of twentieth-century history was the failure of this promise. Far from solving human conflict, the revolution of humanitarian fraternity served merely to increase it. Far from forging ahead into the modern world, the countries that followed this path lost much of their moral or social capital and ended up with an obsolete rusting industry built over a pile of corpses. It became clear that perfecting the human condition was a bit more complicated than it had seemed.

The failure of Communism was consecrated in the fall of the Soviet Union. The remarkable thing is that, as in most cases when prophecy fails, the faith never faltered. Indeed, an alternative version had long been maturing, though cast into the shadows for a time by enthusiasm for the quick fix of revolution. It had, however, been maturing for at least a century and already had a notable repertoire of institutions available. We may call it Olympianism, because it is the project of an intellectual elite that believes that it enjoys superior enlightenment and that its business is to spread this benefit to those living on the lower slopes of human achievement. And just as Communism had been a political project passing itself off as the ultimate in scientific understanding, so Olympianism burrowed like a parasite into the most powerful institution of the emerging knowledge economy—the universities.

We may define Olympianism as a vision of human betterment to be achieved on a global scale by forging the peoples of the world into a single community based on the universal enjoyment of appropriate human rights. Olympianism is the cast of mind dedicated to this end, which is believed to correspond to the triumph of reason and community over superstition and hatred. It is a politico-moral package in which the modern distinction between morals and politics disappears into the aspiration for a shared mode of life in which the communal transcends individual life. To be a moral agent is in these terms to affirm a faith in a multicultural humanity whose social and economic conditions will be free from the causes of current misery. Olympianism is thus a complex long-term vision, and contemporary Western Olympians partake of different fragments of it.

To be an Olympian is to be entangled in a complex dialectic involving elitism and egalitarianism. The foundational elitism of the Olympian lies in self-ascribed rationality, generally picked up on an academic campus. Egalitarianism involves a formal adherence to democracy as a rejection of all forms of traditional authority, but with no commitment to taking any serious notice of what the people actually think. Olympians instruct mortals, they do not obey them. Ideally, Olympianism spreads by rational persuasion, as prejudice gives way to enlightenment. Equally ideally, democracy is the only tolerable mode of social coordination, but until the majority of people have become enlightened, it must be constrained within a framework of rights, to which Olympian legislation is constantly adding. Without these constraints, progress would be in danger from reactionary populism appealing to prejudice. The overriding passion of the Olympian is thus to educate the ignorant and everything is treated in educational terms.

Laws for example are enacted not only to shape the conduct of the people, but also to send messages to them. A belief in the power of role models, public relations campaigns, and above all fierce restrictions on raising sensitive questions *devant le peuple* are all part of pedagogic Olympianism.

Olympianism is the characteristic belief system of today's secularist, and it has itself many of the features of a religion. For one thing, the fusion of political conviction and moral superiority into a single package resembles the way in which religions (outside liberal states) constitute comprehensive ways of life supplying all that is necessary (in the eyes of believers) for salvation. Again, the religions with which we are familiar are monotheistic and refer everything to a single center. In traditional religions, this is usually God; with Olympianism, it is society, understood ultimately as including the whole of humanity. And Olympianism, like many religions, is keen to proselytize. Its characteristic mode of missionary activity is journalism and the media.

If Olympianism has the character of a religion, as I am suggesting, there would be no mystery about its hostility to Christianity. Real religions (by contrast with test-tube religions such as ecumenism) don't much like each other; they are, after all, competitors. Olympianism, however, is in the interesting position of being a kind of religion which does not recognize itself as such, and indeed claims a cognitive superiority to religion in general. But there is a deeper reason why the spread of Olympianism may be measured by the degree of Christophobia. It is that Olympianism is an imperial project which can only be hindered by the association between Christianity and the West.

Consider another rather more obviously imperial project. It appears to be the case that Colonel Gadaffi of Libya wants to fuse Libya with the whole of Africa. This would seem to be an absurd enterprise, given that Libya is small and Africa vast. The Colonel seeks, however, to "melt and merge [Libya] in Africa." The cost of this adventure is in one way catastrophic: Libya would cease to exist. But on the other hand, Libya would in a sense become Africa. It would have the run of all that water, those raw materials, that exploding population, etc. This is the image of a grandiose project of takeover, and it might stand, I suggest, as an image of the Olympian project of turning the whole world into an expression of Western prosperity and human rights. The cost might well be abandoning the particular character of Western civilization as an historic entity, but Olympianism might also be the salvation of mankind.

In reality, of course, you can't give up your identity, because you are what you are. It's a fantasy. You can, however, toss away the scraps of your past that seem to be an impediment to your present ambitions, as some

Olympians have done in apologizing for the Crusades, the Inquisition, the Conquest of the Americas, slavery, and anything else apologizing for which might curry favor with one part of the "Third World" or another. Above all, however, Olympianism seeks to repudiate its own religious basis. The last thing a missionary rationalism needs is a noisy minority reminding outsiders that the project of world justice as currently advanced is a spin-off from Western civilization. Worse, Christianity as a reminder of this fact is exactly the thing likely to provoke irrational resistance to the message. The basis of much of the visceral hatred of Christianity today is that it contradicts the ambition to present the West as the source of pure reason and compassion. Very similar Olympian passions may well account for the rising hatred of Israel, construed as a vehicle of religious dogmatism standing in the way of the West's accommodation with the whole Islamic world.

The Olympian project now takes the form of advancing world government by judicializing political conflicts, and its central instrument is in expanding treaty commitment to human rights and in creating international criminal law. The setback (for Olympians) of Colonel Gaddaffi's Libya becoming the Chair of the U.N. Committee on Human Rights suggests that there is a certain unreality in these international organizations, but Olympians think in the long term. They have, after all, been working on the project since Woodrow Wilson and the League of Nations. Failure in the 1930s was redeemed after 1945 by the creation of the United Nations, which accorded international bureaucracies some power over most of the important political problems. Politicians can often be persuaded to sign uplifting treaties even at the cost of creating problems for their own constitutions. An imagined place in history is a powerful inducement to a politician. The treaties signed soon come to be understood by lawyers and journalists, always keen to expand their power, as another step forward in the process of making a better world.

They are even spoken of as if they constituted international law. Certainly Olympian high-mindedness is a powerful enough card in public opinion to make any denunciation of these instruments by democratic governments a perilous adventure. The concept of "the world community" flattered the West, which was therefore prepared to foot the bills. It is however an empty expression since the world community neither covers the world nor constitutes a community. The Iraq crisis of 2002–2003 made it very clear that the executive element of the "world community" (if there is any) is to be found in the United States. The General Assembly of the U.N. is not to be taken very seriously as a legislature.

Progress, Communism, and Olympianism: these are three versions of the grand Western project. The first rumbles along in the background of our thought, the second is obviously a complete failure, but Olympianism is not only alive but a positively vibrant force in the way we think now. Above all, it determines the Western moral posture towards the rest of the world. It affirms democracy as an ideal, but carefully manipulates attitudes in a nervous attempt to control opinions hostile to Olympianism, such as beliefs in capital or corporal punishment, racial, and other forms of prejudice, national self-assertion—and indeed, religion.

The essence of the Olympian moral posture is a kind of humility. Whatever it has, it is keen to share—technology especially. A just world is an offer to be accepted, not a command to be obeyed. The project being to bring everyone into the world community, Olympians will make whatever sacrifices are required. It will not only pick up the expenses, but abandon anything in its own past that might be a sticking point to non-Western peoples. Humility amounts to the offer of accommodation to others on terms that all sides can agree upon, and the great virtue of the humble is that they can recognize, own up to and apologize for their faults.

Such a moral posture comes naturally to the Olympian because it merely extends to the Third World the precedence accorded to the poor when deciding public policy in the liberal democratic states of the West itself. The old familiar social question—how to deal with the poor—has suddenly turned up in a civilizational context. "The test of a civilization," Olympians somewhat implausibly say to each other, "is how it treats its poor and vulnerable." The rhetoric of Western elites is steeped in self-criticism about the inequalities of contemporary Western societies. Ideally, the Western elites would like to see, or at least imagine they would like to see, an order of things which dispenses, or at least seems to dispense, with inequality, indeed with any form of the exercise of power. The aim of the Olympian project in this area is to replace as the basis of order irrational passions such as fear of punishment. They ought to give way to more rational expedients such as understanding and therapy. As in all versions of the Enlightenment, "education" is central, but one needs distancing quotes around the term "education" to make it clear that we are referring to a process that aims to produce people of a certain type: in other words, not education at all, but training. And the basis of this training will be to make people empirically flexible but morally rigid.

Having developed a welfarist moral and political posture, the Olympian takes easily to expressing the same posture in international affairs. That notably coercive institution the state is now pronounced a survival from the past. The idea of governing has not quite disappeared from politics, but the term "governance" is preferred, not only because it sounds more arcane, but also because it suggests that laws and rules "emerge" out of a society rather than be made by some sovereign body. Rules, laws, edicts, recommendations, and so on turn up in our lives without apparently being touched by human breath; they come from bodies so remote—preferably supranational if not international—that one may take their wisdom for granted. And if there should be muttering about the burdens this concern for the world's poor might impose, Olympians have taught their democratic populations to think of themselves as generous and compassionate to suffering classes of people. They have large funds available for subsidizing the Third World poor in their endeavors to improve themselves. In any case, Western people are extraordinarily generous about helping those who suffer in remote places.

One of the central problems of Olympianism has always been with the nation-state and its derivative, nationalism. A world of nation-states is one of constant potential antipathy. It makes something of a mockery of the term "world community." Hence it is a basic tenet of Olympianism that the day of the nation-state has gone. It is an anachronism. And on this point, events have played into the hands of this project. The homogeneity of these nation-states is a condition of democracy, but it also facilitates the wars in which they have engaged. If, however, homogeneity were to be lost as states became multicultural, then they would turn into empires, and their freedom of action would be seriously constrained. Empires can only be ruled, to the extent that they are ruled, from the top. They are ideal soil for oligarchy. Olympianism is very enthusiastic about this new development, which generates multiculturalism. Those who rule a rainbow society will have little trouble with an unruly national will, because no such thing remains possible. The Olympian lawyer and administrator will adjudicate the interests of a heterogeneous population according to some higher set of principles. Indeed, quite a lot of this work can be contracted out to independent agencies of the state, agencies whose judgments lead on to judicial tribunals in cases of conflict. This is part of a process in which the autonomy of civil institutions (of firms to employ whom they want, of schools to teach curricula they choose, and so on) is steadily eroded by centralized standards. Multiculturalism in the name of abstract moral standards has the effect of restricting freedom across the board.

Like the Libyans in Africa, the Olympians in the West are turning a plural thing like a civilization into a rigid thing like a project. There is a dire purposiveness about the Olympian passion for signing up to treaties and handing power over to international bureaucrats who want to rule the world. Everything down to the details of family life and the modes of education are governed and guided so as to fit into the rising project of a world government. The independence of universities in choosing whom to admit, of firms choosing whom to employ, of citizens to say and think what they like has all been subject to regulation in the name of harmony between nations and peace between religions. The playfulness and creativity of Western societies is under threat. So too is their identity and freedom.

Globalization is having very odd effects on our thinking, but none is more curious than the Olympian project of turning the West's cultural plurality into a homogenized rationalism designed for export to, and domination over, the rest of the world. Turning a civilization into a project by putting everything through a kind of rationalist strainer so as to remove every item that might count as prejudice, bigotry, and superstition will leave Europeans meandering without a compass in a wonderland of abstractions. It reminds one of Aesop's frog, who wanted to be as big as an ox, and blew himself up more and more, his skin becoming thinner and thinner, till he burst.

June 2003

The Phobia of Phobias

John Gross

L ONDON RECENTLY UNDERWENT a visit from Dr. Yusuf al-Qaradawi. A celebrated Muslim cleric, born in Egypt but based in Qatar, he had accepted an invitation to address a conference organized by the Muslim Association of Britain.

Dr. al-Qaradawi (who is barred from entering the United States) is a man of strong views. He condones wife beating. He advocates the persecution—indeed, under some circumstances, the extermination—of homosexuals. He is a fervent supporter of Palestinian suicide bombings, including bombings carried out by children, and he has offered up prayers for the destruction of "crusaders and infidels." (He also maintains that McDonald's and Pizza Hut are part of an international Jewish conspiracy.)

Not surprisingly, the news of his visit to London prompted widespread protests. These were countered by British Muslim spokesmen with reassurances that he was held in high regard by coreligionists for his learning and piety. One or two added that he should in fact be considered a moderate (an alarming thought, if true). And when he arrived in Britain, al-Qaradawi himself was offered a platform by the *Guardian* newspaper—an interview in which he claimed that his views had been completely misrepresented. (The published record says otherwise, however, both in print and on the web.)

Extremist Muslim clerics aren't a novelty in Britain, and the whole episode might have died down quickly if it weren't for the role played by the Mayor of London, Ken Livingstone. As readers who follow British affairs will recall, Livingstone is mayor of the whole of London, all 620 square miles of it. His post, which shouldn't be confused with the ancient and largely ceremonial office of Lord Mayor, was created by the Blair government. One of the advantages it was supposed to confer was that

Londoners would at last feel that they had a First Citizen—someone who could serve, if the need arose, as their spokesman and representative.

And how did the First Citizen comport himself on this occasion? Although many opponents of the al-Qaradawi visit hoped that he would join them in their condemnation, there was a case for his saying nothing. The affair wasn't strictly the mayor's business. But as it is, he chose to intervene. He hosted a press conference for al-Qaradawi at City Hall, welcoming him warmly and sitting through a speech in which the cleric defended "martyrdom" operations. At a second conference, on the rights of Muslim women to wear traditional headdress, he hugged him; he invited him to return to London later this year, and lashed out at critics of the visit as bigoted and xenophobic.

People shouldn't have been altogether surprised. On Israel, Livingstone's record is well known; as they say in the British underworld, he has "form." In the 1980s, when he was head of what was then the city's main administrative body, the Greater London Council, he waged a bitter propaganda campaign against Israel. He said some peculiar things, too. In one interview he asserted that Jews in Britain were organizing a secret network of fascist-style paramilitary groups.

From here to his embrace of Dr. al-Qaradawi some twenty years later was no great step—not as far as the politics of the Middle East are concerned, at least. But it might still seem odd that he shouldn't have felt the need to distance himself a little from the good doctor on other issues. He has always been an outspoken champion of feminists and gay activists. Far milder examples of prejudice against women or gays than al-Qaradawi's would normally incur his wrath. The only conclusion one can draw is that for the time being he regards homophobia and the maltreatment of women as secondary issues. They have been overshadowed in his mind by a greater menace—the phobia of phobias, Islamophobia.

He is hardly alone in this. The idea that Islamophobia is the most dangerous of current social evils had taken root within days, perhaps even hours, of 9/11, and since then it has become widely accepted wisdom. We are constantly warned to be on guard against prejudice toward Muslims. We have inevitably been told that British society is "institutionally Islamophobic."

Islamophobia is a word which means a number of different things, and the confusion which can result suits many of those who use it very well. At one extreme it covers the brutal racism of the BNP (the British National Party) and its supporters. But it is also freely employed to describe virtually any adverse criticism, however well-founded, of Muslim activities. Among educated people (who are probably the only ones who use it) it is a scare word. It serves not so much to denote a phobia as to instill one.

The BNP is an ugly phenomenon, but it remains relatively small and marginal. Meanwhile, the media tend to be chary of highlighting the increasing importance of Muslim pressure in mainstream British politics. Earlier this summer there were shock results in two simultaneous parliamentary by-elections, in constituencies in Birmingham and Leicester. Both seats had previously been held by Labour with solid majorities: in one, they just scraped home against the Liberal Democrats (the only major party whose leadership is firmly against the Iraq war), in the other, the Liberal Democrats defeated them. That the Muslim vote played a significant part in the outcome could hardly be ignored—in both constituencies Muslims comprise around 20 percent of the electorate—but there was rather less reporting of the fact that in both cities the candidates outbid each other in falling in with the views put to them by local Muslim leaders. Those views primarily concerned Iraq and Palestine, rather than domestic issues; in Leicester, just so nobody should miss the point, the tribunal which questioned candidates called itself the "Friends of Al-Aqsa Committee."

No doubt it is important to maintain a sense of perspective. In Britain as a whole, Muslims at present form only around 3 percent of the population. But the proportion seems bound to grow (both through immigration and on account of the higher Muslim birthrate), and in the meantime Muslims stand out by their greater religious commitment. According to official sources, the number of British Muslims attending a mosque at least once a week has now overtaken the number of Anglicans attending church.

This last statistic reveals as much about the Church of England as it does about Islam. The decline of the "C of E" has been a notable feature of English life over the past generation or two. It is a decline shared, in varying degrees, by other Christian denominations in Britain, but in the case of what is still, technically speaking, the Established Church, the repercussions go well beyond questions of religious belief. The Church was until recently one of the central institutions of English society; it did a great deal to give English culture its distinctive tone.

What is particularly sad (and often, alas, also quite funny) is the inanity in which it has been willing to indulge in an effort to win back popularity. The Bishop of London, for instance, has solemnly urged churches to learn from the example of "clubbing." ("There is a sense of belonging and openness to one another and sometimes even what people describe as a mystical experience, induced by the music and dancing . . ." Chemical substances play their part, too: "Ecstasy, the drug, comes with a mystic sign embossed upon the tablets.") And then there is *Good as New*, a new updated version of the New Testament, in which Peter becomes Rocky, Mary Magdalen becomes Maggie,

Barabbas becomes Barry, and Zacchaeus for some reason becomes Keith. Nor is it only names that have been given a makeover. "Thou art my beloved Son, in whom I am well pleased" is transmogrified into "That's my boy! You're doing fine!" It used to be "Woe unto you, scribes and Pharisees!"; now the "Holy Joes and humbugs" are told to "take a running jump."

Strictly speaking, the Church of England isn't responsible for *Good as New*. It is the work of a freelance translator, and is published independently. But it does carry a foreword by the Archbishop of Canterbury, Rowan Williams, in which he describes it as a work of "extraordinary power" and commends it for being "close to the prose and poetry of ordinary life."

Perhaps one shouldn't judge too harshly, at a time when Christianity is increasingly on the defensive. Christians have found themselves up against a human rights culture which insists that they must not only respect other religions, but frequently give way to them as well. Even a Christian playgroup for toddlers is liable to be monitored to make sure that it celebrates non-Christian festivals.

Amid all this, the government is introducing legislation to make the promotion of religious hatred a crime. It is plainly designed to protect Muslims, since other groups are regarded as being protected by existing laws against race-hate, and it will no doubt do some good, but in the light of the looser definitions of Islamophobia that fly around, it also opens up the possibility of serious restrictions on free speech.

At least there is very little chance of the Church of England falling foul of the new law. It has bent over backwards to avoid offending Muslim opinion—maintaining an eerie silence on the persecution of Christians in the Sudan, for instance. Church leaders have also been prominent critics of the war in Iraq, while the entire bench of Anglican bishops recently sent a letter to Tony Blair deploring the influence of "Christian Zionists" (curious phrase) on American policy in the Middle East.

And now Rowan Williams is planning to fly to Cairo to deliver a message of reconciliation in an address at Al-Azhar University on September 11. It takes two to tango, however, and it takes two to reconcile, and it doesn't augur well that Muslim leaders are reported to have welcomed his mission as an opportunity to dispel the ill will created by his predecessor, Archbishop Carey, who earlier this year criticized them for failing to condemn suicide bombers unequivocally. No one doubts Williams's good intentions, but if he doesn't offer criticism as well as praise when he is in Cairo, the chief practical result of his visit will probably be to confirm Islamic terrorists in their conviction that the West is soft and fundamentally weak.

September 2004

Atatürk's Creation

David Fromkin

C AN TRADITIONAL CULTURES in the third world break with the past in order to enjoy modern civilization? Ought they to do so? And at what price? Can a leader persuade or force his nation to make so drastic a change? Questions such as these were brought to the rest of the planet by the Europeans who explored, invaded, and settled the other continents in the years following 1492. Half-a-millennium later, we still are looking for answers to some of them.

I would have said that at least one thing seems clear. It is the apparent truth charmingly illustrated in *Anna and the King of Siam*: that a people cannot be made European—or modern or Western, call it what you will— merely by the fiat of their ruler, no matter how powerful he or she may be. I would have said it, except that it would have not been entirely true. For it is contradicted by the achievement of Mustafa Kemal in creating the modern Turkish Republic. That is what makes Kemal's story of more than intrinsic and historic interest. Indeed it is central to one of the great on-going world dramas: the clash of modern civilizations with religious fundamentalists of various persuasions. Can the cause of modernization be won by politics, and from the top down? Is that what Kemal's story shows? And what, really, was Kemal's story?

Until recently, in English we depended upon the biography by Patrick, Lord Kinross (1964). Although based on wide personal knowledge and experience, as well as many interviews, Kinross's is an uncritical "official" account. It does not cite sources, which therefore cannot be checked. Kinross was a first-rate storyteller, so the book is a good read, but it is unreliable: many a tale sounds as though much improved in the telling. Kinross relied heavily on the mythmaking account Kemal himself provided of his life and times in a six-day, thirty-six-hour speech to his political party in

1927. Kinross accepted this work of imagination as though it were strictly factual.

In the nearly four decades since the Kinross volume appeared, there has been a wealth of publications in Turkish, including many firsthand accounts by Kemal's associates and other eyewitnesses to the events. Some of this was made available to English-speaking readers in a biography by Vamik D. Volkan and Norman Itzkowitz (1984), which, however, suffered from being a "psychobiography," with a focus on psychological analysis of a person whom neither author knew.

For years, those who take an interest in these matters have been waiting for Andrew Mango to complete and publish his biography, which now has appeared and immediately has taken its place as the definitive study (*Atatürk: The Biography of the Founder of Modern Turkey*; Overlook Press, 2002). Born in Istanbul, Mango has been writing about Turkish affairs for more than forty years. He has a mastery of the sources, and so at last we have an account that, episode by episode, is accurate and balanced. It reveals the long suppressed darker aspects of its subject, showing us a far more complex personality than we had seen before. Curiously, however, the main lines of Kemal's policy and accomplishments emerge as having been much the same as we had believed them to be in the past.

Mustafa Kemal was born in about 1880. We are uncertain of the day or month and have to guess even at the season: it may have been spring. Like most Muslims at the time, he bore only one name. He was Mustafa. Later, as a student, he assumed the surname "Kemal" (which means "perfection"). Later still, he obtained from his followers the name "Atatürk" ("Father of the Turks") and was called the "Ghazi": a warrior for Islam or the "Crusader."

In large part he created his own name, and also his own history. He was born in the Balkans. In physical appearance he resembled the Balkan people amongst whom his family lived: Slavs and Albanians. But his parents spoke Turkish as their native language, and when Mustafa became a nationalist he claimed that he descended from Turkish nomads who had settled in the Balkans in the service of their sultan.

Actually there was no such thing as a Turkish ethnicity. Turkish was, if anything, a language group. The Turkish-speaking warrior hordes that poured out of Central Asia beginning a thousand years ago were of mixed blood. Animists at first, they converted over the course of years to Islam. One such war band, the followers (according to tradition) of a certain Osman (hence "osmanlis," or, as they became, "Ottomans"), went on to build an empire that at its height half a millennium ago comprised the Arab-speaking Middle East, North Africa, and Balkan Europe all the way to the gates of Vienna.

The Ottoman Empire was a dynastic state: an assemblage of disparate lands and peoples having in common their subjection to the occupant of the Ottoman throne in Constantinople (today's Istanbul). The empire contained between two and three dozen "nations"—depending upon how nationality is defined. As generation after generation of Turkish warriors settled on the estates that were their rewards for military service, new warriors were recruited from among the conquered peoples, and acquired the Turkish language and the Muslim faith. Bulgarian Christians, thus converted, formed over the years a particularly large—and ever larger—percentage of "Turks."

The Ottoman Empire was a theocracy. It was a Muslim state, not a national one. A common religion provided the overriding loyalty that bound the peoples of the Arab-speaking and Turkish-speaking Muslim world together in one commonwealth. It was elsewhere—in the empire's lands in Christian Europe—that internal turmoil erupted. It was there that the full force of nationalism, unleashed by the French Revolution and Napoleon, was felt. The Ottoman retreat from empire at the start of the eighteenth century became a rout by the end of the nineteenth. It was assumed by outside observers that the disintegration would lead to total collapse. The chancellories of Europe hoped and believed that one day soon the Ottoman Empire would retire from all of its Balkan territories, but they worried that the scramble by the Great Powers to pick up the pieces might destroy the balance of power among them and lead to a general war. This was the famous "Eastern Question" that so bedevilled Great Power diplomacy throughout the nineteenth century. The concern proved to be justified. The assassination of Archduke Franz Ferdinand and his wife in Sarajevo on June 28, 1914, a consequence of the clash between Slavic and German peoples about who should have Bosnia when the Ottomans definitely lost it, led to the First World War.

Mustafa Kemal was born at the frontier: in Salonika, capital city of Macedonia. Salonika (today's Greek city of Thessaloniki) was a city largely Jewish and *Dunmeh* (a Jewish sect that had converted to Islam centuries before). It was a center of Freemason activity. Beyond the effective control of the sultan in Constantinople and his secret police, it was alive with subversive ideas. Macedonia was a province at the edge of the empire, coveted by Greece, Bulgaria, and Serbia, a prey to brigandage, and Ottoman troops sent to garrison Macedonia were subject to disaffection.

Kemal came into the world at a frontier in time. His was the last generation of Ottoman army officers. The autocratic Sultan Abdul Hamid II (1842–1918) instituted reform and modernization in his own despotic way, but lost ground to the advancing forces of imperialist Europe. Kemal and his contemporaries saw the empire dying before their eyes. In their own young lifetimes before the First World War, the empire lost much of North Africa and the Balkans.

Like other ambitious young men with few other opportunities, Kemal sought out a military career. The army provided an education and also an engine of change in an otherwise backwards state. Secret societies provided the only outlet for political expression in Abdul Hamid's domains, and, for evident reasons, the military secret societies proved the most effective. Modernization was the theme of their discourse, and warding off European control was their goal. As a young officer, Kemal played a notable role in secret society affairs, but he was eclipsed by the leaders of a group called the Committee for Union and Progress (CUP), more generally known as the "Young Turkey" party.

In the turbulent Macedonia of 1908, the Young Turks sparked off a revolt, followed by a coup d'état in 1913 that brought them to supreme power. They ruled thereafter with a puppet sultan, a brother of the deposed Abdul Hamid. The most conspicuous of the Young Turks, a self-promoting young officer named Enver who married the sultan's niece and made himself minister of war, was well aware of Kemal's abilities and commanding personality, and jealously made sure that he received only obscure appointments.

In power, the Young Turks were uncertain how to go about modernizing the ramshackle empire. Beforehand, they had committed to a partnership among all the two or three dozen peoples of the empire. The Young Turk triumph therefore was greeted with enthusiasm by those released from Abdul Hamid's tyranny. In Europe, too, there were many well-wishers; the British foreign secretary, Sir Edward Grey, was one of those who hoped the Young Turks would prove to be liberal reformers.

For whatever reason, the CUP government instead opted for the rule of Turkish-speaking Muslims (perhaps 40 percent of the empire's population) over Arab speakers (perhaps another 40 percent) and others. Later Enver was to pursue an imperial fantasy: uniting his Turkish-speaking subjects with Turkish-speaking Central Asia so as to form a Turanian state stretching from the Mediterranean to the Chinese frontier.

In pursuit of yet another fantasy, Enver led his colleagues to enter the First World War—which was entirely unnecessary and in the end cost the empire its existence—and to bet on a German victory, which turned out to be a losing wager. Kemal, though an outsider powerless to change government policy, was never prey to such delusions. He was opposed to the war.

Despite Enver's best efforts, Kemal was given a chance to distinguish himself in the war. It was in 1915, when Allied troops invaded the Gallipoli peninsula, the European shore of the Dardanelles strait that leads from the

Mediterranean via the Sea of Marmara, the Bosporus Strait, and Constantinople to the Black Sea. In overall command of the defense was a German general, Liman von Sanders, and he gave Kemal a battlefield command.

With the eye of a tactical genius, Kemal saw the key position on the peninsula, seized the high ground, and held it. Gallipoli, much written about since in the English-speaking world as an Allied failure and an historic tragedy, is remembered in Turkey as a triumph. Kemal emerged from it, and from the entire 1914–1918 conflict, as a war hero of the Ottoman armies.

The defeated Central Powers—Germany, Austria, Hungary, Bulgaria, and the Ottoman Empire—signed separate surrenders in the autumn of 1918. The Young Turkey leaders fled Constantinople and left the country. The feeble sultan was willing to agree to any terms imposed by the Allies, so long as he was allowed to retain his throne. In the event, these terms were harsh almost to the point of being Carthaginian. After wrangling among themselves for almost two years, the Allies forced the sultan's government to sign the Treaty of Sèvres in the summer of 1920, leaving the Turks very little in the way of self-rule.

In 1919 Kemal left for the interior of Asia Minor—what is now Turkey—on an official commission. He found Turkish army groups there that still were intact. In a move reminiscent of Charles de Gaulle, leaving France for London in 1940 after securing the allegiance to himself of French officers, who ranked above him, in order to carry on the battle, Kemal solicited and obtained the support of the commanders of these army groups. Thus began the War of Independence (1919–1923) that led to the establishment, by Mustafa Kemal, of the Turkish Republic.

Britain, France, and the other main Allies had been forced by domestic public opinion and by sentiment within their armed forces to demobilize soon after hostilities ceased. They therefore commissioned Greece to employ its armed forces to impose Allied terms on Turkey. Greece was a principal beneficiary of those terms. But the landing of the hated Christian Greek soldiers in Asia Minor aroused passion in Turkish-speaking Muslims. Turks turned their backs on the sultan and rallied instead to Kemal's nationalist cause.

In defeating the Greeks, Kemal displayed strategic genius. He personally took responsibility—when nobody else would—for ordering his Turkish armies to abandon strategic locations in order to retreat deep into the interior of the country to give battle where he chose, with backs to the wall.

He also showed himself a master of diplomacy in playing off the Allies—Britain, France, and Italy—against one another, and Communist Russia against all of them. His toughness was evident in his dealings with the Soviets, taking what he needed from then and essentially giving nothing in return. He entertained no illusions about their ideology. He formed an "official" Communist party, loyal to himself, that could be joined by those who genuinely believed in Communism. A different fate was in store for those who took their directions from Moscow. A delegation of Turkish Communist officials that arrived from Russia was murdered. Their bodies were dumped in the harbor of Trabzon on the Black Sea. Local thugs did it, believing it, probably correctly, to be Kemal's desire. Later Kemal's soldiers killed the thugs.

Kemal was supremely disciplined in his approach to politics. In making peace with the Allies in 1922–1923, he resisted the temptation to raise his demands when he won. Early on, he had outlined the terms he felt he needed, and never wavered from them. In this he was the statesman that Talleyrand wanted Napoleon to be—and that Napoleon never was.

The Ottoman Empire had lost its Arab-speaking territories in the war. Apart from a disputed border province in the south (Hatay, which Turkey recovered from French Syria in 1938) Kemal did not want them back. To be a modern country, Turkey would have to be a nation-state. In turn, that required a relatively homogeneous population, living in a coherent territory. To Kemal, the empire was a burden to be cast away. Out of its heart, he cut a cohesive new nation.

A British traveler in Ottoman lands before the First World War began his book, "How many people realize, when they speak of Turkey and the Turks, that there is no such place and no such people?" (Sir Mark Sykes, *The Caliphs' Last Heritage*; 1915.) That is one of the things that Kemal changed. Since 1923, there has been a Turkish state and a Turkish people. And Mustafa Kemal did it.

For Mustafa Kemal the conquering *Ghazi*, fighting the War of Independence was somewhat like riding a tiger. The forces that carried him to victory were not his own, and might well consume him in the hour of triumph. The Muslim mullahs were among the chief supporters of Kemal's revolt, enflamed by the Greek Christian landing. Yet Kemal aimed at disestablishing Islam in Turkey. The Young Turkey network had gone underground in 1918 in the autumn of defeat. It remained intact and provided an organizational structure for the nationalist cause. But its first loyalty was to Enver, who schemed to return to contest Kemal's leadership.

The army was the Ghazi's chief instrument, but its commanders expected to participate in a collegial leadership, while Kemal was a dominating personality who could not tolerate equals. From men as from women, he demanded and expected complete loyalty, unquestioning obedience, and what one can only call worshipful admiration.

Victory over the Allies in 1923 therefore was only the beginning. Mustafa Kemal turned next to the taming of his supporters. In scrupulous detail, Mango provides an account of the distasteful episodes in which Kemal drove old friends, allies, and colleagues out of public life. The low point was reached in purge trials that resulted in the hanging of innocents.

Secure in his position as dictatorial president, with a rubber-stamp parliament, a rubber-stamp single political party, and a firm control of an adoring army, Kemal left administration and details to his admirably efficient prime minister Ismet Inonu. Kemal had accumulated as much power in himself to change his country as any ruler possibly could have. It was, besides, really *his* country: he had created it himself.

Unlike third-world leaders today who argue that they can modernize their countries while at the same time retaining their traditional cultures, Kemal believed it necessary to go the whole way. His program was for Turks to become Europeans, and it was breathtaking in its sweep. He abolished the caliphate, and changed the country from a theocracy to a secular republic. He moved its capital city from Istanbul inland to Ankara. He instituted a unified secular education system. He introduced a civil code and emancipated women. He changed the sabbath from Friday to Sunday. He broke the Islamic ban on reproducing human images; statues and pictures were introduced. So was Western music. He ended the ban on alcohol and encouraged the growth of a wine industry. Sermons were to be delivered in the language of the country, Turkish, and no longer in Arabic. Then there was the change to the Latin alphabet and to Western numerals; the introduction of new words; the literacy drive. The traditional head pieces, the fez and the scarf, were banned. It was a total cultural revolution, imposed by one man's iron will and by the force of an army.

Kemal was a notorious womanizer. Knowing that Andrew Mango would tell the whole story, many have awaited revelations. Rather than stay with one woman, Kemal would try another, and was described as the "chief taster." His adoption of a half-dozen young girls aroused speculation. And his bringing in a black eunuch to serve them aroused gaudy tales. He drank to excess, and died of cirrhosis of the liver.

Mango does tell all, but what is of most interest is what he calls "the forced march to modernity." Can one modernize by marches that are forced? Nowadays a prevailing theory is that the information revolution and other aspects of globalization will bring previously backwards peoples into the modern world: that technology will modernize people, so to speak, from within.

Kemal's approach—commanding people to behave in a modern way—still is being tested. It is the attempt to modernize from without or from above. It has brought Turkey to the verge of being European. But a devotion to religion and to the old ways remains. An elite, especially along the coast, has become thoroughly Western; in the interior there are many who have not.

The army remains faithful to its mission, reflecting its founder both in its strengths and in its limitations. It does not know what to do with a large minority in a nation-state, the Kurds in the Turkish Republic, because Kemal did not know; and it does not know how to expose the religious masses to the rationalist values of the secular world—in other words, to render unto Caesar that which is Caesar's—because Kemal did not know that either.

Kemal was a great soldier, a great diplomat, and a great world statesman. Mango tells us that above all he was a man of the Enlightenment, and "the Enlightenment was not made by saints." He believes that

> Atatürk's message is that East and West can meet on the ground of universal secular values and mutual respect, that nationalism is compatible with peace, that human reason is the only true guide in life.

It says much for the enduring value of his legacy that, despite his great flaws as a human being and the dark side of his dictatorial and often vindictive politics, his army remains loyal to him. Nearly eighty years after he led them to victory, his troops still would follow him to the ends of the earth.

April 2000

From Moses to Musa

Eric Ormsby

I N A BRUTAL antithesis, worthy of some ancient Gnostic, Franz Kafka wrote, "The Bible, sanctum; the world, sputum." In this formulation, the world is something spewed out, a vile off-scouring—quite literally, a "shit-hole" (Scheißtum)—a matrix of infected matter, over against which stands, as its polar opposite, the Word, pristine and incontaminate. Of course, the tuberculosis from which Kafka suffered all his life, and which killed him in the end, gives the second half of his dictum a certain savage poignancy. The distance between sputum and sanctum, only accentuated by the assonance, must be immeasurable; and yet, if this is so, where are we to live? The cruelty of the paradox is not that it disparages the world in favor of the Bible, but that it leaves us no in-between we might comfortably inhabit. Even so, as any attentive reader of Kafka knows, the Bible stands in a subtle continuum with that world of his whose sordid processes and meticulous strictures are as perplexing as anything to be found in Leviticus. On the evidence of his later journals, Kafka often dwelt, if only in daydream, in the land of Canaan; in more prophetic moments, he even saw himself as a latter-day Moses. Moses was permitted to behold, but not to enter, that region of milk and honey; like Moses, Kafka could spy beneath the spittle-lineaments of this fallen world a dimension of existence that moved to the sway of other laws, palpable though hidden from us.

I note this at the outset of a discussion of translation because Kafka's dichotomy seems to me to go to the heart of the enterprise, particularly when a sacred text is involved. In the case of the Bible, translation is unusually thorny (though certain of the same problems vex the translator of the Koran). The meanings of ancient words, questions of textual accuracy, the very weight of centuries of previous commentary and analysis—all these, and other problems, complicate the task enormously; these are the same hurdles that the translator of *Gilgamesh* or Pindar or Lucretius or Kalidasa must somehow leap. But the translator of scripture confronts another order of difficulty.

The difficulty is succinctly exposed in a remark by the historian David Daniel in his superb 2003 study, *The Bible in English: Its History and Influence*, where he states bluntly that "a religion is a revelation of God or it is nothing." If the Bible is just a collection of good yarns or a repository of quaint prescriptions, why should we read it rather than, say, *The Decameron* or *The Arabian Nights* or *The Stories of O. Henry*? The standard answer, of course, is that most of our common heritage, and especially our literature, is incomprehensible without a knowledge of the Bible. True enough—and yet, this cannot really suffice as a reason for immersion in the scriptures. To hunt down the biblical references in "Lycidas" or *Moby-Dick*, while a worthy project, strikes me not only as a diminishment of the Bible but also as a misapprehension of the whole point of reading classic literature. The English and American authors inspired by the Bible from Langland and Chaucer onwards were not composing acrostics for graduate students; they were themselves possessed by scripture in ways we can hardly now comprehend. The force of a biblical allusion lies in the fact that it has been assimilated into the text and is apprehended instinctually by the reader; its impact depends on spontaneous recognition of its source. When Milton speaks of "the pilot of the Galilean lake," it helps me to know the New Testament source of the phrase; the power of the phrase, however, comes not from mere textual recognition but from the more-than-literary authority the words possess.

Moreover, the Bible is enmeshed with the world of human experience in a way that makes it ultimately quite unlike mere literary masterpieces, however it may incidentally resemble them. It teems with exempla who have a strange extra-textual autonomy of their own. For anyone brought up on the Bible, the world quite often seems peopled by Jobs and Josephs, Rebeccas and Ruths and Rachels, and even the occasional Moses. As a child I for one was constantly being admonished by reference to Elijah and the bear or the Prodigal Son, and our neighbors were often apparelled in biblical disguises that would have astonished them; there was more than one long-suffering Jacob or duped Esau and even, in the person of a blowsy good-time girl, a "whore of Babylon." My wretched piggy bank was "the widow's mite" or worse, "the buried talent," and even the scruffy donkey in the petting zoo could in a flash reveal himself "Balaam's ass." Such exempla were not drawn only from the Bible. I got to know quite a few Micawbers and Uriah Heeps as well, not to mention a full array of Snopeses (this was still the South). I would argue, even so, that these personages drew their strength not entirely from the brilliance of their creators, but because they possessed a moral dimension that derived ultimately from biblical precedent, however tacit. They are literary creations who transcend mere literature to become part of life itself.

Robert Alter's new translation of the Hebrew Bible prompts such uneasy thoughts (*The Five Books of Moses: a translation with commentary*, by Robert Alter; W. W. Norton, 1997). His approach is overwhelmingly literary, and even though his premises seem justified by his results (which are generally quite magnificent), a certain uneasiness remains. It would be simplistic, if not misleading, to review a fresh translation of the Hebrew Bible as if it were another new version of Homer or Cervantes, although many of the problems of such translation—technical as well as substantive—are identical. Whether we like it or not, the Bible isn't, and cannot be, a neutral book. Even if it has played no part in one's personal history, its formulations, tales, injunctions, and prohibitions bear on virtually every important human issue, and are still in play today, often excruciatingly so. This is a book people have died for, often haplessly, often bravely. I'm not aware that anyone has gone to the stake over a deviant reading of Proust (or at least, not yet).

That said, Alter's accomplishment is immense. He has produced a translation of the Pentateuch that respects and captures the beauty and majesty of the original; he is unfailingly alert to matters of tone and diction, cadence and tempo, in the Hebrew, to a degree not attained by any previous translator into English. He knows that the virtually unsurpassable King James version tends to doom all rivals; he also knows that translation is too often incorrect both in its interpretations and its tone. Those who proclaim it "inerrant" merely proclaim their own ignorance. His approach therefore has been to model his own version closely on the King James while correcting, modifying, and emending it wherever necessary in accord with philological as well as stylistic dictates. In his translation and in the rich commentary which accompanies it, Alter makes use of the findings and insights of textual criticism, as it has been applied to the biblical text for almost two centuries now, although he is anything but slavish in his acceptance of either its methods or its discoveries. He is as likely to draw on Rashi or David Kimchi or Abraham ibn Ezra as on contemporary exegetes; the results prove that he has been right to do so. Since his guiding principle is aesthetic, he is free to dispense with the picayune quibbling that disfigures so much scriptural commentary; instead, he homes in on the insight—ancient, medieval, or modern—that best illumines the passage at hand from a literary standpoint.

Alter published his translation of Genesis in 1996; he then brought out a version of 1 and 2 Samuel in 1999 under the title *The David Story*. He has now added the remaining four books of what is, rather confusingly, called the *Chumash* (Hebrew), the Pentateuch (Greek), or, quite simply, the Five Books of Moses; that is, the first, and arguably most important, portion of what Jews know as the *Tanakh* (an acronym for *Torah*, *Neviim*, and *Ketuvim*: Torah or "rule," Prophets, and "Writings"). His translations embody the principles which he has been elaborating over decades, in essays and books, as to how one should read the Hebrew Bible. These might be summarized as follows: approach the text as a conscious literary artifact, subject to the same artistic motives and techniques found in other great works of literature; approach it, moreover, as a coherent body of narrative and prescription, not a mere assemblage of disparate texts. Though he accepts emendations to the Hebrew, and even suggests some himself, and though he draws freely on the findings of the "Higher Criticism," his overriding concern is with the Torah as a literary masterpiece, the supreme such masterpiece. His reverence for the Hebrew Bible is not worn piously on his sleeve but rather, exemplified in hundreds of shrewd, astute, profound, and often witty instances of felicitous translation and elegant commentary. His approach has been surprisingly influential; an Orthodox Jewish colleague has told me that Alter's analyses have finally vindicated the traditional view of Moses as the single author of the Five Books against the textual dissecters, a vindication all the more persuasive because it is based on internal evidence.

The chief merit of Alter's now-complete translation lies in his stubborn fidelity to the Hebrew original. This faithfulness is most impressive not merely in his scrupulous accuracy in rendering the meaning of the text, but also in his sensitivity to the shape and sound and timbre and heft of biblical words. He is scathing in dismissing the prevalent practice of translating by context—what he terms "the heresy of explanation"—clinging instead to the relentlessly tangible and physical nature of the original. His tenacity produces wonderful results at times. In Genesis 25:30, when Esau haggles with Jacob over the price of his birthright and is finally tempted by the stew which Jacob, cunning upstart, has prepared, Esau blurts out, "Let me gulp down some of this red red stuff, for I am famished." Esau's exclamation is crude, and crudely rendered, and this is right. Alter comments, "The famished brother cannot even come up with the ordinary Hebrew word for 'stew' (*nazid*) and instead points to the bubbling pot impatiently as (literally) 'this red red.' The verb he uses for gulping down occurs nowhere else in the Bible, but in rabbinic Hebrew it is reserved for the feeding of animals." The text continues, "Therefore is his [Esau's] name called Edom." And Alter comments, "The pun, which forever associates crude impatient appetite with Israel's perennial enemy, is on *'adom 'adom,'* 'this red red stuff.'" The King James, by contrast, translates Esau's outburst as "Feed me, I pray thee, with that same red pottage; for I am faint; therefore was his name called Edom." The only reason I can see for keeping "pottage" is that the phrase has become proverbial (I was always being warned as a child not to "trade my birthright for a mess of pottage"). Otherwise, Alter's rendering is manifestly superior; it makes the old passage spring alive again for us, as though suddenly we were reading the Hebrew itself. The pun on Edom/*'adom* has, of course, been noted before, but through his commentary, Alter gives that too new pith and force.

As it turns out, even the repetition in such a phrase as "red red" is significant, for repetition is a signature feature of biblical style. Alter is rightly caustic about what he calls "the modern abomination of elegant synonymous variation." Throughout his version, with a few exceptions, he retains the repetitive features of the narrative, using his commentary to elucidate the important effect each of these produces. Again, the result has been to strip away the insidious periphrasis that so often muffles the power of the Hebrew in previous translations (including the King James). Alter also defends, and preserves, the parataxis so characteristic of biblical style (all those "ands": "And Jacob saw that there were provisions in Egypt, and Jacob said to his sons, 'Why are you fearful?' And he said . . .")

In this respect I had rather hoped that Alter might restore the mighty opening of Genesis (which the King James version so memorably recreates), but here, rather disappointingly, he follows the interpretation first advanced by the great biblical scholar and exegete E. A. Speiser (of whom, as a translator, he is elsewhere quite critical, and rightly so). Speiser argued that the famous opening verses were not truly paratactic—a sequence of consecutive declarative sentences linked by the Hebrew conjunction *wa* or "and"—but a sentence with a subordinate clause. The King James, echoing the Hebrew, has: "In the beginning God created the heaven and the earth. And the earth was without form, and void; and darkness was upon the face of the deep. And the spirit of God moved upon the face of the waters. And God said, Let there be light: and there was light." Alter translates: "When God began to create heaven and earth, and the earth then was welter and waste and darkness over the deep and God's breath hovering over the waters, God said, 'Let there be light.' And there was light." In my view, this attempt to have it both ways doesn't really work; suspending the phrases within the clausal structure introduces a laxity into the phrasing that misrepresents the original while failing to improve the King James. Nor does the phrase "welter and waste" adequately convey the Hebrew *tohu wa-bohu*. In his notes, Alter suggests that the second word of the phrase is a kind of "nonce term." If so, why not "helter-skelter?" (I'm tempted to suggest "welter-shmelter" but know it hasn't got a prayer.) Alter notes that while "bohu" is meaningless, "tohu" connotes "emptiness" and "is associated with the trackless vacancy of the desert." (He might have noted too that the word is cognate with the Arabic *tīhun*, which does mean "desert.") In the end, even if "without form, and void" isn't ideal—it's a perfect example of Alter's *bête noire*, the "heresy of explanation"—it has the near-invincible advantage of having become embedded in our language, as *tohu wa-bohu* is in Hebrew.

Again, in translating Genesis 2:7, Alter tries to reproduce a famous "etymological pun" in the original. *Adam*—not a proper name here but the generic term for "human"—derives from *'adamah*, "earth" or "soil." Alter cleverly comes up with "then the Lord God fashioned the human, humus from the soil" to give the feeling of the Hebrew. I don't think that this succeeds, for all its ingenuity. "Human" and "humus" aren't connected etymologically; more importantly, the tone is wrong: the collocation of a horticultural with a universal term knocks the pun askew.

Of course, nothing warms the cold heart of a reviewer more than to be able to tweezer out and hold up for display the occasional nit in an otherwise immaculate work. Alter doesn't invariably hit the mark—his translations of biblical poetry are clumsy to my ear—and he makes the occasional factual error. To note but one: when he describes the Hebrew consonant *'ayin*, he describes it as "a glottal stop that might sound something like the Cockney pronunciation of the middle consonant of 'bottle'" and he goes on to characterize it as "a gulping sound produced from the larynx." The *'ayin*, which is still pronounced in Arabic but not in Hebrew, isn't a glottal stop but what linguists call a pharyngeal; students struggling to learn to pronounce it are often advised to mimic a choking camel, not a Cockney.

Alter succeeds best in rendering tone. The majesty of the King James tends to elevate every episode and to lend a deceptive loftiness of tone, even to scabrous passages (in this, it is unlike such forerunners as Wycliffe and Tyndale). Contemporary translations, whether individual efforts such as Speiser's or Edward Everett Fox's bizarre literal rendering (inspired by the German version of Franz Rosenzweig and Martin Buber) or collective productions such as the New English Bible or the Jewish Publication Society's more recent version or—the worst of all, in my view—the ghastly Jerusalem Bible, homogenize the scripture to lethal blandness by the relentless use of conceptual rather than physical language—a modern form of euphemism. Alter's translation in its sheer physicality of word choice and diction shows how fluid in tone and mood the Hebrew original actually is. He alerts us to those moments when the scripture is sarcastic or ironic or downright crude. He is also very good on what he calls the "scary" side of scripture; that is, those moments in which God suddenly displays an inscrutable and murderous aspect of his nature, moments which seem to arise from some earlier and more primitive stratum of belief. Take Exodus 4:24–26, for example:

> And it happened on the way at the night camp that the Lord encountered him [Moses] and sought to put him to death. And Zipporah took a flint and cut off her son's foreskin and touched it to his feet, and she said, "Yes, a bridegroom of blood you are to me." And He let him go. Then did she say, "A bridegroom of blood by the circumcising."

Alter's commentary on this spooky passage—which far surpasses Kafka in both concision and frightfulness—takes up five times as much space as the two verses. Why does God want to kill Moses? What—shades of Josef K.!—is Moses's sin? Is the circumcision some sort of bloody, expiatory substitute? And why the "blood-wedding" overtones? Alter remarks, "There is something starkly archaic about the whole episode. The Lord here is not a voice from an incandescent bush announcing that this is holy ground but an uncanny silent stranger who 'encounters' Moses, like the mysterious stranger who confronts Jacob at the Jabbok ford, in the dark of the night." Alter is especially curious about the "bridegroom of blood" (the King James, following Tyndale, settles, not so successfully, for "a bloody husband") and has much to say that is pertinent on the role of blood in Exodus. Best of all, he respects the enigma without sidestepping its implications; he comments, "The deity that appears here on the threshold of the return to Egypt is dark and dangerous, a potential killer of father or son."

In reading this, and other such disturbing passages throughout the Five Books, I was reminded of a remark which E. M. Cioran made, in an essay on Joseph de Maistre: "You understand nothing about religion if you think that man runs from a fickle or malevolent or even a ferocious god, or if you forget that man loves fear to the point of frenzy." Scripture should startle, should unnerve, us; Alter's translation, unlike blander and more soothing versions, prompts such salubrious shivers in abundance. The literary approach, it turns out, yields other benefits. Alter views biblical personages, not as rigid exemplars, but as characters who undergo transformation over time, growing better or worse according to their vicissitudes or God's unsearchable designs. The gradual delineation of the character of Moses, from foundling to roughneck to stammering emissary of the Almighty, becomes in Alter's hands something at once moving and mighty.

That Alter is exceptionally good at translating the narrative portions of the Torah—what he terms the "Patriarchal Tales" in Genesis, Exodus, Numbers, and Deuteronomy—comes as no surprise. Not only Jacob, but all the ancient personages from Abraham to Moses, from Sarah to Rachel, Leah and Rebecca, emerge from his handling as complex and many-sided figures, with all their shadows intact. Their rough strength, but also their poignancy, comes through, not in a rush but cumulatively; even so coarse a character as Laban reveals new depths. And as in a novel, we witness these prophets and seers and mothers of nations, at once majestic and oddly bumbling, change and grow so that when we encounter them yet again in some new guise—the rough Esau, years later, become a "kind of prince"— the effect is not unlike that of sporadically re-encountering the characters in a novel by Balzac or Proust or Anthony Powell, all novelists who have taught us that character can be comprehended only as a sort of mosaic compounded out of successive, and fragmentary, moments over a whole lifetime. Of course, this aspect of the Torah was always there, and was implicit in earlier translations, but it is perhaps the finest aspect of Alter's accomplishment that it comes through so vividly and freshly in his version.

In Genesis and Exodus, one seems to stand "before the Law," as in Kafka's parable, only to be admitted, unexpectedly and to sovereign bafflement, in Leviticus. Later, bristling with prohibitions, one can proceed to Numbers and Deuteronomy and maybe even catch a glimpse of the Promised Land. Here, though, all is law; and not law in our secular sense, but law governing the most minute and intimate details of daily life, from the rules on permitted and forbidden foods to menstruation and nocturnal emissions to the distinction and treatment of skin diseases to the elaborate protocols of the priesthood and the temple rites. It's a signal trait of this law that its every commandment is equal; the author of Leviticus could never say, *De minimis non curat lex.* Within the jurisdiction of divine law, nothing is trivial. This is Kafka's "sputum world," in all its profuse and suspect detail, brought under sacred sway.

THE ERUPTION of ritual and proscription characteristic of Leviticus occurs throughout the Koran, often in the very midst of the most sublime passages. This is but one of the features of its 114 chapters, or suras, that disconcerts first-time readers. For all its similarities, and debts, to the Hebrew Bible, the Koran is an intrinsically different book. Where the Bible is linear and propelled by narrative, the Koran is circular; it circles insistently over certain spiritual, moral, and cultic themes which recur in an order more akin to music, with its motifs and refrains, than to logic. Its unity comes not from the linear coherence of a historical account but from a certain consistency of voice. That voice may be God's or it may be Muhammad's, but it displays a distinctive timbre, at once earthy and ineffable (and unlike anything else in Arabic), that led Muslims early on to describe it as inimitable and to make that inimitability an article of faith.

We aren't likely to see anthologies along the lines of "The Koran to be Read as Living Literature," such as were once popular with the Bible. The Koran does not lend itself well to this sort of presentation. But such an approach would be more in keeping with the Islamic than with the Jewish scripture, if only because the Koran is explicitly and consciously regarded by Muslims as apronouncement of supreme beauty; the Hebrew Bible is often overwhelmingly beautiful, most notably in the Psalms or the Book of Job, but we don't generally have the impression that its authors were motivated by aesthetic intent. But the beauty of the Koran is held to be a guarantor of its divine origin. "God is beautiful and loves beauty," runs a famous Islamic tradition. One of the most conspicuous aspects of this beauty resides in God's actual speech, which is what the Koran ultimately is believed to be.

The task of the translator of the Koran is easier than that of the biblical translator, for the simple reason that it is impossible. No King James version stands in the way; though earlier English versions, such as those of Arberry, Dawood, Pickthall, Bell, or Yusuf Ali, have their merits, none is completely satisfying. Now the Egyptian-born scholar M. A. S. Abdel Haleem has tried his hand, to impressive effect (*The Qur'an: a new translation*; Oxford University Press, 2004). Abdel Haleem, who teaches at London's School of Oriental and African Studies and is the editor of the *Journal of Qur'anic Studies*, is unusually well qualified; he knows the text inside and out, having memorized it as a child, and he commands a clear and robust English style. His is certainly the best translation to date. It possesses much of the driving urgency of the original; in certain passages it even manages to reproduce the cascading effect of the Arabic, in which phrase builds upon phrase to an incantatory pitch. Here, for example, is his version of sura 22, verses 5–6:

> People, remember, if you doubt the Resurrection, that We created you from dust, then a drop of fluid, then a clinging form, then a lump of flesh, both shaped and unshaped: We mean to make Our power clear to you. Whatever We choose We cause to remain in the womb for an appointed time, then We bring you forth as infants and then you grow and reach maturity. Some die young and some are left to live on to such an age that they forget all they once knew. You sometimes see the earth lifeless, yet when We send down water it stirs and swells and produces every kind of

joyous growth: this is because God is the Truth; He brings the dead back
to life; and He has power over everything.

This is admirably succinct, though wordy compared with the terse original
(literally: "O people, if you are in doubt about Resurrection—lo, We
created you from dust, then from a drop, then from a clot, then from a
gobbet . . ."). And it fails to reproduce one of the signal beauties of the
Arabic: the contrast between the string of inert states (drop, clot, gobbet)
at the beginning and the sudden sprouting of the revivified earth at the end
which is "abuzz" (*ihtazzat* in the Arabic) with growth. Even so, it captures
what Alter would call the "momentum" of the original.

But the impossibility of the task lies in the very nature of the Koran. It
is an "Arabic Koran," as stated in 42:7 and elsewhere. The fact that it is in
Arabic is not incidental but central. And though it is an Arabic of a particular time and place—the early seventh century in the Hijaz—and of a
particular tribe—the Quraysh, of which Muhammad himself was a poorer
member—the language is itself part of the revelation which it conveys. The
Koran is not simply considered to be "inerrant" in content; the style of the
Koran is itself sacrosanct, and not solely its "message." The few audacious
souls who dared to imitate it were cast out as blasphemers and came to
sticky ends. Moreover, the Koran is deemed to be God's actual speech. As
such, it is held, at least by traditional Sunni Muslims, to be "uncreated,"
that is, eternal. In the preface to a 1997 Arabic-English Koran produced in
Riyadh, we read that the Koran contains "the actual words of Allah—not
created, but revealed by Him through the angel Gabriel to a human messenger, Muhammad . . ." Therefore, "the words of Allah can never be translated literally."

Of course, Arabic, like any other language, can be translated, often accurately and sometimes well. But by removing the content of the Koran
from its medium, a fundamental and irreparable distortion occurs. Abdel
Haleem is aware of this problem (for which there is no solution), and does
his best to translate not only accurately but also with a sensitivity to the
penumbra of certain Koranic terms; he supplies brief annotations on individual words, an excellent introduction, and a running commentary
drawn from the immense exegetical literature in Arabic. To give a sense of
the strengths and the limitations of his version, here is an excerpt from sura
29:41–44:

> Those who take protectors other than God can be compared to spiders
> building themselves houses—the spider's is the frailest of all houses—if
> only they could understand. God knows what things they call upon beside

Him: He is the Mighty, the Wise. Such are the comparisons We draw for
people, though only the wise can grasp them. God has created the heavens
and the earth for a true purpose. There truly is a sign in this for those who
believe.

It is a strange and fascinating aspect of the Koran that like certain crystalline
structures, any section taken tends to mirror the whole. Here we find repeated emphasis on "signs." In a certain sense, contrary to popular impression, the Koran is the thinking man's scripture; it is incessantly enjoining
mankind to consider or reflect or ponder. The universe is an immense system of signs, human intelligence an exercise in semiosis. The spider's house
is a sign, as are the heavens and the earth, and signs are meant to induce
understanding. Belief provides the decipherment of creation; unbelief
blinds. This little passage is built upon contrasts: the fragile house of the
spider stands opposed to "the heavens and the earth"; God is wise, and
only the wise grasp His "comparisons"; those who rely on other than God
are set in contrast with "those who believe."

Abdel Haleem tends to engage in Robert Alter's "heresy of explanation." In the Arabic, the sentence which he translates as "God has created
the heavens and earth for a true purpose" reads "God created the heavens
and the earth in truth." What this means has been debated by theologians
and mystics for centuries and has led to some quite finely spun metaphysics.
By settling on "for a true purpose," he has limited the resonance of the
original phrase; he has also committed himself to a particular theological
stance: there is no suggestion of "purpose" in the Arabic; for many Sunni
Muslims, to assign purpose to God's actions is suspect. Again, in translating 22:41, he writes, "God controls the outcome of all events" when the
Arabic says, more simply, "God's is the outcome of events" (or: "the outcome belongs to God"), not necessarily the same thing. In such small
touches throughout his translation, Abdel Haleem acts more as an interpreter than a translator, often imparting tiny, almost inconspicuous, spins
to recurrent phrases.

He is exceptionally good at sorting out the different voices of the
Koran. It is clear in his version when God is speaking to Muhammad or to
Himself, or when Muhammad is speaking either to God or to his flock. In
this respect, in any number of passages, the Koran seems almost to
represent God's interior monologue. Sometimes He even muses over past
events and seems to be offering a gloss on His own actions. For example, in
sura 28, God comments on His decision to rescue the Israelites from Egyptian bondage and says, "We wished to favour those who were oppressed in
that land, to make them leaders, the ones to survive, to establish them in

the land, and through them show Pharaoh, Haman, and their armies the very thing they feared." So prevalent is this tendency throughout the biblical narratives of the Qur'an that it might even be read as a kind of divine editorializing on the prophetic past.

The Koran is even less separable from the world than the Hebrew Bible. Though the Koran is deemed uncreated and eternal, while the world is created and temporal, both contain the signs of divine wisdom, and both are susceptible of exegesis. Once while working in Rabat, I met a young doctoral student who had just published his thesis, a copy of which he gave to me. To my surprise, it was a systematic exposition of the secret correspondences between the verses of the Koran and the natural world; the idea was prompted by the fact that the Arabic word for "verse" and for "sign" is the same (*ayah*). This world is the "lower world" (*al-dunya*) and not to be compared with scriptural revelation, but it too has its chapters and its verses crying out for decipherment. This student would have found Kafka's statement not only comprehensible but perhaps even acceptable. For a world tissued with scriptural interleavings is, in the end, little more than a ghostly palimpsest of the Word.

October 2005

The Legacy of Russell Kirk

David Frum

R USSELL KIRK, WHO died this spring at his home in Mecosta, Michigan, at the age of seventy-five, has left behind an intellectual and literary achievement as huge as it is difficult to categorize. He was not exactly a political theorist, nor really a philosopher, certainly not a historian; and yet his work speaks profound truths about politics, philosophy, and history. An ardent enemy of Communism, he was barely more enthusiastic about the commercial civilization of America. An unrelenting critic of "King Numbers," he championed a Goldwaterite conservatism that owed far more to the populism of Jefferson, Jackson, and Tom Paine than to the prescriptive politics of Edmund Burke and John Adams. A scourge of ideology and abstraction in politics, he determinedly refused to pay any attention to the circumstances and context in which the thinkers he studied had lived. He loved old cathedral towns and country fields, ancient mansions and Gothic universities; he hated cars, television, and shopping malls. For all his patriotism, one has to wonder how comfortable he ever really felt in late-twentieth-century America. "Against the lust for change," Kirk wrote of his admired John Randolph, "[he] had fought with all his talents. And though he lost, he fell with a brilliancy that was almost consolation for disaster." Of course, it wasn't just Randolph he had in mind.

Russell Kirk came of one of the many small-town families hit hard by the Depression. His great-grandfather had founded the little town of Mecosta, and his mother's father had owned a bank, but Kirk attended Michigan State on a scholarship and worked at Ford's Rouge River plant after completing his M.A. at Duke in 1941. Kirk was then drafted and stationed in Utah; according to George Nash, author of *The Conservative Intellectual Tradition in America Since 1945*, Kirk cast his first presidential ballot for Norman Thomas in 1944, to reward the veteran socialist for his steadfast opposition to the Second World War. Released from the army, Kirk resumed his studies and began to publish. In 1951 came *John Randolph of Roanoke*, an enlargement of his M.A. thesis, and in 1953, *The Conservative Mind*. The fame that second book won Kirk enabled him to return to Mecosta and settle in his family's house.

A charming 1992 essay by Edwin Feulner, president of the Heritage Foundation, quotes Kirk's description of the place: "over everything brooded an air of faded splendours, vanished lands, and baffled expectations." The house soon sheltered armies of young conservative scholars, and other, more miscellaneous, guests: "unwed mothers, half-reformed burglars, . . . Vietnamese . . . families, waves of Ethiopians, Poles fled from martial law, freedom-seeking Croats, students disgusted with their colleges, and a diversity of waifs and strays from Progress." (The sarcastic upper-case "P" on "Progress" is a characteristic Kirkean flourish.)

From Mecosta, for four decades, Kirk fired his observations upon the world: two more major scholarly works, *Eliot and His Age* and *The Roots of American Order*, books, essays, ghost stories, lectures, columns for magazines and newspapers. From Mecosta too he cast a sharp and often disapproving eye upon the conservative movement that had sprung up in the years since the publication of *The Conservative Mind*. He disliked libertarians, and apologists for big business, and neoconservatives. He did not mind making enemies: he separated himself from his old friends at *National Review* after 1980, and in a 1988 critique of neoconservatism he let loose the startling observation that "not seldom has it seemed as if some eminent Neoconservatives"—that capital letter again!—"mistook Tel Aviv for the capital of the United States." By the end of his life, he had circled back to his Taftite origins, and joined the opposition to the war in the Persian Gulf.

Kirk's voice echoed less powerfully in those later years than in the 1950s and 1960s. In part, of course, he was the victim of his own success: with conservatives in a position to exercise national political power after 1978, a political thinker who declined to preoccupy himself with the details of public policy—which he left to the "enlightened expediency" of statesmen—inevitably lost audiences to technical experts. Clad in out-of-fashion vested suits, immersed in his old books, smoking (as Feulner says) dark, thick Burmese cigars that looked and tasted like torpedoes, he looked oddly out of place among the sleek Republicans of Reagan-era Washington.

And these stylistic oddities hinted at an even bigger and deeper gulf between Kirk and his Reaganite audience. From the beginning, Kirk had denied key tenets of the American faith. He had openly defended class hierarchies; he doubted the value of technological progress; and, while disliking the growth of the central government, he cared very little for the danger to prosperity and economic growth posed by bigger government. In fact, Kirk regarded "growth," in most cases, as a misnomer for "decay."

> During the late 'fifties and the early 'sixties, I watched in Long Island the devastation of what had been a charming countryside, as dismaying as what was being done to our cities. To make room for a spreading population was necessary: but to do it hideously and stupidly was not ineluctable. Much of the mischief was accomplished by the highways of Robert Moses, generally supposed to be one of the abler of American planners. Speed was everything, speed by automobile from Manhattan to Montauk.

Many thinkers have damned suburbia, but Kirk uniquely dared to reveal the anti-egalitarian implications of the aesthetic critique of American life. "This is my case: there ought to be inequality of condition in the world. For without inequality, there is no class; without class, no manners and no beauty; and then a people sink into public and private ugliness." Ugliness was for him no light accusation. "With Santayana," he said, "I believe that beauty is the index to civilization." By this index, contemporary America scored low. We now live, he bitterly complained in *The Conservative Mind*, in "a world smudged by industrialism, standardized by the masses, consolidated by government."

Nor was Kirk bashful about itemizing the differences between his conservatism and the enthusiastic Jacksonianism found on the right wing of the contemporary Republican Party. He openly disdained populism, denouncing "those who, in the belief that there exists a malign 'elite,' cry, with Carl Sandburg, 'The people, yes!'" As for the Reagan-era project of identifying conservatism's cause as the defense of "democratic capitalism," an optimistic philosophy that commingled high-tech prosperity and ever-widening popular sovereignty . . . well, here's what Kirk had to say about that:

> Previously, even in America, the structure of society had consisted of a hierarchy of personal and local allegiances — man to master, apprentice to preceptor, householder to parish or town, constituent to representative, son to father, communicant to church. . . . This network of personal relationships and local decencies was brushed aside by steam, coal, the spinning jenny, the cotton gin, speedy transportation, and the other items in that catalogue of progress which school children memorize. The Industrial Revolution . . . turned the world inside out. Personal loyalties gave way to financial relationships. . . . Industrialism was a harder knock to conservatism than the books of the French equalitarians. . . .

That the sudden triumph of democracy should coincide with the rise of industrialism was in part the product of intertwined causes; but, however inescapable, it was a conjunction generally catastrophic. Jeffersonian democracy, designed for a simple agrarian people, was thrust upon an acquisitive, impatient, and often urbanized mass of men.

Instead, Kirk throughout his life insisted upon the six "canons" of conservative thought he first identified in *The Conservative Mind*:

1. Belief that a divine intent rules society as well as conscience. . . .
2. Affection for the proliferating variety and mystery of traditional life. . . .
3. Conviction that civilized society requires orders and classes. . . .
4. Persuasion that property and freedom are inseparably connected. . . .
5. Faith in prescription. . . . Tradition and sound prejudice provide checks upon man's anarchic impulse. . . .
6. Recognition that change and reform are not identical, and that innovation is a devouring conflagration more often than it is a torch of progress. . . .

Kirk expressed his major ideas in highly general terms, and so it is hard to know exactly what these six canons imply, especially the final two. When pressed for specifics, Kirk's political advice tended to take the form of negative injunctions.

Conservative people in politics need to steer clear of the Scylla of abstraction and the Charybdis of opportunism. So it is that folk of conservative inclination ought to decline the embraces of such categories of American political zealots or charlatans as I list below:

Those who demand that the National Parks be sold to private developers. Those who declare that "the test of the market" is the whole of political economy and of morals. Those who fancy that foreign policy can be conducted with religious zeal on a basis of absolute rights and absolute wrongs. . . .

Etcetera. Even Kirk's journalism bears only indirectly on the controversies of his day.

Then again, uncertainty about the implications of his ideas in practice may not matter very much: for Kirk was, at bottom, much more concerned with morals and education than with politics as politics is usually understood. He reserved his energies for other themes, themes sometimes absurdly small, but at other times profound and urgent, as in his remarkable essay "The Rarity of the God-Fearing Man."

"We have to begin," Kirk describes himself telling a group of clergymen, "with the dogma that the fear of God is the beginning of wisdom." "Oh no," they replied, "not the *fear* of God. You mean the *love* of God, don't you?"

> Looking upon their mild and diffident faces, I wondered how much trust I might put in such love as they knew. Their meekness was not that of Moses. Meek before Jehovah, Moses had no fear of Pharaoh; but these doctors of the schools, much at ease in Zion, were timid in the presence of a traffic policeman. Although convinced that God is too indulgent to punish much of anything, they were given to trembling before Caesar. . . . Gauleiters and commissars? Why, their fellowship and charity was not proof against a dean or a divisional head. . . .
>
> Every age portrays God in the image of its poetry and its politics. In one century, God is an absolute monarch, exacting his due; in another century, still an absolute sovereign, but a benevolent despot; again, perhaps a grand gentleman among aristocrats; at a different time, a democratic president, with an eye to the ballot box. It has been said that to many of our generation, God is a Republican and works in a bank; but this image is giving way, I think, to God as Chum—at worst, God as a playground supervisor. . . .
>
> In a Michigan college town stands an immense quasi-Gothic church building, and the sign upon the porch informs the world that this is "The People's Church, Nondenominational and Nonsectarian." Sometimes, passing by, a friend of mine murmurs, "The People's Church—formerly God's" . . . From the People's Church, the fear of God, with its allied wisdom, has been swept away. So have I.

Kirk's literary productivity commands awe. He took particular pride in his ghost stories: His spare curriculum vitae modestly omits mention of nearly all his innumerable awards and honorary degrees, except for three that especially pleased him—one of them being the Ann Radcliffe Award of the Count Dracula Society. ("A child's fearful joy in stories of goblins, witches, and ghosts is a natural yearning after the challenge of the dreadful: raw head and bloody bones, in one form or another, the imagination demands.") In all the millions of words he set in print, however, he never amended or retracted any of the thoughts and formulations of the masterpiece he published at age thirty-two, *The Conservative Mind*.

"Professor J. W. Williams kindly read the manuscript of this book; and in his library at the Roundel, looking upon the wreck of St. Andrews cathedral, we talked of the inundation which only here and there has spared an island of humane learning like St. Andrews town." Those words, the opening sentence of the acknowledgments to *The Conservative Mind*, and the first of Russell Kirk's that most of his readers will encounter, demonstrate what a fine literary artist he could be. You might close the book right there, and Kirk would already have stabbed you with a pang of loss and regret. An old cliché has it that a great actor can wring tears out of audience by reading a laundry list. Kirk could summon up nostalgia with a list of place names. "These chapters have been written in a variety of places: in a but-and-ben snuggled under the cliffs of Eigg; in one of the ancient towers of Kellie Castle, looking out to the Forth; in my great-grandfather's house in the stump-country of Michigan; among the bogs of Sligo in the west of Ireland; upon the steps of Ara Coeli, in Rome; at Balcarres House, where what Burke calls 'the unbought grace of life' still abides."

KIRK WAS WRITING in the aftermath of the forty most catastrophic years in the history of Western civilization, and at the beginning of another forty of the most tense and terrifying. It must have seemed to him that everything he treasured had either been pulverized by war or would soon be bulldozed by one form of socialism or another. He strained all his powers to summon up a vision of the Anglo-American past that would stir the imagination, and entice us to preserve as much of the vanished aristocratic age he loved as we possibly could. In form, *The Conservative Mind* appears to be intellectual history. Each of its chapters closely studies the writing of a conservative thinker or group of thinkers: Edmund Burke; John Adams, Alexander Hamilton, and Fisher Ames; Walter Scott and Samuel Taylor Coleridge; Benjamin Disraeli and Cardinal Newman; Irving Babbitt and George Santayana; and many others. In fact, history is the one thing *The Conservative Mind* is not. Kirk repeatedly declares his lack of interest in the tangle of facts and events from which his subjects' ideas emerged. He takes his ideas as he finds them, the way an anthropologist might examine an artifact or a New Critic, a poem. Was John C. Calhoun's dramatic midlife switch from nationalism to sectionalism motivated by his commitment to slavery? Kirk does not inquire.

> The whole grim slavery-problem, to which no satisfactory answer was possible, warped and discolored the American political mind, on either side of the debate, for the earlier two-thirds of the nineteenth century. So far as it is possible, we shall try to keep clear here of that partisan controversy over slavery and to penetrate, instead, beneath the froth of aboli-

tionist harangues and Southern fire-eating to those conservative ideas which Randolph and Calhoun enunciated.

Are we really to take Benjamin Disraeli's flights of political fancy seriously as expressing a distinctive Tory philosophy? It doesn't matter whether we do.

> In truth, Disraeli's positive legislation sometimes was inconsistent with his theory, and in any case inferior to it. His really important achievement, as a political leader, was implanting in the public imagination an ideal of Toryism which has been immeasurably valuable in keeping Britain faithful to her constitutional and spiritual traditions.

No, *The Conservative Mind* isn't history; it is a work of literature meant to achieve political ends.

This isn't to deny that Kirk could produce acute analysis of earlier times when it suited his purposes. Kirk's erasure of Alexander Hamilton—the hero of an earlier generation of conservative Republicans—from the conservative canon shows his historical intelligence at its best.

> It hardly seems to have occurred to Hamilton's mind that a consolidated nation might also be a levelling and innovating nation, though he had the example of Jacobin France right before him; and he does not appear to have reflected on the possibility that force in government may be applied to other purposes than the maintenance of a conservative order. . . . All his revolutionary ardour notwithstanding, Hamilton loved English society as an English colonial adores it. His vision of the coming America was of another, stronger, richer, eighteenth-century England. . . .
>
> [T]hat industrialization of America which Hamilton successfully promoted was burdened with consequences the haughty and forceful new aristocrat did not perceive. Commerce and manufactures, he believed, would produce a body of wealthy men whose interests would coincide with those of the national commonwealth. Probably he conceived of these pillars of society as being very like great English merchants—purchasing country estates, forming presently a stable class possessed of leisure, talent, and means, providing moral and political and intellectual leadership for the nation. The actual American businessman, generally speaking, has turned out to be a different sort of person: it is difficult to reproduce social classes from a model three thousand miles over the water. Modern captains of industry might surprise Hamilton, modern cities shock him, and the power of industrial labor frighten him: for Hamilton never quite

understood the transmuting power of social change, which in its operation is more miraculous than scientific. Like Dr. Faustus' manservant,
Hamilton could evoke elementals; but once materialized, that new industrialism swept away from the control of eighteenth-century virtuosos
like the masterful Secretary of the Treasury. . . .

Hamilton was a straggler behind his age, rather than the prophet of a
new day. By a very curious coincidence, this old-fangled grand gentleman
died from the bullet of Aaron Burr, friend and disciple of Bentham.

Thinkers whom Kirk sought to include, rather than exclude, from his
canon sometimes met, however, more procrustean fates. It's fascinating to
compare, for instance, the exegesis of a single sentence of Edmund Burke's
both by Kirk and by Conor Cruise O'Brien in his recent study, *The Great
Melody*. First, Kirk:

"I heaved the lead every inch of the way I made," Burke observed of his
career, in the *Letter to a Noble Lord*. Heaving the lead is not a practice for
which Irish orators are renowned; Burke's flights of eloquent fancy
everyone knows; and surely Burke did not seem at Hasting's trial, to
frightened Tory spectators, a man sworn to cautious plumbing of the
depths. Yet Burke spoke accurately of his general policy as a statesman, for
he based his every important decision upon a close examination of par-
ticulars. He detested "abstraction"—by which he meant not *principle*, but
rather vainglorious generalization without respect for human frailty and
the particular circumstances of an age and nation. Thus it was that while
he believed in the rights of Englishmen and in certain human rights of
universal application, he despised the "Rights of Man" which Paine and
the French doctrinaires were soon to proclaim inviolable.

Now O'Brien.

The occasion for the composition of *Letter to a Noble Lord* was an attack by
two Whig peers, the Duke of Bedford and the Earl of Lauderdale, in the
Lords on 13 November 1795 on the pension which had been granted to
Burke in the previous year, on his retirement from Parliament. . . . It
enabled Edmund to pay his debts and to be assured, during his last illness,
that his widow would not have to face a life of poverty. . . .

Inevitably, Burke's many enemies, among the Whigs and the radicals,
triumphed. . . . It was the thirty pieces of silver. . . . Burke had received an
enormous amount of abuse and innuendo—more than any other
politician—in his long political career. In *Letter to a Noble Lord* he called it

"the hunt of obloquy, which ever has pursued me with full cry through life." Most of those attacks came from anonymous writers in the corrupt press of the time, faceless and unaccountable tormenters. Burke did not answer those ever. The Duke of Bedford, on the other hand, was a marvelous target. . . .

He was also vulnerable. The Bedford family, since the days of Henry VIII, had been beneficiaries of Crown patronage on a colossal scale. Thus, by attacking Burke's modest pension, the Duke had unwittingly laid himself open to the most devastating *argumentum ad hominem* in the history of English controversy. . . . It contains [in the "heaving the lead" passage], with much else, Burke's grave and succinct rebuttal to the charge of venality that dogged him throughout his life, and has clung to his reputation ever since.

In some respects, obviously, Kirk's reading of the sentence is better. Kirk never even acknowledged, much less succumbed to, the contemporary urge to psychologize and personalize every human utterance. His Burke is a public man, and a public man's public statements are given public meanings by Kirk. Too, Kirk relies only on what he can see in the documentary record; O'Brien's conviction that he possesses some special intuition into Burke's Irish soul that justifies leaps beyond the available facts would have irritated Kirk no end. Even so, and for all that, O'Brien's Burke is a *man*—maybe a badly misunderstood man, but a man all the same. Kirk's Burke is a repository of political wisdom, the author of a series of preternatural insights on which, two hundred years later, a political movement can be grounded.

Russell Kirk has always reminded me of those nineteenth-century Central European historians who promoted national consciousness by writing passionate histories of "nations" that had not existed until those same historians invented them. And just as the nationalist historians manufactured "Croatia" or "Czechoslovakia" out of half-forgotten medieval and baroque fragments, Russell Kirk inspired the postwar conservative movement by pulling together a series of only partially related ideas and events into a coherent narrative—even, although Kirk objected to the word, into an ideology. Kirk did not record the past; he created it. He gathered the words of his political exemplars to answer his burning question:

What is the essence of British and American conservatism? What system of ideas, common to England and the United States, has sustained men of conservative instincts in their resistance against radical theories and social transformation since the beginning of the French revolution?

As a question, of course, Kirk's query takes far too much for granted. Can one in fact fuse the English and American political traditions together in this way? Was the dilemma of the English Tories—how to maintain aristocratic deference in a democratizing society?—truly identical to that of American conservatives in the North—how to maintain the virtues of the founders' way of life in the face of colossal, unexpected wealth and exploding, non-Anglo-Saxon, populations?—and South—how to preserve white supremacy in the face of Northern criticism and an agricultural way of life in an industrial age? But Kirk's question is not a question. It is a prelude to a romantic reading of the past for the purposes of the present. No wonder, then, that *The Conservative Mind* found little favor with professional historians. Writers of the Left may be able to get away with devising "usable pasts": Certainly Michel Foucault and the writers of women's history distort the past for their own polemical purposes on a scale and with a brazen falsity that would have made Kirk gasp. But in the hostile purlieus of the academy, writers of the Right must be more careful.

Yet if Kirk's great work cannot be counted as history, exactly, it ought to be esteemed as something in some ways more important: a profound critique of contemporary mass society, and a vivid and poetic image—not a program, an image—of how that society might better itself. It is, in important respects, the twentieth century's own version of the *Reflections on the Revolution in France*. If Kirk was not a historian, he was an artist, a visionary, almost a prophet. As long as he lived, by word and example he cautioned conservatives against overindulging their fascination with economics. He taught that conservativism was above all a *moral* cause: one devoted to the preservation of the priceless heritage of Western civilization.

December 1994

Remembering the Gulag

Hilton Kramer

T HE FIRST ACCOUNT of the concentration camps that I can remember reading was an essay by Hannah Arendt in the July 1948 number of *Partisan Review* when I was a sophomore in college. What I now mainly recall about my first reading of this essay, "The Concentration Camps," is that I was greatly put off by it. Expecting, somewhat fearfully, to be given a gruesome account of life (and death) in the camps, what I encountered instead was a succession of apodictic abstractions and pronouncements that seemed, to my undergraduate mind, unduly eager to place the whole subject beyond the reader's ability to comprehend it. Innocent as I then was about the details of the camps, this approach nonetheless struck me as an odd way to deal with a human catastrophe on an epic scale.

Rereading that essay today, more than half a century later, I can easily see what had put me off. This is a representative passage:

> The horror of the concentration and extermination camps can never be fully embraced by the imagination for the very reason that it stands outside of life and death. The inmates are more effectively cut off from the world of the living than if they were dead, because terror compels oblivion among those who know or love them. . . . The fear of the absolute Evil which permits of no escape knows that this is the end of dialectical evolutions and developments. It knows that modern politics revolves around a question which, strictly speaking, should never enter into politics, the question of all or nothing: of all, that is, a human society rich with infinite possibilities; or exactly nothing, that is, the end of mankind.

Exactly what it could mean for any human experience to stand "outside of life and death" was never explained. Nor was Hannah Arendt's own response to early accounts of the camps ever in danger of succumbing to "the end of dialectical evolutions and developments." On the contrary, in her case it marked the beginning of an illustrious career as a connoisseur of the totalitarian "dialectical evolutions and developments" that led to the camps.

Two other aspects of "The Concentration Camps" essay are also worth noting. One is Arendt's bizarre insistence on downgrading the importance of eyewitness accounts of the camps.

> If it is true that the concentration camps are the most consequential in-
> stitution of totalitarian rule, "dwelling on horrors" would seem to be in-
> dispensable for the understanding of totalitarianism. But recollection can
> no more do this than can the uncommunicative eye-witness report. In
> both these genres there is an inherent tendency to run away from the ex-
> perience; instinctively or rationally, both types of writer are so much aware
> of the terrible abyss that separates the world of the living from that of the
> living dead, that they cannot supply anything more than a series of
> remembered occurrences that must seem just as incredible to those who
> relate them as to their audience.

There was ample reason to doubt that any of this was true even before the publication of Solzhenitsyn's *Gulag Archipelago* in the 1970s, but with respect to the Soviet camps, anyway, the claim of an alleged "tendency to run away from the experience" is scarcely credible in the light of the abundant firsthand testimony to the contrary. The author of *The Gulag Archipelago* was himself, after all, a zek, as inmates of the Soviet camps were called, and he was also an assiduous compiler of other zeks' personal accounts of their servitude and suffering.

What was true, however, was that the West wasn't especially eager to hear about the Soviet camps, and that for a long time the Soviets were remarkably successful in preventing the circulation of information about them. Even the word "Gulag" does not appear to have made its entry into our English-language dictionaries prior to the early 1970s, almost two decades after the death of Stalin and half a century after the creation of the Gulag itself. It can no longer surprise us, then, to find that another curious thing about Hannah Arendt's 1948 "Concentration Camps" essay is that it paid only the most cursory attention to the Soviet camps even though they had been in existence far longer than their Nazi counterparts—since, indeed, the Bolsheviks' seizure of power in 1917—and commanded vastly greater resources, populations, and territories.

What has to be understood, of course, is that the horrors of the Soviet system had never penetrated the public imagination in this country on anything like the scale that made the Nazis a familiar symbol of evil and criminality. Even as kids Americans of my generation recognized the swastika as an emblem of the "bad guys," if only from the movies we saw and the comic books we read. No Soviet symbol ever acquired a comparable status in the public mind. Nor did Hollywood make any movies about heroic anti-Soviet resistance movements. As Anne Applebaum writes in the introduction to her magisterial study of the Soviet camps (*Gulag: A History*; Doubleday, 2003)—a book that is certain to remain the definitive account of its subject for many years to come—

> The Cold War produced James Bond and thrillers, and cartoon Russians of the sort who appear in Rambo films, but nothing as ambitious as *Schindler's List* or *Sophie's Choice*. Steven Spielberg, probably Hollywood's leading director (like it or not) has chosen to make films about Japanese concentration camps (*Empire of the Sun*) and Nazi concentration camps, but not about Stalinist concentration camps. The latter haven't caught Hollywood's imagination in the same way.

Besides, Russia (as most people still called the Soviet Union) had been an ally in the war against Hitler, and was thus identified in the public mind as somehow belonging to "our" side. In the mainstream media and entertainment industries, the Soviet Union remained exempt from critical scrutiny, and the Gulag did not exist. Yet, as Ms. Applebaum also writes:

> [N]ot all of our attitudes to the Soviet past are linked to political ideology. . . . Many, in fact, are rather a fading by-product of our memories of the Second World War. We have, at present, a firm conviction that the Second World War was a wholly just war, and few want that conviction shaken. We remember D-Day, the liberation of the Nazi concentration camps, the children welcoming American GIs with cheers on the streets. No one wants to be told that there was another, darker side to the Allied victory, or that the camps of Stalin, our ally, expanded just as the camps of Hitler, our enemy, were liberated. To admit that by sending thousands of Russians to their deaths by forcibly repatriating them after the war, or by consigning millions of people to Soviet rule at Yalta, the Western Allies might have helped others commit crimes against humanity would undermine the moral clarity of our memories of that era. No one wants to think that we defeated one mass murderer with the help of another. No one wants to remember how well that mass murderer got on with Western statesmen. "I have a real liking for Stalin," the British Foreign Secretary, Anthony

Eden, told a friend, "he has never broken his word." There are many, many photographs of Stalin, Churchill, and Roosevelt all together, all smiling.

This is why *The Gulag Archipelago* and Solzhenitsyn himself met with such resistance and hostility in this country after his expulsion from the Soviet Union. "Soviet propaganda was not without its effect," writes Ms. Applebaum. "Soviet attempts to cast doubt upon Solzhenitsyn's writing, for example, to paint him as a madman or an anti-Semite or a drunk, had some impact." Let us never forget the infamous passage in George Steiner's *New Yorker* review of *The Gulag Archipelago* in 1974: "To infer that the Soviet terror is as hideous as Hitlerism is not only a brutal simplification but a moral indecency." Nor was Steiner alone in his hostile response to Solzhenitsyn's revelations. The late Irving Howe, who had found so much to admire in Leon Trotsky, took to the pages of *The New Republic* to offer Solzhenitsyn moral instruction on the correct way to think about socialism.

Has anything really changed in our public comprehension—or incomprehension—of the Gulag since the collapse of the Soviet Union and the final dismantling of the Soviet camps? We shall all be in a better position to answer this question when we see what kind of critical reception is accorded to Ms. Applebaum's extraordinary account of the Soviet camps. Or, what is even more important, what impact that reception may have beyond the sphere of the book-review pages of our newspapers and magazines—in the realm of media opinion and public awareness. For make no mistake: *Gulag: A History* is a landmark achievement in the writing of modern history. Until some work of a comparable size is devoted to the millions who have perished under Communist rule in China, this book will remain a model for what is, in effect, a new historical genre: the history, that is, of what may rightly be called an anti-civilization on a colossal scale whose sole claim to distinction has been the degradation and destruction of millions of innocents. In the anti-civilization of the Soviet Gulag in the years 1929 to the death of Stalin in 1953, it encompasses some eighteen million people, four and a half million of whom never returned.

Gulag: A History is not, then, to be mistaken for a comprehensive history of the Soviet Union; it is rather a history of Soviet society's most distinctive institution, described by Ms. Applebaum as

> the vast network of labor camps that were once scattered across the length and breadth of the Soviet Union, from the islands of the White Sea to the shores of the Black Sea, from the Arctic Circle to the plains of central Asia, from Murmansk to Vorkuta to Kazakhstan, from central Moscow to the Leningrad suburbs. Literally, the word GULAG is an acronym, meaning

Glavnoe Uppravlenie Lagerei, or Main Camp Administration. Over time, the word "Gulag" has also come to signify not only the administration of the concentration camps but also the system of Soviet slave labor itself, in all its forms and varieties: labor camps, punishment camps, criminal and political camps, women's camps, children's camps, transit camps. Even more broadly, "Gulag" has come to mean the Soviet repressive system itself, the set of procedures that prisoners once called the "meat-grinder": the arrests, the interrogations, the transport in unheated cattle cars, the forced labor, the destruction of families, the years spent in exile, the early and unnecessary deaths.

It is Ms. Applebaum's distinctive accomplishment to have traced the tortuous history of this anti-civilization in scrupulously documented detail from its Bolshevik beginnings to the Great Terror, the Second World War, the early years of the Cold War, the death of Stalin, the Thaw that followed, the era of the Soviet dissidents, and the final collapse of the Soviet regime. And while *Gulag: A History* is written throughout in a prose that is exemplary for its clarity, its gravity, and its moral candor, it must also be acknowledged that the book is a long and difficult read—difficult, above all, because of the feeling of outrage and despair it induces in the reader. I could not myself get through the chapter devoted to "Women and Children" without pausing to wipe the tears from my eyes more than once. And that is by no means the only section of the book to induce such a response.

For Ms. Applebaum lavishes a great deal of attention on what may be called the social and domestic history of the Gulag—the food that was provided the inmates, the bedding, the hygiene (if it could still be called by that name), the sexual customs and even the romantic attachments that developed in the camps. Worst of all, perhaps, are the accounts of the inhuman work schedules demanded by what she nicely describes as the Camp-Industrial Complex in the Soviet workers' paradise. It is an immense achievement to have written this book. What now remains to be seen is whether our own society, which for so many decades has refused to acknowledge the moral enormity of the Gulag, is even now equal to the challenge of giving this achievement its due.

May 2003

II. Contentions

The Hypocrisy of Noam Chomsky

Keith Windschuttle

There's a famous definition in the Gospels of the hypocrite, and the hypocrite is the person who refuses to apply to himself the standards he applies to others. By that standard, the entire commentary and discussion of the so-called War on Terror is pure hypocrisy, virtually without exception. Can anybody understand that? No, they can't understand it.
—Noam Chomsky, *Power and Terror,* 2003

NOAM CHOMSKY was the most conspicuous American intellectual to rationalize the al Qaeda terrorist attacks on New York and Washington. The death toll, he argued, was minor compared to the list of Third World victims of the "far more extreme terrorism" of United States foreign policy. Despite its calculated affront to mainstream opinion, this sentiment went down very well with Chomsky's own constituency. He has never been more popular among the academic and intellectual left than he is today.

Two books of interviews with him published since September 11, 2001 both went straight onto the bestseller lists (*9-11*; Seven Stories Press, October 2001; *Power and Terror: Post 9/11 Talks and Interviews*; Seven Stories Press, 2003). One of them has since been turned into a film entitled *Power and Terror*, now doing brisk business in the art-house movie market. In March 2002 the film's director, John Junkerman, accompanied his subject to the University of California, Berkeley, where in a five-day visit Chomsky gave five political talks to a total audience of no fewer than five thousand people.

Meanwhile, the liberal news media around the world has sought him out for countless interviews as the most prominent intellectual opposed to the American response to the terrorist attacks. Newspaper articles routinely open by reminding readers of his awesome intellectual status. A profile headlined "Conscience of a Nation" in the English daily *The Guardian* declared: "Chomsky ranks with Marx, Shakespeare, and the Bible as one of the ten most quoted sources in the humanities—and is the only writer among them still alive." *The New York Times* has called him "arguably the most important intellectual alive."

Chomsky has used his status, originally gained in the field of linguistics, to turn himself into the leading voice of the American left. He is not merely a spokesman. His own stance has done much to structure left-wing politics over the past forty years. Today, when actors, rock stars, and protesting students mouth anti-American slogans for the cameras, they are very often expressing sentiments they have gleaned from Chomsky's voluminous output.

Hence, to examine Chomsky's views is to analyze the core mindset of contemporary radicalism, especially the variety that now holds so much sway in the academic and arts communities.

Chomsky has been a celebrity radical since the mid-1960s when he made his name as an anti-Vietnam War activist. Although he lost some of his appeal in the late-1970s and 1980s by his defense of the Pol Pot regime in Cambodia, he has used September 11 to restore his reputation, indeed to surpass his former influence and stature. At seventy-four years of age, he is today the doyen of the American and much of the world's intellectual left.

He is, however, an unconventional academic radical. Over the past thirty years, the left in the humanities has been smitten by high theory, especially neo-Marxist, feminist, and postmodernist philosophy out of Germany and France. Much of this material was arcane enough in its own language but in translation it elevated obscurantism to a badge of prestige. It inundated the humanities with relativism both in epistemology and moral philosophy.

In contrast, Chomsky has produced no substantial body of political theory of his own. Nor is he a relativist. He advocates the pursuit of truth and knowledge about human affairs and promotes a simple, universal set of moral principles. Moreover, his political writings are very clear, pitched to a general rather than specialist audience. He supports his claims not by appeals to some esoteric conceptual apparatus but by presenting plain, apparently factual evidence. The explanation for his current appeal, therefore, needs to be sought not in recent intellectual fashions but in something with a longer history.

Chomsky is the most prominent intellectual remnant of the New Left of the 1960s. In many ways he epitomized the New Left and its hatred of

"Amerika," a country he believed, through its policies both at home and abroad, had descended into fascism. In his most famous book of the 1960s, *American Power and the New Mandarins*, Chomsky said what America needed was "a kind of denazification."

Of all the major powers in the 1960s, according to Chomsky, America was the most reprehensible. Its principles of liberal democracy were a sham. Its democracy was a "four-year dictatorship" and its economic commitment to free markets was merely a disguise for corporate power. Its foreign policy was positively evil. "By any objective standard," he wrote at the time, "the United States has become the most aggressive power in the world, the greatest threat to peace, to national self-determination, and to international cooperation."

As an anti-war activist, Chomsky participated in some of the most publicized demonstrations, including the attempt, famously celebrated in Norman Mailer's *Armies of the Night*, to form a human chain around the Pentagon. Chomsky described the event as "tens of thousands of young people surrounding what they believe to be—I must add that I agree—the most hideous institution on this earth."

This kind of anti-Americanism was common on the left at the time but there were two things that made Chomsky stand out from the crowd. He was a scholar with a remarkable reputation and he was in tune with the anti-authoritarianism of the student-based New Left.

At the time, the traditional left was still dominated by an older generation of Marxists, who were either supporters of the Communist Party or else Trotskyists opposed to Joseph Stalin and his heirs but who still endorsed Lenin and Bolshevism. Either way, the emerging generation of radical students saw both groups as compromised by their support for the Russian Revolution and the repressive regimes it had bequeathed to Eastern Europe.

Chomsky was not himself a member of the student generation—in 1968 he was a forty-year-old tenured professor—but his lack of party membership or any other formal political commitment absolved him of any connection to the Old Left. Instead, his adherence to anarchism, or what he called "libertarian socialism," did much to shape the outlook of the New Left.

American Power and the New Mandarins approvingly quotes the nineteenth-century anarchist Mikhail Bakunin predicting that the version of socialism supported by Karl Marx would end up transferring state power not to the workers but to the elitist cadres of the Communist Party itself.

Despite his anti-Bolshevism, Chomsky remained a supporter of socialist revolution. He urged that "a true social revolution" would transform the masses so they could take power into their own hands and run institutions themselves. His favorite real-life political model was the short-lived anarchist enclave formed in Barcelona in 1936–1937 during the Spanish Civil War.

The 1960s demand for "student power" was a consequence of this brand of political thought. It allowed the New Left to persuade itself that it had invented a more pristine form of radicalism, untainted by the totalitarianism of the communist world.

For all his in-principle disdain of communism, however, when it came to the real world of international politics Chomsky turned out to endorse a fairly orthodox band of socialist revolutionaries. They included the architects of communism in Cuba, Fidel Castro and Che Guevera, as well as Mao Tse-tung and the founders of the Chinese communist state. Chomsky told a forum in New York in December 1967 that in China "one finds many things that are really quite admirable." He believed the Chinese had gone some way to empowering the masses along lines endorsed by his own libertarian socialist principles:

> China is an important example of a new society in which very interesting and positive things happened at the local level, in which a good deal of the collectivization and communization was really based on mass participation and took place after a level of understanding had been reached in the peasantry that led to this next step.

When he provided this endorsement of what he called Mao Tse-tung's "relatively livable" and "just society," Chomsky was probably unaware he was speaking only five years after the end of the great Chinese famine of 1958–1962, the worst in human history. He did not know, because the full story did not come out for another two decades, that the very collectivization he endorsed was the principal cause of this famine, one of the greatest human catastrophes ever, with a total death toll of thirty million people.

Nonetheless, if he was as genuinely aloof from totalitarianism as his political principles proclaimed, the track record of communism in the USSR—which was by then widely known to have faked its statistics of agricultural and industrial output in the 1930s when its own population was also suffering crop failures and famine—should have left this anarchist a little more skeptical about the claims of the Russians' counterparts in China.

In fact, Chomsky was well aware of the degree of violence that communist regimes had routinely directed at the people of their own countries. At the 1967 New York forum he acknowledged both "the mass slaughter of landlords in China" and "the slaughter of landlords in North Vietnam" that had taken place once the communists came to power. His main objective, however, was to provide a rationalization for this violence, especially that of the National Liberation Front then trying to take control of South Vietnam. Chomsky revealed he was no pacifist.

> I don't accept the view that we can just condemn the NLF terror, period, because it was so horrible. I think we really have to ask questions of comparative costs, ugly as that may sound. And if we are going to take a moral position on this—and I think we should—we have to ask both what the consequences were of using terror and not using terror. If it were true that the consequences of not using terror would be that the peasantry in Vietnam would continue to live in the state of the peasantry of the Philippines, then I think the use of terror would be justified.

It was not only Chomsky who was sucked into supporting the maelstrom of violence that characterized the communist takeovers in Southeast Asia. Almost the whole of the 1960s New Left followed. They opposed the American side and turned Ho Chi Minh and the Vietcong into romantic heroes.

When the Khmer Rouge took over Cambodia in 1975 both Chomsky and the New Left welcomed it. And when news emerged of the extraordinary event that immediately followed, the complete evacuation of the capital Phnom Penh accompanied by reports of widespread killings, Chomsky offered a rationalization similar to those he had provided for the terror in China and Vietnam: there might have been some violence, but this was understandable under conditions of regime change and social revolution.

Although information was hard to come by, Chomsky suggested in an article in 1977 that postwar Cambodia was probably similar to France after liberation at the end of World War II when thousands of enemy collaborators were massacred within a few months. This was to be expected, he said, and was a small price to pay for the positive outcomes of the new government of Pol Pot. Chomsky cited a book by two American left-wing authors, Gareth Porter and George Hildebrand, who had "presented a carefully documented study of the destructive American impact on Cambodia and the success of the Cambodian revolutionaries in overcoming it, giving a very favorable picture of their programs and policies."

By this time, however, there were two other books published on Cambodia that took a very different line. The American authors John Barron and Anthony Paul called their work *Murder of a Gentle Land* and accused the Pol Pot regime of mass killings that amounted to genocide. François Ponchaud's *Cambodia Year Zero* repeated the charge.

Chomsky reviewed both books, together with a number of press articles, in *The Nation* in June 1977. He accused them of publishing little more than anti-communist propaganda. Articles in *The New York Times Magazine* and *The Christian Science Monitor* suggested that the death toll was between one and two million people out of a total population of 7.8 million. Chomsky mocked their total and picked at their sources, showing some were dubious and that a famous photograph of forced labor in the Cambodian countryside was actually a fake.

He dismissed the Barron and Paul book partly because it had been published by *Reader's Digest* and publicized on the front page of *The Wall Street Journal*, both of them notorious anti-communist publications, and partly because they had omitted to report the views of journalists who had been to Cambodia but not witnessed any executions.

Ponchaud's book was harder to ignore. It was based on the author's personal experience in Cambodia from 1965 until the capture of Phnom Penh, extensive interviews with refugees and reports from Cambodian radio. Moreover, it had been favorably reviewed by a left-wing author in *The New York Review of Books*, a publication for which Chomsky himself had often written. Chomsky's strategy was to undermine Ponchaud's book by questioning the credibility of his refugee testimony. Acknowledging that Ponchaud "gives a grisly account of what refugees have reported to him about the barbarity of their treatment at the hands of the Khmer Rouge," Chomsky said we should be wary of "the extreme unreliability of refugee reports":

> Refugees are frightened and defenseless, at the mercy of alien forces. They naturally tend to report what they believe their interlocutors wish to hear. While these reports must be considered seriously, care and caution are necessary. Specifically, refugees questioned by Westerners or Thais have a vested interest in reporting atrocities on the part of Cambodian revolutionaries, an obvious fact that no serious reporter will fail to take into account.

In 1980, Chomsky expanded this critique into the book *After the Cataclysm*, co-authored with his long-time collaborator Edward S. Herman. Ostensibly about Vietnam, Laos, and Cambodia, the great majority of its content was a defense of the position Chomsky took on the Pol Pot regime. By this time, Chomsky was well aware that something terrible had happened: "The record of atrocities in Cambodia is substantial and often gruesome," he wrote. "There can be little doubt that the war was followed by an outbreak of violence, massacre and repression." He mocked the suggestion, however, that the death toll might have reached more than a million and attacked Senator George McGovern's call for military intervention to halt what McGovern called "a clear case of genocide."

Instead, Chomsky commended authors who apologized for the Pol Pot regime. He approvingly cited their analyses that the forced march of the population out of Phnom Penh was probably necessitated by the failure of the 1976 rice crop. If this was true, Chomsky wrote, "the evacuation of Phnom Penh, widely denounced at the time and since for its undoubted brutality, may actually have saved many lives." Chomsky rejected the charge of genocide, suggesting that

> the deaths in Cambodia were not the result of systematic slaughter and starvation organized by the state but rather attributable in large measure to peasant revenge, undisciplined military units out of government control, starvation and disease that are direct consequences of the US war, or other such factors.

After the Cataclysm also presented a much more extended critique of refugee testimony. Chomsky revealed his original 1977 source for this had been Ben Kiernan, at the time an Australian graduate student and apologist for the Pol Pot regime, who wrote in the Maoist-inspired *Melbourne Journal of Politics*. What Chomsky avoided telling his readers, however, was that well before 1980, the year *After the Cataclysm* was published, Kiernan himself had recanted his position.

Kiernan had spent much of 1978 and 1979 interviewing five hundred Cambodian refugees in camps inside Thailand. They persuaded him they were actually telling the truth. He also gained a mass of evidence from the new Vietnamese-installed regime. This led him to write a *mea culpa* in the *Bulletin of Concerned Asian Scholars* in 1979. This was a left-wing journal frequently cited by Chomsky, so he must have been aware that Kiernan wrote: "There can be no doubting that the evidence also points clearly to a systematic use of violence against the population by that chauvinist section of the revolutionary movement that was led by Pol Pot." Yet in *After the Cataclysm*, Chomsky does not acknowledge this at all.

Kiernan later went on to write *The Pol Pot Regime: Race, Power and Genocide under the Khmer Rouge 1975–79*, a book now widely regarded as the definitive analysis of one of the most appalling episodes in recorded history. In the evacuation of Phnom Penh in 1975, tens of thousands of people died. Almost the entire middle class was deliberately targeted and killed, including civil servants, teachers, intellectuals, and artists. No fewer than 68,000 Buddhist monks out of a total of 70,000 were executed. Fifty percent of urban Chinese were murdered.

Kiernan argues for a total death toll between April 1975 and January 1979, when the Vietnamese invasion put an end to the regime, of 1.67 million out of 7.89 million, or 21 percent of the entire population. This is proportionally the greatest mass killing ever inflicted by a government on its own population in modern times, probably in all history.

Chomsky was this regime's most prestigious and most persistent Western apologist. Even as late as 1988, when they were forced to admit in their book *Manufacturing Consent* that Pol Pot had committed genocide against his own people, Chomsky and Herman still insisted they had been right to reject the journalists and authors who had initially reported the story. The evidence that became available after the Vietnamese invasion of 1979, they maintained, did not retrospectively justify the reports they had criticized in 1977.

They were still adamant that the United States, who they claimed started it all, bore the brunt of the blame. In short, Chomsky still refused to admit how wrong he had been over Cambodia.

CHOMSKY HAS PERSISTED with this pattern of behavior right to this day. In his response to September 11, he claimed that no matter how appalling the terrorists' actions, the United States had done worse. He supported his case with arguments and evidence just as empirically selective and morally duplicitous as those he used to defend Pol Pot. On September 12, 2001, Chomsky wrote:

> The terrorist attacks were major atrocities. In scale they may not reach the level of many others, for example, Clinton's bombing of the Sudan with no credible pretext, destroying half its pharmaceutical supplies and killing unknown numbers of people.

This Sudanese incident was an American missile attack on the Al-Shifa pharmaceutical factory in Khartoum, where the CIA suspected Iraqi scientists were manufacturing the nerve agent VX for use in chemical weapons contracted by the Saddam Hussein regime. The missile was fired at night so that no workers would be there and the loss of innocent life would be minimised. The factory was located in an industrial area and the only apparent casualty at the time was the caretaker.

While Chomsky drew criticism for making such an odious comparison, he was soon able to flesh out his case. He told a reporter from salon.com that, rather than an "unknown" number of deaths in Khartoum, he now had credible statistics to show there were many more Sudanese victims than those killed in New York and Washington: "That one bombing, according to estimates made by the German Embassy in Sudan and Human Rights Watch, probably led to tens of thousands of deaths." However, this claim was quickly rendered suspect. One of his two sources, Human Rights Watch, wrote to salon.com the following week denying it had produced any such figure. Its communications director said: "In fact, Human Rights Watch has conducted no research into civilian deaths as the result of US bombing in Sudan and would not make such an assessment without a careful and thorough research mission on the ground."

Chomsky's second source had done no research into the matter either. He was Werner Daum, German ambassador to Sudan from 1996 to 2000 who wrote in the *Harvard International Review*, Summer 2001. Despite his occupation, Daum's article was anything but diplomatic.

It was a largely anti-American tirade criticizing the United States' international human rights record, blaming America for the 1980s Iran-Iraq war, accusing it of ignoring Iraq's gassing of the Kurds, and holding it responsible for the purported deaths of 600,000 Iraqi children as a result of post-1991 economic sanctions. Nonetheless, his comments on the death toll from the Khartoum bombing were not as definitive as Chomsky intimated. Daum wrote:

> It is difficult to assess how many people in this poor African country died as a result of the destruction of the Al-Shifa factory, but several tens of thousands seems a reasonable guess. The factory produced some of the basic medicines on the World Health Organization list, covering 20 to 60 percent of Sudan's market and 100 percent of the market for intravenous liquids. It took more than three months for these products to be replaced with imports.

Now, it is hard to take seriously Daum's claim that this "guess" was in any way "reasonable." He said there was a three-month gap between the destruction of the factory and the time it took to replace its products with imports. This seems an implausibly long interval to ship pharmaceuticals but, even if true, it is fanciful to suggest that "several tens of thousands" of people would have died in such a brief period.

Had they done so, they must have succumbed to a highly visible medical crisis, a pandemic to put the SARS outbreak in the shade. Yet no one on the spot, apart from the German ambassador, seems to have heard of it.

Anyone who makes an Internet search of the reports of the Sudanese operations of the several Western aid agencies, including Oxfam, Médecins sans Frontières, and Norwegian People's Aid, who have been operating in this region for decades, will not find any evidence of an unusual increase in the death toll at the time. Instead, their major health concern, then and now, has been how the Muslim Marxist government in Khartoum was waging civil war by bombing the civilian hospitals of its Christian enemies in the south of the country.

The idea that tens of thousands of Sudanese would have died within three months from a shortage of pharmaceuticals is implausible enough in itself. That this could have happened without any of the aid organizations noticing or complaining is simply unbelievable.

Hence Chomsky's rationalization for the September 11 attacks is every bit as deceitful as his apology for Pol Pot and his misreading of the Cambodian genocide.

"It is the responsibility of intellectuals to speak the truth and to expose lies," Chomsky wrote in a famous article in *The New York Review of Books* in February 1967. This was not only a well-put and memorable statement but was also a good indication of his principal target. Most of his adult life has been spent in the critique of other intellectuals who, he claims, have not fulfilled their duty.

The central argument of *American Power and the New Mandarins* is that the humanities and social sciences had been captured by a new breed of intellectuals. Rather than acting as Socratic free thinkers challenging received opinion, they had betrayed their calling by becoming servants of the military-industrial state. The interests of this new mandarin class, he argued, had turned the United States into an imperial power. Their ideology demonstrated

> the mentality of the colonial civil servant, persuaded of the benevolence of the mother country and the correctness of its vision of world order, and convinced that he understands the true interests of the backward peoples whose welfare he is to administer.

Chomsky named the academic fields he regarded as the worst offenders—psychology, sociology, systems analysis, and political science—and held up some well-known practitioners, including Samuel Huntington of Harvard, as among the worst examples. The Vietnam War, Chomsky claimed, was designed and executed by the new mandarins.

In itself, Chomsky's identification of the emergence of a new type of academically trained official was neither original nor radical. Similar critiques had been made of the same phenomenon in both western and eastern Europe for some time. Much of his critique had been anticipated in the 1940s in a book from the other end of the political spectrum, Friedrich von Hayek's *Road to Serfdom*, which identified the social engineers of the welfare state as the greatest internal threats to Western liberty. Chomsky offered a leftist version of the same idea, writing:

> There are dangerous tendencies in the ideology of the welfare state intelligentsia who claim to possess the technique and understanding required to manage our "postindustrial society" and to organize the international society dominated by the American superpower.

Yet at the very time he was making this critique, Chomsky himself was playing at social engineering on an even grander scale. As he indicated in his support in 1967 for the "collectivization and communization" of Chinese and Vietnamese agriculture, with its attendant terror and mass slaughter, he had sought the calculated reorganization of traditional societies. By his advocacy of revolutionary change throughout Asia, he was seeking to play a role in the reorganization of the international order as well.

Hence, apart from occupying a space on the political spectrum much further to the left than the academics he criticized, and apart from his preference for bloodshed over more bureaucratic techniques, Chomsky himself was the very exemplar of the new mandarin he purported to despise.

He was, in fact, one of the more successful examples of the breed. There has now been enough analysis of the Vietnam War to demonstrate conclusively that the United States was not defeated militarily. South Vietnam was abandoned to its fate because of the war's political costs at home. The influence of radical intellectuals like Chomsky in persuading the student generation of the 1960s to oppose the war was crucial in elevating these political costs to an intolerable level.

The result they helped produce, however, was far worse than any bureaucratic solution that might have emanated from the behavioral sciences of the 1960s. From our present vantage point, we can today see the long-term outcome of the choice Chomsky posed in 1967 between the "comparative costs" of revolutionary terror in Vietnam versus the continuation of private enterprise agriculture in the Philippines.

The results all favor the latter. In 2001, the average GDP per head in the Philippines was $4000. At the same time, twenty-five years of revolution in Vietnam had produced a figure of only half as much, a mere $2100. Even those Vietnamese who played major roles in the transformation are now dismayed at the outcome. The former Vietcong General Pham Xuan An said in 1999: "All that talk about 'liberation' twenty, thirty years ago, all the plotting, all the bodies, produced this, this impoverished broken-down country led by a gang of cruel and paternalistic half-educated theorists."

These "half-educated theorists" were the very mandarins Chomsky and his supporters so badly wanted to succeed and worked so hard to install.

As well as social science practitioners and bureaucrats, the other representatives of the intelligentsia to whom Chomsky has long been hostile are the people who work in the news media.

Although his politics made him famous, Chomsky has made no substantial contribution to political theory. Almost all his political books are collections of short essays, interviews, speeches, and newspaper opinion pieces about current events. The one attempt he made at a more thorough-going analysis was the work he produced in 1988 with Edward S. Herman, *Manufacturing Consent: The Political Economy of the Mass Media*. This book, however, must have been a disappointment to his followers.

Media studies is a huge field ranging from traditional defenses of the news media as the fourth estate of the democratic system, to the most arcane cultural analyses produced by radical postmodernist theorists. Chomsky and Herman gave no indication they had digested any of it.

Instead, their book offers a crude analysis that would have been at home in an old Marxist pamphlet from the 1930s. Apart from the introduction, most of the book is simply a re-hash of the authors' previously published work criticizing media coverage of events in central America (El Salvador, Guatemala, and Nicaragua) and in south-east Asia (Vietnam, Laos, and Cambodia), plus one chapter on reporting of the 1981 KGB-Bulgarian plot to kill the pope.

To explain the role of the mass media, Chomsky and Herman offer their "propaganda model." This claims the function of the media is

> to amuse, entertain and inform, and to inculcate individuals with the values, beliefs and codes of behavior that will integrate them into the institutional structures of the larger society. In a world of concentrated wealth and major conflicts of class interest, to fulfil this role requires systematic propaganda.

This is true, they maintain, whether the media operate in liberal democracies or under totalitarian regimes. The only difference is that in communist and other authoritarian societies, it is clear to everyone that the media are instruments of the dominant elite. In capitalist societies, however, this fact is concealed, since the media "actively compete, periodically attack and expose corporate and governmental malfeasance, and aggressively portray themselves as spokesmen for free speech and the general community interest."

Chomsky and Herman argue that these attacks on authority are always very limited and the claims of free speech are merely smokescreens for inculcating the economic and political agendas of the privileged groups that dominate the economy.

The media, they note, are all owned by large corporations, they are beholden for their income to major national advertisers, most news is generated by large multinational news agencies, and any newspaper or television station that steps out of line is bombarded with "flak" or letters, petitions, lawsuits, and speeches from pro-capitalist institutes set up for this very purpose.

There are, however, two glaring omissions from their analysis: the role of journalists and the preferences of media audiences. Nowhere do the authors explain how journalists and other news producers come to believe they are exercising their freedom to report the world as they see it. Chomsky and Herman simply assert these people have been duped into seeing the world through a pro-capitalist ideological lens.

Nor do they attempt any analysis of why millions of ordinary people exercise their free choice every day to buy newspapers and tune in to radio and television programs. Chomsky and Herman fail to explain why readers and viewers so willingly accept the worldview of capitalist media proprietors. They provide no explanation for the tastes of media audiences.

This view of both journalists and audiences as easily-led, ideological dupes of the powerful is not just a fantasy of Chomsky and Herman's own making. It is also a stance that reveals an arrogant and patronising contempt for everyone who does not share their politics. The disdain inherent in this outlook was revealed during an exchange between Chomsky and a questioner at a conference in 1989 (reproduced in Chomsky, *Understanding Power*, 2002):

> Man: The only poll I've seen about journalists is that they are basically narcissistic and left of center.
> Chomsky: Look, what people call "left of center" doesn't mean anything—it means they're conventional liberals and conventional liberals are very state-oriented, and usually dedicated to private power.

In short, Chomsky believes that only he and those who share his radical perspective have the ability to rise above the illusions that keep everyone else slaves of the system. Only he can see things as they really are.

Since the European Enlightenment a number of prominent intellectuals have presented themselves as secular Christ-like figures, lonely beacons of light struggling to survive in a dark and corrupting world. This is a tactic that has often delivered them followers among students and other idealistic youths in late adolescence.

The phenomenon has been most successful when accompanied by an uncomplicated morality that its constituency can readily absorb. In his ruminations on September 11, Chomsky reiterated his own apparently direct and simple moral principles. Reactions to the terrorist attacks, he said, "should meet the most elementary moral standards: specifically, if an action is right for us, it is right for others; and if it is wrong for others, it is wrong for us."

Unfortunately, like his declaration of the responsibility of the intellectual to speak the truth and expose lies, Chomsky himself has consistently demonstrated an inability to abide by his own standards. Among his most provocative recent demands are for American political and military leaders to be tried as war criminals. He has often couched this in terms of the failure by the United States to apply the same standards to itself as it does to its enemies.

For instance, America tried and executed the remaining World War II leaders of Germany and Japan, but failed to try its own personnel for the "war crime" of dropping the atomic bomb on Japan. Chomsky claims the American bombing of dams during the Korean War was "a huge war crime . . . just like racist fanaticism" but the action was praised at home. "That's just a couple of years after they hanged German leaders who were doing much less than that."

The worst current example, he claims, is American support for Israel:

> virtually everything that Israel is doing, meaning the United States and Israel are doing, is illegal, in fact, a war crime. And many of them they defined as "grave breaches," that is, serious war crimes. This means that the United States and Israeli leadership should be brought to trial.

Yet Chomsky's moral perspective is completely one-sided. No matter how great the crimes of the regimes he has favored, such as China, Vietnam, and Cambodia under the communists, Chomsky has never demanded their leaders be captured and tried for war crimes. Instead, he has defended these regimes for many years to the best of his ability through the use of evidence he must have realized was selective, deceptive, and in some cases invented.

In fact, had Pol Pot ever been captured and tried in a Western court, Chomsky's writings could have been cited as witness for the defense. Were the same to happen to Osama bin Laden, Chomsky's moral rationalizations in his most recent book—"almost any crime, a crime in the street, a war, whatever it may be, there's usually something behind it that has elements of legitimacy"—could be used to plead for a lighter sentence.

This kind of two-faced morality has provided a model for the world-wide protests by left-wing opponents of the American-led coalition's war against Iraq. The left was willing to tolerate the most hideous acts of state terrorism by the Saddam Hussein regime, but was implacable in its hostility to intervention by Western democratic governments in the interests of both their own security and the emancipation of the Iraqi people. This is hypocrisy writ large.

The long political history of this aging activist demonstrates that double standards of the same kind have characterized his entire career.

Chomsky has declared himself a libertarian and anarchist but has defended some of the most authoritarian and murderous regimes in human history. His political philosophy is purportedly based on empowering the oppressed and toiling masses but he has contempt for ordinary people who he regards as ignorant dupes of the privileged and the powerful. He has defined the responsibility of the intellectual as the pursuit of truth and the exposure of lies, but has supported the regimes he admires by suppressing the truth and perpetrating falsehoods. He has endorsed universal moral principles but has only applied them to Western liberal democracies, while continuing to rationalize the crimes of his own political favorites. He is a mandarin who denounces mandarins. When caught out making culpably irresponsible misjudgments, as he was over Cambodia and Sudan, he has never admitted he was wrong.

Today, Chomsky's hypocrisy stands as the most revealing measure of the sorry depths to which the left-wing political activism he has done so much to propagate has now sunk.

May 2003

Eric Hobsbawm: Lying to the Credulous

David Pryce-Jones

E RIC HOBSBAWM IS NO doubt intelligent and industrious, and he might well have made a notable contribution as a historian. Unfortunately, lifelong devotion to Communism destroyed him as a thinker or interpreter of events. Such original work as he did concerned bandits and outlaws. But even here there is bias, for he rescued them from obscurity not for their own sake but as precursors of Communist revolution. His longer and later books are constructed around the abstractions of the bourgeoisie and the proletariat and the supposedly pre-ordained class struggle between them, capital and capitalism, empire and imperialism—in short the Marxist organizing principles which reduce human beings and their varied lives to concepts handy to serve a thesis worked up in advance and in the library. This material, needless to say, was derived from secondary sources.

The purpose of all Hobsbawm's writing, indeed of his life, has been to certify the inevitable triumph of Communism. In the face of whatever might actually have been happening in the Soviet Union and its satellites, he devised reasons to justify or excuse the Communist Party right to its end— long after Russians themselves had realized that Communism had ruined morally and materially everybody and everything within its reach. He loves to describe himself as a professional historian, but someone who has steadily corrupted knowledge into propaganda, and scorns the concept of objective truth, is nothing of the kind, neither a historian nor professional.

It becomes quite a good joke that Communism collapsed under him, proving in the living world that the beliefs and ideas in his head were empty illusions, and all the Marxist and Soviet rhetoric just claptrap. This Hobsbawn cannot understand, never mind accept. His best-known book, *Age of Extremes*, published as recently as 1994, still attempts to whitewash Communism as "a formidable innovation" in social engineering, glossing with fundamental dishonesty over such integral features as enforced famine through collectivization and the Hitler-Stalin Pact, and omitting all mention of the massacre at Katyn, the terrifying secret police apparatus of Beria, and the Gulag. At the same time, Hobsbawm depicts the United States "unfortunately" as a greater danger than the Soviet Union. Presenting him with a prestigious prize for this farrago, the left-wing historian Sir Keith Thomas said, "For pure intelligence applied to history, Eric Hobsbawm has no equal." Another left-winger, the journalist Neal Ascherson, held that "No historian now writing in English can match his overwhelming command of fact and source." So much for Robert Conquest, Sir Kenneth Dover, Sir Hugh Lloyd-Jones, Bernard Lewis, and other genuine scholars.

A mystery peculiar to the twentieth century is that intellectuals were eager to endorse the terror and mass murder which characterized Soviet rule, at one and the same time abdicating humane feelings and all sense of responsibility toward others, and of course perverting the pursuit of truth. The man who sets dogs on concentration camp victims or fires his revolver into the back of their necks is evidently a brute; the intellectual who devises justifications for the brutality is harder to deal with, and far more sinister in the long run. Apologizing for the Soviet Union, such intellectuals licensed and ratified unprecedented crime and tyranny, to degrade and confuse all standards of humanity and morality. Hobsbawm is an outstanding example of the type. The overriding question is: how was someone with his capacity able to deceive himself so completely about reality and take his stand alongside the commissar signing death warrants?

Not long ago, on a popular television show, Hobsbawm explained that the fact of Soviet mass murdering made no difference to his Communist commitment. In astonishment, his interviewer asked, "What that comes down to is saying that had the radiant tomorrow actually been created, the loss of fifteen, twenty million people might have been justified?" Without hesitation Hobsbawm replied, "Yes." His autobiography, *Interesting Times: A Twentieth-Century Life* (Penguin, 2005), conveys the same point, only rather more deviously. On the very last page, it is true, he is "prepared to concede, with regret, that Lenin's Comintern was not such a good idea," though for no very obvious reason (except as a cheap shot) he concludes the sentence by cramming in the comment that Herzl's Zionism was also not a good idea. Note that slippery use of "Comintern" as a substitute for Communism itself. The concession, such as it is, is anyhow vitiated by an earlier passage when he attacks America and its allies, bizarrely spelled out as India, Israel, and Italy, and referred to as rich and the heirs of fascism. In this passage he predicts, "The world may regret that, faced with Rosa Luxemburg's alternative of socialism and barbarism, it decided against socialism." (Which leaves Americans as barbarians.) By my count, these are the only two expressions of regret in this long book. In contrast, the October revolution remains "the central point of reference in the political universe," and "the dream of the October revolution" is still vivid inside him. He cannot bring himself to refer to Leningrad as St. Petersburg. Learning nothing, he has forgotten nothing.

The key to this limited personality no doubt lies in his background and childhood. His father was a British subject, though of Central European Jewish origins, and his mother was Viennese. The hazards of his father's career meant that Hobsbawm was born in Egypt, in 1917, though very soon afterwards the family settled in Vienna. In the aftermath of the First War, the time and the place were unpropitious; his father found it hard to make a living as a businessman in Vienna; his mother helped out by doing some writing, including a novel. Both parents died prematurely, and Hobsbawm was brought up by an aunt and uncle in Berlin between 1931 and 1935. At school in that city, he says, he did not suffer any sort of taunting either as a displaced English teenager or as a Jew, but these years induced "the sense of living in some sort of final crisis" and this made him a Communist. When it suits him, of course, he uses his experience of Germany under Hitler to shelter under the convenient label of anti-fascist or socialist.

One of Stalin's major mistakes was to order the German Communists to side with the Nazis against the "social fascists" or Social Democrats, thus consummating Hitler's rise to power. Hobsbawm approved, but he can hardly have understood the implication at the time. A more likely factor determining his Communism, it seems to me, is the remoteness he feels from normal emotions. His parents and their sad lives leave him unmoved. His aunts and uncles are described here with a chilling one-dimensional detachment free from any gratitude for what they did. He also had one sister, younger than he, of whom he says baldly, "She did not share my interests or my life, increasingly dominated by politics." Elsewhere in the book, this sister is written off as "a demonstratively conventional Anglican country matron and Conservative Party activist." He is able to say of himself that his "intellectualism and lack of interest in the world of people" gave him protection. The confession does nothing to mitigate the coldness and inhumanity of such a character.

A scholarship to King's College, Cambridge, refashioned Hobsbawm's life after 1935. A British subject, he was not a refugee, but he was certainly an outsider, and one, moreover, who had the luck to fall into a milieu welcoming to outsiders. King's is one of the most historic English colleges, and one of the richest. Kingsmen have long been a byword for self-satisfaction, quick to attack the privileges they make sure that they are themselves enjoying. In the college was a semi-secret society known as the Apostles, which in the Thirties evolved from embracing a Bloomsbury aestheticism to Communism. Blunt and Burgess and Maclean—as well as other traitors and Soviet agents—had been Apostles slightly ahead of Hobsbawm. It was from this vantage point that Hobsbawm applauded the Hitler-Stalin Pact of 1939, another of Stalin's major mistakes.

As an active and declared Communist, Hobsbawm remained unpromoted in the ranks throughout the war, and was kept stationed in the country. Hardly surprising, though it still rankles with him. He also suggests that his Communism delayed academic preferment, but in fact a telephone call to a colleague at King's was enough to gain him a fellowship there. After that, he became a professor at Birkbeck College, London, another fortress of the left. It was also always plain sailing for him to obtain his visa to the United States, where eventually he taught regularly. The Cold War saw him become a spokesman for Communism, and a visitor to the Soviet Union and its satellites. In this memoir he continues to glide over Stalin and the criminality of Stalinism. Communists allegedly did not recognize the extent of the Soviet camps. Why ever not? Everybody else did. The United States, he holds, was responsible for waging the Cold War, winning what he considers an undeserved victory. An unfathomable contradiction emerges: the Soviet Union was a superpower inspiring a sixth of the globe yet helplessly weak in the face of the supposedly blind and selfish United States.

For Hobsbawm, Khrushchev's denunciation of Stalin at the Twentieth Party Congress in 1956 was a horror. Khrushchev wantonly sullied the October revolution and its dream. (The implication is that if he had only kept his mouth shut Stalinist criminality could have endured indefinitely.) An immediate consequence was the Hungarian uprising that same year, put down by the Soviets with the usual mixture of duplicity and brute force. Most of Hobsbawm's friends left the Communist Party. He himself made a point of staying, out of pride, the refusal to admit that he might be in the wrong. He has the tiresome habit of quoting at length from his own writings, but he carefully makes sure not to quote the letter he published on 9 November 1956 in the Communist *Daily Worker* defending the Soviet onslaught on Hungary. "While approving, with a heavy heart, of what is now happening in Hungary, we should therefore also say frankly that we think the USSR should withdraw its troops from the country as soon as this is possible." Which is more deceitful, the spirit of this letter, or the omission of any reference to it?

In the course of his life, the only people Hobsbawm seems ever to have known were Communist intellectuals like himself, a good many of them privileged people with private incomes. For many years he had a cottage in

Wales on the estate of Clough Williams-Ellis, a rich landowner and baroque architect whose wife Amabel, born into the Strachey family of Bloomsbury fame, was a salon Communist. In a comic mirror-image of the more usual social snobbery, Hobsbawm lets drop, "I refused all contact with the sub-urban petty-bourgeoisie, which I naturally regarded with contempt." That "naturally" is worth a moment's pause.

Of course some of the people he did know tell a story too, a story of political hysteria and frenzy. He was a friend of Jürgen Kuczynski, an East German Marxist, and his sister Ruth, a Soviet agent who was the contact for Klaus Fuchs, who gave the Soviets the drawings for the atom bomb. He was also the friend of Alexander Rado, who ran a Soviet spy network in Switzerland, and finished up in Hungary. And of the Communist theoretician Louis Althusser, who murdered his wife, and E. P. Thompson and Raymond Williams, both Communist writers. (With the latter in 1940 he wrote a defense of the Soviet invasion of Finland.) A female comrade called Freddie was trapped by bomb damage during the London blitz. Thinking that she was about to die, she cried out to the helpers, "Long live the Party, long live Stalin."

Hobsbawm was a contemporary at King's of James Klugmann, already then a Communist, and later a member of the British party's Politburo. His full story remains to be told, but what is known already is a striking il-lustration of the political hysteria surrounding these people, and the harm that this could do. Special Operations Executive was the wartime unit responsible for partisan warfare behind the German lines, and therefore a special target for Soviet infiltration. Security was lax, and Klugmann was able to worm his way into a senior position in the SOE bureaucracy. As the intercepts in the archives now reveal, as a good Stalinist he falsified the reports from agents in the field in Yugoslavia to SOE headquarters, in order to attribute monarchist acts of resistance to Tito's Communists. This in-fluenced Churchill to switch support from the monarchists to Tito, an es-sential step facilitating the Communist takeover of Yugoslavia. At the time of the break with Yugoslavia, Moscow forced Klugmann to write a book denouncing Tito whom he had done so much to empower. This book is a collector's item in the rich library of Communist absurdity, along with the defense by Hobsbawm and Williams of the Soviet invasion of Finland. Hobsbawm's final judgment on Klugmann is: "He knew what was right, but shied away from saying it in public." That "shied away" is also worth a moment's pause. What else did Hobsbawm ever do but shy away from what was right? The Communist Party and its claim to unconditional obedience governed him. "We did what it ordered us to do," he writes. Be-sides, "The Party got things done." The justification is still more childish because he makes sure not to specify or to analyze, and certainly not to criticize, what exactly were these things that the Party got done.

Reduction of human beings and their doings to cerebral figments is the sign of a cold, not to say nasty, character. And Hobsbawm further does himself no favors with his frequent sneering, for instance referring to Orwell not by his literary name but as "an upper-class Englishman called Eric Blair" or applying to American jails the phrase "*univers concentrationnaire*" (originally coined by David Rousset to cover both Nazi and Soviet camps). He multiplies euphemistic observations such as that the odious dictatorship of East Germany was a "firmly structured community" and deserving credit because it held show trials which did not end in executions. He has a passage attacking as "literally senseless" the familiar western Cold War slogan "Better dead than red." Needless to say, this is an inversion of the words, a pure fabrication. Pacifists and Soviet apologists coined the slogan "Better red than dead" in order to persuade the West not to defend itself with nuclear weapons.

Hobsbawm's autobiography brings out the further complicating factor of his Jewishness. His mother apparently told him never to do anything that might suggest he was ashamed of being a Jew. But the relationship between Communism and Jewishness does not allow for anything so simple and straightforward. The theoretical internationalism of the former is in conflict with both the nationalism and the religious separatism of the latter. Some Jews turned to Communism as a release from an identity they did not wish to have for all sorts of reasons, some high and some ignoble. Others became Zionists, who were often deviant Marxists to begin with. Hobsbawm shows the consistent Communist animus against Zionism and Israel, losing no chance to sneer on that score about "the small, militarist, culturally disappointing and politically aggressive nation-state which asks for my solidarity on racial grounds." He boasts of a visit to Bir Zeit University on the West Bank to display solidarity with the Palestinians. Why Palestinian nationalism is valid, and Jewish nationalism invalid, is something else Hobsbawm fails to analyze and explain. Quite crudely, he approves of nationalism in countries which proclaim themselves Communist and anti-American, like Cuba or Vietnam, while rejecting nationalism in countries which are not Communist and are pro-American, like Israel. Whatever he may profess about his mother's recommendation, this makes him in practice thoroughly ashamed of being Jewish.

The welcome given to Jewish intellectuals who denounce their identity is far greater than the welcome for those who assert it in whatever form. Hobsbawm's success is huge. Portentously but for once truthfully, he declares that he is at the center of the establishment. It says much about present-day Britain that the Blair government awarded him the Companion of Honour, a prestigious decoration, and it says much about Hobsbawm that he accepted it. According to *Who's Who*, he holds something like twenty honorary degrees, many from distinguished institutions such as the University of Chicago, Bard College, and Columbia University. He is also the recipient of many other honors including membership in the American Academy of Arts and Sciences.

A companion piece to the dishonest *Age of Extremes*, his memoir has precipitated further cloud-bursts of hyperbole. A history magazine published by the BBC calls him a "key witness" to the twentieth century. "Newsnight" is a flagship BBC television program on current events, and its anchorman, Jeremy Paxman, makes it his trademark to be abrasive. A suddenly oleaginous Paxman called Hobsbawm to his face the greatest historian of the twentieth century. In *The London Review of Books*, Perry Anderson (once editor of *New Left Review*) elaborated in thousands of words on the largeness of Hobsbawm's mind, and the "complex distinction of the life." Not content with that, in the subsequent issue of the *London Review*, Anderson followed up at many times the length with a turgidly Marxoid essay on his hero, criticizing him only for occasional lapses from Party correctness, and—rather surprisingly—for self-importance. (His reward is to be called "remarkably able" in Hobsbawm's book). Even a conservative reviewer, Niall Ferguson, who found fault with Hobsbawm's Communism, nonetheless thought it undeniable that he is "one of the great historians of his generation."

What can be going on? Part of the indulgence shown to Hobsbawm no doubt stems from admirable British civility, and the desire to accommodate even the most unaccommodating Jewish intellectual. And part of it is hagiography, the left on their knees chanting prayers for one another. But more generally here is a hangover from the Thirties, when apologia for Communism swept aside rationality and common humanity. Proof against all evidence, proof against political reality, a fictitious representation of Communism as a benign force retains its hold somewhere in the imagination even of quite intelligent people. The Soviet Union collapsed with hardly a sigh, like gas going out of a balloon, because it was all a lie. Hobsbawm and his supporters will never admit their share in the central intellectual and moral failure of the times. They lost out in the real historical process, but they hope to win the historiography by turning Communism into some spectral romantic myth shimmering tantalizingly above the surface of things, out of range of truth, and therefore fit to be started up all over again. All it takes is what it always took—an unscrupulous character, lack of interest in the world of people, and well-crafted lying to the credulous.

January 2003

Thomas Kuhn's Irrationalism

James Franklin

F OR AN INSIGHT into trends and fads in the humanities world, it is hard to improve on the Arts and Humanities Citation Index. It lists all citations in the major humanities journals—that is, an army of trained slaves keys in every footnote of every article and the computer rearranges them according to the work cited. The compilers of the index examined the records for the years 1976–1983, and issued a report on the most cited works of the twentieth century. The most cited *author* was Lenin, which speaks volumes on the state of the humanities in the West toward the end of the Cold War. But the most cited single works were, in reverse order: in third place, Northrop Frye's *Anatomy of Criticism*; second, Joyce's *Ulysses*; and, well in the lead, Thomas Kuhn's 1962 book, *The Structure of Scientific Revolutions.*

Interest in Kuhn's book has not waned. The Index is now online, and records one-hundred citations to the book for 1999—plus another four-hundred in the Social Sciences Citation Index. To call the tone of most of these citations reverential would be something of an understatement. It is reported that *Structure* is Al Gore's favorite book, and William Safire's *New Political Dictionary* has an article on "paradigm shift," a phrase popularized by Kuhn, which reports both Bush (senior) and Clinton being much impressed with its usefulness.

THE BASIC CONTENT of Kuhn's book can be inferred simply by asking: what would the humanities crowd *want* said about science? Once the question is asked, the answer is obvious. Kuhn's thesis is that scientific theories are no better than ones in the humanities. The idea that science is all theoretical talk and negotiation, which never really establishes anything, is one that caused trouble long ago for Galileo, who wrote:

If what we are discussing were a point of law or of the humanities, in which neither true nor false exists, one might trust in subtlety of mind and readiness of tongue and in the greater experience of the writers, and expect him who excelled in those things to make his reasoning more plausible, and one might judge it to be the best. But in natural sciences whose conclusions are true and necessary and have nothing to do with human will, one must take care not to place oneself in the defense of error; for here a thousand Demostheneses and a thousand Aristotles would be left in the lurch by every mediocre wit who happened to hit upon the truth for himself.

Kuhn's "achievement" was to put the view of Galileo's scholastic opponents back on the agenda. Up to his time, philosophy of science had concentrated on such questions as how evidence confirms theories and what the difference is between science and pseudo-science, that is, questions about the logic of science. Kuhn declared logic outmoded and replaced it with history.

A caricature of his opinions is this: a science, say astronomy, is dominated for a long period by a "paradigm," such as Ptolemy's theory that the sun and planets revolve around a stationary earth. Most work is on "normal science," the solving of standard problems in terms of the reigning paradigm. But anomalies—results the paradigm cannot explain—accumulate and eventually make the paradigm unsustainable. The science enters a revolutionary phase as a new paradigm such as Copernicus's heliocentrism comes to seem more plausible. Defenders of the old order, who cannot accommodate the change and usually cannot even understand the concepts in which it is expressed, gradually die out and the new paradigm is left in control of the field. Then the process repeats. According to the summary in Francis Fukuyama's *End of History*,

> The cumulative and progressive nature of modern science has been challenged by Thomas Kuhn, who has pointed to the discontinuous and revolutionary nature of change in the sciences. In his most radical assertions, he has denied the possibility of "scientific" knowledge of nature at all, since *all* "paradigms" by which scientists understand nature ultimately fail.

As with many caricatures, one finds that the original consists of the caricature with the addition of a number of qualifications; the qualifications render the original inconsistent, and the author's subsequent denials that he had said anything so radical increase further the number of inconsistencies. One observes also that the caricature has a historical career considerably more vigorous than the original, whose qualifications would have lessened its appeal. Besides its simplicity, the caricature makes the story of science into one of the simple emotive plotlines that literary folk find so engaging. It is the story of the *Morte d'Arthur*, of the peaceable order and its aging king, their virtue undermined by internal corruption, falling to the challenge of the vigorous and bloodthirsty young challenger. The plot made Frazer's *Golden Bough* a literary hit decades before, with its stories of tribal chiefs displacing one another with extreme prejudice, and even persuaded the humanities world to take an interest in the doings of Red Deer, among whom the transfer of harems between dominant males is conducted on similar principles. Kuhn's success is also an instance of the enduring appeal of *theomachy*, a mode of explanation which worked so brilliantly for Marx and Freud, and, long before, for Homer. What was previously thought to be a continuous and uninteresting succession of random events is discovered to be a conflict of a finite number of hidden gods (classes, complexes, paradigms, as the case may be), who manipulate the flux of appearances to their own advantage, but whose machinations may be uncovered by the elect to whom the key has been revealed.

Further reasons for Kuhn's success are not hard to find. He gave permission to anyone who wished to comment on science to ignore completely the large number of sciences which undeniably are progressive accumulations of established results—sciences like ophthalmology, oceanography, operations research, and ornithology, to keep to just one letter of the alphabet. That certainly saved a lot of effort. Kuhn's theory also had a special appeal to social scientists. Political scientists, sociologists, and anthropologists recognized Kuhn's picture of disciplines putting the accumulation of evidence to the background while bringing to the fore fights about theory; they were delighted to hear that what had previously been thought an embarrassment was the way it was done in the most respectable sciences. Kuhn even offered something to massage the egos of natural scientists themselves. It might seem at first glance that his claim that most scientists are drones was insulting, but there was a good reason why it was met with the same equanimity one notices in fundamentalist religious circles at the news that only 144,000 are saved. The damned may be a majority, but of course they are other people; every scientist had the opportunity to cast himself as a revolutionary hero of a new paradigm, shamefully ill-used by the establishment. Kuhn's rhetoric incorporated a few further successful ploys, in that "paradigm" was undoubtedly a cute technical term, as technical terms go, and the phrase "normal science" had just the right hint of superciliousness toward the worker bees who are credulously doing the hard work of science. Kuhn's work was the perfect Sixties product, and, since he managed to publish it in

1962, his success was inevitable—indeed, as the philosophers say, overdetermined.

At a more logical level, Kuhn's success depended on certain ambiguities. Even in the caricature above, it is clear how some were essential to Kuhn's plan. What does "unsustainable" mean when said of a scientific theory? In particular, is it a matter of logic or of psychology? If it means that there are a number of observed results that would be unlikely if the theory were true, then one is back in the realm of logic, of the bad old philosophy of science that studied the relation of evidence to hypothesis. Naturally, Kuhn is not keen to emphasize that direction. But if "unsustainable" is a purely psychological matter, a kind of collective disgust by a *salon des refusés* of younger scientists who simply think their elders are too smug, then it is impossible to see why it should have any standing as science. If the old theory is not broke—if its predictions are true, for example, and its explanations coherent—why fix it? Whatever there is to be said for a pure appetite for novelties in the art world, there is no scope for it in science. There, the difficulty of attaining the truth means no one is inclined to pointless exercises in throwing away pearls attained at great expense.

In his new book *Thomas Kuhn: A Philosophical History for Our Times* (University of Chicago Press, 2001), Steve Fuller agrees with the above analysis in only one respect. He too thinks the effect of Kuhn's book was a bad one. But Fuller is a professor of sociology at the University of Warwick, and he has the attitudes that a sociologist would predict for a Midlands professor of sociology. His complaint is that Kuhn was not nearly revolutionary enough, especially in politics. In saying Kuhn's book was the perfect Sixties product, one qualification is possibly needed. Was it sufficiently leftist? Certainly, the suggestion of the blood of old paradigms staining the water had a reddish tinge. But Kuhn gave no attention to the complaints the left wished made about the complicity of science in the military-industrial complex. It was disappointing that after all Kuhn's work in replacing the logic and philosophy of science with its history and sociology he failed to so much as mention the social effects the left wished targeted.

The villain of the piece, according to Fuller, was James Bryant Conant, president of Harvard from 1933 to 1953. His "General Education in Science" program at Harvard, in which Kuhn taught, explicitly aimed to give future policy makers a broad understanding of science. In the era of the atomic bomb, Sputnik and the moon race, of penicillin, DNA, and the pill, it was clear that science had much greater social implications than had been thought only a decade or two before. Conant was one of the "action-intellectuals" who defined America's early Cold War vision, especially in the areas of science and educational policy. Central to it was the National

Science Foundation, which provided large sums for basic research, of the kind that had turned out unexpectedly to be at the basis of the making of the atomic bomb (and in contrast to the kind of science directly aimed at ideologically specified technological ends, like Lysenko's biology and Nazi eugenics).

Conant's preface to Kuhn's first book, *The Copernican Revolution* (1957), linked the decline of Western Europe to its outdated humanities curricula. Yet, he thought, simply teaching humanists a little straight science had not proved effective either. Science tends to lack a storyline or anything that engages the emotions or encourages the taking of sides. "No one admires or condemns the metals or the behavior of their salts," as he justly said. His solution was history. Carefully chosen episodes in the history of science, in early modern times before it had become too complicated, would allow the student to engage with the excitement of discovery, the "interplay of hypothesis and experiment," and the conflict of personalities and ideas. This was the plan Kuhn implemented in his own teaching, and refined in his books. As it happened, it was not an institutionally successful plan at the time. It was not exported to universities other than Harvard, and when Conant became U.S. Ambassador to West Germany, Kuhn was left undefended and in 1955 refused tenure, on the grounds that he was not an expert on anything in particular. General education for humanists at Harvard retreated to the plan of introducing them to a little real science. But the simplified-history-as-moral-lesson scheme certainly had its revenge with the success of Kuhn's book.

In one way, then, Fuller's book bears comparison with Frances Stonor Saunders's *The Cultural Cold War* which described the CIA spending large sums of money to promote such all-American cultural products as Abstract Expressionism. Certainly, Kuhn's vision of science was as disconnected from reality as Pollock and as free from bothersome detail as Rothko, and as likely as either to contribute to civilized values. But Fuller's spin on the story makes it resemble more closely the thesis of Martin A. Lee and Bruce Shlain's *Acid Dreams* (1985) and Jay Stevens's *Storming Heaven* (1987), according to which the drug culture of the Sixties was a CIA plan that went wrong, and the drugs that at first encouraged the rebellions of those times, in the end undermined them by replacing politics with pleasure. Fuller's accusation is that Kuhn was a patio fauvist, a purveyor of gift-wrapped frissons to the intellectual bourgeoisie, chocolate revolutions that exist in the children's-fiction world of theories and paradigms, without import in the real world. Prescinding for the moment from the question of whether the defusing of revolutionary zeal is a good thing, the thesis itself is interesting, as is the more general thesis that postmodern and other "high theory" forms of leftism act mainly to keep revolutionaries off the streets by channeling their mental energies into endless efforts to understand the incomprehensible. Fuller does not present evidence that any particular theorist was diverted by Kuhn from the path of true socialism which he would have pursued otherwise, but he is right to point to the apolitical, or perhaps better the *faux* political, nature of Kuhn's message, both in the original and its caricature. The research community that pursues a paradigm is a political entity, in the sense that it acts to preserve itself and outmaneuver its rivals, but its talk of "revolution" is very harmless; the revolution is in the past, against the previous paradigm, and no present entities have anything to fear from it. Like the violence in a horror film, it's all virtual and it's over when you come out into the light. At least, that is the correct perspective from the outside society, though denizens of the academy who have to compete for grants and students with the powerful lobbies of rampant paradigms may take a less sanguine view.

In pursuing such issues, Fuller writes well about many matters. He is hugely well-informed about cultural theorists of the fifty years before Kuhn's book, and has many illuminating remarks on the influence of such unlikely figures as Piaget and Pirandello, the connection of paradigms with iconographic approaches to art history, the bifurcation of nineteenth-century relativism into anthropological and Nazi wings, and the like. What Fuller does not know anything about is science. Nowhere in his huge output or its bibliographies is there evidence of reading in science, much less hands-on work. Hence he can write things like "lab work in today's world would seem to be little more than a showcase activity—perhaps, like so many tribal rituals, done *primarily* for the benefit of the spectators." Fuller would be well advised to take a break from his frenetic production of big books and spend a year as bottle washer and data analyst in a lab. Perhaps he would find that the logical techniques he uses himself to evaluate the impact of one cultural theorist on another also work in the lab to allow the scientist to know the reaction of one chemical with another. It is unlikely he will take this advice. In fact, he revealingly explains how he has inoculated himself against any such suggestions. Commenting on some other philosophers of science who did spend time in a laboratory, he writes, "Interestingly, no one ever seems to have left his apprenticeship *less* committed to the science in question than when he entered." Many would take this to be indeed an interesting fact, perhaps suggesting that normal human beings find what goes on in labs quite convincing, when they take a close look. Fuller's unthinking use of "interestingly" to express a presumption that what is generally believed *ipso facto* deserves suspicion places him dead center of the post-Sixties generation of "tenured radicals."

It is Fuller's typicality that makes him a valuable witness to the one aspect of Kuhn's legacy that he does agree with, one that has been the most lasting from the point of view of science studies. To the bewilderment of scientists, that field has almost universally followed Kuhn in his substitution of history and sociology of science for logic and philosophy. In particular, the explanation of why some change occurs in science, such as the belief in Copernicus's system replacing belief in Ptolemy's, is required to be in terms of social causes, such as the interests of patrons. This mode of explanation is contrasted with that which refers principally to the better support by the evidence that a later theory has. The contrast in styles of explanation was the crux of the recent "science wars," where books such as Paul Gross and Norman Levitt's *Higher Superstition* (1994) and Noretta Koertge's collection, *A House Built on Sand*, vigorously attacked the "social contructivists," Kuhn's successors, for "relativism." If science was "constructed" at the whim of powerful interests, could it not be just as easily constructed some other way, and thus be "relative" (to one's tribe, education, or community committed to a paradigm)? And would that not be to deny scientific truth entirely? As Richard Dawkins, the biologist noted for his "selfish gene" theomachy, wrote, "Show me a relativist at 30,000 feet and I'll show you a hypocrite." Fuller reveals why this line of reasoning is not making much impact. He, like other constructivist respondents, merely says that constructivists did not deny scientific truths, or assert relativism. Fuller calls his position a "non-relativist constructivism." By this he means that usually different scientists *will* come to agree on what they say about reality, but that the reason for this is not in reality but in the scientists, in particular in their social relations. Human groups have many things in common, so they will naturally agree on many things.

Taking this line, which is an explicit version of what many humanists are doing when they think briefly about science, requires two remarkable argumentative leaps. The first is simply ignoring the critics' argument that constructivism left its adherents no reason to believe any of the deliverances of science, such as those concerning the effects of actions at 30,000 feet. This problem is not resolved by making one's constructivism "non-relativist." If beliefs are fixed by the political requirements of communities on the ground, that gives no reason to trust them at 30,000 feet. The second leap is more insidious and important, and here Fuller makes explicit, for once, the actual *reasoning* that lies at the bottom of the turn to historical and sociological explanation. Since the move to such causal explanations and away from logic is at once so crucial, so baffling, and so rarely argued for, it is worth attending to his presentation. It occurs in his earlier book, *Philosophy of Science and Its Discontents* (1989). His argument—actually, he calls it "a few homely observations," which will put fallacy watchers on high alert—is that "knowledge exists only through its embodiment in linguistic and other social practices"; these in turn are transmitted by communities, and it is hardly likely that a worldview or even a proposition could persist through this transmission. Indeed, Fuller argues that, even if scientific theories were true, they could not cause reliable transmission of themselves.

This argument is the central plank of the social constructivist position. It is also at the center of the shift from logic to history that Kuhn argues for. Although extraordinarily popular, it is a very bad argument—so bad that the philosopher David Stove named it the winner of his "Competition to Find the Worst Argument in the World." It will be familiar to anyone who has studied philosophy: "We can know things only insofar as they fall under our conceptual or linguistic schemes; therefore, we cannot know things as they are in themselves." In other words, our knowledge is fatally flawed just because it is *our* knowledge. This is an argument that has underpinned many irrationalist programs in the history of thought, from classical idealism to the cultural relativism supported by some anthropologists. It is clear why Fuller's argument is a version: he says "We can know things only via causal (social) processes acting on the brains of real scientists, therefore the content of our theories is fully explained by the social factors causing them; that is, we cannot know things as they are in themselves." It says, in the philosopher Alan Olding's telling caricature, "We have eyes, therefore we cannot see." This is why no amount of raging about relativism, skepticism and truth is going to make any impact on constructivists. They will always say, "Those entities in Platonic worlds, like truths and theories, cannot cause belief in themselves. Scientists are *people*, after all, and as such are responsive only to social or similar causes."

Is it clear what is wrong with this argument? If not, an analogy may help. An electronic calculator implements the laws of arithmetic. If we ask why the number 4 is displayed when we punch in 2 + 2, then there is a causal explanation in terms of the circuitry. At a molecule's eye view of the matter it is a complete explanation. But a full explanation must mention the abstract arithmetical fact that 2 + 2 *is* 4, and that the circuitry has been designed exactly to track such facts. It is not as if numbers magically cause electrical effects, but that physical causes and abstract reasons cooperate. It is the same with scientists and the truths they discover. The truth of the inverse square law of gravity is an essential part of the explanation of why that law is believed. For one thing, its truth is what makes true the measurements that provide the evidence for the theory. Of course, there needs to be some philosophical story about why causes cooperate with reasons, as there does in the case of the calculator. But the point of Kuhn and his followers was not to request such a story, but to argue that it must be irrelevant to explaining scientific beliefs. The worst effect of Kuhn, and the one taken up both most unthinkingly and most forcefully across the whole range of disciplines he influenced, has been the frivolous discarding of the way things are as a constraint on theory about the way things are.

It would be good to conclude by recommending a short book, *What Is Science?*, that does things the right way. It takes a robustly objective view of the relation of evidence to conclusion, explains what laws of nature are, briefly shows how measurement, data, statistics, and mathematical models work in science, states which parts of science are well-established and which not, illustrates with engaging episodes in the history of science, and ends with some colorful rudenesses on postmodernist solecisms concerning science. Unfortunately, it does not exist.

June 2000

Looking Backward at
Edward Bellamy's Utopia

Martin Gardner

No man any more has any care for the morrow, either for himself or his children,
for the nation guarantees the nurture, education, and comfortable maintenance
of every citizen from the cradle to the grave.
—Edward Bellamy, *Looking Backward*

L OOKING BACKWARD: 2000-1887, by Edward Bellamy (1850–1898) is far
and away the most popular, most influential utopia novel ever written,
and also one of the worst. In its endless reprintings, it has sold over a million copies and been translated into twenty languages. Soon after its
appearance in 1888, some hundred books were published either attacking
Bellamy's vision of Boston in the year 2000 or defending it. About half of
these books were utopias with such titles as *Looking Ahead, Looking Beyond,*
Looking Within, Looking Forward, all even more preposterous than Bellamy's.

William Dean Howells was so taken by *Looking Backward* that he wrote
two utopia novels of his own, *A Traveler from Altruria* and *Through the Eye*
of the Needle. Both books resemble Bellamy's in their replacement of un-
bridled capitalism by a moneyless socialist state. The English poet and
socialist William Morris was so infuriated by what he called Bellamy's "horrible cockney dream" that he wrote *News from Nowhere* about a less regi-
mented future society with more of an emphasis on crafts than on
machinery. (The most recent fictional spinoffs from Bellamy's utopia are
two novels by the science-fiction writer Mack Reynolds: *Looking Backward*
from the Year 2000 (1973), and *Equality in the Year 2000* (1977). The hero,
named after Bellamy's, goes to sleep and awakes to find a world trans-

formed by nuclear fission energy. Reynolds was an active member of America's Socialist Labor.

Looking Backward had an enormous effect on Eugene Debs and the later American labor and political leaders who called themselves socialists. In an essay "How I Became a Socialist," Debs thanked Bellamy for "helping me out of darkness into light." The book left its mark on such American socialists and liberals as Norman Thomas, Upton Sinclair, John Dewey, Scott Nearing, Lincoln Steffens, Jack London, Charles Beard, Carl Sandburg, and Erich Fromm. Socialist leaders in England and Europe were also influenced by the book. Leo Tolstoy translated it into Russian.

Vernon Parrington, in the third volume of *Main Currents in American Thought*, devoted fourteen pages to a sympathetic account of *Looking Backward*. David Riesman, in his biography of Thorstein Veblen, told how Bellamy's utopia altered the lives of Veblen and his wife, and persuaded Veblen to shift his academic training from philosophy to economics. The engineer Arthur Ernest Morgan, chairman of the Tennessee Valley Authority under Franklin Roosevelt, and for sixteen years president of Antioch University, thought so highly of *Looking Backward* that he wrote Bellamy's first biography. In *Nowhere and Somewhere: How History Makes Utopias and How Utopias Make History* (1946), Morgan discussed the influence of *Looking Backward* on the shapers of Roosevelt's New Deal, especially on Adolf Berle, Jr., whose father was a friend and disciple of Bellamy. "Striking parallels may be drawn," Morgan wrote,

> between *Looking Backward* and various important aspects of New Deal public policy. It may be said with considerable force that to understand the long range implication of the New Deal one must read *Looking Backward*.

Heywood Broun, during his Soviet fellow-traveling phase and before he converted to Catholicism, wrote an effusive introduction to the Modern Library's edition of *Looking Backward*. Bellamy's utopia, Broun wrote, aroused his first interest in socialism. He thought its description of America in 2000 was "close to an entirely practical and possible scheme of life. . . . there is at least a fair chance that another fifty years will confirm Bellamy's position as one of the authentic prophets of our age."

Oscar Ameringer, known as the Mark Twain of American socialism because of his comic wit, had this to say in his autobiography *If You Don't Weaken*:

> Yes, yes, *Looking Backward*. A great book. A very great book. One of the greatest, most prophetic books this country has produced. It didn't make

me look backward, it made me look forward, and I haven't got over looking forward since I read *Looking Backward*.

Krishan Kumar, in *Utopia and Anti-Utopia*, quotes John Dewey:

Bellamy was an American and a New Englander in more than a geographical sense. He was imbued with a religious faith in the democratic ideal. But for that very reason he saw through the sham and pretense that exists or can exist in the present economic system. I could fill pages with quotations in which he exposes his profound conviction that our democratic government is a veiled plutocracy. He was far from being the originator of this idea. But what distinguishes Bellamy is the clear ardor with which he grasped the *human* meaning of democracy as an idea of equality and liberty, and portrayed the complete contradiction between our present economic system and the realization of human equality and liberty. No one has carried through the idea that equality is obtainable only by complete equality of income more fully than Bellamy. Again, what distinguishes him is that he derives his zeal and his insight from devotion to an American ideal of democracy.

Bellamy was a shy, genial, slender, lifelong New Englander. The son of a Baptist minister, he began his career as a journalist. He became an attorney but never practiced. Several of his early novels and a raft of science-fiction tales are now totally forgotten, but *Looking Backward* became an instant bestseller, second in the century only to *Uncle Tom's Cabin*. It has never been out of print. At the moment at least seven editions are available in the U.S., including a two-dollar Dover paperback.

Looking Backward is narrated by Julian West, a rich, politically conservative young man living in Boston in 1887 and engaged to Edith Bartlett. He suffers from insomnia. Because little noises keep him awake at night he builds a soundproof cellar and hires a mesmerist to put him to sleep. A servant is trained to wake him in the morning. While he is in a deep trance-like slumber, his house burns down. The basement vault is not discovered and it is assumed that West died in the fire.

Fast forward to the fall of 2000. Dr. Leete, a retired physician, has built a house on West's former property. An excavation reveals the hidden cellar and within it the perfectly preserved body of West. He has slept for 113 years. This notion of someone entering the future by way of a big sleep had been used many times before—"Rip Van Winkle," for example—and would be used again, notably by H. G. Wells in his dystopia *When the Sleeper Wakes* and by Woody Allen in his 1973 movie *Sleeper*.

After being aroused from his hypnotic trance, West becomes the guest of Dr. Leete, his wife, and his daughter, Edith. West is attracted at once by the "faultless luxuriance" of Edith's figure and her "bewitching" face. The rest of the novel is a detailed account of the brave new world of 2000 in which West is now amazed to find himself. Dr. Leete has an annoying habit of laughing at almost everything that West has to say about nineteenth-century Boston, and Edith blushes at West's slightest remarks. The romance between Julian and this second Edith is embarrassingly mawkish. It turns out that she is the great-granddaughter of the earlier Edith, and there is even a hint that she is West's former fiancée reincarnated. Did Bellamy intend "E. Leete" to be a pun, as Everett Bleiler suggests in his massive *Science Fiction: The Early Years*?

Like Marx's *Das Kapital*, which had little influence on Bellamy,[1] *Looking Backward* gives a fairly accurate picture of the evils of a totally unregulated ·capitalism. The nation's economy in the late nineteenth century was in the grip of gigantic trusts. Graft was rampant in big cities. Labor unions were just getting organized and there were bitter, bloody strikes. The air was dense with coal smoke. Anarchists were blowing up buildings. Everywhere there was enormous wealth alongside slums and miserable poverty.

Julian West's famous allegory of the coach appears in the first chapter of *Looking Backward*. It likens nineteenth-century America to a "prodigious coach" that is being pulled slowly over rough terrain by workers who are harnessed like beasts to a long rope. The coach's driver is hunger. By lashing the workers, hunger forces them to keep pulling. Riding on the coach in comfortable seats are the rich capitalists. When workers faint from hunger, the riders urge them to be patient. If they become injured or crippled, the rich, out of compassion, give them salves and liniments. They agree it is a great pity that the coach is so hard to pull. The gap between themselves and the poor is rationalized by the "hallucination" that they are made of "finer clay" than the rope pullers.

West's account of the vast changes that have taken place in the twen-

---

1 The books that probably had the greatest impact on Bellamy's socialism were *The Coming Revolution* (1880) and *The Cooperative Commonwealth* (1884) by the Danish-born Laurence Gronlund, a promoter of the Socialist Labor Party. The plot of *Looking Backward*, though little else, may have been partly borrowed from a now forgotten utopian novel, *The Diothas or a Far Look Ahead* (1881) by Ismar Thiusen, pseudonym of John MacNie, professor of French and German at the University of North Dakota. The narrator is projected into the far future by mesmerism, where he marries a reincarnation of Edith, his former sweetheart.

tieth century is, as in all utopias, a bizarre mix of hits and misses. Its most spectacular hit is not its vision of America in 2000, but its description of a command economy that strongly resembles the Soviet Union under Lenin and Stalin, especially their dream of the Communist state they believed would follow a temporary but necessary "dictatorship of the proletariat." It's as if West awoke not in Boston but in Lenin's Moscow!

In the early years of the twentieth century, as Dr. Leete informs West, the great monopolies grew larger and more powerful. No violent worker revolution occurred as in Russia. Unregulated capitalism slowly evolved until the state took over the monopolies and all other means of production to become one monstrous trust, the country's sole capitalist and land owner. The profit motive was gradually replaced by a patriotic desire on the part of everyone to serve the government. Political parties, labor unions, banks, prisons, and retail stores all vanished. In the absence of greed, there was no government corruption. Even prostitution became extinct. Everybody loved everybody. Crime faded away except for a few unfortunate souls who are mentally ill. They are treated in mental hospitals.

As in the land of Oz, money has totally disappeared. As the nation's sole employer, the government pays no wages. Instead, it provides each citizen with an annual allotment of goods and services. Everyone carries a cardboard credit card that is punched each time a purchase is made or a service rendered.

Edith takes West to a building where samples of all available goods are on display. Their prices, strictly controlled, are in dollars and cents, but these numbers, like algebraic letters, are no more than symbols to aid government accounting. There is no advertising. A buyer tells a clerk what he or she wants, orders are sent through pneumatic tubes to a warehouse, then the goods are shipped through larger tubes to spots from which they are delivered to houses.

There are no household servants. Washing is done in public laundries. Medical and health care is completely socialized. You may choose your doctor. His pay, in the form of goods, is the same as everyone else, including laborers. Public kitchens provide food for home meals, though most people take their main meal at government-run restaurants.

Prizes go to workers for exceptionally good work. If they refuse to do their job properly they are put in solitary confinement on bread and water. Work hours are short and vacations regular. Those too ill to work are placed in "invalid corps" where they do whatever they can. The lame, sick, and blind all receive the same goods as others. There is no longer a division between rich and poor. From each according to his abilities, as a popular Marxist slogan had it, and to each according to his needs.

The state operates like a vast military complex. Every man is conscripted at age twenty-one to serve as a common laborer. At twenty-four, all persons, male and female, are given tests to determine their natural aptitudes and wishes. State-run colleges train them for a profession. Some choose "brain work" such as music, art, science, writing, and so on. Workers are free later to change jobs and to live where they like. Retirement is compulsory at age forty-five. October 15 is Muster Day on which those of twenty-four enter the work force and those of forty-five are mustered out.

All books and newspapers are published by the government, though there is no censorship and one may write anything he or she pleases. Authors pay for first printings. If a book or periodical sells well, the author receives a royalty in the form of goods. Red Ribbons are awarded to outstanding brain workers.

There is no jury system, no attorneys. Legal decisions are made by judges appointed by the president. State governments have vanished. A congress meets once every five years, though just what it does is unclear because new laws are no longer needed. All schools and colleges are run by the state.

What about religion? There are no churches or clergy, no denominations or sects. Persons are free to express their religious opinions in sermons delivered over a telephone system, but the dominant religion is a vague sort of theism, based on the ethical teaching of Jesus to love God and neighbor, much like the deism of the founding fathers.

Fossil fuels have been replaced by electric power that provides heat and light. The air is free of pollution. Chimneys are nowhere to be seen. Wars have become relics of the past, replaced by what William James called its "moral equivalent," working for a better world. All the world's great nations have become command socialisms with universally honored credit cards. There is free trade, free emigration, and the stirrings of a world government. Everyone speaks a native language and a universal language, the nature of which is not specified. Democracy of a sort exists by voting at various government levels. The president, chosen by a small group of peers, serves for five years.

The novel's plot takes a surprising turn at the end. West falls asleep and wakes up back in nineteenth-century Boston convinced that his visit to 2000 was only a dream. He tries to interest others in his dream's utopia only to be ridiculed and thought mad. He then wakes up to find himself back in Boston in the year 2000, the real world, to marry Edith and live happily as a lecturer on the sins of capitalism.

Bellamy never used the word "socialism," a term he hated because it suggested European influences and violent revolutions. He called his ideology nationalism. It is hard now to believe, but so persuasive was his rhetoric that over 150 groups called Nationalist Clubs or Bellamy Clubs sprang up throughout the land. There was even a short-lived Nationalist Party. Two journals promoting nationalism flourished for a few years: *The Nationalist* (1889–1894), and Bellamy's own monthly, *The New Nation* (1891–1894). There were other periodicals that debated nationalism. The populist movement, embodied in the People's Party, owed a great debt to nationalism.

Not much is said in *Looking Backward* about the role of women in 2000 except that they serve as an auxiliary force in the industrial army under a female general. A much more detailed account of the status of women appears in *Equality* (1897), Bellamy's lengthy sequel to *Looking Backward*. West continues as narrator. The book makes clear that women enter the work place as equal to men in all respects except for participation in athletic games. Edith, for example, works on a farm. Bellamy supported the suffrage movement, and the early feminist leaders considered him one of their heroes.

In *Looking Backward*, Edith dresses in nineteenth-century attire so as not to disturb Julian, who is in a perpetual state of shock over everything he sees. In *Equality*, Edith reveals to Julian the clothes she actually prefers. They are men's suits with trousers. Clothes in 2000 are made of paper and discarded after being worn. Also made of paper are shoes, carpets, sheets, draperies, dishes, even pots and pans. When discarded they are recycled to be used in making other things.

Girls, we are told, take over their mother's last name with their father's name as their middle name. Boys do the reverse. Women have free choice over the number of children they desire, though Bellamy is silent about birth control methods and abortions. The pessimism of Malthus has been answered by a stable world population. Blacks are nowhere mentioned in *Looking Backward*. In *Equality*, in a section headed "The Colored Races and the New Order," it is explained that after the freeing of slaves they were soon absorbed into the new order as equal to whites in all respects, although there continues to be no social "commingling" of the two races.

Equality's chapter 19, "Can a Maid Forget Her Ornaments?" (a quotation from Jeremiah 2:32), is pure Veblen. Women no longer wear rings or other costly jewelry to serve as badges of wealth. Since there is no longer a distinction between rich and poor there is no need for such displays. Conspicuous waste has gone the way of the profit motive. When West mentions that in his day persons actually thought that diamonds and other precious stones were intrinsically beautiful, Dr. Leete's reply could have come straight out of Veblen's *Theory of the Leisure Class*:

"Yes, I suppose savage races honestly thought so, but, being honest, they did not distinguish between precious stones and glass beads so long as both were equally shiny. As to the pretension of civilized persons to admire gems or gold for their intrinsic beauty apart from their value, I suspect that was a more or less unconscious sham. Suppose, by any sudden abundance, diamonds of the first water had gone down to the value of bottle glass, how much longer do you think they would have been worn by anybody in your day?"

One of Bellamy's most successful predictions is what he calls an electroscope. Although its sounds and images come over telephone cables, it is connected to a worldwide network of wires so that it functions exactly like today's television. Not only does it allow home owners to enjoy music, plays, operas, and lectures, but it also permits viewers to see live news events wherever they occur around the world.

Umbrellas have become obsolete because when it rains waterproof canopies are lowered over sidewalks and street corners. Water, electricity, and mail are, of course, free to all households. Horses have been replaced by trains and electric cars. West converses with a young farm lass who is plowing a field with an electric machine. Flesh eating has been abandoned for strictly vegetarian diets.

Several chapters in *Equality* describe West's view of Boston and its suburbs from what is called an "air-car." Submarines are mentioned. Of course, Bellamy could not conceive of atomic energy, although he does mention that past wars were fought by dropping dynamite from air-cars—the "ghastly dew" in a passage quoted from a Tennyson poem about the future. Nor should we fault Bellamy for not anticipating computers, the moon walk, space probes of planets, and all the other wonders of twentieth-century physics, chemistry, medicine, and genetics.

There is nothing about psychic phenomena in Bellamy's two utopia novels, but throughout his short life he was fascinated by the paranormal. Extra Sensory Perception is featured in several of his short stories. "To Whom They May Come" tells of an island where natives communicate with each other only by telepathy, a notion that H. G. Wells exploited in his finest utopia, *Men Like Gods*. *Miss Luddington's Sister*, one of Bellamy's early novels, is about spiritualism.

Always in poor health, Bellamy died of tuberculosis at age forty-eight. Had he lived through the Russian Revolution he would probably have become a dedicated Communist. I do not know whether Lenin or Engels ever actually read Bellamy, although we do know they had only disdain for what they called utopian speculation.

In the final chapter of *Equality*, Dr. Leete does his best to counter the main objections that conservatives hurl against socialism: that it opposes religion, stifles incentives, discourages originality, leads to political corruption, violates civil rights, makes everybody behave alike, and so on. To the incentive objection, Dr. Leete's unconvincing reply is that under socialism the old desire to maximize one's wealth is replaced by the higher incentives of doing one's work well and contributing to the common good. As it turned out, in every twentieth-century nation where a government, Marxist or fascist, took total control of the economy, the result was a cruel dictatorship in which not only did the predictions cited above prove accurate, but millions of citizens were needlessly slaughtered.

There are two big lessons to be learned from Bellamy's vision of 2000. First, though admirable in its indictment of unfettered capitalism and in its enthusiasm for building a better world, it projected a cure as bad as, if not worse than, the disease. Bellamy's two books reveal with great starkness how naïve and simple-minded were the early socialists both here and abroad. They had no inkling of how socialism would soon come to recognize the power of free-market competition and the baleful results of any effort to eliminate it.

Socialism is, of course, a fuzzy word, as impossible to define precisely as capitalism or Christianity. Bellamy's vision has almost no resemblance to the democratic socialism of Norman Thomas, Michael Harrington, Irving Howe, John Kenneth Galbraith, and other leading American socialists, or to any of today's socialist nations in which a rigorous democracy is combined with a mixed economy that is part free market and part government owned or controlled. In the opinion of Milton Friedman and many other conservatives, the United States is now a model of democratic socialism. In *Freedom to Choose*, Friedman points out that every plank in Thomas's platform from the last time he ran for president has been fulfilled and is now accepted by both Democrats and Republicans. The ability of capitalism to overcome its dark past and become more benign was a development that neither Bellamy nor Marx could foresee.

The second lesson to be learned from Bellamy is that the future is unpredictable, with respect not only to science and technology but also to political and economic change. It's a safe bet that the new millennium will swarm with stupendous surprises that no one now is even capable of imagining. G. K. Chesterton opens *The Napoleon of Notting Hill*, a fantasy set like George Orwell's dystopia in 1984, with these wise words:

> The human race, to which so many of my readers belong, has been playing
> at children's games from the beginning, and will probably do it till the

end, which is a nuisance for the few people who grow up. And one of the games to which it is most attached is called "Keep to-morrow dark," and which is also named (by the rustics in Shropshire, I have no doubt) "Cheat the Prophet." The players listen very carefully and respectfully to all that the clever men have to say about what is to happen in the next generation. The players then wait until all the clever men are dead, and bury them nicely. They then go and do something else. That is all. For a race of simple tastes, however, it is great fun.

September 2000

Adversary Jurisprudence

Robert H. Bork

The prophecies of what the courts will do in fact, and nothing more pretentious, are what I mean by law.
—Oliver Wendell Holmes

Every law or rule of conduct must, whether its author perceives the fact or not, lay down or rest upon some general principle, and must therefore, if it succeeds in attaining its end, commend the principle to public attention and imitation and thus affect legislative opinion.
—A. V. Dicey

The nightmare of the American intellectual is that the control of public policy should fall into the hands of the American people. . . . [P]olicymaking by the justices of the Supreme Court, intellectuals all, in the name of the Constitution, is the only way in which this can be prevented.
—Lino Graglia

U NTIL RECENTLY, the name of Charles Pickering was hardly a household word. That changed the moment President Bush nominated the obscure federal trial judge for a seat on a court of appeals. Overnight, Judge Pickering became the latest casualty of the culture wars. There was certainly no good reason why Pickering should not have been elevated to an appeals court. Candidates less qualified have in the past been routinely confirmed by the Senate. He was not. Instead, in a scenario that has become depressingly familiar, he was vilified by the media and anti-Bush partisans. His candidacy was scuttled by a party-line vote in the Judiciary Committee, which denied him consideration by the full Senate where he probably would have been confirmed.

What was surprising about the unfortunate Pickering's travails was the brutality of the campaign against him. We have, alas, become accustomed to such battles over Supreme Court nominees. Until now, however, such battles had not extended to nominations to the lower courts. The immediate explanation, of course, was that the Democratic Party and its allies—People for the American Way, NOW, NARAL, and other left-wing groups—immolated Pickering to warn George Bush that they had the votes in the Committee to defeat any Supreme Court nominees who bore the slightest resemblance to Justices Antonin Scalia and Clarence Thomas.

The political struggle for control of the courts has become open and savage precisely because it is a major part of the war in our culture, a battle for dominance between opposed moral visions of our future. In that battle, Supreme Court Justices are the major prize, but appeals court nominees are also important because those courts are final for all but the tiny sliver of cases accepted by the Supreme Court for review.

The outcome of the struggle for control of the courts will determine the future of the rule of law and hence the prospects for the survival of traditional American culture. The culture war has been best described by James Davison Hunter, who first adapted the term to the American context. On one side are traditionalists who accord a presumption of legitimacy and worth to longstanding sources of cultural authority, sources whose strength is eroded or whose continued existence is brought into doubt by the clamor for liberation of the individual. On the other side are the emancipationists, who are highly critical of constituted authorities and institutions and wish to liberate the individual will from such restraints. That is a process that must have limits if a coherent culture is to survive. Our courts, however, continually test and frequently transgress those limits. The disagreement is not merely philosophical; it is intensely political and generates furious passions. It may be roughly summarized as a battle between the ethos of the student radicals of the Sixties and that of adherence to bourgeois virtues.

THE EMANCIPATIONIST party is led by—in fact it almost entirely consists of—intellectuals, a group that, as Friedrich Hayek noted, "has long been characterized by disillusionment with [the West's] principles, disparagement of its achievements, and exclusive concern with the creation of 'better worlds.'" This destructive utopianism was not too serious as long as intellectuals were an ineffective minority, but they increased in size and influence after World War II, and in the Sixties their values came to predominate.

We are accustomed to manifestations of the liberationist impulse in the institutions controlled by intellectuals: the press (print and electronic), universities, Hollywood, mainline churches, foundations, and other "elite" institutions that engage in shaping or trying to shape our attitudes. Most people, however, do not think of the judiciary—insofar as they think about the judiciary at all—in the same way. They should. Television and motion pictures powerfully influence the direction of our culture but they do not claim to speak with the authority of the Constitution, nor do they possess the judges' power to coerce. In truth, television and motion pictures would not have the unfortunate cultural impact they do if courts had not broken the restraints of enacted law. Behavior and language are now routine that not long ago would have met not only with social disapproval but also with legal sanctions. No doubt public attitudes were changing in any event, but they could not have moved so far and so fast if the courts had not weakened moral curbs and made legal restraint impossible.

As many thinkers have noted, the Enlightenment has had a dark as well as a cheerful legacy. If it bequeathed us greater freedom, it also brought with it an attenuated sense of tradition and weaker attachments to communal, familial, and religious values. Although these disruptions accelerated in the 1960s, their real beginning was the growing view that what one did with one's life was almost entirely a matter of personal choice, owing little to the wishes of family, religion, or community. Today, this disintegration of the culture, and hence of the society, goes by the apparently respectable name of libertarianism, a catchword rather than a philosophy, and one with very unhappy consequences.

To say that this is a general cultural movement that we do not know how to stop or reverse is not to absolve activist courts from their responsibility in causing the damage we see about us. The courts, and especially the Supreme Court, have led the way to cultural dissolution by breaking down the legal barriers that restrain radical individualism. And, in destroying those barriers, an enterprise wicked enough in itself, the Court has also fostered the immoral attitude that the individual will must be completely emancipated, no matter what the cost. The judiciary has in large measure become the enemy of traditional culture. This enterprise of the law deserves the title of adversary jurisprudence.

The political manifestation of the culture war was the 1972 takeover of the Democratic Party by the McGovernites. To put the matter crudely, but by no means inaccurately, since that time the Democratic Party has come to represent the values of the Sixties, while the Republican Party, insofar as it has a pulse, tends to a traditionalist stance on social issues. If it seems odd to refer to politicians as intellectuals, it must be remembered that the term does not signify any particular skill at intellectual work. Ted Turner, Cornel West, and Barbra Streisand qualify; you get the idea. The intelligentsia are influential beyond their numbers because they control the institutions that shape attitudes, ration information, and offer prestige and comfortable lives to the young they recruit. *The New York Times*, Harvard Law School, the Ford Foundation, and NBC's nightly news are a few of many examples.

The performance of the Supreme Court over the past half century follows the agenda of the intelligentsia. The Court majority's spirit is activist and emancipationist: it liberates the individual will in constitutional issues of speech, religion, abortion, sexuality, welfare, public education, and much else. This is what liberalism has become in our time. Judicial activism, a term of abuse flung about freely without much thought, properly refers to the practice of some judges of enunciating principles and reaching conclusions that cannot plausibly be derived from the Constitution they purport to be interpreting. Activism consists in the assumption by the judiciary of powers not entrusted to it by the document which alone justifies its authority. The results are twofold: the erosion of democracy and the movement of the 4:40 culture in a left-liberal direction. If the text, history, and structure of the Constitution no longer guide and confine the judge, he has nowhere to look but to his own ideas of justice, and these are likely to be formed by the assumptions of the intellectualized elites he has known for most of his life and whose approval he very much wants. When the judge's views are claimed, however implausibly, to be based on the Constitution, the legislators and the public are helpless. For better or for worse, on crucial issues, an activist Court, not the Constitution, leads and shapes the culture.

At the apex of all our courts, federal and state, sits the Supreme Court of the United States. Its rulings are not merely final but are highly visible and influential statements of the principles our most fundamental document is said, not always credibly, to enshrine for our governance and contemplation. Though these principles are the same as those on the intellectual class agenda, it must be said that there is more diversity of opinion on the Court than there is in the faculty lounges of the law schools. That fact makes the liberal Left anxious and determined to control every new appointment. So far they have been successful. No matter how many Justices are appointed by Republican presidents, the works of the Warren Court and the victories of the ACLU are not reversed.

The small sampling of cases that can be discussed here nevertheless constitutes a cornucopia of judicial activism: no court could arrive at such results by reasoning from the text, history, or structure of the Constitution. Here, as elsewhere in our national life, attitude trumps reason.

The First Amendment to the United States Constitution is a major focal point of the culture war.

Consider freedom of speech. The First Amendment to the Constitution, dealing with speech and religion, is central to America's understanding of itself and its freedoms. The first words of the Amendment are: "Congress shall make no law respecting an establishment of religion, or prohibiting the free exercise thereof; or abridging the freedom of speech, or of the press."

The Court has since extended these prohibitions from Congress to all federal, state, and local governments. But that is of secondary importance to the explosive expansion it has given the words "speech" and "establishment." It is indicative both of the Court's radically altered importance in cultural matters and of the late rise of the intellectual class that neither the Speech Clause nor the Establishment Clause, adopted in 1791, occasioned Supreme Court review of official acts until well into the twentieth century.

American law concerning freedom of speech, and perhaps much wider areas of constitutional law, has been deformed by the almost irrebuttable presumption of unswerving rationality and freedom of individual choice embodied in Justice Oliver Wendell Holmes's foolish and dangerous metaphor of the marketplace of ideas. That notion made its debut in 1919 in Holmes's much-lauded dissent in *Abrams* v. *United States*. The Court majority upheld the convictions under the Espionage Act of Russian immigrants, self-proclaimed "revolutionists" who distributed circulars in New York City advocating a general strike and urging that workers stop producing ammunition to be used against the revolutionaries in Russia. The theory of the prosecution was that the strike, though not so intended, would harm the war effort against Germany. Holmes would have set aside the convictions on statutory grounds, which would have been entirely proper, but he went on to introduce into the First Amendment an unfortunate assumption:

> [W]hen men have realized that time has upset many fighting faiths, they may come to believe even more than they believe the very foundations of their own conduct that the ultimate good desired is better reached by free trade in ideas—that the test of truth is the power of thought to get itself accepted in the competition of the market.

Holmes certainly knew that horrible ideas are often accepted in the market. The market for ideas has few of the self-correcting features of the market for goods and services. When he wrote, Holmes of course knew nothing of Soviet Communism or German Naziism, but his own experience in the Civil War demonstrated that when ideas differ sharply enough, the truth of one or the other is not settled in the competition of the market but in the slaughter of the battlefield. Nevertheless, the compelling quality of his prose and the attractiveness to intellectuals of the supposed ultimate supremacy of good ideas has served, down to our own day, to make his absurd notion dominant in First Amendment jurisprudence and, more remotely, in other fields of constitutional law.

The metaphor of the marketplace not only assumes the goodwill and rationality of most men who have to choose among the ideas offered, but also, by the nature of a market, the choices, desires, and gratifications of the individual are of first importance. Given that assumption, it is an easy step to the thought that no idea should be kept from the market. Individualism is placed above the welfare of the community, a theme that runs throughout constitutional law.

But Holmes, joined again by Brandeis, elevated that thought to incoherence. *Gitlow* v. *New York* (1925) upheld a conviction under a criminal anarchy statute for publishing a call for the violent overthrow of the government. "If in the long run [Holmes wrote in dissent] the beliefs expressed in proletarian dictatorship are destined to be accepted by the dominant forces of the community, the only meaning of free speech is that they should be given their chance and have their way." This in a case where the defendant urged violent action by a minority to institute a dictatorship that would put a stop to free speech? What happened to the marketplace of ideas? Why, on Holmes's reasoning, were the dominant forces of the community that enacted the criminal anarchy law not allowed to have their way? That they should, on his reasoning, must be the only meaning of free speech. There is an alarming frivolity in these dissents. "If in the long run the belief, let us say, in genocide is destined to be accepted by the dominant forces of the community, the only meaning of free speech is that it should be given its chance and have its way. Do we believe that?," Alexander Bickel asked. "Do we accept it?" Funny little mustached men wearing raincoats stand on street corners preaching obviously crackpot notions that may one day become the policy of a nation. "Where nothing is unspeakable, nothing is undoable."

The themes of the Holmes-Brandeis dissents were ready at hand for adoption by the intellectualized post-World War II Court. After some wavering, the essence of those dissents became the law in *Brandenberg* v. *Ohio* (1969). The Court there reversed the conviction under the Ohio Criminal Syndicalism statute of a Ku Klux Klan leader who made a speech threatening to blacks and Jews, ruling that "the constitutional guarantees of free speech and free press do not permit a State to forbid or proscribe advocacy of the use of force or of law violation except where such advocacy is directed to inciting or producing imminent lawless action and is likely to produce such action." To wait until violence is imminent, of course, is likely to wait too long to prevent it.

WHAT BENEFITS can such speech have in a country committed to representative democracy? The ideas involved, if such expostulations can be called ideas, could be offered in Holmes's marketplace uncoupled from calls to violence. A nation that fears only violence but is otherwise indifferent to fundamental republican principles, as the *Abrams* and *Gitlow* dissents and *Brandenberg* would have it, is unlikely to show persistent determination in defending its culture.

Individualistic relativism appears even more clearly in cases dealing with vulgarity, pornography, and obscenity. The prime example is *Cohen* v. *California* (1971) which overturned a conviction for disorderly conduct of a man who entered a courthouse wearing a jacket bearing the words "F . . . the Draft" (without the ellipsis). The majority opinion by Justice Powell asked "How is one to distinguish this from any other offensive word?" and answered that no distinction could be made since "one man's vulgarity is another's lyric." The Court would never dream of saying that one man's armed robbery is another's redistribution of wealth in pursuit of social justice. (Although, come to think of it, the Warren Court's solicitude for criminals may have come close to that.)

Cohen was just the beginning. The following year the Court decided *Rosenfeld* v. *New Jersey*, *Lewis* v. *New Orleans*, and *Brown* v. *Oklahoma*. Rosenfeld addressed a school board meeting of about 150 people, including about forty children, and on four occasions used the adjective "motherf . . . ing" to describe the teachers, the school board, the town, and the United States. Lewis shouted the same epithet at police officers who were arresting her son. Brown used the same language in a meeting in a university chapel. None of the convictions—for disorderly conduct, breach of the peace, and use of obscene language in a public place—was allowed to stand. The relativism of these decisions seems to reflect a loss of will to maintain conventional standards. The Court refused to allow punishment for the same obscene and assaultive speech that was tolerated by supine university faculties and administrators in the late 1960s and early 1970s. When the faculties collapsed, the universities were corrupted; when the Supreme Court gave way, the national culture was defiled. Now, of course, such language is routine on television and in motion pictures.

Pervasive vulgarity was guaranteed by *Miller* v. *California* (1973) which laid down the conditions under which a state could regulate obscenity. That test is a maze whose center cannot be reached. The most damaging condition is that the work, taken as a whole, must lack serious literary, artistic, political, or scientific value. How can a jury find that *anything* lacks serious artistic value when museums, our cultural authorities on what is art, exhibit Robert Mapplethorpe's photograph of one man urinating in the mouth of another, a picture of the Virgin Mary spattered with dung, and jars of excrement as works of art? There will, in any event, always be a gaggle of professors eager to testify that the most blatant pornography is actually a profound parable about the horrors of capitalism or the oppressiveness of bourgeois culture.

The themes the Court had been developing reached a crescendo of sorts in *United States v. Playboy Entertainment Group, Inc.* (2000). The decision held unconstitutional a congressional statute that required cable television channels "primarily dedicated to sexually-oriented programming" to limit their transmission to hours when children are unlikely to be viewing. The Court majority found the law a restriction on the content of speech that was not justified because there appeared to be less restrictive methods of protecting children.

THE JUSTICES, equating sex and speech, said, "Basic speech principles are at stake in this case." That is a peculiar view of fundamentals since Playboy advertised, as Justice Scalia pointed out in dissent, that its channel depicted such things as "female masturbation/external," "girl/girl sex," and "oral sex/cunnilingus." Most of the speech in such entertainment probably consisted of simulated moans of ecstasy which the females are required to utter in order to excite viewers.

The legislation and the Court both focused on the danger that children would be exposed to erotic sounds or pictures. The Court's discussion centered upon the pleasures of adults. No weight was given to the interest of society in preserving some vestige of a moral tone. "Where the designed benefit of a content-based speech restriction is to shield the sensibilities of listeners, the general rule is that the right of expression prevails, even where no less restrictive alternative exists. We are expected to protect our own sensibilities 'simply by averting [our] eyes.'" Many of the people around us will not avert their eyes, and that fact will certainly produce a moral and aesthetic environment which it is impossible to ignore. We are forced to live in an increasingly ugly society.

Indeed, the Court majority refuted its own avert-your-eyes solution when it said: "It is through speech that our convictions and beliefs are influenced, expressed, and tested. It is through speech that we bring those beliefs to bear on Government and society. It is through speech that our personalities are formed and expressed." Try substituting "consuming pornography" or "watching female masturbation/external" for the word "speech" in that passage and see how persuasive it remains.

Apparently aware that this line of cases has been criticized, the majority opinion essays a rebuttal:

When a student first encounters our free speech jurisprudence, he or she might think it is influenced by the philosophy that one idea is as good as any other, and that in art and literature objective standards of style, taste, decorum, beauty, and esthetics are deemed by the Constitution to be inappropriate, indeed unattainable. Quite the opposite is true. The Constitution no more enforces a relativistic philosophy or moral nihilism than it does any other point of view. The Constitution exists precisely so that opinions and judgments, including esthetic and moral judgments about art and literature, can be formed, tested, and expressed. What the Constitution says is that these judgments are for the individual to make, not for the Government to decree, even with the mandate or approval of a majority.

In a word, what the Constitution says, as interpreted by today's Court, is that one idea *is* as good as another so far as the law is concerned; only the omnipotent individual may judge. A majority may not enact its belief, apparently self-evidently wrong-headed, that the production and consumption of obscenity and pornography work social harms. That is a relativistic philosophy or moral nihilism, if anything is. And it is not the Constitution's philosophy; it is the Court's.

It is not too much to say that the suffocating vulgarity of popular culture is in large measure the work of the Court. The Court did not create vulgarity, but it defeated attempts of communities to contain and minimize vulgarity. Base instincts are always present in humans, but better instincts attempt, through law as well as moral disapproval, to suppress pornography, obscenity, and vulgarity. When the law is declared unfit to survive, not only are base instincts freed, they are also validated.

The triumph of the individual over the community advanced in a new direction in *Texas* v. *Johnson* (1989), a five-to-four decision invalidating federal law and the laws of forty-eight states prohibiting the physical desecration or defilement of the American flag. While chanting insults to the United States, Johnson burned the flag in public to show contempt for this country. He was not prosecuted for his words but only for the burning. Equating an expressive *act* with speech, itself an extremely dubious proposition, Justice Brennan said the government could not prohibit the expression of an idea on the grounds of offensiveness. Unifying symbols are essential to an increasingly divided community, but the strain of individualism in its precedents left the Court majority unable to accept that fact.

The perversion of the First Amendment took the opposite tack when legislative majorities cut at the heart of the Speech Clause by diminishing and biasing political speech.

Buckley v. *Valeo* (1976) upheld portions of the Federal Election Campaign Act that severely limited individual contributions to political campaigns on the theory that large contributions may lead to the corruption of politics or may create a public impression of corruption. Had limits so severe then been in effect they would have made impossible Eugene McCarthy's primary challenge that led Lyndon Johnson not to run for reelection. Yet freedom of political speech is conceded to lie at the core of the Speech Clause.

Any hope that *Buckley* was an aberration that the appointment of new justices would cure was dashed by *Nixon* v. *Shrink Missouri Government PAC* (2000). Missouri law set limits on campaign contributions for state elections that were considerably more severe than the limits set by the federal law. The Court once more held that corruption or the possible appearance of corruption was an adequate ground to regulate contributions. Justice Stevens concurred, insisting on "one simple point. Money is property; it is not speech." A soapbox is also property, not speech, but the speech of an orator in Hyde Park would be much less effective without it. Television equipment, paid for by contributions, is also property, but speech could not reach a mass audience without it. Justice Breyer's concurrence, while conceding that money enables speech, argued that limiting the size of the largest contributions serves "to democratize the influence that money itself may bring to bear upon the electoral process." Real democratization would justify restrictions upon media commentary that is obviously one-sided in support of liberal candidates and policies. Had the speech been pornographic it would have gained greater protection. Those, including the president, who are counting on the Supreme Court to rescue the political process from the excesses of the new campaign finance law may be unpleasantly surprised.

The Court's deformation of the Speech Clause is outdone by its treatment of religion. Tocqueville saw that religion should be "considered as the first of [the Americans'] political institutions; for if it does not give them the taste for freedom, it singularly facilitates their use of it" because it "prevents them from conceiving everything and forbids them to dare everything." That was then. Now the restraints for which Tocqueville praised religion are seen as intolerable limitations on the individual will. The power of religion to prevent and forbid is greatly attenuated and no little part of that decline is due to the Supreme Court's endorsement of intellectual class secularism. This decline, in turn, bears directly upon the Court's interpretation of the freedom of speech, since in that area there is no longer much that cannot be conceived and dared.

The Establishment Clause has spawned a welter of cases, but it is necessary to examine only a few to see the themes that run through them. *Engel* v. *Vitale* (1962) was the first case dealing with a nondenominational prayer initiated by New York school officials. Officially sanctioned prayer had long been a feature of public schooling, but now the Court, perceiving a forbidden establishment of religion, started down a path leading to the official equality of religion and irreligion. In truth, irreligion seems the preferred constitutional value. A year later, *Abington School District* v. *Schempp* (1963) invalidated a Pennsylvania law requiring that the school day begin with a reading of verses from the Bible and student recitation of the Lord's Prayer. Although any student could be excused upon the written request of his parent, the Court said "the breach of [constitutional] neutrality that is today a trickling stream may all too soon become a raging torrent." That was extravagant hyperbole. In all of American constitutional history, the trickling stream has never achieved the status of even a sluggish creek.

The Court said the state must maintain neutrality by "neither aiding nor opposing religion." The long-standing policy, dating back to George Washington's presidency and the first Congress, that the state should favor religion in general was ignored. Faith and atheism may seem now to stand on equal footing, but only faith is barred from official recognition. That may be appealing to many moderns, but it certainly was not the view of those who wrote, the Congress that proposed, and the states that ratified the First Amendment.

So drastic has the antagonism to religion become that *Wallace* v. *Jaffree* (1985) struck down an Alabama statute permitting one minute of silent prayer or meditation in public schools. No one would know whether a student was praying, meditating, or daydreaming. The difficulty, according to Justice Stevens, was that by adding the option of silent prayer, the state characterized prayer as a favored practice.

The Court's treatment of religion became even more draconian in *Lee* v. *Weisman* (1992) which held unconstitutional a rabbi's recitation of a nonsectarian prayer at a middle-school graduation ceremony. Justice Souter disparaged evidence that after adoption of the First Amendment the founding generation encouraged public support for religion, saying that such acts "prove only that public officials, no matter when they serve, can turn a blind eye to constitutional principle." That is an extraordinary dismissal of the evidence that the same Congress that proposed the no-establishment principle also hired chaplains for both Houses and the armed forces, and successfully called upon presidents to declare national days of thanksgiving to God. History is in fact quite clear that the founding generation thought the state could and should encourage religion. The prayer was harmful to plaintiff

Deborah Weisman, the Court said, because public or peer pressure might cause her to stand or at least maintain a respectful silence during its reading. She could constitutionally be required to stand or remain silent during the reading of any other material—the Communist Manifesto, say, or Darwinian theory—so long as it had no hint of religious content. But then such philosophical trickles which have upon occasion become raging torrents are not religious, at least not in the conventional sense.

ONE OF THE MOST extreme examples of anti-religious animus was presented by *Board of Education of Kiryas Joel Village School District* v. *Grumet* (1994). The Satmar Hasidim, who practiced a strict form of Judaism, established a village that excluded all but Satmars. Their children were educated in private religious schools. Federal law entitled handicapped children "the deaf, mentally retarded, and those suffering from various physical, mental, or emotional disorders" to special education services, but a Supreme Court ruling forced them to attend public schools outside the village. Their parents withdrew the children because of "the panic, fear and trauma [the children] suffered in leaving their own community and being with people whose ways were so different." The State of New York responded by constituting the village a separate school district to enable it to provide for itself the special services needed.

The Supreme Court, however, in an opinion by Justice Souter, found this to be a forbidden establishment of religion. Justice Stevens, joined by Blackmun and Kennedy, concurred, offering the advice that "the State could have taken steps to alleviate the children's fear by teaching their schoolmates to be tolerant and respectful of Satmar customs." Teaching grade schoolers to be tolerant and respectful of handicapped, strangely dressed classmates who spoke Yiddish and practiced what the classmates would see as a weird religion would be a Sisyphean task at best. The Justices must have forgotten how cruel children can be to those they regard as even mildly eccentric.

"The isolation of these children," the concurrence went on to say, "while it may protect them from 'panic, fear and trauma,' also unquestionably increased the likelihood that they would remain within the fold, faithful adherents of their parents' religious faith." Why families' freedom to raise their children as they think best should be suspect and what relevance the observation had to the Establishment Clause went unexplained. The concurrence spoke for social atomization.

Justice Scalia, in a dissent joined by Chief Justice Rehnquist and Justice Thomas, wrote that the Grand Rebbe, who brought the Satmars from Europe to escape religious persecution, would be "astounded" to learn that the sect was so powerful as to have become an "establishment" of New York State, and the Founding Fathers would be "astonished" that the Establishment Clause was used to prohibit a characteristically American accommodation of the religious practices of a tiny minority sect. "I, however," Scalia continued, "am not surprised. Once this Court has abandoned text and history as guides, nothing prevents it from calling religious toleration the establishment of religion." (Actually, once text and history are jettisoned, nothing prevents the Court from doing anything it chooses with any part of the Constitution.) Souter inadvertently conceded the point by rebuking Scalia for "his inability to accept the fact that this Court has long held that the First Amendment reaches more than classic, eighteenth-century establishments." Unfortunately for that riposte, the Establishment Clause is a product of the eighteenth century.

The same radical individualism determined the result in *Santa Fe Independent School District* v. *Doe* (2000). The school district authorized two student elections, one to decide whether invocations, messages, or statements should be delivered at home football games and a second to select a student to deliver them. The Court held the school district's policy a forbidden establishment of religion. Dislike of majority rule surfaced in Justice Stevens's opinion for the majority: "[T]his student election does nothing to protect minority views but rather places the students who hold such views at the mercy of the majority. School sponsorship of a religious message is impermissible because it sends the ancillary message to members of the audience who are nonadherents 'that they are outsiders, not full members of the political community, and an accompanying message to adherents that they are insiders, favored members of the political community.'" Religious speech must have extraordinary political power. All of us have heard actual *political* speech with which we heartily disagreed without feeling any the less members of the political community. But where religion is concerned, even imaginary discomfort to a hypothetical individual overrides the reasonable desires of the community.

There is also the issue of feminism. *United States* v. *Virginia* (1996) held 7–1 that Virginia Military Institute, which is supported by the state, could not, under the Equal Protection Clause of the Fourteenth Amendment, remain an all-male school. The school was founded in 1839. The Fourteenth Amendment, designed to protect the newly freed slaves, was not ratified until 1868. Nobody at the time suggested that the Amendment banned single-sex education. In fact, it was not until 1971, over a hundred years later, that the Court first applied the Amendment to an irrational distinction between men and women. The ratifiers would have been aghast that a military school could not be all-male.

VMI featured strict discipline, hard physical performance, and an absolute lack of privacy, something, in fact, very like Marine boot camp. The admission of women required modifications, as they have in every military college. VMI's distinctive character, it was pointed out, would be lost. The Court attached no weight to this prospect. The Court insisted on the abstract equality of men and women in all things, undeterred by the historical meaning of the Equal Protection Clause, the value of well over a century of unquestioned excellence and tradition, and most certainly not by the heretical thought that there might be some areas of life suited to masculinity that feminism should not be permitted to destroy. Masculinity is a highly suspect idea in today's elite culture and it cannot, therefore, be expected to find lodgement in the Supreme Court's version of constitutional law.

There is no limit to what the Court can do with the Equal Protection Clause. As Justice Scalia said in dissent, the "current equal-protection jurisprudence . . . regards this Court as free to evaluate everything under the sun." That is exactly right. Every law makes a distinction between lawful and unlawful behavior. Every law, therefore, produces inequality because some conduct is allowed while other conduct is forbidden. The Court's equal protection jurisprudence thus allows scrutiny of all law to see if it meets the Justices' views of appropriate policy.

It might appear that the Court's theme of equality is contrary to the theme of emancipated individualism, but that is a misunderstanding. Equality denies the right of the majority to impose standards that require some individuals to desist from activities they enjoy. When the clause is applied to erase such distinctions, the individual is liberated, even if we think he ought not to be. Emancipation of the will is then quite selective. One is reminded of the folks who deny the existence of any objective truth or moral standard even while fiercely imposing their truths on others. They are not in fact nihilists, since they clearly believe in something, even if it is only the protection of their own prerogatives. Equality can be a means of breaking down traditional authority so that a new morality may be imposed. Though equal rights authoritarians demand nonjudgmentalism, they are very judgmental about traditionalists who oppose them. The emancipation of the individual will turns out to be about power.

THE INTELLIGENTSIA are not through with VMI. The college has a tradition of a "brief, nonsectarian, inclusive blessing" before the evening meal. The ACLU persuaded a district court to prohibit even that. VMI's superintendent said, no doubt pensively, "Hearing a brief prayer before supper is no more the establishment of religion than the singing of 'God Bless America.'"

True, but he shouldn't have given the ACLU any ideas for an additional lawsuit.

The Court's intervention has also been disruptive in the matter of sexuality. Much of the Court's activism is concerned with sexuality as the abortion cases *Roe* v. *Wade* (1973), *Planned Parenthood* v. *Casey* (1992), and *Stenberg* v. *Carhart* (2000) make clear. The chosen instrument in these cases was the Due Process Clause of the Fourteenth Amendment, which requires that no one be deprived of life, liberty, or property without due process of law. The language obviously requires only fair procedures in the application of substantive law. But in *Dred Scott* v. *Sanford*, a 1857 decision, Chief Justice Roger Taney transformed the identical Due Process Clause of the Fifth Amendment to require that statutes have substantive meanings which judges approve. He and a majority of the Court did not approve of a federal statute which, quite arguably, would have freed a slave taken by his owner to territory where slavery was forbidden. Taney wrote that depriving a man of his property, regardless of procedural regularity, could hardly be called due process. "Substantive due process," an oxymoron, was born.

Regardless of the shame in which it was conceived, and its internal contradiction, substantive due process has proved too valuable for judicial activism to be given up. In 1965, *Griswold* v. *Connecticut* gave birth to the Court-invented and undefined "right of privacy" which in turn spawned *Roe* v. *Wade*, a case which, without even a pretense of legal reasoning, announced a right to abortion. In an opinion of just over fifty-one pages, Justice Harry Blackmun surveyed such subjects as the view of abortion taken in the Persian Empire, the English common law, and by the American Medical Association, before announcing without further ado that the right of privacy was "broad enough" to cover a right to abortion. In *Planned Parenthood* v. *Casey*, the concurring opinion of three Justices, which created a majority to sustain a somewhat modified right to abortion, fashioned a right to "personal dignity and autonomy": "At the heart of liberty"—runs the by-now famous "mystery passage"—"is the right to define one's own concept of existence, of meaning, of the universe, and of the mystery of human life." Though the liberty to be protected is left entirely unclear by this fogbound rhetoric, the mood is certainly one of radical individualism. The three-justice opinion simply refuses to explain what it is talking about, just as *Roe* v. *Wade* did almost twenty years earlier.

Worse was to come. In *Stenberg* v. *Carhart*, the Court struck down a Nebraska statute banning partial birth abortions, a procedure in which a live baby is almost entirely removed from the mother, its skull pierced and its brain vacuumed out, before the carcass is taken from the birth canal. The procedure is morally indistinguishable from infanticide, but the Court majority held that an exception for cases in which the mother's life was otherwise endangered was not sufficient; there must be an exception to preserve the mother's health. Though it is never true that the mother's health would be adversely affected unless a partial birth abortion were performed, the ruling means that such abortions cannot be banned at all. There will always be an abortionist willing to certify that the procedure is essential to health.

In view of the territory the Court has claimed, it is worth examining the title deed composed in the *Griswold* decision. At issue was an ancient and unenforced statute prohibiting the use of contraceptives. Justice William O. Douglas reasoned that various provisions of the Bill of Rights protected aspects of privacy. That being so, the emanations from such rights formed a penumbra from which a larger, unmentioned right of privacy could be deduced. That reasoning assumes that the framers and ratifiers of the Bill of Rights had a sense that there was a more encompassing right which they were unable to articulate and so had to settle for a list of specific guarantees. In this view, the Court must finish the drafting by discerning a meaning the founders could not. The word "hubris" comes to mind. Bogus as it was, Douglas's sleight of hand seemed harmless, but it became the rhetorical cover for the far more serious decisions that followed. It is on that bastardized version of constitutional reasoning that the entire edifice of so-called reproductive rights rests.

The radical individualism of the abortion cases has offshoots. In *Eisenstadt* v. *Baird* (1972), the Court moved beyond the rationale of *Griswold*, which purported to rest upon the marriage relationship, to decide that the same rationale must apply to the distribution of contraceptives to unmarried people. Justice William Brennan announced that "If the right of privacy means anything, it is the right of the *individual*, married or single, to be free from unwarranted governmental intrusion into matters so fundamentally affecting a person as the decision whether to bear or beget a child." It would be quibbling to point out that the right of privacy does not, in fact, mean anything, except what a majority of the Court wants it to mean on any given day. There was, of course, no explanation why the law in question was an "unwarranted" intrusion. The point to notice is that, once more, individualism triumphed over majority morality.

THE COURT'S CONCERN with sexuality has taken it into the subject of homosexual behavior. Justice Harry Blackmun's dissenting opinion in *Bowers* v. *Hardwick* (1986) is perhaps the leading example of judicial insistence upon an individualism so unconfined as to be useless for any practical purpose other than rhetorical bludgeoning. The majority upheld the constitutionality of making homosexual sodomy a criminal offense. Blackmun's dissent dismissed the relevance of prior cases that seemed to confine the claimed "right of privacy" to the protection of the family: "We protect those rights not because they contribute, in some direct and material way, to the general public welfare, but because they form so central a part of an individual's life." This casual dismissal of the family, heretofore considered the most important unit of society, was in keeping with the modern attitudes of the intellectual class. On Blackmun's reasoning, since the individual is all, no-fault divorce must be a constitutional right. But he immediately went on to make matters worse: "[T]he concept of privacy embodies 'the moral fact that a person belongs to himself and not others nor to society as a whole.'" In short, the individual owes nothing to family, neighborhood, friends, nation, or anything outside his own skin, if that would interfere with his own pleasures. The four justices who signed the dissent cannot really have meant that, of course, but the fact that it could be written at all shows how far committed to individualism some of the justices have become.

Romer v. *Evans* (1996) took the next step and overruled *Bowers* without mentioning that case. By referendum the citizens of Colorado amended the state constitution to prevent localities from adding sexual orientation to the list of characteristics—race, sex, etc.—that were protected from private discrimination. The Court struck down the amendment on the theory that it treated homosexuals differently from other protected groups and thus violated the Equal Protection Clause. The rationale can best be described as incoherent. In order to gain legal immunity from private discrimination, homosexuals would have to seek it at the state level while the other groups would not. The fact is, of course, that all statewide or national laws require some groups to go beyond local government in order to change those laws. The Bill of Rights itself states principles that cannot be changed except by constitutional amendment. The most that can be made of *Romer* is that homosexuality is now a subject of special judicial solicitude. Individuals must be free to engage in homosexual behavior regardless of the community's moral standards.

A number of observers predict that within a few years the Court will announce that the principle of equality requires a constitutional right to same-sex marriage. If Jane is free to marry John, why doesn't equal protection require that Fred be equally able to marry John? Two state courts, of course, have already taken that step, to the intense displeasure of their citizens.

Since the Court is a central prize in the culture war, the fight to control it is political, engaging the White House and the Senate. There is, however, an equally important arena consisting of academic lawyers and pressure groups. These are heavily on the side of the emancipationists or liberals. Their tactic is frequently to insist, contrary to obvious reality, that the Supreme Court is dominated by conservatives.

Harvard's Laurence Tribe, for example, calls the current Justices "the most activist in our history." He said that "the astonishing weakness and vulnerability of the majority opinion in *Bush* v. *Gore*, and of the majority opinions in a number of other democracy-denying decisions in whose mold it was cast, are functions in part of the uniquely narrow spectrum of views . . . covered by the membership of the current Court." It must come as a revelation to the Justices themselves to learn that Stevens and Souter advance almost the same views as Scalia and Thomas. Tribe describes the Court's makeup as "four justices distinctly on the right, two moderate conservatives, a conservative moderate, two moderates, and no liberals." Cass Sunstein of Chicago states that today's Court has no liberals, which can only be true if he defines liberals as extreme radicals. Yale's Bruce Ackerman urges the Senate not to confirm anyone nominated by George Bush.

IT IS ONLY on the misunderstanding that the proper function of judges is to advance an ideological agenda that Abner Mikva, once a judge on the court on which I sat and later counsel to President Clinton, can urge the Senate not to confirm any Bush nominees to the Court because that might disturb the "delicate balance on the court on fundamental issues." That "delicate balance" means a Court that is predominantly liberal. In his next sentence, Mikva clarifies the balance he praises by noting, with obvious approval, that the Warren Court, which was heavily liberal, made fundamental changes by substantial majorities. Balance is desirable only when a Republican president might tip the Court in a neutral direction. When liberals say "balance" they mean a Court that will rewrite the Constitution to make it ever more liberal.

It is hard not to think such remarks disingenuous. The Court as a whole lists heavily to the cultural left. A "narrow spectrum of views" hardly describes a Court that though it splits on important cultural issues, almost invariably comes down on the liberal side and whose members regularly denounce one another in heated terms. Tribe himself rebuts his narrow-spectrum description by saying that "the recurring 5–4 majority on the Court on these matters has become a genuine threat to our system of government." How close votes threaten our system of government is unspecified. That Tribe is committed to the judicial activism he decries is demonstrated by his four (at last count) attempts to find an acceptable rationale for *Roe* v. *Wade*. The problem is not that he fails—success is impossible—but that he will not stop trying. Abortion must be a constitutional right even if no one can explain why.

The interest groups of the Left proceed by systematic lying about judicial nominees who adopt the traditional approach of interpreting the Constitution according to its actual meaning. In opposing Judge Pickering, Ralph Neas of the hard-left People for the American Way said, "Achieving ideological domination of the federal judiciary is the top goal of right-wing activists inside and outside the Bush administration." The left wing has discovered an effective tactic of labeling any conventional jurist an ideologue with a right-wing agenda and hence "outside the mainstream."

There is far more diversity of opinion on the Court than is to be found on law school faculties. In the last three decades, as the students of the Sixties became professors, law scholarship has become increasingly left wing and intellectually disordered. Faculties are less and less engaged in scholarship that might conceivably be of use to practitioners and judges or to the reform of legal doctrine. As Harry Edwards, formerly chief judge of the Court of Appeals for the District of Columbia Circuit, put it, "there is a growing disjunction between legal education and the legal profession," which is reflected in the gradual replacement of older, traditional scholars by younger faculty whose work is often so theoretical as to be of little use outside the coterie of like-minded professors who engage in impractical discourse. The division, Edwards says, "is permeated by rancor, contempt and ill will." The newer scholarship is politically motivated: "Many, although not all, of the legal theorists would like to bring about a radical transformation of society. In many cases, their work amounts to an attack on classical liberalism, which they would like to see replaced with a philosophical or political theory that will lead to a much more egalitarian society."

Professor Edgar Hahn, a professor of jurisprudence at Case Western Reserve University, reports, "Reading hundreds of articles in researching a book on legal scholarship confirms that politically correct writing appears with increasing frequency." In the university community, he writes, political correctness "is associated with language modification, oppression studies, race and gender victimization, rejection of the white male canon," which it sees as a culture of "objectivity and rationality." This began with the critical legal studies movement which attempted to deconstruct the intellectual foundations of existing law and traditional legal scholarship, without, however, indicating what might be substituted. A liberal professor states that "critical legal studies is a political location for a group of people on the Left who share the project of supporting and extending the domain of the Left in the legal academy." Hahn says that the advocates of political correctness now come from "Critical Race theorists, composed of Blacks and females, feminists, plus the remnants of the Critical Legal Studies movement." Hahn continued: "One of the more esteemed techniques is the use of personal experiences to convey the emotion and agony of persevering in an alien environment of patriarchy, hierarchy, and objectification." Thus some work of "scholars" consists of storytelling. Their narratives are published in law reviews and have been sufficient for the award of tenure. This intellectual collapse is now praised as "postmodern jurisprudence," a term which itself ought to be an embarrassment to the legal academics involved.

There have emerged almost innumerable competing theories of how the Constitution should be "interpreted." None of these has proved satisfactory to the competing theorists so that now we have reached a state of advanced nihilism in which articles and books are written on the impossibility of all normative theories of constitutional law or the "misguided quest for constitutional foundations." Were these counsels of despair accurate, the only honest conclusion would be that since they cannot make sense of what they are doing, judges should abandon judicial review altogether. That conclusion is never drawn, however. Constitutional law is about power, and professors will never relinquish their bit of that power.

If the legal academy is hopeless, one might suppose that at least some Justices would by now have undertaken a justification for their habitual departures from any conceivable meaning of the Constitution they claim as their authority. But search as one may, the opinions of the Court are utterly devoid of any such attempt. The most the Court has ever offered is the statement that it has never felt its power confined by the original understanding of the document. That much is certainly true, but it is hardly a justification. Persistent invasions of territory belonging to the people and their elected representatives cannot establish an easement across territory that the Constitution assigns to the democratic process.

It is not obvious what, if anything, can be done to bring the American judiciary back to legitimacy in a polity whose basic character is supposed to be democratic. It was once argued that a wayward Court would be corrected by professional criticism. The bar, however, is largely uninterested and academic constitutional commentary is largely intellectually corrupt.

Perhaps there is no remedy for judicial activism, perhaps a preference for immediate victories and short-term gratification of desires is characteristic of the spirit of our times. The public does seem ready to jettison long-term safeguards and the benefits of process for the short-term satisfaction of desires. That is always and everywhere the human temptation. But it is precisely that temptation that a constitution and its judicial spokesmen are supposed to protect us against. Constitutions speak for permanent values and judges are supposed to give those values voice. Instead, representatives of our judiciary are all too often, and increasingly, exemplars of disrespect for the rule of law. That situation is inconsistent with the survival of the culture that has for so long sustained American freedom and well-being. The example of lawless courts teaches a lesson of disrespect for process to all other actors in that system, the lesson that winning outside the rules is legitimate, and that political victory is the only virtue.

Born in Europe, central to the American founding, and fundamental to Western civilization, the ideal of the rule of law no longer commands much more than verbal allegiance. If prophecies of what the Court will do in fact is the meaning of law, then, in cultural matters the law may be predicted by the known personal inclinations of the Justices, nothing more pretentious. That is not the rule of law; it is the rule of judges. It would have been unthinkable until recently that so many areas of our national life would be controlled by judges. What is today unthinkable may well become not only thinkable but also actual in the next half century.

The liberal mindset refuses to recognize that real institutions can never approximate their ideal institutions. The pursuit of the ideal necessarily proceeds by and teaches an abstract, universalistic style of reasoning and legal argument. It leads to an incessant harping on rights that impoverishes political, cultural, and legal discourse. Universalistic rhetoric teaches disrespect for the actual institutions of the nation. Those institutions slow change, allow compromise, tame absolutisms, and thus embody inconsistencies that are, on balance, wholesome. They work, in short, to do things, albeit democratically and therefore messily, that abstract generalizations about the just society bring into contempt.

A Court that in one context after another lays down general principles of emancipation commends that principle to public attention and imitation and thus affects legislative opinion. Many people assume that what is legal is also moral, and they are all too likely to believe that what has been declared unconstitutional is immoral. Resistance to judicial imperialism in the name of the Constitution itself comes to be seen as immoral.

Writing last year in *The Wall Street Journal*, Charles Murray reflected on Arnold Toynbee's thesis about the decline of civilizations. One reliable sign of decline, Toynbee suggested, was when elites began to imitate those at the bottom of society. In robust societies, those at the bottom tend to imitate "their betters"—a phrase whose departure from common usage betokens the degradation Toynbee prophesied. One does not have to look far to see the vulgarization of the elites in contemporary American society. There is no more elite institution in America than the Supreme Court of the United States. The sampling of cases discussed here suggests that the Court is ahead of the general public in approving, and to a degree enforcing, the vulgarization or proletarianization of our culture.

Yet it is precisely that for which the Court is most admired by the intelligentsia and in our law schools. The names of Warren, Douglas, and Brennan are enshrined in the liberal pantheon. Justices who performed their duties more faithfully are often less well-known or even almost entirely forgotten. The career of Chief Justice Morrison Waite is a case in point. Probably not one in twenty law professors and not one in a hundred lawyers even recognizes his name. Yet Professor Felix Frankfurter, in praising Waite, identified the characteristic judicial sin: "When dealing with such large conceptions as the rights and duties of property, judges lacking some governing directions are easily lost in the fog of abstraction." That may be even more true today as the Court multiplies vaguely defined rights.

Frankfurter said that Waite has become

> a dim figure in constitutional history because his opinions are not delectable reading. . . . But the limited appeal of his opinions is due in part to something else—to the fulfillment of one of the greatest duties of a judge, the duty not to enlarge his authority. . . . The distinction between those who are makers of policy and those concerned solely with questions [of the Constitution's allocations] of ultimate power probably marks the deepest cleavage among the men who have sat on the Supreme Bench. . . . The conception of significant achievement on the Supreme Court has been too much identified with largeness of utterance, and too little governed by inquiry into the extent to which judges have fulfilled their professed role in the American constitutional system.

Largeness of judicial utterance is still very much with us. In fact, we are inundated by it and the related multiplication of individual rights that are traceable to nothing in the Constitution. The consequence is severe damage to our politics and our culture. Unless it takes its law from the original understanding of the Constitution's principles, the Court will continue to be an adversary to democratic government and to the morality of our traditional culture.

May 2002

Frantz Fanon: The Platonic
Form of Human Resentment

Anthony Daniels

W HILE BROWSING IN a secondhand bookshop recently, I came across
an English children's story entitled *Although He Was Black*. Readers
might like to complete the title for themselves: although he was black, he
was clean; although he was black, he was honest; although he was black, he
was clever. The last sentence of the book, however, reveals all, and reads:

> Dear old chap, he was one of the whitest fellows I ever knew—although
> he was black!

The dear old chap in question was Sambo, an orphaned black boy
brought to England by a wealthy Englishman called Mr. Darrell who, for a
reason unspecified, had spent some time in Kentucky. His two sons were
expecting him to return with a parrot or a monkey as a present from such
exotic climes, but he brought back Sambo instead, telling his two sons
that

> "I want you each to understand that Sambo is to be kindly treated, al-
> though never allowed to take liberties; the negro is faithful to death if
> properly handled. You will find him most amusing, some of his ways, and
> also his lingo is quaintness itself. Of course, the latter will improve in
> time."

Actually, Sambo's lingo doesn't improve in the slightest, despite his
close and lengthy association with two boys whose highest term of approbation is "Ripping!" When one of Mr. Darrell's two sons is sent to
the attic as punishment for disobedience, Sambo loyally offers to take his
place:

"Might dis dirty ole nigger stop up in de attic 'stead of Massa Hugh? 'Im eat up all de bread and drink de water. Laws, dis chile lub dry bread, sometimes 'im live on it for days in de ole times, and 'pears like jes' de right fing for 'im to be up in de attic."

The book had been awarded as a prize to a child in the Beginner's Class at a Baptist Sunday school in 1944, when Frantz Fanon, the Martinican who posthumously became one of the founders and heroes of Third Worldism—the doctrine that three-quarters of the world's population is pitilessly exploited by the remaining quarter—was fighting for the Free French. (Fanon was decorated for bravery by Colonel, later General, Salan, who eventually became head of the terrorist OAS in the last days of French Algeria.) *Although He Was Black* was not the only book of its kind, then or later. My wife, who is French, remembers reading very similar books as a child in Paris in the 1950s: while across the Channel, I read stories about Billy Bunter, a very fat and rather dim pupil in a minor English public school, who repeatedly translated "*Magna est veritas et praevalebit*" as "Great is the truth and it will prevail a bit" (a profound, if unconscious, insight into the working of the world). Bunter was known as the Fat Owl of the Remove because, short-sighted and wearing thick round spectacles, he spent his entire life scheming to obtain and consume cream cakes. One of his classmates was Harry Jamset Ram Singh, the son of an Indian rajah who, as everyone agreed, was "a white man deep inside," a fact which satisfactorily accounted for his thoroughgoing decency and sportsmanship.

It was not altogether surprising, then, that a member of the audience for Fanon's public lecture in Lyon in the early 1950s on the parallels between black and white poetry should have sought to congratulate him on the excellence of his talk by telling him that "Basically, you're white." He could think of no higher compliment than that: but it was a compliment that had, alas, a less flattering corollary.

It is one of the virtues of David Macey's extremely long, sympathetic but not completely uncritical biography of Frantz Fanon (*Frantz Fanon: A Biography*; Picador Press, 2002) that Mr. Macey should understand the psychological significance of such an event. Fanon was himself never the serious victim of overt French racism, but as a sensitive and intelligent man he must have been profoundly wounded by the disdain and contempt in which members of his race were often held in the metropolitan countries. And in my experience, it is small slights rather than great wrongs that create the bitterest resentment: for such slights intimate that the person delivering them does not consider their recipients to be fully human.

Mr. Macey's book is exceptionally strong on Fanon's Martinican background, a background that explains some of the agonized and agonizing contortions of his first book, *Black Skin, White Masks* (1952). Fanon was born on the French West Indian island in 1925, when society was racially stratified but not segregated. The children of the white elite went to school with the better-off mulattoes and blacks, where they all absorbed an idealistic republican ideology and historiography, with the idea that all men under French rule were equal and endowed with rights, thanks to the Revolution of 1789 and the efforts of Victor Schoelcher, the framer of the 1848 decree that abolished slavery in French territories. Thus Fanon grew up without much awareness of his place in the racial pecking order: he thought he was just a human being. At the same time, however, he was aware of a cultural pecking order: all things French were, by definition, superior and cultivated, and woe betide the child of an aspiring Martinican family caught speaking in Creole rather than in the language of Racine and Corneille.

Fanon's awakening was not so much rude as gradual: it occurred in stages. First came the defeat of France in 1940. The armistice left France still in control of its colonies, including Martinique, which was not only governed by a follower and local avatar of Pétain, Admiral Robert, but also became for a time the base of some of Vichy's fleet, whose sailors were stationed ashore. Not only did their presence put a strain on the fragile economy of the island, but their racist demeanor and conduct came as a shock to blacks brought up to believe in *nos ancêtres, les Gaulois.* Still, what could be expected of a pack of Pétainists and Vichyites?

The second stage in Fanon's awakening occurred when Fanon, with considerable bravery, escaped Martinique to join the Free French. He discovered that, even as he fought for France's freedom, not all Frenchmen were as equal as he had thought. True, he was considered more French than, that is to say superior to, a Senegalese or a North African, but he was not the equal of a white metropolitan Frenchman, and he had the distinct impression that black units were sent into battle first, as cannon fodder. Moreover, white metropolitans were given superior rations and accommodation. This was a discovery from which Fanon never recovered: never again was he to believe that France represented liberty, equality, and fraternity.

The third stage in Fanon's awakening occurred when, demobilized after the war, he gained a scholarship to study medicine in Lyons. Needless to say, because the scholarship was his by right—a law had been passed entitling ex-Free French servicemen to assisted places at university—he saw no reason to be grateful to France for it (an object lesson in the profoundly pernicious effect upon character of the idea of entitlement). But soon after his arrival in France there occurred an incident which he considered much more significant than his scholarship, and of which he made much in *Black Skin, White Masks*. A little girl, accompanied by her mother, sees Fanon and exclaims, "Look, a negro! Look, a negro! Look, a negro! Mum, look at the negro, I'm frightened!"

Having read and admired Sartre, Fanon was well prepared to make a theoretical mountain out of an empirical molehill. The little girl's exclamation demonstrated for him the all-pervasive nature of French racism: for if a little girl expressed fear of the black man at so tender an age, what ideas must she have absorbed from her social milieu?

These were the experiences that sensitized Fanon against French colonialism in Algeria, as previous exposure to allergens sensitize people so that they eventually suffer from anaphylactic shock when re-exposed to the allergen. Fanon went to Algeria to practice as a psychiatrist, and, though he was left-wing in his sympathies, he was merely seeking employment, not revolution, there. He was by all accounts a dedicated doctor, but when the revolt against French rule started it was inevitable that he would sympathize with and eventually adhere to it, putting his medical knowledge at its disposal. Whatever else he might have been, Fanon was definitely not a coward.

But since he has come to be known principally as a political philosopher, as a man of ideas, it is necessary to evaluate his thought independently of his psychological trajectory. Perhaps this is just as well, because the picture of the man that emerges from the 640 pages of this biography is strangely colorless and indistinct, of a man without very definite characteristics apart from his political and medical interests. Fanon manages to appear both passionate and bloodless at the same time, a kind of platonic form of human resentment, redeemed only by the code of medical ethics to which, as far as is known, he always adhered in his dealings with individual patients, even when they were French torturers. From Mr. Macey's book, we learn little of the love affair which resulted in the birth in France of an illegitimate child, abandoned without evidence of regret, or of his marriage to a white woman and of his relationship to their son: perhaps because there is very little to learn. Fanon's intense privacy was part of his colorlessness. He would have wanted to be judged by his ideas and political actions, not by his intimate life.

Mr. Macey is, in my view, far too indulgent to Fanon as a thinker. In the first place, Fanon often expressed himself badly, and in the second, he was hardly capable of sustained argument. As a theorist, he was allusive and suggestive rather than systematic: in other words, lazy. Finally, he was dishonest: more a pamphleteer in support of a cause than a seeker after truth or wisdom.

Fanon's most famous idea, of course, and the one with which he will forever be associated, is that of the healing power of violence. This does not mean that he was a sadist: there is no evidence that he enjoyed watching, hearing about, or inflicting violence. Nor was he a Nietzschean: violence was for him not an end in itself, or a sign of personal election, but a stage through which man had unfortunately to pass. Its purpose was ultimately to bring about a reign of universal milk-and-water benevolence that Nietzsche would have detested and despised. The fantastic unlikelihood of universal brotherhood being brought about by a bloodbath seemed entirely to have escaped him, however. He was so beguiled by the fact that he had had an original thought that he could not bear to give it up merely because it was wrong.

He did not believe in the healing power of any and all violence. His attitude was a bit like that of the Peronist who, on being asked what he thought of torture, replied, "It depends who's being tortured and who's doing the torturing." Healing violence was the prerogative of the colonial oppressed who suffered not only from material exploitation, but also from an inferiority complex brought about by the deliberate inculcation of the idea that the colonialists' culture was vastly superior to their own. In killing a white man, therefore, the colonized were simultaneously ridding them-selves of their material oppressors and of their inferiority complex. When the violence was over, the formerly colonized and the former colonizers would be able to relate to one another as equals. The violence would have liberated the latter as well as the former: for a superiority complex is as psy-chologically unhealthy as an inferiority complex. Henceforth all men would be brothers.

I trust that the shallowness of this view needs no lengthy exposition. Fanon could not face up to the indubitable though uncomfortable fact that some cultures are richer and more advanced than others. An African doesn't need to be tricked into believing that it is more comfortable to ride in a Mercedes-Benz than to walk through the bush barefoot after a herd of goats, nor does he need persuading that his culture played no part whatever in the production of the Mercedes-Benz. He knows that his own culture is inferior, at least in very many directions.

Of course, those who belong to the most advanced material culture are not necessarily superior in other ways, or even the happier for it. And likewise, it is a vulgar error to deduce individual capabilities or characteris-tics—one's own, or those of other people—from the capabilities or charac-teristics of a group or culture. The fact that I am British does not in the least mean I cannot be taught to cook or cannot appreciate good food. But it is nevertheless a part of human psychology to feel the inferiority of one's group as a personal wound. This wound cannot be healed by psychological legerdemain or by violence, any more than the CEO of Ford Motors can make his cars more desirable than BMWs by shooting the CEO of BMW. Such an act might relieve momentary frustration, but would not result in long-term advantages.

Moreover, Fanon knew from his clinical practice that violence did not bring about the effects he elsewhere said it did, either in individuals or in society as a whole. In the chapter of his most famous book, *The Wretched of the Earth*, entitled "Colonial War and Mental Disorders," he provided many startling and interesting case histories, in none of which does violence play anything other than a destructive role. For example, one young Algerian who takes part in the revolt coldbloodedly kills the wife of a known French torturer: the kind of act that Fanon elsewhere recommends as liberating. But the young man is not liberated by his deed: on the contrary, he is tormented by it, and rightly so. His torment is a sign that he retains his humanity, and all Fanon could find to say of this case is that "in our opinion time alone can bring some improvement to the disrupted personality of this young man." This is hardly evidence of the healing power of anticolonial violence.

FANON BELIEVED, at least in theory, in the beneficial effects of indiscriminate slaughter. This followed from his statement that there were no innocent Frenchmen in Algeria, or even in France, and that therefore everyone was "a legitimate target." But when he came across the case of two Algerian boys, aged thirteen and fourteen, who killed their French playmate simply because he was French, he was clearly appalled. He believed that they should have waited until they were adults before they killed their French friends: perfidy being for adults, not children.

Fanon also knew perfectly well that the FLN was not a democratic organization and had no intention of becoming one. Like many guerrillophiles, he penned dithyrambs to the new, more genuine kind of democracy being forged in the crucible of slaughter, but he also knew that the FLN was almost as concerned to eliminate its internal rivals (whom it could definitively defeat) as drive out the French (whom it couldn't). The lust for power is almost always much stronger than the lust for freedom, at least for the freedom of anyone other than oneself. He knew that the FLN committed atrocities, but did not protest or publicize them: for he had, quite literally, defined truth as that which served the revolution:

> Truth is that which dislocates the colonial regime, that which promotes the emergence of the nation. Truth is that which protects the natives and destroys foreigners.

This is the kind of thing a propagandist says, but not a philosopher. Indeed, the open avowal of such an idea should be sufficient to put an alleged intellectual beyond all serious consideration. He is in effect telling the world that nothing he says can be believed: so that even if there were no internal evidence in Fanon's work of economy with the truth, it should be regarded as aesthetes used to regard pig manure before it became transgressive.

Fanon was not the first, nor the last, in the twentieth century to define truth as that which serves a cause. There were many Communists and Nazis who did so. He was not original in this, any more than he was in his guerrillophilia. He was, in effect, the Edgar Snow, Agnes Smedley, and Anna Louise Strong of the Algerian revolution rolled into one. Alas, this particular cast of mind has even yet to disappear: the outbreak of the Zapatista revolt in Chiapas, Mexico, brought it all back, like foot and mouth disease in England.

FANON'S POLITICAL JUDGMENT was naïve at best. Considering he was a psychiatrist, he showed little mistrust of the honeyed words of politicians and little ability to penetrate to their real motives. The most startling example of this was his admiration for, and belief in, Ahmed Sékou Touré, the first President of Guinea. Even in the extensive menagerie of bizarre post-independence African dictators, Sékou Touré was outstanding for his combination of cruelty, megalomania, paranoia, and economic incompetence. I can best capture the quality of his rule by relating a small anecdote.

The former foreign minister of Tanzania, Oscar Kambona, who went into exile in London when he disagreed with the sainted Julius Nyerere over the matter of the one-party state—and who was repaid for his contretemps with St. Julius by the fatal defenestration of his son from an apartment in London by the Tanzanian secret service (a death still not fully investigated by the British authorities for the sake of maintaining good diplomatic relations)—told me that he was traveling one day on the London underground when he found himself next to an African of about his own age.

"Where are you from?" asked his neighbor on the train.

"Tanzania," he replied.

"Ah, Tanzania," said the neighbour, throwing up his arms in admiration. "Great Nyerere! Great African leader!"

Oscar asked the man where he was from.

"Guinea," he replied.

"Ah, Guinea," said Oscar, throwing up his arms in mock admiration. "Great Sékou Touré! Great African leader!"

The man burst into tears. I am no friend of emotional incontinence or display, but suffice it to say that I sympathize entirely with that elderly Guinean on the London underground. His emotion was real enough, as was its cause: for Sékou Touré killed or drove into exile a third of the population of his country, a feat equalled only by Macías Nguema of Equatorial Guinea (both were democratically elected, incidentally).

As for Algeria's own future, Fanon (who spoke no Arabic) was about as good a prophet as Khrushchev was about the future of the Soviet Union.

The question remains as to why a thinker as crude and propagandistic as Fanon should have commanded so wide a following in the West. I well remember the popularity in intellectual circles of the Fanonian argument that those African countries that "liberated" themselves by force of arms, such as Angola and Mozambique, had a better prognosis than those that received their independence peacefully, more or less as a gift, because people who had fought for the independence of their country were politically aware and dedicated unselfishly to the future, had become, in short, Fanon's "New Man." Now, several million lives later, we know better.

Fanon was actually never very popular in France, despite his use of the language of Racine and Corneille: not because his bloodthirsty views were alien to the French left, but because they struck a little close to home. After all, Algeria was a humiliation for France, and the French left, unlike the British, has always been patriotic to the point of nationalism. If France was not militarily defeated, it was defeated politically, and the whole episode was a significant part of the painful contraction of Europe to the western peninsula of its own continent. Moreover, the conscience of the French left was not clear in the case of Algeria: Mitterand was a firm supporter of *Algérie française*, and the French Communist Party believed the uprising in 1954 to be a manifestation of petit bourgeois nationalism, that is to say wholly retrograde. The Algerians had more to hope for from being part of a Communist France than from ruining their country for themselves.

As if this were not sufficient, France dealt with the Algerian episode as it dealt with Vichy: that is to say, by forgetting it as soon as possible and almost pretending it never happened. Thus, although the atrocious methods used by the French forces were well-known and publicized more than forty years ago, they have been re-revealed recently in France with all the appearance of national shock. The re-revelations of French torture in Algeria are to the French what Clinton's presidential pardons were to American liberals.

Fanon was very much a figure for the 1960s: only in that decade could he have achieved his fame, which was almost entirely posthumous (he died of leukemia in 1961, aged thirty-six, shortly before the publication of *The*

Wretched of the Earth). His evident hatred of Europe fitted in well with the exhibitionist self-loathing of the era: a hatred and self-loathing based largely on ignorance. When in Rome, for example, Fanon displayed no interest whatever in the monuments of that marvelous city, in case—I suspect—he were confronted with the astonishing glory of Europe as well as its degradation, a confrontation which would have required him to moderate his views. For he firmly believed that European civilization was raised on a foundation of exploitation of Africa. The ruins of Rome threatened his worldview, and therefore his justification for the violence he had lauded.

In the last analysis, Fanon is more interesting as a sociological phenomenon—both for himself and for the reaction he called forth in the parts of the world he excoriated—than as a thinker. I doubt that anyone will ever again have to undertake Mr. Macey's biographical task, unless, as is unlikely, more evidence comes to light. We can only hope that the concept of laudable violence has been as comprehensively consigned to the past as the nineteenth-century medical concept of laudable pus. And Mr. Macey omits one irony that surely would have made Fanon's life a terrible torment had he lived: it was France, not Algeria, that prospered after the conclusion of the Algerian war of independence. Truly, the Owl of Minerva flies by night.

May 2001

"The Innocents Abroad,"
or the New Pilgrim's Progress

Mordecai Richler

T HE BUSINESS OF getting from here to there has become increasingly
frustrating, even infuriating, and I speak as someone who once adored
traveling, the slaphappy sensation of traipsing down the twisting streets of a
foreign city for the first time, your jaded senses heightened by what Gerard
Manley Hopkins celebrated as "all things counter, original, spare, strange."

Of course nowadays disembark in Moscow, Barcelona, or Tel Aviv, set
out for the main boulevard, and you are bound to be deflated by the
familiar: a McDonald's, a Georgio Armani boutique, a Gucci, a pizza bar,
and a shop called "Wyatt Urp" or "Doge City" [*sic*] specializing in designer
jeans and hand-tooled western boots made by prisoners in China. Over-
priced restaurants will welcome American Express, Visa, and MasterCard.
CNN will be available on your hotel TV, and you can count on the indigenous channel to be showing reruns of "Dallas" or "Cheers," dubbed in
Russian, Spanish, or Hebrew. Mind you, these latter variations on the
familiar can be inadvertently amusing.

Item: in 1951, drifting down the Ramblas in Barcelona, somewhat
footsore, I slipped into a cinema to catch a Joel McCrae western dubbed in
Spanish and, lo and behold, good old reliable Joel moseyed up to a saloon
bar in Tombstone and demanded, "*Uno cognac, por favor.*"

I first crossed the Atlantic, at the age of nineteen, in 1950, on board the
Franconia, outward-bound from Quebec City to Liverpool. In those days
everybody in tourist class on an ocean liner or propeller-driven airplane was
equal, paying the same fare. But nowadays, after you have probably forked
out something like a thousand bucks for your jumbo jet "hospitality" (that
is to say, cattle-class) return ticket to Paris, Rome, or wherever, the odds are
that the three-hundred-pound behemoth shoehorned into the seat beside
you, having promised to fly on a rainy Wednesday while wearing his track

suit with the Day-Glo stripes, most likely has acquired his ticket for $49.95, payable in twelve installments. Furthermore, that price includes four nights in a two-star hotel, a clutch of theater tickets, and coupons that will yield magnums of Dom Perignon in any number of restaurants. And if that isn't enough to put you in a yippee mood, it turns out that fatso, once he has stowed away a ton of "carry-on" luggage under his seat *and* yours, turns out to be a compulsive nose picker or a master of the silent fart, earning *you* dirty looks from everyone in the rows ahead and behind. And, naturally, he is a talker, who wants to know how the world is treating you and where do you hail from?

"Montreal," I once said, on an Air France flight out of New York.

"Gosh. That's my favorite city in the United States."

Freeze out your seatmate, and he retaliates by fishing into one of his bulging flight bags and surfacing with the latest Garfield paperback, which has him quaking with laughter for the next four hours of flight time. The rest of the jet, it goes without saying, is usually filled with shrieking babes, kids playing tag, teenagers jerking their heads in time to the rock beat leaking out of the Walkman clamped to their ears, middle-aged wits who feel entitled to flirt with the stewardesses ("I've got the time, if you've got the place"), and battalions of Japanese tourists, laden with state-of-the-art camcorders, shooting film of cloud formations, of flight attendants propelling drink trolleys, and of each other standing up, sitting down, and performing other astonishing feats.

Then, after bouncing about at thirty-five thousand feet for seven hours, snug as a sardine in a tin, you land, ears throbbing with pain, and line up in an overheated hall to pass through immigration. This will take an hour, maybe more, because either you have arrived just after a flight from Colombia, every passenger a suspected drug smuggler, or there's an obviously impecunious African immediately ahead of you in line, who claims to be a citizen of Finland, and is armed with an inch-thick passport that opens like an accordion and calls for a half-hour examination by the suspicious immigration officer.

Finally, you reach your hotel—smelly, eyes bloodshot—only to be welcomed by the news that they have no record of your reservation or that your room, overlooking a parking lot, won't be ready for another four hours. Never mind. The bar is open, and there you can contemplate the ordeals that lie ahead: all those museums and churches and castles, the snotty waiters you will have to tolerate. Because you are a North American, they will unfailingly check you out to make sure you are wearing shoes, and treat you as if you were about to sample your first glass of wine.

Ah, but it was utterly different—still an amazing, even daring adventure—when the incomparable Mark Twain, born Samuel Langhorne Clemens in 1835, set out on an "Excursion to the Holy Land, Egypt, the Crimea, and Intermediate Points of Interest" on *Quaker City*, a paddle-steamer, sailing out of New York, on June 8, 1867. In Twain's time the world had not yet become a village to be avoided. Escape was still possible and novelty was the happy rule.

"The proprietors of the *Daily Alta Californian*," wrote Twain in his autobiography, "engaged me to write an account of the trip for that paper—fifty letters of a column and a half each, which would be about two thousand words per letter, and the pay to be twenty dollars per letter."

Twain, thirty-two years old at the time, set sail as just another freelance hack, and he returned as the first true master of the American idiom. This he accomplished at a time when, as Stephen Leacock wrote in his biography of Twain, "of American literature there was much doubt in Europe; of American honesty, much more, of American manners more still." But I knew nothing of this when I first came across the writings of Mark Twain, introduced to them, like most boys of my generation, through *The Adventures of Tom Sawyer*, a gift from an uncle.

I would like to claim that reading Twain for the first time made for an epiphany, but it wasn't the case. I was far more taken with *Scaramouche*, *The Three Musketeers*, *The Count of Monte Cristo*, and *Robin Hood*. Settling into bed for the night, I dreamed of humiliating the dastardly Sheriff of Nottingham with my dazzling swordplay, or galloping off with d'Artagnan and his chums, all for one, one for all. Titled ladies were my heart's desire. My problem was I knew kids like Tom Sawyer, who might try to con me into painting their fence. It was familiar and, therefore, couldn't count as literature, like, say, Shelley's "Ode to the West Wind," which I had to copy out ten times after my class master caught me ogling a copy of *Sunbathing* in his Highroads to Reading class.

I WAS A SLOW LEARNER. And so only later, after I had read *Huckleberry Finn* for a second time, did I grasp that I was in the presence of a great writer, somebody who could convey more about the white American's prejudice against blacks in one seemingly effortless colloquial exchange than many a polemicist could manage in ten fulminating, fact-bound pages.

Huck tells Aunt Sally, "It was the grounding of the steamer that kept us back. We blowed out a cylinder head."

"Good gracious. Anybody hurt?"

"No'm. Killed a nigger."

"Well, it's lucky; because sometimes people do get hurt."

The advertisement announcing the sailing of *Quaker City* claimed there would be cabins sufficient to accommodate "a select company" of 150 on a "first-class steamer," which was provided "with every necessary comfort, including a library and musical instruments," as well as "an experienced physician on board." The price per passage, on what was actually America's first venture into mass tourism, a harbinger of the heavy traffic to come, was $1,250 for adult passengers, who were advised that five dollars per day, in gold, would be sufficient to handle their needs on shore.

Anticipating what would be the case in many an over-promoted tour in years to come, the promised shipboard celebrities were notable by their absence. Urgent duties, a bemused Twain noted, obliged the Reverend Henry Ward Beecher to give up the idea, and the Indian wars compelled Lt. Gen. Sherman's presence on the plains.

> A popular actress had entered her name on the ship's books, but something interfered, and *she* couldn't go. The "Drummer Boy of the Potomac" deserted, and lo, we had never a celebrity left!

As with so many of today's so-called "love boats," advertised by photographs of decks adorned with sexy, bikini-clad young women, what *Quaker City* did in fact deliver was a plethora of what my daughter calls cotton-tops, or as Twain had it, venerable people, among them, three ministers of the gospel, eight doctors, sixteen or eighteen ladies, "several military and naval chieftains with sounding titles, an ample crop of 'Professors' of various kinds, and a gentleman who had 'Commissioner of the United States of America to Europe, Asia, and Africa' thundering under his name in one awful blast!" And none of them, I'm sure, suspected that they would be the victims of a rollicking satire that still reads freshly more than a century after its first publication.

In Twain's below decks cabin, which he was to share with a young gentleman, there was room to turn around in, but not to swing a cat. Happily, however, the saloon bar, which the unregenerated dubbed the "Synagogue," was a good fifty or sixty feet long, and the ship's company boasted not one, not two, but five captains.

Having crossed the Atlantic several times myself on modern liners equipped with stabilizers—still a sick-making ordeal in heavy seas—I can only marvel at what Twain and his companions must have endured on their little paddle-steamer. But Twain makes reference to only one Atlantic gale, wherein *Quaker City* "climbed aloft as if she would climb to heaven—then paused an instant that seemed like a century, and plunged headlong down again, as from a precipice."

First port of call was in the Azores, and it becomes instantly clear that the free-wheeling Twain, bless him, is not going to be shackled by political correctness. Oh dear, oh dear. Given today's touchy political climate, I suspect there is sufficient kindling in *The Innocents Abroad* to light a fire of protest under Portuguese, Italians, Moslems, Catholics, Turks, Greeks, feminists, Arabs, American Indians, and other sensitive types. I have no doubt that *The Innocents Abroad*, released today, would be banned in schools, the author condemned as a racist, and possibly, just possibly, finding himself the subject of a *fatwa*.

The Portuguese people of the Azores, wrote Twain, lie, and cheat the stranger, and are "slow, shiftless, sleepy, and lazy." He didn't fancy the women of Tangier:

> I have caught a glimpse of the faces of several Moorish women (for they are only human, and will expose their faces for the admiration of a Christian dog when no male Moor is by), and I am full of veneration for the wisdom that leads them to cover up such atrocious ugliness.

Unaware of what would become modish everywhere today, he added, "They carry their children at their backs, in a sack, like other savages the world over." But Twain did allow that "weak, stupid, ignorant" Abdul-Aziz, Sultan of Turkey, Lord of the Ottoman Empire, was a true representative of a people, which is to say he was "by nature and training filthy, brutish, unprogressive, superstitious."

He was not enchanted by Civitavecchia, which he adjudged "the finest nest of dirt, vermin and ignorance we have found yet, except that African perdition they call Tangier, which is just like it."

Poor Twain was born too soon to appreciate that a "dwarf" is actually a "vertically challenged" person and that "cripple" has been displaced by "physically disadvantaged."

> If you want dwarfs—I mean just a few dwarfs for a curiosity—go to Genoa. If you wish to buy them by the gross, for retail, go to Milan. . . . But if you want to see the very heart and home of cripples and human monsters, both, go straight to Constantinople.

A writer who usually got his priorities right, he was perturbed by the scarcity of whiskey in Constantinople, and didn't much care for the Greeks, Turks, or Armenians in town:

> [Their] morals consist only in attending church regularly on the appointed Sabbaths, and in breaking the ten commandments all the balance of the

week. It comes natural to them to lie and cheat in the first place, and then go on and improve on nature until they arrive at perfection.

Twain was appalled by "the usual assemblage of squalid humanity" that waited outside the pilgrims' camp on the outskirts of Damascus:

> They sat in silence, and with tireless patience watching our every motion with that vile, uncomplaining impoliteness which is so truly Indian, and which makes a white man so nervous and uncomfortable and savage that he wants to exterminate the whole tribe.
>
> These people about us had other peculiarities, which I have noticed in the noble red man, too: they were infested with vermin, and the dirt caked on them until it amounted to bark.

He pronounced Magdala thoroughly Syrian, that is to say, "thoroughly ugly, and cramped, squalid, uncomfortable, and filthy." In Jerusalem, a city of a mere fourteen thousand souls when Twain visited, he inveighed against Moslem rule:

> Rags, wretchedness, poverty and dirt, those signs and symbols that indicate the presence of Moslem rule more surely than the crescent-flag itself, abound. Lepers, cripples, the blind, and the idiotic, assail you on every hand, and they know but one word of but one language apparently—the eternal "bucksheesh."

Twain couldn't know that something like 135 years later the right-wing editor of *The Jerusalem Post*, David Bar-Illan, would brandish Twain's condemnation of Moslem rule as a license for Israel's sole possession of the city.

The majesty of the Sphinx impressed Twain, but not the "corrugated, unsightly mountain of stone" that formed the great pyramid of Cheops. In Cairo, of course, he was immediately surrounded by the usual rabble, demanding bucksheesh. But Twain wasn't nearly as naughty about Cairo as an earlier distinguished visitor, the twenty-seven-year-old Gustave Flaubert, who was there in 1849, and wrote in *Flaubert in Egypt: A Sensibility on Tour* that on his first day in Cairo he was immediately surrounded: "The girls were making imitation fart sounds with their hands. The boy was excellent—short, ugly, stocky: 'If you will give me five paras I'll bring you my mother to fuck. I wish you all kinds of prosperity, especially a long prick.'"

I didn't get to see the Great Pyramid myself until 1992, but, obviously, not much had changed since Mark Twain had come and gone. Approaching the Great Pyramid on foot, my wife and I were instantly besieged by vendors and supplicants, old men and boys, offering T-shirts, posters, sun hats, bottles of mineral water, camel or horseback rides, a helping hand to enter the pyramid—everybody after bucksheesh, the grease that turns the Egyptian wheel. Furthermore, our guide, licensed to speak English, had to be a direct descendant of one Twain had endured. He was contemptuous of the smaller, sometimes crumbling pyramids at Giza: "They was for nobbels or womens and womens not equals mens."

Leading us to the Sphinx, he asked, "Why is it the Sphinx has it head mans and body of lions? It is to show intelligence of mens and muskels of beast togethered."

ONE HUNDRED AND TWENTY-SIX YEARS after it was first published, *The Innocents Abroad* can be read not only for its literary delights, and the pleasures of reading a major writer when he was young and just beginning to flex his muscles, but also as an enduring, no-nonsense guide for the first-time traveler to Europe and the Holy Land.

The grandchildren of the mendacious guides Twain suffered here, there, and everywhere, will still inveigle travelers "into shirt stores, boot stores, tailor shops," where they are entitled to a commission on sales. Perdition catch all guides, wrote Twain, after an experience in Italy with a guide who claimed to be "the most gifted linguist in Genoa, as far as English was concerned, and that only two persons in the city beside himself could talk the language at all." In a memorable exchange, Twain and his chum, the doctor, do manage to get the better of this particular guide, whom they had dubbed Ferguson:

> "Come wis me, genteelmen!—come! I show you ze letter writing by Christopher Columbo!—write it himself!—write it wis his own hand! come!"
>
> He led us to the municipal palace. After much impressive fumbling of keys and opening of locks, the stained and aged document was spread before us.
>
> "What I tell you, genteelmen! Is it not so? See! handwriting Christopher Columbo!— write it himself!"
>
> We looked indifferent—unconcerned. The doctor examined the document deliberately, during a painful pause.—Then he said, without any show of interest:
>
> "Ah—Ferguson—what—what did you say was the name of the party who wrote this?"
>
> "Christopher Columbo! ze great Christopher Columbo!"
>
> Another deliberate examination.

"Ah—did he write it himself, or—or how?"

"He write it himself!—Christopher Columbo! he's own hand-writing, write by himself!"

"Why, I have seen boys in America only fourteen years old that could write better than that."

"But zis is ze great Christo—"

"I don't care who it is! It's the worst writing I ever saw. Now you mustn't think you can impose on us because we are strangers. We are not fools, by a good deal. If you have got any specimens of penmanship of real merit, trot them out!—and if you haven't, drive on!"

Shocks of recognition abound in *The Innocents Abroad*. I am willing to swear, for instance, that the Fergusons Twain suffered in Milan, and elsewhere, were the progenitors of that babbler of statistics who drove my wife and me to Masada, on our extended tour of Israel in 1992. "Their tongues are never still," wrote Twain. "They talk forever and forever . . . they interrupt every dream, every pleasant train of thought, with their tiresome cackling."

Only last year, arriving at a hotel in Paris, I stood by, a helpless victim, as the doorman removed our bags from a taxi, deposited them at the front door and extended his hand for a tip. Then another man carried our bags as far as the registration desk, and extended his hand. Finally, a third man lugged the bags to our room, and held out his hand for the obligatory *pourboire*. So I clapped hands at Twain's description of the avarice he witnessed at Vesuvius:

> They seize a lady's shawl from a chair and hand it to her and charge a penny; they open a carriage door and charge for it—shut it when you get out, and charge for it; brush your clothes and make them worse than they were before—two cents; smile upon you—two cents; bow, with lick-spittle smirk, hat in hand—two cents.

Like Twain, I have visited the Haram al-Sharif (the Noble Sanctuary) in the Old City of Jerusalem, and descended the steps of the Dome of the Rock to gawk at the fabled Stone of Foundation, where, it is claimed, Adam was molded from dust. This is amply proven, wrote Twain, "by the fact that in six thousand years no man has ever been able to prove that the dirt was *not* procured here whereof he was made."

It was on this busiest of rocks, according to legend, that Cain killed Abel, and Abraham, put to the test by Jehovah, prepared to sacrifice Isaac. Jesus is said to have preached here. And this is exactly where Mohammed stopped on his *isra*, his celebrated nocturnal journey to heaven, in which he traveled from Mecca to Jerusalem and ascended to heaven on his horse. "Where Mohammed stood," wrote Twain, "he left his foot-prints in solid stone. I should judge he wore about eighteens."

In his autobiography, Twain wrote that he "did not lean heavily on the *Alta* letters" in composing *The Innocents Abroad*. "I found they were newspaper matter, not book matter." He used several of the letters, ten or twelve perhaps, and claims to have churned out the rest, some two hundred thousand words, in sixty days. On one level, surely, *The Innocents Abroad* was meant as an antidote to the insufferably romantic, cliché-ridden travel books of the period, written by intimidated colonials genuflecting to European culture and exaggerating the charms of the Holy Land. Giving them the raspberry, Twain wrote:

> If any man has a right to feel proud of himself, and satisfied, surely it is I. For I have written about the Coliseum, and the gladiators, the martyrs, and the lions, and yet have never once used the phrase "butchered to make a Roman holyday." I am the only free white man of mature age, who has accomplished this since Byron originated the expression.

Twain was especially scornful of one Wm. C. Grimes, a hack much given to florid descriptions, and another writer, identified only as C. W. E., author of *Life in the Holy Land*, who easily outdid today's most gushing travel brochure in his celebration of the Sea of Galilee, pronouncing it a "terrestrial paradise." The truth of the matter, wrote Twain, is that the Sea of Galilee, stripped for inspection, "proves to be only an unobtrusive basin of water, some mountainous desolation, and one tree."

Familiar as he was with the grandeur, and incredible variety, of the yet untamed American continent, Twain was far from enchanted with Palestine, venturing that it was a hopeless, dreary, heart-broken land. "The hills are barren," he wrote, "they are dull of color, they are unpicturesque in shape." But Twain was alert to beauty whenever he stumbled on it, as he did once in Smyrna, where he observed a passing camel train:

> They stride along these streets, in single file, a dozen in a train, with heavy loads on their backs, and a fancy-looking negro in Turkish costume, or an Arab, preceding them on a little donkey completely overshadowed and rendered insignificant by the huge beasts. To see a camel train laden with the spices of Arabia and the rare fabrics of Persia come marching through the narrow alleys of the bazaar, among porters with their burdens, money-changers, lamp-merchants, Alnaschars in the glassware business,

portly cross-legged Turks smoking the famous narghili, and the crowds drifting to and fro in fanciful costumes of the East, is a genuine revelation of the Orient. The picture lacks nothing.

Mark Twain, then a largely unknown young journalist enjoying a freebie passage, set sail on *Quaker City* at a time when America's best-known humorists were Petroleum Vesuvius Nasby and Orpheus C. Kerr, long since forgotten, as well as Artemus Ward. Possibly trying too hard for knee-slappers, the early pages of *The Innocents Abroad* suffer from being a tad broad, proffering more burlesque than inspired satire. But as the voyage proceeds, Twain's voice starts to emerge, gathering assurance and force. The book begins to soar. The comic genius who will go on to write *Huckleberry Finn* and *Life on the Mississippi* declares himself, staking out a territory.

ONE OF THE JOYS of reading *The Innocents Abroad* is the opportunity it affords us of watching the young Twain liberate himself, and American writing, from the yoke of the European tradition, doing a necessary demolition job on it, and the pilgrims who revere often second-rate pictures, proclaiming them masterpieces.
"O, wonderful!"
"Such faultless drawing!"
"Such feeling!"
The painting of *The Last Supper* was seriously flawed for Twain, because he couldn't tell whether the disciples were Hebrews or Italians.

The Italian artists painted Italian Virgins, the Dutch painted Dutch Virgins, the Virgins of the French painters were Frenchwomen—none of them ever put into the face of the Madonna that indescribable something which proclaims the Jewess, whether you find her in New York, in Constantinople, in Paris, Jerusalem, or in the Empire of Morocco.

With the best of intentions, Jean-Paul Sartre once wrote a foolish polemic denying that there was any such thing as a "Jewish face," but Twain, poor man, didn't realize that identifying "that indescribable something" that proclaims it could one day be adjudged politically incorrect. Mind you, even the most exacting prejudice-sniffer employed by B'nai B'rith's Anti-Defamation League would have his work cut out trying to label Twain an anti-Semite. If anything, he was a Judeophile. In *The Innocents Abroad*, he contrasts the plight of Jews confined to European and Near Eastern ghettos with their fulfillment in America, where, he wrote, they were treated just like human beings, instead of dogs:

They can work at any business they please; they can sell brand new goods if they want to . . . they can practice medicine among Christians. They can associate with them, just the same as one human being does with another human being; they don't have to stay shut up in one corner of the town; they can live in any part of the town they like best . . . they never have to run races naked through the public streets, against jackasses, to please the people in carnival time; [in America] they never have been driven by soldiers into a church every Sunday for hundreds of years to hear themselves and their religion especially and particularly cursed; at this very day, in that curious country, a Jew is allowed to vote, hold office, yea, get up on a rostrum in the public street and express his opinion of the government if the government doesn't suit him! Ah, it is wonderful.

Trading on his satirist's license, overstating his case, Twain extols the pristine quality of Lake Tahoe over one as inconsequential as Lake Como, and the grandeur of his cherished Mississippi opposed to such piddling bodies of water as the Tiber or the Arno, failing to acknowledge the splendor of the bridges over the latter river, or the incomparable beauty of the city it divides. The dull waters of Lake Como, he wrote, would not compare with the wonderful transparence of Lake Tahoe, "where one can count the scales of a trout at a depth of a hundred and eighty feet." Those dark and bloody Florentines, he ventured, "call the Arno a river, and they help out the delusion by building bridges over it. I do not see why they are too good to wade." And the Tiber, he complained, "is not so long, nor yet so wide, as the American Mississippi—nor yet the Ohio, nor even the Hudson."

I must also grudgingly acknowledge that those cultural ruffians who have now taken so vociferously against what they denounce as Eurocentrism do, alas, sometimes make a valid point. Celebrating Columbus, in the Pinta's shrouds, Twain wrote, "he swung his hat above a fabled sea and gazed upon *an unknown world* [emphasis mine]." A world unknown to Europeans, whose pretensions Twain punctures with abandon in *The Innocents Abroad*, but not to the Indians who were rooted there since time immemorial.

TWAIN, A WRITER with an enduring affection for chicanery, and for those who can get away with it, takes obvious delight in the Church of Rome's holiest of Christian relics in the Azores:

We visited a Jesuit cathedral nearly two hundred years old and found in it a piece of the veritable cross upon which our Savior was crucified. It was polished and hard, and in an excellent state of preservation as if the dread tragedy of Calvary had occurred yesterday instead of eighteen centuries ago.

Then, lo and behold, in the Cathedral of Notre Dame, he is shown "some nails of the true cross, a fragment of the cross itself, a part of the crown of thorns." And, in the chapel of St. John the Baptist, in Genoa, there are the relics again.

> We find a piece of the true cross in every old church we go into, and some of the nails that held it together. I would not like to be positive, but I think we have seen as much as a keg of those nails.

But when he finally gets to the Church of the Holy Sepulcher, in Jerusalem, he discovers that the piece of the true cross no longer rests in the niche where they used to preserve it.

> The Latin priests say it was stolen away, long ago, by priests of another sect. That seems like a hard statement to make, but we know very well that it *was* stolen, because we have seen it ourselves in several of the Cathedrals of Italy and France.

The vandalism of the *Quaker City*'s pilgrims, a harbinger of offenses to come, was a recurring embarrassment to Twain. They break off fragments of Noah's tomb; and, in Damascus, from the tomb of Nimrod the Hunter. Servicing their insatiable appetite for souvenirs, they are at it again in Jerusalem, "hacking and chipping away at those arches that Jesus looked upon in the flesh." In Nazareth, coming upon a chapel rising out of a huge boulder, Twain mused, "Our pilgrims would have liked very well to get out their lampblack and stencil-plates and paint their names together with the names of the villages they hail from in America, but the priests permit nothing of the kind." In Egypt, however, the indefatigable pilgrims are at it once more, actually hacking away at the Sphinx.

Were Twain alive today I imagine he would be relieved to know that the Japanese have displaced Americans as Europe's most acquisitive and objectionable tourists. Only last week in the Louvre my wife was unable to even glimpse the *Mona Lisa* in passing. It was surrounded by hordes of Japanese, none of them the least bit interested in looking at the painting, all of them posing to have their pictures taken in turn before it. They were, however, unable to chip away at it, the *Mona Lisa* now sheltered by a glass guard.

A major innovator's work is never done. As I write in London, on

March 24, 1995, I learned from this morning's *Times* that Prince Charles, speaking at the British Council's English 2000 project, has warned against the threat to "proper English" from the spread of the American vernacular, which he pronounced very corrupting. Because of American influence, he said, "People tend to invent all sorts of nouns and verbs, and make words that shouldn't be. I think we have to be a bit careful, otherwise the whole thing can get rather a mess."

Obviously Prince Charles has never read Mark Twain, or Mencken on the American language, or Twain's successors (say, Hemingway, Bellow, Toni Morrison, and Raymond Carver, among others) and is unaware of how they have enriched a living language that is constantly evolving. He should be sent immediately a copy of *The Innocents Abroad*, the American coming-of-cultural-age book, the first major offering of a great writer, which belongs on a small shelf of Twain classics, alongside *Life on the Mississippi*, *Huckleberry Finn*, and *Connecticut Yankee*.

May 1996

Revisionist Lust

Heather Mac Donald

R ECENT VISITORS TO the Smithsonian's Natural History Museum were
greeted with some unpleasant news: the museum was contaminated.
Not by asbestos or toxic chemicals, mind you, but by far more noxious
substances: racism, sexism, and anthrocentrism. To protect the unwary,
warning labels throughout the halls identified which of the museum's
venerable dioramas were infected by which ideological error. "Female
animals are being portrayed in ways that make them appear deviant or sub-
standard to male animals," warned a label next to an exhibit of American
hartebeests. A beloved family of lions at a watering hole was also branded
for sexism, because the standing male and reclining female suggested to the
museum's gender police a pre-feminist division of labor. A leaping Ben-
galese tiger was dismissed as too predatory, a violation of the communitarian animal ethic.

The Natural History Museum is not the only Smithsonian institution
to have rethought its mission in recent years. Next door at the National
Museum of American History, visitors encounter an America characterized
by rigid class barriers, ever-growing economic inequality, predatory capitalists, and oppressed minorities. Several blocks away, curators at the
Smithsonian's American Art Museum are busy exposing art as just another
"social text" masking illegitimate power relations. And across the Mall, Air
and Space Museum curators, still fuming over the cancellation of the
shameful Enola Gay exhibit, whine like grounded teenagers about the old
military fogies now directing the museum who are inhibiting the curators'
revisionist lust.

Anyone who still doubts that the madness currently possessing American universities matters to society at large should take a stroll through
today's Smithsonian. The Institution has been transformed by a wholesale

embrace of the worst elements of America's academic culture. The staples of cutting-edge academic "research"—smirking irony, cultural relativism, celebration of putative victims, facile attacks on science—are all thriving in America's premier museum and research complex, its showcase to itself and to the world. The changes at the Smithsonian are not unique to that institution. Museums across the country have rushed headlong into what may be called the "new museology," based on a mindless parroting of academic fads. But the Smithsonian's embrace of postmodern theory and identity politics is of greatest import, because of the Institution's contribution to America's public identity.

For most of its history, the Smithsonian has been driven by the thirst for knowledge. In 1835, the U.S. chargé d'affaires in London received news of a most unusual bequest. James Smithson, a British aristocrat and amateur scientist, had left his estate of a hundred thousand pounds to the "United States of America, to found at Washington, under the name of the Smithsonian Institution, an establishment for the increase and diffusion of knowledge among men." Smithson, a bastard of august lineage, had never been to America; his gift may have been revenge against his native society for snubbing him for his illegitimate birth, or it may have simply reflected his admiration for the democratic experiment under way across the Atlantic.

Smithson's bequest caused an enormous stir. After eight years of heated debate over its interpretation—suggestions included an agricultural college and an observatory—Congress finally defined the institution in 1846 as a national museum for government collections, a laboratory, an art gallery, and a library.

An explosion in scientific knowledge and America's passionate desire to discover what lay west drove the Smithsonian in the nineteenth century. Smithsonian naturalists accompanied westward expeditions, and returned to the Castle (the Smithsonian's first building) on the Mall with crates of mineral, animal, and vegetable specimens. Smithsonian geologists heroically mapped unknown territory, and Smithsonian ethnographers lovingly chronicled Indian cultures. For the next century and a half, this drive for knowledge would continue, until eventually, the Institution's collections would constitute a veritable library of the world.

In the late 1960s and 1970s, however, while the Smithsonian's scientific research continued apace, its historical and cultural identity subtly changed. As its current curators proudly describe it, the Institution became sensitive to the social and political currents swirling around it—ghetto riots, Vietnam War protests, and women's "liberation." Museums nationwide became terrified of the charge of "elitism," and adopted the media of popular culture to increase their "relevance."

The Smithsonian of the 1970s already looked to the academy for its inspiration, particularly to the new fields of social and cultural history. A 1976 show on immigration at the Museum of History and Technology (since renamed the National Museum of American History) reflected this influence in its acute attention to race and class. Also academically inspired was the Institution's newfound zest for exhibiting the detritus of popular culture, most famously, its Archie Bunker Chair.

But nothing in the 1970s matched the changes ushered in by anthropologist Robert McCormick Adams, who assumed the Smithsonian secretaryship in 1984. Adams had been sold to Congress as someone who would increase the scholarly standards at the Institution, illustrating yet again the utter cluelessness of politicians and ordinary people regarding the academically enfranchised cultural Left. Described by *The Washington Post* as a "happily successful Establishment radical," Adams declared the purpose of museums to be "confrontation, experimentation, and debate"—a politically charged manifesto that pointedly ignored the Smithsonian's mandate to increase knowledge. Adams dictated an aggressive program to "diversify" the Institution, and set out to hire curators, mostly from the academy, that shared his commitment to "critical" scholarship.

The Adams regime (which ended in 1994) perfected the "new museology" at the Smithsonian. The most important principle of the new dogma is "honoring multiple ways of interpreting the world." Curatorial expertise and scientific knowledge are out; "multiple voices" and relativism in all its forms are in. (As we will see, however, only certain "voices" ever seem to get heard.) In furtherance of the "multiple interpretations" principle, the new museologist consults with "the community" in devising exhibits. Moreover, those exhibits must aim to enhance self-esteem: they are designed to increase the ethnic pride of minorities. Concomitant with this redressive principle, a new museological exhibit is grossly ahistorical: it exports contemporary standards of equity to the past in order to make its case against oppression and victimhood seem stronger.

The final two principles of the new museology are contempt for the public, and infatuation with high-tech wizardry. With the exception of these last two tenets, the new museology is directly imported from the academy. The Smithsonian's recent public relations fiascoes all embodied one or more of its principles.

A prototypical new hire of the Adams regime—and classic "new museologist"—was Robert Sullivan, responsible for the warning labels on the Natural History Museum's dioramas. Sullivan was brought to the museum in 1990 as director of public programs, and his existence there is particularly unfortunate, for no museum better embodies the Smithsonian's glorious past. To Sullivan, however, that past is cause for shame and criticism. Sullivan is nothing if not steeped in theory, and he can reel off Foucauldian riffs with the best of them. Natural history museums embody the concept of "Safe Terror," he explains; they were part of the "Victorian campaign of containing wildness." "While the etiquette books were talking of how to conceal, repress, and deny bodily functions of any sort," he says, "natural history museums were created as a place to exhibit such wildness from a safe distance." Among the practices that were being "repressed on the street" while being shown in museums, according to Sullivan, were scarification and tattooing—not heretofore recognized as important Anglo-American traditions. Sullivan's sinister interpretation of natural history museums clashes with their philanthropic origins. Such institutions, their advocates argued, would allow the urban poor, increasingly imprisoned by large industrial cities, to enjoy the "refreshment, humanism, and inspiration" of nature, as one nineteenth-century proponent wrote.

Sullivan shares Foucault's contempt for civilization, which he characterizes as "quote-unquote 'civilization.'" He also has fully imbibed the postmodern academy's skepticism about science (though of course he continues to enjoy its benefits daily). He announced breezily upon his arrival that the "western-scientific-anthropological world view is merely one more alternative way of knowing and encoding the world, no more valuable or accurate, no less ideological or culture-bound, than any other."

A critic espousing such contempt for the achievements of Western civilization is poorly suited to help lead an institution so intimately related to the "western-scientific-anthropological world view." Indeed, Sullivan almost didn't accept the position. As he confided to Frank Talbot, the museum director at the time, "I was so frightened and discouraged by the overwhelming needs I see [at the museum] and the seeming indifference of the visitors." Those annoying visitors, he explained, "don't want to be engaged, empowered, or even educated, [but] just want to be distracted . . . from the dailiness, the tedium, the fear of their lives." But courageous and self-sacrificing fellow that he is, Sullivan manfully accepted the job at the largest research museum in the country, explaining grandiloquently: "We must affirm life, have the courage to name what is intolerable to us, and act against it."

Sullivan immediately set to work "erasing [the museum's] racist belief system." He assembled a gender-race bias task force to "critique exhibits and produce policy and practices manuals on Gender and Race Equity." Faced with budget limits, Sullivan was unable to tear down and replace everything he found offensive about the museum; his second-best solution was the so-called "dilemma labels" (since removed) placed next to the dioramas. "If you couldn't change the exhibits, can you make an exhibit out of the exhibit, and show the cultural values in science?" Sullivan explains, demonstrating his close familiarity with self-reflexive postmodern practice.

Ironically, many of the museum's naturalists had complained for years of *scientific* inaccuracies in some of the exhibition labels, but their complaints went ignored. Science has no constituency, however; politics does.

Sullivan also acted on his announced intention to grant to "minority cultures . . . access to collections and meaningful influence on interpretive points of view." Upon his arrival at the museum, he started a "dialogue" with a radically Afrocentric "community" group that had long complained of the museum's alleged racism. Sullivan invited the group Tu-Wa-Moja to advise the museum regarding planned revisions to its Africa Hall and Human Evolution exhibit.

The result was predictable. The group made life extremely difficult for the archaeologists and anthropologists who had been ordered to find common ground with it; but little else was accomplished. The museum tried to defuse Tu-Wa-Moja's objections to the Africa Hall by putting "dilemma labels" on the exhibits, but the group was not satisfied. In a remarkable symbol of the new museology, Sullivan simply shut down the hall. "Tearing down the hall was a way to build trust," he explains. Leaving it up while the new hall was in development would have damaged the Smithsonian's credibility, Sullivan concluded, because the "community had great mistrust about whether the Smithsonian would redo it in an inclusive way." As a final gesture of "trust," Sullivan allowed Tu-Wa-Moja to film the shuttered hall for its Afrocentric propaganda materials; Leonard Jeffries served as de facto master of ceremonies. The moral of the story is that in order to stoke an ethnic interest group's self-esteem, the new museology demands that everyone else be denied the opportunity to learn from the Smithsonian's collections.

To his credit, Sullivan has not pressured the museum's curators to accept Tu-Wa-Moja's views on the African origins of everything. But why was the group invited in the first place? What did this group of Washington residents know about evolution to justify their advising a team of physical anthropologists, with all the extra labor that that interaction cost the museum, or about Africa to justify their advising cultural anthropologists? The answer, of course, lies in skin color—more specifically, in the racial essentialism that holds that a young, black Washington male is an expert on all things African.

The "community consultation" imperative that brought Tu-Wa-Moja into the Natural History Museum has cast a wider net than just local Afrocentrics. Over one hundred people are advising the museum on its new

Africa Hall, most of them black. Again, the process is extremely time-con-suming. Mary Jo Arnoldi, an African curator at the museum, explained why the community consultations are necessary: "Museums are becoming aware that in a postmodern world, the people you're representing say: how come you're the expert? Sullivan's only echoing what the academy has been talking about for a long time."

The new Africa Hall will be impeccably postmodern. It will tell African "stories" with African "voices." Its theme is not Africa per se, but African identity: over half the hall will be devoted to the "African dias-pora"—peoples of African origin living elsewhere. Geographical divisions of Africa will be minimally included as a grudging concession to visitors who expect it. The new museology has little use for the traditional organizing tools of natural history, such as geography or species classification, which are seen, no doubt, as relics of the "western-scientific-anthropological world view." But what is a natural history museum if not the record of the interaction of humans with a particular patch of the natural world? In an era when Americans' geographical and historical knowledge is shrinking into nothingness, a deemphasis on geography is dangerous.

The old Africa Hall was criticized in the press and the "community" as showing a timeless Africa of quaint or barbaric customs; curators of the new Africa Hall are determined to avoid such charges. "We have to make sure to let people know there are as many Africans in science labs as are working in the fields," says Mary Jo Arnoldi. The self-esteem imperative seems to have overridden truth here: given the backward state of Africa's still largely rural economy, it seems highly unlikely that Africa is producing as many scientists as subsistence farmers. Oddly, when identity groups seek to legitimate themselves, they draw on traditional Western criteria of ac-complishment, such as science, despite the cultural left's disdain for such alienating forms of thought.

To date, Sullivan has been better at shutting things down than putting them up. Occasionally, his revisionist agenda has met with stiff internal op-position. He had tried to remove from the museum's rotunda its famous charging elephant, for example—as a hunting trophy, a symbol for Sullivan of white capitalist aggression. But a passionate protest by the museum's animal scientists shelved the plan. Anyone who cares for museum aesthetics can be glad for that, since Sullivan's suggestions for a replacement included a "large animated programmable globe," illustrating the cardinal truth that while the new museum bureaucrat may be chock full of political opinions, he is absolutely devoid of taste.

But there are large changes in the offing, and readers with a love of traditional natural history museums are advised to visit the Smithsonian soon, before it's too late. Eventually, all of the museum's enchanting human culture halls will be torn down, to make way for the new museological extravaganza "Changing Cultures in a Changing World." This overarching cultural anthropology exhibit will focus on three or four big ideas about "cultural change"—one of the watchwords, along with "global change," of the new thinking.

The ideology of "cultural change" is the antithesis of everything natural history museums once stood for. The naturalists and anthropologists who created those museums wanted to present the vast wonders of the earth in a logical, coherent fashion; they had an enormous respect for details and facts. The Smithsonian's glorious dioramas—the creation of scientists with obvious artistic flair—gave visitors a panoramic, but specific, view of the world's cultures. But museums no longer strive for comprehensiveness or specificity. Instead, the educator's favorite "idea" is paramount. "We have the space to tell four to five potent stories," says Sullivan. "All the dioramas will be gone, we're not worried about covering the same ground." There is considerable irony to this breezy indifference to coverage. Native American activists have attacked the museum for only showing *one* tribe of Eskimos; now, there will likely be none. (In the interim, to respond to Native American complaints, Sullivan will put a video next to the Eskimo diorama showing contemporary Aleut life—a gross and unconscionable violation of the aesthetics of the Americas Hall.)

If the theme of "cultural change" does not highlight specific places and peoples, what then is it all about? Like most everything in postmodern politics it is about "identity." But there is a twist. "Every visitor [to the new hall] should find something about themselves," says Sullivan. Future visitors should find that they are "the culmination of cultural change that makes them the same as every other visitor. They will not meet the exotic other here, they will meet themselves." The unspoken agenda here is that all cultures are equal, and influence each other equally.

The Natural History Museum provides one further contrast between the old and the new museology. The old museology created places of refuge, where visitors could contemplate nature in stillness. The new museology abhors stillness; the key word is "interactivity." The new museum halls are starting to resemble video arcades: recorded voices drone over and over from all corners, TV screens run the same video endlessly, and computers beep and blink before jamming up. For all Sullivan and his ilk's professed distaste for "rational-logical-technocratic society," they are absolutely besotted with gadgetry. An exhibit on marine ecosystems features several video screens embedded in fake rock and tacky plywood, as well as an LED display. On either side of the cluttered exhibit are the traditional bird and mammal halls, featuring such endearing vitrines as "Mammal Parachutes" and "Concealing Coloration." The brilliance and variety of the animals, many collected by Theodore Roosevelt, makes the point about "biodiversity" far more effectively than the beeping, whirring technologies next door. With so splendid a species collection, why would the curators opt for the simulacrum of video?

"Interactive" museum technologies are supposed to allow visitors to "create the meaning" of the exhibit, or, less pretentiously, learn at their own speed. But the new technology is about as interactive as a factory time clock. Typically, the viewer punches a few keys on a computer screen to access data, and the computer spews it out. The answer was predetermined; there is no reason the information could not have been presented in straight graphic format. But the new technology allows curators to feel up-to-date with the information age.

To be sure, there is only so much a new museologist at an old museum can do. Despite the best of revisionist intentions, not all the old exhibits can be junked immediately. To achieve a perfect embodiment of the new museology, one must start from a clean slate. What luck for Secretary Adams that such a slate existed—the last undeveloped piece of land on the Mall. On it, Adams decreed the erection of the National Museum of the American Indian, planned for completion in 2001. The project has sucked money out of existing parts of the Smithsonian, but from Adams's perspective, nothing was too good for the museum, for it would seal his reputation as protector of ethnic identity groups. The American Indian Museum provides an ominous harbinger of museums to come.

The museum was born in racial animus. Its administrator declared early on: "If we do not take responsibility for the work, the white people will win the day. . . . We cannot let some arrogant, racist, or stupid people defeat us." The museum is supposed to be not just *about* America Indians, but by them and for them as well. Museum planners describe American Indians as their "constituency," an overtly political concept. Naturally, a Native American is designing the building; he renews himself for further battles by retreating to his "sweat lodge" in Rock Creek Park.

Anyone eager for a foretaste of this pure new museological creation can get it in the Smithsonian's historic Arts and Industries Building. There, a preview exhibition, predictably called "Stories of the People," is installed. And what a preview it is! The first jolt comes from the wall labels, which use the first-person plural throughout: "As tribal people, . . . we are wonderfully diverse yet essentially similar"; "our Cherokee story is one of balance—men and women, animals and plants, complementing each other's lives." Had a white curator presumed to use the first-person plural, the postmodernists would be busy deploring the "construction" of the viewer as "the Other."

The second jolt from "Stories of the People" is the embarrassing vacuousness of the accompanying texts, many of which seem transcribed from Chinese fortune cookies. "Apache culture is adaptive and reflects the times," reads one. The conceit of "living in balance" with nature pervades the exhibition, though one does wonder about the buffalo run off cliffs by Indians: did they, too, feel in perfect harmony with nature? Even "men and women" lived in balance, as the Cherokee text quoted above claims. Let us recall that that balance consisted of the women doing hard labor domestically while the men hunted and went to war. If an eighteenth-century burgher had made a similar claim for his domestic arrangements, he would be impaled on the stake of false consciousness.

Finally, there is the overtly political nature of the show. The exhibition is a piece of advocacy from start to finish, arguing the validity of Indian legal claims against the U.S. government. The following statement is typical in its clumsy juxtaposition of folksy English translations and hard-nosed legal claims:

> Today, the environment is not as rich as it was before the House on the Water People came. Conflicts between our Tribe and the House on the Water People still exist. The harvest and management of fisheries is a contentious issue, despite court decisions affirming our right to half of the fish in our waters.

Although construction of its new multimillion-dollar taxpayer-financed building on the Mall proceeds apace, there may be little to fill it when it is completed. The museum is depleting its collections under the aegis of the Native American Graves Protection and Repatriation Act of 1990, which governs the return of native remains to tribes. In essence, the museum sent around a shopping list of goodies, asking tribes if they wanted to make a claim on its collections. The claims are becoming increasingly attenuated. Anthropologist Clement Meighan laments: "Adams sold us out. The institution is spending to destroy its collections."

Like the Natural History Museum, the National Museum of American History is firmly tied to the Smithsonian's past; and like the Natural History Museum, it has just as surely betrayed it. Repository for over a century of the nation's tangible heritage, the museum is conducting a fierce revisionist campaign. Like the other Smithsonian museums, it has taken its cue directly from the multicultural-mad, victim-celebrating universities.

The collections at American History originated when the U.S. Patent

Office transferred the contents of its National Cabinet of Curiosities to the Smithsonian in 1858. Included were George Washington's tent and the Star-Spangled Banner. The collections got another boost in 1876, from the Centennial Exposition of 1876 in Philadelphia. The present museum, a windowless battlement possessing all the charm of an airplane terminal, opened in 1964 as the National Museum of History and Technology. Its ground floor, now featuring a noisy, high-tech exhibit about industrial materials, resembles a food court in a large suburban mall. The museum was ominously renamed the American History Museum in 1980, confirming a change of emphasis that was already taking place inside it. While some wonderful traditional exhibits of great hulking machines still stand, the social historical exhibits take an attitude toward technology that is typically ironic and skeptical.

Anyone looking for political history in the museum will be disappointed. It features nothing on the American Revolution or the constitutional conventions, nothing that embodies the ideals that animated the United States. America's presidents? You'll find their shadowy images sticking out from underneath the First Ladies' portraits arrayed across a wall. And tucked back in a tiny case behind an escalator are some presidential possessions, such as Woodrow Wilson's golf clubs and Lincoln's gold cane. Good luck finding the case, however.

Instead of political history, the museum focuses on a congeries of identity groups. Two themes emerge: America's ever-growing inequalities, and the unpleasantness of white people. Take any point in time in the Smithsonian's America, and you will find shocking inequalities that only get worse. After the Revolution: "The gulf between rich and poor, powerful and powerless . . . did not vanish after 1776. . . . Whatever their race or gender, working Philadelphians found that the Revolution had not solved the problems of social and economic inequality." During the nineteenth-century industrial revolution: there was increasing "economic inequality." Turn of the century: "By the 1890s, . . . growing contrasts of wealth and poverty, and rigid racial barriers had created urgent social problems." Modern era: "It is much easier in the United States to be decently dressed than it is to be decently housed, fed or doctored" (quoting socialist Michael Harrington).

What is most striking about the Smithsonian's survey of American inequality through the ages is its utter lack of historical awareness. The curators bring to the past no historical context; they observe and judge the past as if it were simultaneous with the present. The postrevolutionary period was characterized by "social and economic inequality," say the curators. Compared to what? Judged by contemporary European standards, America was the least class-bound society in the world, and would remain so for two centuries. Titles, primogeniture, feudal rights, strict distinction between the nobility and the merchant and servant classes—*those* were the indices of eighteenth-century inequality, and America had cast them off.

Similarly inapt is the observation that during the Progressive era, the "rigid structures of American society were difficult to overcome in building cross-class and interracial alliances." That is an agenda straight out of the 1990s multicultural campus, with its vacuous talk of class consciousness and rainbow coalitions; it has nothing to do with the Progressive agenda.

Nowhere is the Smithsonian curators' self-absorption more apparent than in their treatment of "women's issues." Barbara Clark Smith, a curator, notes scornfully that late eighteenth-century Philadelphians "continued to assume that women of both races would and should be dependent on men." Well, of course they did—"women's lib" was still one hundred and eighty years away! A young student reading such comments will nevertheless come away with the impression that the American past was a shamefully inadequate place.

Even the language used to describe the past is self-absorbed. The "settlement house" movement, wherein social workers helped immigrants assimilate, "enabled women to use gender concepts as a source of empowerment," coos an exhibition on women's social movements. The statement would have been absolutely incomprehensible to an early twentieth-century citizen; it is still meaningless today, rendering it a bona fide product of the academy.

The Smithsonian's assault on the American past doesn't end with its obsessive harping on social and economic inequality. The museum has a far more specific agenda to pursue, and that is against whites. An exhibition on postcolonial society suggests that American history was formed of equal parts white, black, and Indian influence, and a good thing, too, because black and Indian cultures, according to the exhibit, were superior in every way. The first generation of American citizens were social-climbing, ruthless, obsessed with status and power, indifferent to equality, sexist, and, of course, viciously hypocritical in their embrace of slavery. Their victory over Britain was due to the "labors of the African-Americans they enslaved," not, apparently, to their zeal to found a new, classless society.

A display of a Virginia planter's parlor says it all. Droning incessantly above the barren room is a recorded male voice that interprets the space. "Every aspect [of the room] is designed for social advancement," the tape sneers. "The construction of the staircase was *fashionable*, [long pause], *expensive* [long pause], *showy*." The narrator practically spits out the words:

"This is more than just a *room*; this is an elaborate proclamation of prosperity and ambition, the public face of a *man*, [who is] part of a fiercely competitive social system." The planter and his neighbors, the narrator sniffs, used "every occasion to prove themselves *better* [pause], *richer* [pause], more *powerful* than each other."

It is no surprise, then, when we learn later in the exhibit that the planter had murdered his wife. *This* is the family the Smithsonian chose to highlight as a typical early Southern family! Not only were the white citizens slavers and social-climbers, they were also domestic murderers. Now there undoubtedly was a pecking order in postcolonial society. But there is little reason to suppose that early Americans were more socially aggrandizing than potlatching "native peoples" or a king in a slave-trading African dynasty.

The Smithsonian's selection of a New England family is also telling. Did it choose one with a glorious revolutionary past? Not a chance. It selects an opponent of equality and possible Royalist. Merchant Samuel Cotton "disapproved of the notions of equality that were spreading in the northeast." Not only a reactionary, Cotton is also a greedy capitalist: an audio tape ceaselessly reenacts a court hearing that found him guilty of profiteering off the Revolution by overcharging for sugar, molasses, salt, and rum.

Fortunately, there is an escape from this backbiting, petty society: we can visit the Seneca Nation of the Iroquois Confederacy. And suddenly, we reencounter the curatorial "we": "Our ancestors considered it a great transgression to reject the council of their women." Apparently, the Indians deserve a "voice," and the whites do not. This carefully chosen female-centric aspect of Iroquois society contrasts sharply with eighteenth-century white society, wherein women, Clark notes, had more rights as widows than as wives. Whom is she kidding? Does Clark really believe that "gender roles" were less rigid among the bloody Iroquois than in England or America? The "rights of women," a concept even then being debated in England, would have been incomprehensible to the Indians.

There isn't a single myth about the nobility of the oppressed to which Clark doesn't subscribe. "Most African-Americans, Native Americans, and women white Americans . . . studied nature in order to work in harmony with it, not to control it," she declares breathlessly. If Native Americans and blacks did not "control nature," it is because they did not possess the technology and scientific knowledge to do so. African-Americans performed voodoo rituals with animals. Was that more "harmonious" than cultivating livestock?

But the Smithsonian knows no such ambiguity. It presents the so-called "systematic spirit—or deep faith in the power of reason and science" as white man's religion, no more efficacious or valid than the lore of illiterate peoples. Astoundingly, it puts the onus on *white Europeans* to understand native cultures, not vice versa: "Because of cultural bias, Europeans frequently were unable to comprehend the systems by which the knowledge passed from teacher to student in these traditional cultures, and the content of that knowledge." This is balderdash. First of all, if Europeans were "unable to comprehend" the "knowledge systems" of traditional cultures, it was undoubtedly because the high priests who presided over those "knowledge systems" kept them shrouded in mystery, not only to outsiders, but to members of the native culture itself. The notion of the public availability of knowledge and scientific research was a Western creation and a great tool of equality, to boot. It was utterly foreign to primitive cultures, who understood long before Foucault that knowledge (and even the appearance of knowledge) was power.

Second, if "cultural bias" prevented Europeans from understanding the occult mysteries of native "knowledge systems," fairness would require mentioning that illiteracy and scientific ignorance prevented native cultures from understanding Western "knowledge systems." But the Smithsonian sees the deficiency only on the whites' side.

The notion that native peoples lived in "harmony" while whites lived in conflict with the natural world pervades the exhibit. A label in a case on popular science announces darkly: "The air pump subjected nature to unnatural forces." There is no room in Clark's intellectual universe for the joy of experimentation; in her scheme, eighteenth-century popular interest in physics smacks of imperialism, aggression, and probably also racism and sexism. Eli Whitney's cotton gin, an ingenious invention, is simply labelled: "An Engine of Slavery."

The romanticization of native peoples continues in another American History exhibit: "New Mexico: An American Encounter," about the interaction of American Indians and Hispanics, and their fight against white imperialism. The exhibition states that Indian tribes take in tourists because of their "desire to share"; apparently the aggressive marketing of Indian artifacts springs from a similarly disinterested motive. A full-length mirror shaped as a human with a camera hanging from the neck (actually, the camera has been stolen, leaving just a plastic mount) silently accuses the museum visitor of "objectifying the Other." Again, no one is forcing the tourist industry on the Indians. The show glosses over the often brutal missionizing of the Indians by the Spaniards.

Smirking irony is a favorite conceit of academic demystifiers, and it pervades the Smithsonian. It entails liberal use of scare quotes, or implicit scare quotes, to debunk concepts that twenty years ago were quite un-problematic. Echoing Robert Sullivan's theme that middle-class manners are tools of power, the American History Museum questions the most basic mechanisms of American history: assimilation. A section called "Social Service v. Social Control" in the women's reform movement exhibition argues that

> middle class reformers . . . often imposed their concepts of the "American Way" on people.. . . Teaching immigrants and the less fortunate how to "better" themselves involved making judgments of moral and cultural "superiority."

For those immigrants who came over without a proper sense of hygiene, who beat their wives, who took their children out of school to work, that "bettering" process was essential to their social progress. But the adolescent sees all forms of authority as oppressive.

The cynical debunking of core American beliefs doesn't always use scare quotes. Another favorite ploy is the "Americans believed" construction, which introduces a note of irony into what are generally unobjectionable views. A show on the American industrial revolution from 1790 to 1860 subtly mocks Americans' enthusiasm for the new industrial inventions: Americans "believed that economic progress depended on technological advance." Why is this noteworthy, unless we are to understand it as a bizarre belief? But Americans saw daily the impact of technology on the economy. Nineteenth-century Americans' belief in the efficacy of gifted individuals is another howler to the Smithsonian: "Many Americans believed . . . that progress was the work of a few great inventors." One can almost hear curator Steve Lubar's guffaws as he wrote this. A sophisticated social historian such as Lubar understands that such concepts as "greatness" and even the "individual" are just political fictions designed to conceal oppressive power relations.

Curator Lubar also singles out for implicit scorn the "widespread [nineteenth-century] assumption that work was good for people." How repressive, we murmur sympathetically. Even worse, " 'houses of industry' helped to keep the poor busy and out of trouble." How much more humane are the ready welfare benefits that cultivate a huge class of non-working, dependent, and often criminal people!

No museum has better employed academically inspired scorn, however, than Air and Space, and nowhere is the effect more jarring. If ever there were a testament to the power of science, engineering, and mental mastery, it is the Air and Space Museum. Yet as the recent Enola Gay debacle revealed, the museum is now populated by curators and, until recently, a director who sought to debunk technology and military prowess. Pilots and former military men once dominated the museum; today, academic historians rule the place. Secretary Adams orchestrated this change, to bring the museum into line with the academy, which had long derided Air and Space for its allegedly celebratory attitude toward aeronautic technology.

The results of this academic incursion were in long before the Enola Gay controversy. A curator recalls the heady pre-Enola Gay days, when the public hadn't yet noticed the changes underway in the museum: "There was a sense of optimism in the 1980s and 1990s that we could stretch boundaries and do cultural history." A show on World War I fighter pilots argues that Americans have been hoodwinked into a naïve romanticization of air war. Displays of commercial detritus with pilot themes drive home the point that Americans can't tell the difference, say, between Snoopy in his Red Baron flying gear or a Red Baron pizza box and the realities of war. This dour "deconstruction" of popular culture comes right from the academy. A previous exhibit—a wildly popular show on "Star Trek"—also drew on academic fads to reveal the searing social critique in the TV series. The important point about the exhibit devoted to "Star Trek" is not that it represented a crass pandering to popular culture (although it did), but that it found in the series a criticism of racism, sexism, militarism, and, in an earlier draft of the exhibition's script, the Vietnam War.

But nothing, obviously, can match the enormity of the Enola Gay disaster. The true outrage of the project was not that it used spurious analyses to second-guess the military necessity of the atomic bomb, or that its authors chose the fiftieth anniversary of the end of World War II to propound their revisionist views, or even that it portrayed the Japanese as quasi-victims during the war they started with a surprise attack on Pearl Harbor. The true outrage lies in the disgusting condescension and contempt shown to the public and to the war's veterans by the Smithsonian personnel, from Adams on down.

The abortive exhibition presented Hiroshima not as the conclusion of World War II, but as the start of the arms race. To Martin Harwit, director of the Air and Space Museum, the conjunction of the atom bombing of Hiroshima and Nagasaki and the end of the war was purely coincidental. This perspective on the bomb set the stage for the follies to come, guaranteeing that the veterans and the curators would be talking past each other.

From the start, Smithsonian officials held themselves out as the only people sensitive enough to understand the horrors of nuclear war and the anxieties of the nuclear age. Responding to one of the many World War II veterans campaigning tirelessly for the restoration and exhibition of the Enola Gay, Secretary Adams intoned piously: "'Decent respect for the opinions of mankind' requires us also to touch on the demonstrated horror and yawning future risk of the age that the Enola Gay helped to inaugurate." Adams's condescension was not lost on the vet, who shot back that Adams was a "Washington satrap."

Harwit easily matched Adams for self-righteousness. Hand-picked by Adams to bring a critical perspective on strategic bombing to the museum, Harwit, an astrophysicist, was the first director of the museum without a flying or military background. Writing to Japan's ambassador in Washington, Harwit revealed his deep contempt for the public: "Unless the public is willing to understand the events that led to the bombings, and the terrible destruction they wrought, the most valuable lessons that can be learned from history will be lost." The gall of this message is nearly unfathomable. Harwit posits the public as his quasi-adversary, determined to hold on to its blind ignorance in the face of his proffered enlightenment. It is the height of arrogance for Harwit to present himself and his curators, none of whom served in the war, as the repositories of wisdom regarding the "events that led to the bombings."

Even more offensive than the museum's condescension toward the public was its contempt for the veterans. In statement after statement, the museum's personnel caricatured the vets as an annoying, insignificant, self-engrossed interest group in conflict with the public good. In one of the most explosive statements during the public controversy, a curator named Tom Crouch wrote to Harwit: "Do you want an exhibit to make veterans feel good, or do you want an exhibition that will lead our visitors to think about the consequences of the atomic bombing of Japan? Frankly, I don't think we can do both." In his self-exculpatory book, Harwit adopts the same stance, alleging that the vets merely sought to "satisfy their nostalgia" or to be celebrated.

Only someone who had never served in a war could characterize the vets' desire for a public history as "nostalgia" or "feel-good" therapy. Harwit and his curators exemplify the offensive self-righteousness most often found in academia—that of a generation that has lived without sacrifice and that sneers at tradition. Contrary to the Smithsonian's dismissive rhetoric, the vets showed themselves throughout the battle as extraordinarily eloquent, informed, and morally wise.

But few at the Smithsonian seem to have learned anything from the episode (except the current secretary, Michael Heyman, who, upon succeeding Adams in 1994, canceled the original exhibition and fired Harwit). Throughout the Institution, curators and historians stew about the grievous injury done to their intellectual freedom by the cancellation of the show, and complain darkly about continuing censorship. The resentment is strongest, naturally, at Air and Space, which is still licking its wounds. "The outlook in this place is bleak; we can't do anything that's critical of anything, we're so constrained by the political right wing," one curator fumed to me. Note his assumption: his primary goal is to be "critical," not to share knowledge or edify. But even more remarkable is the curator's shocking lack of respect for experience and seniority. "A bunch of seventy-five-year-olds—two world War II vets—are running this place now," he complained, who "bring the mindset of that generation."

Next up at Air and Space: a show on the *Star Wars* trilogy, one of the last Harwit projects still on the books. A bid for popular appeal, to be sure, but don't be surprised to find trenchant social criticism served up as well—perhaps a paean to diversity and sensitivity. In line with the redressive mission of the Smithsonian, Air and Space is also planning an exhibit on the black experience in aviation, following the precedent of a 1994 show on a female aerial acrobat that demonstrated that young girls really *can* triumph against the sexist odds!

If many of the Air and Space curators seek to debunk the alleged myths of flight technology, many curators at the American Art Museum, housed in the splendid neoclassical Old Patent Office Building, are determined to debunk art itself. Ideally, some believe, there would cease to be any distinction between art—what one curator snidely calls "so-called paintings"—and ephemera such as political cartoons. All would be marshalled to the great project of tearing down America's ideals.

Mention of the sublime to some curators provokes a recoil of distaste. In a recent essay on art curating, curator William Truettner scoffs: museum visitors used to believe that works of art "disregard everyday life in favor of expressing what was profound and lasting about the human spirit." Such aesthetic idealism is repugnant to Truettner; he wants to "bring art museum visitors back to earth [and] make them believe that works have more-limited [*sic*] meanings."

Truettner brought the public thuddingly to earth in his much-criticized "The West as America" exhibit of 1991. The show argued that the great heroic canvases of the Western expansion were really about Eastern capitalism, ethnic strife, and greed. Truettner, who has read his Derrida, finds exploitation and despair in the most peaceful of canvases, for the very absence of social strife and oppression from a canvas "has the ironic effect of calling them back to life," he argues.

Truettner's heavy-handed decoding of art violates the interpretive code he professes to follow. Mouthing platitudes about the open-ended nature of meaning, Truettner's interpretations admit of no variation over time; they are presented as the definitive decoding of the canvas. Though he invokes a populist philosophy—everyone can understand art—his bizarre allegorical readings of paintings must appear far more arcane to an average viewer than a formal or moral analysis. Like his colleagues in the academy, he approaches canvases with a checklist of politically correct "issues": if a painting contains a woman, that's a "gender issue." If it contains a black person, that's a "race issue." If it contains a woman *and* a black person, it's time to cash in. Analyzing an 1861 historical allegory called *The Founding of Maryland*, Truettner fills out his scorecard: "The demure colonial wife, her head covered by a blue shawl, looks askance at the three bare-breasted Indian women, raising not only racial but gender issues." If the painting had been half as skilled, presumably the analysis would be identical: the "issues" would be duly noted, and not a word said about the aesthetic qualities of the work.

In the odd world of the museum, curators regard shows as failures if the public innocently enjoys them. A recent show on the nineteenth-century landscape painter Thomas Cole sought to portray the paintings as a reactionary critique of Jacksonian democracy. "We got nowhere with the show," laments one curator. "Visitors just didn't get it." The visitor comment books contained such responses as "Great show! Wonderful paintings!" "Do more shows like this!"—a source of curatorial embarrassment.

A forthcoming exhibition scheduled for March 1999 continues the museum's project of debunking American history and culture. A companion to "The West as America," it will focus on late-nineteenth-century images of New England. Such images, often idyllic, the curators will argue, represent a desperate attempt of whites to hold on to an ideal Anglo-Protestant America, in a time of black migration from the South and ethnic migration from Europe. What else is new?

If aesthetic values are meaningless and transitory, the museum finds enormous value in identity politics. A spate of recent contemporary art shows focused on ethnicity and "political orientation." Serving up the worst atrocities from SoHo, the museum has displayed repulsive installations and tasteless postmodern junk art, such as Pepon Osorro's tacky chandeliers constructed from plastic beads, tiny soccer balls, and cheap knickknacks. As Osorro explains: "My work is socially relevant because that is the need I see in the community." How about the need for a good grammar-school education in using the English language? Isn't that socially relevant?

The museum's acquisitions policy is just as bad, causing some traditional curators to despair that the Smithsonian is selling off its heritage to buy politically correct junk. The Institution's race- and ethnicity-based acquisitions policy is part of a much broader diversity drive. Adams made diversity the centerpiece of his tenure, ordering museum directors to bring in a staff that was more "representative" of the country. "Sometimes these hires worked out, others were dead on their feet," recalls a curator at Natural History. The deadwood is the most likely to have survived, given the difficulties of firing federal employees. The only practical recourse available to a manager of an incompetent employee is to find an unwitting supervisor in another museum and try to palm the employee off on him.

Adams also encouraged the formation of identity-based employee advocacy groups. These have increasingly flexed their muscles regarding the content of exhibitions. The Hispanic lobby seems to be in the ascendancy today. In 1993, Secretary Adams authorized the formation of a Task Force on Latino Issues, charged, in essence, to prove that the Smithsonian is guilty of discrimination. The Task Force was chaired by Raul Yzaguirre, president of the National Council of La Raza, one of the most radical Hispanic advocacy groups in the country.

The Task Force performed exactly as expected. A year after its formation, it published "Willful Neglect," an extraordinarily dishonest report charging the Smithsonian with *deliberately* excluding Latinos from its collections and staff. Count one of the indictment was the absence of a separate museum dedicated to Latinos—ethnically coded museums have now become the primary litmus test of the Smithsonian's ethnic good faith. Like all arguments for Hispanic power, "Willful Neglect" cast a wide net in its definition of Hispanic, including Mexican-, Puerto Rican-, Cuban-, Dominican-, Central American-, South American-, and Spanish-Americans, despite the wide cultural differences between those groups. When I asked the Smithsonian's new counsel for Latino affairs, Miguel Bretos, if these groups really constituted a single identity, he responded with an amazing reinterpretation of American history. A common Hispanic identity was "emerging rapidly," Bretos said: "The American tradition of *E Pluribus Unum* is taking root in the Hispanic community; there is an increasing sense of a common fund of culture that cuts across tribes." That, in a nutshell, describes American ideals today—assimilation no longer means assimilation to a common American identity, but to a heightened ethnic identity.

"Willful Neglect" worked its anticipated magic. The Smithsonian created an entire office dedicated to Hispanic advocacy within the Institution, headed by Bretos. "Basically, Bretos wants a gallery in every museum devoted to Hispanics," says a curator of natural history who has had repeated dealings with him. In a particularly cowardly move, the Smithsonian changed the name of Bretos's office from Latino Affairs to Community Affairs, trying to cover up its partisan nature, though no one within the Institution is fooled.

But the bureaucratic spawn of "Willful Neglect" spilled over beyond the Community Affairs office. Secretary Heyman, in continuing token of his ethnic good faith, empowered two high-level panels to study employment and affirmative action policy, on the one hand, and programming and acquisitions, on the other. Their reports will undoubtedly find grievous gaps in the Smithsonian's efforts to achieve a "diverse" museum.

All this is pretty impressive fallout from a report based on misrepresentation and virtual falsehood. Even its authors backpedal wildly when confronted with its misstatements. "Willful Neglect" charges the Smithsonian with deliberately failing to hire an ethnically proportionate Hispanic workforce. A chart grimly documents the absence of Hispanic curators. Such a charge makes sense only if there is a pool of Hispanic qualified museologists upon which the Smithsonian should have been drawing. I asked Bretos if such a pool exists. He responded: "It's relatively small, which is part of the difficulty of making sure that all the voices are represented." More accurately, the number of Hispanic art history or archeology or aerospace Ph.D.s is probably close to zero, given the continuing problem of low academic achievement among Hispanics. What about lower-level staff, also a target of scathing criticism in the report? "The Smithsonian is at a disadvantage in Washington in attracting Latinos," admitted Bretos, "because it's a first-generation immigrant community." In other words, few qualified Hispanics for clerical work either.

How, then, can you charge the Smithsonian with *willful* neglect, I asked Bretos. He dodged the query. "The question is one of focus: how do you present the narrative of America?" he replied. He laughed: "I wrote poisonous pages regarding the Smithsonian Institution." No wonder he's laughing: these days, there is no better way to end up in a sinecure than to blast an institution with false charges of racism.

The report's allegation that the Institution's collections ignore Hispanic material is just as spurious. Smithsonian archaeologists have been collecting and documenting culture in the Southwest almost since the Institution's founding; a curator at American History has specialized in Hispanic-American material since 1965. And again, the report's authors take a far different line. "The collections from Latin America are incredible," says Bretos. "We are one of the largest Latin American collections in botany and zoology."

The precedent set by "Willful Neglect" is ominous. If the Smithsonian capitulates so spinelessly to ethnic extortion, a parade of other ethnic lobbies will be sure to follow the model of the Hispanics, splintering the Institution further into just so many grievance groups.

Ironically, the only place one can consistently find traditional curating in the Smithsonian these days is in the non-Western art museums—the Sackler and Freer galleries of Asian art and the National Museum of African Art. All three are elegant and understated, displaying art and even ritual artifacts as aesthetic objects, rather than as social texts. Apparently, the concepts of beauty and the sublime are still appropriate for non-Western cultures, while the West is busily deconstructing itself.

The Smithsonian's future is not auspicious. On the positive side, Secretary Heyman, a former chancellor of the University of California at Berkeley, is far more sensitive to the commemorative, celebratory function of a national museum than Robert McCormick Adams ever was, and he has openly questioned the advocacy curating favored by the Smithsonian's academically inspired professionals. His cancellation of the Enola Gay exhibit was welcome. Yet there remain many reasons for apprehension. Heyman vehemently promoted racial quotas at Berkeley; he is continuing race-conscious policies at the Smithsonian, putting further out of reach the ideal of a national museum that transcends race and ethnic differences.

Moreover, Heyman's proposed solution to the controversies that have scorched the Institution recently misdiagnoses the problem. In a speech last year at Georgetown Law Center, Heyman argued that issue-oriented curators should follow the model of the legal system and present both sides of a political debate: "Presenting at least two sides of an important issue, and letting the visitors know exactly what is evidence and what is interpretation, can only enhance broader public understanding."

But the problem with the politicized exhibitions at the Smithsonian is not that they present only one side of an issue; the problem is the manufacture of such specious "issues" in the first place. When William Truettner is spotting his race and gender issues, what possible "other side" could be presented? When the American History Museum sets out to multiculturalize and relativize Anglo-American culture, when it deliberately selects unsympathetic white families to contrast with the virtuous natives, no counterargument is even possible, because the ground of debate is already so skewed. To accept the terms of debate is already to have lost.

Short of a total housecleaning of staff, there is little that can save the Smithsonian from being further engulfed by the poisonous trends of identity politics and postmodern theory. These chic academic assumptions are by now thoroughly ingrained in the Smithsonian's bureaucracy. Ultimately, only a change in the powerful culture of universities can restore America's public culture.

May 1997

Pictures from an Institution

James Panero

[T]he absurdities of Benton were so absurd, and I myself was so thoroughly used to them, that they had come to seem to me, almost, the ordinary absurdities of existence. Like Gertrude, I cherished my grievances against God, but to some of them I had become very accustomed. . . .

Sex, greed, envy, power, money: Gertrude knew that these were working away at Benton . . . exactly as they work away everywhere else.
—Randall Jarrell, *Pictures from an Institution*

A S FAR AS I KNOW, the great novel of graduate-student life has yet to be written. As for the life of the graduate student of art history, a subgenre of subgenres, one finds virgin literary terrain. Kingsley Amis gave us Dixon and Welch, and you could do worse for a model than that. *Lucky Jim*'s archetype of hapless lecturer and dense don may find a good home just about anywhere you are thirty, you are in your fourth year of researching the role of dwarfs in seventeenth-century Spanish portraiture (with a nod toward Veronese), you have spent a fruitless year dilating on Oriental motifs in Regency caricature, and your funding is up for annual review. Evelyn Waugh's poor Paul Pennyfeather from *Decline and Fall*, sent down for indecent behavior ("I expect you'll be becoming a schoolmaster, sir. That's what most of the gentlemen does, sir, that gets sent down for indecent behaviour"), might serve as fair warning for what happens when things turn south, and why a graduate student should avoid attention. David Lodge's campus trilogy with Philip Swallow and Morris Zapp—*Changing Places*, *Small World*, and *Nice Work*—can also do a good turn to any young adjunct professor contending with his generation's Stanley Fish.

But as a guide to studying in the humanities for years on end (which can include a visiting lectureship here or there), Randall Jarrell's *Pictures from an Institution* is the closest one comes to Baedeker's. Jarrell's erudite putdown of Benton, based on the poet's experience teaching at the progressive Sarah Lawrence College for Women in the late 1940s, should be awarded each year as the booby-prize to the most ill-treated graduate student in the realm—a consolation that life at school has always been strange, and that progress can sometimes mean a stampede over your mangled corpse. The life of the mind may be all that and a bag of chips, but it's nothing up against the life of the stomach. The motivating factors of grad-life can be as base as they come.

At the opposite extreme to grad-life is the undergraduate. At my own Benton, Brown University, where I studied art history as a graduate student, and which I had an occasion to revisit, the dew that collects on these princes and princesses is the ichor of Greek mythology. Here a fountain replenishes itself every year with fresh faces. A Rhine flows with red-cheeked Kewpies. Fashionable gamines smell of Kiehl's. Blond tresses sprout Mikimoto. These undergraduates have been imbued with an admiration for their elders and a sinfully sophisticated libido. They are the reason this Benton exists—forget Spanish portraiture and Regency caricature. They need teaching assistants, and whether you know it or not, for them you are to assist. "At Benton they wanted you really to believe everything that they did, especially if they hadn't told you what it was."

The daily psychodrama mostly unfolds in the afternoons, during office hours in the Brutalist building you called home. The slender legs and arms of future filmmakers, auction-house workers, and assistants on the Council on Foreign Relations litter the corridors. Across from your temporary office, a professor in Chinese art slams her door pointedly at your arrival. You press into your fourth decade of life, but you have yet to be accorded the respect that comes from adulthood. The fact that you are the most educated, privileged person who is not a felon or insane to live this far below the poverty line is not lost on you. You take a pauper's pride in penury, as though asceticism has focused you on your studies and weakened you from deviation. The queerness of the situation can be downright pleasurable.

[W]hen I dream I'm back at Benton it's as if I were in a hothouse or a—or with the Lotus-Eaters. I can feel Benton all over me like a warm bath, and I try to move my arms and legs, and I can't and I say to myself, "you've got to get out of here. You've got to get out of here!" and then I wake up.

"To get out of here," you endure strange circumstances. Without teaching assistantships, study carrels, and library privileges, you and your fellow Nibelungs would be out of Nibelheim. Tenured faculty would be forced to grade papers. Alberich would be less than pleased. You can also forget researching Spanish dwarfs for the foreseeable future.

Sometimes friends ask what it was like to study at my Benton, expecting stories of radicalism and ramparts. But of course progressivism on the inside can seem downright conservative. "If Benton had had an administration building with pillars it could have carved over the pillars: *Ye shall know the truth, and the truth shall make you feel guilty.*" And as Gertrude notes in Jarrell's story: "Americans are so conformist that even their dissident groups exhibit the most abject conformity."

As in any institution with a healthy department of semiotics and a school of "modern culture and media," by the nature of subject matter alone a department of art history can seem old-fashioned, no matter how radical the instruction. Compared to the larger field of art history, Benton's department might even be tame. The assumption of progressiveness often leads to a complacency in appropriating the latest in what's new. Radicalism ten years out of date can be as decorous as tea and biscuits. Likewise, the same graduate students who might lament the radicalization of art history still bemoan Benton's retardation in "advanced" teaching. To take an unintended lesson from Roger Kimball's *Tenured Radicals*, if tenure will result from radicalism, then radical they must become. Accommodation is the surest path out of Benton and perhaps the only way to get a job. The border between idealism and a life out of poverty is one that graduate students eagerly line up to cross.

In fact, at the Bentons of the world, the biggest faux pas is not rooted in bad politics but in bad manners. "Almost all the people there were agreed about everything, and glad to be agreed, and *right* to be agreed." No one likes to have bulls run in the china shop. From the most senior tenured faculty member down to the most meager first-year grad student, relationships are built on codependence—and often mistrust. The faculty might yank your funding at any moment. You might try to unionize your fellow grad-students or make a general stink. Meanwhile, everyone badmouths each other in a cosmic circle of who-slept-with-whom-a-decade-ago gossip. It would make a spinster blush. And so it goes.

But somewhere along the line something gives, and most often it is the art that gives.

If you had given a Benton student a pencil and a piece of paper, and asked her to draw something, she would have looked at you in helpless astonishment: it would have been plain to her that you knew nothing about art.

To put it another way, as Waugh writes in *Brideshead Revisited*: "'Charles,' said Cordelia, 'Modern Art is all bosh, isn't it?'"

"'Great bosh.'"

Art needs defending from a great deal of bosh—not necessarily the bosh of modern art, which I rather enjoy—but from the many accepted practices of what one might call anti-art. Every day, the next generation of art historians are rendered incapable of doing a thing about it.

Anti-art was part of my reason for visiting my old Benton. I had been invited to give a talk—not by Benton, but by the Intercollegiate Studies Institute—on why I had left the school's art history program without taking a degree. (I delivered my talk, "Why I Left Brown," on November 9, 2004 in 102 Wilson Hall, Brown Unversity, Providence, Rhode Island.) This was something of a sore subject for everyone involved (in particular, my mother). *Brideshead*, of all books, provided a point of departure for my thinking. A subtext on art underlies this novel, especially if you consider Charles's early comparison between Collins, "the embryo don," and Sebastian.

Without venturing into the superlatives of "Against Interpretation," Susan Sontag's essay "against the revenge of the intellect," I came to wonder if good art history could depend on whether a practice revives art or fossilizes art—between what one might call the Flyte and Collins approaches. I also wondered whether one could see a correlation between the "regenerative" properties of scholarship and the "generosity" (or lack thereof) of the professoriate—both words coming out of the same root for "birth." This is a touchy subject. But when you believe that the achievement of art adds up to more than the sum of the social and material circumstances of its creation, as do I, you have to think that your sense of economy is different from that of a parsimonious don whose approach is to divide up the spoils of production and take most of it for keeps.

The temperament of a critic is, alas, the opposite of today's art historian, and art history could use more critics. I had forgotten how enfeebling the "open" atmosphere of the university had become until I returned to Benton. As an art critic for *The New Criterion*, I rarely encounter a hostile gallery or museum. Except for the boorish Whitney, almost everyone welcomes the attention of a review, however critical. But at a progressive school like Benton, where all the important truths of life have been agreed upon beforehand and heaven is fast on its way to earth, no one wants to hear a peep. Upon the announcement of my talk, rumor has it, the faculty at Benton confabulated, and somewhere along the line it was understood that one professor from the department would attend. Two professors would have confessed genuine interest; zero professors, a sign of intimidation. But one was just enough to keep an eye on things, enforce the silent treatment, and radiate bad vibes.

And so it went off as it did. My talk was loaded with praise for Benton (Benton had accepted me, funded me, and imparted the lesson that academia wasn't for everyone). But minds had been made up. When I approached the lone professor afterwards and offered what we in the real world might call good manners (an extended hand, a "thanks for coming"), the professor responded "it's your trip," turned, and spontaneously combusted. The grad students meanwhile slunk down the side aisles. Although a number of them had sent words of encouragement before my talk, few asked questions after it. All of them—friends and colleagues, I had supposed—declined an invitation to dinner, usually by means of the old mafia trick of speaking with hand cupped over mouth. Whispering, cigarette-smoking shadows, the embryo dons slipped into the night, surely never to make eye contact with me again. They have their priorities at Benton, and criticism isn't one of them. Doubtless they wondered where I went wrong.

December 2004

III. Recuperations

"Realism Coloured by Poetry": Rereading John Buchan

Roger Kimball

Life is barren enough surely with all her trappings; let us be therefore cautious of how we strip her.
—Dr. Johnson, quoted by John Buchan

The life of reason is our heritage and exists only through tradition. Now the misfortune of revolutionists is that they are disinherited, and their folly is that they wish to be disinherited even more than they are.
—George Santayana, quoted by John Buchan

"You think that a wall as solid as the earth separates civilization from barbarism. I tell you the division is a thread, a sheet of glass. A touch here, a push there, and you bring back the reign of Satan."
—Andrew Lumley, in Buchan's *The Power-House*

"R EALLY?" I believe that was my cautious response when a friend urged me to read John Buchan's memoir *Pilgrim's Way*. It was, he said, "a remarkable spiritual testament," or words to that effect. *Hmm.* The source of the recommendation was unimpeachable: one of the most intelligent and least frivolous people I know. Yet I had read Buchan—probably the same books you have: *The Thirty-Nine Steps* (1915), for example, the short, bracing spy thriller (or "shocker," as Buchan called it) in which the dashing Richard Hannay battles a perfidious German spy ring and—after a series of wild, pulse-rattling cliffhangers—emerges triumphant in the nick of time. I had also read *Greenmantle* (1916), the somewhat longer, but still bracing, spy thriller in which the dashing Richard Hannay battles a perfidious German spy ring and—after a series of wild, pulse-rattling cliffhangers—emerges triumphant in the nick of time. I had even read *Mr. Standfast* (1919), the moderately long spy thriller in which a dashing Richard . . . German . . . wild . . . emerges . . . nick of t.

I hasten to add that the preceding sentences are not fair to my experience of reading those books. I gobbled them up gratefully if heedlessly. And that, I suspect, is precisely how Buchan intended them to be read. His biographers make a point of telling us that he disliked talking about his "shockers." He was pleased that people liked them—pleased that they sold—but at bottom they were a bit of a lark, a recreation rather than a vocation.

Buchan once said that if there were six literary categories from "highbrow to solid ivory" he belonged in the middle, to the "high-lowbrow." He understood perfectly that his popular fiction was a species of "romance where the incidents defy the probabilities, and march just inside the borders of the possible." That indeed was part of its attraction. As the critic John Gross observed in his review of Janet Adam Smith's biography of Buchan (1965), "one of the main reasons for enjoying Buchan is because he is so preposterous." But do note that the emphasis here is as much on "enjoyment" as on "preposterous."

In any event, there is nothing that prevents the preposterous from possessing contemporary relevance. I reread *Greenmantle* two years ago, just after al Qaeda destroyed the World Trade Towers. It really is an extravagant period piece. But I am surprised that the book has not made a conspicuous comeback. The story turns on a German effort to enlist and enflame a radical Islamist sect in Turkey, where things are touch and go for the Allies. Sir Walter Bullivant of the Foreign Office summons Hannay and puts him in the picture. "The ordinary man" believes that Islam is succumbing to "Krupp guns," to modernity. "Yet—I don't know," Sir Walter confesses. "I do not quite believe in Islam becoming a back number." Hannay agrees (natch): "It looks as if Islam had a bigger hand in the thing than we thought. . . . Islam is a fighting creed, and the mullah still stands in the pulpit with the Koran in one hand and a drawn sword in the other." Indeed. Later in the book, another character observes,

> There's a great stirring in Islam, something moving on the face of the waters. . . . Those religious revivals come in cycles, and one was due about now. And they are quite clear about the details. A seer has arisen of the blood of the Prophet, who will restore the Khalifate to its old glories and Islam to its old purity.

Greenmantle was published in 1916. Perhaps we've finally caught up with it.

BUCHAN OFTEN DELIBERATELY poached on contemporary historical events and places in his shockers. He was aiming less at verisimilitude than at the piquancy that the appearance of verisimilitude provided. He did it all with a wink. In the dedication to *The Thirty-Nine Steps*, Buchan explains that, convalescing from an illness, he had exhausted his supply of thrillers—"those aids to cheerfulness"—and so decided to write one of his own. He tossed it off in a matter of weeks in the autumn of 1914 and was duly startled by its immense success. (An earlier shocker, *The Power-House*, had been serialized in 1913 but wasn't published in book form until 1916.) A million copies of *The Thirty-Nine Steps* sold, I read somewhere, and that is an old figure. Timing played a part in the huge sale. The book was published in October 1915, early in the First World War. Tales about brave chaps hunting down dastardly German spies had an audience primed and waiting.

But the success of *The Thirty-Nine Steps* was not due to timing alone. It is a remarkable book. Like Mr. Hannay himself, the book hits the ground running and barely stops for breath in the course of its 110 pages. On your mark (first sentence): Hannay, back from South Africa having made his pile, is "pretty well disgusted with life"; he contemplates Albania, "a place that might keep a man from yawning."

> I made a vow. I would give the Old Country another day to fit me into something; if nothing happened, I would take the next boat for the Cape.

Get set (a few pages later): Hannay comes home to find the man with a dark secret he'd met a few days earlier murdered in his apartment. *Go*: Hannay, pursued by both the police (who suspect him of the murder) and the bad guys (who done it), races from London to Scotland, clambers over endless Scottish moors, is caught by the baddies, escapes, and zigzags back by the cliffs of Dover to reveal the secret of the Black Stone. Whew: "All Europe" had been "trembling on the edge of an earthquake." Not to worry: Hannay nabs the spy; England is safe. (In his famous 1935 film version of the book, Alfred Hitchcock took many liberties with the text, but he did manage to preserve Buchan's uncanny union of velocity and menace.)

The Thirty-Nine Steps recounts all this with an urgent but evocative economy. It owes as much to Sir Walter Scott and Robert Louis Stevenson (fellow Scots and two of Buchan's models) as E. Phillips Oppenheim (a less august though no less favored model: "my master in fiction . . . the greatest Jewish writer since Isaiah").

Buchan did not invent a genre with *The Thirty-Nine Steps*. Conan Doyle, Wilkie Collins, Erskine Childers, and others beat him to it. But he did supply some novel furnishings, a distinctive tone and atmosphere instantly recognizable as the Buchanesque. The scholar Robin Winks called Buchan "the father of the modern spy thriller," a genre whose beneficiaries include Graham Greene, Ian Fleming, and John le Carré. The chase scenes, the villain who belongs to the upper reaches of respectable society, the breeding and derring-do of the hero: they're reasonably fresh in Buchan, overripe in Fleming, often a bit rancid in later authors.

BUT THE BUCHANESQUE involved other elements. It has something to do with his breathless plots and flat but somehow compelling characters—not only Hannay (modelled, it is said, on the young Edmund Ironside, later Field Marshall Lord Ironside of Archangel), but also figures like Peter Pienaar, the wiry Dutch hunter; Dickson McCunn, the retired Glasgow grocer; Sir Edward Leithen, the high-powered lawyer. None is three-dimensional; none seems "real"; all are curiously memorable in the context of their actions. I suspect that Buchan would have agreed with—let's see, Aristotle, wasn't it?—that plot is "the first principle and, as it were, the soul of the 'shocker'; character holds second place."

The Buchanesque also has something to do with the way place and landscape are woven into the bones of his stories (*vide* Stevenson here). *John Macnab* (1925) is in the form of a Buchan shocker. But it does not present a tale of high-stakes espionage. Instead, it tells the story of three middle-aged Buchan characters, Sir Edward Leithen, Palliser Yeates, and Lord Lamancha, who, at the pinnacles of their careers, find themselves bored and (like Hannay in *The Thirty-Nine Steps*) "disgusted with life." They need a challenge, the stimulus of danger, what William James called "the moral equivalent of war." So they betake themselves in secret to Scotland, where, under the name of John Macnab, they announce to some local grandees their intention of poaching two stags and a salmon over the course of a few days. The penalty if caught is public humiliation. As the historian Gertrude Himmelfarb observes in her classic essay on Buchan, there is a sense in which "the hunting and fishing scenes, . . . described in great and exciting detail, are not appendages to the plot; they *are* the plot." The relation between man and landscape, his behavior toward the land and its bounty, are part of the moral compact of society. One is not surprised to discover that Buchan was an avid, almost a compulsive walker. Ten, twenty, thirty miles a day—like Richard Hannay or Peter Pienaar, he also clambered over hill and dale, scouring the horizon, registering the lay of the land. Richard Usborne notes in his book *Clubland Heroes* (first published in 1953) that Buchan's characters "are attracted to exhaustion as a drinker to the bottle." It was an attraction that Buchan himself seemed to share.

John Macnab is a *tour de force*—some regard it as Buchan's best novel—

an adventure story in which the McGuffin (to use Hitchcock's term) is deliberately reduced to a minimum: fish and fauna instead of foul play. Yet the result is more than a sprightly, slightly absurd adventure tale. Its theme, as Himmelfarb notes, "is not only the natural and rightful authority exercised by some men by virtue of their breeding, experience, and character, but also the natural and rightful impulse to rebel against authority." That dialectic—the implication of authority and independence, of conformity and innovation—are at the heart of Buchan's worldview.

It is one version of the Tory creed. Democracy, Buchan believes, is all well and good. In fact, he is a passionate democrat. But it is essential to remember that (as he puts it in *Pilgrim's Way*) "Democracy . . . is a negative thing. It provides a fair field for the Good Life, but it is not itself the Good Life." Buchan's view of democracy owes more to Athens than to Jefferson. It is a political arrangement that encourages striving and excellence—the *agon* of superior achievement—but not the levelling imperative of equality. This sobering truth is at the heart of *John Macnab*: "It is a melancholy fact," a character muses, "which exponents of democracy must face that, while all men may be on a level in the eyes of the State, they will continue in fact to be preposterously unequal." All of which is to say that if Buchan is constitutionally a Tory, he practices a slightly seditious—some might just say "Scottish"—redaction of Toryism: its benediction is not upon the pastness of the past but its compact with the energies of the present. Hence Buchan's (qualified) admiration for such robust but un-Toryesque figures as Cromwell, to whom he devoted a biography in 1934:

> His bequest to the world was not institutions, for his could not last, or a political faith, for his was more instinct and divination than coherent thought. It was the man himself, his frailty and his strength, typical in almost every quality of his own English people, but with these qualities so magnified as to become epic and universal.

As this passage suggests, another element of the Buchanesque involves highminded moral earnestness. Usborne notes that there is throughout Buchan's fiction "a slight but persistent propaganda for the decencies as preached by the enthusiastic housemaster—for cold baths, for hard work, for healthy exhaustion in the playing-field, for shaking hands with the beaten opponent, for the attainment of Success in after-life." In *Mr. Standfast* (remember *The Pilgrim's Progress*?), Hannay has a clear shot at the evil Moxon Ivery, who is planning to infect the British army with anthrax. He doesn't fire because Ivery is sitting down and facing away from him: a sportsman does not shoot a man in the back. In *Greenmantle*, when it's clear that the bloody battle of Erzerum is going the right way, Hannay's sidekick Sandy Arbuthnot exclaims, "Oh, well done our side!" It wasn't only Waterloo that was won on the playing fields of Eton.

USBORNE RATHER DEPRECATES the public-school, "success ethic" in Buchan. It is I suppose easy to mock, though perhaps less easy to replace (apart from the cold baths, I mean). Buchan's characters are the best-est, most-est at whatever they do. The financier Julius Victor is "the richest man in the world." Sandy Arbuthnot was "one of the two or three most intelligent people in the world." Everyone has made, or is about to make, a "big name" for himself. Of a character at a dinner party of luminaries, "it was rumored that in the same week he had been offered the Secretaryship of State, the Presidency of an ancient University, and the control of a great industrial corporation." That is business as usual in Buchanland. Likewise Buchan's villains. In *Mr. Standfast*, the good guys are not just hunting bad chaps, they are "hunting the most dangerous man in all the world." Hilda von Einem (*Greenmantle*), Dominick Medina (*The Three Hostages*, 1924), Moxon Ivery (a repeat character): When they are bad, they are very bad indeed (though few are without a redeeming dollop of courage). Buchan was writing a species of romance, not tragedy, but perhaps here, too, he followed Aristotle and aimed at presenting men "better than in actual life." At first blush, anyway, it is easy to see why Buchan was an author approved by parents, teachers, pastors. As Usborne put it, he "backed up their directives and doctrines. Buchan wrote good English. Buchan taught you things. Buchan was good for you."

In fact, I believe that Buchan probably *is* good for you, especially considering the alternatives on offer. The question is whether the Buchan doctrine can still resonate meaningfully. In her essay on Buchan, Himmelfarb described him as "the last Victorian." What she had in mind was that extraordinary British amalgam of seriousness and eccentricity, energy and lassitude, adventurousness and propriety, world-conquering boldness and coddling domesticity; industry, yes; duty, yes; honor, yes; even a certain priggishness—all that but so much more: the whole complex package of moral passion at once goaded and stymied by spiritual cataclysm that made up (in Walter Houghton's phrase) "the Victorian frame of mind." Buchan, son of the manse, occupied a late-model version of that frame as magnificently as anyone.

One tends to think—*I* certainly thought—of Buchan primarily as a writer of thrillers. But that is like saying Winston Churchill was a painter. He did a few other things as well. In fact, Buchan comes closer than almost anyone to fulfilling Sydney Smith's definition of an "extraordinary man":

"The meaning of an extraordinary man is that he is eight men in one man." Born in 1875 in Perth, Scotland, Buchan was the eldest of five children. Buchan père, a minister in the Free Church of Scotland, was, his son later recalled, "a man of wide culture, to whom, in the words of the Psalms, all things were full of the goodness of the Lord"—solemn, perhaps, but with "none of the harshness against which so many have revolted." It was a close family, with the tensions but also the emotional bounty that closeness brings. In *Pilgrim's Way*, Buchan described his father as "the best man I have ever known" and noted that "not many sons and mothers can have understood each other better than she and I"—"indeed," he continues with a smile, "in my adolescence we sometimes arrived at that point of complete comprehension known as a misunderstanding."

THE BUCHAN FAMILY, of decidedly modest means, moved south in 1876 to Pathhead, near the Firth of Forth. Buchan's childhood was instinct partly with the magic of bonny braes and burns, tarns, haughs, and other burry ornaments of the Scottish countryside, partly with the magic of a gentle though unwavering Calvinism. The Bible and *The Pilgrim's Progress* loomed large, rich literary and rhetorical as well as spiritual reservoirs.

Buchan conjectured that his "boyhood must have been one of the idlest on record," yet he managed to get through one or two books.

> Early in my teens I had read Scott, Dickens, Thackeray, and a host of other story tellers; all Shakespeare; a good deal of history, and many works of travel; essayists like Bacon and Addison, Hazlitt and Lamb, and a vast assortment of poetry including Milton, Pope, Dante (in a translation), Wordsworth, Shelley, Keats, and Tennyson. Matthew Arnold I knew almost by heart; Browning I still found too difficult except in patches.

If Buchan was idle, what are we?

In 1888, the Buchans moved to Glasgow. John was educated at Hutchesons' Grammar School and then (from 1892–1895) at Glasgow University, where he studied and became friends with the classicist Gilbert Murray. In 1895, he won a place at Brasenose College, Oxford, an institution of barely a hundred students and known chiefly for rowdiness and prowess at games. Buchan distinguished himself in other areas. He just missed a first in Mods but managed a first in Greats the following year. He won (after a few tries) both the Stanhope and Newdigate Prizes. He was elected President of the Union and, by 1899 when he was graduated, already had six or seven books to his credit, including a novel, a collection of essays, and an edition of Bacon's essays. He was, Janet Adam Smith speculated, possibly the only person in the 1898 edition of *Who's Who* whose occupation was listed as "undergraduate."

Brasenose both extended and mollified Buchan's temperament. Growing up, he recalled in *Pilgrim's Way* (*Memory Hold-the-Door* in England), he instinctively subscribed to Lord Falkland's famous dictum: "When it is not necessary to change, it is necessary not to change." But his exposure to philosophy led him to become "skeptical of dogmas," which he more and more looked upon "as questions rather than answers."

> The limited outlook of my early youth had broadened. Formerly I had regarded life as a pilgrimage along a strait and steep path on which the pilgrim must keep his eyes fixed. I prided myself on a certain moral austerity, but now I came to realise that there was a good deal of self-interest in that outlook, like the Puritan who saw in his creed not only the road to heaven but the way to worldly success. I began to be attracted by the environs as well as by the road, and I became more charitable in my judgment of things and men.

Buchan considered staying on at Oxford and becoming a don or professor. He concluded that he was not sufficiently devoted to any subject to give up his life to it. "I wanted a stiffer job, one with greater hazards in it, and I was not averse to one which offered bigger material rewards." So after four years he traded Oxford for London and philosophy for the law.

IN 1900, BUCHAN was in London working for *The Spectator*, reading for the Bar, and, as always, writing, writing, writing. (One sees different figures for his total output: one plausible sum is 130 books.) In 1901, he was called to the Bar, practiced briefly, but then accepted an offer from Lord Alfred Milner to join him in South Africa. Buchan became a distinguished member of Milner's "Kindergarten," the brilliant young men who helped the British High Commissioner for South Africa establish order in the aftermath of the Boer War and raise the standard of civilization among the natives.

The youth and inexperience of Milner's staff raised eyebrows, but he knew what he was doing. "There will be a regular rumpus and a lot of talk about boys and Oxford and jobs and all that," Milner wrote to a friend.

> Well, I value brains and character more than experience. First-class men of experience are not to be got. Nothing one could offer would tempt them to give up what they have. . . . No! I shall not be here for very long, but when I go I mean to leave behind me young men with plenty of work in them.

Buchan was one such, and South Africa was a revelation to him. For one thing, invested with enormous administrative responsibility during his two years in South Africa, this bookish youth discovered that "there was a fine practical wisdom which owed nothing to books and academies." He met Cecil Rhodes when the great imperialist was at the end of his life. Rhodes was a fount of pragmatic wisdom. "You can make your book with roguery," he told the young Buchan, "but vanity is incalculable."

Buchan was the perfect acolyte for Milner's reformist zeal and benefits-of-Empire campaign. And if Milner discerned great potential in his youthful recruits, at least some of his *Kinder* returned the admiration. Milner, Buchan noted, was an administrative genius. "The drawback to a completely rational mind is that it is apt to assume that what is flawless in logic is therefore practicable. Milner never made that mistake." He possessed an unerring "instinct for what is possible. . . . He could do what the lumberman does in a log-jam, and pick out the key log which, once moved, sets the rest going."

Buchan's stint in South Africa—reading Euripides on the veldt, absorbing that surprising new landscape—plumbed a current of almost mystical feeling that, in fact, is an aspect of Buchan's character often overlooked on account of his worldly competence and the practical can-do bustle of many of his heroes. In South Africa, Buchan reported in *Pilgrim's Way*, he enjoyed "moments, even hours, of intense exhilaration."

> There are no more comfortable words in the language than Peace and Joy. . . . Peace is that state in which fear of any kind is unknown. But Joy is a positive thing; in Joy one does not only feel secure, but something goes out from oneself to the universe, a warm, possessive effluence of love. There may be Peace without Joy, and Joy without Peace, but the two combined make Happiness. It was Happiness that I knew in those rare moments. The world was a place of inexhaustible beauty, but still more it was the husk of something infinite, ineffable, and immortal, in very truth the garment of God.

I cannot recall Richard Hannay expressing such feelings, but they are on view in other books by Buchan—*The Dancing Floor* (1926), for example, or his last, posthumously published novel, *Sick Heart River* (1940, published in America as *Mountain Meadow*).

IN 1903, BUCHAN returned to London, resumed work for *The Spectator* and the Middle Temple, and wrote, among other books, *The Law Relating to the Taxation of Foreign Income* (1905), a work I have no intention of reading. In

1906, he became a partner in the publishing firm of his old Oxford friend Tommy Nelson. The following year, Buchan married Susan Grosvenor, a granddaughter of Lord Ebury, and great-great-grandniece of the Duke of Wellington. It was a splendid match, which brought four children and much happiness. "I have," Buchan wrote toward the end of his life, "been happy in many things, but all my other good fortune has been as dust in the balance compared with the blessing of an incomparable wife." Susan was not rich, but she was well-connected and her marriage came as an agreeable surprise to some. One friend wrote, "So you aren't going to be a fat Duchess after all. I had always looked forward to being given one finger to shake at one omnium-gatherum garden-party by your Grace, and now you're going to marry something like a genius instead."

FROM HIS PERCH in the publishing world, Buchan naturally came into contact with many writers and public figures. "With G. K. Chesterton and Hilaire Belloc and Maurice Baring," Buchan reports with Chestertonian slyness, "I never differed—except in opinion." He knew Kipling and Lord Asquith, Stanley Baldwin and Lord Balfour ("the only public figure for whom I felt a disciple's loyalty").

Pilgrim's Way is a sort of memoir, but an impersonal one; it is less an autobiography than a portrait of an age. With typical decorum, Buchan leaves out of his account contemporaries who were still living. Much of the book is devoted to sketches of Buchan's Oxford friends who died in the War: Tommy Nelson, Raymond Asquith, and Auberon Thomas Herbert, who was a model for Sandy Arbuthnot.

Buchan's recollections are invariably affectionate but seldom uncritical. Of the famous lawyer Richard Haldane, Buchan noted that "to differ from him seemed to be denying the existence of God." Haldane was steeped in the philosophy of Hegel and his arguments, though brilliant, gave to the uninitiated "No light, but darkness visible," as Milton might put it. Buchan recalls one episode when the bench mistook Haldane's use of the word "antinomy" to mean the metal "antimony." It is clear that Buchan admired Haldane. It is also clear that he regarded him as a sort of object lesson in the dangers of Teutonic intellectualization. "A man who has been nourished on German metaphysics," Buchan observed, "should make a point of expressing his thoughts in plain workaday English, for the technical terms of German philosophy have a kind of hypnotic power; they create a world remote from common reality where reconciliations and synthesis flow as smoothly and with as little meaning as in an opiate dream." This is an observation that aspiring graduate students in the humanities ought to memorize and repeat three times daily before breakfast.

Although a man of immense intellectual cultivation, Buchan had his feet planted firmly on the ground. He understood the dangers of political as well as intellectual infatuation. He understood that responsiveness to the unexpected—which means responsiveness to reality—was a key political asset. Of Prime Minister Asquith, Buchan concluded that he possessed "every traditional virtue—dignity, honor, courage, and a fine selflessness. . . . He was extremely intelligent, but he was impercipient."

> New facts made little impression on his capacious but insensitive mind. Whatever ran counter to his bland libertarianism seemed an impiety. I remember, when the audacities of Lytton Strachey's Victorian Studies were delighting the world, suggesting to Mr. Asquith that the time was ripe for a return match. It was easy, I said, to make fun of the household of faith, but I thought just as much fun could be made out of the other side, even with the most respectful and accurate presentation. I suggested a book to be called "Three Saints of Rationalism" on the lines of Eminent Victorians, and proposed for the chapters John Stuart Mill, Herbert Spencer, and John Morley. He was really shocked, as shocked as a High Churchman would be who was invited to consider the comic side of the Oxford Movement.

That "Three Saints of Rationalism" is a volume still waiting to be written.

"EXPERIMENTALISM" IN ART (or life) had little appeal for Buchan. In the the late Teens and early Twenties, he made an effort to read his contemporaries. "Alas! I had put it off too long. My ear simply could not attune itself to their rhythms, or lack of rhythms." T. S. Eliot's poetry he regarded as "a pastiche of Donne" that reproduced "only his tortured conceits. . . not his sudden flute notes and moments of shattering profundity." Still, Buchan's intelligence admitted the merits of the great modernists, though his heart did not respond. On Proust, for example: "I disliked his hothouse world, but it was idle to deny his supreme skill in disentangling subtle threads of thought and emotion." Buchan befriended T. E. Lawrence ("a mixture of contradictories which never were—perhaps could never have been—harmonised") and Henry James. Although he did not care for James's late novels ("tortuous arabesques"), he "loved the man" and "revelled in the idioms of his wonderful talk."

Once Buchan acted as host at a relative's country house where James was a guest. He knew that James, like most sophisticated New Englanders of his day, would appreciate a good Madeira. The house had a wonderful cellar. Buchan promised James something special.

He sipped his glass, and his large benign face remained impassive while he gave his verdict. I wish I could remember his epithets; they were a masterpiece of the intricate, evasive, and non-committal, and yet of an exquisite politeness. Then I tasted the wine and found it swipes. It was the old story of a dishonest butler who was selling famous vintages and replacing them by cheap stuff from a neighbouring public house.

On another occasion, an aunt of Buchan's wife, the widow of Byron's grandson, asked Buchan and James to examine the archives in order to write an opinion on the quarrel between Byron and his wife. Over the course of a summer weekend, Buchan and James "waded through masses of ancient indecency, and duly wrote an opinion. The thing nearly made me sick, but my colleague never turned a hair. His only words for some special vileness were 'singular'—'most curious'—'nauseating, perhaps, but how quite inexpressibly significant.'"

When Buchan was five years old, he fell out of a carriage and fractured his skull when the back wheel rolled over his head. He spent the better part of a year in bed recovering, but Buchan himself attributes a long run of good health to the episode. Before, he had been "a miserable headachy little boy"; afterwards he was in a nearly continuous bloom of health until 1911. From then until his early death in 1940, Buchan was beset by painful stomach problems. The onset of World War I found him in bed for three months recovering from an operation for a duodenal ulcer.

Buchan was too old for the infantry, but he served the war effort well, first as a correspondent in France for *The Times*, then working for Lord Beaverbrook as Director of the Department of Information and, briefly, as Director of Intelligence. In order to keep the presses of Thomas Nelson and Sons running, he also undertook *Nelson's History of the War*, which was published in twenty-four volumes from 1915–1919. I have read in several places that Buchan's quota was 50,000 words a fortnight. That depressing number works out to 5,000 words a day, Monday through Friday. Try it sometime, especially when you are Director of your country's intelligence service, raising a family, and writing a clutch of novels and a volume of verse. Buchan's *History* is no piece of makework, either. For sheer narrative verve, it may outdo even Churchill's multivolume history of the Great War. Buchan had a genius for making military operations clear to the layman. Writing as events were unfolding, in the confusing smoke-and-mirrors chaos of war, he nevertheless managed to see beyond sorties, troop movements, and individual campaigns. His deep reading in history allowed him to keep the larger picture in view. The larger picture concerned civilization: its requirements and enemies. Summing up toward the end of his final volume, Buchan optimistically suggests that one benefit of the war was to have shaken the world "out of its complacency." The ensuing years showed how resilient a trait is human complacency. We are never done with it—a fact that Buchan implicitly acknowledged when he observed that "The world is at no time safe for freedom, which needs vigilant and unremitting guardianship."

Andrew Lownie said in his biography of Buchan, *The Presbyterian Cavalier* (2003, David R. Godine), that the War left Buchan "physically and emotionally shattered." That seems to me to overstate things. He suffered the loss of many close friends (including Tommy Nelson, who fell at the Somme). His stomach problems had become chronic. But shattered men do not continue turning out the books; they do not become Director of Reuters, as Buchan did in 1919, or buy and restore a manor house, as Buchan did with Elsfield near Oxford that same year. In 1927, when he was first elected Conservative MP for Scottish Universities, Buchan was working on five books. In 1929, he finally resigned from Nelson's. A few years later, he was created High Commissioner to the General Assembly of the Church of Scotland, the representative of the Crown to the Church. (In 1929, Buchan had co-authored *The Kirk in Scotland*, so he was prepared by industry as well as background for the pomp-filled post.) The apex of Buchan's public career came in 1935 when he was created Baron Tweedsmuir of Elsfield and was appointed Governor General of Canada, a post he held until his death in Ottawa in February 1940.

BUCHAN WAS SCHOOLED to an intelligent toughness—to an independence bred in reverence—that would twist and bristle in the self-self-self moral atmosphere of today. There was a strong streak of lyricism in his make up, yet candor and forthrightness were among the primary virtues he cultivated. Heckling, he noted with some pride, was an art "pursued for the pure love of the game" in the Border Country. Candidates were sometimes heckled to a standstill by their own supporters. Buchan recalled an incident shortly after Lloyd George's Insurance Act had been introduced. A speaker was defending the welfare policy on the grounds that it was a practical application of the Sermon on the Mount. A shepherd rose to chivvy the speaker:

> "Ye believe in the Bible, sir?"
> "With all my heart."
> "And ye consider that this Insurance Act is in keepin' with the Bible?"
> "I do."
> "Is it true that under the Act there's a maternity benefit, and that a

woman gets the benefit whether she's married or no?"

"That is right."

"D'ye approve of that?"

"With all my heart."

"Well, sir, how d'ye explain this? The Bible says the wages of sin is death and the Act says thirty shillin's."

Of the Border folk he represented in Parliament, Buchan said he particularly admired their "realism coloured by poetry, a stalwart independence sweetened by courtesy, a shrewd kindly wisdom." These were qualities that by most accounts Buchan himself embodied.

One cannot read far into the commentary on Buchan, however, before encountering some stiff criticism of some of his attitudes and language. The criticism resolves into three main charges. Buchan was a colonialist, a champion of the British Empire. Buchan was a racist: he said and believed unpleasant things about Negroes. Buchan was an anti-Semite: he said and believed unpleasant things about Jews.

On the first matter, Buchan must stand guilty as charged, though "guilty" is assuredly not the right word. Buchan was a partisan of the British colonialist enterprise; he did believe in the civilizing mandate of the British Empire. The only question is whether that is something of which Buchan ought to have been ashamed. In fact, what was already crystal clear in the early 1900s when Buchan was with Milner in South Africa has become sadly, grimly reinforced in recent decades: everywhere Britain went benefitted immensely from its wise and beneficent intervention. Were there mistakes? Yes. Were there unnecessary cruelties, stupidities, miscalculations? You bet. But the British colonial adventure was an incalculable gain for the colonized. The British brought better hygiene, the rule of law, better schools, roads, industry, manners. Santayana was right about the colonial rule of the Englishman: "Never since the heroic days of Greece has the world had such a sweet, just, boyish master. It will be a black day for the human race when scientific blackguards, conspirators, churls, and fanatics manage to supplant him." What's happened in Africa in the period of decolonization—better call it rebarbarization—is stark evidence that Santayana was right.

BUT WHAT ABOUT the other charges against Buchan? In *Mr. Standfast*, when Richard Hannay is asked to pose as a pacifist, he objects: "there are some things that no one has a right to ask of any white man." You'll find similar locutions salted through Buchan's novels. You'll also find, as you will in the novels of Mark Twain or Joseph Conrad (for example), the use of the word "nigger." Is that objectionable? Today it would be. Indeed, a few decades ago a publisher refused to re-issue Buchan's adventure novel *Prester John* (1910) because of the "N" word.

You will find similar language about Jews. At the beginning of *The Thirty-Nine Steps*, Franklin Scudder is ranting about the international Jewish conspiracy and conjures up the evil figure of the mastermind behind the scenes, a "little white-faced Jew in a bath chair with an eye like a rattle-snake." Of course, Scudder is potty and winds up a few pages later with a knife in his back. But Buchan's portrayal of Jews, at least in his early novels, is not glamorous. With some exceptions, they are rag dealers or pawnbrokers or else nefarious anarchists or shady financiers. There are exceptions—Julius Victor, for example, "the richest man in the world," who is a thoroughly noble chap. But then he is described by the dyspeptic American John S. Blenkiron as "the whitest Jew since the apostle Paul." It was meant as praise, but still . . .

Buchan's biographer Lownie said that "It is difficult to find any evidence of anti-Semitism in Buchan's own personal views." Well, maybe. It's much more likely that—up to the 1930s, anyway—Buchan was anti-Semitic (and anti-foreigner) in the way nearly everyone in his society was. At the time, Gertrude Himmelfarb notes, "Men were normally anti-Semitic, unless by some quirk of temperament or ideology they happened to be philo-Semitic. So long as the world itself was normal, this was of no great consequence. . . . It was Hitler . . . who put an end to the casual, innocent anti-Semitism of the clubman." And by the time the Nazis came along, Buchan had abandoned any casual aspersions against Jews in his novels. Moreover, he publicly denounced Hitler's anti-Semitism in 1934. (Which was one reason, no doubt, that he was on the Nazi's post-invasion list of people to be imprisoned for "Pro-Jewish activity.") Like Milner, Buchan was ardently pro-Zionist, and his name was later ceremoniously inscribed in the Golden Book of the Jewish National Fund.

Buchan wrote at a time less constrained than ours by the imperatives of political correctness. He didn't try to second-guess his audience. He had confidence not only in his knowledge, but also, as Himmelfarb observed, in

> his opinions, attitudes, intuitions, and prejudices. What he wrote for the public was what he felt in private; he did not labor for a subtlety or profundity that did not come spontaneously, or censor his spontaneous thoughts before committing them to paper. He had none of the scruples that are so inhibiting today. He was candid about race, nation, religion, and class, because it did not occur to him that anything he was capable of feeling or thinking could be reprehensible. . . . What some have con-

demned as insensitivity or condescension may also be taken as a forthright expression of opinion—or not so much opinion, because that is to dignify it as a conscious judgment, but rather impression or experience.

In *The Three Hostages*, Sandy Arbuthnot gives voice to feelings of exasperation that, I suspect, come close to Buchan's own feelings:

"The old English way was to regard all foreigners as slightly childish and rather idiotic and ourselves as the only grown-ups in a kindergarten world. That meant that we had a cool detached view and did even-handed unsympathetic justice. But now we have to go into the nursery ourselves and are bear-fighting on the floor. We take violent sides, and make pets, and of course if you are *-phil* something or other you have got to be *-phobe* something else."

It was precisely that unreasoning attachment to ideology—to the grim nursery of human passions—that Buchan resisted.

HIMMELFARB DESCRIBED BUCHAN as "the last Victorian" because the world that could nurture such a character has long since vanished. But one may hope that Buchan will have successors, for the creator of Richard Hannay, Sandy Arbuthnot, and the others was a great and potent friend of civilization. Robin Winks remarked that "What Buchan feared most was unreasoning passion"—that, and the complacency which renders passion toxic. In his biography of Augustus (1937), Buchan wrote that the Emperor's "true achievement . . . is that he saved the world from disintegration." At the end of his life Buchan saw the world once again threatened by a storm of irrational violence and hatred. Yet again it was revealed that (as his character Dickson McCunn put it) "civilisation anywhere is a very thin crust." Nevertheless, what Buchan feared above all was not "barbarism, which is civilisation submerged or not yet born, but de-civilisation, which is civilisation gone rotten." In his posthumously published memoir, he describes a "nightmare" world in which science had transformed the world into "a huge, dapper, smooth-running mechanism."

Everyone would be comfortable, but since there could be no great demand for intellectual exertion everyone would be also slightly idiotic. Their shallow minds would be easily bored, and therefore unstable. Their life would be largely a quest for amusement. . . . Men would go everywhere and live nowhere; know everything and understand nothing. . . . In the tumult of a jazz existence what hope would there be for the still small voices of the prophets and philosophers and poets? A world which claimed to be a triumph of the human personality would in truth have killed that personality. In such a bagman's paradise, where life would be rationalised and padded with every material comfort, there would be little satisfaction for the immortal part of man. It would be a new Vanity Fair. . . . The essence of civilisation lies in man's defiance of an impersonal universe. It makes no difference that a mechanised universe may be his own creation if he allows his handiwork to enslave him. Not for the first time in history have the idols that humanity has shaped for its own ends become its master.

Buchan thought the dictators of the 1930s and 1940s had paradoxically "done us a marvellous service in reminding us of the true values of life," awakening men to the dangers of complacency.

YET BUCHAN KNEW THAT, whatever questions the war answered, the compact of routinization and unruly passion—the marriage of hyper-rationalization and irrationality—was a problem that transcended the savagery of war. It was a problem built into the nature of modernity. How *that* problem would be solved—or, rather, how that unthinking version of life was to be avoided, for it was not a problem susceptible of any one solution—was something Buchan regarded with a mixture of foreboding and faith. He regarded the extinction of eccentricity, the homogenization of the world with a distaste bordering on horror. What he feared was failure bred in success: "a deepening and narrowing of ruts" that technological and economic success regularly brought in their wake. "The world," he wrote toward the end of *Pilgrim's Way*, "must remain an oyster for youth to open. If not, youth will cease to be young, and that will be the end of everything." Buchan speculated that "the challenge with which we are now faced may restore us to that manly humility which alone gives power." The campaign against genuine individuality is much further advanced today than it was in 1940 when Buchan wrote. We seem further than ever from the "manly humility" he prescribed. Which is one reason that rereading John Buchan is such a tonic exercise. His adventures are riches that help remind us of our poverty. If, as Montaigne wrote, admonition is the highest office of friendship, that counsel is a precious bounty.

September 2003

Who Was Simon Raven?

Brooke Allen

NOVELISTS WHO achieve a cult status write, by definition, for a narrow and usually specialist readership, and while their books are not for everyone, they attract certain passionate partisans. One cult figure, the English novelist, journalist, and television writer Simon Raven (1927–2001), did not reach a mass audience or even attain a very broad readership among the upper middle class and the intelligentsia; but then, he never exerted himself very far to do so. "I've always written for a small audience consisting of people like myself," he remarked, "who are well-educated, worldly, skeptical and snobbish (meaning that they rank good taste over bad). And who believe that nothing and nobody is special."

"People like myself": there are few of them left, for Raven was one of a breed that was dying in his youth and is now all but extinct. Not that well-educated, worldly, skeptical, and snobbish people have entirely disappeared, only that Raven's own type is no longer to be seen: his was not an earnest agnosticism but a robust eighteenth-century paganism. A civilized man should, he believed, "reject both enthusiasms and faiths, if only because of the ridiculous postures, whether mental or physical, which they require." This philosophy was allied with a deep contempt for the egalitarian moral code of postwar England with its namby-pamby unwillingness to offend. He himself suffered from no such diffidence.

Raven's offensiveness did not grow from bile or melancholy but from extreme high spirits. From earliest youth, he reveled in the role of outrageous provocateur and exuded what one of his school contemporaries, Gerald Priestland, recalled as a "Luciferian aura." "Brilliant when he could be bothered, handsomely copper-headed but with a world-weary slouch and drawl, [he] moved through Charterhouse trailing an odour of brimstone." Noel Annan felt him to be one of the rare "liberators" some of us are lucky enough to encounter during our lives: "Simon was one of those very assured undergraduates who by their example liberate their contemporaries from the shackles of family, school or class."

Raven was the author of thirty-four books (as well as many radio and television plays, essays, and reviews), but his reputation today rests almost entirely on his ten-volume *roman fleuve*, *Alms for Oblivion* (1964–1976). His undertaking has inevitably been compared with Anthony Powell's *Dance to the Music of Time*, also in ten volumes, as it deals with the same social milieu (but a generation younger) and touches on the same themes of time and mutability.

> I wanted to look at the upper-middle-class scene since the war, and in particular my generation's part in it. We had spent our early years as privileged members of a privileged class. How were we faring in the Age of the Common Man? How *ought* we to be faring?. . . Would the high-minded lot stoop to conquer? . . . And what about their unscrupulous confreres? No Queensberry rules for them, so they had a flying start. But Fate has a way of bitching things up just when you least expect it.

Many of *Alms for Oblivion*'s protagonists attended the same public school, served in the same regiment (the dashing and aristocratic Earl Hamilton's Light Dragoons), and read Classics or History in a more or less desultory manner at the same Cambridge college (Lancaster, a thinly disguised version of King's). The novels, which, unlike Powell's, jump back and forth in time, take the characters from school (*Fielding Gray*, 1967) to the Army (*Sound the Retreat*, 1971, and *The Sabre Squadron*, 1966), the "corridors of power" (*The Rich Pay Late*, 1964, and *Friends in Low Places*, 1965), scenes of international intrigue (*The Judas Boy*, 1968), student unrest during the Sixties (*Places Where They Sing*, 1970), the movie business and an excursion into American Philistia (*Come Like Shadows*, 1972) and finally to nemesis and impending age (*Bring Forth the Body*, 1974, and *The Survivors*, 1976).

English *romans fleuves* of the last century have tended to be elegiac, for obvious reasons. The horror of World War I, the breakdown of traditional society during the interwar years and its complete reinvention in the postwar period were deeply traumatic to the upper middle class from whose ranks so many serious novelists came. Siegfried Sassoon's and Ford Madox Ford's novel sequences record that trauma with bleak eloquence. *A Dance to the Music of Time*, subtly, and Evelyn Waugh's *Sword of Honour*, rather less subtly, lamented the end of what their authors perceived as a stable social order. Simon Raven tried, intermittently, to be elegiac too, for he bitterly regretted the decay of the ritualistic, male-oriented society in which he grew up and to whose institutions—public school, Army, cricket, university—he was romantically attached.

But Raven was a little too cynical to pull off an affecting elegy. He was the Petronius of his generation, a cold-blooded satirist whose characters were compilations of various appetites and ambitions rather than living beings: if his novels were to be represented graphically, they would perhaps constitute a crude, cartoonish, somewhat pornographic decorative frieze rather than aspiring to the Poussinesque melancholy of Powell's elegant books. And the resemblance to Petronius extends to the personal as well as the literary, with Tacitus's description of the author of the *Satyricon* perfectly applicable to the unregenerate Raven: "By his dissolute life he had become as famous as other men by a life of energy, and he was regarded as no ordinary profligate, but as an accomplished voluptuary. His feckless freedom of speech, being regarded as frankness, procured him popularity."

Simon Raven occasionally wrote about his life, most notably in *Shadows on the Grass* (1981), a memoir which has the dubious distinction of being, in the opinion of E. W. Swanton, "the filthiest book on cricket" ever written. ("Can I quote you on that, Jim?," Raven asked eagerly.) But even more delightful is Michael Barber's *The Captain: The Life and Times of Simon Raven* (1996), a wonderfully hilarious biography which is, rather sadly, better than anything Raven himself ever wrote. But since the persistence of the Raven cult is due more to Raven's personality than to his gifts, which were beguiling but minor, this is acceptable, and Barber more than does his subject justice. His affection for the disreputable writer is obvious, and it is impossible for his reader not to share it, for Raven, for all his vaunted snobbery, intolerance, and amorality, was essentially a sweet man.

Simon Arthur Noel Raven was the grandson of a Victorian industrialist who had made a fortune in the manufacture of socks. His father, Arthur, lived off this fortune and frittered it away over the course of his life until there was very little left for Simon and his two younger siblings. Raven describes his childhood as "middle-class, for which read respectable, prying, puritanical, penny-pinching, joyless."

His intelligence and precocious facility with the classical languages was evident very early, and he won the top scholarship to Charterhouse, where his academic success continued. Raven never ceased to be grateful for his classical education, which imparted not only a tremendous verbal facility, thanks to constant exercises in translation, but a comprehensive and multi-layered worldview. The upper layer, a schoolmaster's version of Hellenism that was propagated in the public schools, Raven described in the following manner in *The Decline of the Gentleman* (1961):

First, the truth must be sought honestly and with intelligence on every level, and must be prized above convenience and even perhaps above freedom itself, because it is not made by man but exists independently of him. . . . One comes at the truth by logic, patience, and fairmindedness. From which it follows, by extension, that one should always be *moderate*. . . . With moderation comes tolerance. . . . Being free meant that you were not "*servile*," i.e. . . . that subject to the general good you did not have to do anything against your will and must not, as a point of honour, do anything for monetary gain. . . . Pericles expressed stern views about women: They should be heard of, he said, neither for good nor ill. . . . [T]he Greeks strongly disapproved of inflated pride. . . . They took the view that anyone who became too pleased with himself or thought himself too clever would be punished by the gods with disgrace and ruin.

This simplified and sanitized Hellenism was developed for the purpose of civilizing cross public schoolboys, and designed to harmonize with Christianity: the Greeks were presented as proto-Christians, lacking only the knowledge of Christ to make them perfect. But there were layers beneath layers, and to those with sufficient intellect and curiosity the classical authors also delivered an unsanitized, definitely un- and anti-Christian message, entirely subversive of public school values; Raven sucked this up greedily.

Here was Horace, openly boasting of how he ran away from a battle. Tacitus, quietly equating enthusiasm with stupidity. Thucydides, grimly announcing that the only law of human affairs was "Necessity." Lucretius, recommending regular one-night stands as a way of securing immunity from passion, which was simply the unwholesome and ridiculous product of suppressed or thwarted lust. Catullus, advocating sex with women or sex with boys, whichever you fancy at the time, because there is no such thing as right or wrong in this context. . . . *All* of them insistent that you take what pleasure you can from this world because only superstitious fools believe in the existence of the next.

Both versions of Hellenism were to mold his character. He remained, from school days on, doggedly pagan, "ready," as he put it, "to back Greek reason against 'revealed truth' any day of the week." In all his novels he honored Greek themes—the irresistible forces of Retribution and Necessity are often given a central position, and he did not underestimate the power of the Furies—and understood that the gods must be placated; but he had little use for God the Father or His putative son: "Christ asked for everything he got," remarks Captain Detterling, one of the many characters in *Alms for Oblivion* who tend to serve as mouthpieces for the author's own thoughts. The best Raven was ever to say of Christianity was that Anglicanism at any rate is "a quiet and decent superstition, as they go, offering a wide choice in decoration and no poisonous enthusiasms."

Raven was a brilliant schoolboy but in no way a model one, for he took the advice of Lucretius and Catullus rather more literally than his masters would have liked. Sexually, he had catholic tastes, no inhibitions whatever, and scant respect for the moral code imposed by the school. He made countless conquests among the other boys and enjoyed "a number of experiences," as he later boasted, "far more erotic (and poetic) than the perfunctory grabbing and snatching and jerking depicted on Greek vases." Raven's school adventures are depicted in *Fielding Gray*, the most autobiographical novel in *Alms for Oblivion*, but X-rated as the novel is, the reality seems to have been even more so. In the end even the tolerance of Charterhouse's long-suffering headmaster was exhausted, and Raven, although he had won his First XI Cricket colors and a scholarship to King's, was expelled.

For a few weeks, he said, he felt "like Adam and Eve did when they had to do a proper day's work." Like his alter-ego Fielding Gray, he had hoped and expected to become "a wining and dining don. A witty, worldly, *comfortable* don." Would Cambridge still have him? He was now to learn one of the most important lessons of his life: "I got a commission, joined clubs and took up my place at King's as if nothing had happened. People just giggled when they learnt I'd been sacked for 'the usual thing.' . . . One trembled in fear of the last trump and all that sounded was a wet fart."

With his compulsory term of military service impending, Raven joined the Parachute Regiment and was soon shipped to Bangalore as an Officer Cadet. In this capacity Raven set the pattern for his later behavior as an officer in the Regular Army: "He had this romantic, Edwardian view of what being a subaltern entailed," said Raven's Charterhouse and Army friend James Prior (later Lord Prior, longtime Cabinet Minister under Margaret Thatcher and the model for *Alms for Oblivion*'s opportunistic Peter Morrison). "It was vital to look the part—carry a swagger stick and wear kid gloves. . . . You were there to lead your platoon over the top in the event of a fight. Otherwise, it was a case of 'Carry on, sergeant.'"

But it was 1947 and the Raj was winding up its business in undignified haste; "One got a crash course in the sudden fall of Imperial greatness," Raven remarked. It was a richly symbolic historical moment at which Raven was given a ringside seat, and the novel it produced, *Sound the Retreat*, is the finest volume of *Alms for Oblivion*: full of irony, compassion (a rare quality in Raven's work), and featuring the strongest and most memorable character in the sequence, the colorful Muslim officer Gilzai Khan.

Raven duly took his place at King's in 1948. The post-war climate was anti-elitist and leveling, rife with progressive dogma, and King's was particularly "pink" in shade; one might have thought that Raven, with his rapidly hardening conservative attitudes, would have rebelled. Yet as he acknowledged, the college's very pinkness presented distinct advantages to himself: "Nobody minded what you did in bed or what you said about God, a very civilized attitude in 1948."

Raven was undiscriminating in his sexual tastes, and Cambridge offered these more scope than Charterhouse had done: one disgruntled Newnham girl was overheard saying, "I'm not going to bed with Simon ever again. One day it's Boris, then a choral scholar, then it's me, then it's back to Boris again. No!" Raven was a promiscuous bisexual who on balance favored boys and young men over women. Nevertheless, he managed to knock up a recent graduate, Susan Kilner.

This was a potential disaster, for he prized his independence above everything else. (Two of his early novels, *Doctors Wear Scarlet* [1960] and *Close of Play* [1962], feature characters who take this desperate need for personal independence to violent extremes.) So, as Raven remembers it, "I said, 'Right ho, I'll marry you. That'll keep your family happy. But I won't live with you—ever.' Very caddish of me, I agree. But I knew, you see, that if ever there were a born bachelor, it was me. And Susan accepted this. She was a brick." Although he kept in touch with Susan and their son, Adam, for the rest of his life, and would eventually foot the bill for Adam's education, they did not seriously impinge on his resolutely single life.

At the end of his undergraduate career Raven was awarded the Studentship (that is, graduate fellowship) he coveted. But extended scholarly endeavor turned out, perhaps not surprisingly, to go against his nature. "Scholarship was one thing, drudgery another. I very soon concluded that nothing would induce me to read, let alone make notes on, hundreds and hundreds of *very, very, very* boring books."

How then to make a living? Raven was by now earning a small income reviewing books for the *Listener*, under the aegis of the legendary J. R. Ackerley, but his first novel had been rejected, business ("money-grubbing") was beyond the social Pale, and schoolmastering was impossible, "because I was on every blacklist in existence." He ended up joining the Regular Army with backdated seniority, attaching himself to the smart King's Own Shropshire Light Infantry.

Raven spent three years in the Army, serving in Germany (his experiences there would go into *The Sabre Squadron*) and in Kenya against the

Mau Mau (a conflict which, fictionalized, became the backdrop for his first novel, *The Feathers of Death* [1959]). He looked at the British Army, even in its decline, in a highly romantic light: "although there was more in him of Alcibiades than Achilles," comments Barber, "he retained a sentimental attachment to the Homeric ideal."

It became rapidly apparent that he was far too lazy to make a decent field commander. "I loved the Army as an institution and loathed every single thing it required me to do," he later said. A brother-officer remembers that "Captain Raven settled down to organize his life, believing that ability to delegate authority was the true mark of a leader of men. He speedily delegated 100% of his." His most significant achievements were to effect an improvement in the food, and to set up "a rough and ready knocking shop" for the men. A middle-class man trying to lead an upper-class life, he ran up massive debts and had to leave the Army hurriedly: he would later recreate his ejection from the cozy Regiment into a cold world in his 1959 novel *Brother Cain*.

"And so, at the age of thirty," Raven wrote in *The Decline of the Gentleman* (1961), "I had successively disgraced myself with three fine institutions, each of which had made me free of its full and rich resources, had trained me with skill and patience, and had shown me nothing but forbearance and charity when I failed in trust." He now fell back on his last resource: writing. "For in a literary career there was one unfailing advantage: No degree whatever of moral or social disgrace could disqualify one from practice—and indeed a bad character, if suitably tricked out for presentation, might win one helpful publicity."

He embarked on a rackety, hand-to-mouth Grub Street life, described fairly faithfully in the early career of Tom Llewellyn, the unwashed intellectual in *Alms for Oblivion*. He enjoyed some success, but his weakness for gambling, drinking, and overeating quickly took control of his life, and physical deterioration followed apace. J. R. Ackerley provides a memorable portrait of the prematurely aging Raven:

> A disaster has happened to him, I fear [Ackerley informed E. M. Forster]; he has got plump. His one-time crowning glory, that abundant Titian hair, crinkles thinly and gingerly now above a fat pink face, with creases of fat about the eyes. . . . Suede boots, and a loose, short, shapeless, not very clean camel-hair coat—or would it be called duffle? He looked like the kind of person who asks for a light in the Long Bar of the Trocadero and to whom one replies with only a regretful mutter as one edges away. . . . He has his intelligence still, and indeed his charm and warmth of manner, but I did not accompany him to his homosexual club.

Raven seemed set on a course of complete self-destruction, but salvation now appeared in the guise of his publisher, Anthony Blond. "This is the last hand-out you get," Blond told him. "Leave London, or leave my employ." Blond offered his feckless client generous terms: if he would move at least fifty miles from London, Blond would pay him a steady £15 and settle the following bills: dentist, tailor, nightly dinner at a restaurant and, within reason, wine merchant. Raven obeyed without a moment's argument, moving to Deal, in Kent, where his brother Myles was teaching at a preparatory school. He was, to his own surprise, immediately happy.

The removal from London revealed a surprising side to Raven's character: the steady worker. The rake who lived for pleasure disappeared and was replaced by a worker bee of extremely regular habits. He would write all morning, read in the afternoons, dine at a nearby hotel and spend the evening at the local pub with Myles and his schoolmaster friends. Under this regimen he produced a huge quantity of work.

His motto was "Art for art's sake, money for God's sake," and not all of his large output was of the highest quality. He took on the daunting task of producing a second *roman fleuve* for instance, *The First-Born of Egypt*, only for financial reasons. It was a continuation, of sorts, of *Alms for Oblivion*, but Raven had long since run out of ideas and material and was excruciatingly bored during the writing process ("How can I go on with this?" he frequently asked himself. "Please God, let me win a football pool"); the boredom shows, badly, in the final product. But somewhere along the way Raven had acquired a professional attitude, and his television plays, notably the BBC adaptation of Trollope's *Palliser* novels and other adaptations of books by Iris Murdoch, Nancy Mitford, and Aldous Huxley, were very fine indeed. He possessed in fact a natural gift for adaptation, a technical skill he likened to translating in and out of Latin.

In middle age he preferred, by his own admission, "a good dinner to a good fuck." When in funds he enjoyed treating his friends to expensive meals, paying the bill with a flourish: when out of them he never economized *too* radically. A friend remembers him, in dire straits, saying "Well, dear, I'm going to be hellish mean. I'm not going to take anyone out to dinner." "What about you?" said the friend. "Are you going to go on taking yourself out to dinner?" "Oh yes, dear, I'm not going to be *miserly*."

RAVEN SPENT HIS last years in Sutton's Hospital, an alms house for impoverished old gentlemen, long connected with Charterhouse, which gave precedence to "decrepit or old Captaynes either at Sea or Land" and "Souldiers maymed or ympotent." It was hard to get a place there, and although at this point Raven was certainly "ympotent" he was neither decrepit nor maimed. But he managed to talk his way in, and so ended his days contentedly enough, in yet another all-male club.

Although he readily and even happily admitted to being no gentleman, Raven revered the gentleman as an ideal and mourned his passing, for the modern age, he believed, had rejected the gentleman and everything he represented. "Gentlemen can now only behave as such, or be tolerated as such, in circumstances that are manifestly contrived or unreal," he asserted in *The Decline of the Gentleman*: in anachronistically hierarchical institutions, that is, like the military.

He illustrates this contention in the career of Peter Morrison, one of the protagonists of *Alms for Oblivion*. Morrison has all the trappings of the gentleman, certainly. The eldest son of an old East Anglia family, Morrison inherits substantial estates, distinguishes himself in the Indian Army at the time of Independence, enjoys a happy and monogamous marriage, and serves for many years as a Conservative M.P., eventually becoming Minister of Commerce. Yet he is subtly, without even knowing it himself, a hypocrite and an opportunist, and always manages to further his own interests while leaving his "honour"—a flexible term in his case, as in most of ours—intact. "Oh, he likes to do the right thing," observes Detterling; "to be seen to do the right thing, and even to believe it himself, if he possibly can. But he's got a lot of shit in his tanks."

Morrison's antipode is the Machiavellian journalist and politician Somerset Lloyd-James (thought by many readers to resemble Raven's former schoolfellow Lord Rees-Mogg). Lloyd-James also comes from a "good" family and has received a gentleman's education, but unlike Morrison he feels no obligation to uphold the gentleman's creed: he is openly unscrupulous and grasping, relishing the brute struggle for power and influence. A practicing Catholic, he habitually resorts to Jesuitical casuistry in dubious justification of whatever shady deal he might have in mind at the moment.

In their early thirties, the two men compete for the Conservative candidacy for the Parliamentary seat of Bishop's Cross. Morrison is in every way the superior candidate—*apparently*: three years previously, during the Suez crisis, he had resigned from Parliament because, while he disapproved of the government's actions, he didn't want to show a lack of support for the Army, to which he remained loyal: it was a complicated matter of personal conscience, in other words, surely commendable, showing rare delicacy in a politician. But while Morrison congratulates himself, others can see behind the façade of high principle. Fielding Gray castigates Morrison as "a pompous, self-satisfied prig. All this prate about duty and honour and loyalty, and not a row of beans to show for it." Sir Edwin Turbot, a Whitehall power-broker, opines that "Lloyd-James is pretty foul, I grant you that. But he does things. He doesn't sit around moaning about his honour." And the political grandee Lord Canteloupe, one of Raven's finest and most robust creations, frankly prefers working with a "howling shit" like Lloyd-James: "For the great thing about shits," he reflects, "was that they got on with it (provided the price was right) and didn't ask damn silly questions."

Idealism and realism are at war throughout *Alms for Oblivion*, with Raven reserving all the heavy artillery for use against idealism. ("Idealists are far more dangerous than criminals," says the mathematician Daniel Mond, the only character in *Alms for Oblivion* who can be said to represent the Good. "Criminals stop when they've got what they wanted. Idealists never stop because they can never attain their ideal.") Lord Canteloupe, the personification of appetite and greed, is the series's great realist, for better and for worse. He makes his first appearance in *Friends in Low Places*: having turned the grounds of his Stately Home into a profitable theme park, in the manner of the Duke of Bedford, he receives an offer to advise the government on a project for morally uplifting public entertainment. His ideas on the subject are worth quoting:

> "Now what about this? Government-sponsored caravan sites for holidays. Make a filthy mess of some well-known beauty spot—they'll love that— and then publish a lot of balls about The People enjoying its Rights in the Countryside, that kind of blab. Jam the bloody caravans as close together as possible—you know how they love being crowded—make a song and dance about being good neighbours, give a prize for the best behaved family, and perhaps throw in compulsory P.T."

Lord Canteloupe is manifestly *not* a gentleman: he is an aristocrat, a class for which Raven shows little mercy. "Whereas the gentleman always seeks to deserve his position," Raven observed, "the aristocrat, disdainful and insouciant, is quite happy just to exploit it." A rare (and refreshing) bird among conservative English authors of the last century, Raven displayed no romantic nostalgia for an aristocracy in picturesque decline.

Alms for Oblivion contains quite a number of selfish aristocrats, like Canteloupe, and pseudo-gentlemen, like Morrison: what it does *not* contain are very many *real* gentlemen. In fact these are so thin on the ground that one is tempted to wonder whether in Raven's scheme of things the genuine article actually exists, or is, instead, merely an intellectual abstraction. A few characters fit the bill in the moral department, but none of them, significantly, is an *English* gentleman in the traditional sense: Daniel

Mond, a Jew; the Muslim Gilzai Khan; Tom Llewellyn, of lowly Welsh origins; Piero, a teenaged Italian prostitute. Fielding Gray, who claims to live by the code of officer and gentleman, is far too tainted a character to qualify as the latter.

Raven's *Weltanschauung*—what one friend called his "Regency, cynical, materialistic outlook"—made for some fine comedy, but its limitations became evident when something more was called for, real emotion or strength. He always maintained that his classical education had inoculated him against love. He was probably right, but the resulting immunity did not always work to his advantage. The lack of love harms his writing: all his books share a tiresome coarseness and a tendency to sentiment. No one in all the enormous cast of *Alms for Oblivion* is the least bit emotionally affecting, except for the gallant and witty Gilzai Khan. As for the female characters, they are all of one type, the slavering nymphomaniac: Raven's was a man's world, and he could see women only as unwelcome intruders.

At one point in the sequence Raven has Fielding Gray articulate his professional creed.

> "I never said I was an artist. I am an entertainer. . . . I arrange words in pleasing patterns in order to make money. I try to give good value—to see that my patterns are well wrought—but I do not delude myself by inflating the nature of my function. I try to be neat, intelligent and lucid: let others be 'creative' or 'inspired.'"

Is this how Raven saw his own writerly task? For the philosophy is spurious, of course: entertainers, if they are any good, must also be artists, and a lack of creativity or inspiration is just as fatal to their results as it would be to a more artistic (*un*entertaining?) writer. Raven too often makes the reader feel that he is simply setting up some formal and hypothetical situation and then inserting his characters into it.

Michael Barber compared Raven's work with a ball at Versailles: "all that pomp and glitter and finery while the chamber pots overflow in every corner." Raven's fascination with smut for its own sake is undoubtedly entertaining, but in the end it contributed to the work's one-dimensionality. His friend Christopher Moorson thought the novels were like a weird combination of Henty and Huysmans. "Reading these," he observed to Anthony Blond, "is like eating your way through a cake which is made of chestnuts, and covered with layers of cream and treacle." To which Blond replied: "Yes, *and* covered with shit, my dear."

April 2003

The Seriousness of Yvor Winters

David Yezzi

Though night is always close, complete negation
Ready to drop on wisdom and emotion,
Night from the air or the carnivorous breath,
Still it is right to know the force of death,
And, as you do, persistent, tough in will,
Raise from the excellent the better still.
—Thom Gunn, "To Yvor Winters, 1955"

W ITH A FEW WEIGHTY exceptions, the bulk of poetry's greatest critics in America in this century have also been its practitioners. Such poet-critics, many associated (rightly or wrongly) with the New Criticism, brought to their writings on verse an artisan's supple hand and the fruits of a rigorous apprenticeship in the craft of making poems: the essays of each, like windows at Chartres, display their sponsors' guild affiliation some way in the corner. As critics, they hove close to the nuances of poetic facture; as poets, to a scholar's exhaustive knowledge of the progress of poetry in English.

TAKE AS A MEASURE of the relative wealth of first-rate poetry and poetry criticism in the Thirties and Forties the initial volume of John Crowe Ransom's *Kenyon Review* (1939), which featured work from Randall Jarrell, Allen Tate, R. P. Blackmur, Yvor Winters, Muriel Rukeyser, John Berryman, and Robert Lowell (who, like Jarrell and Berryman, was still in his twenties). That the ranks of poet-critics today have thinned seems inevitable given the breadth of that antecedent outpouring; to be sure, the standard has been borne into the Nineties, in America and elsewhere—not least of all by Seamus Heaney, Donald Hall, and Joseph Brodsky—but the diminution is palpable all the same.

If this falling off constitutes an injury to poetry, the added insult is the unavailability of much of the writing from that fecund earlier period. As a corrective, *The Advocates of Poetry: A Reader of American Poet-Critics of the Modernist Era* (University of Arkansas Press, 1996), a collection of essays by American poet-critics after T. S. Eliot and Ezra Pound, has been edited by R. S. Gwynn, himself an essayist and poet. In addition to pieces by several poet-critics already mentioned, returned to the spotlight are works by Robert Penn Warren, Louise Bogan, Robert Hayden, Kenneth Burke, Elder Olson, Delmore Schwartz, and John Ciardi. As Gwynn points out in his Introduction, a situation no longer exists where the dual role of the poet-critic is seen as a responsibility, where, in Lowell's words, critics such as "Allan Tate, Eliot, Blackmur, and Winters . . . were very much news. You waited for their essays, and when a good critical essay came out it had the excitement of a new imaginative work."

OF THESE, Yvor Winters, perhaps, has fallen furthest. This is a great shame, for it is just Winters's brand of seriousness and his emphasis on reason in poetry that contemporary verse sorely wants. The current neglect may have as much to do with his crabbed, sometimes contradictory and dogmatic style. Winters's stern call for a "moral poetry" was provocative, while his more cracked judgments earned him the opprobrium of many who, like Stanley Edgar Hyman in *The Armed Vision* (1947), saw Winters as "an excessively irritating and bad critic of some importance."

Randall Jarrell was likewise divided in his estimation of Winters. From one side of his mouth he pronounced in *The New York Times* that "Winters' clear, independent and serious talent has produced criticism that no cultivated person can afford to leave unread." And from the other, in an unpublished lecture lately exhumed for an issue of *The Georgia Review*, Jarrell suggests that Winters's criticism

> should be classified, in his own terms, as a startlingly neoprimitive variety of neoclassicism, since in it he pretends to a simplicity, a simple-mindedness, that is not naturally his but that has been imported from another age at the great cost of everyone concerned. Mr. Winters' critical method reminds me of Blake and his wife sitting naked in their garden, pretending to be Adam and Eve.

Of Winters's "The Experimental School in American Poetry," which Jarrell notes has "been praised as the critical feat of the time," he gripes, "There is a sort of brutal frivolity about it: it is so disorganized, arbitrary, and obviously inadequate as to be unworthy both of the subject and Mr. Winters."

Hyman, too, picks up on this brutal strain in Winters, whose method he locates in the broad scythe-strokes of the evaluator. Lesser poets (who often had the greatest reputations) were mown down in order that others more in line with Winters's view of poetry might flourish. When weighing the value of a particular poet, Winters proceeded with the imperiousness of, as Denis Donoghue has euphemistically put it, "a mind assertively made up." As Hyman notes, Winters's poetic taxonomies could be perfunctory in the extreme: "He gives only his conclusions, almost never with any evidence approaching adequacy, and in a form in which it is not possible to argue with him or even understand what he is trying to say." What's more, the evaluative critic "can be saved from falling into either priggishness or pontifical foolishness only by being invariably right. There should be no need to point out that Winters is hardly that."

The litany of Winters's more eccentric *obiter dicta* has been well rehearsed by Hyman and others: he felt, for example, that Charles Churchill, "the greatest poetic talent" of the mid-eighteenth century, was wrongfully passed over for Collins and Gray; F. G. Tuckerman and Jones Very were, along with Dickinson, two of the three "greatest poets of the nineteenth century" (take *that* Keats, Wordsworth, et al.); Edith Wharton's novel *The Age of Innocence* is superior to any one novel by Austen, Melville, or Henry James; Robert Bridges is a better poet than Eliot, Hart Crane, William Carlos Williams, or Marianne Moore; while the poetry of T. Sturge Moore, a correspondent and friend of Yeats, outstrips that of his prominent pen pal.

If Winters exalted some unexpected candidates to his personal pantheon, he regularly barred those generally thought to be of the first water. While by no means exhausting the list, René Wellek has compiled a roster of Winters's broadest condemnations. A snippet from just those dealing with the nineteenth century argues that "Coleridge . . . is 'merely one of the indistinguishably bad poets of an unfortunate period,'"; "Tennyson 'has nothing to say, and his style is insipid'; Browning is 'fresh, brisk, shallow, and journalistic'; Arnold 'sentimental to the point of being lachrymose.'" Here one perceives the glint of genuine insight flashing from those bared teeth, though the uniformity of Winters's denouncement of the nineteenth century is unlikely to find many wholeheartedly sympathetic readers.

The poet Robert Pinsky, who studied with Winters at Stanford University, recounts the ridicule the "Old Man" faced even from some of his own students. In the twentieth section of Pinsky's poem "Essay on Psychiatrists," a defiant, self-aware Winters is ventriloquized through the voice of the professor:

. . . "I know why you are here.

You are here to laugh. You have heard of a crazy
Old man who believes that Robert Bridges
Was a great poet; who believes that Fulke

Greville was a great poet, greater than Philip
Sydney; who believes that Shakespeare's Sonnets
Are not all that they are cracked up to be. . . ."

Winters was loyal to his favorite students, however, often crediting them
with knitting together the strands of a rational, plain-spoken poetic, which
had been frayed so violently by the associative tendencies of the Romantic
tradition. Winters makes room at the top of his critical ladder for students
and colleagues such as Thom Gunn, J. V. Cunningham, Edgar Bowers, N.
Scott Momaday, Donald Stanford, and his wife, Janet Lewis—a few of
them excellent poets, but a dubious, nepotistic list. In turn his students
have lauded their mentor in book-length studies and essays, as well as in
memoirs by Gunn, Donald Hall, and Turner Cassity. As a tribute, Pinsky
dedicated his critical work *The Situation of Poetry* to Winters.

Never wanting for detractors, Winters's reputation has to a large extent
had to rely for its perpetuation on a claque of devoted disciples, increasingly so as the whole generation of critics succumbed to an ebbing of interest in their brand of criticism. Nevertheless, as both a description of its
enduring ills and a prescription for regaining much that has been lost to the
lyric tradition in English, Winters's bitter pill is our long-overlooked and
strongest medicine.

Born on October 17, in Chicago, (Arthur) Yvor Winters (1900–1968)
grew up in Eagle Rock, California, with his parents and maternal grandmother, who taught him to read, at the age of four, out of the works of
Macaulay. In 1917 he became a founding member of the University of
Chicago Poetry Club, though his undergraduate studies were interrupted in
the fall of 1918 by the onset of tuberculosis. A fair-weather cure brought
him eventually to St. Vincent's Sanatorium (and later to Sunmount Sanatorium) in Sante Fe, where, despite the distance, Winters maintained contact with his Chicago circle, including Janet Lewis, his future wife. Lewis,
herself a poet of considerable accomplishment, had joined the Poetry Club
in 1919. When she, too, was diagnosed with tuberculosis, Winters arranged
for her to tutor at Sunmount in exchange for her residence there in 1922.
He took a B.A. and an M.A. in Romance languages and Latin from the
University of Colorado—the place again dictated by his health. In 1935

Winters received his Ph.D. from Stanford, where he would remain as a teacher until 1966. His seven major critical works were from these years: *Primitivism and Decadence: A Study of American Experimental Poetry* (1937); *Maule's Curse: Seven Studies in the History of American Obscurantism* (1938); *The Anatomy of Nonsense* (1943) — these first three gathered in 1947 as *In Defense of Reason*; *Edwin Arlington Robinson* (1946); *The Function of Criticism: Problems and Exercises* (1957); *Forms of Discovery: Critical and Historical Essays on the Forms of the Short Poem in English* (1967); and the posthumous *Uncollected Essays and Reviews* (1976).

Winters began, however, as a poet. During his years in sanatoriums, he wrote the majority of the poems that would compose his first two collections, *The Immobile Wind* (1921) and *The Magpie's Shadow* (1922). In these books, Winters followed the Imagist tradition of Pound and had, by the time of his first book "definitely given up rhymed verse except for short excursions." (For this and for further biographical material, see the exhibition catalogue *The Strength of Art: Poets and Poetry in the Lives of Yvor Winters and Janet Lewis*, prepared by Brigitte Hoy Carnochan [Stanford University, 1984].) For the young poet, free verse was "more interesting and more challenging. I truly believe that it can be used for practically anything for which one can use rhymed." It was at this time that he characterized poetry as escapism: "a permanent gateway to walking oblivion." As the poet and critic Dick Davis has pointed out, though, Winters quickly repented such youthful vagaries and turned "from oblivion to definition," adding that his work had "also taken on a moral dimension": "the verse he admired and wrote in his early twenties was arational, minimal, and concrete; his later work is rational, discursive, and to a large degree abstract."

This extreme about-face was not only galvanizing, it was permanent; Winters would remain on this tack through his last published works of poetry and criticism. The shift toward the rational, while worked out over some years, was relatively abrupt, given how thoroughly it pervaded every aspect of his thought and practice. If Winters's newly won opinions put readers on their guard in the Thirties, they would fairly provoke riots in classrooms today. When asked by Stanford professors at his orals if he was an absolutist, Winters replied, "Yes, I am, relatively speaking," which was to say that compared to his adjudicators he certainly was. In the Introduction to *Primitivism and Decadence*, he mapped his territory as an anti-Romantic and a combatant of relativism:

> The Romantic theory of human nature teaches that if man will rely upon his impulses, he will achieve the good life. When this notion is combined, as it frequently is, with a pantheistic philosophy or religion, it commonly

teaches that through surrender to impulse man will not only achieve the good life but will achieve a kind of mystical union with the Divinity: this for example is the doctrine of Emerson. Literature thus becomes a form of self-expression. . . .

The theory of literature I defend . . . is absolutist. I believe that the work of literature, in so far as it is valuable, approximates a real apprehension and communication of a particular kind of objective truth.

Emerson was Winters's long-standing *bête noire*, a propounder of such untenable notions as "no man, no matter how ignorant of books, need be perplexed in his speculations." Winters characterized Emerson's view of art as resting "on the assumption that man should express what he is at any given moment." The dangers to poetry from self-expression of this kind are both technical and thematic: the poet is caught between the rocks of a first-thought-best-thought brand of automatism, where every word is judged worthy that reflects a "spontaneous impression," and the whirlpool of ideas linked only by loose association, where "extemporary performances" overbear the desire to deepen one's understanding through carefully reasoned contemplation.

Emerson receives such exhaustive attention from Winters in part because he is American, and thereby a localizer of Romanticism, but Emerson is not the watershed of such views, merely a tributary onto native soil. Winters traces the antirational tradition—the genesis of which he places in the early 1700s—to two basic doctrines:

the sentimentalism of the third Earl of Shaftesbury (later summarized by Pope, along with other ideas, in the *Essay on Man*), and the doctrine of the association of ideas, a psychological doctrine having its beginnings in Hobbes and formulated by Locke, a doctrine translated into literary theory by Addison and discussed interminably in the eighteenth century.

To say nothing of the nineteenth, where, for Winters, such ideas undermined an entire school of poets who had turned away from the study of experience through reason. The rise of the subjective view of art in the eighteenth century was radicalized in the nineteenth as Romanticism, of which Emerson's is an extreme American version. As far as Winters was concerned, of the Romantic poets the less said the better—unless, of course, one spoke up to denigrate them.

Perhaps haunted by the excesses and death of his friend Hart Crane (whom he called "a saint of the wrong religion"), Winters identified the psychic destruction at work on three centuries of poets:

From the eighteenth century onward, and not, so far as I can recollect, before, we have had a high incidence of madness among poets of more or less recognized talent: Collins, Gray, Chatterton, Smart, Blake, and others later; the same thing happens in other languages. A psychological theory which justifies the freeing of emotions and which holds rational understanding in contempt appears to be sufficient to break the minds of a good many men with sufficient talent to take the theory seriously.

According to Winters, Crane was a genius who "ruined his life and his talent by living and writing" in the shadow of "the two great religious teachers of our nation," Emerson and Whitman. In 1932, the same year Crane ordered a large breakfast before vaulting over the side of an ocean liner, Winters published his only short story, "The Brink of Darkness," which has taken on the resonance of a spiritual manifesto. In it he describes a "hostile supernatural world," at once pernicious and unknowable, in which darkness hovers just beyond the illumination of the rational: "It was as if there were darkness evenly underlying the brightness of the air." This darkness he would later relate to such practices as hedonism, obscurantism, associationism, and incontinent emotionalism. In "Notes on Contemporary Criticism" (1929) from *Uncollected Essays*, Winters puts a diamond point on these "insidious" forces:

> The basis of evil is in emotion; Good rests in the power of rational selection in action, as a preliminary to which *the emotion in any situation must be as far as possible eliminated, and, in so far as it cannot be eliminated, understood*. . . . the end is a controlled and harmonious life [italics mine].

It is important to note that what Winters called for was not the complete eradication of emotion (an impossibility) but the elucidation of it. As his chief weapon against corrosive emotionalism, reason became a tenet of faith for Winters. What skulked outside the purview of the rational, the obscuring darkness at the margins of experience, held the supreme threat. His was not, however, a denial of such murky realms; in fact, far from being an innocent with regard to the deleterious darkness lying beyond reason, Winters keeps watch on just that verge of benightedness.

Winters's view of poetry, "the art of saying something about something in verse," can be condensed to one often-quoted statement: "The poem is a statement in words about a human experience." Even this simple aphorism, he realizes, draws a distinct line in the sand when "most of the philosophers of this century have been nominalists of one kind or another; they have written extensively to prove that nothing can be said in words, because words are conceptual and do not correspond to reality." Winters points out, however, that if reality or "the realm that our ancestors took to be real" is an illusion, it nonetheless follows certain set laws that we violate at our peril. It is in this realm that "we pass our daily lives, including our moral lives. . . . this illusion is our reality. I will hereafter refer to it as reality."

For Winters, poetry—and, in its concision, lyric, especially—is the highest linguistic expression because, in addition to the denotative aspects of words emphasized in other forms of writing, poetry makes particular use of the connotative ones, the two together composing the "total content" of language. For Winters, the purpose of poetry is to describe experience as precisely as possible. Connotation in poetry, then, acquires a "moral" dimension—to preserve clarity, connotation or "feeling" must be carefully controlled:

> The artistic process is one of moral evaluation of human experience, by means of a technique which renders possible an evaluation more precise than any other. The poet tries to understand his experience in rational terms, to state his understanding, and simultaneously to state, by means of the feelings we attach to words, the kind and degree of emotion that should properly be motivated by this understanding.

Though Winters used the term "morality" in various ways, this passage illustrates his reigning principle for how a poem should convey human experience. Here, the term "morality" refers to a fairly technical process of choosing the appropriate words for evaluating a given subject. Romantic poetry often employed associative logic, fuzzy revery, and words emotionally in excess of their subjects. The "moral" Wintersian poet controls emotion, releasing it through restraint. He aims to match the argument of the poem to the proper degree of emotion.

The critic's detractors who feel that Winters, through his adherence to reason, has squelched emotion have lost the gist. The connotations inherent in language are expressive of emotion; to this extent emotion is a great part of the point. The "morality" of poetry as Winters understood it lay in how emotion was not obliterated but managed. Emotion in excess of the motivating argument was contrary to the purpose of poetry, as it obscured the experience under consideration: "In so far as the rational statement is understandable and acceptable, and in so far as the feeling is properly motivated by the rational statement, the poem will be good."

What Winters considers the moral or "ethical" nature of poetry, though, has opened him up to misinterpretation. In *The New Criticism* (1941), John Crowe Ransom bobbles Winters's argument, suggesting that "if there is a poem without visible ethical content, as a merely descriptive poem for example, I believe he thinks it is negligible and off the line of real poetry." Winters fired back in his essay on Ransom from *The Anatomy of Nonsense*—he rarely missed an opportunity to rebut his detractors in print—that, yes, ethical interest is the sole poetic concern, but a descriptive poem in its contemplation of some small nook of human experience perforce contains a moral element that it is the poet's job to evaluate. "Morality" in poetry, as Winters intends it, then, is a slippery beast. The morality of a poem is not confined to any ostensible ethical subject matter, but is found in the degree to which the poem adds to our accurate apprehension of experience.

This point may be clarified by looking at Winters's estimation of the infamously randy John Wilmot, Earl of Rochester (1647–1680). For Winters, it is not the lascivious earl's subject matter that determines his poems' moral qualities. Execution is all. Poetic "morality" lies in the propriety of emotion and the logical precision with which the poem is rendered. Even when Rochester writes of his debauchery in "Upon Drinking in a Bowl," there is grace and wit enough for Winters to recommend it as fine poetry—though one might hesitate to recount its rather louche topics. Opposed to this, Winters indicts other poems by Rochester on similar themes which "have a grossness of feeling comparable to his worst actions." The bad poems are not reprehensible for their content, but for their slipshod rendering of experience. Here Winters displays a distinct lack of squeamishness. In a similar vein, he counters Ransom's surprise that Winters should approve of Baudelaire given that his flowers are, after all, "flowers of evil": "The 'logical materials' of much of Baudelaire are no more evil than the materials of Shakespeare. The topics of both men are bad enough, for both explore human experience rather far; both depict evil as evil and make us know it as evil."

In the course of a reading life, one often stumbles on excellent prose writers never before encountered; such discoveries, however, are less likely in poetry. First-rate poetry is a more manageable quantity. Unlike with prose, it is possible to read all, or virtually all, of the decent verse in the language. Winters had done just that, and, having developed a basis for evaluation, proceeded in his last book, *Forms of Discovery*, through the entire history of poetry in English. The best section from this book, perhaps Winters's greatest single essay, began as a piece on sixteenth-century verse for *Poetry* and was expanded to chapter length and retitled "Aspects of the Short Poem in the English Renaissance." Save the "post-Symbolist" poetry of Wallace Stevens, which Winters deems the most versatile in the language, the poems of the Renaissance were for Winters unequaled, the peak from which he perceived a long decline.

True to form, Winters's critique of the poetry of the late sixteenth and early seventeenth centuries flouts convention and has the distinction of reclaiming an entire strain of early lyric poetry, namely that of the plain style. C. S. Lewis, in his Oxford *English Literature in the Sixteenth Century Excluding Drama*, rightly identifies the two major movements of the sixteenth century, the "Drab" and the "Golden." Winters recognizes in Lewis's choice of terms, however, the standard prejudice, which favors the "sugared" Petrarchanism of Sidney and Spenser over the native plain style of Barnabe Googe, George Gascoigne, Sir Walter Raleigh, and Ben Jonson. Lewis, he says, "blames modern scholars for approaching the period with Romantic prejudices, but he sees the entire poetry of the period in terms of a Romantic prejudice: he likes the pretty so profoundly that he overlooks the serious."

Winters's seriousness is his abiding characteristic. With regard to Horace's two-fold description of the purpose of poetry, to delight and instruct, Winters's preference seems clear. Take as an example of the plain-style seriousness that Winters championed this sixteenth-century lyric by Googe, "Of Money":

> Give money me, take friendship whoso list,
> For friends are gone come once adversity,
> When money yet remaineth safe in chest,
> That quickly can thee bring from misery.
> Fair face show friends, when riches do abound;
> Come time of proof, fare well they must away.
> Believe me well, they are not to be found
> If God but send thee once a lowering day.
> Gold never starts aside, but in distress,
> Finds ways enough to ease thine heavyness.

While very good, this is not among the greatest poems of the plain style (better would be Jonson's "To His Son" or Gascoigne's "Woodmanship"), yet it is typical in certain appealing respects. Such poems, for Winters, are good because they display themes "broad, simple, and obvious, even tending toward the proverbial, but usually a theme of some importance; a feeling restrained to the minimum required by the subject; a rhetoric restrained to a similar minimum" as opposed to the Petrarchan use of "rhetoric for its own sake." The argument of the poem is painstakingly logical and precise. The rhythm is restrained in its careful adherence to the metrical norm, a heavily stopped line, and a strong caesura.

Googe's tone expresses, here, a good degree of worldly melancholy which one suspects Winters valued, though it is for the poems of spiritual melancholy that he reserves his highest praise—Jonson's "To Heaven," George Herbert's "Church Monuments," and Fulke Greville's "Down in the depth of mine iniquity." For Winters, Greville in particular endeavored "with some consistency to employ the Petrarchan refinements, or such of them as he needed, on matter worthy of them." It is telling, I think, of Winters's own sensibility that he quotes the following passage from Greville, who wrote of himself in a life of his close friend Sir Philip Sidney:

> For my own part I found my creeping genius more fixed upon the images of life, than the images of wit, and therefore chose not to write to them on whose foot the black ox had not already trod, as the proverb is, but to those that are weather-beaten in the sea of this world, such as having lost sight of their gardens and groves, study to sail on a right course among rocks and quicksands.

The black ox of melancholy that had trod on Winters's critical writing finds in his poems its fullest and most affecting expression, yet his poetry, even more than his criticism, has fallen off the literary radar. In his review of Winters's *Collected Poems* (1960), Robert Lowell calls him "an immortal poet, a poet of great kindness and stamina." Lowell is perspicacious in naming many of Winters's finest efforts: "Time and the Garden," "John Sutter," "To a Military Rifle 1942," "A Dream Vision," "Sir Gawain and the Green Knight," "Hercules," and "The Marriage." Denis Donoghue assents to this list and offers several more: "Inscription for a Graveyard," "A Prayer for My Son," "A Fragment," and "A Testament." Then there is "The Slow Pacific Swell," to my mind his best.

To these fine poems one might add others such as "A Grave," included in *Collected Poems*. The poem begins, as does Herbert's "Church Monuments," with the contemplation of a grave, where the deceased waits alone "Under a little plaque": "There is no faintest tremor in that urn./ Each flake of ash is sure in its return" ("How tame these ashes are, how free from lust," Herbert writes). And, as with Herbert, the certainty of death prompts thoughts of mending one's life:

> What has he found there? Life it seems is this:
> To learn to shorten what has moved amiss;
> To temper motion till a mean is hit,
> Though the wild meaning would unbalance it;
> To stand, precarious, near the utter end;
> Betrayed, deserted, and alone descend,

Blackness before, and on the road above
The crowded terror that is human love;
To still the spirit till the flesh may lock
Its final cession in eternal rock.

Anyone skeptical as to Winters's access to emotional power need only reread the passage beginning "Betrayed. . . ." He continues:

Then let me pause in this symbolic air,
Each fiery grain immobile as despair,
Fixed at a rigid distance from the earth,
Absorbed each motion that arose from birth.
Here let me contemplate eternal peace,
Eternal station, which annuls release.
Here may I read its meaning, through the eye
Sear with effort, ere the body die.
For what one is, one sees not; 'tis the lot
Of him at peace to contemplate it not.

The poem hinges on movement. The "motion" of life in the earlier stanza suggested by the words *moved, motion, unbalance, precarious,* and *To still,* is countered with the stasis of death in *pause, immobile, fixed, rigid.* The contemplation of death affects a deathlike stillness in the speaker, from which vantage point he may look on life. The final couplet relates a bitter paradox: when one is in the throes of life, one cannot see life; when one is dead, the "wild meaning" is no longer a concern.

Winters's poems never hesitate to swing for the outfield wall. They do everything poems these days ought not to do: they tackle subjects other than the self, grapple with universals, follow strict prosodic norms, command a bold rhetorical tone, eschew imagery for abstraction, favor edification over pleasure. They are, in Winters's phrase, "Laurel, archaic, rude." If Winters's poems are forgotten, they have themselves to blame. They are extreme measures for poetry's present ills. Likewise, while its often unorthodox judgments can be hard to swallow whole, Winter's criticism reclaims for poetry a passionate control, and a spareness suited to our perennial concerns. After Winters, every line and every word may be held responsible to standards of emotional clarity. As with Rilke's archaic torso, or Winters's own "A Grave," when each of today's more fashionable, self-expressive, and wildly emotive poets looks on Winters's work, there is but one heartfelt message: you must change your life.

June 1997

The Last Critic?
The Importance of F. R. Leavis

Paul Dean

To AMERICAN READERS the name F. R. Leavis (1895–1978) may signify little more than half-remembered phrases and controversies—the Great Tradition, the Two Cultures—now surely, it might be thought, relegated to literary history. In England, Leavis's influence has waned but his name still evokes strong reactions, as the reviews of Ian MacKillop's new biography show (*F. R. Leavis: A Life in Criticism*; Allen Lane/The Penguin Press, 1995.) Leavis is variously described as "neurotic," "petty," "authoritarian," "impossibly haughty," exhibiting "suppressed hysteria" or "crazed paranoia"; he is mocked as "the good doctor," surrounded by "disciples," his life "claustrophobically book-based." As for his critical achievements, we hear from one writer that "he was often conspicuously wrong," from another that he made "often extraordinarily dumb judgements about fiction, such as the absurd idea that *Lady Chatterley* is better than *Women in Love*"—a valuation Leavis made in 1930 and withdrew in 1955 and again in 1961. Yet another reviewer refers to *Dickens the Novelist* (1970) as Leavis's "last major work," although there were three books left to come, all of them important. Of course, the reviewers all agree that the man they are treating with such personal contempt, patronizing distortion, and simple inaccuracy was fantasizing when he voiced the opinion that he was being misrepresented, or that some people considered themselves his enemies, or that the London literary establishment was out to get him. "They say I have persecution mania," he remarked once. "Comes of being persecuted, you know." An unimpeachable source.

Not that such viciousness was rare during Leavis's lifetime. Dr. MacKillop tells the story of the meeting which was arranged, at Leavis's request, to discuss the appointment of someone of whom he disapproved to the lectureship established in his honor after he had retired from full-time teaching at Cambridge. One of those turning up to the meeting, John Newton, said that he wanted to call Leavis a liar. Someone else said that this might kill Leavis: Newton replied, "Yes, but at least he'd die in the truth." I remember these (to me) shocking words whenever I read of Leavis's "vindictiveness."

I saw him only once, in 1972 when, persuaded to make the journey by a former pupil who was a senior faculty member at my university in the north of England, he came to give his lecture "Reading Out Poetry." The lecture room was packed to overflowing. At the appointed hour Leavis, then seventy-seven and looking it, was ushered in, still wearing a shabby fawn raincoat over his jacket. After the chairman's introduction he took from his briefcase a dog-eared manuscript which he began to read in a semi-audible monotone—a deliberate ploy, I later discovered, to frustrate those who had come expecting a "performance" rather than out of genuine interest in what he had to say. Nevertheless, there *was* a performance at one point. In pursuit of his contention that to arrive at a satisfactory reading-out of a great poem was in itself an act of interpretation, challenging all one's resources of intelligence and sensitivity, Leavis did some reading-out with interpolated commentaries. Eventually he came to the last speech of Othello. This prompted him to explain how he despised actors who treated Shakespeare as providing them with an opportunity to display their "eloquence"; and he mentioned with particular scorn Sir Laurence Olivier, whose performance as Othello had reportedly been influenced by Leavis's essay on the play. Then, raising his head and raking the room with still-magnificent eyes, he jerked out in increasingly *forte* bursts: "Olivier! That . . . old Etonian. . . *golden-voiced* . . . NARCISSUS!" (Olivier was not of course an old Etonian— Leavis was typecasting.) Since this was the only sentence everyone had been able to hear, there was laughter and applause. Leavis subsided, resuming his former quiet delivery. At the end of an hour he broke off with a weary gesture—"I must end there, my voice has gone." The chairman, somewhat nervously, invited questions. There were none. How could there be?

I didn't find the lecture impressive. I had only been at university a year, and didn't have the intellectual equipment to make a qualified judgment on Leavis. Worse, I didn't know I wasn't qualified, and mocked with the others. Only in reading him, subsequently, have I come to realize how well he described himself, in that lecture, when he characterized the good reader as

> the ideal executant musician, the one who, knowing it rests with him to re-create in obedience to what lies in black print on the white sheet in front of him, devotes all his trained intelligence, sensitiveness, intuition,

and skill to re-creating, reproducing faithfully what he divines his composer essentially conceived.[1]

Dr. MacKillop's is not an authorized biography. Denied access to crucial papers, he falls back too much on secondhand testimony, and his coverage of Leavis's life is patchy (for instance, there is no mention of the one visit Leavis and his wife made to the United States, in 1966). Much of his material necessarily consists of academic minutiae which could only be made gripping by a livelier style than his. Moreover, when he comes to the indisputably painful episodes in the lives of Leavis and his wife, Dr. Mac-Killop is compromised by a delicacy of feeling perfectly proper to an ex-pupil (which he is) but not ideal in a biographer. In the end, of course, the emphasis ought to be on what in fact Leavis achieved as a literary critic: but even here MacKillop, like almost everyone else, slights or ignores the books of the 1970s. His book is better than nothing, and it expands valuably the perspectives of the collection of essays edited by Denys Thompson, *The Leavises: Recollections and Impressions* (1984). However, it makes no reference to some important biographical essays published since then. It certainly does not represent a definitive account of Leavis's life and works.

Leavis was Cambridge born and bred. His father, a Victorian rationalist and "centre of human power" (the son's phrase), kept a piano shop opposite the gates of Downing College, which was later to be Leavis's center of operations for so many years. He went up to Emmanuel College, Cambridge, in 1914 on a scholarship to read history. After a year he joined the Friends' Ambulance Unit, in 1915, and was present at the Somme—an experience, rarely afterward alluded to, which left an indelible memory. It's not difficult to imagine how monstrously unreal academic History must have seemed to him on his return to Cambridge in 1919. He switched to English, then in its infancy as a degree subject, and graduated with first-class Honours in 1921—an achievement all the more astonishing when we know that his father died, following an accident, on the morning of his first examination paper. Despite his good degree, Leavis was not seen as a strong candidate for one of the scarce research fellowships. He embarked on a Ph.D., then a distinctly lowly career move for an aspiring academic. His thesis, on the relationship between literature and journalism in the eighteenth century, was supervised by the flamboyant professor of English

---

1 The lecture may be found in a posthumously published volume by Leavis, *Valuation in Criticism and Other Essays*, edited by G. Singh (Cambridge University Press, 1986). This also contains the first essays Leavis contributed to *The Cambridge Review* at the start of his career.

(and ex–Fleet Street man) Sir Arthur Quiller-Couch, and examined by George Saintsbury. It's striking to think of these sturdy Victorian figures, born respectively in 1863 and 1845, giving their blessing to Leavis's work; but then a case could be made for his being, in curious ways, closer to their world than might first appear.

After receiving his doctorate in 1924, Leavis must have thought a move to a lectureship would be swift; but circumstances went against him, and perhaps not only those, for Quiller-Couch had written privately of his pupil's "Self-Sufficiency" as an ominous trait: "no good fortune would easily equal his sense of his deserts." He subsisted on freelance teaching—"hand-to-mouth disease" as I. A. Richards called it—for a number of colleges; one of his pupils, Queenie Roth, became his wife in 1929. Dr. MacKillop cannot, for many reasons, do full justice to the figure of Mrs. Leavis. She was a more confidently ambitious person than her husband, and on the novel, in my view, a greater critic than he. Her Ph.D. thesis, published in 1932 as *Fiction and the Reading Public*, had been supervised by I. A. Richards, but relations between them, already uneasy, broke down when he failed to support her after her parents bitterly opposed her intention to marry outside the Jewish faith. Despite a string of brilliant scholarly publications (now mostly gathered in three volumes of her *Collected Essays*, published by Cambridge University Press), she never attained an official university teaching post; instead she continued freelancing, as well as playing a major role in the editing of *Scrutiny*, contributing officially and unofficially to her husband's books, and bringing up three children. Leavis was rather in awe of her; he described her as "the embodiment of passionate will," and once exclaimed, "They talk of the atom bomb—there's enough energy in my wife to blow Europe to pieces!" Certainly she worked with amazing intensity, especially when one remembers that she was for years gravely ill. Not all the biographical facts about Mrs. Leavis are available, and speculation would be impertinent, but there is enough to warrant the detection of a psychological pattern of rejection which became more pronounced with time.

For years the Leavises watched as their contemporaries, and eventually their juniors, blossomed in careers while they languished. Dr. MacKillop is surprisingly reluctant to endorse Leavis's belief that his progress was blocked by enemies within the Faculty. How else are we to explain the facts: that his appointment in 1932 was followed—in 1936—by only a part-time university lectureship which was not made full time until 1947, promotion to Reader (the next grade below full Professor) coming in 1959 when he was three years away from retirement? It was a ludicrously mean way in which to reward his achievements. Not until retirement did honorary chairs, at Wales and York, come his way; he endured years of financial hardship, with damaging consequences for his pension, on top of family problems (his wife's ill health, the breakdown and estrangement of one of their sons). In the face of all this he worked unremittingly, never taking a sabbatical term or a proper holiday, and publishing his last book at the age of eighty-one. Thereafter, until his death two years later, he slowly declined into senility. Dr. MacKillop gives a harrowing account of this sad period, during which Mrs. Leavis reported Leavis as saying, "I am wretched. I am in despair." He would often tell his pupils that Blake died singing. He himself, alas, did not.

Why should a life which was, in many ways, so uneventful have been so stormy? Leavis's temperament, like his wife's, was not an easy one, and not well suited to the kind of academic life which flourishes in England. University teachers, not only at Cambridge, often value good manners more than the disinterested pursuit of the truth, and laugh (because of embarrassment and deep-buried guilt) at people who "take it all too seriously." No one took it more seriously than Leavis. Unfailingly courteous and sympathetic, by all accounts, to his pupils, he was not urbane, and saw no need to be polite to colleagues whom he felt to be in error or worse. He was a tireless antagonist—"Eight stone, fighting weight" he would say of himself proudly—and unbeatable in discussion. He never simply won: he annihilated. His sense of professional responsibility offended the Cambridge worship of "good form"; he wouldn't play the game, wouldn't be hypocritical for the sake of getting on with people. The inevitable accusations of paranoia combined with his and Mrs. Leavis's suspicion of former friends and colleagues; there were accusations of betrayal and painful scenes from which no one emerged with credit. The fascination of reviewers with these battles, however initially understandable, becomes ultimately tedious. Who, at this distance of time, has the right to adjudicate such disputes? What we know of the facts makes us certain that the cost in personal terms for all concerned was ruinous. Is that not enough?

No estimate of Leavis's criticism can ignore its origin in the classroom: as Dr. MacKillop excellently says, "His teaching was a way of being a person" (though little of the individuality of that teaching is conveyed in the biography). The charges of narrowness often brought against him are unsustainable: he wrote about far more authors than people realize (over thirty in *Revaluation* alone), and had read far more authors than those about whom he wrote—not just in English, either. As a teacher, however, he had responsibilities toward students whose time was limited. Most undergraduates would barely have time to read—*really* read, not just skim-and-look-at-the-criticism—the major works of English literature, let alone those "strangely neglected" minor figures. Almost all Leavis's books were worked out in classroom and lecture hall, a fact which must be borne in mind when considering their self-imposed limitations and economies. One must add that he despised colleagues who crammed students for the examinations, and that he insisted on a far wider range of reading than was usual ("Cultivate promiscuity" he would say picturesquely)—but he would not waste his pupils' time on irrelevancies. Everything he himself had to say was fresh and firsthand. An undergraduate noted of his lectures in 1928, "the fact that his arguments are always founded on the works of the authors themselves makes them unassailable on their own premises"—clearly this was both novel and exasperating!

In the crudest terms for measuring a teacher's success—examination results—Leavis must be rated highly, though the consistently good performance of his pupils led to jealousy and to the first whisperings about cliques and disciples; in less definable but more important terms his influence reverberated far beyond the specific texts to which he was addressing himself. His teaching was a mode of life, of thought; something Dr. MacKillop hints of in saying that he "allowed students to experience the pains of seriousness" (this appears in the review-caricatures as joyless Puritanism). Profiting from the autonomy of colleges within the Cambridge system, Leavis, secure at Downing, could defy his critics and carry on teaching as he wished. That this did not always work to his pupils' advantage, in worldly terms, is undeniable; denied permanent posts at Cambridge, they frequently went abroad. Yet it is absurd of Marius Bewley (who applied Leavis's ideas extensively to American literature) to complain, as Dr. MacKillop records, that Leavis should have thought more about the consequences of his actions on students who "have expended years, energy, and money, to study with him, and enlarge his reputation." If that was their aim, they should have reconsidered the propriety of their motives. Conversely, no real teacher imagines that the goal of his work is an enhanced reputation—as if that mattered! Leavis is the only great critic who has earned his living as a teacher: and we are all his pupils.

Leavis's writing will not fit into neat classifications, but four broad phases can be distinguished. In the first—the period of his early pamphlets and of *New Bearings in English Poetry* (1932) and *Revaluation* (1936)—he was mainly preoccupied with rewriting, under Eliot's influence, the history of English poetry from the seventeenth to the twentieth centuries, and with sketching his view of the nature and purpose of university education. In the second he turned his attention to the novel, probably at his wife's instigation; this is the period of *The Great Tradition* (1948) and *D. H. Lawrence, Novelist* (1955). From the time of his lecture *Two Cultures: The Significance of*

C. P. Snow (1962) Leavis sought a more eclectic treatment of literary, educational, and social issues; the central focus remained literature but the perspective from which he commented was enlarged, so that *English Literature in Our Time and the University* (1969) is quite different from *Education and the University* (1943), just as *Dickens the Novelist* (1970, with Q. D. Leavis) is quite different from the book on Lawrence. This phase of Leavis's work, the "higher pamphleteering" as he called it, reaches its apogee in *Nor Shall My Sword: Discourses on Pluralism, Compassion, and Social Hope* (1972). The fourth and final phase is in many ways the most interesting of all. It consists of two books, *The Living Principle: "English" as a Discipline of Thought* (1975), and *Thought, Words, and Creativity: Art and Thought in Lawrence* (1976), to both of which *Nor Shall My Sword* acts as a curtain-raiser. Here Leavis branches out into areas of thought which must be described— despite his resistance to the term—as philosophical. Such a grouping of his books leaves out of account, of course, the collections of essays *The Common Pursuit* (1952) and *"Anna Karenina" and Other Essays* (1967) as well as much of his writing in *Scrutiny* and some posthumously published material (Dr. MacKillop gives a full list). I shall try to say something briefly about each phase in turn.

Leavis was much struck by Eliot's early critical works *The Sacred Wood* and *Homage to John Dryden*, as well as by Eliot's poetry, and he hailed Empson's *Seven Types of Ambiguity*, in a review, as containing "more of the history of English poetry" than in any other book he knew. Empson's own poetry, too, was unusually impressive. (Yet later, as Dr. MacKillop reports, he would say, "If you want a character study of Empson, go to Iago.") *Revaluation* and *New Bearings* accepted Eliot's catchphrase "dissociation of sensibility" as corresponding to something real in social and literary history during the seventeenth century: and they reflected, although in a less intense and pyrotechnic fashion, Empson's insistence on analysis as the route to understanding. The nineteenth century was seen as a diversion from the genuine in poetic language (Leavis would later argue that poetry in this period is to be found in the novel rather than in the formal verse); Eliot and Pound had rediscovered the strengths of seventeenth-century poetry—its complex fusion of tones, its wit which was not joke-making but the detached yet engaged play of cultivated minds over the widest range of human experience, its subordination of metric to the cadences of the speaking voice—and had managed to apply it in poems which, far from being pastiche, were unmistakably modern in their idiom and preoccupations. Victorian dream-worlds had been ousted by Metaphysical nervous strength. This view entailed a reconsideration of the "mellifluous" tradition coming down from Spenser through Milton to Tennyson. Those poets were not (as is often said) simply dismissed, nor was their classicism written off. Many early English teachers at Cambridge were classicists by training, and assumed that the evaluative criteria they were in the habit of applying to Greek and Latin verse could be transferred to English verse: Leavis maintained that this would lead to little beyond "aesthetic" (a word he detested) appreciation which absolved the aesthete from critical thinking. Milton comes alive, for instance, when he is close to Shakespeare in part of *Comus*, in ways which are absent from his attempts to imitate Latin verse in English; a comparable alertness to Shakespeare's language would benefit Milton's critics too, Leavis hints.

Read without *a priori* assumptions these books can still teach us, not only about the specific passages and poets they discuss, but more broadly about what it is to have one's own grasped history of English literature—not something mugged up from text books but an indwelt possession. How to achieve this was also Leavis's concern in his educational writings of this period, *How to Teach Reading* (1932), a response to Ezra Pound's *How to Read* which elicited from Pound a characteristic riposte ("*balls and shit*"), and *Education and the University*. Despite the widespread assumption that Leavis had no sense of history or was nostalgic or sentimental about it—that he was a "refugee in a never-never-land of the past" in J. H. Plumb's sneering phrase—it is plain from his "Sketch for an 'English School'" in *Education and the University* that his historical sense was both cultivated and extraordinarily delicate. It is true that he had no time for "literary history" as "background" (and showed in controversies with F. W. Bateson and W. W. Robson how vacuous "historical scholarship" was when it was made to substitute for criticism), but he emphatically believed that a literary critic should be educated about history. What he asserted was that, while literary texts could never stand by themselves, context-free (so that the common assimilation of Leavis to the New Critics in America is a bizarre mistake), yet there were criteria of relevance to be observed, and in the end the critic's judgment, however well-informed by other considerations, was a literary one. However, he wanted English departments to act as "liaison-centres" for the humanities in universities, providing in the texts a focus in which specialists could meet, contributing from their different perspectives. Tireless in campaigning for this ideal to be put into practice, he nonetheless sensed, as a realist, that he fought a losing battle. As early as 1970 he warned against

> the more and more matter-of-course view that a university is so much plant
> that should be kept in full production all year round, its staff made to *earn*
> their salaries, and its management governed by strict cost-efficiency recommendations.

Twenty-five years ago this might have seemed melodramatic: now it is sober fact. That is how a modern university is run, in Britain and America. Leavis knew, as we do, that in such an establishment no education can take place.

Before leaving this first group of Leavis's writings I ought to stress how much Eliot's practice, as well as his criticism, mattered to Leavis. He had early given offense to the Cambridge establishment in his first published article, "T. S. Eliot—a Reply to the Condescending" (1929). "The Condescending" was F. L. Lucas, a don at King's College who had reviewed *For Lancelot Andrewes* as "a pleasant little volume written by a man who is evidently fond of reading . . ."! Leavis saw that Eliot's concept of tradition and of the dynamic relationship between the poetry of the past and of the present—his idea of literature as an *order*, an organic whole—offered the solution to the problem of establishing a critical judgment as more than merely personal, a problem Leavis wrestled with all his life. His discussions of Eliot in *New Bearings* and *Education and the University*, which take in the poetry up to the first three of the *Quartets*, are more approving than his later re-assessments, and his personal contacts with Eliot were never easy (he believed himself to be the "other" of the vision in *Little Gidding*). Eliot was the figure against whom, and in opposition to whom, Leavis was always defining himself. He would have reacted with mixed feelings to this appraisal appearing in a magazine called *The New Criterion*.

On the first page of *The Great Tradition* Leavis remarked wryly that "the view . . . will be . . . attributed to me that, except Jane Austen, George Eliot, James, and Conrad, there are no novelists in English worth reading." He was right. What he actually said was that, given the quantity of novels available, a reader needs some sense of where the highest achievements lie if what is valuable in the rest is to be identified. To suggest the distinctive nature of the great in prose fiction, Leavis coined the phrase "the novel as dramatic poem"—dramatic because it gives a direct presentment of its themes, and poem because, in the nineteenth century, the essentially poetic uses of English are found elsewhere than in formal verse. Image and symbol, Leavis shows, are structuring devices in the novel too, and prose rhythm (understood as a flexible instrument) can be as intense a means of control as meter. Leavis's analyses of George Eliot, James, Conrad, Lawrence, and, later, Dickens—together with shorter pieces on Bunyan, Twain, Tolstoy, and Forster—constitute a genuinely original achievement. Henry James was the only notable precursor, and his preoccupation with technique restricted his perspective. Leavis, together with his wife, made the case for the great novelists' being concerned, not (or not only) with offering a "realistic" depiction of society, but also, through that depiction, with making a critique, a diagnostic analysis, of it. Thus Lawrence and Dickens descend from Blake in their exposure of the impersonal mechanisms with which modern "civilization" blights the spiritual health of the individual; thus James, like Jane Austen, has the wit to make of social comedy a vehicle for enquiring into individual integrity; thus Twain raises a local dialect to the status of poetry, and through the persona of the uneducated states the potential of any sensitive being for fineness of soul.

In 1962 Leavis achieved his most spectacular, and unwelcome, bout of publicity in his lecture on C. P. Snow—a reply to Snow's own lecture of 1959, "The Two Cultures and the Scientific Revolution," which had deplored the ignorance of science shown by "literary intellectuals," dubbed "Luddites" and accused of willfully obstructing technological, and therefore social, progress:

> They still like to pretend that the traditional culture is the whole of "culture," as though the natural order didn't exist. As though the exploration of the natural order was of no interest either in its own value or its consequences. As though the scientific edifice of the physical world was not, in its intellectual depth, complexity, and articulation, the most beautiful and wonderful collective work of the mind of man.

Leavis's reply was so scathing that the publishers were advised it contained libelous statements. They sent the text to Snow who, to his eternal credit, insisted that it "must be printed exactly as it stood." When it appeared, Leavis was magisterially rebuked for rudeness by George Steiner and Lionel Trilling, and even had to suffer a would-be lethal put-down from Edith Sitwell—"Dr. Leavis only hates Charles because he is famous and writes good English!" The outrage centered on Leavis's dismissal of Snow's claims to be taken seriously as a novelist—which he was right in saying are nonexistent. What was ignored was his wider contention that Snow was naïve to lament the "divide" between what he perceived as two cultures when, in fact, "there is only one culture," of which science is a part as much as literature. Dr. MacKillop makes a useful distinction between the language *of* science and discourse *about* science: "The discourses of and about literature need not be inherently alien to the discourse of individuals; discourse about science need not be alien either; but the discourse *of* science certainly is." Leavis was not setting himself up as an enemy of scientific research; how could he, knowing he had no training which would give him the right to comment? What he said was that science, like every other branch of intellectual activity, is an enquiry by the human mind, not by some impersonal ("collective" to use Snow's word) entity external to, or absolved from, human procedures and responsibilities. Nor did Leavis expect that literary critics could meet scientists on their own terms. He *did* expect a critic to be able to address intelligently the human consequences of scientific discovery; and he could point to Blake and, again, Dickens as creative writers who had done so.

Puzzlingly, Leavis did not cite the essay on Snow by the physical chemist and philosopher Michael Polanyi, which he must have known. Here is authoritative support from a qualified scientist:

> If I yet agree that there is a gap, and a dangerous gap, between science and the rest of our culture, it is not such deficiencies as the ignorance of thermodynamics shown by literary people, mentioned by Charles Snow, that I have in mind. Even mature scientists know little more than the names of most branches of science. This is inherent in the division of labour on which the progress of modern science is based, and which is likewise indispensable to the advancement of all our modern culture. . . . To do away with the specialization of knowledge would be to produce a race of quiz winners and destroy our culture in favour of a universal dilettantism. . . . The mechanistic explanation of the universe is a meaningless ideal. . . . The prediction of all atomic positions in the universe would not answer any question of interest to anybody.

From 1962 onward much of Leavis's effort went into applying this perception which he shared with Polanyi, that what is threatened in a world dominated by technology (and the world of the 1960s was barely affected by it compared to ours) is the belief in the irreducibility of the individual human being. As Leavis says:

> Science is obviously of great importance to mankind; it's of great cultural importance. But to say that is to make a value-judgement—a human judgement of value. The criteria of judgements of value and importance are determined by a sense of human nature and human need, and can't be arrived at by science itself; they aren't, and can't be, a product of scientific method, or anything like it. They are an expression of human responsibility.

So, when assured by an ingenuous philosophy don that "a computer can write a poem," Leavis replied that that was something he *knew* to be impossible. So it is, and the "analogy" between the human brain and the computer (which depends upon the mistaken equation of "brain" with "mind") is one of the most insidiously misleading examples of modern sophistry.

Dr. MacKillop is right to stress that, ultimately, Leavis and Snow were engaged in "a conflict over history." I mentioned earlier that Leavis is often derided for being nostalgic or sentimental about a past "organic society" to which he allegedly wanted everyone to return. As a former History scholar, and survivor of the Somme, Leavis is the last person in danger of glamorizing the past. Snow equated history with progress: Leavis knew that it was more complex than that. He could point to literature as evidence that a seismic change in society and social relations had occurred, beginning in the mid-seventeenth century, accelerated by the industrial revolution, and making (literally) a quantum leap in our own time; but when he did so it was not to hanker after old certainties but to assert the irrevocableness of what had gone.

> We can't restore the general day-to-day creativity that has vanished; we shall have no successor to Dickens. But we *have* Dickens, and we have the English literature that (a profoundly significant truth) Dickens himself had, and more—for there is the later development that includes Lawrence. There *is* English literature—so very much more than an aggregation or succession of individual works and authors. It reveals for the contemplation it challenges—in its organic interrelatedness reveals incomparably—the nature of a cultural continuity, being such a continuity itself.

(We see here that, however scathing he may have been about Eliot's "Tradition and the Individual Talent," Leavis did owe it a debt.)

In his final trilogy of books, *Nor Shall My Sword*, *The Living Principle*, and *Thought, Words, and Creativity*, Leavis, astonishingly for a man in his eighties, broke new ground, taking up a long-gone discussion with René Wellek. In his classic essay "Literary Criticism and Philosophy" (1937, reprinted in *The Common Pursuit*) Leavis had addressed Wellek's objection that he did not make explicit the theoretical bases of his criticism. His answer was simple: he couldn't; he wasn't a philosopher, and his premises were found only as his work exemplified them. But he added, "There is, I hope, a chance that I may in this way have advanced the theory, even if I haven't done the theorising"; and in *Education and the University* he had been rash enough to call *Burnt Norton* "the equivalent in poetry of a philosophical work" doing "by strictly poetical means the business of an epistemological and metaphysical inquiry." He can't have been satisfied with the equivocal nature of this comment, and in the 1970s found himself confronted by trendy dons recommending Wittgenstein to literary students, and by an apparent merger between literary criticism and linguistics (the first British flirtation with structuralism). Leavis, whose uneasy relationship with Wittgenstein is recorded in one of his finest essays,[2] sought for something which would be of genuine use at the undergraduate level in equipping students philosophically—for he couldn't believe Wittgenstein would be profitable—and found Michael Polanyi's essays *Knowing and Being*, edited by Marjorie Grene, which, with Polanyi's major treatise *Personal Knowledge* and Grene's own book *The Knower and the Known*, became essential reference points to him. They helped him to his final verdict on Eliot, the hundred-page commentary on *Four Quartets* in *The Living Principle*, and to his final statement of why Eliot was a lesser writer than Lawrence.

Grene and Polanyi mounted an attack upon Cartesian dualism. My mind, they insisted, is the mind of my body, and my body is the body of my mind. I as a person am my-mind-and-my-body, all five words receiving equal stress. All being, therefore, is indwelling—both *in* the body, tacitly, and focally *through* it to the external world ("external" *faute de mieux*—since my experience of the world must be interiorized before it is truly mine). "Life" exists, consequently, only in individual lives, and can't be aggregated, quantified, or reduced to statistics in Gradgrind fashion. All thinking is done by individual minds, but also collaboratively (*not* collectively) in the human world; and language—also the collaborative creation of human minds—is the medium of *all* thought. In Polanyi's words, "An exact mathematical theory means nothing unless we recognize an inexact nonmathematical knowledge on which it bears and a person whose judgement upholds this bearing."

This chimed in with problems Leavis had been pondering for years, notably the nature of judgment. "A judgement is personal, or it is nothing": but it also aspires to be more than personal, to have probative force, albeit in a non-scientific way. Where did judgment stand, epistemologically? Where, indeed, did literature stand? Already, in his reply to Snow, Leavis had begun to speak of "the Third Realm"—

> that which is neither merely private and personal nor public in the sense that it can be brought into the laboratory or pointed to. You cannot point to the poem; it is "there" only in the re-creative response of individual minds to the black marks on the page. But—a necessary faith—it is something in which minds can meet.

Critical discussion becomes a paradigm of this re-creation, collaborative and creative: and English literature as an organic whole, like the

---

2 "Memories of Wittgenstein" (1973), reprinted in *The Critic as Anti-Philosopher*, edited by G. Singh (Ivan R. Dee, 1998).

individual works which compose it,

> can have its life only in the living present, in the creative response of in-
> dividuals, who collaboratively renew and perpetuate what they participate
> in—a cultural community or consciousness.

Text, body of texts, the university department teaching them—all, analogi-
cally, are inhabitants of the Third Realm, "to which all that makes us human
belongs." (Some commentators have sought to make connections between
Leavis's Third Realm and Karl Popper's World Three, as expounded in
Popper's *Objective Knowledge* [Clarendon Press, 1972]—indeed Popper himself endorses this position. Leavis however denied any influence, and
reflection will show that the apparent similarities are superficial.)

IN HIS LAST TWO BOOKS Leavis presented creative works, those of Eliot and
Lawrence above all, as, heuristically, achievements of "thought," of a nonmathematical, anti-philosophical kind (that is, not *opposed*, but *antithetical*,
to philosophy). Lawrence's is the greater triumph because, unlike Eliot, he
accepted the spirit of anti-Cartesianism, living in and through the body.
Eliot's conception of Christianity led him to fear and, in crucial ways, deny
the body, setting the spirit over and against it; his paradoxical—and self-
contradicting—denial of the value of "merely" human creativity stems from
the same feelings. When he writes in *The Dry Salvages*, "The hint half
guessed, the gift half understood, is Incarnation," he hardly knows what he
is affirming: for if the Incarnation means anything it means that physical
matter is redeemed, or at least redeemable. It was Lawrence, not Eliot,
however, who saw this most clearly.

Leavis consistently denied that he was contributing to philosophy, but
it is hard to see how this last stage of his work falls outside that category—
without at any time ceasing to be literary criticism. His discomfort with
Wittgenstein, and his professional dislike of seeming to slight the specialist
skills of a fellow-academic in another discipline, may have made him
excessively cautious. Then, too, one wonders if he in some sense saw Wittgenstein as the equivalent in philosophy of himself in criticism. The teaching of both was overheard monologue in effect, and some of Wittgenstein's
personal traits as evoked by Leavis (his "disinterested regardlessness," for
instance, which could manifest itself as "a disconcerting lack of consideration," or his innocence which was often mistaken for cruelty) sound almost
autobiographical. Wittgenstein wrote in *Culture and Value*:

> A teacher may get good, even astounding, results from his pupils while he

is teaching them and yet not be a good teacher; because it may be that, while his pupils are directly under his influence, he raises them to a height which is not natural to them, without fostering their own capacities for work at this level, so that they immediately decline again as soon as the teacher leaves the classroom.

He is, I suspect, thinking of himself here; at times, reading the passage, I think of Leavis too. In the nature of things, Leavis's experiences, like his judgments, couldn't be lived through by anyone else; and although there are distinguished pupils of his in many walks of academic life—the art historian Michael Baxandall, or the philosopher and musicologist Michael Tanner—he cannot really be said to have left any successors. His life's work was "what was done, not to be done again."

Why, in conclusion, does Leavis matter? I propose the following theses, baldly stated: (1) He changed the way we read—poetry especially, but also the novel—not by pontificating about hermeneutics but by leaving an array of brilliant readings of particular works, readings which are not hermetic "practical criticism" exercises (a term he disliked—"practical criticism is criticism in practice"). No critic before Leavis had paid such close attention to words and their connections with ideas. (Perhaps Coleridge comes closest, but his brilliance was undisciplined.); (2) He provides a shining example of the way a mind can teach itself to develop. He emancipated himself from the influence of Eliot and, after fifty years, furnished the drastic limiting critique which "placed" his former mentor, in the process doing innovative work on the nature of thought and language; (3) He virtually invented (in conjunction with Mrs. Leavis) the criticism of the novel and the subject of cultural studies; (4) In his debates with the Marxists in the 1930s and with Snow and others in the 1960s, he vindicated the autonomy and dignity of literature as an activity of humanity which gives a vital context to *all* thinking, including the scientific and mathematical; (5) His conception of the university—the boldest since Newman's—although now rendered unrealizable by the degeneration of universities into business corporations, stands as a reminder of what higher education could be, and a rebuke to the reality; (6) In keeping *Scrutiny* going for twenty years, he made possible the publication of major work on English literature from Chaucer to the present day, plus French and German literature, philosophy, sociology, music, history, education, and politics; (7) His conception of the Third Realm, and his use of Grene and Polanyi, enabled him to make original and fruitful connections between literary criticism and philosophy, and contributed to the anti-Cartesian reassertion of the integrity of the individual human being; (8) All these are general points. They take no account of his work on individual authors: Arnold, Blake, Coleridge, George Eliot, T. S. Eliot, Hardy, Hopkins, James, Johnson, Lawrence, Marvell, Milton, Pope, Twain, and Wordsworth, to name the most obvious.

For what other critic this century can equal claims be made? To those who deny that Leavis matters, or that his importance is historical merely, all one can do is point to the evidence and ask the question.

In a sense, however, he *has* a historical importance, hinted at in my title—he is "the last critic," the last to have a coherent understanding of what literature and criticism were, the last to have the intellectual equipment to fulfill the critic's function. If he was the product of a particular historical moment, which has now passed with him, his greatness in meeting its challenges seems only more marked now: and if criticism as he understood it has ceased to exist, so much the worse for criticism—and literature. What is written by most university teachers of "English" now answers to no conception of criticism that Leavis would recognize: and those teachers' pupils are their successors. The future for the causes that Leavis gave his life to is unfathomably dark. When I listened to him in 1972, I was already aware that my own university teachers were, on the whole, a mediocre bunch; but I had no inkling of what now seems to me absolutely certain: that, however poorly served it was, my generation was the last which had the privilege of receiving an education at university at all.

January 1996

The Intimate Abstraction of Paul Valéry

Joseph Epstein

Always demand proof, proof is the elementary courtesy that is anyone's due.
—Valéry, *Monsieur Teste*

THE NAME Paul Valéry carries its own music. For those who know something of what lies behind it, the music deepens, is suggestive, and always richly complex. ("Complex," said Ravel, about his own artistic aims, "never complicated.") To know Valéry only from his melodious but difficult poems—"Le Cimitière marin," "La Jeune Parque," and others—turns out to be to know him scarcely at all. "Poetry," he wrote, "has never been a goal for me—more an instrument, an exercise, and its character derives from this— an artifice—product of will." Poetry provided him with fame, but he found his real intellectual stimulation elsewhere.

Today, Valéry is perhaps best known for his aphoristic remarks, in- evitably both brilliant and running against received opinion. Glimpse Valéry's name on the page and one knows something immensely clarifying, possibly life-altering, awaits. "Everything changes but the avant-garde" is one example. "The future, like everything else, is not what it used to be" is another. "History is the science of things which do not repeat themselves" is a third. Without too much effort, one could record three or four hundred Valéryan remarks of equal charm and intellectual provocation.

"Remarks are not literature," Gertrude Stein is supposed to have said to Ernest Hemingway. She was wrong; all depends on the quality of the remarks. But then Stein's stricture would not much have bothered Paul Valéry, who did not think "literature" a purely honorific word. For him literature is a construct, made for entertainment, instruction, excitation, and many other things that are not quite the truth. "There's always a rather sordid side to literature," he wrote in his *Cahiers*, "a lurking deference to one's public. Hence the mental reservations, the ulterior motives basic to every form of charlatanism. Thus every literary production is an 'impure' product."

Although Valéry came to public notice as a young poet, what most interested him was the intellectual operation of the mind; the search for the truth about the way the mind works in cerebration, the mechanics of its functioning, was his main passion. He sought, as he himself late in life put it, "to know the substratum of thought and sensibility on which one has lived." In his *Cahiers*, again, he wrote: "I would like to have classified and clarified my personal forms of thought, and learned to think within them in such a way that each new thought bore the imprint of the whole system generating it and was unmistakably a modification of a well-defined system."

The way Valéry went about this enterprise is not the least astonishing thing about this extraordinary man. After a lustrous beginning as a poet— he met and early fell under the influence of that saint of modernism, Stéphane Mallarmé—he stopped writing poems for twenty years, beginning in 1892, when he was twenty-one. While making a living for a wife and children through employment with the French War Ministry and later as private secretary to one of the chief executives for the Paris financial conglomerate Agence Havas, he worked out his ideas, chiefly in private, in 261 notebooks which he wrote during the early morning hours.

Harry Kessler, in his journals, described the middle-age Valéry as resembling nothing so much as a French marquis. French to the highest power though Valéry has always seemed, from the accent *aigu* in his name to the chill clarity that he invariably brought to matters of the highest abstraction—*Ce qui n'est pas clair, n'est pas français*—Valéry's father, a customs officer, was Corsican and his mother came of a northern Italian family. His upbringing was in the French Mediterranean sea-coast city of Cette. He was, like Baudelaire, Henry James, and so many literary men who went on to have unconventional points of view, rather a poor student; most of his serious reading was done away from school. He thought of a naval career, but was washed out by his insufficient math; he went to law school at the Université de Montpellier, where he developed a serious interest in science and mathematics and began writing poems. He met Pierre Louÿs, later author of erotic novels written in a Hellenistic vein, who introduced him to the poetry of Mallarmé.

When Valéry sent Mallarmé a few of his poems, the older man returned them with the comment that "the gift of analogy along with adequate music are already yours and they are all that count." Mallarmé later wrote that one of Valéry's early published poems "charms me." Valéry, meanwhile, after having moved to Paris, became part of the coterie of young poets and *bellelettristes* who met to discuss literary questions at Mallarmé's apartment on Tuesdays.

But on the night of October 4, 1892, in Genoa, Valéry had a vision, an epiphany, one doesn't quite know what to term it, but on that night he decided to forego a standard literary career and instead concentrate his intellectual power on what one can only call pure thought. (He later wrote that "there are few poets who do not go through a fundamental crisis between the ages of twenty and thirty, one in which the destiny of their gift is at stake.") He wanted to know how thought works, what it is based on, its underpinnings, the fundamental mechanisms of the mind itself. This did not mean that Valéry withdrew from society; not at all. He was something of a literary man about town. Nor did he cease publication altogether. He published a few poems. He wrote *Monsieur Teste*, his portrait of a man coolly distanced from common concerns by his detached, scientific standards of truth, and *An Introduction to the Method of Leonardo da Vinci*, his study of perhaps the only man in history who did both first-rate science and art.

In a letter to his Harvard teacher J. H. Woods, T. S. Eliot remarks that there are two ways to make a great literary success in London. One is through ubiquity, to publish constantly and everywhere; the other is to publish seldom but, when doing so, always to dazzle by making "these things perfect in their kind." Eliot of course chose this latter path, and so, in a more extreme way, did Paul Valéry.

But, somehow, even with his greatly limited publication, everyone seemed to know about the brilliance of M. Valéry. André Gide was a close friend and a longtime correspondent. Valéry saw Cocteau and Degas and the publisher Gaston Gallimard regularly. His wife, whom he married in 1900 (and with whom he had three children), was the niece of Berthe Morisot and a cousin to Edouard Manet. He knew Ravel and Debussy. André Breton, the main figure in French Surrealism, asked him to be best man at his wedding. "I think I met him [Valéry] for the first time in 1921 or 1922 at a reception by the Princesse de Polignac," Igor Stravinsky recalled in *Memories and Commentaries*. "He was small—about my own height, in fact—quick, quiet (he spoke in very rapid, *sotto voce* mumbles), and gentle. His monocle and *boutonnière* made him seem a dandy, but that impression dissolved as soon as he began to talk. Everything he said was instinct with wit and intelligence."

At the urging of Gide and Gallimard, Valéry returned to writing verse in 1912, and, in attempting to round out a volume of verse for publication, he wrote "La Jeune Parque," a poem of 512 lines that made him a poet of great fame not only in France but throughout Europe. But fame is one thing, fortune, for a poet, quite another. In 1922, after the death of his patron Edouard Lebey, at Agence Havas, he had to scramble for a living. Scrambling meant becoming a literary man-of-all-work: giving talks, doing bits of teaching, writing introductions to other people's books, and the rest of it.

In 1925, Valéry was appointed to fill the seat at the Académie Française of Anatole France. In a dazzlingly ironic reception address upon ascending to membership, he lightly mocked his predecessor and made plain how the changing of the guard of literature had taken place:

> Blessed are those writers who relieve us of the burden of thought and who dextrously weave a luminous veil over the complexity of things. Alas, gentlemen, there are others, whose existence must be deplored, who have have elected to strike out in the opposite direction. They have placed toil of the mind in the way of its pleasures. They offer us riddles. Such creatures are inhuman.

Valéry was of course speaking of himself and his own difficult writing. He also got in a shot about a French society "notable for its inability to find for the intellectually gifted man an appropriate and tolerable place in its gigantic and crude economy." The French seem to understand such mockery and do not let it get in the way; they take it in stride, make no real changes, and move on, business as usual. For Valéry, this meant treating him very much as what used to be called an establishment figure, without his ever having an establishment financial base.

> Please include me [he wrote in connection with being asked to serve on yet another award committee] among those who are weariest of delivering oracles. In the course of this past week, I have spoken a dozen times before thinking. On one occasion, I was asked to name the most beautiful line of verse in our language; on another, I narrated the greatest day in my life; I offered opinions on State reform and on votes for women. I nearly even issued a pronouncement on the comma! The truth is, my good man, that I am past admiring my brain for all the wonderfully various things it had no idea it contained.

Honors continued to come to him until his death in 1945: President of the French P.E.N. Club, an honorary doctorate from Oxford, the post of Administrator of the Centre Universitaire Méditerranéen de Nice, a leading member of the Committee on Intellectual Co-Operation of the League of Nations and later of its Permanent Committee on Arts and Letters, Professor of Poetics at the Collège de France. He was long considered the unofficial poet laureate of France; he referred to himself, in 1932, as "a kind of state poet." His intellectual connections widened, and he knew people as diverse as Joseph Conrad and Rabindranath Tagore, Eliot and D'Annunzio, Pirandello and H. G. Wells. The wonder is how he managed to escape the Nobel Prize.

Valéry wrote no more poems after 1926. His two main periods of poetic production were between 1887–1892 and 1912–1922. "After each period," Roger Shattuck has written, "came twenty years of highly active 'silence' in prose." Such was his intellectual skill that, despite his complaints about all the official hackwork he had to turn out, the truth is that he was incapable of writing anything really dull. The source of this skill was in the daily work on his *Cahiers*. From his early twenties until his death, Valéry began each day, arising between 5:00 and 6:00 A.M., aided by coffee and cigarettes, in the act of cerebration, writing out those of his thoughts that he felt were worth preserving. Ultimately, these came to a body of work of 26,000 pages, constituting twenty-nine volumes in a facsimile edition and two volumes in the Pléiade edition of his works.

Much of this material has never been available in English, though an enticing portion was published in the volume titled *Analects* in the splendid fifteen-volume English-language edition of Valéry that Jackson Matthews edited for the Bollingen Foundation. Valéry has always been fortunate in his editors, and perhaps in none more than Matthews, who gave the better part of his adult life to making him available to the small number of readers who do not negotiate the French language with complete ease but who are capable of appreciating both the importance and the pleasure that Valéry's work gives.

Now an English-language version of the full *Cahiers*, under the title *Cahiers/Notebooks*, has begun, scrupulously and skillfully edited by three Valéry scholars, Brian Stimpson, Paul Gifford, and Robert Pickering. The first two volumes are currently available, in a handsome edition in English under the aegis of the international publisher Peter Lang. Valéry seems to have struggled with the question of how to organize all this material in a systematic way; and felt unsure at times whether it ought even to be published at all. Five volumes are planned for this English edition, the last three more scientific and philosophical (another word that was no honorific in Valéry's vocabulary) than these first two, which are more literary and, in a distant sense of the word, personal. The project is a genuine contribution to scholarship and even more to the history of thought in the twentieth century.

Rilke once remarked that what drew him to Paul Valéry's writing was the "finality" and "composure" of its language. His lucidity on complex subjects is what excites; his ability to capture the essence of the questions, issues, and problems that the rest of us find puzzling if not impenetrable is what amazes—and that he was able to do so with an almost assembly-line regularity is itself astonishing.

What gives Valéry's prose its gravity, lucidity, and chasteness is what he excludes from it. He disliked irony, except in conversation, and felt that it chiefly gave a writer an air of superiority, adding that "every ironist has in mind a pretentious reader, mirror of himself." He also had a distaste for eloquence, "because eloquence has the form of a mixture, adapted to a crowd. It has not the form of thought." He cared more for precision than profundity, and precision was only accessible through the utmost clarity: "the kind that does not come from the use of words like 'death,' 'God,' 'life,' or 'love'—but dispenses with such trombones." No trombones, no trumpets, no brass section in Valéry's prose; a solo cello, deep strings played under perfect control and superior acoustical conditions, is all we ever hear.

Add to this his intellectual contempt for politics, which he felt took on life *en masse*, or in its coarsest possible form. "I consider politics, political action, all forms of politics, as inferior values and inferior activities of the mind," he wrote. Politics is the realm of the expedient, the rough guess: "crude, vain, or desperate solutions are indispensable to mankind just as they are to individuals, *because they do not know*." In politics, he wrote, "by a trick of inverted lights, friends see each other as enemies, fools look impressive to the intelligent, who in turn see themselves as very tiny indeed." Politics calls, inevitably, for the polemic, which carries its own peril: "that of losing the power of thinking otherwise than polemically, as if one were facing an audience and in the presence of the enemy." Valéry could think of nothing in the realm of thought "madder" or more vulgar "than wanting to be right," which is of course what politics is chiefly about.

He had no greater regard for history. "The *true character* of history," he wrote, "is to play a part in history itself." He thought of it as sheer story-telling, with the added danger of "invitation to plagiarism," which entails repeating earlier historians' stories, always "a fatal invitation." He wrote: "*History teaches us . . . History will judge . . .* That's a myth in two nonsenses." He especially disliked the grand dramatizers of history—Michelet is a notable example—and he believed that "history finally leads to politics, just as Bacchus used to lead to Venus."

Although his own quest was sometimes described as philosophical, philosophy, too, was, for Valéry, yet another shaky enterprise; "hearsay," he called it, and pronounced metaphysics "astrology with words." Religion, he felt, "provides people with words, acts, gestures, and 'thoughts' covering the predicaments in which they are at a loss what to say, to do, or to imagine." A man tends "to deny what he is unable to affirm (express)," and so religion, inadequate as a mode of thought, at least provided a shield against our deep ignorance about the basic questions of existence. He was himself not averse to using the world "soul," though he said he was interested in "collecting *minds* only." Valéry does not say much about his own views on religion, but he was prescient enough, more than half a century ago, to write: "The religious debate is no longer between different religions; but between those who believe that *belief* has some sort of value and those who don't."

Anyone who reads through these *Notebooks* and through Valéry's work generally will notice how seldom he quotes, or even mentions other writers. In an essay called "French Thought and Art," he descants for thirteen pages with the mention of only a single name, that of Montesquieu, and this brought in only tangentially. This is another sign of the purity of his lucubrations. "Names," he wrote, "are only made to send us back to things, yet they too often save us the journey."

As by now will be evident, Valéry sought a position of maximum detachment for his own efforts to understand the functioning of the mind. "No one has stood back from everything and everyone more than I have." he wrote. "I'd like to turn them all into a spectacle—and rid myself of everything but my own way of looking." His *Notebooks* are neither journals nor a diary, nor even, in the sense in which most writers, Henry James perhaps primary among them, use notebooks to record impressions and ideas later to be developed in one's novels, plays, or poems. "Here is no merely private record of personal hopes, fears, and aspirations, no chronicle of deeds and days, still less is it (as Journals from Rousseau to Gide had commonly been) the public confession of, or apology for, an intimate self," as Paul Gifford writes. Instead the *Notebooks* constitute, as Gifford accurately calls it, "a laboratory of thought." Valéry uses them to work through his intellectual dissatisfaction with modes of thinking that we have all inherited, and in the attempt to break through them he tries, in these many pages, to understand why, in their faultiness, they appeal to us.

Cool and impersonal though Valéry's *Notebooks* at first might appear, in the end it is difficult to imagine anything more personal than this work. T. S. Eliot famously said that poetry "is not the expression of personality, but an escape from personality." But the more impersonal serious writing attempts to become, the more personal it seems. This may be owing to the mysteries of style, which is a way of looking at the world, and no one had a more original way of looking at the world than Valéry, which of course is what gave him his distinctive style. His is a style of thought, rather than of manner, thought marked by skepticism, penetration, and a taste and talent for useful paradox. The deeper, the more abstract his thought, the more intimate he could be.

Characteristically, Valéry disapproves of the words "deep" or "depth" to describe thinking. He held that "only what is on the surface can have meaning," by which he can only have meant that, if one has the intelligence to read the surface accurately, one will easily enough discover what lies beneath it. "Being 'deep,' getting to the bottom of things," he writes, "is nothing. Anybody can dive; some, however, are caught in the water weeds of their abyss and die there, unable to break free." In his *Notebooks*, sometimes one is required to put on the scuba-diving equipment. Behind his quest for the way the mind works was the deeper search for human potential—that is, only when we know how our mental operations work will we know of what we are capable.

"By scrutinizing the inner structures and workings of the self," Brian Stimpson writes in the introduction to the English edition of the *Notebooks*, "and by employing the most advanced tools of scientific analysis, [Valéry] might, so he hoped, at once free himself from the tyranny of ideas and emotions and formulate a unitary mathematically expressed model of mental functioning, a rigorous, comprehensive understanding of the mind and its products." Valéry didn't, no one will be shocked to learn, achieve this, or even come anywhere near close. "What Valéry has done, had to be attempted," said Henri Bergson, his very grammar acknowledging the element of noble defeat. Valéry himself came to have a more modest view of his own enterprise: "Personally," he wrote, "I regard thought as a sort of 'nexus of possibilities' which, operating between these two states [a question and an answer], and by means of certain disciplines, can render useful services as a catalytic." Reading through Valéry's works, I have come to regard him as both catalytic and as prophylactic, simultaneously evoking thought and guarding against shoddy thinking and unearned intellectual confidence.

In a famous formulation, Valéry wrote that "The mind is a moment in the response of the body to the world." One might think that the triad of mind, body, and environment and their effect on one another would be easily enough plotted and traced, but they are not. And to raise the question of mind, of what is behind our thinking and how it really works, is, as Valéry knew, "to call everything into question." In a brief essay called "I Would Sometimes Say to Mallarmé," he wrote: "Why not admit that man is the source and origin of enigmas, where there is no object, or being, or moment that is not impenetrable; when our existence, our movements, our sensations absolutely cannot be explained; and when everything we see becomes indecipherable from the moment our minds come to rest on it." Valéry did admit it; and in his *Notebooks* he attempted to investigate why this was so.

Of the various divisions among thinkers, I have always been partial to that between thinkers whose strength is in their ideas (Marx, Freud, to a much lesser power Orwell) and thinkers whose strength is in the texture and subtlety, the sensibility, of their minds (Montaigne, Henry James, Santayana). The former win their way in the world, then die out; the latter, always less dramatic in their presentation, are wiser and their work tends to last longer. Valéry is among the sensibility thinkers. "I don't construct a 'System,'" he reports in his *Notebooks*. "My system—is me," And later he writes: "Just think!—The stock of ideas on which the majority of 'cultured' people live is the legacy of a specific number of individuals, all of whom were moved and inspired by philosophic and literary vanity, and by the ambition to govern other minds and seek their approval and their praise." This may seem very radical, but Valéry would have viewed it as traditional, for, as he wrote, "in all great undertakings, tradition, in the true sense of the word, does not consist of doing again what others have done before, but in recapturing the spirit that went into what they did—and would have done differently in a different age."

If one doesn't read Valéry in the hope of finding yet another false key to unlocking the room containing all the world's mysteries, one does read him, or at least I read him, to remind me what genuine thought looks like. I also read him because, as he writes, "From 1892 onwards I've felt and maintained a hatred and scorn for Vague Things, and have waged relentless war on them my whole life long. They are the things which cannot stand up to sustained attention, without being reduced to having no existence beyond the name which one thinks denotes them; things which either evaporate the more you think about them, or change into objects of thought for which quite different names are appropriate." If a few examples of such "things" are wanted, try, just for size, the Class Struggle or the Oedipus Complex. "I don't like those minds," Valéry wrote, "even vast and powerful ones, whose thoughts are incapable of being taken to a certain level of precision." Think of Ralph Waldo Emerson; now reverse him and you have Paul Valéry.

"My life's ambition," Valéry wrote, "has only ever been to stir a little interest in minds that are not easily satisfied." One hopes, of course, that one possesses such a mind. Another requisite for an appreciation of Valéry is a mind excited by style. Style, my guess is, functioned for him as a filter through which nonsense was strained. Karl Kraus once described a journalist as "someone who, given time, writes worse." So with Valéry: when he wrote longer he often wrote worse. His lordly lucidity is most impressive when most concise "A machine is matter that has been trained," he wrote. "A lyrical poem is the unfolding of an exclamation," he wrote. "Optimists write badly," he wrote.

Valéry's was the art of precise formulation. His powers of formulation made him one of the great naturally aphoristic writers of the last century. Unlike other French aphorists, *les moralistes*, his aphorisms touch on serious and delicate matters but almost never on moral questions. "My son," he confided to his *Notebooks*, "I'll bring you up very badly for I'm incapable of giving you precepts that I don't understand." Elsewhere he added: "I know the value of *good* and *evil*. I feel very pleased when I do *good* because I recognize evil so strongly—and because I recognize even more strongly the irrelevance of these notions." By "irrelevance," my suspicion is, he meant his inability to do much about good or evil in the world. Valéry claimed to despise proselytizing, and there is no reason to disbelieve him.

His own mind operated above the level of ideas. You will find few words in Valéry that end in i-s-m; and those that he does use he brings in only to mock. Symbolism is an example, for "Symbolist" was the label attached to the poets clustered around Mallarmé when he, Valéry, was young. "It is impossible to think *seriously* with such words as Classicism, Romanticism, Humanism, Realism, and the other -isms. You can't get drunk or quench your thirst with the labels on bottles."

Although Valéry tended to be less than impressed with the novel—"reading stories and novels helps to kill second- or third-class time"—his was in many ways the view of a superior novelist. In an essay called "Descartes," he wrote: "My own view is that we cannot really circumscribe a man's life, imprison him in his ideas and his actions, reduce him to what he appeared to be and, so to speak, lay siege to him in his works. We are much more (and sometimes much less) than we have done."

Valéry's formulations, brilliant in themselves, often provide the added pleasure of provoking useful disagreement. "Our most important thoughts are those which contradict our feelings," he wrote. True enough though that seems, it seems even truer the other way round: our most important feelings are those which contradict our thoughts. "A writer is 'profound,'" Valéry claimed, "when what he says, *once translated from language into unambiguous thought*, compels us to think it over for a perceptible, and rewarding, period of time." Valéry's own writing passes that test, again and again.

The only standard of truth that Valéry was able to invoke was that of science, especially mathematics. The man who when young was unable to set out on a naval career for want of mathematical ability later developed a passionate fascination for the beauty of mathematics and an intense interest in neuroscience. His personal library provides evidence that, as he grew older, he read more science than literature. Among his friends were Poincaré and Niels Bohr; Einstein was someone he met on a number of occasions. His heroes were men, beginning with Leonardo da Vinci, in whom thought and action were one, from Napoleon to Lord Kelvin. Although he was no more than a reasonably well-informed dilettante in scientific matters, scientists came to have a high opinion, as his niece Judith Robinson-Valéry has put it, of his "precise and strategic grasp of what is at stake in their own research." In early positing the inextricability of the triad of Mind, Body, and World in influencing human thought and conduct, Valéry can even be said to have been anticipated much work in modern neurology that was still to come.

The task Valéry set himself was that of re-cognition—to "re-cognate, to rethink things afresh," and to work through them shorn of the conventional wisdom supplied by politics, history, and rhetoric. "'Opinions,' 'convictions,' and 'beliefs' are to me like weeds—confusions," he wrote. He claimed that he wrote "to test, to clarify, to extend, not to duplicate what has been done." He sought his own definitions, more precise than any to be found in dictionaries. "I notice in passing," he wrote to his friend André Gide, "that it is the vague idea that is most generally understood—and that a man is taken to be obscure as soon as he is precise." He also knew that in human beings "cognition reigns but does not rule."

Not everyone felt that Valéry's great project was worthwhile. Some even felt it an evasion. Stravinsky thought he was "altogether too fascinated by the processes of creation" and too worshipful of the power of intellect, and regretted that he failed to spend more time at his poetry than in solitary cerebration. Invited to write about Valéry by Hubert Benoit, St. John Perse felt that Valéry had been mistaken not to set his thoughts in order "with a view to make a definite statement of them," and instead "dissipated his gifts, for lack of real control and of ability to follow through, and also for lack of a really demanding vitality."

Valéry himself was far from thinking his enterprise a grand success. He was in the uncomfortable position of being everywhere revered yet knowing his own shortcomings. "I'm afraid," he wrote in the *Notebooks*, "I might be beginning to find a feeling of vanity in me—thinking I'm something—which until now was quite foreign to me." He goes on to say that this feeling is pleasant to the taste, "like certain kinds of poison," but that he knows he hasn't obtained "what I would have desired from the world." What he desired can only have been a lucid presentation of the function of the mind, a magnum opus, *The Art of Thinking,* he once called it, saying it was a book "which has never really been written; nor was anyone ever to write it."

Instead he left behind these 261 notebooks, filled with his thoughts on everything from the composition of poetry to the relation among body parts to recognition of the beautiful to the connection between dreams and intellectual discovery ("sleep and ye shall find") to negative hallucinations (not seeing things that are there), and a catalogue of other items, at whose vastness I have only been able to hint at here. In the end, though, he understood that "the essential object of the mind is the mind. What it pursues in its analyses and its construction of worlds, what it tracks down in heaven and on earth, can only be itself."

Valéry was too wise not to know that, when his life was over, his work was incomplete. He had set out to do for intellection what Dante had done for the spirit and Balzac for men and women in society—to write, in fact, a Comedy of the Mind. People who put themselves to a reading of his *Notebooks* will recognize them as an unfinished masterpiece, but he would have thought otherwise and eschewed the word "masterpiece," for in an entry in those *Notebooks* he remarks that what other people judge a successful work may seem a defeat for the author; and he also believed that, though what he discovered was not without its importance, people were unlikely to be able to decipher it from his notes.

"Everything I've accomplished all my life since I was twenty, consists of nothing other than a kind of *perpetual preparation*, *without purpose*, without end . . . without practical or external goal," he wrote. He also claimed that everything done outside his *Notebooks* was "my *artificial* work—the result of obligations and external impulses. And this must be understood if anyone wants to understand anything about me—there's nothing essential—or necessary—in any of it." But his every morning's work—"between lamp and dawn," as he once described it—sharpened his mind, so that even the least dutiful official talk he gave, introduction he wrote, journalistic query he responded to shimmered with intelligence and was free of falsity.

Some minds, Valéry wrote, "have the merit of seeing clearly what all others see confusedly. Some have the merit of glimpsing confusedly what no one sees as yet. A combination of these gifts is exceptional." He was himself in possession of this combination, but, then, he was an exceptional man. Reading him gives you the sense of fog lifting. His writing makes you feel, as he himself wished to feel, that you see things no one but you (and he) has seen. One of the keenest pleasures of reading derives from being in the close company of someone more thoughtful than you but whose thoughts, owing to the courtesy of clarity, are handsomely accessible to you. Paul Valéry provides this pleasure more delectably than any writer I know.

March 2003

Milton Avery: Then and Now

James Panero

In the new art we can trace two main currents; in one synthesis predominates, in the other analysis; the latter preponderates enormously. Indeed, this is the direction in which abstract art has tended to develop ever since the Renaissance.
—Julius Meier-Graefe, 1908

Why talk when you can paint?
—Milton Avery

M Y FIRST ACQUAINTANCE with the work of Milton Avery (1885–1965) was indirect. In Christmas 1982, a color-rich, half-abstract landscape of a mountain scene—a catalogue-cover reproduction of it anyway—landed on my parents' coffee table. At this point, the total understanding of my world encompassed 1) the five blocks around my apartment, 2) the television lineup of Channel Thirteen, and 3) Central Park. To this was added 4) *Red Rock Falls* (1947) from 1982's Avery retrospective, prepared by Barbara Haskell for the Whitney Museum. Avery's waterfall flowed through my childhood with the drip of a bathroom faucet.

UNTIL I STARTED researching a show now at The Phillips Collection ("Discovering Milton Avery: Two Devoted Collectors, Louis Kaufman and Duncan Phillips"; February 14–May 16, 2004), and I found *that* book, the whole experience was a sort of broken memory. There could be worse introductions to art than *Red Rock Falls*, or even its reproduction. Perhaps what I most remember is that I rarely grew tired of it; the ten thousandth glance was as engaging, or as frustrating, as the first. *Red Rock Falls* seems simple, but it refuses to give up its secrets. Depending on what you want art to do, I suppose, this refusal can either be construed as a painting's greatest compliment or its harshest critique.

Red Rock Falls is made up of six fields of color: blue (water), purple (riverbank), brown (cliff), orange (hill), green (mountains), and pink (sky)—the image of the actual painting, which is in the Milwaukee Art Museum, so blends into the memory of my faded, sun-damaged reproduction that you must bear with me. A pattern of cross-hatches—not too regular—runs though the orange and brown regions. The blue varies as the waterfall joins the river. Other than that, the colors are creamy and slightly mottled yet distinct from one another. The riverbank relaxes in its purple splendor all the way up to the foothills of the green mountains, which rub against the pink sky. The brown cliffs slip between the orange hill and the blue river.

The shapes tease at one another. The sky presses down on the mountains, which are packed against the hill. The riverbank sprawls out and pokes left into the narrowing river. This river does not so much flow down as shoot up, from lower left to upper right. It widens at one corner to form a body that thins into an attenuated neck (choked at its most vulnerable spot by the riverbank). This neck then leads to a head—the waterfall—that sits up and forms the flattest part of the canvas, here in the shape of a C. The notch in the C might be the river flowing around a rock in the cliff face. It might just as well be a mouth, wide open and yelling. (Is it because of the pushy riverbank? Is it shouting over the noise of the falls? Could it be producing the noise of the falls itself?) The brown cliffs hang down around this head like a mat of hair. The red hillside to its left: a fancy veil fluttering in the breeze.

That might be Wednesday. On Thursday, that head could become a hand reaching up to grab the green mountain—or is it holding it back? On Friday, back to the head again, but this time of a monster. Saturday is something different: the river becomes sky as seen though the beak of a tropical bird, a detailed closeup of Toucan Sam facing left, flat as a pancake. And on Sunday? It is a waterfall flowing over red rocks. Such are some conscious impressions. The corners of my eyes have their own, no doubt wilder, thoughts on the matter.

Milton Avery was fond of saying "Why talk when you can paint?" The quip sounds like a toss-off—a Yankee way of shushing the room. But I doubt whether Avery could have offered a more forthright statement about his artistic position. In Avery's case, I think, the reasons went beyond New England reticence. He believed that his paintings said everything he needed to say, and that was that.

There lies a deep urgency in what Avery could create. The passage of time has only helped flesh out these qualities. While much of what seemed avant-garde in the past looks dated, Avery still resonates. The history of art is not a series of facts, of course, but a battleground of styles. How did this play out in the art of the twentieth century? On one side: tone, volume, depth, illusion, narrative, and an art that is as much literary as aesthetic. The opposing style: based in color, spiritual in an entirely different manner (one might say non-evangelical), and rooted most directly in Symbolism, synesthesia, tone poetry, and the art of the 1890s. Here the unity of painting predominates. The interlocking flatness and harmonies of shape and color take precedence over subject matter. The painting itself *is* subject matter. Within this vein, most notably as a colorist, Milton Avery has proved to be a central figure in twentieth-century art.

When Social Realism was riding high in art in the 1930s, Avery once remarked, "Either I am crazy or they are crazy." He might have said the same thing in the 1920s, surrounded by the nativist style of the "American scene"—following the collapse of modernist art as championed by Alfred Stieglitz and Arthur Dove—or in the early 1950s, when his younger disciples, including Mark Rothko, Adolph Gottlieb, and Barnett Newman (they all met him in the late 1920s and early 1930s), began writing manifestos to the *Times* and took up pure abstraction. It must speak to an artist's continued relevance when he is supposedly "surpassed" on numerous occasions for completely different reasons.

Avery's laconic disposition and lack of political engagement were often mistaken for simpleness. It is rumored that he never voted. In the late 1930s, he gave up a job in the Easel Division of the Works Progress Administration/Federal Art Project because he resisted signing the obligatory pauper's oath. John Maynard Keynes: no thanks. But Avery was not a social outsider or a naif. He was known for his keen sense of humor. He led what must have been the most stable family life of any artist in the twentieth century, due in no small part to the steadfastness of his wife, Sally. She served as the Averys' breadwinner first by drawing sketches for a publication called *Progressive Grocer* and then, after 1940, as the illustrator for a popular weekly column in the *New York Times Magazine* called "Child and Parent," for which she earned $100 a week. In 1925, the year they met, Avery moved to New York. He gave up his odd jobs in manufacturing, third-watch shifts at the Travelers Insurance Company, and the conservative art schools he had been attending around Hartford, Connecticut. In New York he dedicated himself to art full time. He was forty—an artist with no reputation, no money, no means of high-level employment, but he was someone with prodigious, unabated output. Although he joined the esteemed Valentine Gallery in 1935—the American representative of

Matisse—and received stipends from various sources, Avery was never really a money-making artist, partly because of some predatory dealers. Roy Neuberger, for example, speculated at bargain basement prices on a cache of Avery's work from Valentine Dudensing in 1943, the year Avery left the gallery. Neuberger soon turned the work around to great profit and cut Avery out of the deal.

In 1926, the Averys moved into an artists' complex called Lincoln Arcade on the Upper West Side of Manhattan, on what is now part of Lincoln Center (as it happens, a block and fifty-odd years away from my parents' coffee table). The Averys' next-door neighbor was Stuart Davis. Marcel Duchamp, Francis Picabia, and Jacques Villon were familiar visitors to the building. Here Avery primed his own canvases and learned to thin his pigments with turpentine. It was said he could make paint last longer than anyone. The Averys regularly welcomed other artists at their apartment, including Gottlieb and Rothko. Both eighteen years his junior, these artists—along with William Baziotes and Theodoros Stamos—directly drew on Avery's work. With Rothko and Gottlieb talking through the night, Milton listened and sketched his guests. Sally cooked the hamburgers. Perhaps Milton was most talkative when he was reading aloud. This was his family's common and affordable form of entertainment; the reading list included Melville, Proust, Thoreau, Stevens, and Eliot—not too shabby. On Saturdays they all went to the galleries. In the summers it was off to Gloucester, Massachusetts, towns in Vermont, the Gaspé Peninsula, Quebec, or a road trip to Yellowstone and California. With their daughter, March, in tow, it could have been a scene out of Norman Rockwell.

Avery did not lead a storied public existence. This was not from lack of artistic passion, as some might claim, but from a completeness of vision matched with an intensity of discipline. He developed and matured as an artist, especially from 1940 on. Yet even as it appeared that his style—colorist, impressionist, always representational—was on the wane, as happened more than once, he did not stray from his general aesthetic direction. Hilton Kramer, who wrote the first monograph on Avery in 1962, remarked that it was "in Avery's aesthetic rather than in his biography that the key to his achievement will be found." Avery was so private that he falsified, successfully, the date of his own birth by eight years, relocating his birth year from 1885 to 1893 so as to court his younger wife. This detail was only uncovered in 1982 by Barbara Haskell. That white lie, she notes, was probably the only time this straightforward and one might even say modest painter exaggerated his lot in life.

If Milton Avery rarely discussed his work, the critics had no hesitations. His reputation was hashed out in the papers and the critical press with increasing frequency, especially from the late 1950s through his death in 1965 and after. For those seeking The Next Big Thing, Avery was chronically out of touch. He arrived in New York, just at a time when Stieglitz was closing up shop at his famous 291 Gallery, with what one might call a European style of modernism, not Cubism but more like Post-Impressionism mixed with the Hudson River School. In the 1920s, Avery was a colorist when few wanted color; in the 1930s, he was a hazy impressionist when the world wanted hard detail; in the 1950s, he was a representationalist when all-over abstraction was the rage. Despite the bad timing, the critic for the old *New York Sun*, Henry McBride, was one of Avery's earliest champions, writing over twenty reviews between 1928 and 1951. McBride often urged collectors to purchase Avery's work and was influential in placing him at Valentine Gallery. He wrote of one show in 1936: "it is a fine and natural talent that he has, though not easily defined. He is a poet, a colorist and a decorator; so excellent in each of these diversions that he might exist on any one of them; yet I presume that being a poet will eventually be his strongest claim." Edward Alden Jewell, the critic for *The New York Times*, was not so generous. He wrote in 1932: "The fact that Milton Avery sticks, season after season, to his mysterious—or, as the case may be, his mildly exasperating—paint theories, makes one feel that he is perfectly sincere. These often grotesque and sometimes rather gruesome forms of his must mean something pretty definite to him."

Bad as this treatment was, the most lasting damage to Avery's reputation came from comparisons to Matisse. Many critics considered Avery derivative of Matisse. Avery was certainly aware of Matisse because of their connection to Valentine Gallery, and McBride was in fact the first to make the comparison in 1940. One critic called Avery "the Matisse of puritanism." Frank Getlein wrote in *The New Republic* in 1966: "The French Master wished to make an art as comfortable as a good armchair, and he succeeded. The American's art is more nearly described as a swim in the ocean off Maine." Sally Avery, in one interview, keyed in the differences: "Matisse was a hedonist and Milton was an ascetic. . . . That is the opposite of French sensibility. . . . Milton's nudes are the purest nudes you ever came across, where . . . Matisse's have an erotic quality."

Sally Avery was Milton's first critical champion and his best observer. She once remarked of her husband: "The subject of his drawing was not the object of his drawing. It could have been anything." In a seminal essay on Avery in *Arts Magazine* in 1957, Clement Greenberg agreed and acknowledged that he once underestimated the artist. Comparing Avery to Dove, Arnold Friedman, John Marin, and Marsden Hartley (whom Avery painted more than once), Greenberg wrote:

Fifteen years ago, reviewing one of his shows at Paul Rosenberg's in *The Nation*, while I admired his landscapes, I gave most of my space to the derivativeness of the figure pieces, that made up the bulk of the show, and if I failed to discern how much there was in these that was not Matisse, it was not only because of my own imperceptiveness, but also because the artist himself had contrived not to call enough attention to it. . . . Avery's is the opposite of what is supposed to be a typical American attitude in that he approaches nature as a subject rather than as an object. One does not manipulate a subject, one *meets* it.

Ultimately, it was Milton Avery himself who let his interests be known. In 1931, he gave a rare interview to the *Hartford Courant* that, very early in his career, identified his position with pinpoint accuracy:

the canvas must be completely organized through the perfect arrangement of form, line, color and space. Objects in the subject matter, therefore, cannot be painted representatively, but they must take their place in the whole design. . . . To those who do not see the aim of the artist, the effect seems to be a distortion . . . but to the painter it is simply the result of a planned organization of all the elements that enter into a painting in the space of the canvas. El Greco elongated his figures for the same reason.

There have been many artists as well as critics of modernism who have shared these painterly concerns. The achievement of Milton Avery can be found in the way he was able to articulate his faith in "the organization of all the elements" with an economy of means and, more significantly, with his color palette—different from both Bonnard and Matisse. He crafted *Red Rock Falls* through an ideal of interlocking shapes and colors that, I now realize, allows for a special form of dynamism. Even its checkered hatchmarks, as though sewn with a piece of thread, tie this work together.

The mid-size show at The Phillips Collection, "Discovering Milton Avery: Two Devoted Collectors, Louis Kaufman and Duncan Phillips," presents a wide range of Avery's oeuvre. Louis Kaufman, a violinist, played on the soundtracks of some of Hollywood's most famous films, including *Gone with the Wind* and *Casablanca*; he was also the first person to make a recording of Vivaldi's "Four Seasons." In 1928 he purchased the first work Avery ever sold, *Still Life with Bananas and a Bottle* (1928). He and his wife, Annette—who at ninety helped organize this show—developed a close friendship with the Averys that lasted forty years. During this time they received many paintings and sketches from Avery, and the two also sat for a number of portraits.

Paired to the Kaufman collection are the acquisitions of Duncan Phillips, who was Avery's first institutional buyer. In 1929 he acquired *Winter Riders* (1929) from a dealer for his new Washington gallery. This is more significant than it may appear. One of the great ironies of American collecting is that while Americans collected the French modernists ahead of the French, Americans often ignored the American school.

Rounding out the show is a handful of Avery's famous large colorist works of the late 1950s and early 1960s, on loan from the Milton Avery Trust. These canvases constitute a magnificent conclusion to the exhibition and shed additional light on the earlier work collected by Phillips and Kaufman.

What I noticed from this exhibition, some of it purchased for collection, other work received as gifts, is how haltingly and sometimes falteringly Avery's style developed: compare the Matisse-like portrait of *Annette in a Green Dress* from 1933 with the distilled forms of *Annette Kaufman in a Black Dress*. Painted in 1944, *Black Dress* looks new even today while *Green Dress* appears fussy and, yes, derivative. There are also many drawings, sketches, and some exquisite drypoints here, crafted on discarded copper plates from *Progressive Grocer*, that reveal Avery's deft achievements in line, which often rival his skills as a colorist.

It is as a colorist, nevertheless, that Avery most influenced the artists and critics around him. Roger Fry, in *Transformations* (1926), rightly predicted the importance of color in the art to come: "as colour becomes incorporated into the integral plastic expression the principles which underlie its evocative power will claim a more conscious and deliberate investigation." Hans Hofmann maintained that "Avery was one of the first to understand color as a creative means. He was one of the first to relate colors in a plastic way." At Avery's memorial service in 1965, Mark Rothko famously remarked: "There have been several others in our generation who have celebrated the world around them, but none with that inevitability where the poetry penetrated every pore of the canvas to the very last touch of the brush. For Avery was a great poet-inventor who had invented sonorities never seen or heard before. From these we have learned much and will learn more for a long time to come." With quiet harmonies of color and line, Avery's lessons continue to instruct.

May 2004

Philhellene's Progress:
Patrick Leigh Fermor

Ben Downing

I have carried the soldier's musket, the traveler's stick, the pilgrim's staff.
—Chateaubriand

T HE CAPTIVE MUST have been exhausted and afraid, but when, on the fourth day of his grueling forced march across Crete, he saw dawn break behind Mount Ida, the sight was so beautiful that it brought to his lips the opening of Horace's Ode I.ix: "*Vides ut alta stet nive candidum/ Soracte,*" (In J. V. Cunningham's translation, "See how resplendent in deep snow/ Soracte stands.") he murmured. Then, just as he trailed off, one of his captors came in to take the poem over, reciting the rest of its six stanzas. At this, the captive's startled eyes slanted down from the peak to meet those of his enemy, and, after a long thoughtful silence, he pronounced, "*Ach so, Herr Major.*" For the captive was a German soldier—the commander of the island's garrison, no less. General Karl Kreipe (to give him his name) had been abducted on April 26, 1944 by a band of Greek guerrillas led by two English commandos. Over the next three weeks, the kidnappers picked their way across Crete, eluding the thousands of Nazi troops who hunted them, until eventually they were met by a British boat and whisked to Cairo, where Kreipe was handed over and the two commandos promptly awarded the D.S.O. One of these men was W. Stanley Moss, who in 1950 published a riveting account of the escapade, *Ill-Met by Moonlight*, later filmed by Michael Powell. The other was a certain Patrick Leigh Fermor. Disguised as a shepherd and (like Zeus in his Cretan boyhood) living largely in caves, he had spent much of the previous two years on the island organizing the resistance. Leigh Fermor it was who finished the quotation.

But where had he, who'd never completed high school, learned Horace so well? Had Kreipe asked him this, Leigh Fermor could have answered, savoring the irony, that he'd committed the odes to memory during his teenage *Wanderjahr* a decade earlier, when, just after Hitler's rise to power, he'd walked clear across Germany (among other countries) with a volume of Horace for his vade mecum, often reciting the poems to himself as he tramped. About that experience he'd not yet written a public word, and would not do so for many more years. Similarly he held off recounting his aubade with Kreipe. At last, however, in the 1970s, he broached the subjects of his continental traverse and, in an aside to that account, of his fleeting bond with Kreipe. Some things are best waited for: the book in which Leigh Fermor set these matters down, *A Time of Gifts* (1977), along with its sequel, *Between the Woods and the Water* (1986), represent not only the capstone of his career but, in my opinion, the finest travel books in the language and a pinnacle of modern English prose, resplendent as Soracte or Ida in deep snow.

The deplorable fact that most Americans, even well-read ones, have never even heard, as I also had not until recently, of a figure who in Britain (to say nothing of Greece, where he lives to this day) is revered and beloved as war hero, author, and bon vivant; who is, in Jan Morris's words, "beyond cavil the greatest of living travel writers"; and who, in those of the historian John Julius Norwich, "writes English as well as anyone alive"—all this spurs me to correct our oversight of the sublime, the peerless Patrick Leigh Fermor.

HIS TURBULENT EARLY life is recounted in the introduction to *A Time of Gifts*. Shortly after his birth in 1915, his mother and sister went to join his father in India, while he was left behind "so that one of us might survive if the ship were sunk by a submarine." For four years he was billeted with a Northamptonshire farming family, an experience that proved "the opposite of the ordeal Kipling describes in *Baa Baa Black Sheep*." A halcyon period, this, but the taste for boisterous freedom he acquired in the fields made for trouble later on: "Those marvelously lawless years, it seems, had unfitted me for the faintest shadow of constraint." Especially intolerable to him were academic strictures of any kind, and there ensued a long series of dust-ups and expulsions, hilariously related. At ten he was sent to "a school for difficult children," among which misfits he lists

> the millionaire's nephew who chased motor-cars along country lanes with a stick, the admiral's pretty and slightly kleptomaniac daughter, the pursuivant's son with nightmares and an infectious inherited passion for

heraldry, the backward, the somnambulists . . . and, finally, the small bad hats like me who were merely very naughty.

As Leigh Fermor observes, "English schools, the moment they depart from the conventional track, are oases of strangeness and comedy."

That "conventional track" was given one last stab when he, having narrowly passed his Common Entrance exams, entered King's School, Canterbury. For a time all went smoothly, but soon he was back to raising adolescent hob. "'You're mad!,' prefects and monitors would exclaim, brows knit in glaring scrum-half bewilderment, as new misdeeds came to light. . . . Frequent gatings joined the miles of Latin hexameters copied out as impositions." (Today such a scapegrace would no doubt be diagnosed with A.D.D. and put on ritalin.) His housemaster, in a report, described him as "a dangerous mixture of sophistication and recklessness." The last straw was almost literally that, a vegetable transgression: he conceived a violent crush on a local greengrocer's daughter—a townie, as it were—and while his affair with this "sonnet-begetting beauty" never progressed beyond handholding, it was, once found out, too much for the school authorities. He was promptly sacked.

At loose ends, he went through the motions of preparing for Sandhurst. Soon, however, he slid into a dissipated life of partying with "the remainder, more or less, of the Bright Young People, but ten years and twenty thousand double whiskies after their heyday." He lodged with Beatrice Stewart, a friend and model to Sargent, Sickert, Augustus John, and others. "I had a vision of myself, as I moved in, settling down to writing with a single-minded and almost Trollopian diligence." But the ceaseless on-site bacchanalia put paid to his ambitions for the moment. Frustration mounted and was capped by despair. What to do next?

Then, at a stroke, he hatched a fantastic plan to "set out across Europe like a tramp—or, as I characteristically phrased it to myself, like a pilgrim or a palmer, an errant scholar, a broken knight or the hero of *The Cloister and the Hearth*!" (Helen Waddell's recently published *The Wandering Scholars* also must have fired his imagination.) On foot, he would follow a mostly riverine course, along the Rhine and then the Danube; and as for his final destination, it could only be Constantinople, as he persists in calling Istanbul. "These certainties sprang from reading the books of Robert Byron; dragon-green Byzantium loomed serpent-haunted and gong-tormented." By luck, he even managed a link with Byron when his friend Mark Ogilvie-Grant bequeathed to him the rucksack he had carried while accompanying Byron around Mount Athos. Thus talismanically kitted, he set sail for the Hook of Holland in December 1933.

To the Netherlands, soon crossed, Leigh Fermor devotes only a few pages. Here he documents that peculiar *déjà vu* provoked by moving through an intimate world that hundreds of Dutch canvases have faithfully adumbrated—of *being* in a painting:

> So compelling is the identity of picture and reality that all along my path numberless dawdling afternoons in museums were being summoned back to life and set in motion. Every pace confirmed them. Each scene conjured up its echo. The masts and quays and gables of a river port, the backyard with a besom leaning against a brick wall, the chequer-board floors of churches—there they all were, the entire range of Dutch themes, ending in taverns where I expected to find boors carousing, and found them.

Such reveries were brought up short by the sight of swastikas at the German border. Leigh Fermor's treatment of Germany, whose capacity for barbarism he later felt at close quarters, is remarkably evenhanded. He never lets subsequent events retroactively embitter his memories of that winter, and is quick to acknowledge the praiseworthy aspects of German life, in particular the "old tradition . . . of benevolence to the wandering young," of which he gratefully took advantage. Still, there were hints of the catastrophe to come, as when, at some *Bierstube*, the talk would take a sudden, awkward turn:

> In all these conversations there was one opening I particularly dreaded: I was English? Yes. A student? Yes. At Oxford, no? No. At this point I knew what I was in for.
>
> The summer before, the Oxford Union had voted that "under no circumstances would they fight for King and Country." The stir it had made in England was nothing, I gathered, to the sensation in Germany. I didn't know much about it. In my explanation—for I was always pressed for one—I depicted the whole thing as merely another act of defiance against the older generation. The very phrasing of the motion—"fight for King and Country"—was an obsolete cliché from an old recruiting poster: no one, not even the fiercest patriot, would use it now to describe a deeply-felt sentiment. My interlocutors asked: "Why not?" "Für König und Vaterland" sounded different in German ears: it was a bugle-call that had lost none of its resonance. What exactly did I mean? The motion was probably "pour épater les bourgeois," I floundered. Here someone speaking a little French would try to help. "Um die Bürger zu erstaunen? Ach, so!" A pause would follow. "A kind of joke, really," I went on. "Ein Scherz?" they would ask. "Ein Spass? Ein Witz?" I was surrounded by

glaring eyeballs and teeth. Someone would shrug and let out a staccato
laugh like three notches on a watchman's rattle. I could detect a kindling
glint of scornful pity and triumph in the surrounding eyes which declared
quite plainly their certainty that, were I right, England was too far gone in
degeneracy and frivolity to present a problem. But the distress I could
detect on the face of a silent opponent of the régime was still harder to
bear: it hinted that the will or the capacity to save civilisation was lacking
where it might have been hoped for.

Not even these omens, though, could dampen his surging enthusiasm.
By Ulm, he was in full aesthetic ferment. The town's minster is remembered
thus:

> The clustered piers, which looked slender for so huge a place, divided the
> nave into five aisles and soared to a network of groins and ribs and liernes
> that a slight architectural shrug would have flicked into fan tracery. But it
> was the choir-stalls that halted one. A bold oaken outburst of three-
> dimensional humanism had wrought the finials . . . into the life-size tor-
> sos, in dark wood, of the sybils: ladies that is, dressed in coifs and wimples
> and slashed sleeves and hatted in pikehorn headdresses like the Duchess's
> in *Alice in Wonderland*. They craned yearning across the chancel towards
> Plato and Aristotle and an answering academy of pagan philosophers ac-
> coutred like burgomasters and led by a burgravial Ptolemy wielding a
> wooden astrolabe.

Then, in Munich, he became close with a family of exiled Estonian
aristocrats, through them gaining entry to a rarefied network of Central
European country-houses. Letters on his behalf were fired off to schlosses
all along the way, and these missives "unloosed cornucopias of warm and
boundless hospitality when I caught up with them." Hopping like a latter-
day Rilke from castle to castle (and mildly reproaching himself for having
abandoned his ideal of scroungy vagabondage), he glimpsed a whole gen-
teel world teetering on the cusp of extinction. Here he is being regaled by a
kindly old count in Austria:

> As I listened, the white gloved hand of the Lincoln green footman poured
> out coffee and placed little silver vermeil-lined goblets beside the Count's
> cup and mine. Then he filled them with what I thought was schnapps. I'd
> learnt what to do with that in recent weeks—*or so I thought*—and I was
> picking it up to tilt it into the coffee when the Count broke off his narra-
> tive with a quavering cry as though an arrow from some hidden archer

had transfixed him. "NEIN! NEIN!," he faltered. A pleading, ringed and almost transparent hand was stretched out and the stress of the moment drove him into English: "No! No! Nononono—!" I didn't know what had happened. Nor did the others. There was a moment of perplexity. Then, following the Count's troubled glance, all our eyes alighted simultaneously on the little poised silver goblet in my hand. . . . His anxiety had been for my sake, he said apologetically. The liquid wasn't schnapps at all, but incomparable nectar—the last of a bottle of liqueur distilled from Tokay grapes and an elixir of fabulous rarity and age.

Further on, in Slovakia, he was hosted by the marvelously named Baron Pips, who put him on to Proust. In Budapest—we've now shifted, by the way, to *Between the Woods and the Water*—he caroused with the local *jeunesse dorée*; and when he set out across the Great Hungarian Plain, he found still more drawbridges lowering at his approach: "word of the hazard moving across the south-east Alföld [i.e., the Plain] must have got about and thank God I shall never know whether it loomed as a threat or a bit of a joke." Crossing into Transylvania, he found himself swept up into a strange quaint universe of Magyar squires, all chafing under the Treaty of Trianon, which had left them marooned in Romania. (For a magisterial account of Germano-Romanian life in the same period, see *The Snows of Yesteryear* by Gregor von Rezzori; 1989.) "The prevailing atmosphere surrounding these kastély-dwellers conjured up that of the tumbling demesnes of the Anglo-Irish in Waterford or Galway, with all their sadness and their magic. . . . They lived in a backward-looking, a genealogical, almost a Confucian dream and many sentences ended in a sigh." His picture of this isolate elite, haunted by "phantoms of their lost ascendancy," is unforgettable, as witness the following inventory:

> All through the afternoon the hills had been growing in height and now they rolled into the distance behind a steep and solitary hemisphere clad to the summit with vineyard. We turned into the tall gates at the foot of it and a long sweep of grass brought us to a Palladian façade just as night was falling. Two herons rose as we approached; the shadows were full of the scent of lilac. Beyond the french windows, a coifed and barefoot maid with a spill was lighting lamps down a long room and, with each new pool of light, Biedermeier furniture took shape and chairs and sofas where only a few strands of the original fabric still lingered; there were faded plum-coloured curtains and a grand piano laden with framed photographs and old family albums with brass clasps; antlers branched, a stuffed lynx pricked its ears, ancestors with swords and furred tunics dimly postured. A

white stove soared between bookcases, bear-skins spread underfoot, and . . . a sideboard carried an array of silver cigarette-cases with the arms and monograms of friends who had bestowed them for standing god-father or being best man at a wedding or second in a duel. There was a polished shellcase from some Silesian battle, a congeries of thimble-sized goblets, a scimitar with a turquoise-encrusted scabbard, folded news-papers—*Az Ujság* and *Pesti Hírlap* sent from Budapest, and the *Wiener Salonblatt*, an Austrian *Tatler* full of pictures of shooting parties, equestrian events and smart balls far away, posted from Vienna. Among the silver frames was a daguerreotype of the Empress Elizabeth—Queen, rather, in this lost province of the former Kingdom—another of the Regent dressed as admiral of a vanished fleet, and a third of Archduke Otto in the pelts and the plumes of a Hungarian magnate. Red, green and blue, the squat volumes of the *Almanach de Gotha* were ready to pounce.

Despite their dislocation, these gentlefolk never failed to exude, he found, "charm and *douceur de vivre.*" As spring ripened into summer, and as he pushed further into Romania, he joined in their gay round of parties and excursions. Also flings: this magic season culminated for him in a brief yet torrid affair with a married Hungarian woman, Angéla. Zipping around Transylvania in a touring car with Angéla and his friend István, his bliss was such that even the news of Dollfuss's assassination, filtering in from Austria, cast but a momentary pall. Finally he tore himself loose from this idyll, reverting to his hobo ways as he headed up into the Carpathians, where he became the guest, successively, of backwoods Gypsies and Jews. (A rabbi's bonhomie especially delighted him: "I had thought I could never get on friendly terms with such unassailable-looking men.") Descending from the mountains to the spa town of Baile Herculane to seek out a friend of István, he indulged in one last gilded frolic before sailing down a gorge of the Danube known as the Iron Gates, which is where the second volume ends.

It is difficult, even quoting extensively as I have, to convey the almost preternatural copiousness of these two books. There are disquisitions on everything from the *Landsknecht* (a Renaissance infantryman) to the *chibook* (a Turkish pipe) and everyone from the Jazyges ("an Iranian speaking branch of the Sarmatians mentioned by Herodotus") to the Uniats (a Greco-Catholic sect), from St. John Nepomuk to Vlad the Impaler; vivid evocations of Bavarian beerhalls, Slovak red-light districts, and countless other milieux; and razor-sharp, affectionate, often uproarious sketches of the oddballs Leigh Fermor met along the way. These include a Frisian Is-lander given to speaking garbled neo-Elizabethan—"Among good and luckless men," he warned, "there is no lack of base ones, footpads and knaves who never shrink from purloining"—and a Romanian count, famous as an entomologist, whose Scottish nanny had left him muttering things like "I hae me doots." Far from surfeit, the effect of so much muchness is a cumulative magnificence, building up in golden passage after golden passage.

Yet what of the more than forty-year gap between journey and tale? How can Leigh Fermor possibly *remember* all this? One answer is that he took extensive notes at the time, and has since retraced parts of his route. Another is that he's added a lot: there are great reams of learning here that not even the most precocious teenager can have mastered. But still. Wisely, he negotiates this narrative dilemma by ignoring it; never does he wring his hands and fret, in effect, "Well, admittedly I didn't know such and such *back then*." That he often embellishes, that he credits to youth what properly belongs to riper age, hardly needs acknowledgment, and so commandingly articulated is his point of view that one doesn't think to question it. In fact, this overlay of adult sensibility vastly enhances the account, investing it with a rich patina.

But it's the boy who predominates. Few writers catch as well as Leigh Fermor the raw jubilation of youth, and fewer still render it so infectious. As he advances into a deepening enchantment, so goes the reader headlong with him. Schlosses and minsters, barons and counts, Gypsies and Jazyges, Tokay and *chibook*: all contribute to the spell, yet what matters more is how all these are felt, the way each fillips along the boy's cultural education—his *Bildung*, if you will. Many books implicitly concern the windfall lessons of travel; these explicitly do. Their narrative treats, ultimately, of grace; it's the story of how Leigh Fermor put juvenile ignominy behind him and gained, in its place, mature knowledge and confidence.

This whole ameliorative dimension of *A Time of Gifts* and *Between the Woods and the Water*, combined with the profusion and sweep of their prose, makes the books, by the end, overwhelmingly beautiful and satisfying. Small wonder they've inspired younger writers—such as Jason Goodwin, author of *On Foot to the Golden Horn*—and pilgrims to follow in Leigh Fermor's tracks. When he finishes his trilogy, it will constitute one of the great sequences in modern literature. I gather that John Murray, Leigh Fermor's publisher, fields, on average, one call per week from a fan desperate to know when the last volume is expected. (John Murray keeps strikingly handsome clothbound editions of most of Leigh Fermor's books in print in England. Penguin does the same with paperbacks, but, inexplicably and unforgivably, does not distribute them in the United States.)

Leigh Fermor's activities over the next few years remain murky to me; he alludes to them here and there, but only vaguely. He took part, apparently, in an anti-royalist revolt in northern Greece, attaching himself to a cavalry regiment. According to his schoolday friend Alan Watts, the famous proponent of Zen, in this period he also "visited the monks at Mount Athos, which he discovered to be an elaborate homosexual organization, and then spent a year as the lover of a Rumanian princess." I'm unsure about the princess part, but it does seem that Leigh Fermor lived for a while—two years, in fact—with a family in Moldavia, until the war forced his departure. Post-bellum he began roving again, this time in the Caribbean and Central America, before eventually settling in the Peloponnese, where he lives with his wife in a house he designed and built (architecture being one of his main preoccupations).

His remaining works can be neatly halved: there are three full-dress travelogues and three minor productions. Of these latter, the earliest is a suave novella, *The Violins of Saint-Jacques* (1953), which concerns a *Titanic*-meets-Mount Pelée disaster: during Mardi Gras, a volcanic Caribbean island erupts, then sinks, leaving one survivor. Next came *A Time to Keep Silence* (1957), a short volume about monasteries and my favorite of this group. A sample:

> According to a rumour widespread in France, Trappist monks greet each other daily with the words: *Frère, il faut mourir*, and a mythical agendum in the duties of a monk is the digging of his own tomb, a few spadefuls a day. Another legend represents all Trappists as the authors of atrocious and undetected crimes, preferably the murder of their fathers and mothers, for which only the long penance of Trappist life can atone. Most sinister of all is the theory that the marshy country in which Cistercian monasteries are usually situated is chosen so that the vapours of the swamps may speed their inhabitants to an early grave. Even the name encourages such fables: the unwary traveller advances, the Trappe swings open, he drops into the dark, he is caught.

Last of the triad is *Three Letters from the Andes* (1991), a very slight affair indeed and not particularly recommended.

As for the major books, *The Traveller's Tree* (1950) recounts Leigh Fermor's jaunt in the Caribbean. Though often superb, it falls short of his best European work; his manner somehow suits the New World less than the Old. Then there are his two prodigious books about Greece, *Mani* (1958) and *Roumeli* (1966), both of them stuffed to bursting with Hellenic arcana. *Roumeli* features some quintessentially Leigh Fermorian adventures, including visits to the Sarakatsáns, a mysterious nomadic people, and the Kravarites, a remote community of mendicants and hustlers who speak a private language ("the odd ethnological rock-pools of Europe" have always fascinated him), as well as an errand to Missolonghi to retrieve a pair of Lord Byron's shoes. Still, the clear choice here is *Mani*, Leigh Fermor's other flat-out masterpiece.

THE MANI, A BACKWARD, hardscrabble region of the southern Peloponnese, would seem a tough row for a writer to hoe. But, like Norman Douglas in *Old Calabria*, Leigh Fermor turns up, in this unpromising place, a fine trove of history ("It is a little known fact, recorded in the *Wars* of Procopius, that Genseric, King of the Vandals, after he had conquered Carthage, purposed to invade the Mani") and folklore:

> Belief in the prophetic importance of dreams, a pan-Hellenic superstition, is even stronger here than in the rest of Greece. In Greece, one 'sees' a dream, but the exegesis of what one sees varies from region to region. In the Mani, in unconscious conformity with many modern theories, it goes by opposites. The dream-taste of sweetness or the sight of sweet things — cakes or a honeycomb, for instance — spell poison and bitterness; flowers mean sorrow . . . eggs — the symbol of paschal concord — foretell high words and a quarrel. . . . To have meaning, a dream must be short — a sort of illuminating flash. Long dreams are attributed to indigestion and discounted. . . . If a dream seems totally irrelevant it may be the case of a wrong address, as they are sometimes delivered by mistake to people with the same name as the true destinatory. The dreamer must try and find out the real addressee and hand the dream over.

Nancy Mitford, in a letter to Evelyn Waugh, once sniffed about Paddy (as he's universally known) "wasting his excellent language on Greek peasants." How dreadfully *déclassé*! True, he does sometimes wax rather misty over the manifold virtues of rural Greek character. But when sticking to custom he's crystalline:

> Often, from its inception, one is able to predict the whole course of a village conversation, what topic will unleash another, where the sighs and the laughter will come, the signs of the cross and the right hand displayed palm outwards and fingers extended in anathema; where heads will be shaken or the edge of the table struck in indignation with the index-finger doubled up. They unfold with the inevitability of ritual. . . . Many an hour of hilarity is really a long game of conkers and there is a strange pleasure for the experienced in observing the punctilio of stroke and counterstroke.

Along with this kind of hominess, there is, as ever, plenty of pyrotechnic display. One of Leigh Fermor's key obsessions remains Byzantium, which he can scarcely mention without a sigh of Yeatsian nostalgia. Even in *The Traveller's Tree*, he manages to stumble, in a Barbados churchyard, on the grave of Ferdinando Palaeologus, a seventeenth-century descendant of Constantine XI. The Mani provides far broader license for his Byzantine excurses:

> Very often, wandering in the wilder parts of Greece, the traveller is astonished in semi-abandoned chapels . . . by the subtlety with which the painter has availed himself of the sparse elbow-room for private inspiration that the formulae of Byzantine iconography allow him: a convention so strict that it was finally codified by a sixteenth-century painter-monk called Dionysios of Phourna. He formalized the tradition of centuries into an iconographic dogma and deviation became, as it were, tantamount to schism. He it was who made the army of saints and martyrs and prophets identifiable at once by certain unvarying indices—the cut and growth of saints' beards, their fall in waves or ringlets, their smooth flow or their shagginess. . . . He regulated—it was more the ratification of old custom than the launching of new fiats—the wings that anomalously spring from the shoulder blades of St. John Prodromos, and placed his head on a charger in his hands as well as on his neck. He stipulated the angle at which a timely sapling, springing from the ground, should redeem the nakedness of St. Onouphrios from scandal.

Yet another of Leigh Fermor's hobbyhorses is costume, of whose history and lexicon he evinces a knowledge almost unseemly in a heterosexual male; clearly a fashion plate himself, he can't resist cataloging the dress of everyone he comes across. In *Mani*, we are treated to a spectacular digression on two kinds of hats, the *gudjaman* and the *ishlik*, both worn by Phanariot hospodars in the Danubian principalities of the Ottoman Empire. "What is the origin of these sartorial freaks?," Leigh Fermor wonders aloud, then lets fly with conjectures that reach into Persia and Muscovy and that adduce, among others, Filarete, Piero della Francesca, and Pisanello—all by way of illustrating "the Byzantine passion for strange hats." We also hear of the *fustanella*, a white skirt once worn by Greek men:

> Under King Otto and Queen Amelia, the fustanella and all its attendant finery, with superbly Byronic costumes for ladies-in-waiting, was the official court dress. When he was Greek Minister in Paris the great Kolletis . . . would often wear it, and the Goncourt journals speak with admiration of

his presiding fully-kilted over delicious banquets of *agneau à la pallikare*. . . .
Wittelsbach eccentricity, and a touching loyalty to the country he adopted,
impelled King Otto to affect the fustanella in Bavaria after his abdication. It
is thus clad that we may think of him among the fir trees and neo-gothic
pinnacles of Neuschwanstein and Hohenschwangau.

Finally there are, as always, remembrances of drinks past:

> The stone flags of the water's edge, where [we] sat down to dinner, flung
> back the heat like a casserole with the lid off. On a sudden, silent decision
> we stepped down fully dressed into the sea carrying the iron table a few
> yards out and then our three chairs. . . . The waiter, arriving a moment
> later, gazed with surprise at the empty space on the quay; then, observing
> us with a quickly-masked flicker of pleasure, he stepped unhesitatingly
> into the sea, advanced waist deep with a butler's gravity, and, saying
> nothing more than "Dinner-time," placed our meal before us. . . . Diverted
> by this spectacle, the diners on the quay sent us can upon can of retsina till
> the table was crowded. A dozen boats soon gathered there, the craft
> radiating from the table's circumference like the petals of a marguerite.
> Leaning from their gently rocking boats, the fishermen helped us out with
> this sudden flux of wine.

Almost as much toping goes on in Leigh Fermor as in Hemingway, and his
wassails sound like far more fun than Papa's.

Of all the sweeping judgments one might pronounce on the literature
of the century just departed, fewer can be ventured more confidently than
that the British dominated travel writing. Admittedly, the term itself is
baggy and unappealing; Leigh Fermor himself, as did his close friend Bruce
Chatwin, abominates it. (Chatwin's latest biographer, Nicholas Shakespeare, describes Leigh Fermor as Chatwin's "last guru" and "a man of
action and of knowledge to a degree that Bruce envied." Chatwin's ashes are
buried near the Leigh Fermors' house.) But whatever one chooses to call
the form, the British knack for it is undeniable. Consider first the many
authors admired mostly for their peregrinations, even a short list of whom
surely must include (by order of birth) Norman Douglas, H. M. Tomlin-
son, Apsley Cherry-Garrard, Freya Stark, Robert Byron, Peter Fleming,
Wilfred Thesiger, Eric Newby, Norman Lewis, Jan Morris, Colin Thubron,
Bruce Chatwin, Jonathan Raban, and Redmond O'Hanlon. And now add
those known chiefly for other work, but who've produced travel writing of
note: Belloc, Maugham, Forster, Lawrence, West, Huxley, Ackerley,
Pritchett, Waugh, Greene, Isherwood, Auden, and Durrell, to name only a

few. It seems almost obligatory, in fact, for British men and women of letters at least to dabble in the genre, which ranges in nature from perilous exploration of Antarctica (Cherry-Garrard) or Arabia (Thesiger) to setting up adorable house in Provence (you know who), and in length from the brisk metropolitan sketches of Morris to the hulking immensity of West's *Black Lamb and Grey Falcon*.

As for what makes the British so adept, such speculations are beyond the scope of this essay. I would remark, however, that the signal feature of their travelogues is an emphatic, often prickly individualism. (This extends even to studiously ignoring each other when they meet in godforsaken places. Just so, A. W. Kinglake greets another Englishman in the Sinai with no more than a tip of his cap, "as if we had passed in Pall Mall." In *Brazilian Adventure*, Peter Fleming shamefully confesses to having saluted a compatriot deep in the Amazon.) The impression of forceful and idiosyncratic personality is stronger with them, the attack more distinct. And of course the humor is matchless. Whether they purvey the imperious comedy of taking no guff from the natives or the gentler sort which derives from exposing their own blunders—Fleming, Newby, and O'Hanlon are self-skewering masters of ineptitude—British travelers can make the wretchedest, most hazardous trek seem an occasion for mirth.

Of these tendencies Leigh Fermor seems to me both the apotheosis and, in important ways, the opposite. Supremely independent and amusing he is, to be sure. But where the prevailing temper leans, by degrees, toward the skeptical, the tart, even the downright cantankerous—Douglas, Byron, and Raban (splendid writers all) are three very different examples of this—he is sanguine, cheerful, tolerant. At bottom he's an incorrigible romantic in several senses of that overtaxed word. It shows in his passionate exuberance; his love of pageantry and heraldry; his "minnesinger disposition" (as Iain Moncreiffe dubbed it); the dashing, gallant quality to everything he does and writes; and, above all, the free rein he gives to fancy and imagination. But Leigh Fermor's is a romanticism primarily of fact, which anchors his wildest fantasias and of which he possesses a stupefying store. Nor does there cling to his erudition the least stale whiff of pedantry or cant; his is the limber, rangy, magpie learning of the true autodidact, of a man who's never come within a mile of a university.

And then there's his prose. Unmistakable, without obvious antecedents, and fairly leaping off the page, the style of Patrick Leigh Fermor is a thing to make us mere hacks despair; for liveliness, momentum, and sheer, unfailing felicity of expression, there are few in the language to equal him. (Those of ascetic taste will find him purple. They are to be pitied.) At once relaxed and highly wrought, his prose moves to a cantering rhythm all its own and blithely flouts certain proprieties. No model for schoolboys, it is, to borrow Leigh Fermor's epithet for Robert Byron, "uncircumspect"—a prolix, run-on, spendthrift style, rife with exclamation marks and polysyndeton. It points up a basic yet crucial obligation of style in general: that it convey personality and point of view. What makes Leigh Fermor's style so remarkable isn't its flourishes of rhetoric or niceties of phrasing, choice though these may be, but how fully it bears out his robust character, how perfectly suited an instrument it is to him, and him alone.

Not only other writers may find themselves humbled. Fellow ramblers too. Next to Leigh Fermor, who is able, at any point on the map, both to notice and to put into play so formidably much, one cannot help but feel somewhat lumpish and incurious, like a rank package tourist. Yet this soon wears off. At communicating pleasure he is nonpareil, and one quickly catches his fever. For me, he captures uniquely the excitement, meaning, and value of travel; one learns how to travel better by reading him.

Which isn't to suggest that he has little to offer the sedentary. Even if you rarely quit your couch and opine, with Emerson, that travel is a fool's paradise, you are bound to enjoy Leigh Fermor purely as a historian, albeit of eccentric stripe. His great subject, to the extent he can be said to have one, is, quite simply, Europe. Brought alive in his pages as in no others known to me are the continent's heroes and villains, courtiers and peasants, wars and *belles époques*, faiths, tongues, buildings, garments, even tools: a whole ramified civilization of infinite nuance and cross-currents. Also the landscape in which all this unfolds—not just nature, though certainly that, but a sort of peopled, transhistorical topography.

Quite a mouthful! What I mean is better shown than told, so I'll conclude by citing two last passages. Here's Leigh Fermor in *Mani*, watching a cruise ship pass offshore:

> The liner followed the same path as many a Phoenician galley and many a quinquereme; heading northward in the invisible groove of Harald Hardraada's ships, sailing shield-hung and dragon-prowed from the Byzantine splendour of Mickelgaard for grey northern fjords.

And here he is in *A Time of Gifts*, gazing out across Slovakia but ruminating on landscape generally:

> The shift of mountains and plains and rivers and the evidence of enormous movements of races gave me the feeling of travelling across a relief map where the initiative lay wholly with the mineral world. It evicted with drought and ice, beckoned with water and grazing, decoyed with mirages

and tilted and shifted populations . . . steering languages, breaking them up into tribes and dialects, assembling and confronting kingdoms, grouping civilizations, channelling beliefs, guiding armies and blocking the way to philosophies and styles of art and finally giving them a relenting shove through the steeper passes.

The kind of mineral push, perhaps, that brings incongruously together, on a Greek mountainside, a German and an Englishman, communing at riflepoint over the verses of a long-dead Roman.

January 2001

Lord Acton: In Pursuit of First Principles

Gertrude Himmelfarb

A LMOST FIFTY YEARS ago, introducing my biography of Lord Acton, I wrote: "He is of this age, more than of his. He is, indeed, one of our great contemporaries." A decade and a half later, in an essay on Acton, I described him as being "totally out of sorts with his times"—but I no longer ventured to claim him for our times. Today, almost a century after his death, he seems to me to be even more out of sorts with our age than with his. His governing passions were liberty and morality, religion and history. If he found them all defective in his age, he would have been far more dismayed by what we have made of them.

Yet it is one of the many paradoxes of this extraordinary man that today he is a hero to so many people of such different persuasions and dispositions—liberals and conservatives, libertarians and traditionalists, Catholics, non-Catholics, and non-believers. An eminent Chicago-school economist, after professing the greatest admiration for Acton, once asked me, in all seriousness, how a man so brilliant, so learned, so utterly devoted to the cause of liberty, could also be a pious Catholic. One might more justly ask how a man so averse to the postmodernist spirit of our times can continue to be published, read, and quoted—and not only his celebrated aphorism about power. There are currently four substantial volumes of his essays and lectures in print and eight books (including my own) about him. The Acton Institute, under the energetic direction of Father Robert Sirico, sponsors lectures and monographs promoting his name and ideas. And now we have the first full biography of Acton, not an intellectual biography but a conventional one.

There are good reasons why such a biography has been so long delayed, among them the reluctance of the family, until recently, to make available correspondence critical of the Catholic Church. But the main reason may lie with Acton himself, who passionately believed in ideas as the moving force in history and whose own life was so dramatic a testament to the power of ideas that it naturally lends itself to intellectual biography and commentary. The present work by Roland Hill (*Lord Acton*; Yale University Press, 2000) is welcome, not only because it is meticulously and comprehensively researched—Hill is an English journalist who has written a book worthy of a professional historian—but also because it fleshes out little-known details of his personal life and relationships, his travels, financial difficulties, and the like. No less important, it inspires us to return to Acton's own writings and to reevaluate a mind that is far more complicated and challenging than we may have thought.

The barest account of Acton's life helps explain one of the most curious facts about him, that this eminent Victorian (his life was almost coterminous with the reign of Queen Victoria) was even more untypically Victorian than were other eminent Victorians. In a sense, Acton was not a Victorian at all, because he was not really an Englishman. By birth, education, and disposition, he was thoroughly cosmopolitan. The Actons were descended from an old English family of squires and baronets, the estate at Aldenham in Shropshire dating back to the early fourteenth century. In the eighteenth century Sir Richard, the head of the family, converted to Catholicism, and other members of the family, also converts, sought their fortunes abroad. With the death of Sir Richard, the title and estate reverted to a John Acton who was then the prime minister of Naples. John's eldest son, Richard, married Marie, the only daughter of the Duke of Dalberg (the Dalbergs, residing in the Rhineland, held the premier dukedom in the Holy Roman Empire) and of his wife, who came of an ancient Genoan family. The Dalbergs, like the Actons, had wandered from their ancestral home, one of them becoming a nationalized French citizen during the Napoleonic Wars and a peer of France after the restoration. It was into this multinational, multilingual family that the son of Richard and Marie, John Edward Emerich Dalberg Acton, was born in Naples in 1834.

Acton's father died when the boy was only three, and his mother's remarriage brought the family into yet another, very different social milieu. Lord Leveson, later the second Earl Granville, met Marie Acton in Paris, when he was Under-Secretary for Foreign Affairs in the Whig government and his father was the British ambassador to France. (The Dalbergs, who were part of Talleyrand's entourage, and the Actons, who maintained a house in the faubourg St. Honoré, spent the "season" in Paris.) If Acton proved to be an untypical Victorian (if a Victorian at all), his stepfather was the quintessential Victorian aristocrat, a member of one of the grand Whig—and, of course, Anglican—families. The marriage was not without its tensions, for Acton's mother was a devout Catholic, as was her son, who resisted the social life and political career that his stepfather thought natural and proper.

At every point, Acton's life reflected the complexities and anomalies of his heritage. Refused admission to three Cambridge colleges because he was Catholic, he pursued a decidedly un-English course of studies at Munich under the tutelage of the eminent Catholic theologian Johann Ignaz von Döllinger; when he went to Cambridge toward the end of his life it was as the Regius Professor of Modern History. His first position was as editor of the *Rambler*, a small Catholic journal; his last as editor of the monumental *Cambridge Modern History*. As a young man, on the urging of his stepfather, he reluctantly served in parliament for one undistinguished term; later, as the friend and adviser of Prime Minister Gladstone, he entertained the hope of a cabinet post, but received instead the position of Lord-in-Waiting to the Queen, the most onerous of his duties being dining with the Queen and royal family. He was relieved of that task by his appointment (not by Gladstone but by his successor, Rosebery) to the Regius Professorship, whereupon he delivered an inaugural lecture so allusive and abstruse that reviewers complained that they could not understand it.

These are only the more superficial paradoxes and ironies of Acton's life. Others are more serious, even tragic. A pious Catholic, for whom membership in the church was, as he said, "more than life itself" (Hill describes him as a man of "childlike faith"), he found himself passionately engaged in one of the most contentious Catholic events in modern times, the controversy over the doctrine of papal infallibility; very nearly excommunicated as a result, he was spared that fate by his influential political connections. A liberal, who was as zealously devoted to liberty as to religion, he had as little in common with the laissez-faire, utilitarian mode of liberalism prevalent in his day as with the welfare-state liberalism of our own. And a historian, who was perhaps the most learned and intellectually ambitious of his generation, he is known today as the author, so to speak, of the most famous book that was never written, *The History of Liberty*, and as the inventor of the aphorism (generally misquoted), "Power tends to corrupt and absolute power corrupts absolutely."

The most dramatic, indeed climactic, event in Acton's life was his battle against the doctrine of papal infallibility. He was well prepared for that battle by his theological and historical studies in Munich, his earlier conflict with the English Catholic hierarchy over his editorship of two liberal Catholic journals, and his relationship with Granville and Gladstone which gave him a special standing at the time of the Vatican Council. And he carried the scars of that battle throughout his later life, as is evident in his falling out with his mentor Döllinger, his sense of intellectual frustration and isolation, and his failure to write what should have been his magnum opus, the history of liberty. Long before the end of his life, he began to speak privately of this work as his "Madonna of the Future," a reference to Henry James's story of an artist who devotes his life to the creation of a single masterpiece which after his death is exposed as a blank canvas.

ᵃCTON WAS IN ʳOME when the Vatican Council met in 1870 and, although a layman, was influential in formulating the case against infallibility, publicizing it within the council and to the outside world, and coordinating the activities of the minority of bishops who opposed the doctrine. Papal infallibility, he insisted, was a perversion of both history and religion; it could only be supported by denying the spirit of Christianity, falsifying the history of the church, and subverting the legitimate relationship of pope and church. He delivered that uncompromising message to Catholics and non-Catholics alike. In an influential English journal, he wrote:

> The passage from the Catholicism of the Fathers to that of the modern Popes was accomplished by willful falsehood; and the whole structure of traditions, laws, and doctrines that supports the theory of infallibility, and the practical despotism of the Popes, stands on a basis of fraud.

Acton never deviated from that position, even after the promulgation of the doctrine when he formally professed obedience to the church, being careful, however, not to profess belief in the doctrine of infallibility itself. He bitterly reproached those Catholics, like Newman, who had also opposed the doctrine and had then, all too easily, in Acton's opinion, submitted to the church. More serious, and far more painful, was his disillusionment with Döllinger, who refused to submit and was excommunicated. But even he, Acton believed, did not appreciate the enormity of the doctrine itself, for by objecting to it on theological rather than historical grounds, he implicitly sanctioned all the evils in the "pre-July Church"— that is, before the promulgation of the doctrine.

The shadow of infallibility hovered over Acton the rest of his life, dominating his thinking not only about the church, but also about all of philosophy, politics, and history. Before the Vatican Council he had eulogized Edmund Burke as "the law and the prophets," the "teacher of mankind," the exponent of a "purely Catholic view of political principles and of history." One can hear the unmistakable echo of Burke in Acton's defense of the South at the time of the American Civil War and in his criticism of the abolitionists for exhibiting an "abstract, ideal absolutism, which is equally hostile with the Catholic and with the English spirit"—very different, Acton maintained, from the church, which sought to "reform mankind by assimilating realities with ideals, and accommodating herself to times and circumstances."

After the Vatican Council, as Acton's judgments of Döllinger and Newman became harsher, so did his judgment of Burke. The pragmatic, accommodating, "Catholic" Burke was now rebuked for encouraging men to "evade the arbitration of principle," to think of politics "experimentally," as an exercise in "what is likely to do good or harm, not what is right or wrong, innocent or sinful." For Acton, Burke became the quintessential, opportunistic Whig as opposed to the principled liberal. In his notes and letters he made much of this distinction between Whiggism and liberalism. Where the Whig revered "legality, authority, possession, tradition, custom, opinion," the liberal respected only "what ought to be, irrespective of what is." The Whig believed in the "repression of the ideal," the liberal in its affirmation. "The Whig governed by compromise; the Liberal begins the reign of idea." "To a Liberal, all the stages between Burke and Nero are little more than the phases of forgotten moons."

The *History of Liberty* was meant to trace the development of this idea of liberalism. Bits and pieces of that history survive: in two lectures on the history of freedom in antiquity and Christianity, delivered in 1877 to a local historical society and published in their journal; in a score of essays and reviews on a variety of subjects in the following decades; and in his lectures on the French Revolution delivered in Cambridge in the late 1890s and published posthumously as a volume. These essays and lectures are full of brilliant analyses and insights, recondite facts, provocative assertions, and a host of references to wide-ranging and often obscure sources. It would take a corps of researchers to elucidate all of his cryptic allusions: "the greatest man born of a Jewish mother since Titus" (identified elsewhere as the German statesman and philosopher Friedrich Julius Stahl—but did Titus have a Jewish mother?), or "the most prodigal imagination ever possessed by man" (the Renaissance poet Ariosto). An industrious young historian could embark upon a career by documenting and amplifying a single one of Acton's essays, or even one of his dense paragraphs. The whole adds up to a story so complicated that it defies easy summation or generalization. And it becomes even more complicated when these lectures and essays are supplemented by the vast amount of notes that reflect not only the extraordinary breadth and depth of his scholarship, but also the boldness and passion of his ideas.

Early in the lecture on antiquity, Acton cited, seemingly approvingly, the "famous saying of the most famous authoress on the continent" (Mme de Staël) that liberty is ancient and despotism modern. He then qualified that assertion so abundantly that little was left of it. The great contribution of the Greeks was the principle of representation, government by consent. But by failing to limit the power of the sovereign people or to provide for any law superior to the lawgiver, the principle of democracy undermined the principle of liberty. "The vice of the classic State" (Acton apologized for the anachronism) "was that it was both Church and State in one. . . . In religion, morality, and politics there was only one legislator and one authority." That fatal flaw was corrected by Christianity, whose dictum, "Render unto Caesar . . ." gave to the civil power "a sacredness it had never enjoyed, and bounds it had never acknowledged," thus laying the ground for "the repudiation of absolutism and the inauguration of freedom." Civil liberty was the result of the ensuing conflict between church and state, each aspiring to absolute authority and each limited by the other. The Middle Ages furthered the cause of freedom by extending representative govern-ment, abolishing slavery, recognizing the right of insurrection, and acknowledging duties "superior to those which are imposed by man." But even before the Reformation, and still more after, the church undermined freedom when it became the instrument of the ruling monarchs. Thus the kings of Spain appropriated the tribunal of the Inquisition, and the ab-solute monarchy of France was built up by "twelve political cardinals." "In the ages of which I have spoken," Acton sadly observed toward the end of his lecture on Christianity, "the history of freedom was the history of the thing that was not."

IN ANTIQUITY AND CHRISTIANITY, Acton saw the first tentative overtures toward freedom, but only in modernity did it emerge in its true nature. Protestant sects in seventeenth-century England discovered that "religious liberty is the generating principle of civil, and that civil liberty is the neces-sary condition of religious." But not until the American Revolution had "men sought liberty knowing what they sought." Unlike earlier experiments in liberty, which had been tainted by expediency, compromise, and interest, the Americans demanded liberty simply and purely as a right. The three-pence tax that provoked the revolution was three-pence worth of pure principle. "I will freely spend nineteen shillings in the pound," Acton quoted Benjamin Franklin, "to defend my right of giving or refusing one other shilling." Acton himself went further. The true liberal, like the Ameri-can revolutionist, "stakes his life, his fortune, the existence of his family, not to resist the intolerable reality of oppression, but the remote possibility of wrong, of diminished freedom." The American Constitution was unique in being both democratic and liberal. "It was democracy in its highest perfection, armed and vigilant, less against aristocracy and monarchy than against its own weakness and excess. . . . It resembled no other known democracy, for it respected freedom, authority, and law."

The French, unhappily, did not follow the example of the Americans. In his lectures on the French Revolution, Acton traced the course of events and the logic of ideas by which the revolution, starting with the promise of liberty, ended in tyranny and terror. (Those who deplore Acton's failure to fulfill his potentialities as a historian sometimes overlook this substantial volume. It is all the more remarkable because it is the work not of a specialist on the French Revolution but of one for whom this was only one of many interests, and by no means the major one.) The two fatal flaws in this revolution were the predilection for violence, which exhibited itself as early as the attack on the Bastille, and the commitment to the idea of equality: "The passion for equality made vain the hope of freedom." Unlike the Americans, who wisely complemented their declaration of rights with a mixed constitution, the French permitted nothing to stand in the way of equality. In a passage reminiscent of Tocqueville, Acton explained the potential for tyranny in democracy:

> It is bad to be oppressed by a minority, but it is worse to be oppressed by a majority. For there is a reserve of latent power in the masses which, if it is called into play, the minority can seldom resist. But from the absolute will of an entire people there is no appeal, no redemption, no refuge but treason.

This barebones summary of Acton's *History of Liberty* is almost a travesty of the original; it does not begin to convey the complexity and density of his lectures and essays. And the subject is further complicated by his views of history in general—the writing of history as well as the actuality of history. The audience at his inaugural lecture on "The Study of History" may have found much of it obscure, but there is no mistaking the moral fervor that inspired it and the moral burden it laid upon the historian. The historian, Acton declared, is a "hanging judge."

> The weight of opinion is against me when I exhort you [the student of history] never to debase the moral currency or to lower the standard of rectitude, but to try others by the final maxim that governs your own lives, and to suffer no man and no cause to escape the undying penalty which history has the power to inflict on wrong. . . . Opinions alter, manners change, creeds rise and fall, but the moral law is written on the tablets of eternity.

The idea of a moral law that is absolute and immutable is a recurrent, almost obsessive, theme in his notes and correspondence. Murder is the "low-water mark," the ultimate, objective fact that carries with it the ultimate, objective moral judgment. Historians who fail to abide by this test are more culpable than the murderers, for they are imperilling history as well as morality. "History ceases to be a science," Acton warned us, if the moral currency is debased.

History as "science"—Acton did not at all mean by this what latter-day positivists do, for his science, so far from being morally neutral ("value-free," we now say), was predicated on a moral absolute. His instructions to the contributors to the *Cambridge Modern History* have been much cited and derided. The idea of a "scientific" history written by scholars so objective as to be virtually anonymous seems quixotic in itself, and it is even more so when conjoined to the idea of a universal history, which was to be not so much a history of nations as a history of ideas, an "illumination of the soul." To Acton there was nothing utopian in these ideas, for both derived from a morality that was fixed and absolute. "The inflexible integrity of the moral code is, to me, the secret of the authority, the dignity, the utility of history."

IT IS THIS VIEW of history that lies behind the much quoted, and misquoted, maxim about power. It is not *all* power that corrupts, but power that *tends* to corrupt; and it is only *absolute* power that corrupts absolutely. Although Acton was careful to introduce such qualifications— "tends," "almost always," "in most cases," "the uncounted majority"—they are overshadowed by the passion of the idea itself:

> Great men are almost always bad men, even when they exercise influence and not authority: still more when you superadd the tendency or the certainty of corruption by authority. . . .
>
> The experience of history teaches that the uncounted majority of those who get a place in its pages are bad. . . . The Men of the Time are, in most cases, unprincipled, and act from motives of interest, of passion, of prejudice cherished and unchecked, of selfish hope or unworthy fear. . . .
>
> History is not a web woven with innocent hands. Among all the causes which degrade and demoralize men, power is the most constant and the most active.

This view of history is hardly conducive either to the pursuit of liberty or to the writing of a *History of Liberty*. One can account for Acton's failure to write that history by saying of him what he said of Döllinger, that "he knew too much to write." Or one can cite Acton's lament when he discovered that even Döllinger did not share his moral views (Döllinger having criticized the church for its "errors" rather than "crimes"):

> I am absolutely alone in my essential ethical position, and therefore useless. . . . The probability of doing good by writings so isolated and repulsive . . . is so small that I have no right to sacrifice to it my own tranquillity and my duty of educating my children.

But the problem is more fundamental still. It lies in an idea of liberty so morally rigorous, so absolute, that it could not be implemented, still less sustained, without fatal consequences.

THE ABSOLUTENESS of that idea is sometimes explicit, more often implicit, in his essays and lectures, but his notes carry it to its ultimate conclusion—to revolution as the culmination of absolute liberty. Liberalism inaugurated the "reign of ideas," and "the reign of general ideas [is that] which we call the Revolution." So too, the liberal theory of history, which requires that "what ought to be" take precedence over "what is," implies nothing less than a "revolution in permanence." His notes repeat this theme again and again:

> The principle of the higher law signifies Revolution. . . .
> Liberalism essentially revolutionary. Facts must yield to ideas. Peaceably and patiently if possible. Violently if not. . . .
> The story of the revolted colonies impresses us first and most distinctly as the supreme manifestation of the law of resistance, as the abstract revolution in its purest and most perfect shape.

"Revolution in permanence"—shades of Trotsky's "permanent revolution"! And shades of the French Revolution, whose degeneration from a "Republic of Virtue" into a Reign of Terror Acton so graphically described. But even as he was lauding this idea of liberty he was acutely aware of the perils of any idea so absolute.

> Government by Idea tends to take in everything, to make the whole of society obedient to the idea. Spaces not so governed are unconquered, beyond the border, unconverted, unconvinced, a future danger. . . .
> Government that is natural, habitual, works more easily. It remains in the hands of average men, that is of men who do not live by ideas. Therefore there is less strain by making government adapt itself to custom. An ideal government, much better, perhaps, would have to be maintained by effort, and imposed by force.

It might have been Burke who wrote this trenchant criticism of "government by idea." But then it was not Burke who was trying to write a *History of Liberty*. A Burkean (or Whiggish, as Acton would say) *History of Liberty* would be difficult enough; an Actonian (or liberal, again in Acton's sense) is impossible—and especially an Actonian one that had lingering traces of Burkeanism. Acton's *History of Liberty* invites comparison with Croce's *History as the Story of Liberty*. If the latter was written (and published), it was perhaps because Croce had all the confidence of a philosophical idealist whose ideals were immanent in history, whereas Acton had all the *angst* of an ethical idealist whose ideals were always being violated by history.

If my Acton is a more complicated, more tragic figure than Roland Hill's, it is perhaps because any conventional biography of a man like Acton, the drama of whose life was entirely the drama of his ideas, inevitably mutes that drama—domesticates it, as it were, by placing it in the context of the more mundane aspects of life. A conventional biographer is necessarily limited in the amount of space and attention he can give to ideas as dense, convoluted, often inconsistent and ambiguous as Acton's. Yet Hill's Acton, although blander than mine, is essentially the same Acton, an Acton "out of sorts" with his age and, even more, with ours. If Acton found his contemporaries insufficiently committed to the absolute value of truth and morality, what would he have made of those in our own time who have only the most relativistic sense of those values, or, worse, of those who dismiss and deride the very ideas of truth and morality as illusory, pawns in the struggle for power and "hegemony"?

Yet Acton does speak to us today—to those of us, at least, who are also out of sorts with our times. Whatever reservations we may have about his views on one or another subject, rereading him today is exhilarating, stimulating, illuminating, and often wonderfully prophetic. Historians may quarrel with his excessively idealistic interpretation of the American Revolution, but not with the contrast he draws between the American and French revolutions. We may find fault with an absolute liberty that has, as its necessary corollary, revolution, or an absolute morality that takes murder as its "low-water mark," or a view of the historian as a "hanging judge." But a generation that has experienced the horrors of totalitarianism and the atrocities of the Holocaust can appreciate, as his contemporaries could not, the importance he attached to the principles of liberty and morality. And we may well marvel at his extraordinary prescience in warning us against evils that have become all too real—the corrupting effects of power, or the despotic implications of "government by idea," or the potential for illiberalism in movements, such as nationalism, that most liberals of his time thought entirely commendable. Hill quotes the historian G. M. Trevelyan who, in his autobiography published after World War II, confessed that he had found Acton "always interesting, but sometimes strange": "I remember, for instance, his saying to me that States based on the unity of a single race, like modern Italy and Germany, would prove a danger to liberty; I did not see what he meant at the time, but I do now!" (That conversation took place some fifty years earlier, well before the First World War, let alone the Second.)

Catholics today have special reason to admire Acton. If they were once discomfitted by his trenchant criticisms, not only of the doctrine of infallibility, but also of the Inquisition and a multitude of other "crimes" committed by the church, they will now find him at least partially vindicated by their highest authority. Pope John Paul II's first major address in the new millennium was a plea for forgiveness for "the past and present sins" of the "sons" and "brothers" of the church. This "purification of memory," as the pope put it, recalls Acton's insistence upon the need to restore the true history of the "pre-July" as well as the "post-July" church. Moreover, Acton's special kind of "liberal Catholicism" is much more in the spirit of John Paul II than of those who generally assume that label. Acton did not wish to alter or dilute the dogmas, rituals, or traditions of the church; indeed, he opposed the "Old Catholic" sect that Döllinger joined because it did just that. Acton's liberal Catholicism consisted in reconciling the church with science and secular learning, observing the separation of church and state, and respecting the civil and political liberties of individuals.

"I never had any contemporaries," Acton once said. He would be pleased to know how many he now has. For dissidents today, he stands as an exemplar of intellectual courage, recalling us to first principles that are even more unfashionable today than they were in his time, and challenging us to reconsider how those principles may be incorporated into the practical realms of ethics and politics.

June 2000

Surtees and Money

Timothy Congdon

MONEY AND LITERATURE have an awkward relationship. Most authors are very human and like to be well paid. Yet authors also have a tendency to distinguish between literature as an art form and writing as a way of making a living, and they put literature on a higher plane of existence than the vulgar and repetitive accumulation of wealth. Despite the undoubted genuineness of their private efforts to improve their own fees and royalties, many authors in public deprecate the materialism of modern society. In October 2000, the Institute of Economic Affairs, a London-based think tank, published a book on *The Representation of Business in English Literature*. In a foreword, the institute's director, John Blundell, asked, "Why does the novelist, the writer of fiction, spit at the market, despise its institutions such as private property and the rule of law, and try to bite off the hand that feeds him?" The book provoked some irritation in such publications as *The New Statesman* and *Prospect*.

BUT AN ARGUMENT could be made that the use of literature to attack market institutions was a twentieth-century mistake. There may be intellectual mopping-up still to do, but few now question the superiority of liberal democracy and the market economy to the totalitarian, planned, and state-owned alternatives. In this respect the twenty-first century is more like the nineteenth century than its immediate predecessor. Some literature of the nineteenth century may therefore seem closer to us than much that was written in the twentieth century. In trying to find a drama to comment on the bubble economy of 1999 and 2000, the British Broadcasting Corporation chose Trollope's *The Way We Live Now* in preference to anything written in the previous hundred years. Trollope's novel had originally been a response to the speculative excesses of the early 1870s, years when a burst of

314

American railroad construction stimulated a boom in the trans-Atlantic economy of the day.

Robert Surtees[1] has much in common with two better-known Victorian novelists, Dickens and Trollope, and he may have had some influence on Dickens. (Surtees was born in 1805, Dickens in 1812. Surtees's *Jorrocks' Jaunts and Jollities*—a series of comical episodes loosely linked by a tour of parts of England—is said to have suggested the original plan of *Pickwick Papers*.) All three novelists lived in an individualistic society with low taxes and small government, akin to the self-image (although not entirely the reality) of modern America. They were not embarrassed by money, either their own or other people's. Surtees and Trollope accepted the inequality of mid-Victorian England as part of the human condition, and in Surtees's case he saw the inequality as the by-product of a game, the always entertaining moves and counter-moves of the market economy. If people want to return to equilibrium after the stock market nonsense of the late 1990s and its crazy redistributions, Surtees's comments on the mid-Victorian economy will seem contemporary, as well as refreshingly funny and agreeably unsentimental. Surtees deserves to be remembered as England's anticipation of Mark Twain.

Literary criticism is often rather snooty about Surtees. In the third edition of Benet's *Reader's Encyclopedia*, his books are dismissed as "of minor literary value," although they are acknowledged as preserving "the spirit of the old English sporting life." Volume six of the *Pelican Guide to English Literature*, which covers the period from Dickens to Hardy, mentions him three times, but places his work in "the mounds of the talented, readable, amusing or historically interesting" novels, not with "the handful of 'great' novels." In many surveys of Victorian literature he is not noticed at all. But it is undeniable that, in one respect, Surtees's achievement matched that of the acknowledged leaders of Victorian fiction. Like them, he imagined a world—or, at any rate, he imagined an England—which was inhabited by people who are recognizably his characters and could not be the characters of any other novelist. So there is a Surteesian "England," just as there is a Barsetshire and a Dickensian "England."

Surtees's England contained a large number of markets. There were markets in horses, markets in financial instruments, markets in stocks and shares, markets in houses, even markets in matrimony. It was in and through these markets that his characters not only bought and sold, but

---

1 The republished works of Robert Surtees are available from The Robert Smith Surtees Society, Manor Farm House, Nunney, near Frome, Somerset BA11 4NJ, U.K.; telephone +44 (0) 1373 836937; online at www.room101.co.uk/r.s.surtees-society.

also lived and died, triumphed and failed, and cheated or were cheated. Indeed, the hallmark of Surtees's England was that cheating was routine in transactions of all kinds. Surtees is usually seen as the definitive novelist of Victorian horses and hunting, but a case can be made that his writings are unrivaled in their candid, pitiless, and very amusing accounts of deception, fraud, and outright swindling. His distinctive subject was horse-trading, where "horse-trading" is to be understood in both the literal and metaphorical senses. Surtees was the greatest novelist of the fib and the whopper. To suggest that cheating was routine in Surtees is not to say that it was unconstrained. The extent of cheating was limited by law and custom, and—perhaps most important of all—by the sanction of social disgrace. But the markets of Surtees's England were almost wholly unshackled by government regulation; they had few official or quasi-official organizations whose express task was to prevent certain types of behavior between otherwise free individuals.

A fine debating point is whether Surtees's Englishmen and -women thought more about money than about horses. At any rate, the market in horses is the obvious starting point for a discussion of his attitude toward money. Before the appearance of any of his novels, Surtees had published *The Horseman's Manual* in 1831. At that time, just before the coming of the railways, England's bloodstock was a vital capital asset. Despite the rather general title, *The Horseman's Manual* was a specialized monograph on the law relating to the buying and selling of horses. Its focus was the law of warranty, the law—in other words—of the representation by buyers to sellers of the attributes of the things—whether animal, vegetable, mineral, or financial—to be sold. The book referred to and analyzed forty-seven common law cases, and would presumably have helped Surtees in his career if he had remained a solicitor. In the event his brother died in 1831, and he became heir to the family estate, with the leisure to write novels for his own enjoyment, as well as that of his readers. The question of how horses are to be described before, during, and after transactions became a perennial theme in his fiction.

The character of Mr. Sponge was Surtees's main fictional vehicle for displaying his knowledge of horse-dealing. *Mr. Sponge's Sporting Tour*, published as a serial between 1849 and 1851, has been described as "his first real success." In its early pages Surtees noted that "hunting men . . . are all supposed to be rich," but Mr. Sponge most certainly was not. "That Mr. Sponge might have lost a trifle on the great races of the year, we don't mean to deny, but that he lost such a sum as eighteen hundred on the Derby and seven on the Leger we are in a condition to contradict, for the best of all possible reasons, that he hadn't it to lose." In fact, Mr. Sponge makes a living, just about, by persuading other people to buy horses at prices well above their true value. As an excellent horseman, he is well-equipped to demonstrate a horse's qualities and to conceal its faults.

In his first major transaction he does a deal with Mr. Buckram, the owner of a strong but vicious hack called Hercules (or "Ercles," in the vernacular). Mr Sponge's bargain with Buckram was a so-called "jobbing deal." In detail, it was a rather complex rent-to-buy scheme, in which he has to pay an initial ten guineas a month for the use of Hercules, but is then confronted "with a sort of sliding scale of prices if he chose to buy." The price of Ercles is "fixed at fifty [pounds], inclusive of hire at the end of the first month and gradually" rises "according to the length of time he kept him beyond that."

Two chapters later Mr. Sponge has found his victim, Mr. Waffles of Laverick Wells, a young man about to inherit a large fortune who "had not the slightest idea of the value of money" or indeed of horses. After impressing Mr. Waffles at a meet of the Laverick Wells hunt, Mr. Sponge dupes Waffles's agent, the hapless Caingey Thornton, into believing that he paid 250 guineas for Hercules. He offers to sell the horse for 300 guineas. Thornton accepts the price and proposes payment with a post-dated check signed by Mr. Waffles. Sponge prefers a "stiff," which seems to have been a bill of exchange. Thornton agrees and tells Sponge "to draw at three months, and Mr. Waffles will accept, payable at Coutts." The bill is handed over and Caingey Thornton takes possession of Hercules. The phrase "takes possession," rather than "takes control," is used deliberately, as the immediate results of the transaction are both highly dramatic and very destructive, and are excellently portrayed in one of the R. S. Surtees Society's postcards. Hercules, for all his virtues, was not too much concerned about the legal niceties of ownership. After three "most desperate bounds" with Mr. Thornton in the saddle and two more for the hell of it, he "crashed right through Messrs Frippery and Flummery's fine plate-glass window, to the terror and astonishment of their elegant young" customers, "who were busy arranging their ribbons and finery for the day."

Surtees's transactions in horses sometimes involved the exchange of hard cash and sometimes of checks, but—as *Mr. Sponge's Sporting Tour* shows—settlement was often in bills of exchange. Although the bill of exchange may be an exotic instrument at the start of the twenty-first century, it was a commonplace to the British upper and middle classes of the mid-nineteenth century. In essence, it was an IOU, with a promise to pay in legal tender (coin of the realm or Bank of England notes) at a future date. As long as the debtor had an undoubted ability to pay, the IOU could pass from hand to hand and be used to make payments several times before its ultimate redemption. Of course, someone taking a bill in payment would not be given full face value, partly because of the risk of default and partly to allow for interest costs. Bills three months, six months, or longer before redemption were "discounted," at times very heavily.

Bankers in mid-Victorian England could take deposits and make loans in the same way as their modern counterparts, but many of them were in a rather different business. They bought bills at a discount and made their profit when the bill was delivered for full value as it fell due. These bill specialists operated in the City of London, particularly in Lombard Street, where they were known as "discount houses." In some instances they carried out an extensive banking business, taking deposits from other banks and maintaining close links with the Bank of England. But often the bill specialists were quite small, having only one banking parlor which was in their homes. Two examples in Surtees are Mr. Hall in *Young Tom Hall* and Old Goldspink in *Plain or Ringlets?*. Surtees's views on the ethnic origins of this sort of banker were openly prejudiced and, to the modern liberal mind, highly unattractive. Of course, many of them were Jewish, but the Jews were not Surtees's only target. Old Goldspink is characterized as "one of the cautious money-scraping order of bankers, as distinguished to [sic] the go-ahead Scotch school, who run a-muck at everything."

Obviously, the activity of bill discounting required a robust preparedness to say "no," as well as a good understanding of interest-rate trends and an intimate knowledge of the credit-worthiness of particular individuals. Surtees assures his readers that Jorrocks's bills "were as good as his bank notes," but—in saying this—he implies that the generality of bills were inferior to bank notes. The uncertainties of bill finance made it an excellent subject for fiction. As the bill could pass through several hands in successive chapters, it was an ideal topic to sustain the reader's attention in the serialized novels of mid-Victorian England.

Chapter XXIX of *Plain or Ringlets?* describes "a quiet, innocent evening" in which Old Goldspink's son, Jasper, is fleeced by a gang of professional card-sharpers, led by the loathsome Mr. O'Dicey. After a few hours of very one-sided play, Mr. O'Dicey remarks, "Credit is the soul of commerce, and why not of cards? let us see how each of us stands, and then we can talk about settling." The card-players then resolve themselves "into a finance committee, and the process of IOU-ing and UOMe-ing" commence. At this stage Jasper's losses amounted to £4,000.

Mr. O'Dicey proposes—since he protests himself sorry to win money off young men—that "we all join in a double or quits toss." After various coughs and murmurs the cards are played. "Jasper turned up the Queen of Hearts, which O'Dicey immediately capped with the King of Spades, and, of course, the debt was doubled." O'Dicey's accomplices quickly find the stamps and other requirements to make the document legal and extract Jasper's signature for £8,000, even though his father had "charged him never to put his name to anything." So Jasper has written a bill of exchange, effectively against his father's firm, to the tune of £8,000—about half a million pounds (or almost $750,000) in terms of the money of 2000—after a quiet, innocent, and very expensive evening of cards.

Given the scale of the transaction and the audacity of the fraud, the reader might expect Surtees to discuss the bill's final destination in the next chapter. But he leaves the matter alone for several chapters, just as with a typical bill the debtor would postpone payment for a number of months. In fact, it is only twenty chapters later that the bill is presented to Goldspink's institution, the Mayfield Bank. Old Goldspink quickly understands what has happened and considers taking the card-sharpers to court, but he fears that the magnitude of the sum and the attendant publicity might precipitate a run on the bank. "At last he made up his mind to pay and be done with it." Ironically, a run on the bank occurs much later in the book and the bank goes under, ostensibly for a different reason. Nevertheless, the damage from his son's gambling debts must have severely undermined the bank's solvency.

Gambling makes an appearance in several of Surtees's novels, even if the fate of the Goldspinks and the Mayfield Bank was perhaps the most poignant. One of Surtees's more appealing characters is Mamma in *Ask Mamma*. Readers familiar with the novel will know that Mamma started life as Miss Emma Willing, a humble seamstress, who made a good first marriage to a wealthy merchant and became Mrs. Pringle, and was then widowed and made an even better second marriage to the Earl of Ladythorne. As a servant early in her career she found that "though fine ladies like to be cheated, it must be done in style." She also found that in dire circumstances—for example, after their husbands had gambled nearly all the money away—fine ladies might indulge in a little cheating themselves. After she joined "the Hon. Mrs. Cavesson's service late in the day, when all the preliminaries for a smash had been perfected, her fine sensibilities and discrimination enabled her to anticipate the coming evil and to deposit her mistress's jewellery in a place of safety three quarters of an hour before the bailiffs entered."

The alternations of fortune in Surtees's England could be drastic but should not be exaggerated. The mid-Victorians were not always losing money by being cheated, by having feckless children, or by gambling. They could in fact hold their wealth in a wide variety of forms, some of them very safe. Surtees's novels have an abundance of references to assets and to the problems of "investment management," as it would be called nowadays. As Britain's economy became richer, more cosmopolitan, and more complex, it became host to a remarkably wide assortment of financial securities and tangible possessions. In his imaginings of great wealth, Facey Romford conjectures that his uncle's fortune contains "bills, bonds, post obits, IOUs." The abolition of the Corn Laws in 1846 and the embrace of free trade led to the influx of an exotic range of consumer durables, some of which have retained value and over 150 years later are still being bought and sold as antiques. Mr. Jorrocks' villa in *Handley Cross* had a "Honduran Mahogany table" and a Turkey carpet, while its stock of provisions included "Copenhagen cherry-brandy" as well as the more familiar "Dundee marmalade."

Surtees's views on portfolio selection are occasionally made explicit. It seems he was a cautious investor, with a deeply ingrained scepticism about the latest money-making fad. The most fundamental choice in mid-Victorian England was among the safety of "the funds" (i.e., government debt, particularly Consolidated stock or "Consols"), the relative safety of land and mortgages on land, and the riskiness of equities and other asset types. Broadly speaking, the yield on Consols was a stable, predictable, and reliable 3 percent. This was not much, but—in a society where long-run price stability was an established fact—it was a real return. Facey Romford sought his first employment as master of fox hounds in the Heaviside Hunt country. It had little industry or enterprise, but the people enjoyed a solid rural prosperity. In Surtees's words, "they might be called a 3 percent sort of people in contradistinction to the raving capacity of modern cupidity."

Surtees gave many examples of such "modern cupidity," before his investors retreated to the safety of government debt or property. In the new speculatively built spa town of *Handley Cross*, the self-appointed "Master of Ceremonies" Captain Doleful has tried his hand at being a coal merchant, which was judged by Surtees to be "an unprofitable speculation." Doleful sold up when it did not work and "sunk his money in an annuity." (The annuity would have been paid by an insurance company, holding mortgages and government debt to meet the liability.) In *Mr. Sponge's Sporting Tour*, the Jawleyfords were embittered by their investments in railways, "at whose bright lights" the family "had burnt its fingers." In order to retain Jawleyford Court, they have to curb their expenses and keep them in line with their fairly secure rental income. On the whole, the 1840s and 1850s were years of considerable agricultural prosperity and rising rents, and investment in land generally gave better returns than investment in gilt-edged securities. Nevertheless, at one point in *Ask Mamma* Surtees opines "a man who has no taste for land or horses should have nothing do with either. He should put his money in the funds."

Surtees was a significant landowner himself. It was very understandable that in the early 1840s he should be opposed to the abolition of the Corn

Laws. *Hillingdon Hall* is full of entertaining characters and events, and remains a viable read at the start of the twenty-first century. It appeared in serial form in 1844, and was intended as a satire on the Anti-Corn Law League. The aristocracy feared that the influx of cheap corn would cut farm incomes, and so lead to a reduction in rents and the value of land. As agricultural improvement was one way to anticipate the evil, the novel pokes much fun at Jorrocks' efforts in this direction. Jorrocks had made his fortune as a London-based merchant in tea and groceries, but in advanced middle age his love of hunting tempted him to set himself up as a country gentleman. He bought Hillingdon Hall, described as "quite a specimen of the old-fashioned manor-house." When told of his rural neighbors' wish to elect him as Member of Parliament, Jorrocks protests at the cost of living in London and asked them to consider "'ow 'appy I am in the country, tendin' my flocks and 'erds, guanoin' and nitrate o' soberin' my land, and all that sort of thing." He nevertheless lets his name go forward as a candidate against the Marquis of Bray, who represents the Duke of Donkeytown's interests. The reader is led to assume that successive Dukes of Donkeytown have regarded the seat as a pocket borough for several generations.

The Sellborough election in *Hillingdon Hall* has not made such an impression on English-speaking culture as the Eatanswill election in *Pickwick Papers*, perhaps because Surtees took the satire too far. Agricultural improvement was a more straightforward theme in *Ask Mamma*, where Major Yammerton turns round an over-mortgaged estate by draining the land with the proceeds of a government loan and greatly increasing its productivity. (*Ask Mamma* was published in 1858, after more than a decade in which the free import of food had been reconciled with high agricultural incomes.) But—in both *Hillingdon Hall* and *Ask Mamma*—Surtees was frank about the ethical standards of the English farming community. In *Hillingdon Hall,* Jorrocks is cheated by Joshua Sneakington, his estate manager, and so brought to "the unpleasant conviction that there were as big thieves in the country as in London," including the City of London. In *Ask Mamma*, Surtees was more general in his comments, averring that the occasional difficulties caused by the repeal of the Corn Laws led tenants to renege on their obligations. In his words, the "probing of pockets showed that in too many cases the reputed honesty of the British farmer was . . . mere fiction; for some who were thought to be well-off now declared that their capital was their aunt's, their uncle's, or their grandmother's, or someone else's."

The discussion of farming in *Hillingdon Hall* and *Ask Mamma* reflected Surtees's own experience. According to Norman Gash, author of a 1993 study of "Robert Surtees and Early Victorian Society," Surtees took his place "among the more active and sensible landlords of his day." The references to tiles in the Sellborough election speeches were not rhetorical. The 1840s and 1850s saw extensive drainage work, often financed—like Major Yammerton's—by government loans made possible by the Public Money Drainage Act of 1846. The loans were available at 3.5 percent, less than the commercial rate. An evident implication is that the typical return on farming was well above the 3 percent received on government securities, but both land-owning and the pursuit of farming itself (as a tenant) were quite risky, although not as risky as railway or coal-mining investments. Land had to give a higher return than government securities and other investments a yet higher return still, if they were to find a permanent place in investors' portfolios. Part of the explanation for the excess return on these other assets was the risk of being cheated. There was an obvious need for lawyers to define and protect property rights, although Surtees was as cynical about their ethical standards as he was about other professions.'

Plain or Ringlets? and *Ask Mamma* are Surtees's most extended treatments of the marriage market. The central theme of *Ask Mamma* is—in effect—the choice of strategies for making a "good" marriage, where the excellence of the marriage is to be judged largely by the financial uplift enjoyed by the schemer. In Surtees's novels the female philosophy of matrimony is simple and unsentimental: women marry in order to maximize their living standards. One chapter in *Ask Mamma* has the brazen title "Money and matrimony." As already noted, Miss Willing (later Lady Ladythorne and the Mamma of the novel's title) had a good first marriage which took her from the position of servant into that of the merchant middle class and an even better second marriage which advanced her into the aristocracy. The son by the first marriage—Fine Billy—goes to stay at the Earl of Ladythorne's castle to learn about hunting in the county of Featherbedfordshire. Fine Billy is introduced to the dashing "equestrian coquette" Miss de Glancey as "the richest commoner in England," but Mamma writes to her son, "Beware Miss de Glancey. . . . *She hasn't a halfpenny.*"

In fact, at this stage in the novel the Earl of Ladythorne is still unmarried, and Miss de Glancey has eyes for him as well as for Fine Billy. Surtees does not give precise contractual details, but hints that some investors have even put up money in a scheme to promote a match between de Glancey and Ladythorne. Presumably the most important projected expenditure in this example of venture capital is a horse and fine clothes. "Miss de Glancey of Half-the-watering - places - in - England - and - some - on- the- Continent . . . had induced a part of England's enterprizing sons to fit her out for an expedition against the gallant Earl of Ladythorne under the Limited Liability Act." The reference to the Limited Liability Act may seem gratuitous, but it again reflects Surtees's interest in contemporary political and financial developments. Of course, the marriage market—unlike other markets—was a parasitic zero-sum game. To the extent that one party gained, another party lost.

Ask Mamma is cynical and materialistic about marriage, but at least Surtees did not mention specific amounts of money in the Miss de Glancey enterprises. In his search for a bride in *Plain or Ringlets?* Mr. Bunting does not take such a relaxed view of matters. After his unsuccessful pursuit of Miss Wingfield "somewhere in Cumberland," Mr. Bunting is sent a lawyer's bill, "made out in a rather vindictive acrimonious way," for £43.13s.4d. "So what with a twenty guinea diamond ring that the young lady had forgotten to return along with his letters and poetical effusions, together with the seven pound odd he had spent in equestrian exercise, he had got a long way into a three-figure note."

In one respect the prominence of money and matrimony in mid-Victorian fiction reflects social mobility. The Victorians were fascinated by good and bad marriages, because they did lead to large changes in personal fortunes and position. The triumph of Miss Willing in *Ask Mamma* may have been exceptional, but Surtees's novels are crowded with characters who leap or plunge several ranks in the social hierarchy because of the marriages they make. The theme of marriage between aristocrat husband and commoner wife appears in *Hillingdon Hall* as well as *Ask Mamma* and demonstrates the flexibility and openness of Victorian society. Big differences in investment returns are part of the reason for the changing distribution of income and wealth, but stake-holding and position-taking in the marriage market also play a role.

Nevertheless, the zero-sum character of the marriage market restricted the potential gains. From the point of view of society as a whole, the considerable effort devoted to it was unproductive and wasteful. Mrs. Thomas Trattles in Roseberry Rocks, the locale for the pursuit of Miss McDermott in *Plain or Ringlets?*, makes a living from taking commissions on introductions between possible marriage partners, "and was always ready in the mediating way, . . . to adjust differences, recommend houses, engage musicians or attend dinner parties on the shortest notice." No doubt the Mrs. Trattles of this world served a useful function, but there were limits to the demand for the services provided by such people. Surtees had no illusions about the ultimate worth of matrimonial intermediaries. Mrs. Trattles was "truly invaluable" for "fanning a flirtation" and "was frequently retained on both sides."

Mid-Victorian Englishmen and -women were well aware of the riskiness of their lives. Chapter XV of *Handley Cross* features a conversation between Jorrocks' servants and the staff of the Dragon Inn. They know that their employment prospects are unpredictable, their pay is likely to be late, and the probability of being cheated in everyday purchases is high. While conditions were therefore uncertain for those without property, enough has already been said about the investment risks facing the propertied Victorian middle class. England in the middle of the nineteenth century lacked social security to comfort the working class and financial regulation to protect the middle-class saver. People had to look after themselves, and they knew it. In Jorrocks' words to the Handley Cross hunt ball, "Honesty is of no use to licensed 'oss dealers. Every man supposes they are rogues and treats them accordingly."

To the modern reader, Surtees's England may seem tough, harsh, and unfair, but it has an important economic advantage over the industrial societies of the early twenty-first century. The lightness of regulation saved on two kinds of cost. First, it allowed society to dispense with regulatory bureaucracy. Relatively few people were involved in preventing other people from doing things which, left to themselves, they genuinely wanted to do. Relatively more people could therefore get on with doing what they wanted to do or—in other words—with actual productive work. Secondly, the costs of complying with regulation were negligible. Of course, dealing in second- or third-hand horses, like that in second-hand cars today, was intrinsically difficult to regulate. But—in the modern world with vast cross-border capital flows—so also are transactions in financial securities, but that does not prevent governments and official agencies introducing a vast apparatus of rules, rule-makers, and rule-enforcers to supervise such transactions.

The mid-Victorian age is commonly represented as the heyday of *laissez-faire*. The characters in Surtees's novels are indeed mostly self-reliant, self-starting, and self-made, however indifferent their standards of financial probity. They knew that they might be cheated every day of their lives, and that they had to be alert and careful. To that extent the need for government and regulation was less than in the twentieth century. No one living in early and mid-Victorian England could have any doubts that financial success—in the zero-sum games of marriage and gambling, and in the risky games of investing—was largely a matter of luck; the distribution of income and wealth was not equitable or fair in some abstract sense, and it most certainly was not a reflection of "social justice." But that did not stop the Victorians playing the exciting money-making games of a dynamic and growing economy. Whether they ended as winners and losers, they provided Surtees with the vast amount of source material he assembled in his wonderful novels.

June 2002

The Legacy of Donald Francis Tovey

James F. Penrose

What is new in the artistic spirit of revolt . . . is its bitterness and its universal range. . . . I may venture to assert that today it has, as it seldom had before, the aspect of a grievance. The mildest, and therefore perhaps the most serious form of the grievance, is that the load of classical tradition has long been so heavy as to repress further creative impulse. . . . What I do believe to be fundamentally wrong is every attitude towards Classical masterpieces that does not make them a stimulus instead of an oppression.
—D. F. Tovey, *Stimulus and the Classics of Music* (1914)

THE NINETEENTH-CENTURY violinist Joseph Joachim thought that Donald Francis Tovey knew more about music than either Brahms or the Schumanns. Pablo Casals went one better by publicly acknowledging Tovey as one of the very greatest musicians of all time. The critic (and former bank clerk) Ernest Newman grudgingly admitted that Tovey's pianism was "in a class with Busoni." Which all goes to show that few things in life are more perishable than an artistic reputation.

Tovey's public career spanned the four decades from the death of Queen Victoria to the onset of the Second World War. He was a living example of the truth of Samuel Butler's tag that genius is the "supreme capacity for getting its possessors into trouble of all kinds and keeping them therein so long as the genius remains." Tovey's performances as a pianist and conductor were followed with polite consternation (by the musical public) and asperity (by the English critics). His recital programs were long and complex. Audiences accustomed to some nice preludes, a song-without-words or two, a sonata, and some waltzes were bludgeoned from their seats by Tovey's three-hour, five-sonata programs. There was no respite during intermissions: the pianist provided his own mammoth program notes (sometimes over a half-inch thick and over twenty-four thousand words long), replete with musical quotations, literary allusions, and an oddball sense of humor. After his appointment to the Reid Chair at the University of Edinburgh, Tovey founded his own orchestra and over the next twenty-four years transformed it into an important, if idiosyncratic, cultural resource. But public success was countered by abundant personal woe; his health deteriorated early, his first marriage dissolved with his wife's sanity, and he was forever harried by his teacher, Sophie Weisse.

There is little sense of repine, however, in his magnum opus, the six-volume *Essays in Musical Analysis* (1935–39), an exuberant and masterly commentary on the great and not-so-great works of the classical-music canon (a seventh volume was added posthumously, in 1944). This is his legacy, along with his eleven-odd other books and his superb performing editions of *The Well-Tempered Clavier* and the Beethoven piano sonatas and cello sonatas. Yet it is not the only legacy Tovey would have us treasure: he believed (with justification) that what he regarded as his greatest achievements, the opera *The Bride of Dionysus* and his massive Cello Concerto, were on the fast-track to obscurity.

Donald Francis Tovey (as he signed himself, even as a boy) was born at Eton on July 17, 1875, the second son of the Reverend Duncan Tovey and his formidably eccentric wife. Tovey's father was a noted classical scholar and entirely unmusical. One day, the Reverend mentioned to his son that it was strange that the archeologist Otto Jahn should have the same name as the author of a life of Mozart. When Donald mentioned that archeologist and author were one and the same, the old man contemptuously exclaimed: "Nonsense! A great scholar like Otto Jahn writing on such stuff as music! Impossible!" Donald was educated at Northlands, a school near Egham run by Sophie Weisse, a German emigrée. Miss Weisse recognized her five-year-old charge's talent when she heard him sight-sing Schubert's *Heidenröslein*, complete with modulations. Miss Weisse realized that her life's work was sitting on her lap: little Donald would have a great career and she would have little Donald, auxiliary rights and all.

No detail was spared in providing the child with the finest musical education in England. He was taught counterpoint by James Higgs and Sir Walter Parratt, composition by Sir Hubert Parry. Orchestras were rented for his conducting lessons. Christmas and Easter gifts for the eight-year-old were orchestral scores or volumes of piano music. Surprisingly, there is little evidence that the boy felt any distaste for this suffocating routine. At Northlands, Tovey was fussed over and cosseted ("like Achilles in Scyros,"

Edward Dent dourly noted), encouraging his already Learish traits: Fritz Busch was to comment on Tovey's "savage neglect of his clothes" and describe how Tovey would "lie his clothes on the floor so that in the morning he had only to slip back into them." By his nineteenth year, Tovey was already a seasoned recitalist and performer. His training was effectively finished by Brahms's great friend Joseph Joachim, who, until his death in 1907, regularly performed with the young man and introduced him to the greatest musicians of the time as their equal.

Donald Tovey matriculated at Balliol in 1894. Mythology notwithstanding, Oxford was hardly some exquisitely refined Athens-on-the-Cherwell. It better resembled the wild rowdiness of Scone College in Evelyn Waugh's *Decline and Fall*. Musicians were particularly favored targets. During one performance by the Holywell Orchestra, the first violinist's Cremona was destroyed by an orange. Notices were posted requesting that "dogs not be brought to the concerts." The shy and unpretentious Tovey was exempted from the musician-baiting, as he was much liked and admired by Oxford hell-raisers, who called him "The Tove"; Hilaire Belloc, Maurice Baring, and the Orientalist Denys Bray became his good friends. Tovey spent much of his time at Oxford composing and performing, but his preoccupation with these activities caused his examination results to suffer. Tovey took a Third in Greats in 1898 and retired both with his degree and a case of acute appendicitis. During his recovery, his nurse, Miss Weisse's mother, wrote frequently to her daughter to complain about Tovey's practice habits.

The Tovey trinity of pianist, composer, and writer made its debut in London with four long Thursday programs in November 1900. Tovey played Bach and Beethoven and accompanied members of the Kruse Quartet in his own Piano Trio, Piano Quartet, Piano Quintet, and Cello Sonata, among other works. Critical reception ranged, as it was to do for his entire career, from the ecstatic ("a new Schumann") to the derisory ("unconscionably dull"). Until the last years of his life Tovey's playing was described by the press as "cold" or "chilly," his *Essays* as "complex and obscure," and his compositions as the work of a man who knew too much about music to be a good composer, whatever that might mean. Tovey's performance style was indeed analytical, much like the performance styles of many of today's noteworthy pianists. In the Golden Age of pianism, however, when Paderewski's success was measured (according to one malicious critic) by the number of damp seats in the house, analysis wasn't good box office.

Tovey's compositions run to some forty opus numbers, though there are gaps in numbering and chronology. Strongly influenced by the Viennese, particularly Brahms, Tovey has a distinctive, lyric voice. This is evident as early as the *Balliol Dances*, op. 11, for piano duet, a delightful collection of waltzes dedicated to his tutor, Ernest Walker, and the pianist F. S. Kelly. The first five dances in the set date from Tovey's Oxford days while the remainder were composed sometime after; the work moves from youthful exuberance to a noble and touching conclusion. The Clarinet Sonata, op. 16, dating from 1906, is another lovely example of Tovey's youthful work and remained a favorite of the composer. The somber and controlled *Gluck Variations*, op. 28, composed in 1913 after a period of great crisis, are telling in their cool poignancy. The chamber works presented in his first London recitals are particularly impressive and were frequently performed by Mandyczewski and Busch.

Tovey's opera, *The Bride of Dionysus* (née *Ariadne*), took him over twenty years to bring to the stage. The opera moved the irascible Miss Weisse to new heights of indignation when she berated Tovey's collaborator, the poet Robert Trevelyan (who had finished *his* part of the job years before), for writing a useless libretto "and ruining all Donald's work." Though Fritz Busch admired the work and scheduled it for revival at Glyndebourne in 1940, those plans were stilled by the war and the opera has remained silent to this day. The Cello Concerto, which was written for Pablo Casals, and the Piano Concerto have fallen into desuetude. Casals once recorded the Cello Concerto, and despite its deficient sonic quality, the recording shows the nobility and pathos of the work. Unpublished or long out of print, these works deserve their posthumous certificates of rehabilitation.

During the first ten years of the century, Tovey's musical schedule became progressively more frantic. He added to his extensive teaching and performance commitments by acting as performer and organizer for three annual series of subscription concerts. He was also commissioned to write the musical articles for the legendary eleventh edition of the *Encyclopaedia Britannica*. The pace of his activities caused him to be often ill with stress and overwork. In his mid-thirties, Tovey began to show a certain quirk of personality, peculiar for one constitutionally so kind and understanding—an opaque insensitivity. In its mildest form, this could be rather endearing. When the visiting Ernest Walker asked Tovey for some bedtime reading, he was handed a volume of the *Bach Gesellschaft*. Though Tovey had been Fritz Busch's houseguest for six months, he was astonished to hear that Mrs. Busch was about to give birth. Sir Henry Wood remarked that after a long and tiring recital which finished with the arduous first book of Brahms's *Paganini Variations*, Tovey misread the warmth of his departing audience's applause as he sat down and played through Book Two.

Its virulent form produced less amusing results. Tovey discarded friends who criticized Miss Weisse, and trivial matters frequently provoked violent outbursts of temper. Tovey also appeared to have difficulty sensing when his interest in the opposite sex was not returned. But his greatest misadventure occurred when he insinuated himself into the Casals–Suggia *ménage* in 1912.

Two years after Joachim's death, Tovey was still bereft when his friend Edward Speyer introduced him to Pablo Casals in October 1909. In Casals, Tovey found Joachim's spiritual and artistic avatar. The two were soon performing throughout Europe, often playing Tovey's music. At the time, Casals was co-habiting with the Portuguese cellist Guilhermina Suggia, who is sometimes quaintly described as his "common-law wife." But in 1912, when the three were on holiday together in Spain, something happened. Suggia "played with fire . . . and certainly Tovey showed that unhappy lack of *Menschenkenntnis* which Miss Weisse had long deplored," wrote Tovey's pupil and biographer, Mary Grierson, in marvelously elliptical fashion.[1] Casals threw Suggia out of the house and Tovey's pathetically inept attempts to heal the breach resulted in the two men being estranged for over a decade. To round the month out, Tovey's father suddenly died. The pianist canceled his performances for the rest of the year, broke from Miss Weisse, and left England for Aix, where he was to remain until 1914.

War and an unexpected academic vacancy drew Tovey back to Britain. Over Miss Weisse's forcibly expressed disapproval, Tovey applied for the Reid Professorship at the University of Edinburgh and was awarded the position in July 1914, less than a month after his application. Two years later he married, again to thunderous tirades from Miss Weisse. The marriage, however, was a disaster. Unknown to Tovey, his bride-to-be was mentally unstable, and soon after the marriage she began frequently commuting across the borderline of sanity. Mrs. Tovey's behavior produced certain sympathetic vibrations in her husband; in 1920, Tovey composed a three-part song called *The Mad Maiden's Song* and later became enamored of a bizarre and ponderous instrument called the Moor Coupler Duplex Piano, on which he played duets with himself. He spent hours with this monstrosity and arranged to give a recital on the instrument at Oxford, which was only canceled when the instrument could not be delivered to the hall. Pictures of Tovey around the time show a shocking change from the handsome if somewhat shambling figure of the mid-Teens to the drawn and staring vision he had become by his divorce in 1922.

---

1 Grierson's hagiographical *Donald Francis Tovey* (Oxford University Press, 1950) remains the standard life of Tovey.

Though he commented acidly and often on its musical climate, Tovey found something of a niche in Edinburgh. His academic schedule permitted him time to concertize and compose while the didacticism that so bewildered his hapless London audiences bore fruit in the teaching of two generations of students and in the creation and nurturing of the Reid Orchestra. The Reid served as Tovey's musical laboratory, not so much for his own works but for the investigation and display of those compositions that Tovey thought truly mattered. The program notes for many of those works were to be eventually collected in six slim blue volumes as the *Essays in Musical Analysis*.

Despite their impeccably dry and forbidding title, the *Essays* contain some of the wittiest and most captivating writing ever done on musical subjects. That includes the famously amusing Berlioz of the *Memoirs*, whom Tovey flicks aside by remarking that while Berlioz is good reading, "we need not go to him for information about anything but his own state of mind as he would like us to conceive it." Tovey is perpetually at pains to remind us that the *Essays* were born to the practical function of enlightening his conservative and suspicious Edinburgh audience, not fond of surprises, less fond of innovation, and least fond of all of parting with the coin-of-the-realm to fund the cost of more horn and wind players and rehearsal time, all of which the Reid so desperately needed.

While the *Essays* are ostensibly grouped by genre, Tovey is the first to admit the informal nature of his divisions. The symphonic form is treated in its classical examples in Volume I and in the first half of Volume II. The remainder of the second volume deals with symphonic variations and orchestral polyphony (chiefly Bach). Volume III divides its discussion of the concerto between classical works based on the *ritornello* (orchestral introduction)—chiefly the Mozart concerti—and the variation-based works descended from the Mendelssohn E-minor Violin Concerto. Volume IV, "Illustrative Music," is a collection of studies (often extremely amusing) of Romantic-period program music, while Volume V deals with vocal music and Volume VI rounds out with "Miscellaneous Works." The subject of the seventh volume is chamber music and deals with the *Goldberg Variations*, the *Art of Fugue*, the *Diabelli Variations*, and other kings-of-the-road.

It is not giving too much of the plot away to reveal that Tovey considered Bach, Beethoven, Mozart, and Brahms to be at the center of his musical solar system. The other forty-five composers treated in the *Essays* orbit around this central cluster, with Berlioz being somewhere past Jupiter and Saint-Saëns being the musical equivalent of Pluto. Though Tovey may frown upon technical shortcomings, the inclusion of a work in his exclusive club belies any rough justice meted out. Tovey's principles of selection and evaluation are straightforward and apparent, and while it is unfair to attempt to summarize those principles in a sentence, the reader of the *Essays* will quickly become aware of Tovey's interest in how structure and technique operate effectively to direct dramatic flow. Tovey was the last, however, to insist on form for its own sake; his teacher, Parry, insisted that Tovey analyze works "point to point" and not ever to fit the work to Procrustean principles of construction.

The fact that relatively few twentieth-century composers are featured in the *Essays* has been held against Tovey as evidence of some form of critical arteriosclerosis. Certainly Stravinsky, Prokofiev, and Bartók are not discussed in the *Essays*, though half of the composers featured there were Tovey's contemporaries. If anything, this statistic suggests Tovey to be at least as progressive as many present-day music directors and conductors who are firmly rooted in the works of bygone days. Moreover, those alleging arrested development overlook the fact that certain of Tovey's favorites, like Bruckner and even Brahms, were by no means as popular then as they are today; others, like Röntgen, Voormolen, and Zador, are even now still largely unknown. Tovey used the *Essays* to justify the quixotic task of keeping his subject works in the repertory. He called himself "counsel for the defense."

Tovey reminds us several times that the *Essays* contained no modern works because of his rather limited resources in Edinburgh; indeed, he would not conduct Mahler's works for years precisely because of the technical weaknesses of the Reid. Strauss's works are difficult for they "bristle with technical abnormalities" not made easier as Strauss "drives through his musical traffic like a road hog." Production of highly complex, non-traditional works like *The Rite of Spring* or Bartók's Concerto for Orchestra was far beyond the resources of an orchestra limited to weekly six-hour rehearsals. Of course, to those so inclined, the *Essays* may be read as a reactionary, rear-guard movement against the Moderns. Others might find it excessively critical to fault Tovey for his silence rather than for what he did in fact say. Certainly Debussy, Holst, Sibelius, and Vaughan Williams had no cause for complaint.

Volume I starts out with Tovey's somewhat disingenuous ground rules. He says that the *Essays* are "certainly not designed for continuous reading"—but nobody, as used to be said in another context, can read just one. "Nor . . . can [they] pass for a work of reference"—yet Tovey scrutinizes a vast range of compositions. He insists the *Essays* are not a complete system of criticism—though even during his lifetime Tovey epigones quoted him as the ultimate critical authority. Tovey wrote most of the *Essays* spontaneously, and he impishly admits that he owes a debt of gratitude to that "most emancipating intellectual maxim of our times, viz. *History is what you remember.*"

Brahms, Haydn, Mozart, Schubert, and Mendelssohn are all discussed in Volume I, but pride of place goes to Beethoven. Tovey's *précis*-form description in Volume I of Beethoven's Symphony no. 9 in D Minor blooms into a forty-five-page exposition in Volume II. Like most of the *Essays*, this study divides into a prefatory commentary followed by a musical description. Tovey begins with a description of the origins of the Ninth Symphony and captures our attention with the intriguing speculation that, had Beethoven survived the chill that eventually killed him, the choral writing of the last movement would have ignited a fourth developmental period in Beethoven's output "distinguished by a body of choral work fully equal in power and perfection to the symphonies and string quartets." Tovey then treats us to some of his most serious and striking writing when he addresses the subject of time in music as the correlative of size in architecture. Tovey explains that one of the greatest features of that great symphony is Beethoven's conjuring up in a very few bars the impression of immense size and distance through proportion in time and scale of tone. (This same sensitivity to Time and Space is also evident in Tovey's treatment of Schubert's C-Major Symphony.) Tovey then provides an expansive description of each movement, saving his best for the Finale. "In the Ninth Symphony, Beethoven's plan is to remind us of the first three movements . . . and to reject them one by one as failing to attain the joy in which he believes." The structural complexities of the Ninth Symphony are handled with masterly ease and lightness, and Tovey's unabashed admiration and affection for the work are apparent.

In Volume II, Tovey's remarks on Schumann's B-flat Major Symphony, op. 38 (the "*Spring*"), show his benevolent understanding of that composer. "It may safely be said that no orchestra ever earned its reputation by its interpretation of Schumann. . . . As for a brilliant performance, that would be an outrage on Schumann's holiest intimacy. . . . The inner content of this music is a perpetual springtime of youthful enthusiasm; the externals are robed in an old dressing gown and carpet-slippers amid thick clouds of tobacco smoke." We also see his sense of humor at its most donnish: "When Shakespeare called springtime 'the only pretty ringtime' he obviously referred to Schumann's happy use of the triangle in the lighter passages."

Volume III is perhaps the densest of the set with its introductory study on the Classical Concerto. Here we see Tovey in overdrive as he first delineates the structural distinctions between the classical symphony and the classical concerto, then leads us to an analysis of the concerto form itself beginning with a most arresting image: "Nothing in human life or history is as thrilling or of more ancient or unusual experience than the antithesis of the individual and the crowd; an antithesis . . . which has been of no less universal prominence in works of art than in life." Tovey takes the form back to the arias of Alessandro Scarlatti and shows us how the form developed "as the contrast of a single voice and the chorus of instruments." In all, some forty-six works are discussed in Volume III, divided between the ritornello-based classical form and the more modern variation-based type. In his study of the Mendelssohn Violin Concerto, Tovey, like the rest of us, shows the adaptability of a good line when he recycles a witticism ("as ascribed by a Master of Balliol to the British schoolboy") made in his edition of *The Well-Tempered Clavier*: "no nonsense is too enormous to be a possible translation from a classical author."

For some, the best way to go about reading the *Essays* may be to start with Tovey's dislikes rather than his enthusiasms. Tovey's other side, that of the acid, take-on-all-comers, take-no-prisoners stylist, is nowhere more apparent than in his treatment in Volume IV of Berlioz's *Harold in Italy*, based on Byron's *Childe Harold*.

Matters get off to a brisk start. "There are excellent reasons for reading *Childe Harold's Pilgrimage*," writes Tovey airily, "but among them I cannot find any that concern Berlioz. . . except for the jejune value of the discovery that no definite elements of Byron's poem have penetrated the impregnable fortress of Berlioz's encyclopedic inattention." After a few remarks about the random nature of the *idée fixe*, he cocks the gun by innocently describing an instrumental technique pioneered in the youthful *Rob Roy*, which Berlioz claimed to have had burnt. Then Tovey starts shooting in earnest: "In Berlioz's vocabulary 'burnt' means carefully preserved, so that an admiring posterity can discover evidence of the truth of Oscar Wilde's assertion that a true artist lives in a series of masterpieces in which no progress whatever can be discerned." It doesn't stop there, either.

But rehabilitation is not long in coming; Tovey's reservations about Berlioz the man are softened by his opinion about Berlioz the composer. "But—and this is a very big but—Berlioz, whose genius for ornamentation has always been recognized, also had a genius for composition. Two causes have prevented the recognition of this: first, that he notoriously failed to learn anything his masters tried to teach him; and, secondly, that almost everything they tried to teach him was wrong." Though Berlioz "cannot develop a theme [but] only submit it to a process aptly described . . . as 'rabbeting,'" Tovey admits that the process bears excellent results. What is the secret of Berlioz's success? "He is a born perorator, and everything leads up to his perorations. But notice that everything does genuinely lead up to them; he does not perorate upon a vacuum. He cannot argue, he cannot meditate . . . But he can sum up and pile on the agony or the exultation." Tovey then proceeds to a movement-by-movement description of *Harold*, citing and commenting upon characteristic themes and embroidering the whole with his wry commentary. Then, as now, Tovey's irreverence to their hero caused Berliozians no small degree of ire, but Tovey, excellent counsel that he is, seldom gets into a hole he can't get out of: "He is big enough to stand our poking a little fun at him; and I am sorry if the out-and-out Berliozians are not."

Volume VI begins with a highly interesting study on "Linear Harmony." The range of the rest of the volume is astonishing, especially when it is noted that much of the material that Tovey discusses was not then available on record. Much, in fact, is still not. The volume begins to close with a highly amusing essay on "Wagner in the Concert Room," which addresses the "bloody chunks" problem confronted by conductors performing extracts from Wagner's operas. The penultimate chapter, "Retrospect and Corrigenda," is a characteristic blend of the genial, the grave, and the waspish as Tovey admits to a fault, embellishes a point—or drives one home. He signs off to his critics with a shrug: "Peace be to their wastepaper baskets and to mine."

Throughout the Thirties, Tovey was in failing health, with an unreliable heart and with gouty hands that made playing stretches miserable even when possible. He had suffered at least two heart attacks when the violinist Jelly d'Aranyi, Joachim's niece and Tovey's old friend, approached Tovey with a most peculiar story. Miss d'Aranyi said that while attending a séance given in London by Baron Erik Palmstierna, the spirit of Robert Schumann appeared and told her (in mangled German) that it was his personal wish that she play his Violin Concerto. Tovey's reputation was such in those days that it extended to the hereafter, for when the nonplussed Miss d'Aranyi replied that she knew of no such concerto, the spirit told her to ask Tovey about it, which she did. Joachim had once told Tovey about the work and the decision of Clara Schumann, Brahms, and Joachim not to publish it because of its apparently uneven merit. The unpublished score was retrieved from its resting place in the State Library in Berlin per additional spiritual directions. Schumann apparently had further thoughts on his manuscript, for at the next séance he directed Miss d'Aranyi to rework parts of the solo writing, which she again did with both Schumann's and Tovey's approval. "Who did this? It is excellent. It is altogether Schumannesque!" said Tovey, in tones resembling the Reverend Collins. For all of the gravity of the matter, as reported in Palmstierna's book *Horizons of Immortality*, the non-musical world was irreverent, but Tovey would not give an inch. "I assert my positive conviction that the spirit of Schumann is inspiring Jelly d'Aranyi's production of Schumann's posthumous Violin Concerto. The sense in which I make this assertion is my own private affair," he barked in a letter to *The Times*.

In June 1939, around the time Volume VI of the *Essays* was published, Tovey wrote to Mary Grierson, saying that "the ground got up and hit me on the nose." He was admitted to Westminster Hospital in London in July, but was evacuated for war reasons back to his country house at Hedenham in Suffolk, far away from bombardment in London and far away from medical help. He died on July 10, 1940, a week before his sixty-fifth birthday.

We read Tovey for his exposition, for his beautiful Austenian prose, but above all for his intuition and musical judgments. His genius was to convey through the written word the fleeting and magical impressions that music, that most evanescent of arts, evokes. Tovey succeeded brilliantly because he understood both the limitations of criticism and his own abilities as a musician. In aspiring not to scholasticism but to art, Tovey conjures up in us the brief, hair-raising sensation of greatness—not just of the subject work, but also, quite possibly, of his own writing. The result is that the *Essays in Musical Analysis* are among the greatest collections of writings on music.

Jean Sibelius once remarked that no one ever raised a statue to a critic. The most famous critic of all, Eduard Hanslick, is notorious for the magnitude of his gaffe in viewing Wagner as a destructive influence in Western music. In this century, Ernest Newman, Tovey's nemesis, sought with others to establish a system of scientific criticism, grounded in quasi-scientific principles, seeking to bring some sort of objectivity to the art of criticism. None of these men have their statues, and quite probably none of them ever shall. Donald Tovey, on the other hand, realized that criticism, like the music it seeks to understand, is an art form, and that good criticism is just as indefinable and just as real as good music. Until the City of Edinburgh gets around to erecting Tovey's statue, the *Essays in Musical Analysis* will serve as a very nice monument indeed.

November 1994

Missing Mister Abbott

Mark Steyn

G EORGE ABBOTT WAS not, in any sense, a political dramatist, but, in the mid-Fifties, he was asked to stage a rally for Adlai Stevenson—an odd choice considering it was Abbott's 1950 hit *Call Me Madam* which gave Eisenhower his campaign song, "They Like Ike." Anyway, he said yes and went down to Madison Square Garden only to find that the Democrats invariably turned up late for rehearsal, which he hated, and, worse, hadn't learned their lines. He withdrew from the rally.

It's tempting to see this as some sort of political metaphor. At any rate, it exemplifies Abbott's approach to his art: he was a practical man of the theater, open-minded about content because he understood that what counts is how efficiently you serve it. I dimly recall saying as much in these pages a few months ago; in fact, since September, I seem to have cited Abbott almost every month, which is strange when you consider the man was 107. But on Broadway these days the only people who aren't dead are incredibly old, and it seemed eerily fitting that the oldest of the lot endured even as everything around him crumbled, including the theater Broadway named in his honor, the George Abbott—now a parking lot. In 1993, while the Great White Way was celebrating its centenary, Abbott was upstate, rewriting *Damn Yankees*. "What's the new script like?" I enquired. "Hard to say," he replied, "but it's better than what most 106-year-old writers are doing."

Is anything true on Broadway anymore? Take this alleged centenary: there's a playhouse on Broadway marked on a city map of 1735; Niblo's Garden was built at Broadway and Prince Street in 1828; Lester Wallack made his Broadway debut at a Broadway theater called the Broadway Theatre in 1847. But, like a faded starlet, Broadway insists on lying about its age. Still, if we take this typical bit of trashy marketing opportunism at face value, Abbott was older than Broadway and, if only because so little else has survived, came to be seen as its embodiment: he made his acting debut at the Hudson in 1913 in a play called *The Misleading Lady*; he's still playing eighty-two seasons later a few hundred yards away in the soulless precincts of the Marriott Marquis; and his first hit as a playwright was titled, with a neatness historians can only marvel at, simply *Broadway*—a wonderful Jazz Age melodrama full of gangsters and showgirls that seems in its vernacular rowdiness the very essence of New York theater.

But sometimes the exception proves the rule. The personification of Broadway was very un-Broadway: he wasn't Jewish or homosexual or East Coast or gushily theatrical; he didn't live in the past and he didn't bullshit; he dressed formally and his nickname was an anti-nickname—Mister Abbott. Many of his protégés were variously Jewish homosexual East Coast gushy nostalgic bullshitters, but, even then, they didn't seem *that* Broadway at first glance. To pluck a creative team at random, Jerome Robbins, Leonard Bernstein, Betty Comden, and Adolph Green are revered today as Broadway bluechips. But, in 1944, who'd have thought that a ballet choreographer, a symphony conductor, and a couple of Greenwich Village satirists had a Main Stem musical in them? Mister Abbott did, and I don't think any other Broadway director (were there any other Broadway directors in 1944?) could have maintained the balancing act needed to pull off *On the Town*.

In our collective memory, we remember the show opening with three sailors bursting ashore and hymning the city: "New York, New York, a helluva town!"—because it *sounds* like an opening number. In fact, the evening begins on the docks, with a languorous long-lined almost-spiritual, "I Feel Like I'm Not Out of Bed Yet," which leads to the big-town valentine via some harsh, dissonant "hurry music." This is the show's way of signaling its musical vocabulary, its symphonic ambitions, its way of being honest with the audience. What's wrong with most plays and musicals can usually be traced to something in the first ten minutes, something which sends the audience's expectations off in the wrong direction and leaves them feeling short-changed when they're not fulfilled.

I cite Abbott a lot because, whenever something goes awry at Playwrights Horizons or the Paramount, some elementary piece of Abbott stage savvy pops into my head, and I mourn the lost connection between operational competence and art. For the sake of example, look at *Show Boat*. The 1927–1928 Broadway season saw the first nights of 264 new plays and musicals. On one night, December 26, there were eleven openings, of which *The White Eagle* was typical: the Earl of Kerhill's brother is on the lam, holed up in the West disguised as a cowhand and romancing an Injun girl called Silverwing. But the following night *Show Boat* opened, and the night after that Edna Ferber and George Kaufman's *The Royal Family*, and a couple of weeks later Eugene O'Neill's *Strange Interlude*. *Show Boat* and *Strange Interlude* alone justify the other 262. Today, a season's worth of openings barely scrapes into double figures. But it's a delusion to think you can slice off the lower levels of the pyramid without affecting the heights the top brick can reach. Abbott worked with great artists, professional craftsmen, and inferior hacks, and he did his best by all of them.

He refined his skills on farce, on *Room Service* and *Three Men on a Horse* and *Boy Meets Girl*. Farce is the most logically demanding form of theater, the most disciplined, and Abbott applied those disciplines when he returned to melodrama, when he moved into musicals (at the age of forty-eight), and when he resumed acting for a landmark production of Thornton Wilder's *The Skin of Our Teeth* in 1956. He had no theories about theater, but, when it came to specifics, he was full of good advice: "I always find that the most successful comedy songs come from a line in the book. If you're looking for an idea for a comic song, find the line in the play that gets the biggest laugh and make it into a song. Reprise the line as a song." There's one answer to second-act problems, and when Jule Styne, Comden and Green were in Boston with *Bells Are Ringing* (1956) that advice saved the show. This is play-making on the hoof, but you can only do it if you've dissected the structures of drama. The younger generation gave it fancier names—the "integrated musical," the "concept musical"—but Abbott was the first to understand the ways in which you could bind book and score together, and the first to appreciate the need for stylistic cohesion.

The night of his death I happened to be in London at *The Three Lives of Lucie Cabrol*, a John Berger story adapted by Théâtre de Complicité. This play has had extraordinary reviews, but all I could hear, from the center of the stalls, was the deafening restlessness of an audience not getting it. As we shuffled back up the aisle, much of the conversation was preoccupied with the question of why, having chopped real logs with a real ax, the actors subsequently tossed imaginary hay with imaginary pitchforks. Was it deliberate? wondered one theatergoer. And, if so, what was its significance? Or perhaps they couldn't afford pitchforks? Which is odd, because they could afford the ax and logs and trickling water and a lot of empty boots. So maybe it was just carelessness? (One of the many things that we last habitués of legit are supposed to make allowance for.) Either way, the effect was the same: the lack of consistency in staging language distanced us from the drama. If you're wondering about the boots, well, that was the opening: the lights go down, and we see the stage strewn with pairs of empty boots, and we think, "Ah, empty boots" and flip mentally through the International Harmonization Directive on Dramatic Symbolism until we come to Footwear, Unoccupied: "Of course! Death!" And sure enough the play opens with a little speech on death.

As Abbott was wont to say, "Cut the kindergarten stuff." Symbols are something the audience should be left to come across: the empty boots business might conceivably be fresh halfway through a play set in a boot factory whose workers have been conscripted—but only if we're allowed to find it for ourselves. A play which opens with the image is telegraphing the audience that it's so complacent it's going to labor the obvious remorselessly. Having figured that boots equals death, my mind wandered to Abbott's opening for *The Pajama Game* (1954):

> This is a very serious drama. It's kind of a problem play. It's about Capital and Labor. I wouldn't bother to make such a point of all this except later on if you happen to see a lot of naked women being chased through the woods, I don't want you to get the wrong impression. This play is full of *symbolism*.

In a few lines, Abbott has distilled the show's spirit. If you don't care for it, fine, leave now; but at least, forty minutes into Act I, you can't complain you've been misled. The day before he died, Mister Abbott was working on a new production of *Pajama Game* and dictating rewrites—but not of the opening speech.

The three most successful directors of the post-Abbott generation— Jerome Robbins, Hal Prince, Bob Fosse—all worked on *Pajama Game* in one capacity or another, and all learned from him. "More directors, writers, composers, lyricists and performers have come out of the Abbott atelier than from any other single figure in the history of the American theater," says Prince, who came to work for Abbott half a century ago and, in the 1995 White Pages, is still listed as sharing an office in Rockefeller Center with him. "It's not because he's lived to 106, but because he's so secure about himself that he's not begrudging in his generosity and encouragement." He served as "apprentices' sorcerer" to talents as disparate as George Balanchine, to whom in 1936 he permitted the then unheard-of billing "Choreography by . . ?"; and Nora Ephron, whose letters home from college he turned into a hit play in 1963; and Styne and Bernstein, Comden and Green, Robbins and Fosse and Prince, Frank Loesser and Garson Kanin, Gwen Verdon and John O'Hara, Gene Kelly and Stanley Donen, Sammy Cahn and Morton Gould, Carol Burnett and Natalia Makarova, Shirley MacLaine and Liza Minnelli, Adler and Ross, Bock and Harnick, Kander and Ebb; and Stephen Sondheim's first show as composer . . . Abbott's family tree extends through his own work to *Born Yesterday* and *Guys and Dolls* and *Fiddler on the Roof* and *Evita* and *Sweeney Todd*. Nine decades after Mister Abbott had his first play produced, it's difficult to find a Broadway musical which hasn't been written or staged by an Abbott graduate—hit or flop, *Phantom* or *Cyrano*, *Kiss of the Spider Woman* or *The Red Shoes*, *Passion* or *The Will Rogers Follies*.

But just as representative of "the Abbott touch" is Clifford Goldsmith. Who? Clifford Goldsmith, b. 1900, Aurora, N.Y., d. 1971, high-school nutritionist. Goldsmith had one good idea for a get-me-to-the-junior-prom farce, he wrote it up, Abbott fixed it, produced it, and staged it, and *What a Life* became one of the most successful plays of the day, and then a long-running radio series. Goldsmith never had another hit; presumably he went back to the high-school nutrition business, whatever that is. But, like Philip Dunning (*Broadway*), Maurine Dallas Watkins (*Chicago*), Ann Preston Bridgers (*Coquette*), and a dozen other one-hit footnotes to theatrical history, he had his moment—thanks to Abbott.

He respected hits, and had little time for the notion of the "undeserved flop." Once, I mentioned to him how much I'd enjoyed his unsuccessful update of the Frankenstein story, which he co-wrote and directed off-Broadway at the age of 102. "That's what I call wasted time," he snapped, and returned to what he considered more fruitful areas of conversation. At 102, a guy can't afford wasted time—especially in an arena where they now figure the average musical takes eight years from page to stage. Abbott's successors transformed popular theater into art—and forgot to take the audience with them: the heirs to Abbott and Rodgers gathered all their expertise, all their technique, and lavished it on *Passion* and *The Petrified Prince*. The theater needs hits: it was because Abbott had given Prince three in a row that the young producer could afford to take a chance on *West Side Story*; Abbott's production of *A Funny Thing Happened on the Way to the Forum* gave Sondheim the financial cushion to indulge himself with *Pacific Overtures* and *Assassins*. Hardcore Sondheim groupies tend to look on *Forum* (1963) as an aberration: good grief, it ran three years and made piles of money; best not to mention it. For them, the real Sondheim was born the following year. *Anyone Can Whistle* was his first cult flop—nine performances and out—and inaugurated the composer as we know him today, a genius too special for the expense account set, the bridge & tunnelers and all the other dummies who'd rather be vegged out at *Hello, Dolly!* But Sondheim himself in his more generous moments points out that *Forum* is, if you give it a moment's thought, one of his most formally experimental works. For one thing, it's the only musical farce that's ever worked. It's difficult to musicalize, say, Feydeau because there's too much plot to fit any songs in, and, if you try to use songs in the traditional Rodgers-and-Hammerstein sense, it all gets too relentless. *Forum* uses the songs as a respite: instead of, as in a musical play, advancing the situation or illuminating character, they bring the play juddering to a halt; they're a chance to stand still and catch your breath. Only Abbott could have taken a one-set no-romance anti-musical and made it seem such an obvious, natural hit.

You find this throughout his career. He delivered hits, but *On Your Toes* (1936), only his second musical, was the first Broadway show with a dramatically integrated ballet; *The Boys from Syracuse* (1938) was the first Shakespearean musical; *Pal Joey* (1940) was the first with an antihero; *On the Town* (1944) was the first with a symphonic score; *Look, Ma, I'm Dancin'* (1948) was the first dance musical; even *Wonderful Town* (1953) has a musicalized dinner-party scene far more radical than anything Bernstein wrote when he moved into opera proper with works like *A Quiet Place* . . . Abbott never indulged innovation; it's not its own justification. But would Rodgers have gone on to do *Oklahoma!* and *Carousel* if Abbott hadn't shown him, in their five shows together, that musicals could have their own dramatic integrity?

At a 100th-birthday seminar, an earnest drama student asked him, "Mister Abbott, when did the theater first become tainted by commercialism?" "Sixteen hundred one," he replied, "when Shakespeare said to Burbage, 'Now let's get this show to a bigger theater.'" Abbott was as confident cutting Shakespeare as Comden and Green, and here *is* a funny thing: as the years go by, *Kiss Me, Kate* and *West Side Story* seem more and more products of their era, and no great threat to the originals; but, in transforming *The Comedy of Errors* into *The Boys from Syracuse*, Abbott streamlined the structure, loosened up the comedy, and ended up improving on Shakespeare. Ever since, the most successful versions of *The Comedy* have always given the impression that they'd much rather be doing the musical; Shakespeare directors have devoted most of their energies to finding substitutes for Rodgers and Hart, drafting in everyone from Sir Arthur Sullivan (London, 1952) to the calypso balladeer Cy Young (Bristol, 1960); the best production of recent years—Trevor Nunn's for the RSC —threw in the towel and decided what the hell, let's do a musical.

A couple of seasons ago, Dame Judi Dench staged *The Boys from Syracuse* at the Open Air Theatre in Regent's Park and this is what she did: as the three ladies are doing "Sing for Your Supper," she brought on a man dressed as a giant chicken; unable to stage the song, she decided instead that the song needed help. The trouble with the contemporary theater is that its stagers are all giant chickens: rather than convince you of the material, they panic, and distract you from the material with irrelevant flim-flam. Abbott never did. In New Haven with *Call Me Madam*, he suggested that Irving Berlin write another contrapuntal number, like one he remembered from forty years earlier, "Play a Simple Melody." Berlin came back with "(You're Not Sick) You're Just in Love." Abbott and Robbins were so confident of the song that they told Berlin it would be sung unstaged: no lights, no dancing, nothing to get in the way. It stopped the show. Conversely, struggling with a campy romp called *Out of This World*, he junked Cole Porter's "From This Moment On." Last year, I asked him how he could possibly have done such a thing. "I'd do it again tomorrow," he growled. "It slowed the show." He was the first director to bring dramatic considerations to musical structure: it had to be the right song in the right place.

It made a difference that he was a writer/director in a writer's theater. Before Abbott, directors were traffic cops: they looked after the star and moved people on and off. Today directors are the only stars left: the '94 *Show Boat* stars Hal Prince; in 1927, who knew or cared who directed it? (Zeke Colvan.) Abbott was amused by the trend: when Robbins, on *West Side Story*, introduced the now standard billing of "Entire Production Conceived, Choreographed And Directed By . . ." —and in a box, too—Abbott commented: "That's like saying 'Entire Part Of Mother Played By Lizzie Flop.'" He knew that, in a theater where the directors are the stars, you soon run out of anything to direct. At the Public Theatre, Prince has devoted a year of work, almost thirty actors, and three-quarters of a million dollars to *The Petrified Prince* and run up against the limits of his power. In the end, the property matters: there *is* a difference between Kern and Hammerstein or Sondheim, on the one hand, and Michael John LaChiusa, on the other, and the slickest stager in the world can't hide it. "Feel/ If you can feel/ Then you can speak/ Shout/ Rise . . ." just isn't worth Prince's trouble.

Fashions change, but, years after they went their separate ways, Prince respected Abbott enough to always arrange a private full-dress performance of his shows before his mentor. So Abbott would sit fifth-row center, and the cast would play *Cabaret*—in three acts. "Put it in two acts," said the old play doctor afterward. Prince did, and you marvel today at how, structurally, it could ever have been otherwise: the first-act finale, where the waiters sing their sweetly beguiling "Tomorrow Belongs to Me" and then you see for the first time their swastikas, seems so obviously the first-act finale you can't believe it took Abbott to point it out. "He doesn't think in terms of what is now called the concept," Prince told me, "but he thinks about the arc. He knows the trajectory of a show, which is why he's had so few disasters in a lifetime in the theater. He was the master of American farce comedy but there is never a dishonest moment on the stage. Characters are always consistent with their character. He never slams a door for the sake of slamming a door, he slams it for a reason. His shows are honest, peppy, energetic—*really* energetic, and that's another thing I learned from him. There's so much phony energy in the theater: people think that by running around in circles like a crazed tiger, you're displaying energy, and, in fact, you're not. You can have energy in the stillest place in the world, and he knew that." Even as he organized and disciplined comedy and musicals, Abbott never confused tempo with speed. We bury him at a time when that mistake has become routine. Jerry Zaks's heartless burlesques of *Guys and Dolls* and *Anything Goes* are full of "phony energy," and, even as the director's heaped with honors, you wonder: if these weren't revivals, if we didn't already love them, would Zaks's stagings persuade us of their merits?

From its concoction of fake centenaries to its obsession with revivals, we know that Broadway wishes it could turn the clock back. But all it can do is fake it. Abbott took the most stylized and artificial forms of theater—farce and musicals—and filled them with recognizable Americans in street clothes. Perhaps it's more difficult than it sounds, at least to judge by the grim cartoons of Zaks & Co. Or perhaps all the "lively arts" eventually devour themselves: like pop music and TV, Broadway has acquired too much of a back-catalogue to be anything other than self-referential and postmodern. Abbott liked to quote the one about holding a mirror up to life; today, shows are about shows, not life. He grew up in Wyoming; he worked as a cowboy, and one of his early acting roles was as a cowboy; to Hal Prince and others, he looked like Gary Cooper. Certainly, he shared both Cooper's famous economy of language and his integrity. It was fascinating to watch him in San Diego, in the theater night after night, those bright piercing eyes fixing the stage, anxious to whip *Damn Yankees* into shape for Broadway. At dinner before the opening, he filled the glass of his friend, the dancer Natalia Makarova. "How's the wine?" he asked. "So-so," she said. A few moments later, she enquired how the show was. "Same as the wine," he said. Abbott's was an American life, and a life in the theater: from ranches and brothels to Tonys and Pulitzers. And, to the end, the old play doctor was still trying to work out how to fix the play. Would that we could.

March 1995

The Other Other Frost

William Logan

THERE HAVE ALWAYS been good reasons to ignore Robert Frost. The most traditional, the most metrically and morally conservative of modern poets, he was in a strict sense the last American poet of the nineteenth century (twelve at the death of Dickinson, he entered Dartmouth the year Whitman died). He could be hidebound and narrow and backward-looking, his Yankee landscape the agrarian fantasy of a Southern Democrat—not John Crowe Ransom or Allen Tate, but Andrew Jackson. The land he celebrated (not just the physical landscape but the moral landscape) was already gone, if it had ever existed. No American poet has created a more profound pastoral than Frost—profound because we'd like to believe it was a real place, not just the landscape of poetry.

Part of Frost's despair was his knowledge that his world was gone (when the terms of Frost's world were gone, the people remained). Many of his best poems take loss as their theme—sometimes as private and as crippling as anything in American literature. He was a ruined melancholic, and the dark gestures of his late Romanticism make him a moodier and far more difficult figure than Stevens, or Eliot, or Pound—compared to Frost they are shining untroubled aesthetes. They took America as a hypothesis; he took it for what it was—Frost told the stories that Whitman only suggested.

Frost was a poet of missed chance, of failed opportunity, of regret and cold disappointment. Of all the moderns he is the one we have not come to terms with, yet part of the problem has always been Frost himself. He did so much to emphasize, to publicize and receive honorary Ph.D.'s for, his own worst instincts, to make himself the cracker-barrel Yankee sage people were glad to take him for, a kind of Grandma Moses on the deck of the *Pequod*, that we shouldn't be surprised if now it is almost impossible to take him for anything else. More than forty years ago Randall Jarrell wrote two marvelous essays of rehabilitation, "The Other Frost" and "To the Laodiceans," arguing for the gloomy, hard, human Frost ("human" was a favorite Jarrell word), the Frost of "The Witch of Coös," "Provide, Provide," and "Home Burial." Most of the poems Jarrell favored are now part of our Frost—but instead we have two Frosts, a farmer schizophrenic, half Vermont maple-syrup and half raw granite, an old man of the mountains people can take home to dinner.

Each of these Frosts serves the idiom of our beliefs—we need the one to believe that poetry is good, the other to believe that poetry is true. Each version is a fact, but each is also a bias confirmed by the partiality of a reading. Frost was at times a bad philosopher, a man who wore his morals on his sleeve, and as he grew older he convinced himself he was a *philosophe* of masques and fables—he almost became a fable himself (or an apophthegm dreaming it was a fable). For sententious observation, homespun morals, complacent sentiment, and barn-idle philosophizing (the kind a cat does, tangled in a ball of yarn), you can't go much further than the later Frost. By the time John F. Kennedy asked him to read at the 1961 Inaugural, Frost was more a monument than half the equestrian statues in Washington—a brass-necked cold calculation, standing proudly on all fours. Has any major poet written a worse poem about America than "The Gift Outright"? It contains every part of Frost's terrible sentiment for the Land, America, the Past, for Ourselves, for the general myth that replaces the mangled event—even the best line, "To the land vaguely realizing westward," drowns in the horror of all that is left unsaid.

When "Home Burial" and "The Death of the Hired Man" can sit comfortably in high-school anthologies, no longer cruel rural dramas but complacent period pieces, perhaps it is time for a different Frost, one not so easily lost to high-mindedness. There is need for a Frost less dramatic and more demonic, a Frost of impermanent mood, whose own moods seemed a confusion to him (hence his reliance on, his attraction to, codes of behavior, morals, blind jurisprudence, the otherworldly forces that might set the world in order, or strip it to raw design).

Jarrell wanted people to read Frost, to suffer from his range and his terrors, and what is permanent in Frost now includes many of the poems Jarrell salvaged from neglect: "The Witch of Coös," "Neither Out Far Nor In Deep," "Home Burial," "Acquainted with the Night," "Design," "Provide, Provide," "An Old Man's Winter Night," and "Desert Places." (Even "After Apple-Picking" and "The Gift Outright," poems I can't imagine anyone liking. I may as well admit that my taste is different from Jarrell's—I don't like "Directive," I don't think "Provide, Provide" an "immortal masterpiece," though I like it well enough, and I despise "The Gift Outright." Every reader should have a list of the Frost poems he can't abide.)

IF JARRELL'S FROST was the Frost of interior and melancholy, of moral observation and metallic cunning, he was also the Frost whose monologues and scenes tended toward sentiment (a poet a lot like himself, in other words). I would like to propose what might seem impossible after Jarrell, a list of a dozen or so of Frost's best poems rarely seen in anthologies and likely to be new to most readers. Here is the list: "The Code," "A Hundred Collars," "The Bearer of Evil Tidings," "Snow," "Place for a Third," "The Exposed Nest," "The Fear," "Spring Pools," "The Thatch," "Sand Dunes," "The Strong Are Saying Nothing," "The Draft Horse," "The Silken Tent," and "Willful Homing." This is a list of moral ambiguity and suspended grief, of stark horror and shy confusion—if Frost was a confusion to himself, we should, part of the time, be as confused and surprised by the Frost we read.

"The Code" starts with three men haying a field under an advancing thundercloud:

There were three in the meadow by the brook
Gathering up windrows, piling cocks of hay,
With an eye always lifted toward the west
Where an irregular sun-bordered cloud
Darkly advanced with a perpetual dagger
Flickering across its bosom. Suddenly
One helper, thrusting pitchfork in the ground,
Marched himself off the field and home. One stayed.
The town-bred farmer failed to understand.

The farmhand's action is as abrupt as a scrawl of lightning, and the rest of the poem sets out to explain it. Silence has the force of speech in Frost, but this is one of the few places where silence is interpreted. The opening lines might seem just an excuse for a story, the story the remaining farmhand goes on to tell about another haying, another farmer who offended the code—in a more straightforward mood (even a rambling storyteller like Frost generally got on with things) the prologue could have been dispensed with. But the action is not just about the code, it is in code—a tale is required to explain the tale. The poem's lovely, lopsided organization is rougher and more accidental than in Frost's conservative dramas—the reader almost requires doubt about the form, as an imitative action. Only gradually is it clear that the second tale is in code as well—that the second farmhand is delivering a genial threat.

> "But the old fool seizes his fork in both hands,
> And looking up bewhiskered out of the pit,
> Shouts like an army captain, 'Let her come!'
> Thinks I, D'ye mean it? 'What was that you said?'
> I asked out loud, so's there'd be no mistake,
> 'Did you say, "Let her come"?' 'Yes, let her come.'
> He said it over, but he said it softer.
> Never you say a thing like that to a man,
> Not if he values what he is. God, I'd as soon
> Murdered him as left out his middle name.
> I'd built the load and knew right where to find it.
> Two or three forkfuls I picked lightly round for
> Like meditating, and then I just dug in
> And dumped the rackful on him in ten lots.
> I looked over the side once in the dust
> And caught sight of him treading-water-like,
> Keeping his head above. 'Damn ye,' I says,
> 'That gets ye!' He squeaked like a squeezed rat.
> That was the last I saw or heard of him.
> I cleaned the rack and drove out to cool off."

"I went about to kill him fair enough," the hand says later—he can afford to be so casual (death is often casual in Frost) because he knows his actions were understood, part of the code, never written down, by which men get along with one another. The farmer didn't die, but he earned his life at the cost of a lesson. The force of the poem is in the implicating conduct of different stories: the squall of violence when the farmhand throws down his pitchfork, the patient explanation of the second farmhand (a code of courtesy here), the town-bred farmer's incomplete understanding of what he's been told, the silent courtesy of the threat which the remaining farmhand delivers. The farmer has been warned—that is part of the code, too. Frost lets each of these stories rustle over the others (he knows something about literary codes as well); but the poem would never be effective without his warm feeling for the way men work, their stiff prides and dishonors, the lies they tell themselves.

The texture of those prides is in the texture of the details, the force that starts as invention and ends as a kind of second life: that "bewhiskered" farmer, about to be whiskered in hay; the ominous way the farmer "said it over, but he said it softer"; the almost meditative construction (*more codes*), "I'd as soon/ Murdered him as left out his middle name"; the further meditative gesture of the farmhand picking "lightly round" the hay (how lovely to describe it as a kind of meditation); and that terrible sound, that terrible image, of the farmer squeaking "like a squeezed rat" (there is danger throughout—recall that "perpetual dagger" in the storm cloud). Running through the poem, as in the best of Frost, is the haunted echo of men's speech. Frost's pentameter is always too dependent on monosyllables, like the speech of most men, and here and there the lines are posed or stilted; but most of a century later these sound like men talking, not like men writing.

A "Hundred Collars" starts in a similar offhand way—a man misses a train, is forced to lodge at a local hotel, but the hotel is full. He doesn't want to share a room—he doesn't *want* to, and Frost conveys with typical economy the apprehension that rises in such a man on such a night. He'd like to know who's in the room already:

> "Who is it?"
>
> "A man."
>
> "So I should hope. What kind of man?"
>
> "I know him: he's all right. A man's a man.
> Separate beds, of course, you understand."
> The night clerk blinked his eyes and dared
>   him on.
>
> "Who's that man sleeping in the office chair?
> Has he had the refusal of my chance?"
>
> "He was afraid of being robbed or murdered.
> What do you say?"
>
> "I'll have to have a bed."

His resistance collapses, but not before he endures the delicious malice of the night clerk (the whole point of "A man's a man" is that it isn't true—a man's a man until he's a murderer). It's an old traveler's fear. Frost has to specify the separate beds—that should remind us not only of the close quarters earlier travelers had to tolerate, but of the scene in Chapter 3 of

Moby-Dick, where Ishmael has to share a bed with Queequeg at the Spouter-Inn (the landlord there is more considerate—when Ishmael is reluctant, he starts to plane down a rough bench). It's one of the most gripping scenes in American fiction—the exhausted young man, reconciled to a bed with the strange harpooner (who's off somewhere selling a shrunken head); the young man finally in bed in the freezing room, on a mattress that seems "stuffed with corn-cobs or broken crockery"; Ishmael awoken by the entry of Queequeg (tattooed like a checkerboard, still holding the unsold head), who gets into bed smoking his tomahawk and then wildly threatens the young man he finds there. When Ishmael wakes the next morning, Queequeg's arm is thrown over him "in the most loving and affectionate manner."

Melville's scene turns maternal and comic there, and the trust between Ishmael and Queequeg is sealed by their night together. Frost has only a scholar and a subscriptions agent to work with, and he toys longer with the dread. The agent is named Lafe.

> The Doctor looked at Lafe and looked away.
> A man? A brute. Naked above the waist,
> He sat there creased and shining in the light,
> Fumbling the buttons in a well-starched shirt.
> "I'm moving into a size-larger shirt.
> I've felt mean lately; mean's no name for it.
> I just found what the matter was tonight:
> I've been a-choking like a nursery tree
> When it outgrows the wire band of its name tag.
> I blamed it on the hot spell we've been having.
> 'Twas nothing but my foolish hanging back,
> Not liking to own up I'd grown a size.
> Number eighteen this is. What size do you wear?"
>
> The Doctor caught his throat convulsively.
> "Oh—ah—fourteen—fourteen."

Every gesture is alive with threat—the half-naked man talks of being "mean lately," talks of choking (a scholar the least sensitive to language would flinch at the latent violence). We're delighted with the unease which Frost so easily manufactures—but we're uneasy too. Frost sets the reader even with the characters—we're given no more information than the Doctor, and we must feel our way as clumsily. Lafe wants to know his collar size because . . . because he wants to give the Doctor a hundred old collars. But we're frightened to take anything from those we fear—what would be generosity seems only a further threat, perhaps even a trick. Frost has taken his character into the worst of fear—and then Lafe offers to take off the Doctor's shoes! Each clumsy action allows a new misinterpretation. The Doctor's poised to run away—but Lafe's only worried about the landlord's sheets. (Who but Frost, his eye on the meanness and misgivings, would pause for the beautiful line where Lafe, though half-naked, seems *to be* his shirt, all "creased and shining"?)

Eventually they find themselves in hobbled conversation, which leads to one of Frost's typical passages of observation, plain and circumstantial, but with the consuming conscience of character:

> "It's business, but I can't say it's not fun.
> What I like best's the lay of different farms,
> Coming out on them from a stretch of woods,
> Or over a hill or round a sudden corner.
> I like to find folks getting out in spring,
> Raking the dooryard, working near the house.
> Later they get out further in the fields.
> Everything's shut sometimes except the barn;
> The family's all away in some back meadow.
> There's a hay load a-coming—when it comes.
> And later still they all get driven in:
> The fields are stripped to lawn, the garden patches
> Stripped to bare ground, the maple trees
> To whips and poles. There's nobody about.
> The chimney, though, keeps up a good brisk smoking.
> And I lie back and ride."

How calmly and warmly and suggestively this is rendered, like harvest scenes from a medieval calendar—or like Wordsworth's first view of London in *The Prelude*. There's that beautiful surveyor's phrase, "the lay of different farms"; the simplicity of feeling in "I like to find folks getting out in spring"; the long patience of "There's a hay load a-coming—when it comes," even if we now think "a-coming" a bit corny (corny, but country); the visual fable of "The fields are stripped to lawn"; and then Brueghel's barren landscape of winter. It's not important to the poem—it's just there, like the landscape, the way that the characters are just there, accidentally thrown together and forced to make something like peace. So many of Frost's effects are almost negligent, as if they just happened. The scholar remains wary even at the last—that is *his* character. All his knowledge is no use in judging men—even when Frost disliked men like the Doctor, it was with fondness and understanding. That was what they were—and Frost's poetry is about the way men are. It would take so little for the Doctor just to accept the collars, yet all he can say is, "But really I—I have so many collars." (This is one of many times that Frost's meter allows a trembling hesi- tation of emphasis.) "There's nothing I'm afraid of like scared people," says Lafe.

Frost knew when to let a poem go—in his best poems the ending comes as a slight shock, as if the poem *couldn't* be over (in his worst the reader feels the poem shouldn't have begun). The actions seem to move beyond the end of the lines—this is an old trick in fiction, but how many poets have used it well? Fiction wouldn't have served Frost's temper (if he'd been a novelist he might have written something awfully like *Ethan Frome*), but when we place him it must be alongside those moody gothics Hawthorne and Melville, the New England geniuses of guilt and redemption, and failures to redeem. Something of the violent Fate that moves their fiction moves through his verse, but it is a Fate blinder and more callous. Here is "The Draft Horse":

With a lantern that wouldn't burn
In too frail a buggy we drove
Behind too heavy a horse
Through a pitch-dark limitless grove.

And a man came out of the trees
And took our horse by the head
And reaching back to his ribs
Deliberately stabbed him dead.

The ponderous beast went down
With a crack of a broken shaft.
And the night drew through the trees
In one long invidious draft.

The most unquestioning pair
That ever accepted fate
And the least disposed to ascribe
Any more than we had to to hate,

We assumed that the man himself
Or someone he had to obey

Wanted us to get down
And walk the rest of the way.

This is the Frost who makes readers uncomfortable. We ought to be able to call it an allegory—but no allegory suggests itself (or, rather, the allegories are too simple for the savagery). The murder of the horse is so abrupt, so unforeseen, that the murderer seems more than just part of that unknowable agency that makes life harder (no memory "keeps the end from being hard," Frost wrote in "Provide, Provide"). The couple, with their faulty lantern and fragile buggy, with the wrong horse, are destined for trouble—and how Frost loved those scary old woods. (One critic asked— this is the sort of question critics *should* ask—why the couple had hitched a draft horse to a buggy. The answer should have been obvious—because they had to.) Frost knew more about depravity than any American writer after Melville and before Faulkner—and he had a cellar knowledge of our irrational fears (Frost tells us the man stabbed the horse *deliberately*; but first, in the way he grips the horse's head, Frost shows us deliberation). This is the Frost people don't *want* to care for, and yet look how compellingly the poem ends. The couple don't curse their fate; they're so unquestioning they seem slightly stupid. Yet isn't this a philosophy, a kind of clear religion, not "to ascribe/ Any more than we had to to hate"? As readers we know we wouldn't act this way, and we're not finally sure that we *should* act this way—but we're not sure we *shouldn't*, either. That makes Frost strange, and us, in our settled, suspicious natures, ill at ease.

Frost's simplicity is deceptive, because it deepens so pitilessly into complication. When we say a man is complex, we mean we're not sure of his responses; and in Frost we're often measured by the way we read. Consider "Sand Dunes," a poem that starts so plainly it hardly starts at all:

Sea waves are green and wet,
But up from where they die
Rise others vaster yet,
And those are brown and dry.

They are the sea made land
To come at the fisher town
And bury in solid sand
The men she could not drown.

She may know cove and cape,
But she does not know mankind

If by any change of shape
She hopes to cut off mind.

Men left her a ship to sink:
They can leave her a hut as well;
And be but more free to think
For the one more cast-off shell.

Without the title, the first stanza might be opaque; but the shore is where waves die, and the dunes rise from the tide-line. "They are the sea made land"—this might be mere ingenuity, a metaphor of sand, but Frost's idea is more peculiar: the dunes are the macabre way the sea will conquer the fishermen it hasn't been able to drown. (Dunes *could* bury a village—I saw them bury a cemetery once.) Even here, when Death and Fate and the Sea all seem inexorable, the poem hasn't finished. The sea isn't clever enough! If Frost were a worse poet, he'd linger here, and tell us that men can abandon a philosophy or an idea—but he doesn't. His men are like hermit crabs—he *says* they'll be freer to think, but we remember that for hermit crabs life is just one abandoned shell after another.

"SAND DUNES" is a trial piece for a poem more poignant and more Stygian, "Neither Out Far Nor In Deep"—think of the syntactic organization of the last stanzas. It shows how good Frost can be when he isn't great, and how disturbing and not quite settled even his settled endings are. Frost is always catching his readers out—he is a poet disastrous to underestimate (even in his late poems there are words, lines, sometimes a stanza or two, that have the old rough homemade truth in them).

No one thinks that the sea really has designs on the land—or no one would think it, if Frost hadn't said so. His fantasies have a primitive agency, a primitive terror—and don't men act at times *as if* they believed what Frost is only whimsical about? His poems require not that we believe them, but that we know we could believe them if we were different—that is, if we were Frost. This slight offness or strangeness lets his readers take as pleasant fiction what would otherwise be unpleasant truths, though that doesn't make the truths less unpleasant. "The Bearer of Evil Tidings" might have been written by Kipling—it is no more than a fantasy about a cliché:

The bearer of evil tidings,
When he was halfway there,
Remembered that evil tidings
Were a dangerous thing to bear.

So when he came to the parting
Where one road led to the throne
And one went off to the mountains
And into the wild unknown,

He took the one to the mountains.
He ran through the Vale of Cashmere,
He ran through the rhododendrons
Till he came to the land of Pamir.

This seems to be a poem about cowardice; but by one of those reversals that drive Frost's poems into the blackness of our psychologies, it is really about prudence.

She taught him her tribe's religion:
How, ages and ages since,
A princess en route from China
To marry a Persian prince

Had been found with child; and her army
Had come to a troubled halt.
And though a god was the father
And nobody else at fault,

It had seemed discreet to remain there
And neither go on nor back.
So they stayed and declared a village
There in the land of the Yak.

Frost is good about religion—his distrust is wolfish and cagy. The Christian religion *has* to say that its god was the father of Jesus—otherwise there would be no religion. The Oriental army advances under a similar suspension of disbelief; but acts in just that bothersome human way Frost loves, accepting enough to believe, doubting enough not to go on or back. (As readers we know that Frost is still thinking Christian thoughts.)

And that was why there were people
On one Himalayan shelf;
And the bearer of evil tidings
Decided to stay there himself.

At least he had this in common
With the race he chose to adopt:
They had both of them had their reasons
For stopping where they had stopped.

As for his evil tidings,
Belshazzar's overthrow,
Why hurry to tell Belshazzar
What soon enough he would know?

Few things escape Frost's brutal wryness here (though look at how deli-
cately he suggests that other shelves have other stories). *They had both of
them had their reasons*—this doesn't mean that the reasons are good or
honorable. The reasons for sacrifice (honor, integrity, loyalty to country or
king) are never argued here—Frost knows all about them already. It is the
small salvation of the slightly disreputable case that interests him. After all,
the news would have had no effect on the outcome—Belshazzar was already
overthrown. The poem might have stopped just before the last, throwaway
stanza; but then it wouldn't have drifted beyond our expectations. A reader
almost forgets that those evil tidings had somewhere to get to. That is the
cold form of Frost's genius, and genius allows no pity for Belshazzar.

Frost's poems often find something human but distasteful in knowledge and belief—not just religion's set beliefs, but the beliefs men have to
accept to get from one day to another. He recognizes that belief can be a
weakness, that strength often requires a restraint. "The Strong Are Saying
Nothing" ends there, but it starts in a casual, causal, haphazard way.

The soil now gets a rumpling soft and damp,
And small regard to the future of any weed.
The final flat of the hoe's approval stamp
Is reserved for the bed of a few selected seed.

There is seldom more than a man to a harrowed piece.
Men work alone, their lots plowed far apart,
One stringing a chain of seed in an open crease,
And another stumbling after a halting cart.

To the fresh and black of the squares of early mold
The leafless bloom of a plum is fresh and white;
Though there's more than a doubt if the weather is not too cold
For the bees to come and serve its beauty aright.

Wind goes from farm to farm in wave on wave,
But carries no cry of what is hoped to be.
There may be little or much beyond the grave,
But the strong are saying nothing until they see.

How lovely that "rumpling" in the first line is, and how ambiguous that "harrowed" later on. There is much in the loneliness of the way these men work, in that farmer "stumbling after a halting cart." The brilliance of Frost's poems is often in these acts of notice, in the contrast between the harrowed soil (retaining the decay in that other sense of "mold") and the white plum blossoms. Frost isn't a poet for mere beauty. The beauty of the plum tree comes ripe with disaster: if the weather is too cold for the bees, the beauty will not be served with plums. It's as if to say, "Beauty is all very well, in its place, but what's really important is the homely old plum." This isn't the point of the poem, but it leads to the point by a roundabout way. Farming is the faith and hope of seeds, the religion of what comes after—suddenly we're in a poem about death. Frost's farmers don't trust anything they can't see. It might be tempting to predict a crop, and for many men it's tempting to predict what lies beyond the grave. It takes a kind of strength, Frost is saying, to resist from hope—those harrowed fields are bleak and biblical.

Frost could barely think of beauty without thinking of death. At times it made him arch and melodramatic, those two sins of Romantic character (there's a self-congratulatory cruelty to the end of the mawkish "Out, Out—"—the boy probably died from bad doctoring and an overdose of ether); but usually he just suffered his understandings, half sad and half stoic. He knew how much death cost the people who survived, how much even the prospect of death cost them. The odd little poem "Not to Keep" is about a wounded soldier, sent home to his wife. She thinks that they've escaped, that the war is over for them; but she cannot see his wound. Finally she has to ask, and he has to tell her—the wound is severe enough to send him home, but not to keep him home. He has to go back to war.

Frost is a master of what people have to endure for one another. The visual arts have never been much good at showing what people say without saying, but in "Not to Keep" it is all there in a line or two. (The movies cheat and use music, and perhaps you could say that de la Tour cheated with light and with significant glances.) It's easy to forget how much Frost does not say in his poems, how much power lies in his reticence.

Frost was unashamed of writing as a man (not for other men, but about other men), in a way that would almost be impossible now. The women in Frost's poetry usually stand apart from the action, like a Greek chorus—and yet we've had few poets who understood women better. How many wonderful women he created as characters: the wife in "The Death of the Hired Man" and the wife in "Home Burial," the Witch of Coös and the Pauper Witch of Grafton, the wife in "The Fear" and the depressed wife in "A Servant to Servants," the mother in "The Housekeeper," the wife of "In the Home Stretch." There's a fine anthology to be made merely from Frost's women, merely from Frost's wives (Frost must have been a bit afraid of women—in the dialogues, the women usually come off better than the men). Frost wasn't ashamed of being a man, and that gave him an understanding of women—not *the* understanding, but an understanding that can only come from liking what women are. It shows in poems like "The Silken Tent."

> She is as in a field a silken tent
> At midday when a sunny summer breeze
> Has dried the dew and all its ropes relent,
> So that in guys it gently sways at ease,
> And its supporting central cedar pole,
> That is its pinnacle to heavenward
> And signifies the sureness of the soul,
> Seems to owe naught to any single cord,
> But strictly held by none, is loosely bound
> By countless silken ties of love and thought
> To everything on earth the compass round,
> And only by one's going slightly taut
> In the capriciousness of summer air
> Is of the slightest bondage made aware.

The language here (that "sunny summer breeze," that "gently sways at ease") doesn't have the considered simplicity of the best of Frost—Frost hovered around clichés so often that sometimes he just lit on them. From the middle of the poem onward, however, this metaphysical conceit (how rarely that plain old lover-of-metaphysics Robert Frost chose to be metaphysical) gains from the force of its slightly self-conscious, off-the-shelf poetic language; and the concentration of the final three lines can scarcely be equalled. Reading those lines, the reader finds something pulling taut in him, too. The awkwardness is an homage to feeling, as it was in Hardy.

This doesn't mean that Frost understood all women, or even specific women. Many of his best poems recognize the mystery between women and men—the mystery that is misunderstanding. The insignificant incident of "The Exposed Nest" starts in that kind of misunderstanding:

You were forever finding some new play.
So when I saw you down on hands and knees
In the meadow, busy with the new-cut hay,
Trying, I thought, to set it up on end,
I went to show you how to make it stay,
If that was your idea, against the breeze,
And, if you asked me, even help pretend
To make it root again and grow afresh.
But 'twas no make-believe with you today,
Nor was the grass itself your real concern,
Though I found your hand full of wilted fern,
Steel-bright June-grass, and blackening heads of clover.
'Twas a nest full of young birds on the ground
The cutter bar had just gone champing over. . . .

The woman wants to make it right, somehow (how many opportunities this poem gives to modern critics, those crippled descendants of Freud). Few passages in Frost are as rich with the inevitability of death as "your hand full of wilted fern,/ Steel-bright June-grass, and blackening heads of clover." The couple are trying to do the impossible, to restore the entire field so the mother bird won't abandon the nest. The field has a mortal beauty, like a Van Gogh; but Frost isn't interested in that. He sees "The way the nest-full every time we stirred/ Stood up to us as to a mother-bird/ Whose coming home has been too long deferred." There isn't much time for these nestlings—and the couple don't know if their meddling will make things worse. They work on anyway.

We saw the risk we took in doing good,
But dared not spare to do the best we could
Though harm should come of it; so built the screen
You had begun, and gave them back their shade.
All this to prove we cared. Why is there then
No more to tell? We turned to other things.
I haven't any memory—have you?—
Of ever coming to the place again
To see if the birds lived the first night through,
And so at last to learn to use their wings.

The poem abandons the nestlings, as the couple did, when everything that could be done had been done—even if they'd done the wrong thing. Without quite saying so (Frost's poems are expert in not quite saying so), the poem has sketched the boundary of this couple's lives: the way the man assumes the woman is playing; the way he wants to show her how to do what she's doing (*just like a man*, we might think now); the way the end acknowledges not just that there are other matters, but that some matters must be abandoned. That some things need to be left alone insinuates darkly into these lives—there is a risk to what kindness can do, a risk and a limit. But sometimes you have to be kind anyway.

The men and women in Frost often stare bleakly past each other. It's not that they have too little to say, but that they have too much. Those birds, or birds very much like them, disturb the complacent rage of the speaker in "The Thatch." He has stormed out of his thatched cottage, into the winter rain, and won't come back until his wife puts out the bedroom light. She won't put out the light until he comes in. Their cast-iron mulishness might last forever—it has the inevitability of myth (Frost is good about the mean things that make us mulish—however leathery the moral quality in his souls, he sees their weakness, too). But . . .

> as I passed along the eaves,
> So low I brushed the straw with my sleeves,
> I flushed birds out of hole after hole,
> Into the darkness. It grieved my soul,
> It started a grief within a grief,
> To think their case was beyond relief—
> They could not go flying about in search
> Of their nest again, nor find a perch.
> They must brood where they fell in mulch and mire,
> Trusting feathers and inward fire
> Till daylight made it safe for a flyer.
> My greater grief was by so much reduced
> As I thought of them without nest or roost.
> That was how that grief started to melt.

He didn't mean to bother those birds, didn't mean to add their hardship to his; but that's the way anger is (it's no use arguing with Frost that anger isn't always this way). The innocent suffer, sometimes without knowing the cause of suffering. The man can do nothing to repair the injury, and there's a naked recognition in that remarkable line, "It started a grief within a grief" (a line that echoes in the scarring ambiguity of "brood"). Frost tended to jingle in couplets (his ear grew unsure when his rhymes were too close together), but here the jingling underlines the absurdity of a man standing out in the rain to prove a point. And some of those rhymes are canny—that hollow, eaten-out "soul" is rhymed with "hole"; the "grief" is intimately bound, not with "relief," but with "beyond relief."

Those tangles of grief and regret between men and women, regret and sometimes the kindness of regret, radiate in odd directions. In "Place for a Third" (what an awful maker of titles Frost was—sometimes they're slapped on like gummed labels), a man wants to respect his wife's dying wishes. She's had three husbands, he's had three wives; and she doesn't want to lie with the other women.

> One man's three women in a burial row
> Somehow made her impatient with the man.
> And so she said to Laban, "You have done
> A good deal right; don't do the last thing wrong.
> Don't make me lie with those two other women."
>
> Laban said, No, he would not make her lie
> With anyone but that she had a mind to,
> If that was how she felt, of course, he said.
> She went her way. But Laban having caught
> This glimpse of lingering person in Eliza,
> And anxious to make all he could of it
> With something he remembered in himself,
> Tried to think how he could exceed his promise,
> And give good measure to the dead, though thankless.

It's a surprise to him, "This glimpse of lingering person" (what a judicious, delighting phrase); but he wants to give to the dead just measure, or measure more than just. He thinks of buying her a plot of her own:

> He'd sell a yoke of steers to pay for it.
> And weren't there special cemetery flowers,
> That, once grief sets to growing, grief may rest;
> The flowers will go on with grief awhile,
> And no one seem neglecting or neglected?
> A prudent grief will not despise such aids.

This is typical of Frost. Laban will grieve, but he'll be practical, too. How can we not admire a character whose complications come so coiled in pathos, whose trivial economies lie next to absurd generosities? (That yoke of steers is a sacrifice—they had to be *trained* to the yoke.) He thinks of a better way of satisfying his duty, and his love: he'll bury her next to the boy she first loved, who lived in a neighboring town. He finds the grave (it's marked *John, Beloved Husband*, but we're never told where John's wife lies—that may be another story), and Laban goes to plead his case before the dead man's sister.

> The sister's face
> Fell all in wrinkles of responsibility.
> She wanted to do right. She'd have to think.
> Laban was old and poor, yet seemed to care;
> And she was old and poor—but she cared, too.
> They sat. She cast one dull, old look at him,
> Then turned him out to go on other errands
> She said he might attend to in the village,
> While she made up her mind how much she cared—
> And how much Laban cared—and why he cared.
> (She made shrewd eyes to see where he came in.)

Here the run of shortened sentences follows the short reversals of a mind at odds. She's shrewd, but not heartless. Finally she can't consent; and she tells Laban through a closed screen door (how good Frost was at paltry details). The reason's so funny it's almost sad: "'There wouldn't be no sense./ Eliza's had too many other men.'" The poem might have ended there, but it can't—it would *be* a bad joke. Laban goes back to his first plan, to buy Eliza her own plot: it "gives him for himself a choice of lots/ When his time comes to die and settle down." That "settle down" is terrifying. Frost's disquiet about the afterlife usually revealed a disquiet about our arrangements in this one; and death here is "settling down" in a way we usually don't like to think of (earlier, death is made almost willful—"She went her way"). We understand too little of people if we don't appreciate how they can be canny and caring at the same time—and the abyss that remains between them.

Frost's poetry is one long exploitation of a fairly limited notion about character, and yet to the limitations what a rare and brush-fine rendering he brings. There is more truth in Frost's simplicities, his love of morals and homilies and examples, than in all the dull rattle of autobiography on which our poetry now subsists (*This was my life*, our poems protest, as if having a life were the same as having art). How interested Frost seems in other people—and yet how interesting that makes *him* seem. The problem is not that Frost is too simple for us; it's that we are too simple for him.

"Snow" is another of Frost's wretched claustrophobic dramas. There's a blizzard. The Coles have been wakened by a visitor, a preacher trying to get home after a prayer meeting. He's named Meserve, one of those cross-grained back-country names, and he's a preacher in some back-country Christian sect. He calls his wife to tell her he's still on the way. The couple want him to stay the night, but they can't make themselves make him stay; and he's stubborn enough to go on (stubborn enough to have gone to town to preach on such a night). Much of the poem consists of the couple squabbling, in a half-fond, half-irritated marital way—the poem is almost as long as "The Waste Land." Meserve goes out to the barn to check his horses, and when he comes back they plead with him to stay.

> Meserve seemed to heed nothing but the lamp
> Or something not far from it on the table.
> By straightening out and lifting a forefinger,
> He pointed with his hand from where it lay
> Like a white crumpled spider on his knee:
> "That leaf there in your open book! It moved
> Just then, I thought. It's stood erect like that,
> There on the table, ever since I came,
> Trying to turn itself backward or forward,
> I've had my eye on it to make out which:
> If forward, then it's with a friend's impatience—
> You see I know—to get you on to things
> It wants to see how you will take; if backward,
> It's from regret for something you have passed
> And failed to see the good of. Never mind,
> Things must expect to come in front of us
> A many times—I don't say just how many—
> That varies with the things—before we see them.
> One of the lies would make it out that nothing
> Ever presents itself before us twice.
> Where would we be at last if that were so?
> Our very life depends on everything's
> Recurring till we answer from within.

The symbol is too available here—the book is no doubt the Bible. (What other book, likely to lie open in a farmhouse, has pages so thin they might stir in the lightest breeze—and what else does Meserve "heed"? And yet why doesn't he name it?) The preacher's hesitation makes the moment less certain; he can't say when we'll see the way things are, and there's more than a shiver of apocalypse in his speech—a preacher who thinks about what comes again (which our lives depend on, when we will "answer from within") is half thinking of the Second Coming. The couple don't much like Meserve, and they're angry with him because they're afraid for him (if he dies in the blizzard, they'll feel responsible). There's something else, something not quite said in the poem—the wife and Meserve were apparently friendly as children. The couple go back and forth with him, and she makes one last attempt:

> "But why, when no one wants you to, go on?
> Your wife—she doesn't want you to. We don't,
> And you yourself don't want to. Who else is there?"

> "Save us from being cornered by a woman.
> Well, there's—" She told Fred afterward that in
> The pause right there, she thought the dreaded word
> Was coming, "God." But no, he only said,
> "Well, there's—the storm. That says I must go on.
> That wants me as a war might if it came.
> Ask any man."

How crafty Frost is. He wants Meserve to surprise us, but it's more of a surprise if we know the *expected* answer—making sure causes a delay, and delay heightens the expectation.

Meserve goes off into the blizzard. "It's quiet as an empty church without him," the husband says. He means to say only that the storm of Meserve's presence having passed, they are left in a strange silence. But Meserve is a preacher, and they are left in the church a preacher has abandoned. They are still *inside* a church—the church of their wintry home, their narrow tight religion of each other. And yet that church feels forsaken—as if the god (the word Meserve hasn't said) has passed out of it, too. We know that when a church is empty, the god's still there; and yet an empty church can feel less than spiritual, just an empty warehouse. What devastating resonances this simple line lets loose, and how long it takes to explain poems that so simply explain themselves.

Hours later Meserve's wife calls—he still hasn't returned. The couple descend to new guilt; they admire and despise Meserve for being what he is. They try to ring her back, but she's left the phone off the hook. (This is an early village party-line system—her number's 21, just two digits, and when her phone's off the hook they can hear the sounds in her house without ringing her.) Then Meserve calls—he's come home. The couple should be relieved, but they're not, quite. A tremor has gone through their lives. Perhaps they'll just forget it. The nearness of death; the icy white desolation of the night (Meserve remembers something he heard a boy say: "You can't get too much winter in the winter"); the runty and nearly repulsive Meserve, down to the lovely, horrible description of his hand, "Like a white crumpled spider"—it's a winter nightmare, all below-freezing anxiety. Frost knows not to let the couple subside into forgiveness, or rise to pure irritation. Frost used dialogue as well as Eliot or Joyce—he may be nineteenth-century in his philosophy (early Frost sounds as if it were written before Darwin), but he's modern in his voices. Eliot caught something of the Twenties when his characters spoke, but Frost's characters are almost our contemporaries.

I don't have space—though I wish I had space—to discuss that wintry companion piece, "Willful Homing"; or that mysterious poem "The Fear" (with that wonderful line, "I saw it just as plain as a white plate"); or the ending of "A Brook in the City," where the hidden won't stay hidden (Freud might have written such a poem, if he hadn't *been* a poem). Let me end, since I've lingered so long in the bleaker regions of Frost, with something almost springlike, "Spring Pools":

> These pools that, though in forests, still reflect
> The total sky almost without defect,
> And like the flowers beside them, chill and shiver,
> Will like the flowers beside them soon be gone,
> And yet not out by any brook or river,
> But up by roots to bring dark foliage on.
>
> The trees that have it in their pent-up buds
> To darken nature and be summer woods—
> Let them think twice before they use their powers
> To blot out and drink up and sweep away
> These flowery waters and these watery flowers
> From snow that melted only yesterday.

The pools reflect the whole sky because the forest leaves haven't come on (the "defect" would be the thin high branches). Their nearly faultless reflections, like barely scratched mirrors, must give way to a darker nature. The darkness in the forest means only the leaves; but we know what Frost *really* means. He was such a plain poet in his words (he so rarely tried for those "poetic" effects of sound and usage which most poets live on like the air—a plant that does that is an epiphyte), but such a devious man in his lines. This doesn't mean that he couldn't be ornamental when he chose—there's that beautiful chiasmus here, "These flowery waters and these watery flowers," and think of the ornate line from "The Black Cottage," "A buttoned haircloth lounge spread scrolling arms." But also think how later in that poem the minister rises briefly into "poetry," and then stops, as if embarrassed. Few poets have ever caught such power in plain speech; Frost's lines bear their ideas without the distraction of ornament, or with the least ornament necessary for the democracy of argument (how tangled the notions in the simple "pent-up" buds here—they're all raw DNA, with empires to build).

The complications are in the shrewdness of the said. How could the summer woods have that kind of fairy-tale darkness? There is no evil, and yet the loss of the pools is a minor kind of evil, just because it is a loss. "Let them think twice," Frost asks, but we know they won't, and can't. The snow has melted into pools, the pools melt away into foliage—the competing forces are just a long chain of sources, of dying supersessions. And yet something remains to be mourned, if we remember how transient our lives are, about to vanish with the silence of the pools. It takes a hard nature to be grateful for the use our lives are to others. Frost knew that necessity as a form of regret.

Frost was a vain and arrogant man, and some of his humility is merely vanity. But some of it is humility, too. He knew his poems might not always be of use—he knew his life had not been much use to those he loved. When we tire of "Birches" and "Mending Wall," of "After Apple-Picking" and "The Road Not Taken" and "Stopping by Woods on a Snowy Evening," of "Nothing Gold Can Stay" and "Fire and Ice" and all the other poems anthologized into the thick crust of our memories—after we have tired of these, there is another Frost, and another. The good in Frost often lies so close to the sentimental and bad, it is difficult to remember that some of the best-loved poems are the best, just as some are the worst and most trivial.

I've wanted here to be like Frost, to be a noticer of common things, of the uncommon in the common. Many of the poems in this other other Frost have caught the eyes of scholars (occasionally only to be dismissed—one weighty critic thought "The Code" and "A Hundred Collars" were "fatuously obvious"), but that has not saved them from general neglect. A reader who hasn't gone beyond the white picket fence of the poems everyone knows by heart will find in Jarrell's essays a remarkable unknown Frost (not quite as unknown now as then), and I hope another unknown Frost here. And I haven't had a word for the grim poverty of "The Housekeeper," for the chilling anecdote of "The Vanishing Red," for "The Ax-Helve" or the strange fable of "Paul's Wife" or the rough comedy of "Brown's Descent," for all the secret bitterness and knowledge in "Fireflies in the Garden," for "The Mountain" (I might as well nominate all of *North of Boston*) or the brilliantly handled monologue of "The Black Cottage" (which Jarrell likes and then calls "lesser") or "On Going Unnoticed."

Frost is a Vermont-granite original. He is strange in the way that Whitman is strange: inconsistent, knowing and yet unknowable, likely to go off on goose chases, self-satisfied and yet raging against self-satisfaction, moral and honest (even when a little immoral and dishonest), his bad jumbled with his good, and yet finally and unconsciously and proof-bright American, representative of even the striving, sentimental, blank and blinkered parts of being American. An art like Frost's is not just the residue of the country he inhabited, it is the factual prelude to that country's imaginative acts. If we want those strange citizens of the next millennium to know what it was to be American in the last centuries of this one, we could do worse than to bury, in Camden or Keokuk or Fresno, in Tie Siding or Pensacola or Hanover or Fort Smith, a lead box with the collected poems of Walt Whitman and Robert Frost.

June 1995

What Happened to Aldous Huxley?

John Derbyshire

M ETAPHYSICS IS OUT of fashion. There is, as department-store sales assistants say, not much call for it nowadays. The word "metaphysics" does not even occur in the index of the current bestseller about human nature, Steven Pinker's *The Blank Slate*, nor does Professor Pinker's text betray any interest in the topic. Most of us, if challenged to disclose our metaphysical beliefs, would probably offer a part-baked dualism. Yes, certainly there is an outer reality, "the universe," made up of material objects whose behavior, thanks to four hundred years of diligent scientific inquiry, we can understand, or at any rate predict, in fine detail. And yes, there is an inner reality, "the self," comprised of mental objects about which science has much less to say, and some irreducible core of which, we are inclined to think, exists independently of the material world. Those of us who are up to date with developments in neuroscience, or who have read Tom Wolfe's famous article on the subject ("Sorry, but your soul just died," in the December 1996 issue of *Forbes ASAP*) are uncomfortably aware of the relentlessness with which researchers have been shrinking the size of that core, but we live in faith that they will never succeed in eliminating it altogether. Professor Pinker, who is very up to date indeed in these matters, plainly does not share that faith, hence his utter neglect of matters metaphysical.

Living as we do in such an un-metaphysical age, we are in a poor frame of mind to approach the writer who said the following thing, and who took it as a premise for his work through most of a long literary career.

> It is impossible to live without a metaphysic. The choice that is given us is not between some kind of metaphysic and no metaphysic; it is always between a good metaphysic and a bad metaphysic.

Aldous Huxley published his first book, a collection of poems, in 1916, shortly after his twenty-second birthday. He died in November 1963, a few weeks after having brought out his twentieth book of essays. (He actually died on the day John F. Kennedy was shot.) At that point Huxley's published work also included three more poetry collections, eleven novels, five short story collections, two travel books, two biographies, a play, some collaborative work on movie scripts, and a mass of fugitive journalism. It was the essays, though, that were the essential Aldous Huxley for a large part of his readership. A star-struck young visitor at the Huxleys' California house in 1939 wrote that: "I had been bitterly disappointed with [Huxley's sixth novel *Eyeless in Gaza*] and unsympathetic to religious experiences, but of course it was Aldous of the Essays, . . . gentle, inquiring, fascinating, and fascinated too with every fact, every thought, hesitatingly brought out with the amazed inflection of his voice."

Huxley's essays have now been gathered together in six volumes by Robert S. Baker of the University of Wisconsin at Madison and James Sexton of Camosun College in British Columbia. The first volume appeared two years ago; the last, covering the years 1956–1963, has just come out (*Complete Essays: Volume VI, 1956–1963*, by Aldous Huxley, edited with commentary by Robert S. Baker and James Sexton; Ivan R. Dee, 2003). Here, in a uniform edition, are not only the essays Huxley published in book form, with his two travel books included for good measure, but also scores of magazine and newspaper pieces previously accessible to the general reader only with difficulty. Title notwithstanding, the *Complete Essays* is not absolutely comprehensive, and does not claim to be. None of Huxley's earliest articles for the *Athenaeum* or the *London Mercury* are here, and a few later pieces I would have liked to see—the 1944 *Harper's* piece on Sheldonism (see below), for example—are missing.[1] This is, though, a good representative collection, gathering between hard covers the whole sweep of Huxley's thought, as it developed across forty-four years.

All of Huxley's biographers begin by pointing out that his bloodlines were distinguished, but somewhat oddly mixed. His paternal grandfather was Thomas Henry Huxley, the great Victorian biologist, best remembered for his victory against Archbishop Wilberforce in the 1860 debate about

---

1 According to Huxley's biographer Sybille Bedford, "In 1919, in the course of the eight months-odd he was working for the *Athenaeum*, Aldous contributed 29 signed articles and 171 anonymous notices and reviews to the paper, did 8 articles for the *London Mercury* and some reviews." Bedford's biography, which first appeared in two volumes in 1973, has been reissued in a single volume by Ivan R. Dee, 832 pages, $24.95 (paper).

evolution. Known as "Darwin's bulldog," T. H. Huxley advocated scientism—that is, the belief that there is no area of human experience or understanding into which science will not eventually advance, or which the scientific method will be unable to explain. He seems to have coined the word "agnostic," and used it to describe his own position on the mysteries of mind, spirit, and creation. Aldous's mother was a granddaughter of the great evangelical headmaster Dr. Thomas Arnold, the "Doctor" in *Tom Brown's Schooldays*, originator of the "muscular Christianity" style of boarding-school education for boys, and father of the poet Matthew Arnold (who was, therefore, Aldous Huxley's great-uncle). Dr. Arnold was an intensely religious man, who, when headmaster of Rugby, was reported to break down and weep openly in front of the whole school at the story of Christ's Passion.

To what degree these antecedents, or his consciousness of them, shaped Aldous's own thinking, is a matter of some interest, the more so since eugenics—a respectable field of discussion and inquiry until tainted by association with Nazi "race science"—is a key topic in Huxley's best-remembered novel, *Brave New World*, published in 1932. The following things, at least, can be said with certainty: Aldous Huxley was raised in a family that took intellectual inquiry very seriously indeed, he maintained a lifelong interest in science, and he treated the religious instinct with utmost respect.

The high summer of Victorian scientific optimism in which Aldous's grandfather had basked was long gone by the time Aldous reached intellectual maturity. So—thanks in part to Grandpa Huxley's efforts—was the social atmosphere in which serious intellectuals, at any rate in the Anglo-Saxon countries, could base programs for social reform on evangelical Christianity, as Dr. Arnold had. The second and third decades of the twentieth century were notoriously an age of failed gods and shattered conventions, to which many thoughtful people responded in obvious ways, retreating into nihilism, hedonism, and experimentalism. Literature became subjective, art became abstract, poetry abandoned its traditional forms. In the "low, dishonest decade" that then followed, much of this negativism curdled into power-worship and escapism of various kinds.

Aldous Huxley stood aside from these large general trends. Though no Victorian in habits or beliefs, he never entered wholeheartedly into the spirit of modernism. The evidence is all over the early volumes of these essays. *Ulysses*, he declares in 1925, is "one of the dullest books ever written, and one of the least significant." Jazz, he remarks two years later, is "drearily barbaric." Writing of Sir Christopher Wren in 1923, he quotes with approval Carlyle's remark that Chelsea Hospital, one of Wren's creations, was "obviously the work of a gentleman." Wren, Huxley goes on to say, was indeed a great gentleman, "one who valued dignity and restraint and who, respecting himself, respected also humanity."

In his thirties, in fact, Huxley comes across as something of a Young Fogey. "I have grown shameless. . . . I can watch unmoved the departure of the last social-cultural bus—the innumerable last buses which are starting at every instant in all the world's capitals. I make no effort to board them, and when the noise of each departure has died down, 'Thank Goodness!' is what I say to myself in the solitude." Those remarks preface a horrified review of the first non-silent movie to strike box-office gold, *The Jazz Singer*.

> A beneficent providence has dimmed my powers of sight, so that, at a distance of more than four or five yards, I am blissfully unaware of the full horror of the average human countenance. At the cinema, however, there is no escape. Magnified up to Brobdingnagian proportions, the human countenance smiles its six-foot smile, opens and closes its thirty-two inch eyes, registered [*sic*] soulfulness or grief, libido or whimsicality with every square centimeter of its several roods of pallid mooniness. . . . For the first time I felt grateful for the defect of vision which had preserved me from a daily acquaintance with such scenes.

Considering that he is thought of nowadays largely as a herald for some soon-to-arrive future of hedonism via genetic manipulation, Huxley could be remarkably old-fashioned.

That "defect of vision" for which Huxley offered ironic thanks was in fact one of the great determinants of his life, constraining his movements in the world and keeping him out of military service during World War I. It began in 1911, when, at the age of seventeen, he was afflicted with a disease of the eyes (eventually diagnosed as *keratitis punctata*, an inflammation of the corneas) that for several months rendered him actually and completely blind. Huxley reacted to this disaster with heroic fortitude. Sent home from Eton, he took up Braille and used it to pursue his studies. He even taught himself to play the piano, with one hand on the keyboard and one on the Braille music sheet. He wrote his first novel while blind (it was never published), and spoke of his affliction only to crack jokes about it. His cousin Gervas Huxley came into his room one bitter winter morning to be greeted with: "You know, Gerry, there's one great advantage in Braille, you can read in bed without getting your hands cold."

Huxley's later description of the state of his eyesight at the time he went up to Oxford in 1913 was as follows: "I was left . . . with one eye just capable of light perception, and the other with enough vision to permit of my detecting the two-hundred foot letter on the Snellen chart at ten feet." Under these circumstances, the recollections of his Oxford coevals are astonishing. Gervas, in a comment one feels obliged to read twice to make sure one has got it right, reported that: "He had read a great deal while he was blind—working on his own, he read a lot of things, like French, which we didn't know." Raymond Mortimer, who was a freshman with Huxley, described him as: "formidably sophisticated . . . dazzling.. . . The erudition: he had read everything." Huxley graduated with a first in English, having done all the reading for his degree with the aid of a powerful magnifying glass.

To have passed through such a crisis, at just the age when one is reading with the most attention and absorption, emerging on the other side of that crisis to impress the brilliant young undergraduates of pre-World War I Oxford as a person who had "read everything," was a stunning intellectual achievement. I do not think there is any question that Aldous Huxley regarded the life of the intellect with utmost seriousness, and worked very hard at keeping his own mind well-furnished. He read slowly and doggedly, but constantly, all through his life. Here he is writing to George Orwell in 1949, when the latter, or his publisher, had sent a courtesy copy of *Nineteen Eighty-Four*. "It arrived as I was in the midst of a piece of work that required much reading and consulting of references [presumably this was *Themes and Variations*, reproduced in Volume V of this *Complete Essays*]; and since poor sight makes it necessary for me to ration my reading, I had to wait a long time before being able to embark on *Nineteen Eighty-Four*."

The greatest impact of Huxley's near-blindness was on his scientific interests. He had originally intended a career as a doctor, until the problems with his sight put an end to the possibility. He might indeed have made a fine research scientist—an astronomer, perhaps, or a physicist. He felt himself to be that way inclined. "If I could be born again and choose what I should be in my next existence, I should desire to be a man of science. . . . [E]ven if I could be Shakespeare, I think I should still choose to be Faraday." It is very easy to imagine Huxley as the more thoughtful kind of scientist, perhaps turning in later life to the writing of good popular books about the origins of life and the future of the human race, like Freeman Dyson, or producing occasional startling science fiction novels, like Fred Hoyle. He sought out and enjoyed the company of scientific professionals—the astronomer Edwin Hubble, after whom the space telescope is named, was a close friend from 1937 until his sudden death (sitting in his car, in his driveway) in 1953.

Huxley was, I believe, a rather pure specimen of the natural-born scientist, equipped with the scientist's tireless curiosity and passion for classifying. *Point Counter Point*, the best of his literary novels, is almost comically a "novel of types"—the equivalent of Ponchielli's opera *La Gioconda*, which has six precisely equiponderant roles, one for each major vocal category. Unfortunately, the early failure of his sight denied Huxley the rigorous disciplines of the laboratory and the peer review. This threw him back on much more speculation *about* science than working scientists— young ones, at any rate—generally go in for, and thence toward the metaphysical imperative I stated up above. Edwin Burtt's *Metaphysical Foundations of Modern Science* was a favorite book. Huxley enthused about it in a 1925 letter to his father. He recommends it to the reader twelve years later, in the book of essays titled *Ends and Means*, and again in the 1946 collection *Science, Liberty and Peace*. This is also the book we find on the lap of Philip Quarles, Huxley's fictional self-portrait, when he is crossing the Red Sea by steamship in *Point Counter Point*. Burtt, whose dates were 1892–1989, was a Professor of Philosophy at the University of Chicago when he published *Metaphysical Foundations* in 1924, bent on seeking what he called "an adequate philosophy of the mind" through a study of scientific revolutions and the thinkers who brought them about. Burtt's interests, prefiguring Huxley's, later turned to Eastern religion: his 1955 anthology of Buddhist scriptures is still in print today.

The frustration of Huxley's natural scientific bent also had at least one malign consequence: a much too uncritical attitude toward fringe and crank sciences, especially those that offered some hint of a connection to the world of the spirit. He was an early enthusiast for the work of Dr. J. B. Rhine of Duke University, which Huxley believed had established the reality of extra-sensory perception. Huxley's 1954 essay in *Life* magazine probably did more than anything else to bring Rhine's "results" (which rested on a misapplication of the rules of statistical inference) to the attention of the broad general public. J. W. Dunne's "experiments with time," which involved sifting through one's dreams for episodes of precognition, got Huxley's attention. So did dianetics, which was later incorporated into Scientology. Huxley and Maria, his first wife, had three or four sessions with L. Ron Hubbard.

The body-typing theories of William Sheldon, the academic psychologist who gave us the words "endomorph," "mesomorph," and "ectomorph," were another enthusiasm. Sheldon taught that every human physiognomy could be placed somewhere on a body-type triangle, with these extremes at its three vertices. Associated with each component of body type was a characteristic personality, which Sheldon named, respectively, "viscerotonic," "somatotonic," and "cerebrotonic." These words are scattered through Huxley's books, and must be very baffling to readers now, when Sheldon's theories have sunk into academic oblivion. Huxley classified himself as an extreme cerebrotonic ectomorph: he stood six feet four—perhaps another point of affinity with Hubble, who was six feet five.

HUXLEY IS MAINLY remembered by the general public now for having written *Brave New World*, one of the two great admonitory novels of the twentieth century. It used to be, and for all I know may still be, a common classroom exercise for high school seniors to read Huxley's novel together with Orwell's *Nineteen Eighty-Four*, and then to express and justify an opinion about which is a more probable future for the human race. Huxley himself seems to have been in two minds about the matter. In his essay on the French metaphysician François-Pierre Maine de Biran (another "extreme cerebrotonic," by the way), Huxley notes that Orwell's forecast "was made from a vantage point considerably further down the descending spiral of modern history than mine, and is probably more nearly correct." However, in the 1949 letter to Orwell, Huxley argued that his own imagined future was the more probable one.

Most of us would agree with this latter opinion, I think. The great terror-despotisms of mid-century are a fading memory now. Their style lingers on in some minor Third World hellholes in Africa or Arabia, but nobody bothers much about that. Those are barbarous places, of which little better can be expected. The shocking thing about the Nazi and Soviet terrors was that they had planted themselves in civilized European nations, the nations that had brought forth Goethe, Beethoven, Tchaikovsky, and Tolstoy. If such things could happen there, they could happen anywhere—or, as in Orwell's novel, everywhere.

As Lenin and Hitler recede into history, the idea that a civilized nation can descend so deep into a totalitarianism maintained by fear seems less and less plausible. Huxley's dystopia, by contrast, is all too plausible. Indeed, the unsettling thing about Huxley's imagined future is that it is not easy for a modern reader to say what, exactly, is so bad about it. To be sure, we maintain our democracy, religion is still alive, and our inclination to join up in pairs and raise our own children seems to be ineradicable. In many other respects, though, we have settled happily into the infantile hedonism of *Brave New World*. Re-reading that novel recently after many years, I suddenly realized why it is that I find the current hit TV show *Friends* so unwatchable. In the World State of the year 632 After Ford, would not Phoebe, Chandler & Co. be model citizens? In the terms of that great Dostoyevskian exchange between the Savage and the Controller at the end of Chapter 17 in Huxley's masterpiece, we have come down pretty firmly on the side of the Controller, and trust to science to cope with whatever unpleasant consequences may attend our choice.

"What?" questioned the Savage, uncomprehending.

"It's one of the conditions of perfect health. That's why we've made the v.p.s. treatments compulsory."

"v.p.s.?"

"Violent Passion Surrogate. Regularly once a month. We flood the whole system with adrenalin. It's the complete physiological equivalent of fear and rage. All the tonic effects of murdering Desdemona and being murdered by Othello, without any of the inconveniences."

"But I like the inconveniences."

"We don't," said the Controller. "We prefer to do things comfortably."

So do we, so do we.

Orwell was an essayist as accomplished as Huxley, though in a very different style. The two men barely knew each other, their closest contact having occurred in 1917–1918, when Huxley taught at Eton, where Orwell was a pupil. The letter of thanks for *Nineteen Eighty-Four* seems to have been the only one from Huxley to Orwell; I do not know of any in the other direction. Huxley was of course an established writer while Orwell was shooting elephants on behalf of the Indian Imperial Police. I counted twenty-four references to the older man in *The Collected Essays, Letters and Journalism of George Orwell*, including a couple of prize say-*what?* Orwellisms. Sample, from a letter to Richard Rees: "You were right abt Huxley's book [*Ape and Essence*]—it is awful. And do you notice that the more holy he gets, the more his books stink with sex. He cannot get off the subject of flagellating women."

Orwell included Huxley among those writers he described as "inside the whale," that is, looking out at the world through a thick transparent layer of insulating blubber. The *Complete Essays* amply confirm this. Huxley does his conscientious best with social and political issues, but can never stay moored to plain fact for long. Soon, after a perfunctory paragraph or two, he soars off into lofty abstraction. This makes Huxley's social and political writing very tedious to read. Compare his detached, colorless description of a visit to a coal-mining region, recorded in the essay "Abroad in England," with the vivid immediacy of Orwell's similar excursions in *The Road to Wigan Pier*. Similarly, while Gandhi's assassination inspired one of Orwell's finest essays, it brought forth no lengthy relections from Huxley, only some offhand remarks at the beginning of *Ape and Essence*. This is particularly striking since Huxley was a pacifist and admirer of Gandhi, while Orwell regarded the sage with mild contempt. Huxley seems not to have noticed Pearl Harbor, though he was living in California at the time.

So what *was* Huxley's metaphysics? His first sustained attempt to express his outlook in writing was the aforementioned 1937 book of essays, *Ends and Means*, reproduced here in its entirety. "It is a dull book," said Evelyn Waugh, reviewing it. He added: "There is no reason to suppose that in ten years' time [Huxley] will hold any of the opinions he holds today."

In this latter opinion, Waugh was mistaken. In fact, so far as metaphysics was concerned, Huxley seems at this point to have settled into the views that he held to for the rest of his life, and which led him to those well-known experiments with mind-altering drugs he conducted from 1953 onwards. (In the last hours of his death from cancer, Huxley asked for, and got, injections of LSD. He died under the influence.) *Ends and Means* is about a great many things—war, politics, religion, economics, and the beginnings of a concern with what we should nowadays call "the environment"—but it is all rooted in metaphysics. I took that starting quote in my second paragraph from *Ends and Means*.

Huxley adopted a philosophical outlook based on mysticism, most especially on Hindu and Buddhist concepts. There exists a single universal consciousness, the "Mind at Large," of which individual selves are manifestations, extrusions into the world of space, time, and language. It follows that our individual consciousnesses, our private selves, are in principle capable of apprehending the whole of reality. In *Doors of Perception*, Huxley quotes with approval the British philosopher C. D. Broad: "The function of the brain and the nervous system is to protect us from being overwhelmed and confused by this mass of largely useless and otherwise irrelevant knowledge, by shutting out most of what we should otherwise perceive." Mind at Large, says Huxley himself, "has to be funneled through the reducing valve of the brain and nervous system." The contents of this much-reduced awareness are then encompassed and fixed (in the chemical sense: "to make nonvolatile or solid") by language, so that they are, by definition, all that language can cope with. Connoisseurs of pseudoscience will spot the parallels with dianetics here, though Huxley had formed his ideas long before Hubbard launched his own system on an unsuspecting world in the May 1950 issue of *Astounding Science Fiction*.

The ethical problem raised by this outlook—the fact that the Mind at Large is impersonal, and therefore ethically neutral—is dealt with in *Ends and Means* by traditional Vedantic and Buddhist arguments. Though ultimate reality is neither good nor evil in itself, it is only by practicing goodness that one can hope to attain any real acquaintance with that reality. My impression, however—and I had better confess here that I find metaphysics tiresome, and may not have grasped the full subtlety of Huxley's exposition—is that the ethical side of things was never well thought out. The Huxley-mouthpiece character in the 1939 immortality novel *After Many a Summer Dies the Swan*, for example, argues that evil is intrinsically inherent in time, and that only by escaping from time can one approach goodness. It seems that in order to attain the sole state in which goodness dwells, we must practice goodness. . . . But, as I said, it may be my own understanding that is deficient here.

All of this was, in Huxley's case, pure intellection. He told Rosamond Lehmann in 1961 that he had never had a religious experience. He did not actually like religion, as a social phenomenon. "One is all for religion until one visits a really religious country." (He seems to have India in mind here.) Huxley took lessons in Indian techniques of meditation from Swami Prabhavananda at the Vedanta Society in Hollywood. He was not, though, willing to accept the Swami as a guru, nor to join with him in devotions to Hindu gods. Huxley was in fact strongly averse to the notion of religion grounded in culture. He sought the universal, the common denominator of religious experience. Writing of Simone Weil, he dismisses as irrelevant the question of whether or not she knew Sanskrit.

> [T]he Upanishads are not systems of pure speculation, in which the niceties of language are all important. They were written by Transcendental Pragmatists, as we may call them, whose concern was to teach a doctrine which could be made to "work," a metaphysical theory which could be operationally tested, not through perception only, but by a direct experience of the whole man on every level of his being. To understand the meaning of *tat tvam asi*, "thou art That," it is not necessary to be a profound Sanskrit scholar. (Similarly, it is not necessary to be a profound Hebrew scholar in order to understand the meaning of, "thou shalt not kill.")

One is not surprised to recall that this is the author who, thirty years earlier, had become the first (I feel pretty sure) to have a character in a novel mention Wittgenstein.

In this context, Sybille Bedford's account of Huxley's U.S. naturalization interview makes curious reading. The McCarran Act of 1952 had denied citizenship to any person who refused to bear arms for other than religious reasons. Aldous was a pacifist, and said so at the interview. Was he a religious man? asked the interviewing judge. "Aldous said that he was indeed a religious man; his opposition to war, however, was an entirely philosophical one." This particular metaphysical circle was never squared to the satisfaction of the immigration authorities; though he lived in the

United States for the last twenty-six years of his life, Huxley never did get citizenship, and died a subject of the Crown.

Huxley himself, in the preface to a 1959 collection of his essays, gave it as his opinion that: "Essays belong to a literary species whose extreme variability can be studied most effectively within a three-poled frame of reference. There is the pole of the personal and autobiographical; there is the pole of the objective, the factual, the concrete-particular; and there is the pole of the abstract-universal." He goes on to elaborate a sort of Sheldonian classification for essayists, with Charles Lamb at the first vertex of the triangle, Macaulay at the second, and Bacon sharing the third with Emerson and Dr. Johnson. (I note in passing the absence of Hazlitt from this preface, and indeed from Huxley's works altogether. This seems odd to me. I should have thought the intellectual affinity quite strong.) Essayists of real genius, Huxley goes on to say, are those like Montaigne, who can roam easily between all three poles.

My impression is that Huxley saw himself as dwelling at that third pole with Bacon, Emerson, and Johnson. If I am right about this, he misjudged himself, as artists often do. Going through these essays now, decades after their first appearance, the "abstract-universal" writings make pretty dull reading. Even at the time they were published, in fact, they struck some very discerning readers that way, as Evelyn Waugh's remark illustrates. (*Ends and Means* is almost solidly "abstract-universal.") Huxley was actually at his best with some literary, artistic, or historical material to comment on, or when traveling.

The 1956 essay collection titled *Adonis and the Alphabet* offers especially rich pickings here. If the publisher of these volumes will forgive my saying so, in fact, I think a person who wanted to form a first acquaintance with "Aldous of the Essays" could do worse than find a second-hand copy of *Adonis*. (The *Adonis* essays are in Volume V of this set.) That comes with a slight qualification. By this stage of Huxley's life, metaphysics had become a hobbyhorse, and many of the essays end with a little coda, relating the principal theme to the need for "direct experience of the basic fact of the divine immanence," or "knowledge of the Whole within." After a few encounters with this sort of thing, though, the reader learns to disregard these metaphysical flourishes, rather as one does the compulsory moment of sappiness at the end of a traditional TV sitcom, and just enjoy the body of the thing.

Here in *Adonis* is the essay titled "Ozymandias," the strange, atmospheric tale of the short-lived Llano del Rio socialist commune, where "everything that ought not to have been done was systematically done." Here is "Hyperion to a Satyr," an amusing and instructive discourse on dirt,

halitosis, and cognate topics. Here is a wittily and, to this musical ig-
noramus, inexplicably fascinating piece on the Neapolitan composer Carlo
Gesualdo (1560–1613), whose first marriage had an abrupt ending when the
lady took a lover. Gesualdo broke into his wife's room, slew her and her
lover, then "took horse and galloped off to one of his castles where, after
liquidating his second child (the one of doubtful paternity), he remained
for several months . . . to avoid the private vengeance of the Avalos and
Carafa families."

Adonis also has some fine travel pieces. The title essay, in fact, was
inspired by a visit to the site of ancient Byblos. Huxley was quite an accomplished travel writer, and four of these six volumes have separate
sections headed "Travel." (I should explain that the general system of organization adopted by the editors has been to group the essays in each
volume under three or four broad thematic headings, breaking up the
original volumes of essays as necessary.) He early developed a fine contrarian attitude toward the great spectacles of the tourist trail. Of the Gold-
en Temple of the Sikhs: "Holiness and costliness make up for any lack of
architectural merit. For architecturally the temple is less than nothing." This
is merely a warm-up for his assault on the Taj Mahal:

> [I]ts elegance is at the best of a very dry and negative kind. Its "classicism"
> is the product not of intellectual restraint imposed on an exuberant fancy
> but of an actual deficiency of fancy, a poverty of imagination. One is struck
> at once by the lack of variety in the architectural forms of which it is com-
> posed. . . . When the Taj is compared with more or less contemporary
> European buildings in the neo-classic style of the High Renaissance and
> Baroque periods, this poverty in the formal elements composing it be-
> comes very apparent.

Any idea that Huxley's failure to appreciate the Taj Mahal might have been
due to his limited eyesight is soon dispelled by reading his art criticism,
most especially, I think, the earlier pieces in this line. Poor as his eyes may
have been, they did not hinder him from developing a comprehensive
knowledge of art, built on a sound esthetic sense. (Nor, come to think of it,
from marrying a very beautiful woman when he was young and penniless.)
Huxley sketched and painted as a hobby, at least into his early forties. All
his writing is sprinkled with judiciously-chosen metaphors from art, as in
this crisp piece of travel writing from *Beyond the Mexique Bay*. The location
here is Honduras.

> We came back from the ruins to find the entire population of Copán clus-

tered round our aeroplane, like a crowd of Breughel's peasants round a crucifixion. Some were standing; some, with the air of people who had come out for a long day's pleasure, were sitting in the shade of our wings and picnicking. They were a villainous set of men and women; not Indian, but low *ladino*, squalid and dirty as only a poverty-stricken half-caste, with a touch of white blood and a sense of superiority to all the traditional decencies of the inferior race, can be dirty and squalid. Before the doors of the cabin stood half a dozen ruffians, looking like the Second Murderers of Elizabethan drama, and armed with genuinely antique muskets of the American Civil War pattern. The local police.

What is left of all this now? Those "objective, factual, and concrete-particular" essays aside, *Brave New World* aside, and the (to my taste) much faded ironical charm of the early fiction likewise, what else is there in Huxley's work that can be read for enlightenment or inspiration by a person of our time? I am sorry to say that I think the answer is: very little. Whether this speaks worse of Huxley, or of us, I am not sure.

The abiding impression one is left with after reading through 2,907 pages of Huxley's nonfiction writing is one of *seriousness*. That is not, I hasten to add, the same as unrelieved earnestness. Huxley was not a humorless man, as the early novels and short stories amply testify, and the lighter essays occasionally confirm. His style included something of a talent for throw-away apothegms: "Ignorance is no deterrent to the hardened journalist," for example. He was a satirist of genius; the description of the California cemetery in *After Many a Summer* must surely have given Evelyn Waugh the idea for his own dark comedy *The Loved One*. Huxley had, in fact, a well-developed sense of the absurd, and that conviction—I always associate it with G. K. Chesterton, though it is of course more widespread—that the universe is radically weird. Comments to this effect turn up again and again in Huxley's writing: "the astonishingness of the most obvious things," "the unutterably odd facts of human experience," etc. He was much tickled to find, when typing one day, that his left hand had slipped from "c" to "v," giving him the phrase: "the human vomedy."

Huxley described himself as "by temperament extremely anti-social," but he was not anhedonic, and the pleasure he took in art, literature, close friendships, and the ordinary processes of life, are plain to see in his writings. He was, though, a bookish intellectual with chronically poor eyesight, and his pleasures were mostly of the private and interior kind. "Fulfilled, domestic duties are a source of happiness, and intellectual labor is rewarded by the most intense delights," he wrote in 1931. "It is not the hope of heaven that prevents me from leading what is technically known as a life of pleasure; it is simply my temperament. I happen to find the life of pleasure boring and painful."

This fundamentally serious nature manifested itself in a lifelong concern with the question: How should we live? The reason for the current irrelevance of most of Huxley's thinking is that, over the past fifty years, the Western world's educated middle classes have arrived at an answer of their own that satisfies the great majority of them fairly well, and this answer implicitly repudiates most of Huxley's ideas.

We should live, we have decided, in modest hedonism, tempered and constrained by a similarly modest respect for traditional moral precepts, these latter encapsulated, for those of us so inclined, in established religious observances. We entrust the keeping of the peace to armies and diplomats, not to idealists. We entrust our social order to policemen and judges, not to hopes for universal moral improvement. We seek personal fulfillment in work, hobbies, child-raising, and service to others, not in the pursuit of Nirvana. If we want to read about human types, we pick up *Psychology Today*, not a novel. For the latest insights into human nature, we go to Professor Pinker, not to writers of literary essays. Mind-altering drugs? They mess up your life. Demographic or ecological catastrophe? We'll science our way out of it. Metaphysics? Hey, we don't even understand *physics* any more! Leave that stuff to the experts, they'll sort it out.

Undoubtedly there is a worm in this rosy apple somewhere. In human affairs, there always is. The End of History is invariably an illusion; when one chess game stops, another starts immediately. This cheerful embourgeoisement of the world will proceed for a few more years, then take a wrong turn somehow, spreading misery and desperation among people raised in comfort and security, as the traumas of 1914–1945 did to Huxley's generation. Until then, though, we are not in a very serious frame of mind, and seriousness on the Huxley scale does not much interest us.

February 2003

IV. Discriminations

Does Abstract Art Have a Future?

Hilton Kramer

It is hard to tell if abstract painting actually got worse [after the 1960s], if it merely stagnated, or if it simply looked bad in comparison to the hopes its own accomplishments had raised.
—Frank Stella, *Working Space*, 1986

I T MUST BE acknowledged at the outset of these observations that the question of whether abstract art has a future is anything but new. The question of abstraction's future has been raised many times in the past. Historically, the question of abstraction's future is as old as abstraction itself, for the birth of abstract art some ninety years or so ago immediately prompted many doubts about its artistic viability. No sooner did abstract art—particularly abstract painting—make its initial appearance on the international art scene in the second decade of the twentieth century than the doubts about its future course began to be heard.

Many good minds have raised such doubts, and many benighted minds have done so as well. There are highly accomplished artists and critics who have taken sides on the question, as well as respected museum curators, art collectors, and art dealers. Over the course of time, in fact, debate about the future of abstract art has been an equal-opportunity enterprise to which the smart and the dumb, the advanced and the reactionary, the informed and the misinformed have all been eager to make a contribution.

I have a particularly vivid memory of an evening in 1954 at the Artists Club in New York when no less an eminence than the late Alfred H. Barr, Jr., the founding director of the Museum of Modern Art, announced that the age of abstraction was drawing to a close and would now be succeeded by, of all things, a revival of history painting. The occasion was a panel discussion on what was then called the "New Realism." It was organized by John Bernard Myers, the irrepressible director of the Tibor de Nagy Gallery, which represented a number of the painters under discussion—among them, Larry Rivers, Fairfield Porter, and Grace Hartigan.

The Artists Club had been founded, of course, as a forum dedicated to the advancement of Abstract Expressionism. It was therefore inevitable that Barr's provocative pronouncement—and indeed, the very subject of the panel—would be greeted with a vociferous mixture of skepticism and hostility. It had clearly been Johnny Myers's intention to create such a stir on that occasion, for he knew very well that public controversy would have the effect of making some of the figurative painters he represented better known to the art world. He also knew that Barr had just acquired Rivers's *Washington Crossing the Delaware*, a modernist version of Emanuel Gottlieb Leutze's well-known nineteenth-century history painting in the Metropolitan Museum, for MOMA's permanent collection, and could therefore be counted upon to acclaim Rivers's picture as a significant development on the contemporary art scene.

To discuss this controversial development, however, Myers had deliberately convened a panel that could be relied upon to be evenly divided about the significance of Rivers's painting. Joining with Barr in extolling the virtues of *Washington Crossing the Delaware* and the shift in direction it was said to represent was Frank O'Hara, already well established as a poet and art critic. Opposing this view, not surprisingly, was Clement Greenberg. Although he had praised Rivers's earlier work, Greenberg clearly had a low opinion of both *Washington Crossing the Delaware* and Barr's claims on its behalf. Relations between Greenberg and Barr had never been anything but icy, and Greenberg remained, in any case, firm in his often-stated belief that abstraction represented what he characterized as the "master current" of the modernist era.

I was the fourth member of the panel, a newcomer to the art scene whose sole claim to attention on that occasion was an essay I had recently published in *Partisan Review* that was highly critical of Harold Rosenberg's theory of "Action" painting, then a hot topic in the art world. This criticism of Rosenberg, then an arch rival of Greenberg's for the critical leadership of the New York School, had the effect of allying me on the panel with Greenberg even though some exhibition reviews I had lately contributed to *The Art Digest* were unmistakably sympathetic to a wide range of contemporary figurative painting. I didn't think much of Rivers's *Washington Crossing the Delaware*, however, and much as I admired Alfred Barr, I didn't believe that a revival of history painting was either imminent or even possible. Like many first-rate art historians, critics, and connoisseurs, Barr was better at codifying the past than at predicting the future.

I mention all this as a reminder that some of the harshest criticisms of abstract art, and some of the direst predictions of its demise, have come from within the ranks of the modernists themselves. In the 1950s, few living persons could rival Alfred Barr in his knowledge and understanding of abstract art, yet he seems genuinely to have come to believe that its end was nigh—and indeed inevitable. In the 1960s, Philip Guston, after winning considerable acclaim as a convert to Abstract Expressionism, won even greater acclaim for loudly denouncing abstraction in favor of a pictorial style derived from comic-strip and other populist images. Then in the 1980s came Frank Stella's Charles Eliot Norton Lectures at Harvard, *Working Space*, with its litany of contemporary abstraction's repeated failures to produce an art that we had any reason to admire. Stella, too, looked to populist imagery for inspiration—in his case, urban graffiti—with results that are depressingly familiar.

Given this checkered history, in which so many gifted people have said so many foolish things about abstract art—and we haven't even mentioned the openly declared enemies of abstraction—why does one feel compelled to raise the question of its future yet again? I think there are several good reasons for doing so. One is that by any objective measure, the place occupied by new developments in abstract art on the contemporary art scene—what we see in the galleries and museums and read about in the mainstream press and in the art journals—by this measure, the place occupied by new developments in abstract art is now greatly diminished from what it once was.

In this country, certainly, you have to go back to the 1950s and 1960s to recall a time when new developments in abstract art had shown themselves to have the effect of transforming our thinking about art itself. This is what Kandinsky, Mondrian, Malevich and others accomplished in the early years of abstract art. It was what Pollock, Rothko, de Kooning, and others in the New York School accomplished in the 1940s and 1950s. And, for better or for worse, it was what Frank Stella, Donald Judd, and certain other Minimalists accomplished in the 1960s.

I don't myself see anything comparable to this group impact on aesthetic thought happening at the present moment. I haven't observed anything of comparable magnitude occurring in the realm of abstract art since the 1960s. Let me underscore here that I am speaking about group impact on aesthetic thought, about art movements and not about individual talents. I am speaking about the impact of abstract art—or more specifically, abstract painting—on cultural life. That kind of impact on cultural life can rarely be achieved by an individual talent working in isolation from a group of like-minded, or similarly-minded, talents.

I think there is a reason why the place occupied by abstract art is now so radically diminished not only on the contemporary art scene but in cultural life generally. At least I have an hypothesis as to the cause or causes of the diminished power and influence that abstraction has suffered since the acclaim it met with and the spell it cast in the 1960s. And let me be clear once again about what I mean in speaking of abstraction's diminished powers. I mean its power to set the kind of agenda that commands the attention of new and ambitious talents—and at times, indeed, even the emulation of established talents.

Before speculating about the causes of this diminution in what may be called, for want of a better name, movement abstraction, I think it important to recall something that has been central to the aesthetic history of abstraction itself—specifically, its inevitably symbiotic relation to representational art. As all of us know (but sometimes forget), abstract art—especially abstract painting—derives, aesthetically, from representational painting. Whatever the degree of purity abstraction can be said to attain, it cannot make claim to a virgin birth. If abstract painting could be said to have a genetic history, its DNA would instantly reveal its debt to some representational forebear. Whether abstraction derives from Cubism or Impressionism or Fauvism or Neo-Impressionism or Expressionism or some combination of these developments, its antecedents are traceable to the aesthetic vitality of representational painting. This is true of abstract sculpture, too—for abstract sculpture comes out of abstract painting—specifically, Cubism and Cubist collage.

In my own speculations about the fate which movement abstraction has suffered in our own day, two specific developments seem to nominate themselves as the cause or causes of our current impasse. The larger and more general cause is the fate of painting itself—its fate as a factor in cultural life generally as well as in the life of art. If we look back on two recent developments—the series of exhibitions at the Museum of Modern Art called "MOMA 2000" and the transformation of the Tate Gallery in London into two really bizarre institutions—Tate Britain and Tate Modern—we are obliged to recognize two things: (1) that on both sides of the Atlantic, abstract art has been marginalized by the institutions that were formerly in the vanguard of its public support and presentation, and (2) that painting itself is well on its way to being similarly marginalized.

It was certainly striking that in the vast logistical planning that went into the organization of the "MOMA 2000" exhibitions, no place was accorded to the birth and developments of abstract art. There were plenty of examples of abstract art in the separate little shows that constituted "MOMA 2000," but those examples were in every case presented to the public on the basis of their subject-matter, their so-called content, and not on the basis of their abstract aesthetic. John Elderfield, one of the curators involved in the organization of "MOMA 2000," at least had the decency to acknowledge this perverse treatment of abstraction as a failure of thought, but elsewhere in the voluminous texts that accompanied "MOMA 2000" the aesthetic history of abstraction was consigned to oblivion.

At Tate Modern in London, there was also a discernible hostility to all aesthetic considerations, for painting and sculpture of every persuasion were similarly presented to the public on the basis of their thematic "content." And in the Tate Modern's initial blockbuster exhibition—a real horror called "Century City: Art and Culture in the Modern Metropolis"—painting could scarcely be said to have been given even a marginal status. In the section devoted to New York, for example, the twentieth century was represented by work from the period 1969–1974 with the principal focus on Andy Warhol, Lynda Benglis, Vito Acconci, Adrian Piper, Gordon Matta-Clark, and Mary Miss. There were no paintings, abstract or otherwise. Even in the sections devoted to Vienna 1908–1918 and Paris 1905–1918, where paintings could not be avoided, they were presented as a kind of tribal art of interest for its social content and political imagery.

In my own thinking about this fateful shift of priorities away from the aesthetics of painting, both abstract and representational, in favor of a political, sexual, and sociological interest in art-making activities, two historical developments—one within the realm of art itself, the other in the larger arena of intellectual and cultural life—appear to have shaped the situation in which we find ourselves. In the art world, the emergence of the Minimalist movement, which has been so central in determining the fate of abstract art since the 1960s, went so far in diminishing the aesthetic scope and resources of abstraction that it may in some respects be said to have marked a terminal point in its aesthetic development. At the same time, in the larger arena of cultural life, the fallout from the 1960s counterculture left all prior distinctions between high art and pop culture more or less stripped of their authority. It was hardly a coincidence that Minimalism and Pop Art made their respective debuts on the American art scene at the very same moment. However they may have differed in other respects, they were alike insofar as each constituted a programmatic assault not only on the Abstract Expressionism of the New York School—their initial target—but also on the entire pictorial tradition of which the New York School was seen to be a culmination.

It was left to Donald Judd, the most militant of the Minimalists, to spell out exactly what was at stake in this project to sever all ties to the cultural past. About what Judd contemptuously called "the salient and most objectionable relics of European art," he was nothing if not explicit: "It suits me fine," he said in a radio interview in 1964, "if that's all down the drain." He clearly meant it, too, for what was needed, in his view, was an art that would radically occlude all connection not only with the great traditions of the distant past but also with the kind of latterday modernism that he had come to regard as the depleted remnants of a moribund culture. For Judd, art itself had become a utopian project.

There is a passage in an essay by Lionel Trilling—"Aggression and Utopia," published in 1973—that neatly defines the spirit that came to govern this utopian project and so much else in the Minimalist movement. Never mind that Trilling was writing about a Victorian utopian romance— William Morris's *News from Nowhere*. His admonitory analysis of its utopian vision applies with uncanny accuracy to the Minimalist project. This is the key passage:

> the world is an aesthetic object, to be delighted in and not speculated about or investigated; the nature and destiny of man raise no questions, being now wholly and finally manifest. . . . [I]n Morris's vision of the future, the judgment having once been made that grandiosity in art is not conformable with happiness and that Sir Christopher Wren had exemplified radical error in designing St. Paul's, the race has settled upon a style for all its artifacts that is simple and modestly elegant, and no one undertakes to surprise or shock or impress by stylistic invention.

This, in my view, is the Ground Zero from which the aesthetics of abstraction has not yet recovered.

December 2002

The Epidemiology of Evil

Theodore Dalrymple

N O ONE FEELS CALLED upon to explain, or explain away, his good deeds or qualities, which are taken to arise from his essential being as naturally and irresistibly as a river from its source, but most people feel the necessity when it comes to their bad deeds or moral failings. That is why the problem of evil is so much more compelling than the problem of good, for evil—especially one's own—is assumed to be against the natural order of things. Ever since Rousseau, man has been born not with original sin, but with original virtue. The question therefore arises as to how beings so inherently good often turn out to be so horribly bad.

One way of solving the problem is by appeal to the phenomenon of doubling. At least once a week, usually more often, a patient in my clinic describes himself to me as a Jekyll and Hyde. The assumption always is, of course, that the Jekyll is the real him or her, while the Hyde is an intruder, alien, or interloper. The transformation from Jekyll to Hyde is often effected, as it is in the novella, by a chemical substance, though one less cinematic than that described by Stevenson:

> The mixture, which was at first of a reddish hue, began, in proportion as the crystals melted, to brighten in colour, to effervesce audibly, and to throw off small fumes of vapour. Suddenly and at the same moment, the ebullition ceased and the compound changed to dark purple, which faded again more slowly to a watery green.

How that passage takes me back to my adolescent days in the chemistry lab, when we would heat and mix chemicals just for the thrill of releasing gaseous iodine, a violet vapor whose transience in that state introduced us to the bittersweet impermanence of excitement, pleasure, and beauty.

No, the substances that transform (or are alleged to transform) our modern Jekylls into Hydes are alcohol, cannabis, and cocaine. The transformative effect, however, is not purely pharmacological: for many a Jekyll and Hyde has told me that a quantity of alcohol taken as beer does not have the terrible consequences for his character as the same quantity taken as whiskey. I suspect that it is the knowledge, or rather rumor, of Stevenson's gothic tale that is the really necessary ingredient for the transformation.

Even the most unliterary people, who have never read a book in their lives, make use of the Jekyll and Hyde metaphor, and perhaps it is not surprising therefore that some of the subtleties of the story are lost in the self-serving use to which it is put by them. Interestingly, those who are unfortunate enough to live with a self-proclaimed Jekyll and Hyde also refer to the story, as if it provided a true physiological explanation of the changes that come over their loved, or loved and feared, one. I've heard "He's a Jekyll and Hyde character" as often as I've heard "I'm a Jekyll and Hyde character."

In the mouth of the wrongdoer, the metaphor is, of course, an exculpatory one. Its function is to allow a person to do evil and yet think of himself as essentially good. Intoxication with alcohol or cannabis has another great advantage: when severe enough, it destroys, or rather prevents, memory for events, and it is difficult to feel truly guilty for acts which one does not remember having committed. It allows the miscreant to say, as many have said to me, "It's not me (Jekyll) who did those things, because they are not the kind of things I (Jekyll) do." No, it was someone else; in short, Hyde. Ergo, I (Jekyll) am innocent.

As for the person who claims that her lover is a Jekyll and Hyde, the metaphor serves to preserve and justify her love for him, despite all the evidence that he is unworthy of it. The transformation being a physical or a physiological one, he cannot truly help himself. His evil is therefore to be pitied rather than condemned; he may strangle his lover occasionally ("But not all the time, doctor"), yet he retains his inner core of goodness. Therefore he is essentially lovable; and therefore also it is not absurd that she remains with him, which—for a variety of reasons—is what she wants and is determined to do.

Stevenson's *Strange Case of Dr. Jekyll and Mr. Hyde* was not the first tale of doubling in Scottish literature, of course. In some ways, its forerunner, *The Private Memoirs and Confessions of a Justified Sinner*, published anonymously by James Hogg sixty-two years earlier, in 1824, is even more illuminating as a source of our modern penchant for gnostic psychobabble. It has not entered the popular consciousness as Stevenson's *Strange Case* has done; no patient has ever said to me, "I'm a Robert Wringhim, doctor";

there are too many ambiguities in the story, the style is too convoluted, the resort to Scots dialect too frequent, for any line, scene, or character from it to have become universally recognized.

Robert Wringhim is the son, possibly the natural son, but possibly also the adopted son (the text does not make it entirely clear), of the Reverend Wringhim, a fierce Calvinist churchman, and Mrs. Colwan, herself something of a religious fanatic, who is the estranged wife of a hedonistic Scottish lowland landowner, George Colwan, by whom she has a legitimate son, also called George. George Junior and Robert are temperamentally opposite, as well as rivals and (in Robert's eyes, at least) enemies. George takes after his father, Robert after the Reverend Wringhim.

Robert is convinced by the Reverend Wringhim that he is one of the saved, according to the Calvinist doctrine of predestination. Thereafter, the ground having been laid for his success, the devil in human form approaches Robert. He has the power to take on the appearance of whomever he addresses: he is the universal double, a faculty suggesting that the devil resides within all of us. Robert, however, mistakes his double for a genuine theological and moral guide. He persuades Robert to begin the great work of ridding the world of the ungodly, and together they kill a good and inoffensive preacher called Blanchard. Subsequently, Robert pursues his brother and finally kills him, inherits the family estate, and leads a debauched existence, though the book does not make it entirely clear whether it is Robert himself who commits all the crimes, his true alter ego, or the devil disguised as Robert.

What Hogg does make clear are the moral consequences of believing in original—that is to say, predestined—virtue. The Reverend Wringhim tells Robert

> how he had wrestled with God . . . not for a night, but for days and years . . . on my account; but that he had at last prevailed, and had now gained the long and earnestly desired assurance of my acceptance with the Almighty, in and through the sufferings of his Son. That I was now a justified person . . . my name written in the Lamb's book of life, and that no by-past transgression, nor any future act of my own . . . could be instrumental in altering the decree. "All the powers of darkness," added he, "shall never be able to pluck you again out of your Redeemer's hand."

This is a belief that does not necessarily provide a strong incentive for virtue, to put it mildly, and it is not a coincidence that the devil seeks shortly afterwards to reinforce it. The devil says:

"Now, when you know, as you do (and as every one of the elect may know of himself) that this Saviour died for you, namely and particularly, dare you say that there is not enough merit in His great atonement to annihilate all your sins, let them be as heinous and atrocious as they may? And, moreover, do you not acknowledge that God hath pre-ordained and decreed whatsoever comes to pass? Then, how is it that you should deem it in your power to eschew one action in your life. . . none of us knows what is pre-ordained, but whatever is pre-ordained we must do, and none of these things will be laid to our charge."

The man who is saved can therefore do as he pleases, and remain thoroughly saved. Rousseauvian man, who is good by his essential nature, can do evil and yet remain at heart good. A famous, or rather infamous, speech by Himmler to senior SS officers in Posen in 1943, is the ne plus ultra of this line of thought:

> Most of you will know what it means when a hundred corpses lie together, when five hundred or a thousand are lying there. To go through all this . . . and yet remain decent men. . . . This is a glorious page in our history, a page which has never been written and which can never be written.

The man who commits genocide thus preserves his inner core of goodness and decency, which can no more be destroyed by a hard day's slaughter than can Robert Wringhim's election be overturned by his conduct.

What Rousseau did, then, was merely to democratize Calvinist election (he wasn't a Swiss for nothing, after all). The Calvinist elect were a small and elite, if not necessarily happy, band of men; for Rousseau, every man was elect merely by virtue of drawing breath, because he was a member of the human species, even if the veneer with which society subsequently covered him concealed his essential goodness.

In fact, my patients who explain their own evil conduct by reference to Jekyll and Hyde exactly overturn the meaning not only of the *Strange Case* itself, but also of its Scots forerunner, *The Private Memoirs and Confessions*. Both Hogg and Stevenson make it clear that, far from being extraneous to the characters of Robert Wringhim and Henry Jekyll, evil is intrinsic to them, and by extension, to the whole of humanity. They believe in original sin, not original virtue.

In the case of Robert Wringhim, not only does his belief in his own moral election predispose him to the commission of evil, but he is bad by his very nature. His account of his childhood and adolescence, for example, makes it clear that he was born both envious and unscrupulous, with a tendency to hypocrisy and bearing false witness. When a serving man of the Reverend Wringhim "discovered some notorious lies that I had framed . . . my cheek burned with offence rather than shame." And he then exults in denouncing him, for the sake of revenge, to the Reverend Wringhim.

In his youth, Robert Wringhim is in competition with his brother (or half-brother). George Colwan is the kind of boy who is at ease with himself and others, who is popular and, while no dunce, is a sportsman *moyen sensuel*. Robert seeks to compensate for his own awkwardness, and awareness that he will never equal George in social graces, by academic prowess. In order to do this, of course, he has to be the best scholar in his class; no other position but the top will do. Unfortunately, good scholar though he is, there is a boy in his class who is greatly and effortlessly more gifted than he, called M'Gill. In order to achieve preeminence, he brings M'Gill down by a series of subterfuges and dirty tricks.

This raises the question whether men choose doctrines, or doctrines choose men, in accordance with their temperaments. It is clear that Robert Wringhim is temperamentally predisposed to the doctrine of election by predestination because it is a convenient mask for his own unscrupulousness. Even before the Reverend Wringhim tells Robert that he is one of the chosen, and his double, the devil, leads him yet further astray, he uses religion as a cover for his envy. "I strove [academically] against him [M'Gill] from year to year, but it was all in vain; for he was a very wicked boy, and I was convinced he had dealings with the Devil." In other words, any means of destroying him were theologically justified, though it takes very little to see that Robert is not intent upon punishing evil but in advancing himself. Robert's sense of election and entitlement to do wrong precede his adoption of the doctrine of predestination in all its fullness.

So Hogg, *pace* my Jekyll and Hyde patients, is not saying that evil is external to man, that it requires an external force to lead him astray to perpetrate it. He is saying that there is evil in the heart of man, evil that finds expression if the wrong doctrines are propagated and adopted, and if the man with a natural propensity to evil finds or is found by an evil genius, within him or without. But he leaves one aspect of the mystery of evil as mysterious as he found it: for why should Robert Wringhim have been born with an evil temperament, as the book implies? The devil tries his blandishments with the good preacher, Blanchard, whom he and Robert eventually kill, but to no effect, because Blanchard is a good man who is proof against the devil's wiles. Why should Blanchard be as naturally good as Robert Wringhim is naturally bad? And if a man is good by nature, is he good at all, given that virtue depends on the existence of choice? To what extent, in other words, are we responsible for our own temperaments?

A closer reading of Stevenson's *Strange Case* than most of my patients ever give it who invoke Jekyll and Hyde to explain their own evil provides a partial answer. For them the fact that they sometimes turn into Hyde is an illness, an involuntary departure from their normal state, which of course is that of Jekyll. But in Stevenson's parable, it becomes harder and harder for Hyde to turn back into Jekyll. Once he has been Hyde for too long, the transformative chemicals lose their power, and have to be taken in ever larger doses before they both lose their efficacy altogether and can no longer even be obtained: in short, Jekyll has become Hyde permanently. "The powers of Hyde seemed to have grown with the sickliness of Jekyll." In other words, if you practice evil, you become evil. Character is habit.

Moreover, Jekyll does not start out as a paragon of virtue. He is, he informs us, 90 percent virtuous (and it is not given to many of us, after all, to be more virtuous than that). The evil is already within him, waiting to pounce, as it is within all of us. The chemicals do not *create* the evil—they release it from the chains in which virtue has hitherto imprisoned it. Jekyll is a very fortunate man, blessed with money, high intelligence, and great gifts, and he starts out with decent sentiments and principles. But once he gives in to the attractions of evil, he decisively changes the balance between good and evil within him.

This is not what my patients mean when they say they are Jekyll and Hyde characters. What they mean is that they are Jekyll (not 90 percent good, but 100 percent good, à la Rousseau), and that an external force over which they have no control turns them to absolute evil to which they have no natural propensity. Thus, a self-proclaimed Jekyll and Hyde will describe what he does that is bad or evil: he puts his hand around his girlfriend's throat, for example, and squeezes, or pulls her across the room by her hair, or shatters her jaw, or blacks her eyes, and so forth, not once, but repeatedly, many times, over periods of years, joyously, and then will blandly assert that "It's not me, doctor, I don't do those things."

Who is it, then? Why, Mr. Hyde, of course. And Mr. Hyde is as invasive, as extraneous to the normal course of things, as pathological in the literal sense, as a brain tumor. What does one do with a brain tumor? One finds a neurosurgeon to excise it. Similarly with Mr. Hyde—one seeks a sweet, oblivious antidote to exorcise him.

It is curious how a work of literature such as Stevenson's *Strange Case* should have supplied a universal metaphor, and yet one that is almost always used in a sense precisely the opposite of the meaning that a deeper consideration of the story itself might suggest. Far from implying that evil is an alien force over which we have no control—that invades us as an alien—Stevenson is telling us that our capacity for evil will be indefinitely enlarged, until it overwhelms us utterly, if we make a habit of indulging in it. To claim to be a Jekyll and Hyde character is not a mitigating but an aggravating circumstance.

Could it even be that a misguided notion of the meaning of Jekyll and Hyde has actually contributed to the prevalence of evil in Western societies? I know of no studies in the epidemiology of evil, but my impression (admittedly derived from the rather peculiar circumstances of my medical practice) is that evil, at least in the sphere of daily social relations, grows ever more prevalent. Perhaps I have merely reached the age of despair, when youthful optimism seems shallow and callow, but yet the willingness with which people explain evil away by reference to Jekyll and Hyde, as a putative neurological condition, has never been greater.

Only today, for example, I was consulted by a patient who had tried to kill herself because she had found her boyfriend in bed with another woman. As he had spent several years accusing her of infidelity, to the extent that he would allow her out of her house only on sufferance, and then provided that she dress as unattractively as possible, this was too much for her, and she swallowed the nearest pills.

"Has he ever been violent to you?" I asked, knowing the answer in advance.

Well, not very violent. He had hit her many times. He had once split her lip and "cracked" (as she put it) her jaw.

"But of course," I said, "when he's nice, he's very nice."

"Yes," she said. "He's a real Jekyll and Hyde."

It crossed my mind that perhaps she would have had a clearer-sighted view of her own situation if Stevenson had never written his story, if Jekyll and Hyde had never entered popular consciousness. Could it be that no knowledge of literature is better than a misunderstanding of literature?—a question at least worth considering as we contemplate the condition of our humanities departments?

September 2004

The Hunter Gracchus

Guy Davenport

O N APRIL 6, 1917, IN a dwarfishly small house rented by his sister Ottla in the medieval quarter of Prague (22 Alchymistengasse—Alchemists' Alley), Kafka wrote in his diary:

> Today, in the tiny harbor where save for fishing boats only two ocean-going passenger steamers used to call, a strange boat lay at anchor. A clumsy old craft, rather low and very broad, filthy, as if bilge water had been poured over it, it still seemed to be dripping down the yellowish sides; the masts disproportionately tall, the upper third of the mainmast split; wrinkled, coarse, yellowish-brown sails stretched every which way between the yards, patched, too weak to stand against the slightest gust of wind.
>
> I gazed in astonishment at it for a time, waited for someone to show himself on deck; no one appeared. A workman sat down beside me on the harbor wall. "Whose ship is that?" I asked; "this is the first time I've seen it."
>
> "It puts in every two or three years," the man said, "and belongs to the Hunter Gracchus."

Gracchus, the name of a noble Roman family from the third to the first centuries B.C., is synonymous with Roman virtue at its sternest. It is useful to Kafka not only for its antiquity and tone of incorruptible rectitude (a portrait bust, as may be, on a classroom shelf, at odds and yet in harmony with the periodic table of the elements behind it), but also for its meaning, a grackle or blackbird; in Czech, a *kavka*. Kafka's father had a blackbird on his business letterhead.

The description of Gracchus's old ship is remarkably like Melville's of the *Pequod*, whose "venerable bows looked bearded" and whose "ancient decks were worn and wrinkled." From Noah's ark to Jonah's storm-tossed boat out of Joppa to the Roman ships in which St. Paul sailed perilously, the ship in history has always been a sign of fate itself.

The first Hunter Gracchus

A first draft, or fragment, of "The Hunter Gracchus" (the title of both fragment and story are Max Brod's) is a dialogue between Gracchus and a visitor to the boat. Gracchus imagines himself known and important. His fate is special and unique. The dialogue is one of cross-purposes. Gracchus says that he is "the most ancient of seafarers," patron saint of sailors. He offers wine. "The master does me proud." Who the master is (Gracchus doesn't understand his language) is a mystery. He died, in fact, "today" in Hamburg, while Gracchus is "down south here." The effect of this fragment is of an Ancient Mariner trying to tell his story to and impress his importance upon a reluctant listener, who concludes that life is too short to hear this old bore out. In the achieved story the interlocutor is the mayor of Riva, who must be diplomatically attentive. The authority of myth engages with the authority of skeptical reason, so that when the mayor asks, "Sind Sie tot?," the metaphysical locale shivers like the confused needle of a compass in "Ja, sagte der Jäger, wie Sie sehen."

A Victorian pentimento

Between writing the two texts now known as "The Hunter Gracchus: A Fragment" and "The Hunter Gracchus," Kafka read Wilkie Collins's novel *Armadale*, which ran serially in *The Cornhill Magazine* from 1864 to 1866, when it was published with great success and popularity. A German translation by Marie Scott (Leipzig, 1866) went through three editions before 1878.

Along with *The Woman in White* (1860) and *The Moonstone* (1868), *Armadale* is one of the three masterpieces of intricately plotted novels of melodrama, suspense, and detection that made Collins as famous as, and for a while, more famous than Dickens.

Although its plot contains a ship that has taken a wrong course, and turns up later as a ghostly wreck, a sudden impulse that dictates the fate of two innocent people (both named Allen Armadale), it is the novel's opening scene that Kafka found interesting enough to appropriate and transmute. Collins furnished Kafka with an ominous arrival of an invalid on a stretcher, with a ghastly face and matted hair, who is carried past the everyday street life of a village—including "flying detachments of plump white-headed children" and a mother with a child at her breast—to be met by the mayor.

Collins's scene is set at a spa in the Black Forest (home of the Hunter Gracchus in the "Fragment"). He has a band playing the waltz from Weber's *Der Freischütz*, which must have struck Kafka as a serendipitous correspondence. Among the archetypes of the Hunter Gracchus is the enchanted marksman of that opera. In Collins it is a guilty past that cannot be buried. The dead past persists. Kafka makes a crystalline abstract of Collins's plot, concentrating its essence into the figure of Gracchus, his wandering ship, his fate, and the enigmatic sense that the dead, having lived and acted, are alive.

Collins's elderly, dying invalid is a murderer. He has come to the spa at Wildbad with a young wife and child. In the last moments he must write a confession intended to avert retribution for his crime from being passed on to his son. *Armadale* is the working out of the futility of that hope.

Kafka, having written a dialogue between Gracchus and an unidentified interlocutor, found in Collins a staging. Gracchus must have an arrival, a procession to a room, an interlocutor with an identity, and a more focused role as man-the-wanderer, fated by an inexplicable past in which a wrong turn was taken that can never be corrected.

De Chirico

The first paragraph of "The Hunter Gracchus" displays the quiet, melancholy stillness of Italian *piazze* that Nietzsche admired, leading Giorgio de Chirico to translate Nietzsche's feeling for Italian light, architecture, and street life into those paintings which art history calls metaphysical. The enigmatic tone of de Chirico comes as much from Arnold Böcklin (whose "Isle of the Dead" is further down the lake from Riva). (For *nicceismo* in Böcklin and de Chirico, see Alberto Savinio's "Arnold Böcklin" in *Operatic Lives* and de Chirico's *Memoirs*. Savinio is de Chirico's brother.) Böcklin's romanticism of mystery, of dark funereal beauty, is in the idiom of the Décadence, "the moment of Nietzsche." Kafka, like de Chirico, was aware of and influenced by this *Stimmung* of a new melancholy that informed European art and writing from Scandinavia to Rome, from London to Prague.

Kafka's distinction is that he stripped it of those elements which would quickly soften into Kitsch.

"Zwei Knaben saßen auf der Quaimauer und spielen Würfel." Two boys were sitting on the harbor wall playing with dice. They touch, lightly, the theme of hazard, of chance, that will vibrate throughout. "History is a child playing at knucklebones," said Heraclitus two and a half millennia earlier, "and that child is the whole majesty of man's power in the world." Mallarmé's "Un coup de dés jamais n'abolira le hasard," with its imagery of shipwreck and pathless seas, was published when Kafka was fourteen, in 1897. "God does not play at dice," said Einstein (whom Kafka may have met at a Prague salon they are both known to have attended). Kafka was not certain that He didn't.

There is a monument on this quay, a "säbelschwingende Held," a sword-flourishing hero, in whose shadow a man is reading a newspaper. History in two *tempi*, and Kafka made the statue up, much as he placed a sword-bearing Statue of Liberty in *Amerika*.

A girl is filling her jug at the public fountain. (Joyce, having a Gemini in the boys, an Aquarius in the water jug, and a Sagittarius in the monument, would have gone ahead and tucked in a full zodiac, however furtively; signs and symbols have no claim on Kafka, who wrecks tradition rather than trust any part of it.)

A fruitseller lies beside his scales (more zodiac, Libra!) staring out to sea.

Then a fleeting Cézanne: through the door and windows of the café we can see two men drinking wine at a table "in der Tiefe," all the way at the back. The owner is out front, asleep at one of his own tables.

Into this de Chirico high noon comes a ship, "eine Barke," "silently making for the little harbor." The sailor who secures the boat with a rope through a ring wears a blue blouse, a French touch that makes us note that two French words have already turned up (*quai* and *barque*). It's the late, hard, spare style of Flaubert, as in the opening paragraphs of *Bouvard et Pécuchet*, that Kafka is taking for a model, and improving upon.

Gracchus, like Wilkie Collins's Armadale, is brought across the quay on a bier, covered by a large Victorian shawl, "a great flower-patterned tasselled silk cloth" perhaps taken from Collins's carpet speckled with "flowers in all the colours of the rainbow," and like Armadale, he seems to be more dead than alive.

Gracchus's arrival is strangely ignored by the people in the square, as if he were invisible. A new set of characters—a committee of innocents—take over: a mother with a nursing child, a little boy who opens and closes a window, and a flock of biblical doves, whose associations with fated ships fit Kafka's diction of imagery, Noah's dove from the ark, and Jonah's name ("dove" in Hebrew).

The mayor of Riva arrives as soon as Gracchus has been carried inside a yellow house with an oaken door. He is dressed in black, with a funeral band on his top hat.

Fifty little boys

These "fünfzig kleine Knaben" who line up in two rows and bow to the Bürgermeister of Riva when he arrives at the house where the Hunter Gracchus has been carried remind us of Max Ernst's *collages*, or Delvaux's paintings; that is, they enact the surrealist strategy of being from the dream world, like Kipling's hovering ghost children in "They" or Tchelitchev's children in *Cache-cache*.

Another horde of children, girls this time, crowd the stairs to the court painter Titorelli's studio in *The Trial*. Their presence is almost as inexplicable as that of the boys. They live in the mazelike tenement where Titorelli paints judges and brokers gossip about cases in process. They are silly, provocative, brazen pests. Like the boys, they line up on either side of the stairway, "squeezing against the walls to leave room for K. to pass." They form, like the boys, a kind of gauntlet through which the mayor of Riva and K. have to pass to a strange and unsettling encounter.

In December 1911 Kafka, having witnessed the circumcision of a nephew, noted that in Russia the period between birth and circumcision was thought to be particularly vulnerable to devils for both the mother and the son. "For seven days after the birth, except on Friday, also in order to ward off evil spirits, ten to fifteen children, always different ones, led by the *belfer* [assistant teacher], are admitted to the bedside of the mother, there repeat *Shema Israel*, and are then given candy. These innocent, five- to eight-year-old children are supposed to be especially effective in driving back the evil spirits, who press forward most strongly toward evening."

At the beginning of *Armadale*, the Bürgermeister of Wildbad in the Black Forest, awaiting the arrival of the elder Armadale ("who lay helpless on a mattress supported by a stretcher; his hair long and disordered under a black skull-cap; his eyes wide open, rolling to and fro ceaselessly anxious; the rest of his face as void of all expression . . . as if he had been dead"), is surrounded by "flying detachments of plump white-headed children careered in perpetual motion."

In 1917 Kafka wrote in his journal: "They were given the choice of becoming kings or the king's messengers. As is the way with children, they all wanted to be messengers. That is why there are only messengers, racing through the world and, since there are no kings, calling out to each other the messages that have now become meaningless." (There is another sentence—"They would gladly put an end to their miserable life, but they do not dare to do so because of their oath of loyalty"—that starts another thought superfluous to the perfect image of messenger children making a botch of all messages.)

All messages in Kafka are incoherent, misleading, enigmatic. The most irresponsible and childish messengers are the assistants to K. in *The Castle*. (They probably enter Kafka's imagination as two silent Swedish boys Kafka kept seeing at a nudist spa in Austria in 1912, always together, uncommunicative, politely nodding in passing, traversing Kafka's path with comic regularity.)

The new myth

Despite Kafka's counting on myths and folktales about hunters, enchanted ships, the Wandering Jew, ships for the souls of the dead, and all the other cultural furniture to stir in the back of our minds as we read "The Hunter Gracchus," he does not, like Joyce, specify them. He treats them like ground water which his taproot can reach. Even when he selects something from the midden of myth, he estranges it. His Don Quijote, his Tower of Babel, his Bucephalus are transmutations.

Hermann Broch in his introduction to Rachel Bespaloff's *De l'Iliade* (1943, English translation as *On the Iliad*, 1947) placed Kafka's relation to myth accurately, beyond it as an exhausted resource. Broch's was one of the earliest sensibilities to see Joyce's greatness and uniqueness. His art, however, was an end and a culmination. Broch's own *The Death of Virgil* may be the final elegy closing the long duration of a European literature from Homer to Joyce. In Kafka he saw a new beginning, a fiercely bright sun burning through the opaque mists of a dawn.

> The striking relationship between the arts on the basis of their common abstractism [Broch wrote], their common style of old age, this hallmark of our epoch is the cause of the inner relationship between artists like Picasso, Stravinsky, and Joyce. This relationship is not only striking in itself but also by reason of the parallelism through which the style of old age was imposed on these men, even in their rather early years.
>
> Nevertheless, abstractism forms no *Gesamtkunstwerk*—the ideal of the late romantic; the arts remain separate. Literature especially can never become completely abstract and "musicalized": therefore the style of old age relies here much more on another symptomatic attitude, namely on

the trend toward myth. It is highly significant that Joyce goes back to the *Odyssey*. And although this return to myth—already anticipated in Wagner—is nowhere so elaborated as in Joyce's work, it is for all that a general attitude of modern literature, as, for instance, in the novels of Thomas Mann, is an evidence of the impetuosity with which myth surges to the forefront of poetry. However, this is only a return—a return to myth in its ancient forms (even when they are so modernized as in Joyce), and so far it is not a new myth, not *the* new myth. Yet, we may assume that at least the first realization of such a new myth is already evident, namely in Franz Kafka's writing.

In Joyce one may still detect neo-romantic trends, a concern with the complications of the human soul, which derives directly from nineteenth-century literature, from Stendhal, and even from Ibsen. Nothing of this kind can be said about Kafka. Here the personal problem no longer exists, and what seems still personal is, at the very moment it is uttered, dissolved in a super-personal atmosphere. The prophecy of myth is suddenly at hand.

Prophecy. All of Kafka is about history that had not yet happened. His sister Ottla would die in the camps, along with all of his kin. *Ungeziefer*, the word for *insect* that Kafka used for Gregor Samsa, is the same word the Nazis used for Jews, and *insect extermination* was one of their obscene euphemisms, as George Steiner has pointed out.

Quite soon after the Second World War it was evident that in *The Castle* and *The Trial*, and especially "In the Penal Colony," Kafka was accurately describing the mechanics of totalitarian barbarity.

Perpetual oscillation

Kafka, Broch says in the Bespaloff introduction, had "reached the point of the Either-Or: either poetry is able to proceed to myth, or it goes bankrupt."

Kafka, in his presentiment of the new cosmogony, the new theogony that he had to achieve, struggling with his love of literature, his disgust for literature, feeling the ultimate insufficiency of any artistic approach, decided (as did Tolstoy, faced with a similar decision) to quit the realm of literature, and ask that his work be destroyed; he asked this for the sake of the universe whose new mythical concept had been bestowed upon him.

In "the blue notebooks" Kafka wrote: "To what indifference people may come, to what profound conviction of having lost the right track forever."

And: "Our salvation is death, but not this one."

Kafka's prose is a hard surface, as of polished steel, without resonance or exact reflection. It is, as Broch remarked, abstract ("of bare essentials and unconditional abstractness"). It is, as many critics have said, a pure German, the austere German in which the Austro-Hungarian empire conducted its administrative affairs, an efficient, Spartan idiom admitting of neither ornament nor poetic tones. Its grace was that of abrupt information and naked utility.

Christopher Middleton speaks (in a letter) of "the transparent, ever-inquiring, tenderly comical, ferociously paradoxical narrative voice that came to Kafka for his Great Wall of China and Josephine the Singer: Kafka's *last* voice."

The paradox everywhere in Kafka is that this efficient prose is graphing images and events forever alien to the administration of a bureaucracy. Middleton's remark happens in a discussion of the spiritual dance of language.

I'm reading about Abraham Abulafia, his "mystical experience," theories of music and of symbolic words. There was a wonderful old Sephardic Rabbi in Smyrna, Isaak ha-Kohen, who borrowed and developed a theory, in turn adopted and cherished by Abulafia, about melody, a theory with obviously ancient origins, but traceable to Byzantium, melody as a rehearsal, with its undulatory ups and downs, of the soul's dancing toward ecstatic union with God: to rehearse the soul, bid your instrumentalists play . . . so melody is a breathing, a veil of breath which flows and undulates, a veiling of the Ruach (spirit). When you listen to recent recreations of Byzantine music, the theory seems more and more childish, but the facts it enwraps become more and more audible—even the *touching* of flute-notes and harp strings enacts the vertiginous conspiracy, the "letting go," out of any succession of instants into an imaginable *nunc stans*, an ingression into "the perfect and complete simultaneous possession of unlimited life" (as dear old Boethius put it). Oddly enough, this (what's "this"?) is the clue to the narrative voice (I conjecture) . . . that came to Kafka for his Great Wall of China.

What Kafka had to be so clear and simple about was that nothing is clear and simple. On his deathbed he said of a vase of flowers that they were like him: simultaneously alive and dead. All demarcations are shimmeringly blurred. Some powerful sets of opposites absolutely do not, as Heraclitus said, cooperate. They fight. They tip over the balance of every certainty. We can, Kafka said, easily believe any truth and its negative at the same time.

Lustron und Kastron

Gracchus's *Lebensproblem*, as the Germans say, is that he cannot encounter his opposite and be resolved (or not) into Being or Nonbeing, as the outcome may be.

Opposites do not cooperate; they obliterate each other.

In 1912, at a nudist spa in Austria, Kafka dreamed that two contingents of nudists were facing each other. One contingent was shouting at the other the insult "Lustron und Kastron!"

The insult was considered so objectionable that they fought. They obliterated each other like the Calico Cat and the Gingham Dog, or like subatomic particles colliding into nonexistence.

The dream interested Kafka; he recorded it. He did not analyze it, at least not on paper. He knew his Freud. There are no such words as *lustron* and *kastron* in Greek, though the dream made them Greek. If we transpose them into Greek loan words in Latin, we get *castrum* (castle) and *lustrum* (the five-year-recurring spiritual cleansing of Roman religion). Both words are antonyms, containing their own opposites (like *altus*, deep or high). *Lustrum*, a washing clean, also means filthy; the *cast-* root give us *chaste* and *castrate*. And *lust* and *chaste* play around in their juxtaposition.

At the nudist spa Kafka records, with wry wit, the presence of the two silent Swedish boys (they will, I think, become the clownishly stupid assistants in *The Castle*) whose handsome nudity reminded him of Castor and Pollux, whose names strangely mean Clean and Dirty (our *chaste* and *polluted*). These archetypal twins, the sons of Leda, Helen's brothers, noble heroes, duplicates of Damon and Pythias in friendship, existed alternately. One lived while the other was dead, capable of swapping these states of being. They are in the zodiac as Gemini, and figure in much folklore, merging with Jesus and James.

When Gracchus claims in the "Fragment" that he is the patron saint of sailors, he is lying. Castor and Pollux are the patron saints of sailors, the corposants that play like bright fire in the rigging.

Pollux in Greek has a euphemism for a name: Polydeukes (The Sweet One). When the Greeks felt they needed to propitiate, they avoided a real name (as in calling the avenging Fates the Eumenides). Pollux was a boxer when all fights were to the death.

Dirty and clean, then, *tref* and *kosher*, motivated Kafka's dream. The insult was that one group of nudists were both. Kafka was a nudist who wore bathing drawers, a nonobservant Jew, a Czech who wrote in German, a man who was habitually engaged to be married and died a bachelor. He could imagine "a curious animal, half kitten, half lamb" (derived from a photograph of himself, age five, with a prop stuffed lamb whose hindquarters look remarkably like those of a cat). He could imagine "an Odradek," the identity of which has so far eluded all the scholars.

We live, Kafka seems to imply, in all matters suspended between belief and doubt, knowing and ignorance, law and chance. Gracchus is both prehistoric man, a hunter and gatherer, and man at his most civilized. He thinks that his fate is due to a fall in a primeval forest, as well as to his death ship being off course.

Kafka could see the human predicament from various angles. We live by many codes of law written thousands of years ago for people whose circumstances are not ours. This is not exclusively a Jewish or Muslim problem; the United States Constitution has its scandals and headaches. Hence lawyers, of whom Kafka was one. He dealt daily with workmen's accidents, and their claims for compensation. What is the value of a hand?

His mind was pre-pre-Socratic. His physics teacher had studied under Ernst Mach, whose extreme skepticism about atoms and cause and effect activated Einstein in quite a different direction.

Walter Benjamin, Kafka's first interpreter, said that a strong prehistoric wind blows across Kafka from the past. There is that picture of a Bushman on the wall which Gracchus can see from his bed, "who is aiming his spear at me and taking cover as best he can behind a beautifully painted shield." A Bushman who has not yet fallen off a cliff and broken his neck.

"Mein Kahn ist ohne Steuer, er fährt mit dem Wind, der in den untersten Regionen des Todes bläst."

This is the voice of the twentieth century, from the ovens of Buchenwald, from the bombarded trenches of the Marne, from Hiroshima.

It was words that started the annihilating fight in Kafka's dream, meaningless words invented by Kafka's dreaming mind. They seem to designate opposite things, things clean and things unclean. Yet they encode their opposite meanings. The relation of word to thing is the lawyer's, the philosopher's, the ruler's constant anguish. The word *Jew* (which occurs nowhere in Kafka's fiction) designates not an anthropological race but a culture, and yet both Hitler and the Jews used it as if it specified a race. "The Hunter Gracchus" inquires into the meaning of the word *death*. If there is an afterlife in an eternal state, then it does not mean death; it means transition, and death as a word is meaningless. It annihilates either of its meanings if you bring them together.

The language of the law, of talking dogs and apes, of singing fieldmice, of ogres and bridges that can talk—everything has its *logos* for Kafka. (Max Brod recounts a conversation between Kafka and a donkey in Paris.) Words are tyrants more powerful than any Caesar. When they are lies, they are devils.

The purity of Kafka's style assures us of its trustworthiness as a witness. It is this purity, as of a child's innocence or an angel's prerogative, that allows Kafka into metaphysical realities where a rhetorical or bogus style would flounder. Try to imagine "The Hunter Gracchus" by the late Tolstoy, or by Poe. The one would have moralized, the other would have tried to scare us. Kafka says, "Here is what it feels like to be lost."

As Auden noted, *as if* in Kafka is treated as *is*. To bring *is* to bear on Kafka's *as if* will only annihilate them both.

Fifty children in two rows

We cannot read "The Hunter Gracchus" without being reminded of all the refugee ships loaded to the gunwales with Jews trying to escape the even more packed cattlecars to Auschwitz, turned away from harbor after harbor.

One of the arrangers of some of these ships was Ada Sereni, an Italian Jewish noblewoman whose family can be traced back to Rome in the first century. In September of 1947 she was involved in secret flights of Jewish children from Italy to Palestine. A twin-engine plane flown by two Americans was to land at night outside Salerno. Ada Sereni and the twenty-year-old Motti Fein (later to command the Israeli Air Force in the Six Day War) were waiting with fifty children to be taken to a kibbutz. As the plane approached, the fifty were placed in two rows of twenty-five each, holding candles as landing lights in a Sicilian meadow. The operation took only a few minutes, and was successful. The children were in orange groves the next morning. "An der Stubentür klopfte er an, gleichzeitig nahm er den Zylinderhut in seine schwarzbehandschuhte Rechte. Gleich wurde geöffnet, wohl fünfzig kleine Knaben bildeten ein Spaller in langen Flurgang und verbeugten sich."

The SS wore black gloves.

Death ships

Kafka does not decode. He is not referring us to Wagner's "Flying Dutchman" or the myth of the Wandering Jew, or to the pharaonic death ships that had harbors built for them in the empty desert, or to the treasure ships in which Viking lords were laid in all their finery, or to the Polynesian death ships that glided from island to island collecting the dead, or to American Indian canoe burials, or to Coleridge's Ancient Mariner, or to any of the ghost ships of legend and folktale. There is a ghostly hunter in the Black Forest. Kafka's ability to write "The Hunter Gracchus" is evidence of what Broch meant when he said that Kafka is the inventor of a new mythology.

Sind Sie tot?

At Auschwitz it was difficult to tell the living from the dead.

Raven and blackbird

Poe's mind was round, fat, and white; Kafka's cubical, lean, and transparent.

Riva

When Max Brod and Kafka visited Riva in September of 1909 it was an Austrian town where 8,000 Italians lived. It sits on the northwest end of Lake Garda. Baedeker's *Northern Italy* for 1909 calls it "charming" and says that "the water is generally azure blue."

Aion

Time in Kafka is dream time, Zenonian and interminable. The bridegroom will never get to his wedding in the country, the charges against Joseph K. will never be known, the death ship of the Hunter Gracchus will never find its bearings.

Circadian rhythm

The opening of "The Hunter Gracchus" is a picture of urban infinity. There is always another throw of the dice. Another newspaper is being printed while today's is being read; a bucket of water must soon be refilled;

the fruitseller is engaged in "the eternal exchange of money and goods" (Heraclitus on the shore shaping the sea, the sea shaping the shore); the men in the café will be there again tomorrow; the sleeping man is in one cycle of his circadian rhythm. Play, reading, housekeeping, business, rest: it is against these ordinary peaceful things that Kafka puts the long duration of Gracchus's thousand years of wandering, a cosmic infinity.

A kind of paradox

Reality is the most effective mask of reality. Our fondest wish, attained, ceases to be our fondest wish. Success is the greatest of disappointments. The spirit is most alive when it is lost. Anxiety was Kafka's composure, as despair was Kierkegaard's happiness. Kafka said impatience is our greatest fault. The man at the gate of the Law waited there all of his life.

The hunter

Nimrod is the biblical archetype, "a mighty hunter before the Lord" (Gen. 10:9, Jer. 16:16), but the Tegum, as Milton knew, records the tradition that he hunted men ("sinful hunting of the sons of men") as well as animals. Kafka was a vegetarian.

Motion

Gracchus explains to the mayor of Riva that he is always in motion, despite his lying as still as a corpse. On the great stair "infinitely wide and spacious" that leads to "the other world" he clambers up and down, sideways to the left, sideways to the right, "always in motion." He says that he is a hunter turned into a butterfly. There is a gate (presumably heaven) toward which he flutters, but when he gets near he wakes to find himself back on his bier in the cabin of his ship, "still stranded forlornly in some earthly sea or other." The motion is in his mind (his *psyche*, Greek for "butterfly" as well as for "soul"). These imaginings (or dreams) are a mockery of his former nimbleness as a hunter. The butterfly is one of the most dramatic of metamorphic creatures, its transformations seemingly more divergent than any other. A caterpillar does not die; it becomes a wholly different being.

Gracchus when he tripped and fell in the Black Forest was glad to die;

he sang joyfully his first night on the death ship. "I slipped into my winding sheet like a girl into her marriage dress. I lay and waited. Then came the mishap."

The mistake causing Gracchus's long wandering happened *after* his death. Behind every enigma in Kafka there is another.

"The Hunter Gracchus" can be placed among Kafka's parables. Are we, the living, already dead? How are we to know if we are on course, or lost? We talk about a loss of life in accidents and war, as if we possessed life rather than life us. Is it that we are never wholly alive, if life is an engagement with the world as far as our talents go? Or does Kafka mean that we can exist but not be?

It is worthwhile, for perspective's sake, to keep the lively Kafka in mind, the delightful friend and traveling companion, the witty ironist, his fascinations with the Yiddish Folk Theatre, with a wide scope of reading, his overlapping and giddy love affairs. He undoubtedly was "as lonely as Franz Kafka" (a remark made, surely, with a wicked smile). We have, however, no record of his enacting a melancholy character.

And some genius of a critic will one day show us how comic a writer Kafka is, how a sense of the ridiculous very kin to that of Sterne and Beckett informs all of his work. Like Kierkegaard, he saw the absurdity of life as the most meaningful clue to its elusive vitality. His humor authenticates his seriousness. "Only Maimonides may say there is no God; he's entitled."

February 1996

Partying on Parnassus:
The New York School Poets

John Simon

D AVID LEHMAN'S *The Last Avant-Garde: The Making of the New York
School of Poets* (Doubleday, 1999) examines the lives, work, and influence of John Ashbery, Frank O'Hara, Kenneth Koch, and James Schuyler
in what seems to be order of importance. To put my cards on the table, as
Lehman would have a critic do, I declare that none of these poets has written what I would call a single poem of any importance, although some of
them have written plausible light verse.

Lehman states the problem succinctly:

> Though he is America's best-known poet, with a strong readership in
> Britain and a larger international following than any of his contem-
> poraries, Ashbery remains an issue and for some a litmus test. A respected
> editor declared that one cannot like both Ashbery and Philip Larkin, and
> though I feel that one can, I understand the logic of her position. Ash-
> bery's poetic assumptions are the opposite of Larkin's. Larkin set store by
> his sincerity and his control; Ashbery by his fancy and his abandon. If your
> sense of literary tradition extends from Keats and the Romantics to Emer-
> son and Whitman and from there to Wallace Stevens, Ashbery's your man;
> if, on the other hand, you derive your sense of tradition from Thomas
> Hardy and William Butler Yeats, Ashbery will seem a renegade.

Except that I would not abandon Keats and the Romantics to the other
camp, and would not limit my tradition to Hardy and Yeats, I agree with
this assessment, and especially with the "respected editor." To like what I
consider anti-poetry as much as poetry bespeaks not catholicity but wishy-
washiness, which, to be sure, has been enshrined as a virtue in our time.
Does my attitude, then, entitle me to review Lehman's book?

It would be a sorry state of affairs in which, say, books on religion could be reviewed only by true believers. There are at least two sides to every question, and a critical dialogue should be just that—a dialogue. Surely Lehman would not be content with preaching only to the converted and gathering their encomia in his collection plate.

So, by way of further laying down of cards, let me state my idea of poetry. It comprises music, painting (imagery), insight, and pregnancy or memorableness of utterance, the first two, of course, in a special sense. Ambiguity, too, may be a legitimate device, but it should not be confused with the mainstay of much New York School (henceforth NYS) stuff: openness to infinite, arbitrary, private readings—*quot homines, tot sententiae.* That way lies formlessness, dissolution, anarchy, and, yes, madness, when free association, becoming too free, hurtles into dementia.

By accepting such scot-free association, anything the NYS poets tossed off or elucubrated could be proclaimed poetry. That these poets were closely associated with some painters (mostly of the NYS of painting) and some composers explains one of their major fallacies: the bland assumption that the procedures of the other arts could be readily appropriated by poetry, so that, for instance, the techniques of Jackson Pollock and John Cage could be applied to writing poems.

Lehman's book divides into three main parts, although he acknowledges only two. He begins with an introductory section acquainting us with the early days of his four poets at Harvard and elsewhere, and the New York literary and art scene in the Forties and Fifties—an avant-garde at odds with contemporary modes in art and life. Next come individual sections on each of the four poets, in which, however, a lot about other poets and artists figures as well. In the third part, "The Ordeal of the Avant-Garde"—although the ordeal seems to me that of the readers—we get affiliations, influences, cross-fertilizations, the work of some of the painters as both painters and poets, also the roles of some art critics, and the most recent developments involving both the heirs of the NYS and rival movements.

Lehman has been a journalist, poet, and teacher, and displays some of the virtues of each profession. He is well-read and readable, knows most of the poets and some of the painters personally, and tells good anecdotes. We also get a sense of the hangouts some of these figures frequented, and probably just enough about their personal relations as well.

John Ashbery (born 1927), Frank O'Hara (1926–1966), Kenneth Koch (born 1925), and James Schuyler (1923–1991): three out of four of them went to Harvard, three out of four wrote professional art criticism, and three were, or are, homosexual. But even in these respects there was no real odd man out. We read, "The painter Alex Katz delighted Schuyler by refusing to believe him when he said that he had attended [without graduating] Bethany College in West Virginia. 'Nah, you're Harvard,' Katz said." Koch, who has not written art criticism, "wrote plays partly for the pleasure of collaborating with painters who did the sets." And though he was the one heterosexual in the group, his friend and collaborator Larry Rivers recalled that he "talked and acted as gay as the rest."

Lehman is at his best documenting the numerous collaborations on poems, plays, and even fiction among these poets, usually in pairs, thus conveying the sense of a school. But he fails to note that, with very few exceptions (and even those not usually in the top bracket), such collaborations have proved artistically negligible.

In further pursuit of honesty, let me mention that I graded Ashbery's papers in Harry Levin's "Proust, Mann & Joyce" course at Harvard, as I did those of his classmates Donald Hall and Robert Bly. All three poets got straight As. I got to know Ashbery—slightly—only later, when we were fellow critics at *New York* magazine. I also run into him at parties. I find him reserved, civilized, and witty, dangerous only when he picks up a pen—or, actually, typewriter—to write a poem. I once reviewed his *Tennis Court Oath* unfavorably, but I did not, as Lehman claims in another book, and Richard Howard alludes to in *Alone with America*, call it garbage. I merely quoted from the autobiographical poem "Europe" the line "He had mistaken his book for garbage," adding that "I do not think it is up to us to know better than the poet."

I knew Koch at Harvard equally slightly. He did me the kindness of getting a couple of my poems into the *Harvard Advocate*, on whose board he was. Frank O'Hara I would glimpse around Harvard, and probably spoke to at the Poets' Theatre, where he was very active and I acted in two plays. I never laid eyes on James Schuyler, and for a long time knew him only as the librettist of Paul Bowles's *Picnic Cantata*, an LP of which I own and enjoy.

I must also state that the review of Ashbery's play *The Compromise* in the Cambridge broadsheet *Audience* was not, as Lehman speculates, by me; everything I published there was signed, as the byline was one's only recompense. I learn from Lehman that this review, though mostly favorable, elicited an "Ode," jointly written by O'Hara and Schuyler, that starts out lampooning me and then proceeds to one of the "harmonious workings of two 'quite singular' sensibilities." The best lines, as quoted by Lehman, begin: "if I did go out on the fire escape and piss on myself in the rain/ which is, I suppose, the male equivalent of a good cry/ I might not ever want to come in again/ I would be emptying myself forever like a masthead for love." Who, I wonder, in this harmonious outpouring, is the pisser on the fire escape, O'Hara or Schuyler? For all their kindred sensibilities, they were not, after all, Siamese twins.

To be sure, some of the NYS poets had, as I learn from the book, uncanny resemblances: "On different occasions both Ashbery's mother and O'Hara's companion were fooled [on the phone] into thinking that one was the other." Even in the flesh, with her back turned, Mrs. Ashbery once mistook Frank for her son. And sure enough, many a NYS poem could have been written by another member of the group.

Which is not to say that there are no salient differences. French, of which they were fond, has apt terms for all four of our poets—what I would call the 4F categories. For Ashbery, *fumiste*; for O'Hara, *flâneur*; for Koch, *farceur*; and for Schuyler, "who was prone to psychotic fits [and] spent most of his life in and out of psychiatric institutions," *fou*. Let me investigate them, and Lehman's treatment of them, one by one. If what follows is more a polemic than a review, let me point out that Lehman's book is more a panegyric than a serious work of criticism.

For Ashbery—whom the poet-critic Thomas M. Disch refers to as "the poet-laureate of spaciness," whom James Dickey called "a very difficult and perhaps impossible poet," and about whom William Arrowsmith wrote, "I have no idea most of the time what Mr. Ashbery is talking about or being. . . his characteristic gesture is an effete and cerebral whimsy"—Lehman has nothing but praise. In *Beyond Amazement*, a collection of essays about Ashbery that he edited and contributed to, Lehman declared, "Ashbery's poetry [is] far from inaccessible; on the contrary, it could be said to open up a path of entry to whole areas of consciousness that could not otherwise be reached."

In *The Last Avant-Garde*, Lehman holds up many poems and passages from Ashbery for our admiration. Here, from what is described as one of his "most admired" poems, is the beginning:

They dream only of America
To be lost among the thirteen million pillars of grass:
"This honey is delicious
Though it burns the throat"

And hiding from darkness in barns
They can be grownups now
And the murderer's ashtray is more easily—
The lake a lilac cube

He holds a key in his right hand

"Please," he asks willingly,
He is thirty years old. . . .

It seems that "it is possible to read this haunting poem as an allegory about
the poet's relationship to Pierre Martory." Martory was Ashbery's lover for
some of the ten years the poet lived in Paris. How such a relationship lends
itself to allegory—and just what here is allegorical as opposed to, say,
aleatoric—is not explained. But to give you a sense of Lehman the exegete,
take "the strangeness of the adverb in the line '"Please," he asks willingly,' is
not easily explained, and that is one of its virtues." What its other virtues
are, we are not told.

Now here is something from a later piece, "A Love Poem," one of "the
great works of [Ashbery's] maturity":

> The dripping is in the walls, within sleep
> Itself. I mean there is no escape
> From me, from it. The night is itself asleep
> And what goes on in it, the naming of
> the wind. Our notes to each other, always
>   repeated, always the same.

Such marvels came from Ashbery "for more than thirty years, as long a
stretch of sustained creative productivity as any American poet has enjoyed." And why not, if one considers Ashbery's method, as described in an
earlier Lehman book, *The Line Forms Here*: "Ashbery approaches his
typewriter once a week or so to write poetry, confident that he will tap his
unconscious in the very act of tapping the keys." And "should the phone
ring during the hour or so . . . he'll welcome the interruption—and allow it
to modify the poem in progress."

Lehman's hero-worship of the NYS's *chef d'école* is often ludicrous bordering on the pitiful. When Ashbery goes to France on a Fulbright, he is
"like the hero in a medieval romance embarking on a test, a quest, and an
adventure." When W. H. Auden, not caring much for either O'Hara's or
Ashbery's submission to the Yale Younger Poets Series in 1956, nevertheless
had to choose between them, he "was as though thrust into the position of
God choosing between the gifts of Cain and Abel." And Lehman adds,
"The competition for Auden's nod stands somewhere behind the epistolary
quarrel between O'Hara and Ashbery on the question of which of the two
was more like the James Dean figure in Elia Kazan's *East of Eden* (1956)."
Lehman devotes the next three pages to the running argument between
two silly queens (my term) about who looked more like James Dean.

Gush like "brilliant," "seminal," and "diabolically clever" proliferates. "Ashbery's poems," we read,

> defeat the analytical methods. . . . Like mysterious equations in which the terms take on multiple values, they cannot be easily reduced to syllogisms. The effort to make conventional sense of the poems would be wasted; rather, the reader should approach them without preconception, or with the willingness to allow expectation to be dashed. ["Please," we should say willingly.] For Ashbery . . . the poem is the performance of experience rather than the commentary on the experience. [By that token, the performance of a sexual act, say, is a poem. Does it even have to be written down?] So radical a departure from the norm is this that critics today are still catching up with poems Ashbery composed nearly half a century ago.

Personally, I have given up trying to catch up with them; I prefer to keep a safe distance.

The reader can conclude from what I have quoted, or from any poem of Ashbery's he might open by way of *sortes Vergilianae*, that all this is sheer camping, sheer nonsense, or, as the French would call it, *fumisterie*. A *fumiste* is, literally, an oven repairman or chimney sweep. The fin-de-siècle wits, with regard to all the smoke and obfuscation, turned the word into argot for a fake artist or pretentious poetaster, or, as the Larousse has it, a *mystificateur, mauvais plaisant*. Or an Ashbery. We read, "Poems are 'going on all the time in my head and I occasionally spin off a length,' Ashbery has said." That's the old sausage machine method: you let the meat be ground a while, then you arbitrarily cut it off, wrap it in casing, and presto, a sausage—I mean, a poem.

But Ashbery's greatness is not confined to his poetry. His "incidental literary criticism adds more to our literary knowledge than any score of scholarly dissertations." That may indeed be true when you consider Lehman's idea of a scholarly dissertation. After quoting from a poem of O'Hara's in which "the most ordinary of activities seems endowed with a nobility"—to wit "the Manhattan Storage Warehouse,/ Which they'll soon tear down. I/ used to think they had the Armory/ Show there"—Lehman comments, "A thesis could be written on O'Hara's error." I dare say twenty such might begin to equal one piece of Ashbery's incidental criticism.

What, however, about Lehman's criticism? In *The Last Avant-Garde*, he speculates a good deal about a relationship between Ashbery's titles, with which the poet begins, and their texts, with the text of a poem having apparently nothing to do with its title. He must have forgotten his interview with Ashbery, in which the poet pronounced,

Very often my poems diverge from the areas or concerns the title has announced, and I think it's profitable in this way to add a further dimension to poetry. I mean, one can write a poem "To a Waterfowl" [as Ashbery has done, stooping to despoil poor Bryant] that has nothing to do with waterfowls, and the reader is obliged to consider the poem as somehow related to the subject indicated only in the title.

If this is not *fumisterie*, I don't know what is: not only writing the poem to a cheaply prankish title, but also erecting a whole *ars poetica* on this campy procedure. To be sure, Lehman opines, "camp, like any other style, can furnish the technical means to ends that are serious and complex." Accordingly, he reports seriously that "Ashbery persuaded Koch that 'shapely as an amoeba' was a better simile than 'shapeless as an amoeba.'" This is what Lehman calls "the poets [getting] a contact high from one another." With equal seriousness, he quotes Ashbery: "As I have gotten older, it seems to me that time is what I have been writing about during all these years when I thought I wasn't writing about anything." Proof, I think, that one should always trust one's first impressions.

ABOUT FRANK O'HARA, Lehman has scarcely less reverential things to say, although none as poignant as this sentence: "O'Hara's father died while he was at Harvard, and his journals of the period show him in a soul-searching mood." (Given Lehman's faulty syntax, one wonders how this poetical father, dying at Harvard as a mere youth, found time for marriage, procreation, and soul-searching.) Son Frank, however, was an unsoul-searching *flâneur*. Most of his poems are street poems (derived from Apollinaire's *poème promenade*) in which O'Hara records his *flâneries*, or else "list poems" in which he enumerates whatever comes to his mind with perfect Whitmania. "Personal Poem," for example, begins with a walk at lunchtime, then describes meeting up with LeRoi Jones. They walk and eat together as the poem continues:

> we get some fish and some ale it's
> cool but crowded we don't like Lionel Trilling
> we decide. We like Don Allen we don't like
> Henry James so much we like Herman Melville. . . .

and ends:

> I wonder if one person out of the 8,000,000 is
> thinking of me as I shake hands with LeRoi

and buy a strap for my wristwatch and go
back to work happy at the thought possibly so

Note the absurd use, or lack, of punctuation and the inane enjambment that, as the NYS fantasizes, turns prose into poetry. But Lehman evaluates, "So casual and spontaneous is this poem, so committed to the rhythms of actual speech, that the reader may not even hear the closing rhyme. And that is as it should be: the music is at the heart of the noise, the poetry something subtle in the midst of all that seems wildly antipoetic." The poem is thirty-four wildly antipoetic lines long, but ends with two lines rhyming, albeit so discreetly we may not even notice it, and indeed shouldn't. Yet the rhyme is "the music at the heart of the noise," the hidden poetry for whose sake we must put up with thirty-two lines of noise. What Lehman fails to mention is that all thirty-four lines, rhyming or not, are equally banal.

THERE IS NO END to the grandiose claims Lehman makes for the Four Horsemen of the NYS. Thus a verse about a bank teller, "Miss Stillwagon (first name Linda I once heard)," "has an interest beyond the sass in the speaker's voice, it helps evoke a once commonplace situation remote from us today, used as we have been to automatic teller machines and the universal American first-name basis." The source of the line is "The Day Lady Died," a putative elegy for Billie Holiday. It is not until the concluding five lines of the poem that O'Hara remembers Lady Day, which Lehman justifies as putting "the poem into the company of other great elegies, notably Milton's 'Lycidas.'" So, too, we learn that "O'Hara's poetic preoccupation with Miles Davis . . . and with Billie Holiday . . . is evidence less of white-negroism than of peerless aesthetic taste." The grand conclusion is "it could be said that if all that survived of 1959 was 'The Day Lady Died,' then historians a century hence could piece together the New York of that moment." Note the poor grammar and syntax, and poorer judgment.

Gilding by association, as in O'Hara-Milton, is one of Lehman's favorite ploys. Kenneth Koch's "poems are unthinkable without a meat-and-potatoes diet of Ovid, Ariosto, Lorca, Pasternak, Mayakovsky, and a dozen French poets," though Lehman doesn't make clear for whom this diet is prescribed: the poet, the reader, or both. He situates Koch in the tradition of satire's "greatest practitioners," Pope and Byron, as he elsewhere brackets Schuyler with Montaigne. Koch's poetry "demands to be read in the context of . . . Rabelais, Lord Byron, Lewis Carroll, and Oscar Wilde," even as Ashbery is "in the visionary company" of Wordsworth, Emerson, and Stevens. O'Hara and Schuyler "revised the lyric model" of Whitman,

Crane, and Williams, and "Ashbery resembles Kierkegaard in the quality of his irony."

Such gilt by association climaxes in the comparison of Koch's two circus poems, "Circus" and the much later "Circus II," which Lehman uses both in class and in public lectures. To choose between them, it seems, is to choose, as Lehman asks his hearers to do, "between art and life. In terms derived from William Blake," one stands for innocence, the other for experience. "In Schiller's terms, the first 'Circus' is naïve, the second sentimental. . . . In Wallace Stevens's terms, the first represents the principle of the imagination, the second that of reality." Indeed, "the second is like Koch's version of Coleridge's 'Dejection Ode.'" All this show apropos of two poems by our *farceur* from which I quote:

> "What is death in the circus? That depends on if it's spring. Then, if elephants are there, *mon père*, we are not completely lost. Oh the sweet strong odor of beasts which laughs at decay! Decay! Decay! we are like the elements in a kaleidoscope But such passions we feel! bigger than the beaches and Rustier than harpoons." After this speech the circus practitioner sat down.

And the second:

> I never mentioned my friends in my poems at the time I wrote The Circus
> Although they meant almost more than anything to me
> Of this now for some time I've felt an attenuation
> So I'm mentioning them maybe this will bring them back to me
> Not them perhaps but what I felt about them
> John Ashbery Jane Freilicher Larry Rivers Frank O'Hara
> their names alone bring tears to my eyes. . . .

As to which of the poems is greater, Lehman avers, "I know the answer, but my lips are sealed," surely an aporia worthy of Jesting Pilate.

It should not surprise us that Lehman, as he says, decided to become a poet when taking his only writing course ever as a Columbia sophomore from Koch, and also by reading Donald Allen's notorious anthology *The New American Poetry*—and especially O'Hara's "Why I Am Not a Painter" contained in it. This "made poetry seem as natural as breathing, as casual as the American idiom, and so imbued with metropolitan irony and bohemian glamour as to be irresistible." He does not, however, tell us what made him also espouse literary criticism, samples of which follow.

"Koch, our funniest poet, has had the misfortune to be a protean genius at a moment when the lyric poem is the be-all and end-all of verse and is mistakenly held to be incompatible with the spirit of comedy." It is elementary knowledge that comic verse has never fallen out of esteem, but is held, now as before, to be light verse rather than poetry, with the exception of Pope and Byron, Chaucer and some epigrams by Rochester and Belloc. Koch, whose entire output traffics in sometimes funny, sometimes unfunny burlesque verse, has not been critically shortchanged.

Now here is Lehman on James Schuyler, whose "Freely Espousing" is "a brief statement of his poetics." For Schuyler, "who is sparing with figurative language, the literal description suffices more often than not, making similes seem supererogatory." So Lehman quotes admiringly from the abovementioned poem: "The sinuous beauty of words like allergy/ the tonic resonance of/ pill when used as in/ 'she is a pill'/ on the other hand I am not going to espouse any short stories in which lawn mowers clack." After quoting from another Schuyler poem, "there is a dull book with me,/ an apple core, cigarettes,/ an ashtray," Lehman comments, "the unembellished 'apple core' is sufficient to suggest the mythic dimensions of another lost garden paradise."

This kind of associative diarrhea is frequent. Koch told a student that "The Lost Golf Ball" would be a good title for an abstract painting because, though people looking for the ball would not find it, "they'll look more closely at the painting." From this, Lehman leaps to these lines of Schuyler's: "Kenneth Koch/ could teach a golf ball/ how to write pantoums," as if this juxtaposition shed critical light on either poet. Similarly, from among questions "as compelling today as when Koch first asked them," Lehman cites "Is there no one who feels like a pair of pants?"; Lehman then finds a "shared aesthetic" in the following from "Personism," O'Hara's poetic manifesto: "that's just common sense: if you're going to buy a pair of pants you want them to be tight enough so everyone will want to go to bed with you." A manifesto all right, but not exactly a poetic one.

Again, the ending of Schuyler's "Korean Mums" is "a notable example of an allegory emerging from literal truth": "what/ is there I have not forgot?/ or one day will forget;/ this garden, the breeze/ in stillness, even/ the words, Korean mums." But does not all allegory take off from a literal meaning, and just what is allegorized here? Lehman perceives "a case of exact identity between 'the words' and what they mean." Is *that* the allegory then? Lehman probably knows, but once again prefers to keep mum. Or mums.

Here is a further example from Ashbery, who "does to conventional syntax what Robespierre did to the monarchy." "When the poet remarks . . . that we . . . 'have been given no help whatever/ In decoding our own man-size quotient and must rely/ On second-hand knowledge' the *hand* in that phrase vibrates with meaning, like the sound of one hand clapping." Has exegesis ever been more elucidating? So, too, when O'Hara writes "to be more revolutionary than a nun/ is our desire, to be secular and intimate/ as, when sighting a redcoat, you smile/ and pull the trigger," Lehman helpfully explicates that it "is conceivable that the 'redcoat' O'Hara envisions was a coat of red paint," though I am more inclined to see it as a coat to be worn over skintight pants making everyone want to go to bed with you.

But then Lehman lauds crazy Schuyler for seeing "the poetic possibilities of the laundry list," as in this "quintessential" passage, "unglib, fresh, and free of fake language," from the poem "Things to Do": "Walk three miles/ a day beginning tomorrow./ Alphabetize./ Purchase nose-hair shears./ Answer letters./ Elicit others./ Write Maxine./ Move to Maine./ Give up NoCal./ See more movies./ Practice long distance dialing." How odd that Lehman doesn't see NoCal as a tribute to a fellow *fou*, Robert Lowell. But Lehman's sharpest moment comes when, in Gertrude Stein's *Stanzas of Meditation*, much admired by Ashbery, he notes that "in one poem . . . Stein places periods in the middle of sentences—an experimental move that still seems fresh today." Fresh? I'd say downright impudent.

There are, moreover, errors of every stripe. *Cadavre exquis* is not a "one-line poem"; Baudelaire is not the inventor of the prose poem, which harks back to Bertrand and Guérin, if not indeed to Evariste Parny. You cannot write "neither true or false" in good English, any more than *bête noir* in either English or French. We read that the NYS poets' pleasure would have been diminished if any of them "felt that the others' approbation were automatic." Lehman makes the common error of using *paraphrasing* to mean twisting someone else's phrase around for effect; he often misuses *supernal* for something like sublime, and he subliterately employs *critique* as a verb.

Again, a steady refrain does not *orchestrate* a poem. In a sentence about Pierre Reverdy, the singular *poetry* makes a poor antecedent for the plural "their enchantment." *Astrological* is misused for astronomical. "O'Hara's 'exoticism' of blacks" is extremely clumsy. Baudelaire's *mauvais vitrier* is a *bad* glazier, not an *evil* one, and the prose poem wherein the glazier occurs does not end with cries of "Life is beautiful!"—*Vivre en beauté* means "live in high style." But then Lehman's French allows for *jeu du* [*sic*] *paume* and *Bibliotheque de l'Arsénale* [accent missing, *arsénal* feminized], his Italian Hispanicizes Francesco Parmigianino into *Francisco*; his German takes *Schadenfreude* to mean envy.

But Lehman is at his least appealing in his continual aggrandizing, as when Ashbery becomes a "hero in a fantastic tale," because a bookstore he bought something from supposedly vanished without a trace when he next looked for it. So Koch is a "poet of the highest originality" because he "has revived the epic and the drama as viable vehicles for verse [surely that statement has been stood on its head] and revealed an uncanny knack for marrying unusual forms to unconventional matter." It takes only a cursory glance at Koch's verse drama or verse epic (and isn't epic ipso facto verse?) to ascertain the hopelessness of each. As for pantoums and sestinas, they can no more be helped by unconventional matter than that matter can be ennobled by marriage to them.

David Lehman studied with Kenneth Koch, who "convert[ed] a generation of Columbia students into sorcerer's apprentices." He was the colleague of John Ashbery both on the faculty of Brooklyn College and at *Newsweek*, where he reviewed books and Ashbery art. With *The Last Avant-Garde*, he proffers a collegial and sorcerer's apprentice tribute to them and their NYS fellows. Whether he has rendered a similar service to his readers remains open to doubt.

In *The Line Forms Here*, Lehman wrote, "For many of us, any key or code to the poems—however ingeniously put forth—might well work to diminish rather than enhance our delight." Ashbery's poetry "induces [a] state of mystified alertness that only the most intense esthetic experiences can afford." One of Ashbery's most cited and debated nonsense phrases, "Murk plectrum," may have finally acquired its critical counterpart in Lehman's murk spectrum.

October 1998

A Satyr Against Mankind

Stefan Beck

NOVELISTS TODAY TEND to be pretty bloodless creatures. Look at their bios: they're mostly workshop professors or M.F.A. hatchlings. They review their peers' books, sit on grant panels, give readings and interviews, and, during their free time, cook up soft-boiled bores to pay their children's tuition.

None of that for Michel Houellebecq! The French author, lately of *The Possibility of an Island*, is an old-style *enfant terrible*: more lecherous than Pepys; more bibulous than Hemingway; more wretched than his own dim lodestar, H. P. Lovecraft (*The Possibility of an Island* by Michel Houllebecq; Knopf 2006). Here, for illustration's sake, is what Emily Eakin wrote for *The New York Times* of her visit to Houellebecq:

> Houellebecq answered the door in stocking feet . . . and ushered me into the living room. He curled up in a chair with a pack of Silk Cuts and a bottle of Jim Beam and hardly moved for the entire weekend. . . .
>
> By the time we sat down to dinner—in the living room—he was too inebriated to eat. He picked at his boiled crab and got some of it on his sleeve. His head began to nod; his eye-lids drooped. But for the first time all day, he looked almost cheerful. "I am the star of French literature," he slurred. "The most radical one of all." He reached over and petted my knee. "What's your name again?" he mumbled. "How would you like to be in my erotic film?"

Despite that drunken boast, he's as self-loathing and -destructive as they come, a fellow for whom razor blades and cyanide tablets would be perfect stocking stuffers. In his book-length canticle *H. P. Lovecraft: Against the World, Against Life*, he writes matter-of-factly, "Of course, life has no meaning. But neither does death" (*H. P. Lovecraft: Against the World*, by Michel Houellebecq; Believer Books, 150 pages, $18).

Then why write so much?

Houellebecq has produced five books—a few of them bestsellers—to say nothing of his Lovecraft treatise, a great deal of poetry, and articles not translated into English. He's earned the praise of *The Wall Street Journal* and the Irish novelist John Banville; he's been denounced by the *Times* critic Michiko Kakutani and is disdained by the French literary establishment.

In 2001, the BBC made a documentary about him, of which the *Guardian*'s Suzie Mackenzie wrote, "I don't remember a single frame in which Houellebecq appears with another human being, though there is a scene of him in a stairwell throwing a ball at his revolting corgi."

In 2002, Houellebecq, having told the magazine *Lire* that Islam is "the dumbest religion," was brought on trial in Paris for "inciting religious hatred." He denied that he hates Muslims, but maintained his "contempt" for Islam and proclaimed the Koran's literary mediocrity.

In an amusing turn, Houellebecq confessed that he'd never read the French penal code. "It is excessively long," he quipped, "and I suspect that there are many boring passages." He was acquitted.

So he's a hell-raiser, and seems to enjoy it. His books have sold in the hundreds of thousands; he seems to enjoy writing them. The question, then, is, "Why isn't this man smiling?"

The short answer is that Houellebecq's novels describe the decay both of the civilized world and, on a smaller scale, of individual human relationships. For Houellebecq and his dismal characters, the life of man is solitary, poor, nasty, brutish, and long.

In the early pages of Houellebecq's first novel, *Whatever* (a fitting, albeit inaccurate, translation of its pompous French title, *Extension du domaine de la lutte*), his nameless narrator tells us that he isn't concerned with "varying states of soul, character traits, etc." His aim, rather, is

> to prune. To simplify. To demolish, one by one, a host of details. In this I will be aided by the simple play of historical forces. The world is becoming more uniform before our eyes; telecommunications are improving; apartment interiors are enriched by new gadgets. Human relationships become progressively impossible, which greatly reduces the quantity of anecdote that goes to make up a life.

Call it fair warning. The last thing Houellebecq's books deliver is quantity *or* quality of anecdote; indeed, they are catalogues of life's most mundane, not to say Sisyphean, activities: getting drunk, watching television, preparing frozen dinners, and getting drunk again.

In keeping with this, both *Whatever* and Houellebecq's second book, the best-selling *Elementary Particles*, begin at the sort of dull, insufferable office party that lucky readers will recognize only from sitcoms and movies. The scene in the former case is especially dispiriting, and, in that regard, emblematic of the world Houellebecq intends to show us. The narrator silently endures an inane conversation between female co-workers, about their "right" to wear miniskirts ("The last dismaying dregs of the collapse of feminism," he thinks to himself). Then he passes out: "On waking I realized I'd thrown up on the moquette. . . . I concealed the vomit under a pile of cushions, then got up to try and get home. It was then that I found I'd lost my car keys."

Things go from bad to worse; for Houellebecq, life is rarely more than a succession of humiliations. When he returns to the area for his car the next day, he can't find it: "Every street looked to be the one. The Rue Marcel-Sembat, Rue Marcel-Dassault . . . there were a lot of Marcels about." This, it turns out, is rather like the feeling of reading Houellebecq's oeuvre: you're going round in circles, and there are a lot of Michels about.

Reading a Houellebecq novel—and this is perhaps most true of *Whatever*—is like reading the author's own hateful, defeated (but often very funny) diary. *Whatever*'s narrator is a software technician; Houellebecq was a software technician. Several of the narrator's colleagues were Houellebecq's colleagues. (He hasn't even changed their names.) And, as Houellebecq is happy to admit, the narrator's unhappy preoccupation with sex is *very* much the author's own. Concupiscence may be his most notorious quality.

When his narratives detour from day-to-day misery, they arrive in the thick of pure pornography—where he is always the star. This is curious, of course, given that he is inclined to blame false freedom—the intellectual and sexual "liberations" of the 1960s—for much of what is manifestly wrong with Western societies. Sex, specifically sex with women far younger than he, is the only thing that makes Houellebecq (and his surrogates) the least bit happy, if happiness it be. (The *Times* profile quoted above claims that Houellebecq sleeps with about two dozen women per year, with his wife's enthusiastic approval.)

Both *The Elementary Particles* and *Platform* revolve around this proclivity. (*Whatever* does as well, but to a lesser extent.) Houellebecq regards sex as another aspect of human interaction that has been conquered by "market forces," and thereby cheapened, made into a source of "injustice" and shame. In *The Elementary Particles*, he writes of Bruno, one of the protagonists:

> While he was a teenager, the fierce economic competition French society had known for two hundred years abated. . . . But human beings are quick to establish hierarchies and keen to feel superior to their peers. . . . Unexpectedly, this great middle class of laborers and office workers—or, rather, their sons and daughters—were to discover a new sport in which to compete. . . . Patrick Castelli, a young French boy in his class, succeeded in fucking thirty-seven girls in the space of three weeks. Over the same period, Bruno managed to score zero. In the end he flashed his prick at a shop assistant in a supermarket; luckily, the girl broke out laughing and did not press charges.

In *Whatever*, we meet Bernard, a grotesque virgin doomed to lonely agony by these viciously competitive mores. In *The Elementary Particles*, the two half-brothers Bruno and Michel suffer through equally pathetic lives. Bruno, a priapic, frustrated loser, winds up in an institution; Michel, a molecular biologist disgusted with mankind, works toward the creation of a superior species. *Platform*, the most controversial but least ambitious of Houellebecq's books, settles for clinically detailed descriptions of a sex tourist's Third World "adventures." It is not difficult to identify a progression toward greater and greater prurience and provocation.

Platform culminates in an Islamist terrorist attack that presages the Bali nightclub bombings, but it has no other merit. Houellebecq is correct to attack the threat posed by Islamic fundamentalism, but he does nothing to decry the immorality that so horrifies the West's enemies. Rather, he wallows in it. Michel in *The Elementary Particles* was, like Houellebecq himself, abandoned by an appallingly self-serving hippie mother. ("Houellebecq" is the surname of the author's beloved grandmother, who cared for him during his childhood years.) But neither the character nor his creator takes any practical lesson from his tragedy. He becomes the thing he hates.

From *Whatever* to *Platform*, the only god to which Houellebecq pays obeisance is despair. It's no wonder he adores Lovecraft, the nihilistic progenitor of what Houellebecq calls a "rigorously material" brand of horror. He writes of Cthulhu, Lovecraft's memorably ridiculous octopus-headed, bat-winged monster: "What is Great Cthulhu? An arrangement of electrons, like us. . . . From his journeys to the penumbral worlds of the unutterable, Lovecraft did not return to bring us good news."

In other words, not only does nothing exist beyond our material world, but also—and worse still—all this world can offer us is violent and unrelenting terror. Yet what, exactly, qualifies Houellebecq to talk about the hopelessness of *our* world?

He is honest, "authentic." This may *truly* be the last refuge of the scoundrel, but at least it affords us a clear picture of the way he conducted his research. The man seems to have limited his interactions with women to bars, package resorts, and sex clubs. This is, if true, more or less like basing one's judgment of mankind on life in a whorehouse.

Houellebecq has immersed himself in the ugliest expressions of human nature, and he expects us to accept that this represents all there is. The fact that so many people who know better—from their own experience—are willing to play along is without question the most upsetting aspect of his fame. Consider Banville's conclusion to a slavering appreciation in the April/May 2005 issue of *Bookforum*: "If we are to take him at his word . . . [Houellebecq] achieves a profound insight into the nature of our collective death wish." Does Banville himself really feel that death wish? And even if he does, do *we*?

What is true of some is not true of all, and to assume the contrary would be mere laziness on the part of the author and his partisans. Of course, Houellebecq doesn't assume any such thing. He may be genuinely despondent, but his insistence that this is man's natural state is pure marketing.

As for his fans, they only fake faith in his contrarian and degenerate ethos; they certainly don't live it. But why? Morbid curiosity, as with the hordes of housewives who swooned for James Frey's phony addiction chronicles? And if they appreciate "profound insight" into the "death wish," whether personal or collective, why don't they ask of their authors that they discourage it, that they hold up something in its stead? Maybe because they conceive of it as nothing more than a frightening curiosity, something to be marveled at and then put safely back on the shelf. Maybe it merely titillates—the mean and shabby appeal of pornography.

Whatever the case, Houellebecq is weeping all the way to the bank.

His latest effort, *The Possibility of an Island*, essentially confesses this (*The Possibility of an Island*, by Michel Houellebecq; Knopf, 352 pages, $24.95). Houellebecq's narrator is, for a change, not Michel but Daniel—an innocent in the lion's den. He is an outrageous, foul-mouthed comedian, who reveals himself at the outset: "To give some context, here is one of the jokes that peppered my shows: 'Do you know what they call the fat stuff around the vagina?' 'No.' 'The woman.'"

Daniel, like Houellebecq, knows full well that he's a carnival barker, exploiting for profit the willful stupidity of his audience, its greedy appetite for the very nihilism that will destroy it. He expands: "I managed to throw in that kind of thing, whilst still getting good reviews in *Elle* and *Télérama*."

One can draw an easy parallel between Houellebecq and the late Hunter S. Thompson: Houellebecq's life, much like Thompson's suicide, would be a valuable object lesson were his enthusiasts not so blind to its meaning, or lack thereof. The best that can be said of Houellebecq is that this latest work (probably his last commercially successful one, since the scam of rewriting the same book again and again can hardly sustain itself) insults and rejects his readers in just the way that they deserve.

In short, *Island* redeems Houellebecq, by shining pitiless Klieg lights on the premeditated squandering of his career. The book is his first to treat the real problem behind his and the West's decline, honestly and responsibly: the fetishization of youth and novelty. One of his funniest and deadliest passages appears when Daniel is interviewed by a writer for a women's magazine similar to *Cosmopolitan*. She tells Daniel of her boss's concept for a new publication:

> The following morning, I passed by his office, and he explained a little bit more. The magazine was to be called *Lolita*. "It's a question of a gap in the market . . ." he said. I understood more or less what he meant: *20 Ans*, for example, was bought mainly by fifteen- or sixteen-year-old girls, who wanted to be emancipated in all things, sex in particular; with *Lolita*, he wanted to find the opposite gap in the market. "Our target readership starts at ten years old . . ." he said, "but there is no upper limit." His bet was that, more and more, mothers would tend to copy their daughters.

The notion that what appeals to a ten-year-old girl will appeal to a fifty-year-old woman isn't misogyny; it is, to anyone with even a passing familiarity with the fashion and "lifestyle" magazine trade, a patent fact. It is the natural *reductio* of the trouble we're in: a world in which nothing frightens more than the prospect of growing older, less desirable, less relevant to the interminable bustle of sexual commerce.

The pathos of Houellebecq is that, however completely he understands this condition, he allows himself to be governed by it. He hates himself for being a withered ghoul. He frets incessantly over the decline in his sexual potency. Where a more mature and reasonable man would pursue marriage, children, and family, he desperately chases chemicals and sexual experiences to artificially prolong his youth. (These lead only to embarrassment and heartbreak: "I had left my coitus cream in Lutétia, and this was my first mistake . . . I sensed she was a little disappointed.")

There's nothing new or modern about fear of the twilight years. What's new is the undignified manner in which people like Michel Houellebecq shuffle toward the end. Simply, he's a coward.

Still, he isn't to be written off entirely. Our times offer numerous, un-precedented opportunities for degeneracy, and few know these and their consequences more intimately than those who let themselves be de-molished. He has something to tell us by his poor example.

Island is the product of a man who wishes it could have been other-wise, and who admits that desire, however obliquely, for the first time.

The book echoes *The Elementary Particles*, Houellebecq's earlier sojourn into science, in that it is a work of science fiction: "Daniel" is in fact "Daniel1," the first of a long series of super-rational clones created through the work of a religious cult called the Elohimites. The narration of the book alternates between Daniel1 and his distant, less entertaining successor, Daniel25.

(The Elohimites are based, to amusing effect, on the real-life Raël Movement, a UFO- and cloning-based "religion" founded by a French former performer and racecar driver, Claude Vorilhon. Categories in the "Frequently Asked Questions" on Rael.org include "Where is Eve, the clone baby?" and "I read in the papers that you have orgies. Is it true?" Houellebecq's attraction to the Raëlians—he reportedly "flirted" with the cult—couldn't be more obvious.)

The Daniels have a dog, reconstituted each time a Daniel dies, called Fox. Fox is, for Houellebecq, love personified. Even in the first pages of *Island*, he writes, "The advantage of having a dog for company lies in the fact that it is possible to make him happy; he demands such simple things, his ego is so limited. Possibly, in a previous era, women found themselves in a comparable situation."

In the London *Telegraph*, Tibor Fischer writes, "Houellebecq seems to have reached that Brigitte Bardot state of disillusionment where only dogs are truly admirable," but there is more to it than that. The little dog is not the last thing left for Houellebecq to love—it is, it certainly seems, the first thing he has loved in a long time. And *Island* shows a faint but unmistak-able change in its author's demeanor. Houellebecq has given up a little bit of his hatred for curiosity. Here is the great insight of Daniel25, speaking of the race to which he belongs:

> Our collective history, like our individual destinies, therefore appears, compared to that of the humans of the last period, peculiarly calm. . . . Daniel1 lives again in me, his body knows in mine a new incarnation, his thoughts are mine; his memories are mine; his existence actually prolongs itself in me, far more than man ever dreamed of prolonging himself through his descendants. My own life, however, I often think, is far from the one he would have liked to live.

Houellebecq's characters, like most deeply unhappy or suicidal people, lack imagination. They cannot posit an existence other than the one they're in, the one they hate. Houellebecq, likewise, is good at describing what he hates—but struck dumb when it comes time to name what he could love. ("Young girls" don't count.) So it's no small thing for Daniel25 to refer to the life his predecessor "would have liked to live." It's a nod toward the dream, the *domaine de la lutte*, to recall the French title of *Whatever*.

In that book, the narrator writes:

> Your total isolation, the sensation of an all-consuming emptiness, the foreboding that your existence is nearing a painful and definitive end all combine to plunge you into a state of real suffering.
> And yet you haven't always wanted to die.
> You had to enter the domain of the struggle. . . . You long believed in the existence of another shore; such is no longer the case.

By the time Daniel25 comes into being, no one searches for another shore, because there is no longer any ocean to cross. But he is correct to guess that no one would prefer that life, devoid of struggle, to which he and the other neohumans are doomed. (Lest Houellebecq's position on that point be in doubt, he shows us that the Elohimite future—a dystopia whose hedonism, even, lacks the vigor of Huxley's—was purchased, as the Radiant Future always is, with blood and lies.)

It was never either "peculiar calm" or life eternal that Daniel1 desired, only the possibility of happiness. But one man's failed or abandoned hunt for happiness, if the game is rigged from the start, is not literature. It's a propaganda of defeat.

Michel Houellebecq has banked on defeat for so long that he cannot even inch away from it without checking himself. With *Island*, he comes close to disowning his commercialized despair—but finds he has nothing to offer in its place. A suggestion, by way of a passage in *Whatever*. Our narrator is speaking of his psychiatrist:

> She took me to task for speaking in general, overly sociological, terms. This, according to her, was not interesting: instead I ought to try and involve myself, try and "get myself centred."
> —But I've had a bellyful of myself, I objected.

Have you, Michel? So have we all. But you're not dead yet, and it's never too late, after all, to try something different.

March 2006

McKim, Mead & White's Architectural Citizenship

Michael J. Lewis

ERNEST HEMINGWAY ONCE declared that "all modern American literature comes from one book by Mark Twain called *Huckleberry Finn*," a
claim so provocative that Lionel Trilling based an essay on it. Was it indeed
possible that Twain's picaresque adventure could be so influential? For
Trilling, the answer was yes, not because of its racial or social themes but
because of its language. Previously, antebellum America "was inclined to
think that the mark of the truly literary product was a grandiosity and
elegance not to be found in the common speech," hence the recurrent passages of stilted grandiloquence on the part of Cooper, Poe, and Melville.
But while "the language of ambitious literature was high and thus always in
danger of falseness, the American reader was keenly interested in the
actualities of daily speech." This meant, to a large extent, dialect, that instrument that is embarrassing to modern sensibilities but which for nineteenth-century America was limitlessly expressive of regional, class, and
racial meaning. Thought vulgar, dialect was shunned by self-consciously
literary writing, but humorous writing suffered no such inhibition.

Trilling's account can be extended to American architecture. There too
a similar stilted provincialism prevailed through the nineteenth century, its
mock Venetian storefronts and haughty Renaissance villas standing at prim
attention. But beneath the awkward grandiloquence, as with American
English, there lay a vernacular reality of remarkable hardiness and vitality.
Already practical builders had devised the cast iron front, the passenger
elevator, the balloon frame, and, by the early 1880s, the steel skeleton. The
American building, in fact, was novel and original in virtually every aspect
but the façade that was draped across it. It took Louis Sullivan and Frank
Lloyd Wright to strip away this drapery and to make buildings whose ar-
chitectural prose spoke the reality of construction, without straining after

imagined European standards. In this respect they are Twain's architectural counterpart.

Such an understanding of American architecture, however persuasive or attractive, cannot be kind to McKim, Mead & White, the firm founded in 1879 by Charles F. McKim, William Rutherford Mead, and Stanford White. Works such as the Boston Public Library, the Morgan Library, or their masterpiece, New York's Pennsylvania Station, are exercises in architectural formality of the most exacting sort. Far from shunning European standards of refinement and taste, these were perhaps the first American buildings to meet them. But a brilliant provincial is still a provincial, and the architects did not even have Cooper's excuse of having no indigenous models who might have shown him a better way. For when construction began on Penn Station in 1905, Sullivan had long since developed the modern steel-framed skyscraper (1891) and Frank Lloyd Wright had already created the Prairie Style house (1901). It is the blithe indifference to these developments on the part of McKim, Mead & White that constitutes the modernist indictment against them.

Of course, the event for which they are most famous has nothing to do with architecture at all: the murder of Stanford White. His killer was Harry Thaw, a young Pittsburgh millionaire who had the great misfortune to marry Evelyn Nesbit, the most alluring artist's model of her day. (She had been memorialized by, among other artists, Charles Dana Gibson, creator of the Gibson Girl.) On their honeymoon, Thaw learned that White had seduced her and kept her as a mistress; at the time of her seduction she was sixteen. Humiliated, Thaw decided to take his revenge in as public a manner as possible.

No celebrity murder, certainly not the squalid ones of recent memory, has matched the élan of White's. On June 25, 1906, he attended the debut of a cabaret entitled *Mamzelle Champagne*, performed on the rooftop cabaret of the old Madison Square Garden at Fifth Avenue and Twenty-sixth Street, a building he himself had designed. Just as the lead singer began to croon "I Could Love a Thousand Girls"—subsequently a detail of infinite delight to the tabloid press—Thaw approached the table where White sat and shot him three times. As he fell, his last sight would have been Augustus Saint-Gaudens's *Diana of the Tower*, the building's lovely weathervane that depicted the bronze goddess, nude and proud as she released her arrow.

The murder has exerted a perennial fascination on the public which did not subside when Thaw was acquitted for reasons of insanity in 1908. It was the subject of the 1955 film *The Girl in the Red Velvet Swing*, starring a young Joan Collins as Nesbit, as well as of the E. L. Doctorow novel *Ragtime*, also made into a film. White's death was memorable for it seemed to encapsulate the guiding principle of his life—the pursuit of beauty—in a particularly poignant way, even to his death at the feet of *Diana*, that banner of beauty. But it was also of a piece with his architecture. To unsympathetic critics, at least, it seemed to embody precisely what was wrong with the firm: they made frivolous buildings for frivolous people, costume architecture for debauched socialites, their Roman arcades masking both their steel framework and the squalid carryings-on within. The scandal and changing architectural fashions did their work. By the 1920s, the conventional wisdom was that McKim, Mead & White were mere façade architects. Their work seemed a quaint curiosity—difficult, to be sure, but not relevant, like painting on vellum or Morris dancing.

This conventional wisdom rested in large part, ironically, on the building that was their finest achievement, Penn Station. The commission came when A. J. Cassatt, the enterprising engineer who headed the Pennsylvania Railroad, decided to tunnel underneath the East River, something that could not be done before the invention of smokeless electric trains. Passengers would now glide swiftly into New York without the cumbersome transfer to ferryboats that formerly burdened the trip. There they would emerge from twenty-one subterranean tracks into a station of gargantuan proportions, a prodigy that stretched 780 feet between Seventh and Eight Avenues, and 430 feet from Thirty-first to Thirty-third streets. This station would greet arriving passengers as a portal to the city, although of a radically new sort, placed not at the periphery of the city but at its center. In program and essence, nothing could be more modern. Yet rather than evoking the industrial audacity of the undertaking, the architects enveloped the building's steel skeleton in a Roman colonnade of pink granite and clad its interior in Roman travertine.

Of course, the ancient world had no train stations, but it did have one large public building with multiple paths of movement: the Roman bath, a massive complex of vaulted public halls and various pools of different temperature. McKim had inspected the ruins of the Baths of Caracalla in 1902, when researching the design of the Mall in Washington, D.C., and he had even paid Italian urchins to wander about in it, so that he might study its capacity to move and orient a crowd. Now he based the central waiting room of his station on the bath's great tepidarium, enlarging it 20 percent in the process, and letting its broad passages welcome pedestrians to their track platforms rather than to tepid pools and steam rooms.

McKim, Mead & White believed that creative classicism—classicism informed by history, archaeology, and modern engineering—could solve any architectural problem that the contemporary world might offer. Penn Station was a demonstration of that philosophy; its demolition was a gleeful renunciation of it. In 1963, the railroad decided to destroy it, condemning it as a spurious copy of a Roman monument. An appalled architectural community, including such stalwart modernists as Louis I. Kahn and Philip Johnson, protested to no avail. The station was razed down to track level, keeping intact only the circulation system (something which not even an age of functionalism could improve upon). Its demolition was swiftly recognized as one of the most tragic acts of cultural vandalism in American history, summed up in Vincent Scully's oft-quoted lament for the station: "Through it one entered the city like a god. One scuttles in now like a rat."

The loss of Penn Station had far-reaching consequences, not only bringing about the rehabilitation of McKim, Mead & White but also launching the influential historic preservation movement. But while its willful destruction has been universally decried, it must be taken seriously, for it was based on principle. It was itself a form of architectural criticism, criticism of a rather muscular sort, rooted in a clear understanding of the task of architecture, and its duty to society and to the present. Without addressing this understanding, and without grounds stronger than mere nostalgia or a fashionable aversion to modernism, there can be no fair assessment of McKim, Mead & White. For we will never be able to praise them as definitively as our predecessors renounced them.

The conventional image of McKim, Mead & White as academic classicists is unfair. It is true that their office was the principal finishing school for American classicists, their alumni including Cass Gilbert, Whitney Warren, Henry Bacon, John Russell Pope, and both members of Carrère and Hastings; hundreds of other former draftsmen flooded into offices across the country. And it is true that the refined civic classicism that dominated the period from 1890 to about 1940 was in large measure created and guided by their example. But they themselves were hardly academics at all (collectively, they spent a total of but three years in a school of architecture). And they came by their classicism honestly, by a circuitous path through the Victorian period styles, which made their classicism the product of a quest and not of indoctrination.

Charles Follen McKim (1847–1909) was the son of a prominent Philadelphia Quaker, an abolitionist who helped launch the *Nation* magazine, which at its founding was the voice of radical Republicanism. The journal's art critic was the architect Russell Sturgis, an ardent Gothic Revivalist whose moralistic conception of art and architecture came verbatim from John Ruskin. After McKim withdrew from Harvard after an unhappy year, Sturgis offered him a berth in his office. McKim agreed, spent the summer of 1867 as an apprentice, and decided that architecture was to his liking. He sailed to Paris and enrolled at the École des Beaux-

Arts, where architecture was viewed not as a moral but as an aesthetic affair. Students were thoroughly grounded in the discipline of the floor plan, which was meant to embody the logic of the entire building in diagrammatic fashion. McKim's marvelously lucid plan for Penn Station has its origin in this education.

He remained in Paris from 1867 to 1870, when he returned to the United States and the office of H. H. Richardson, an architect with a similar Harvard/Paris pedigree. There McKim met a fellow draftsman, Stanford White (1853–1906), like McKim a redhead but otherwise a young man of a different temperament entirely. White was the son of the New York critic and bon vivant Richard Grant White (a regular in the *Nation* as well), from whom he evidently acquired his charm and panache and rather elastic understanding of the marital state. Stanford joined Richardson's office as a teenager, on the strength of his father's connections and his own precocious drawing skills. All of his training occurred on the job.

Richardson was in a formative phase when McKim and White were with him, emerging from the thicket of High Victorian eclecticism to arrive at his own personal style, a bold and brawny modern Romanesque that crystallized during the design and construction of Trinity Church, Boston (1872–1877). Both McKim and White assisted with this remarkable building. It showed that the two great architectural cultures of the nineteenth century, previously thought to be mutually exclusive, might be reconciled, and that the picturesque tradition of England might be brought under the academic discipline of France. For McKim, who had been caught between these two systems of thought, the synthesis was a revelation.

Another revelation was the odd way that Richardson ran his office. Chronically ill and bedridden for days on end, he delegated the development of a design to his assistants, coaxing it to refinement through verbal criticism and swift explanatory sketches. He was also notoriously reluctant to provide a binding design in advance, preferring to visit a building under construction and to judge it in the round, like sculpture, refining its details as it rose. In McKim's subsequent practice, these quirks of the Richardson method became a kind of theology.

So unlike were the temperaments of McKim and White, aesthetic and personal, that a third party was essential, if only to diffuse the element of personal contest in the creative exchange. This leavening agent—the Ringo, as it were, in the Lennon-McCartney collaboration—was William Rutherford Mead (1846–1928), a figure so bland that he was affectionately nicknamed "Dummy" by his partners. Mead was the son of a lawyer from Brattleboro, Vermont, and like McKim he spent a term in the office of Russell Sturgis. He too had literary connections: his sister married William Dean

Howells, the novelist and essayist, for whom the firm designed one of its earliest houses. (Howells repaid the favor by burlesquing White in *The Rise of Silas Lapham*.) Mead handled office administration, and although he was characteristically self-effacing—he once joked that his sole duty was to keep McKim and Mead from "making damn fools of themselves"—he was in fact a fluent planner in his own right, as his floor plan for the Rhode Island Capitol shows.

Such was the triumvirate of McKim, Mead & White, which was formed in 1879. For the first decade of their practice, their fame rested almost exclusively on their domestic architecture. These resolutely vernacular buildings were informed by two extended sketching tours, one in 1877 devoted to the colonial architecture of New England and another the following year along the Rhône to Avignon and Nîmes. Looking at their early work, it is easy to see the lingering shadow of Richardson, particularly in the muscular abstraction of such buildings as the Low House in Bristol, Rhode Island (1887), the entire house treated as one broad shallow gable whose eaves nearly touch the ground. Or the Lovely Lane Methodist Church in Baltimore (1883), whose burly stone tower tapers expressively like the entasis of a Doric column. By the middle of the 1880s, the architects were already drifting toward classicism (in part because they were now winning more formal civic commissions), but the lessons of free composition stayed with them: an appreciation for the abstract force of a sculptural shape, an ability to compose freely in spatial terms, and a feel for chromatic effects.

In 1887, McKim, Mead & White received the commission for the Boston Public Library, which changed the course of their career. It was their first large public building, and on its planning and construction they lavished eight years, studying and restudying its details. Such a deliberate, measured pace was more characteristic of the architectural culture of Europe than that of America, where construction was a pragmatic affair, shaped by the demands of commercial speculation and unrestrained by official standards of taste and decorum. Also novel was the building's rich decorative program of painting and sculpture, with contributions from Saint-Gaudens, John Singer Sargent, and Daniel Chester French. Here the architects seem to have been inspired by Richardson's Trinity Church, which stood across Copley Square and also had a sumptuous program of mural painting, and which they evidently sought to match.

Long before the Boston Public Library opened in 1895 it had decisively altered the course of McKim, Mead & White's career. In place of their languid summer houses there now came an avalanche of monumental civic commissions: the Rhode Island State Capitol (1891), the Agriculture Building at the World's Columbian Exhibition in Chicago (1893), both Columbia and New York universities (both begun in 1894), and the critical expansion of the Metropolitan Museum of Art (1904). In these projects, the exceptionally dynamic collaboration of McKim and White came into its own.

Of course architecture, more than any other of the creative arts, is congenial to collaboration. Any building of complexity is designed incrementally, from idea sketches to preliminary proposals to the finalized contract drawing—and until the actual start of construction, all of these might be discarded and the process of study begun again. At the same time, a design is refined as the drawing increases in scale. The earliest sketches are thumbnails and are diagrammatic but at each successive restudy they are drawn as larger scale, reaching one quarter inch to a foot, one inch to a foot, and occasionally, in the case of ornamental detail, one to one. With each enlargement of scale, new aesthetic issues are raised, as a feature that was but a line in a thumbnail sketch expands to become a wide band, requiring detailing and development. Because of this sequential working process, verbal criticism is possible—even essential—at every stage, for which reason the studio critique is the essence of architectural education.

Unless such criticism is brought to bear, unless a design is rethought and refined at successively larger scale, the resulting building will have a rather bald and schematic character, looking merely like an enlarged model of itself. But McKim and White brought an extraordinary aesthetic intelligence to the process of mutual criticism, and their personal presence during the development of the design accounts for the exquisite quality of their best work. Each project was handled by a different partner—McKim, for example, had the Morgan Library, the University Club, and Columbia University, while White had New York University, the Knickerbocker Trust Company, and the Goelet Building (where *The New Criterion* is published, in fact). Yet whichever partner was principal designer, the other served as design critic, switching roles depending on the building, like seasoned actors trading Othello and Iago on alternate nights.

This process of mutual criticism was extraordinarily beneficial, for despite all the concord that existed between McKim and White, their personalities were diametrically opposed. McKim was a planner of brilliance and logic, his plans marked by a superb legibility that is visible even at a glance; his flair was for the gracious orchestration of movement through space. Modern French architecture seemed insufficiently virile to him, and as his career progressed he aspired more and more to the severe clarity of ancient Roman architecture.

In this was a certain chilly correctness, the orderly antiquity of the grammarian, for McKim was the very opposite of a sensualist. The roots for this may lie in his Quaker childhood. There survives a revealing letter from his student days in which his mother takes him to task for his newly acquired architectural lettering: "Charlie darling, why does thee make those horrid square capital letters . . . ? I should advise thee to keep to a plain round clear hand as the one to commend thy writing to all sensible persons." If a sensuous appreciation of texture and form is acquired early in life, this was clearly not the household in which to learn it.

White, by contrast, was a designer of intuition rather than logic. His genius was in the refinement of surfaces, the sensuous treatment of all that would reach the eye. For academic platitudes he had only contempt; when an assistant complained that his rooms could not be aligned along an axis, White famously exploded, "Damn it all, *bend* the axis." If McKim affected classical antiquity, White was drawn to the Italian Renaissance in its most sumptuous manifestation, outfitting his buildings with polished marbles, fabrics, tooled leather, and sumptuous ceilings that he extracted like teeth from Italian palaces, implanting them on Fifth Avenue.

Out of this pairing, a perfectionist grammarian and a free-spirited voluptuary, emerged a creative collaboration of unusual power. It is easy to see why McKim retreated from active design shortly after White's death, turning the office over to the junior partners who produced clever but cautious imitations of the firm's early work for another generation or so.

The essential tension in McKim, Mead & White, that between logic and feeling, lends their work depth and density, a certain laminated richness in which differing sensibilities are applied to the same problem. Such a quality was rare in American architecture, which historically had evoked its European models as image rather than substance. In the antebellum era its principal sources were print materials, either woodcuts or books, which gave to replicas a flat and graphic quality, a trait that was only intensified by the American habit of building in planar materials such as boards or brick. Here, too, the literary parallel as suggested by Trilling is striking. In his 1948 essay "Art and Fortune," he contrasts the rich density of characters and social classes found in European novels with the thinness of their American counterparts. American characters such as Captain Ahab and Natty Bumppo did not exist in a complex world in which social relations and social class locked them into a network of fraught relations and obligations with others; lacking the property of "substantiality," they were instead "mythic because of the rare fineness and abstractness of the ideas they represent." The very same terms might be used to describe a Greek Revival house, idealized and abstracted from the pages of a Greek pattern book.

But substantiality, in literature as well as architecture, was precisely what the post–Civil War generation now ardently desired. Transatlantic

travel had become routine and part of the normal flow of fashionable summer life. The cultured traveler who had inspected and admired the real
thing was no longer satisfied with mere cardboard approximations of
European architecture; he expected a physical recreation in tangible
materials. For White, with his peculiar gift for the tactile, the timing was
right. And indeed, the hallmark of all of the firm's civic buildings was their
intense corporeal presence, like that of sculpture. McKim made large-scale
plaster models of his important designs, and photographed them to
evaluate their heft and massing. Even this was not enough. For the Boston
Public Library and Penn Station, he built full-size mock-ups of the wall and
cornice, and hoisted them into place on site, so that he might gauge the
boldness of relief and the strength of the shadows, and adjust the proportions by eye. It was a trick he had learned from Michelangelo, who had
done the same with the Farnese Palace.

To the critics of McKim, Mead & White, this fastidious refinement of
detail might be said to represent all that was wrong with the classical
revival: its academicism, elitism, and criminal indifference to modern technology. In this view, they are to be condemned for ignoring the pioneering
achievements of Louis Sullivan and, already evident by 1901, of Frank
Lloyd Wright. But this is to condemn Henry James for not being Theodore
Dreiser. Sullivan and Wright indeed solved brilliantly the problems they set
out to solve, but these represented only one lobe of modern life. There was
another that they scarcely addressed at all, and which their architectural
realism perhaps could not address.

The hallmark of early modernism, paradoxically enough, was at once a
heightened objectivity and a heightened subjectivity. The objectivity lay in
the acute attention to the facts of a building, its program, and its construction. Sullivan's skyscrapers expressed these facts with eager bluntness: the
large commercial windows below, the stacked stories of identical offices
above, the cage of the steel piers. But they were no utilitarian boxes, and
their urgent factuality was offset by an equally urgent subjectivity. Sullivan's
buildings were intensely personal in character, so much so that they might
be taken as surrogates for the architect. Or so Sullivan wrote about them,
invoking the idea of the heroic individual self, the lineage that runs from
Rousseau through German romanticism to Coleridge, Emerson, and
Whitman (to whom he once wrote a fawning mash note).

The typical buildings of Sullivan and early Wright were precisely those
that lent themselves to this sort of treatment, swaggering commercial
towers and the private houses of self-made businessmen. But for McKim,
Mead & White this was not an option. Buildings such as a state capitol or
city library, a university or museum of art, are collective in nature and

reflect a consensus, a shared understanding of society, of art, or of history; they were public documents rather than personal manifestos. (This helps explain McKim's instinct always to place their design on a historical basis, colonial in the early years, and classical in the later, and also his leadership in forming the American Academy in Rome.)

In architecture, as with literature and art, a full century must pass before a reputation settles into lasting form; until then everything still swims in the surf of current events. It has been a century since the creative partnership of McKim, Mead & White came to an end, and it has become abundantly clear that their rank is very high indeed. Their libraries, museums, universities, and other civic buildings, as a corpus, form one of the enduring accomplishments of American culture. These institutions were themselves still in a formative stage, and the buildings McKim, Mead & White made for them helped to crystallize their identity. Their solutions invariably became exemplars of their type, as when a dozen state capitols modeled themselves on the example of Rhode Island's. One no longer feels the need to ritually disavow their classicism. If they did not seek modernist solutions for these buildings, it was because this was not a realm for the principled modernist dissent of Sullivan and Wright; their task was rather one of definition and consolidation, and it is here their achievement lies.

It is an oddity that Charles McKim, William Mead, and Stanford White represented three of America's principal founding cultures, those of Quaker Philadelphia, Puritan New England, and mercantile New York, dominated by the high society of its Episcopalian elite. Each had its distinctive architectural tradition and cultural sensibility, each of which, though in less distinct form, is still palpable today. In some strange way, they were able to amalgamate those traditions, refining away regional peculiarities and personal idiosyncrasy to produce work of national character, which no longer looks like the fashionable output of an overworked design factory, but something like the collective achievement of a high civilization.

September 2006

Balanchine's Castle

Laura Jacobs

THIS WINTER, *Jewels* reappeared in New York City Ballet repertory the way it does every few years, like a mirage of overwhelming majesty, a floating castle set amid fairy forests and ancient icecaps, a castle guarding its secrets. (*Jewels* was performed five times between January 6 and January 24, 1998, at the New York State Theater, Lincoln Center.) The night before the first performance, NYCB held a seminar on *Jewels* for its Guild members. Dancers from the ballet's premiere on April 13, 1967—Conrad Ludlow, Suki Schorer, and Edward Villella—were onstage to speak about that night, those steps, the rehearsals, and, of course, the ballet's choreographer, George Balanchine. The moderator, *Ballet Review* editor Francis Mason, began by explaining that Balanchine had a PR angle when he conceived *Jewels*: he thought Van Cleef & Arpels might foot the bill (lo, City Ballet got not a sou). It was also to be just one ballet, but when Balanchine began working, his idea grew. Soon there were two ballets, then three. In rehearsal, the work was referred to as "Jewels," but on the night of the premiere it went untitled because management was still waffling over what to call this strange evening. The three sections, however, were called "Emeralds," "Rubies," and "Diamonds."

The rehearsal title won out, and *Jewels* became famous as the "first three-act plotless ballet." Its sheer size was dazzling. As Ludlow explained at the seminar, "We were in transition still from City Center [to the New York State Theater at Lincoln Center] and I think that was one of the purposes of the ballet, part of the concept—the gigantic scale." Balanchine wanted to show that his dance and his dancers could fill this larger stage.

"There was a kind of pandemonium in the theater that night," said Suki Schorer, recalling that it wasn't until the premiere that the dancers knew they were taking part in a masterpiece. In *The New York City Ballet*, Lincoln

Kirstein writes, "*Jewels* has been an unequivocal and rapturous 'success' since its introduction; the very title sounds expensive before a step is seen." Rich is how *Jewels* really looks, and not so much in terms of money (the sets are minimal, parures of gemstones pasted on a bare backdrop). *Jewels* is immediately sensuous, saturated, a pleasure-dome decreed. Its crystal and glycerine surface is magic, but inside you begin to sense shadows, murmurs, and the undertow.

Indeed, the audience at the Guild Seminar seemed to be in a state of "I know, but I don't know what I know," for question after question was put to the dancers, each one ignoring the fact of *Jewels*'s plotlessness. Did Balanchine explain what was happening in *Jewels*? Did he tell you what it meant or was about? ("Rubies," Villella was told by Mr. B, was "about twenty minutes.") Did he discuss your character, your role? No, no, and no, came the answers. The castle was still guarding its secrets.

Jewels doesn't demand that you dissect it. It can be enjoyed as pure spectacle, beginning with the colors. The lighting design of Ronald Bates and the costumes of Madame Karinska work in brilliant complicity. Bates makes palpable poetic weather of his lighting, which Karinska's costumes either sink into ("Emeralds") or bounce out of ("Rubies") or refract ("Diamonds"). And so the French opaline greens that soften and blur the edges of "Emeralds" create a plush and pillowy space, a netherworld love nest. The sharp red of "Rubies" practically vibrates against a cindery light; it's a red with black in it, royal and radical at once. And the snow-crystal radiance of "Diamonds" is underlit with a blue as pale as a vein in a slim white wrist.

Karinska's costumes are knockouts. The tutus vary—long and misted in "Emeralds," hip-short and heraldic in "Rubies," stiff sprays in "Diamonds"—but all the bodices, whether green, red, or white, are glittering armatures, intricately seamed and encrusted with jewels, part Tennyson, part Dior. These bodices are fascinating. That reverse décolleté, a passementerie of jewels curving *under* each breast like baroque scrollwork, leaves the bosom naked (actually, sheathed in nude fabric). It's an odd and erotic eye-catcher, suggesting maidens framed in high windows, awaiting the troubadour's song. That song is different in each section, and thus *Jewels*'s faceting begins.

Much has been written about the three parts or panels of *Jewels*, and they can be differentiated with ease. "Emeralds" is French, set to romantic Fauré, dreamy and somnambulistic. "Rubies" is American, neoclassical Stravinsky, nervy and voracious. "Diamonds" is Imperial Russia, palatial Tchaikovsky, tender and at times ecstatically elegiac. You can keep *Jewels* in these compartments, and read it as a lavishly illustrated monograph on

Balanchine's lifelong preoccupations, circa 1967: his experimentation with national styles of classical dancing, his exploration of his own aesthetic affinities—with Paris and Petipa, with Stravinsky and Tchaikovsky. You can even pop out a panel and perform it solo, as has been done with "Rubies" all around the world. But the wholeness of *Jewels* is also the power and glory of *Jewels*.

The score for "Emeralds" was pieced together by Balanchine from incidental music that Gabriel Fauré composed for two plays: Maurice Maeterlinck's *Pelléas et Mélisande* (1898) and a Shakespeare adaptation called *Shylock* (1889). It combines impressionist washes of sound, perfumed and yearning, with simple woodcut melodies that seem sprung from medieval lore. "Emeralds" finds Balanchine deep in the poetic realm of Coleridge and Keats—it's an enchanted forest filled with Darke Ladies—and within the compositional genre of hunt and vision scenes (*Swan Lake*, *The Sleeping Beauty*). It is a work of trance and transparency. You feel you can reach through the green of "Emeralds" and grasp nothing.

What explains this disconnection? To begin with, the pyramidal dance structures of "Emeralds"—its solos, duets, pas de trois, and ensembles— suggest a fairy court on the order of *A Midsummer Night's Dream*, and yet not one but two women are at the top: a first ballerina and, a faint shade beneath her, a second. The Paris Opéra-trained Violette Verdy originated the first role, and put her stamp on a solo that is like no other solo in Balanchine ballet. Intimate, bright, it's an aria of upper-body animation, hands, arms, and shoulders preening, self-regarding, scintillating—a Jewel Song. This ballerina wraps herself and her thoughts in pure port de bras (a Verdy specialty). She seems lost in some fantasy—or found—we do not know. The second ballerina also has a solo, but she is more famous for the "walking duet," a measured, measureless passage—on pointe—along a winding path in which she is supported by a man of whom she is unaware.

Verdy's solo is, in cinematic lingo, the ballet's establishing shot, for with this solo *Jewels* fixes on a pervasive Balanchine preoccupation—the unknowable woman. The second ballerina seconds it. The inequality of these two roles may be that the first is awake and the second asleep. Together, the two add up to a single ambivalence, a sensibility torn or in flux, like Titania in her two states (self-possessed, then spellbound by Oberon), or those twins in confusion, Hermia and Helena ("I have found Demetrius like a jewel/ Mine own, and not mine own"). "Emeralds" ends with three men down on one knee like knights who have dismounted, their eyes sweeping the path for signs of her, the troubled ideal.

In "Rubies" the men have remounted— they're chess knights (and pawns)—and the girls are fillies, tomboys, pinups, Broadway gypsies,

Gypsy Rose Lees, the whole high-kicking, gear-stripping gamut of leggy American allure. Stravinsky's percussive score, Capriccio for Piano and Orchestra, is syncopated like rush hour, then cocktails: you hear the subway rumbling underneath, feel neon Broadway and New York noir take over. In response to the "Rubies" = America equation, Balanchine has said "I did not have that in mind at all." Nevertheless, the first glittering glimpse of "Rubies"—its cast holding hands upstage in a paper-doll arc, poised on pointe—never fails to draw a gasp of appreciation from the audience. It's a city skyline at night, the Big Apple ablaze.

It is in "Rubies" that you clearly see Balanchine using his jeweler's tools, concentrating on the angled body positions of classical dance—écarté, effacé, croisé—and throwing in épaulé, an upper-body arrangement that pulls the arms and torso in prismatic opposition to the lower body, creating a kind of dynamic duality, directional energies at cross purposes. All this was in "Emeralds," but subliminal, cloaked in haze and dew. "Rubies," so overtly athletic, is more pointed. Substitute leotards for those rich red Karinskas with their clacking plackets, and "Rubies" could take its place in Balanchine's black-and-white wing, next to the quantum physics of *The Four Temperaments* and *Agon*.

As in "Emeralds," there are two female leads in "Rubies," but this time one is a true principal, the other a soloist. The lead was originated by tiny Patricia McBride, the second by bigger Patricia Neary. "Rubies" belongs to McBride, but where she seems to be cozily throned in the pas de deux, that sirenlike second girl runs roughshod through the ballet, hitting cheesecake poses that drive the male corps mad. In one graphic sequence four men dive at her in succession, each grabbing a wrist or an ankle. They proceed to manipulate her into split *penchées* and leg extensions, again along the grammatical cuts of *effacé* and *écarté*. Mantrap or manhandled? This role is always cast with a "tall girl." Her M.O. is seduction, and she is the "Rubies" theme writ large.

For smack at the center of "Rubies" is an encounter sui generis, a Genesis—the pas de deux originated by McBride and Edward Villella—and smack at the end of that is a tree. Not literally, but the pas de deux finishes with McBride standing downstage, her arms splayed like branches, Villella snug behind her and climbing around. In a nursery rhyme of intertwining limbs, Villella finally opens out a hand and McBride drops something invisible into his palm. It's that other apple of course, "Rubies" red.

The brilliance of McBride was that with her sinuous, spiky style she turned original sin into a one-woman show: in "Rubies" she's Eve *and* the serpent, the apple *and* the tree. Balanchine leads us to man's first story of seduction with a more recent story straight out of the ballet canon, though again McBride is the only ballerina who's truly shown it to us. The sensation of black one feels in the red of "Rubies" is none other than Odile, the black swan from *Swan Lake*, the imposter-swan who seduces the prince away from gentle white swan Odette, and destroys his life. There is a diagonal in "Rubies" straight out of the Black Swan pas de deux, as well as other Odile-isms—her distorted and dominating attitudes, her relentlessly pull on the man. McBride danced this pas de deux with come-hither casualness, a faux-swan insinuation and feline triumph. In "Rubies," Balanchine sees Woman as forbidden fruit, eternal Eve, downfall.

"Diamonds" has been called an "Odette fantasy," and as a friend recently observed, it feels like the fifth act—a wish fulfillment—of four-act *Swan Lake*. Actually, Tchaikovsky's Symphony No. 3, from which the music is taken, was composed in the summer of 1875, just months before Tchaikovsky began work on *Swan Lake*. There are links between the two scores in key and orchestration, almost as if Tchaikovsky were tuning up for *Swan Lake*, testing the waters (still cold), and feeling his way into the forest. Certainly Balanchine hears it this way. The pas de deux in "Diamonds" refracts imagery from the pas in *Swan Lake*'s Act Two: the vow of love, Odette's arrowy path (so like the winding path in "Emeralds"). In this act of *Jewels*, there is only one ballerina—Suzanne Farrell. She is aware of her isolation and the windswept forces around her.

Farrell was Balanchine's growing obsession throughout the 1960s, and when he choreographed *Jewels* the obsession was in full bloom. In a *New Yorker* essay on *Jewels* published in 1983, Arlene Croce writes, "If I had to guess how the piece was made, I'd say that Balanchine worked backward from the pas de deux of Diamonds. . . ." This is an assessment of Farrell's power as creative muse. Croce also describes how in "Diamonds," mixed in with the Odette iconography, there are pawing steps and forward extensions that allude to the unicorn in the Cluny tapestries. Croce's view is supported by Farrell herself, who writes in her autobiography of 1991, *Holding On to the Air*, of how Balanchine took her to the Musée de Cluny to see the Lady and the Unicorn tapestries. Of the sixth tapestry she writes: "He loved the title *A Mon Seul Désir* ["To My Only Desire"] and said he wanted to make a ballet for me about the story of the unicorn." It seems safe to say that "Diamonds" is that ballet, or rather, that *Jewels* is, that it was the white glow of the unicorn that Balanchine chased into the forest, only to find himself in a thicket of haunting and hunted creatures. Claude Debussy himself began at the end when he composed, with permission from Maeterlinck, the opera *Pelléas et Mélisande*. The first thing he wrote was the climactic Act Four love duet, as if to make for himself a white light at the end of the tunnel—which he needed because the forests of *Pelléas et*

Mélisande are so thick and dark that "there are places where you never see the sun." What are these forests but the human psyche? And what is light but love? And who is Mélisande?

"ONLY THE MOST BEAUTIFUL emeralds contain that miracle of elusive blue," wrote Colette in *Gigi*. And it is through elusive blue we must travel if we are to grasp *Jewels*, through Fauré and Debussy and Maeterlinck to the deep-sea mystery of Mélisande, the ingenue-soprano who has kept opera lovers guessing for almost a century. She is the central question of Maeterlinck's play, for she herself will give no answers. We, along with Golaud, the older man who marries her, know only where he found her. Maeterlinck's stage direction reads: "*A forest. Mélisande discovered at the brink of a spring.*" It could be Balanchine's stage direction for "Emeralds." Mélisande is lost and weeping, has dropped the crown she was wearing into the spring, and will later drop her wedding ring there as well (a Freudian slip of the fingers). Pelléas is Golaud's younger half-brother, and he has instant affinity with Mélisande, which becomes love and leads to his death at the hand of Golaud. Where Pelléas believes in "the truth, the truth, the truth," Mélisande offers evasion, as if unversed in human rules. She nurses a secret sorrow, and is allied with water, fountains, the sea.

What—not who—is Mélisande, may be the better question. There are those who believe she is one of the water sprites immortalized (and they are immortal, unless they mix with humans) in Friedrich, Baron de la Motte Fouqué's story *Undine* (1811). Also, the name Mélisande is very like Mélusine, the undine of a famous French fairy tale. (Mélusine marries a human on the terms that he must never interrupt her privacy. Breaking the terms, he enters her chamber and finds her transformed, playing in a pool. She leaves him.) And in Debussy's *Pelléas et Mélisande*, a work of ravishing irresolution begun in 1893 and premiered in 1902, the closest the composer comes to a true aria occurs when Mélisande lets her otherworldly hair fall from a window. Mermaids are known for two things—their long hair and their song.

Although "Emeralds" has been likened to a tapestry, to chivalric France, to green earth, it has always been described with liquid images. Verdy commented on its "underwater quality," and Kirstein described it as a "submarine summer-green garden." In his book *George Balanchine*, Richard Buckle reports that in 1958 Balanchine had discovered the music of Fauré and imagined a "tipped ballroom" behind a scrim with "a projection of the sea . . . which pulsates." It not only makes musical-textual sense that the first ballerina in "Emeralds" is an undine, it also makes sense choreographically. In Verdy's solo, it is easy to see a woman modeling bracelets and tiaras.

When asked if Balanchine ever mentioned such jewelry, Verdy answered, "No. No bracelets." Might we not as easily see Undine or Mélusine in her imaginative element, wearing water droplets like gems? In fact, it was only during this season's round of *Jewels* that those Karinska costumes—so charming, so puzzling—struck me with new depth. That bare bosom, accentuated by gemwork, and those bodices so tightly seamed and sheathed beneath, recreate the naked flash and surge of mermaids.

"Rubies" is more Lorelei Lee than Undine, the golddigger with no regrets (*rubies* are a girl's best friend). But in "Diamonds" the green-blue waters of "Emeralds" turn to frost and ice. Tchaikovsky's hunting horns seem to answer the far-off horn calls in "Emeralds." Furthermore, Balanchine knew that the watery theme of *Swan Lake*'s Act Two—the lakeside pas de deux—was not original to *Swan Lake*. Tchaikovsky recycled it from an earlier, failed opera, *Undina*. Balanchine has given Farrell some swan queen flutterings, yet she also reiterates the undine port de bras of Verdy's solo, with a heightened, perhaps frightened emphasis. Where Verdy drew delight from her invisible spring center stage, Farrell draws strength and scale.

Move in close and *Jewels* acts more like a solitaire under a spotlight, a single gem glinting a spectrum of hue and allusion. *Jewels* is knee deep in French Symbolists, Mallarmé as much as Maeterlinck. Listen closely to Fauré and you hear Debussy's tumescent woodwinds, Mallarmé's *faune* stretching in the leaves, wondering "Loved I a dream?" *Jewels* takes up the tensions of the Symbolists, who took up the symbols of the Romantics before them—their use of the half-human to understand the human, their sense of the dislocation between possession and privacy, infatuation and freedom. *Jewels* is a vision touched with myths of transformation, with the conflicting impulses of escape and rescue. That the mermaid swims through all channels of *Jewels* is yet another flash of recognition: mermaids have always symbolized the free flow of the mind, the sea of the subconscious. The questions whispered in these waters and woods are the stuff of Balanchine's dreams, and they are unanswerable: To what extent can you possess a woman, a wife, a ballerina? To what extent can you possess your only desire without killing it?

There is an alternate view to Mélisande's identity, and its meanings move deep and dark under *Jewels*. This analysis also comes by way of the opera. If Mélisande has dropped her crown into the spring, the obvious next question is, who gave her the crown? She says, "It is the crown he gave me. . . . I will have no more of it! I had rather die." The scholar Henri Barraud identifies Mélisande as one of Bluebeard's ex-wives escaped from his castle. Or perhaps she is a wife to be. One of Charles Perrault's more rigid and unforgiving stories (it's hard to call it a fairy tale), *Bluebeard's Castle* connects with *Pelléas et Mélisande* in its atmosphere of hot and cold unknowns, its Symbolist portents ripe with erotic suggestion. Another link is Maeterlinck himself. He wrote a version of the tale called *Ariane et Barbe-Bleue*, and he named one of the wives Mélisande.

In brief, *Bluebeard's Castle* is the story of old Bluebeard's young bride, who, in order to know him better, asks for keys to the seven locked doors in his castle. He gives her all the keys, but as a test of fidelity forbids her opening the seventh door. In some versions of *Bluebeard's Castle*—Béla Bartók's opera of 1918, for instance—the keys are given with no stipulations, only foreboding. In eerie empathy, Bartók's staging accompanied the opening of each door with a wash of color—*Jewels*-like lighting effects in red, blue-green, gold, and bright white. Beyond the doors are rooms, each room a facet of Bluebeard's wealth. We see one by one the torture chamber, the armory, the house of jewels, the garden, Bluebeard's lands, a Lake of Tears. Finally, from the seventh room, three ex-wives emerge, the loves of Bluebeard's dawn, noon, and evening. This new wife must take her place behind the seventh door as the wife of Bluebeard's nights.

Violette Verdy once coached Suki Schorer in her role in "Emeralds" and passed on the story she'd invented for herself. "It happens in a bedroom," Verdy insisted. Schorer, imagining a glorious Parisian apartment, repeated this interpretation to Balanchine, who replied "No it doesn't." But Verdy's instincts ring true. *Jewels* does feel like a castle full of rooms, doors opening onto air. Without imposing Bluebeard too rigidly on Balanchine, you *can* see the kingdom's gardens and woodlands in "Emeralds." As for the torture chamber and armory, that would be blood-red "Rubies." At the seminar, Villella made no bones about the fact that his role in "Rubies" was a "gut cruncher," aerobically brutal. He asked Balanchine to change a long stretch that left him gasping for breath, and got one hardly helpful rest in the wings. And I go back to that moment in which the tall girl is manacled by four men, then drawn and quartered.

"Diamonds" is the sixth room, the Lake of Tears, for, as we know from the Act Two mime of *Swan Lake*, Odette resides in the lake made of her mother's tears. And "Diamonds" is the seventh room, too. Like Bluebeard, Balanchine had wives throughout his life. In 1967, when Balanchine was sixty-three, there were three ex-wives alive (plus one common-law ex, Alexandra Danilova); he was currently married to his fourth wife, Tanaquil Le Clercq; and was in love with the woman he wanted to be the fifth, the twenty-one-year-old Farrell. She was his Hope Diamond, the ballerina in *Jewels* who doesn't share the stage with a second because she was all women, all enchantments—unicorn, swan, undine—in one.

When Balanchine choreographed *Jewels*, he did not know Farrell would refuse him. They were still in the flush of their affinity, and the finale he put on "Diamonds"—not the actual suicide-apotheosis of *Swan Lake*, but a wedding coronation—reflects his hope for a happy ending. In her autobiography, Farrell tells of how she and Mr. B. went to Van Cleef & Arpels and, "while cameras clicked away, George and M. Arpels threw priceless jewelry at me. They even took the crowns of Empress Josephine and the Czarina out of the vault and put them on my head. We were like children locked in a candy store." Or in the third room, the house of jewels.

Farrell didn't wish to stay locked in. Balanchine's ardor grew. He wanted to have and to hold, and in 1969, in an act of escape, Farrell married a dancer her own age, Paul Mejia. The couple was banished.

Filling the ballerina roles of *Jewels* once the first ladies left them has always been a company challenge, though these days it can feel more like a confrontation. The bigness of *Jewels* requires clarity and an air-cushion of commitment around that clarity. The romance of *Jewels* requires delicacy. Yet how small so many performances feel today.

Unlike McBride in "Rubies" and Farrell (who came back in 1975) in "Diamonds," both dancing their roles well into the 1980s, Verdy left NYCB and "Emeralds" in the Seventies. The most crucial ballet in *Jewels* because it is the one that casts the spell, "Emeralds" today is a scent without complexity, a profound evocation reduced to prettiness. It has been this way for a long time, and people have been complaining ever since Verdy left, though I've never forgotten Stephanie Saland in the role, smoky and remote. Neither Miranda Weese nor Kathleen Tracey was up to her level of imaginative interest, let alone Verdy's, though I had great expectations for Weese, who has been quietly sublime in some of the more stylistically distilled Balanchine roles—in the first movement of *Symphony in C*, for example, and the first movement of *Brahms-Schoenberg Quartet*—and who is the only young NYCB principal with upper-body sophistication.

Weese in "Rubies" was another story. While Margaret Tracey had great glitter, she tired visibly, showing chinks. Wendy Whelan had wit and snap, yet there was no sense of seduction, or, as critic Robert Greskovic put it, "no silk." Weese, however, put silky and sinful together, adding her own prancing élan. The longer she was on stage, the stronger and more tonally secure she got—and she took the audience with her. I've never seen a bare back used to such effect in this ballet. It somehow magnified her serenely correct carriage, which in turn called attention to her reserves of stillness, a facet of true musicality and something very rare in ballet today (though it didn't used to be rare). In start-and-stop "Rubies," Weese showed what a decisive, dramatic impact a full stop can have. In the three *Jewels* I saw,

"Rubies" was the ballet that caught the audience—its energies are cracklingly coherent in the computer age—and it was Weese's "Rubies" that plugged in.

Darci Kistler and Kyra Nichols took turns with difficult "Diamonds." Both have performed it before, and both have recently had first babies, which is to say there is a built-in subtraction of strength. In Kistler, too much subtraction. She satisfied herself with effects (a halo here, a silvery spin there) but caught no current of sustained concentration. She now looks little, and brittle, in the face of Tchaikovsky's grandeur, unable to find herself in the fine skeins of the soliloquy or to take might from the music's ascent. Nichols, however, not as technically tight as she has been in the past, connects on ever higher levels, bringing to "Diamonds" a moving and magisterial sense of float. She's the last Balanchine ballerina on the roster, and the hush of her upper body attests to it. She's royal, Tolstoyan, unspooling arabesques and pirouettes in the white-marble corridor of Tchaikovsky's Scherzo, snow moving out of her way in drifts. She has made "Diamonds" her own lonely winter palace.

A final note. During the guild seminar, Edward Villella, who is now the artistic director of the Miami City Ballet, the only company other than NYCB ever to stage a complete *Jewels*, told of how he had invited all three ballerinas—Violette Verdy, Patricia McBride, and Suzanne Farrell—to coach his ballerinas in their roles. He praised the commitment and skill of all three equally. And then he paused, angled his body toward the audience, and moved into a more searching key, as if to grapple with something difficult. It was his opinion that Suzanne had become too serious in her devotion to Balanchine, serving his memory and coaching his ballets as if she were wearing a mantle, and maybe it was too much. That Villella was compelled to voice this particular feeling, saying what has been unsaid, in the context of this particular ballet—is it not another murmur from the house of *Jewels*, a sigh from the seventh door? Farrell didn't marry Balanchine in his lifetime, but she has become the wife of his night.

March 1998

Travels in "The Waste Land"

Adam Kirsch

ACCORDING TO THE calendar, *The Waste Land* is more distant from us today than *In Memoriam* and *Leaves of Grass* were from T. S. Eliot when he completed his masterpiece in 1922. Yet as Eliot himself proved, poetic time, like Einsteinian time, is relative. Dante and Donne, he argued in his essays, were closer to the twentieth-century poet than Tennyson and Whitman. By the same token, even though *The Waste Land* has been making Aprils cruel for eighty-three years, it remains more modern than any poem written since.

The appearance of Lawrence Rainey's scholarly new edition of the poem—*The Annotated Waste Land with Eliot's Contemporary Prose*—serves to sharpen this paradox. Here is a book of 260 pages built on a poem of 433 lines—a text-to-commentary ratio appropriate to the Bible or the Greek classics. More than any previous editor, Rainey provides the reader with every resource that might help explain the genesis and significance of the poem. He offers a chronology of its composition, from Eliot's first passing reference to "a poem that I have in mind," in November 1919, through its simultaneous publication in *The Criterion* and *The Dial* in October 1922. He offers notes on the verse and notes on the notes, including full English quotations of the sources Eliot alludes to or leaves untranslated.

Most innovatively, Rainey includes ten prose pieces that Eliot published during the composition of *The Waste Land*, ranging from canonical essays like "The Metaphysical Poets" and "Andrew Marvell" to ephemeral journalism, like the "London Letters" Eliot wrote for the American *Dial*. He reproduces, as in an encyclopedia article, a series of illustrative photographs—the Cannon Street Hotel, haunt of the Smyrna merchant Mr. Eugenides; the interior of St. Magnus Martyr church, with its "splendour of Ionian white and gold." He even prints the music for "That Shakespearian Rag," with its trashy, immortalized lyrics: "That Shakespearian rag, most intelligent, very elegant."

All of this adds up to the most imaginative and useful edition of *The Waste Land* ever published. Yet the result is not, as with most scholarly endeavors, to fix and familiarize the subject, to make it just one more item in the catalogue of knowledge. As Rainey says—quoting John Peale Bishop, who read the poem with wonder when it first appeared—*The Waste Land* remains "IMMENSE. MAGNIFICENT. TERRIBLE."

In fact, the poem may be stranger today than it has ever been. On the one hand, it now appears unmistakably a product of its time, full of dated references, falsified prophecies, and obsolete novelties; parts of *The Waste Land* are as redolent of the 1920s as the silent-movie and vaudeville effects it so brilliantly incorporates. Yet it also remains genuinely surprising, creating before our eyes the very atmosphere and vocabulary of modernness. Next to *The Waste Land*, the best works of later generations—*Life Studies*, *Questions of Travel*, *The Whitsun Weddings*, right down to the most distinguished books of the last few years, like *The Orchards of Syon* and *The Bounty*—seem positively traditional in their metric and lyric assumptions. *The Waste Land* is like one of those receding stars revealed by an orbiting telescope—an event in the past that we can never catch up to.

All of these paradoxes are implied in the oxymoron that no discussion of *The Waste Land* can avoid: "modern classic." Indeed, the best way to approach the poem today may be through a dissection of the concept of the modern, which Eliot did so much to create. For the prose texts included in Rainey's edition, along with Eliot's other influential essays, reveal that his vision of modernism was actually a compound of two very different ideas. Each of those ideas had a revolutionary power, and helped to inaugurate the poetic era in which we are still living. But while one of them is sound and still valuable, the other was flawed from the beginning, and has become increasingly burdensome. And they can both be seen in action, with all their good and ill effects, in the laboratory of modernism that is *The Waste Land*.

As every reader of Eliot's essays knows, the goal of his early criticism was to commit literary parricide. His constant theme is the debility of the nineteenth-century English poetic tradition, the tradition of Shelley, Tennyson, and Swinburne; it is only by deposing this etiolated dynasty that Eliot and his peers can ascend their throne. The Victorians are always Eliot's polemical target, whether he is writing about Andrew Marvell ("the effort to construct a dream-world, which alters English poetry so greatly in the nineteenth century . . . makes a poet of the nineteenth century, of the same size as Marvell, a more trivial and less serious figure"), or John

Dryden ("where Dryden fails to satisfy, the nineteenth century does not satisfy us either; and where that century has condemned him, it is itself condemned"), or the Metaphysical poets ("Tennyson and Browning are poets, and they think; but they do not feel their thought as immediately as the odour of a rose").

The ambiguity in Eliot's revolutionary poetics arises when he must explain the reason for his dissatisfaction with his immediate predecessors. The superficial explanation, and therefore the one that was easiest for later poets and critics to assimilate, is that the Victorians failed because they were not up-to-date enough. They did not accurately reflect the times they lived in, but retreated into a "dream-world" of verbal opiates. To be successfully modern, poets must courageously confront the modern world, as Eliot declares in the famous peroration of "The Metaphysical Poets": "We can only say that poets in our civilization, as it exists at present, must be *difficult*. Our civilization comprehends great variety and complexity, and this variety and complexity, playing upon a refined sensibility, must produce various and complex results."

In other words, a civilization different in kind from any that has come before demands a new kind of poetry. This idea appears again and again in the previously uncollected essays included in Rainey's edition. "Art," Eliot declares in his July 1921 "London Letter" for *The Dial*, "has to create a new world, and a new world must have a new structure." In the September 1921 "Letter," he praises Stravinsky for having succeeded in this absorption of the new: the "Rite of Spring," he writes, "did seem to transform the rhythm of the steppes into the scream of the motor horn, the rattle of machinery, the grind of wheels, the beating of iron and steel, the roar of the underground-railway, and the other barbaric cries of modern life." In this quasi-Futurist vision, the best poet is the one with the toughest alimentary tract, able to suck nutrition from the hard rind of the twentieth century.

This is the principle at the heart of modernism, for which the modern is no longer a premise but an ideology. It was an especially tempting idea in a century when technological changes were constantly accelerating. After all, if poetry must assimilate "the scream of the motor horn," why not every subsequent development—the roar of the airplane, the static of the television, the whine of the modem? Doesn't it follow that poetry must remake its own technologies just as often? It was by this logic that the twentieth century produced an endless series of avant-gardes, which, like Fibonacci numbers, had to summarize and transcend all their predecessors.

But Eliot's charge that the nineteenth century was not modern enough is only superficially an argument about up-to-dateness. After all, the lodestars of his criticism are poets of the fourteenth and seventeenth centuries; in his Clark lectures, published as *The Varieties of Metaphysical Poetry*, he drew a plumbline from Dante through Donne to Laforgue and, by implication, himself. What all these poets had in common was not modernity but a certain kind of intrepidity—the quality Eliot describes in "Prose and Verse," the richest of the essays excavated by Rainey, as "courage and adventurousness in tackling anything that had to be expressed." "Great poetry," he writes still more explicitly, "capture[s] and put[s] into literature an emotion." And the poets Eliot admires are those who captured experiences, sensations, and states of being that had never before been brought into poetry. Such poetic pioneers were, in another illuminating phrase from "The Metaphysical Poets," "engaged in the task of trying to find the verbal equivalent for states of mind and feeling."

Poetry of this kind, what might be called the poetry of discovery, is only superficially related to modernism. Both types of poetry are in pursuit of some sort of novelty; but the poet of discovery wants something new to literature, something that has never been adequately expressed before, while the modernist poet believes he must find something new in life or in "civilization." When Eliot castigates the Victorians, it is really their failure of discovery, not their failure of contemporaneity, that infuriates him. Thus, in "Prose and Verse," he objects to Milton and Tennyson on the grounds that they wrote "language dissociated from things," language that was not a "verbal equivalent for states of mind and feeling" but merely "a style quite remote from life."

For Eliot, then, stylistic innovation is not something that must be undertaken self-consciously, in order to produce a novel effect. It should be the natural result of a poet's attentiveness to new subjects, new feelings, new complexions of consciousness. And this kind of discovery continues to be what we value highest, both in the poetry of our own time and in the poetry of the past. Eliot remains our most influential critic, even in these days of his seeming eclipse, because we instinctively assent to his demand that each poet offer us a sense of reality—or, to use Matthew Arnold's phrase, a criticism of life—which we cannot find in any other poet. For the age of Johnson, a poet's merit lay in his mastery of conventions; for the age of Eliot, the poet can be a master only if he puts those conventions to new uses.

Is it possible, and worthwhile, to disentangle the two principles that are conflated in Eliot's criticism? The best way to answer that question is to return to Eliot's masterpiece, and to its strange double existence in the past and the future of poetry. For *The Waste Land* now appears, after several generations of reading and interpretation, to be a combination of two kinds of novelty—the "period" modernism of the 1920s, with its swagger and pose, its urban nihilism and fashionable despair, and the enduring newness of Eliot's own spiritual and musical discoveries.

Not that these two species can be simply distinguished, line by line. Take, for instance, the most famous of literary clairvoyantes, Madame Sosostris. Her pack of Tarot cards is one of the necessary binding elements in Eliot's fragmentary poem. "The drowned Phoenician sailor" prepares the way for Phlebas, whose appearance in Part IV creates one of the poem's most effective shifts of tone—an eerie submarine interlude between the "burning" of "The Fire Sermon" and the "stony places" of "What the Thunder Said." (Ezra Pound's sure editorial touch, so surprising in so erratic a poet, prevented Eliot from cutting the whole of Part IV: Phlebas, Pound advised, "is needed ABSoloootly where he is.")

Similarly, Madame Sosostris's "one-eyed merchant" looks forward to Mr. Eugenides, in Part III, and her "Those are pearls that were his eyes. Look!" returns to terrible effect in the neurotic dialogue of Part II. The whole Sosostris episode helps to create that illusion of hidden coherence which gives *The Waste Land* its mythic power—even though, as Eliot himself acknowledged in 1956, it is finally no more than an illusion: "I regret having sent so many enquirers off on a wild goose chase after Tarot cards and the Holy Grail."

Yet Madame Sosostris is also a manifestation or a casualty of one of the most dated impulses in *The Waste Land*, Eliot's attack on twentieth-century "decadence." Her fashionable spiritualism, we are meant to see, usurps the traditional prestige of religion, and preys on the insecurities of a rootless bourgeoisie: Mrs. Equitone, the fortune-teller's client, announces her lack of conviction in her very name. Later, in *Four Quartets*, Eliot would again name those who "haruspicate or scry" as agents of spiritual confusion.

From this point of view, Madame Sosostris belongs with the poem's other emblems of modern depravity: the predatory Mr. Eugenides, who tries to arrange an assignation at the Cannon Street Hotel, and the "young man carbuncular," "one of the low" whom a levelling capitalism has allowed to get above himself. Together, they vividly evoke Eliot's sense of a world in which traditional boundaries—of nation and religion, sex and class—have collapsed, leaving sterility and anxiety in their wake. This is, of course, one of the most sinister tropes of the interwar period, and sheds a great deal of light on Eliot's attraction to anti-Semitic stereotypes (in "Burbank with a Baedeker: Bleistein with a Cigar" and "Gerontion") and his sympathy for a protofascist figure like Charles Maurras. Possibly it was only Eliot's turn to Christianity, in the late 1920s, that prevented these tendencies from developing into the fanatical rage for order that was Pound's downfall.

Madame Sosostris, one might say, is a Tiresias-figure in a way Eliot never intended, at once a Joycean myth and a Spenglerian demon. And that same ambiguity runs through the whole of *The Waste Land*. At certain moments, Eliot seems to be staging his despair, in order to call attention to the moral strenuousness that allegedly distinguishes the moderns from the Victorians — their determination, as he puts it in the brief essay "The Lesson of Baudelaire," "to arrive at a point of view toward good and evil." The famous passage beginning "What are the roots that clutch" has something of this histrionic quality, as does the evocation of "hooded hordes swarming" in Part V. Then, too, Eliot's allusiveness can seem programmatic, as though written to fulfill the prescription of "Tradition and the Individual Talent": "a feeling that the whole of the literature of Europe from Homer and within it the whole of the literature of his own country has a simultaneous existence and composes a simultaneous order." Many of Eliot's allusions are magically effective, seeming to spring without premeditation from his auditory imagination, but others are showily eclectic, including the flourished "shantihs" that conclude the poem.

Where *The Waste Land* is still unquestionably vital, however, is in that element of poetry which can never be forced or forged: its music, and especially its rhythm. It was Eliot who established, by precept and example, that the rhythm of a poem is just as important a tool of discovery as its subject and diction. Nothing is more eloquent of a poet's individuality, or more essential to his conquest of experience for art, than the patterns of nerve and thought recorded in his voice. "A poem," Eliot avows in "The Music of Poetry," "may tend to realize itself first as a particular rhythm before it reaches expression in words." That may be why some of the best and most convincing passages in *The Waste Land* approach as nearly as possible to pure rhythm:

> If there were water
> And no rock
> If there were rock
> And also water
> And water
> A spring
> A pool among the rock. . . .

Or, again, from the song of the Thames-daughters in Part III:

> The river sweats
> Oil and tar
> The barges drift

With the turning tide
Red sails
Wide
To leeward, swing on the heavy spar.

In fact, it might be possible to discern the essence of Eliot's artistic and spiritual biography strictly from a study of his evolving rhythms. Such a study would also show how Eliot captured for poetry the sound and movement of whole areas of human experience.

Even today, almost a century later, adolescence is still the plangent hesitation of *Prufrock*; sexual disgust is the stern bite of *Sweeney Among the Nightingales*; spiritual quest, with its necessary doubt and self-suspicion, is the spiralling repetition of *Four Quartets*. And *The Waste Land* is all of these and more, including something that cannot be precisely named—except as the signature in verse of T. S. Eliot's unrepeatable genius.

April 2005

The Drop Too Much:
Emerson's Eccentric Circle

James W. Tuttleton

*The magnificent dreamer, brooding as ever on the renewal or reedification of the
social fabric after ideal law, heedless that he had been uniformly rejected by every
class to whom he has addressed himself and just as sanguine and vast as ever; —
the most cogent example of the drop too much which nature adds of each man's
peculiarity.*

—Emerson on Amos Bronson Alcott

I WAS MUCH TAKEN with the image of the young Ralph Waldo Emerson,
convalescing in Florida in the winter of 1827, playing "a kind of poor man's
golf by propelling green oranges with his stick along the beach at St. Augus-
tine." Equally surprising was the verbal snapshot of the elderly Emerson, in his
seventies, wrapped in a shawl on a cool evening, enjoying conversation and
remarking "the singular comfort" of a good cigar. Somehow such pastimes
seem much too human, material, and commonplace for America's greatest
idealist thinker. America's most peculiar thinker, too, by Carlos Baker's lights.
In any case, such colorful imagery and verbal precision—as well as sharp
characterization and a fine gift for storytelling—are hallmarks of Baker's new
major biography, posthumously published, called *Emerson Among the Eccentrics* (Viking, 1996). Baker was a longtime Professor of English at Princeton
and author of *Hemingway: A Life Story*; *Shelley's Major Poetry: The Fabric of a
Vision*; and *The Echoing Green: Romanticism, Modernism, and the Phenomena of
Transference in Poetry*. He was also the author of four volumes of fiction and
two of poetry, which may account for his splendid literary gifts. Baker died in
1987, before he could finish *Emerson Among the Eccentrics*, but it was so nearly
complete that the rescue of the manuscript and the appearance of the work,
however belated, constitute a publishing event of some importance.

Baker's intention in writing this compendious study of Emerson's life is suggested by notes for the book he drafted in the early 1970s. His aim, he wrote, would be

> to write what will amount to a new biography of Emerson, developed by reference to some of his leading friendships, chiefly but not exclusively literary. These will include Alcott, Edward Thompson Taylor, Jones Very, Margaret Fuller, Thoreau, Hawthorne, Theodore Parker, Walt Whitman, Mary Moody Emerson, Charles Newcomb and Ellery Channing. Through [Emerson's] connections with these, it should be possible to watch the unfolding of his religious, literary, and political ideas, his changing views of nature, man and God; to show how his friends reflected, contradicted, partly diverged from, or zealously misrepresented his philosophical and ethical teachings; to use their views to throw light on his, and his to throw light on them in a program of spiritual ecology, complicated by the fact that he both half-created the climate of opinion by which he was nurtured, while partly adapting his opinions to the ideological environment which local and national events thrust upon him.

As may seem evident from these remarks, Baker's design was conceived long before the present requirement that biography and literary criticism must reflect a politically correct position on race-class-gender victimization. What he has given us here is a solid, old-fashioned composite biography of some of the most interesting figures in the American Renaissance. But the plan also outlines too tall an order, involving the recreation of something like the whole intellectual and artistic culture of the Concord-Cambridge-Boston triangle from the 1830s to the 1880s—the era of Transcendentalism, or "The Newness," and its aftermath. Thus, while it is no surprise to learn from James R. Mellow's informative introduction that *Emerson Among the Eccentrics* was a half-century in the making, the book cannot be said to have fulfilled completely its ambitious intent. It is, however, a major recreation of Emerson's world from which the general reader and the specialist alike will profit.

It was Baker's theory of biography that "one cannot take the measure of a man from disjunctive episodes lifted from his youth or old age; biography is the study of the whole man in the context of time." If Emerson can't really be measured apart from the context of his time, what was that context like? Baker's answer is confident: Emerson created for himself a context of friendships involving a host of eccentrics, and to know him fully is to take the measure of these peculiar people who flocked to, circled about, and deeply affected him. Hence the subtitle of the book: *A Group Portrait.*

For all its six hundred pages, *Emerson Among the Eccentrics* does not really capture Emerson in youth. The group biography begins in about 1830, with Emerson in his late twenties, on the verge of his resignation from the Unitarian ministry in Boston and about to become the Transcendental poet and philosopher who will announce: "I unsettle all things. No facts are to me sacred, none are profane; I simply experiment, an endless seeker, with no past at my back." His first wife, Ellen, has died of consumption, and he has since been remarried to Lydia Jackson and will soon begin a family, including the children Waldo, Ellen, and Edward. I mention these family details because Baker is particularly good at bringing alive the internal dynamics of the extended family, which included (at the outset) Emerson's mother, his Aunt Mary Moody, and his brothers Charles and Edward. Such a method fulfills Emerson's belief that

> if a man wishes to acquaint himself with the real history of the world, with the spirit of the age, he must not go first to the state-house or the court-room. The subtle spirit of life must be sought in facts nearer. It is what is done and suffered in the house . . . in the temperament, in the personal history, that has the profoundest interest for us. The great facts are the near ones.

Emerson's second wife, Lydia, whom he promptly renamed Lidian (but always called "Queenie"), got more than she bargained for in marrying so distinguished a literary figure. Emerson had inherited a substantial sum from the estate of his first wife, and, in due course, he was to earn even more as a writer and lecturer. But his celebrity—and their growing family—brought into the household a larger and larger group of friends and acquaintances each of whom made some kind of claim upon her husband and on their resources of time and money. Overnight visitors were a constant in Concord; and some of them, like Margaret Fuller (who was in love with Emerson) stayed for weeks or even months. And at times the whole responsibility of the household devolved upon Lidian, as Emerson was absent on long lecture tours. At one point the young Henry David Thoreau also lived in their household, at the top of the second-floor stairs, serving for more than two years as the household major-domo and general factotum assisting Lidian in running the establishment.

Emerson, usually ensconced in his scriptorium, was so given over to *solitude* that he invited these friends into his house out of a need for *society*—the two extremes representing the poles of his consciousness. Indeed, he encouraged many of his admirers to move to Concord just to be near him. Elizabeth Peabody called the Emerson household "The Mount of

Transfiguration," in view of what it supposedly did to those who visited there.

It is a small wonder, then, that the beautiful and elegant wife Lidian Emerson developed some major quirks in dealing with her new husband and his peculiar friends. She was not Emerson's intellectual equal, had little interest in his more abstruse metaphysical inquiries, and could not compete with some of the intellectual women— like Caroline Sturgis and Margaret Fuller—who pursued Emerson with a spiritual hunger that now seems indistinguishable from the erotic. Lidian reflected the stress of her situation by neurotic, anorexic, perhaps even bulemic behavior. She was, in any case, often depressed, dyspeptic, given to emotional outbursts, rail thin, obsessed with odd diets like poppies and oatmeal, and generally suspicious of ordinary food. She was so cadaverous that her friends called her the "walking skeleton," and she insisted that the food we don't put into our mouths does us more good than the food we do. If some of her odd mannerisms surprised their friends, Emerson was silent and kept the sweet independence of his own soul.

Emerson was doubtless flattered by the attention of the young Harvard graduate Thoreau, who so fully incarnated the Emersonian principles of self-reliant individualism, the doctrine of perpetual revelation, and reverence for nature as the manifestation of the divine indwelling spirit. "Thoreau gives me in flesh and blood and pertinacious Saxon belief, my own ethics. He is far more real, and daily practically obeying them, than I," Emerson observed. He wrote a splendid character sketch of Thoreau, describing the youth as short in stature, but "firmly built, of light complexion, with strong, serious blue eyes, and a grave aspect." Outdoors, Thoreau wore "a straw hat, stout shoes, strong gray trowsers, to brave scrub oaks and smilax and to climb a tree for a hawk's or a squirrel's nest. He waded into the pool for the water-plants, and his strong legs were no insignificant part of his armor." Baker adds that Thoreau was astonishingly hirsute, with arms "thickly matted with fur, like the pelt of an animal." So committed was Thoreau to the out-of-doors, so completely was he taken up with the wildness of things, especially while living out at Walden Pond, that Emerson and the children called him "the Oneida Chief."

But Thoreau was a true eccentric, and in time Emerson was to become vexed with his young protégé, complaining of "the Personality that eats us up." Thoreau chilled "the social affections" by contradicting everything one said, whether casually, or seriously, in conversation. "'On hearing any proposition,' Emerson wrote, 'his first instinct . . . was to controvert it,' and in a manner 'never affectionate but superior, didactic,' scornful of the 'petty ways' of his interlocutors, 'like a New England Socrates at his most eristic.'"

Emerson was to complain that "all his resources of wit and invention are lost to me in every experiment, year after year, that I make, to hold intercourse with his mind. Always some weary captious paradox to fight you with, and the time and temper wasted." The bickering, in the long run, wasn't worth it. But to Thoreau, being self-reliant seemed to require it.

Baker was of the opinion that Thoreau was in love, at least platonically, with Lidian Emerson. And it is true that, after he moved out of the Emerson household, Thoreau wrote her some letters very tender, rather exalted, and utterly transcendental in feeling. But however that may be, it is clear that Thoreau was contending, largely in vain, against a powerful, authentic genius. A great many people—James Russell Lowell in *A Fable for Critics* among them—dismissed Thoreau as a mere clone of the master:

> How he jumps, how he strains, and gets red in the face
> To keep step with the mystagogue's natural pace . . .
> Fie, for shame, brother bard; with good fruit of your own,
> Can't you let Neighbor Emerson's orchards alone?

Indeed, not only was Thoreau's thinking often indistinguishable from Emerson's, at times so was his handwriting. (For some years a Thoreau manuscript was misattributed to Emerson, so nearly identical were their holographs.) Thoreau is well worth reading on his own, especially in *Walden*, but the similarities are there. What seems evident is that Thoreau's only way of dealing with so formidable an influence as Emerson was continually to contradict him. This devotion to Emerson's doctrine of self-reliance became a tic, then a bad habit, and finally a contentious character trait. "Thoreau wants a little ambition in his mixture," Emerson concluded. What he lacked was the ambition to be himself, someone truly great: "instead of being the head of American Engineers, he is captain of a huckleberry party."

Of particular interest is Carlos Baker's portrait of the eccentric Edward Thompson Taylor, whose extemporaneous homilies at the Seaman's Bethel in North Square in the 1840s offered the liveliest sermons in the state. "Father" Taylor—an "old-fashioned, shouting, hallelujah Methodist"—was called to minister to whatever sailors were in port. He was one of those shadowy peripheral figures mentioned in many biographies and literary histories, but here he comes into his own as the master of religious verbal pyrotechnics. Emerson was drawn to anyone exhibiting evident inspiration. Taylor preached to "rough sailors in red shirts in the central pews, and at the sides and in the gallery all manner of visitors: women and children, pale young unitarian ministers, Harvard intellectuals, the seriously devout, and the merely curious, all of them eager for another demonstration of Father

Taylor's prowess." Baker quotes Emerson to the effect that "there was no snoozing in the Concord Lyceum while Taylor stood at the lectern. 'The wonderful and laughing life of his illustration keeps us broad awake,' Emerson wrote. 'A string of rockets all night.'" Emerson was so taken with Taylor that he studied his manner closely, only to become disillusioned and conclude that, after all, there *was* no manner; it was all verbal smoke and mirrors, *sui generis*, a personality acting with spontaneous enthusiasm, rapt in religious ecstasy. The "utter want and loss of all method, the ridicule of all method" in his sermons, "bereaved" them, Emerson thought, of an intellectual power they might have had. Still, this colorful maker of homespun nautical metaphors was very nearly Emerson's "perfect orator," and his flamboyant sermons later won him a commendation in Emerson's essay "Eloquence."

Perhaps even more like Emerson in religious sensibility was the improvident transcendental seer and progressive educator Amos Bronson Alcott. Married to Abigail May and father of the young "celestials" Anna, Louisa May, and Elizabeth Alcott, this eccentric attained a kind of dubious celebrity as an "Orphic Poet" and founder of the Temple School on Tremont Street in Boston. Emerson was enchanted with Alcott's idealism, copied many of his aphorisms and sayings into his notebook, and praised him everywhere as the incarnation of otherworldly spiritual genius.

Elizabeth Peabody (Hawthorne's sister-in-law) and Margaret Fuller were Alcott's sometime teachers, and the children who attended his school were some of the most hapless innocents ever victimized by an idiosyncratic American educational theory. (Alcott emphasized conversation as a means of educing the children's already intuited knowledge of truth—even for subjects of which they could not possibly have had any understanding.) In one term, he conducted some conversations with the children on the Gospels. When Miss Peabody published her *Record of a School* (1835), with Alcott's blasphemous dialogues with the eight-year-olds about Jesus, the parents withdrew the children in outrage, and Alcott was well-nigh finished as a schoolmaster. His whole life long Alcott spent his time devising one failed enterprise after another. One of the most famous instances of Alcott's "continuous scuffling with untoward circumstances" was his creation of the short-lived commune Fruitlands.

The Unitarian minister William Ellery Channing, learning that Alcott had sunk to supporting his family by chopping wood and plowing fields, wrote Elizabeth Peabody that "such a combination of day labor and high thought made this man 'the most interesting object in our Commonwealth.'" Doubtless thinking of the Scottish poet Burns, Channing hailed Alcott as "Orpheus at the Plough." Emerson linked him with "Apollo serving among the herdsmen of Admetus." After anonymously paying Alcott's rent bill of $52 per annum for some time, Emerson claimed that "Alcott was valuable enough to be 'maintained at the public cost in the Prytaneum,'" and even at one point launched a fund to ameliorate the Alcotts' condition, laying out $500 of his own money so that they could go to Europe.

While Emerson admired and supported so staunch a Transcendentalist ally, he eventually came to see that Alcott had zero national influence and had in fact become something of a local joke. He also came to bridle at Alcott's fatiguing monumental ego. In 1848 Alcott protested to Emerson: "You write on the genius of Plato, of Pythagoras, of Jesus, of Swedenborg, why do you not write of me?" But why should such egotism have surprised Emerson? Alcott was only following the Emersonian admonition: "Trust thyself: every heart vibrates to that iron string." Eventually the Alcott girls got old enough to support their egotistical father and hapless mother. But Louisa May, who brought in considerable cash with her gothic romances and *Little Women*, had the last word on her father's otherworldly improvidence in a satirical reminiscence of Fruitlands called "Transcendental Wild Oats" (1873).

Other important oddities in Baker's gallery of eccentrics include Jones Very, Ellery Channing, and Channing's sister-in-law Margaret Fuller. Emerson's celebration of Channing as a rising young poet of genius is solid evidence, if any were needed, that Emerson was a saintly and generous man who simply had no ear for verse. Yet year after year he praised (and even published in *The Dial*) the effusions of a poetaster who could write (of Caroline Sturgis, in "The River"):

> Sweet falls the summer air
> Over her form who sails with me;
> Her way, like it, is beautifully free,
> Her nature far more rare;
> And is her constant heart of virgin purity.

If verses like these struck Emerson as having "a certain wild beauty immeasurable" that caused "a happiness lightsome and delicious" to fill "my heart and brain," Margaret Fuller was blunt in telling Caroline Sturgis: "Of Ellery's verse I think not much." And when she took over editorship of *The Dial,* she rejected his poems. She thought not much of her brother-in-law the man either, since Ellery played the role of an infantile, temperamental, romantic poet, abusing her sister Ellen by wandering off on any mere whim, abandoning her to the ladies at lying-in time, and failing to support her financially.

The poets Ellery Channing and Jones Very were both drawn to Emerson by virtue of his verse, his moral vision, and his religious ecstasy—an ecstasy reported if not really experienced. But in Very's case, it *was* felt: he was, Emerson thought, a true ecstatic. Very had distinguished himself as a tutor in Greek at Harvard and had begun to make a name for himself as a critic of classical poetry and as a poet himself. But Very's students began to remark his quite odd behavior; and when he invaded the study of Henry Ware, a professor at the Harvard Divinity School, and announced that the Second Coming was at hand and was "*in him*," Harvard moved immediately to put the boy on a medical leave. In Salem, where Hawthorne had lived in his youth, Very marched right into people's homes, declared himself to be the Messiah come again, and acclaimed his sonnets as directly inspired by God. Doubtless Very had heard the Emersonian admonition in "The Divinity School Address": "Yourself a newborn bard of the Holy Ghost, cast behind you all conformity, and acquaint men at first hand with Deity." Unfortunately, like Allen Ginsberg, the deranged Very believed it could be done.

From this distance it appears that not the Deity but dementia possessed Jones Very; but his Transcendentalist friends were disposed to be tolerant of his strangeness. Emerson invited him into his house for five days, observed and talked to him, and judged Very "'profoundly sane' and wished all the world 'were as mad as he.'" Ellery Channing—doubtless thinking of the Coleridgean term for intuition, said that the young poet had "not lost his *Reason*" but "his *Senses*." Elizabeth Peabody claimed that Very's frenzy was a temporary event "caused by overtaxing his brain in the attempt to look from the standpoint of Absolute Spirit." And Bronson Alcott concluded that Very was merely "diswitted in the contemplation of the holiness of Divinity." And so he was. Baker remarks that Very "was the same man who asserted, quite seriously, that he felt it an honor to wash his own face, since it was the outward temple of the inward spirit."

In the fall of 1842, Emerson struck the note of ambivalence that always resounded when he wrote about either solitude or society. He could not make up his mind whether he did, or did not, want these friends about him. "What obstinate propensity to solitude is this? I fancied that I needed society and that it would help me much if fine persons were near, whom I could see when I would, but now that C[hanning] and H[awthorne] are here, and A[lcott] is returning, I look with a sort of terror at my gate."

One source of terror was the frequent visitor Margaret Fuller, his co-editor of *The Dial*, who had become wildly unsettled by Emerson's liberationist theology of love. Bright and ugly, Margaret was the ripest peach on the bough. But as no husband had yet plucked her from the branch, she had set her sights on Emerson. In *Memoirs of Margaret Fuller Ossoli* (1852), he was to write that she was "like the queen of some parliament of love, who carried the key to all confidences." But he had to impound the key in their case, to stop her from trying to eroticize their relationship. Lidian was likewise a distinct obstacle to Margaret's claiming Emerson's heart. "Nothing makes me so anti-Christian, and so anti-marriage," Margaret confided to her diary, "as these long talks with Lidian." No wonder, since Lidian was extolling the sacramental nature of marriage and the wickedness of trying to seduce another's husband.

What is remarkable about a great many of Emerson's eccentric friends is how acidly they competed with each other for his attention and approval, often carping and criticizing each other to him, with the effect, as Baker puts it, that "Emerson's long dream of a cooperative assemblage of gifted individualists was . . . rapidly dissipated by their inability to get along with one another." But their asperity with each other was sometimes matched by their vexation with the master himself, who was intent on preventing any undue intimacy. Emerson answered them by writing an essay, "Friendship," in which he told his disciples that friendship was ideally a relationship between two large formidable natures who were "mutually beheld, mutually feared." The friend was to be "to thee for ever a sort of beautiful enemy, untamable, devoutly revered, and not a trivial conveniency to be soon outgrown and cast aside." The relationship with this beautiful enemy was to be entirely spiritual: "It is foolish to be afraid of making our ties too spiritual, as if so we could lose any genuine love." In another place (again, probably thinking of Fuller), he writes, "Leave this touching and clawing. Let him be to me a spirit. A message, a thought, a sincerity, a glance from him, I want, but not news nor pottage." But in fact too close a relation, for Emerson, was dangerous:

> Though I prize my friends, I cannot afford to talk with them and study their visions, lest I lose my own. It would indeed give me a certain household joy to quit this lofty seeking, this spiritual astronomy, or search of stars, and come down to warm sympathies with you; but then I know well I shall mourn always the vanishing of my mighty gods.

Emerson was fully aware that his friends considered him aloof, but in one of his most remarkable statements, he told them in "Friendship" that "the condition which high friendship demands is ability to do without it."

Margaret Fuller's letters to Emerson exaggerate Lidian's holiness and her own readiness for some self-defining, extravagant, even sexual action. "Who would be a goody that could be a genius?" she asked in her journal (implicitly rejecting the patriarchal adage: "Be good sweet maid, and let who will be clever"). Fuller was also pre-emptively absolving herself for whatever evil that men might afterward accuse her of doing. By 1845 she was openly advocating the socialist (or Fourierist) line on marriage, declaring the holy institution to be oppressive to women and productive of spousal violence, infidelity, infanticide, and the marital uses of arsenic. *Women in the Nineteenth Century* (1845) was the opening volley in the century's feminist movement, and Margaret celebrated it by abandoning New England, with its "bloodless men," and moving to New York, where she worked briefly for Greeley's *Herald Tribune*. Italy was the final field of her activities, for there, during the Risorgimento, she became an activist for the revolutionist Mazzini, and had a probably illegitimate child with Giovanni Ossoli, an impoverished Italian aristocrat. After the collapse of the revolution, the three of them died in a shipwreck off Fire Island in 1850.

There were a great many other eccentrics in Emerson's world whom Baker has engagingly sketched in here. One is Theodore Parker, the polymath abolitionist Unitarian minister who set a standard for learning and moral courage none of the others could match. Another is Walt Whitman, the lower Broadway incarnation of Emerson's idea of the poet, the beginning of whose career the Sage had so generously saluted. Thoreau went down to New York and met Whitman; he found him to be "an extraordinary person," one "full of brute power." Alcott found him less appealing, describing Whitman as "broad-shouldered, rouge-fleshed, Bacchus-browed, bearded like a satyr, and rank." If Whitman didn't bathe often enough for Alcott, Emerson was likewise embarrassed to have Whitman's "pomes" turn priapic in "Children of Adam" and "Calamus." This led E. P. Whipple rightly to complain that *Leaves of Grass* "had every leaf but the fig leaf." A third oddity was Charles Newcomb, a rich Roman Catholic whose religious fanaticism was too much for his fellow Brook Farm denizens—especially since Newcomb "decorated his room with ferns, rushes, and pictures of Jesus and selected Catholic saints, and persisted in reading aloud from the church litany at all hours of the night." Baker remarks that "for reasons that remain obscure he insisted on wearing gloves and a veil as he slept."

This last detail is suggestive of Hawthorne, the Salem solitary who, in the 1840s—before his marriage to Elizabeth Peabody's sister Sophia—also lived for a time at Brook Farm. Hawthorne in due course found ridiculous the transcendental socialism of his high-minded companions at the Farm. He also kept a very wary distance from Emerson, even satirized him for living in cloud-cuckoo land in "The Celestial Railroad" and "Earth's Holocaust," and wrote a biting critique of the Brook Farm communitarians in *The Blithedale Romance*. It was Hawthorne who first noticed the oddity of the Emerson circle, describing Thoreau and Ellery Channing as among "those queer and clever young men whom Mr. Emerson (that everlasting rejecter of all that is, and seeker for he knows not what) is continually picking up by way of genius."

For Hawthorne, none of this circle had in greater superfluity "the drop too much which nature adds of each man's peculiarity" than Emerson himself. In his own time Emerson had a reputation for sublime sanity, an equilibrium of spirit and a serenity of soul beyond that of any other man. But Emerson was at times more eccentric than his friends. Granted that he was grief-stricken at the death of his first wife, Ellen, a beautiful young woman who died of consumption in 1831. But what are we to make of this bald entry in his journal, some *thirteen months later*: "I visited Ellen's tomb and opened the coffin"? His reasons for so ghoulish an act are not explained in the journal.

Moreover, in 1857, long after his young son Waldo had died from scarlet fever—a death memorably eulogized in that remarkable poem "Threnody"—Emerson recorded in his notebook: "I had the remains of my mother and of my son Waldo removed from the tomb of Mrs. Ripley to my lot in 'Sleepy Hollow.' The sun shone brightly on the coffins, of which Waldo's was well preserved—now fifteen years. I ventured to look into the coffin. I gave a few white-oak leaves to each coffin, after they were put in the new vault, and the vault was then covered with two slabs of granite." Nothing else is said of this event in the journal. But Baker remarks that "at home he told his daughter, Ellen, that he had opened Waldo's coffin. He did not elaborate, although he could hardly have helped recalling the day in 1832 when he had opened the coffin of that other Ellen whose name his eldest daughter bore."

What accounts for such abnormal acts? Was it mere morbid curiosity? A wish to see what time and decay had done to his image of his beloved wife and child? Since death had no spiritual reality for Emerson, did he hope to find some confirmation of the primacy of soul? Was it a desire to reconcile himself to death by seeing what had happened to their physical bodies? In the absence of fact, there can be no end to speculation of this kind, but, whatever answer one may produce, most of us will feel that Emerson's behavior was distinctly eccentric, if not pathological.

Because Emerson was one of the greatest writers America has produced, the tendency to hagiography in his friends and admirers has become infused into much of the literary criticism written about him. Baker's work is salutary in reminding us that mixed with Emerson's genius were traits of character and oddities of behavior that most men would regard as strange indeed. Beyond that, however, is a matter that Baker does not develop. And that is the negative impact, on American culture, of the transcendental doctrines Emerson espoused.

I am not referring here to the doctrine of self-reliance, which most parents teach their children quite naturally, though not perhaps in so absolutist a degree. I refer to what happens in a culture like ours when institutions *as such* are attacked as vicious, when people are told that the church and temple, the college and the political party, the Red Cross, the employee's union, and the veteran's group (and so forth) are all unnecessary organizations and are indeed inimical to one's self-development, and that all one needs to do is to consult one's own inner oracle and act out one's own inner imperative, however antisocial it may be. To be told, Do your own thing, is for most people, it seems to me, ultimately disorienting and will leave them floundering and adrift and (even worse) determined—such is the Emersonian imperative—to *act out* their idiosyncrasies, to distill to the last "the drop too much which nature adds of each man's peculiarity." The 1960s represented, in my view, a widespread, disastrous, vulgar translation into action of such Emersonian doctrines, a sort of Age of Aquarius reincarnation of the 1830s "Newness." It produced some colorful personalities and genuinely eccentric communitarian "lifestyles" worthy of Fruitlands. But we have still not recovered from that decade's more sinister attack on the foundations of American culture and the moral life. We still have not directly challenged the Emersonian belief that there is no standard of right and wrong outside the self. And we have not recovered from his assault on the institutions by which we naturally and rightly organize our educational, political, religious, social, and intellectual life. It is through these institutions alone (however imperfect they may be) that jointly and mutually we implement our most deeply held convictions about the national life.

May 1996

Are Emotions Moral?

F. H. Buckley

ON OCTOBER 2, 2002, A SNIPER shot and killed James D. Martin in the parking lot of Shoppers Food Warehouse in Wheaton, Maryland. Martin was fifty-five and lived in the middle-class suburb of Silver Spring, Maryland. There were no witnesses or suspects and nothing to suggest a motive for the crime. Over the next three weeks, the sniper struck thirteen more times. The victims were ordinary people from the Washington area, middle class for the most part, male and female, white, black, Hispanic, and Asian.

The sniper attacks traumatized Washington. A few weeks before, we had observed the first anniversary of September 11. The anthrax investigation was ongoing and many Washingtonians expected another terrorist attack. We read stories of how chemical and nuclear weapons could be smuggled into the United States and set off near a federal building. Some of us thought that the sniper was a Moslem fanatic—and it turned out we were right.

During the three weeks, we all hunkered down. Because the sniper had struck at motorists filling up their cars, people crouched in front of gas stations. Some service stations installed canvas sheets to shroud the pumps, and husbands tanked up their wives' cars. People stayed off the streets, and public events were cancelled. Before the sniper was caught, some worried about whether he would disrupt the local November elections. In Maryland, the sniper attacks became an issue in the contest for governor. The Democratic nominee, Kathleen Kennedy Townsend, bore a famous name and was favored to win in a heavily Democratic state. Her gun control views weighed against her, however, and the victory of her Republican opponent was in part attributed to the sniper. Townsend's efforts to portray herself as tough on crime didn't wash—even when she said that executing the sniper by lethal injection would be an "absolute no-brainer."

The criminal investigation was in the hands of Charles Moose, the Montgomery county chief of police. Throughout the three weeks, we listened on tenterhooks as local radio stations cut away to one of Moose's frequent press conferences. Moose had little to offer but the encouragement that whatever could be done was being done. It wasn't much, but it helped. Moose is an emotional person, and we were reassured that he took the crisis every bit as seriously as we did. He didn't have to tell us that he was doing everything in his power to arrest the sniper—we knew it from his voice.

We liked it that Moose didn't speak to us in technobabble. We liked it when he showed his contempt for the snipers. We especially liked it when he blew up at the *Washington Post* for prematurely revealing a lead. And we liked it when he cried as he described the sniper's attack on a child. "Our children do not deserve this. Shooting a kid. I guess it's getting to be really, really personal now."

All of this took place more than a year ago. The snipers were caught on October 24, 2002 and are now on trial. The sense of terror is gone, and Chief Moose is gone too, hounded out of his job by the *Post* for the book he wrote about the hunt for the snipers.

As our fears have receded, so too has the desire to punish the snipers. In the heat of the moment even Kathleen Kennedy Townsend wanted a summary execution. A year later we feel much less emotional about it all, and we have been willing to let justice take its course. By delaying the trial a year, the criminal justice system has itself sought to dampen the emotional response to the killings.

Criminal defense work is not unlike running out the clock in basketball. The goal is to delay the trial through a plethora of motions until the impulse to punish disappears. Rich defendants can run the clock for years, particularly if they are before a *fainéant* judge. Poorer defendants usually come to trial more quickly. The difference greatly advantages the O. J. Simpsons. I feel less angry about the snipers than I did a year ago, much less upset about O. J. Simpson than I did ten years ago. And I feel positively benign about Bluebeard the Pirate.

Other rules of criminal procedure are aimed at weakening the impulse to punish. In the sniper case, the venue of the lead defendant's trial was moved to Virginia Beach, 200 miles from any of the killings, in order to find a dispassionate jury. Defense lawyers also employ their right to dismiss jurors in order to empanel people who will identify with the defendant and not the victim. The very structure of the American courtroom contributes to the sense that we're all in this together. There is no prisoner's box, as there is in England. Nor is the person on trial referred to as the prisoner, as he is in England; or the accused, as he is in Canada. Here he is simply the defendant, as though he were being sued for breach of contract.

The contest between the individual and the state in a criminal trial is an unequal one, and the consequences of getting it wrong more troubling in criminal than in civil matters. In the language of statisticians, the danger of false positives is greater than that of true negatives. Blackstone expressed the same idea in more familiar language. "It is better," he said, "that ten guilty men go free than one innocent man be found guilty." That is why criminal procedure stacks the deck against the prosecutor. The standard of proof is not the civil burden of the balance of probabilities; instead it is the much more exacting standard of proof beyond a reasonable doubt. A good many people are found civilly liable where there was a reasonable doubt about their negligence; and an equal number are acquitted of crimes which they likely committed on a balance of probabilities.

The difference in the burden of proof reflects the libertarian bias in our common law inheritance, and we should not want to change it. What is new are the procedural devices which defense lawyers employ to delay trials until the emotional need to punish is extinguished. That was not part of Blackstone's law. Eighteenth-century trials were conducted expeditiously, as were the executions after a capital sentence was rendered. Blackstone insisted upon the need to get on with it, as delay would weaken the emotional impact of the law.

What Blackstone understood, and what we have forgotten, is that the wheels of justice are oiled by emotion. We do not punish because the wrongdoer treated others as means and not ends, or because he has negative net-present value on some utilitarian calculus. Abstract theories of justice dull us to the difference between the criminal and his victim and cannot compensate us for the economic and psychic costs of punishing a wrongdoer. We need something more, something provided only by the emotional release that comes from punishing the guilty. We punish because the criminal act was loathsome and the criminal himself hateful.

James Fitzjames Stephen, the Victorian jurist who drafted the Canadian Criminal Code, thought that our morality and criminal law were founded upon an emotional response to wrongdoing. Like John Stuart Mill, Stephen was a member of a prominent liberal, intellectual family. His brother was Leslie Stephen and his niece Virginia Woolf. But Stephen's utilitarianism took a very different form from that of Mill. So far from deprecating social norms, as Mill did, Stephen celebrated them, and in *Liberty, Equality, Fraternity*, written a decade after Mill's *On Liberty*, he argued that "the custom of looking upon certain courses of conduct with aversion [is] the essence of morality." (See Roger Kimball, "James Fitzjames

Stephen v. John Stuart Mill", *Experiments Against Reality*; Ivan R. Dee, 2002.)

Mill's bloodless liberalism had little place for emotion. Consider, said Stephen, the way in which Mill handled the delicate question of what shall be done with a person who, after due deliberation, decides to become a pimp. Mill opposed the imposition of legal sanctions for acts which did not cause harm to others, and where is the harm to others when the transactions are consensual on all sides? Yet, in the end, Mill came down on the side of proscription, for the most delicate of reasons.

> Although the public, or the State, are not warranted in authoritatively deciding, for purposes of repression or punishment, that such or such conduct affecting only the interests of the individual is good or bad, they are fully justified in assuming, if they regard it as bad, that its being so or not is at least a disputable question: That, this being supposed, they cannot be acting wrongly in endeavouring to exclude the influence of solicitations which are not disinterested.

This is poor stuff. Mill's harm-to-others principle has not been violated by the pimp, and we are left with a specious argument which Stephen mercilessly satirized. Here again is Mill, this time as interpreted by Stephen:

> Without offence to your better judgment, dear sir, and without presuming to set up any opinion against yours, I beg to observe that I am entitled for certain purposes to treat the question whether your views of life are right as one which admits of two opinions. I am far from expressing absolute condemnation on an experiment in living from which I dissent (I am sure that mere dissent will not offend a person of your liberality of sentiment), but still I am compelled to observe that you are not altogether unbiased by personal considerations in the choice of life which you have adopted. . . . I venture, accordingly, though with the greatest deference, to call upon you not to exercise your profession.

Stephen has a shorter way with the pimp.

> You dirty rascal, it may be a question whether you should be suffered to remain in your native filth untouched, or whether my opinion about you should be printed by the lash upon your bare back. That question will be determined without the smallest reference to your wishes or feelings; but as to the nature of my opinion about you, there can be no question at all.

Stephen's argument from repugnance has recently been revived in the debate over cloning. There may be excellent prudential reasons why the prospect of cloning a person is dangerous, but Leon Kass, the chair of the Presidential Council of Bioethics, has advanced a very different kind of argument, based on natural feelings of disgust.

> We are repelled by the prospect of cloning human beings not because of the strangeness or novelty of the undertaking, but because we intuit and feel, immediately and without argument, the violation of things that we rightfully hold dear. Repugnance, here as elsewhere, revolts against the excesses of human willfulness, warning us not to transgress against what is unspeakably profound. ("The Wisdom of Repugnance", *The Ethics of Human Cloning*; AEI Press, 1998)

The belief that our emotions and instincts, including the sense of disgust, are coded with compelling information about how we should live was also a theme of Lionel Trilling's *Middle of the Journey*. Trilling's novel described John Laskell, a man of thirty-three who is recovering from a near-fatal illness at the summer home of his friends Arthur and Nancy Croom. The period is the mid-1930s, and the Crooms are people of the Left. Indeed, many readers thought Trilling had meant to portray Alger and Priscilla Hiss, since Trilling's Gifford Maxim is clearly Whittaker Chambers. The Crooms are solicitous of Laskell's health but uncomfortable with any reminder that he nearly died. They are progressives who instinctively sense that any talk of death is a counter-revolutionary negation of the future. Instead, they place their faith in the proletariat, as represented in their sly and brutish handyman, Duck Caldwell. "He's a very important kind of person," Nancy tells Laskell, "even if you don't consider him just personally." The Crooms are intellectuals and mistrust emotions, but bristle with hatreds they cannot acknowledge. They detest Maxim for breaking with the Communist Party, but call him insane. And when Caldwell cruelly strikes his child and unwittingly causes her death, Laskell and the Crooms are repulsed by him without understanding why. It is left to Maxim to explain that those who fail to recognize their repugnance to evil can become its willing accessories.

The argument from our emotions is Burkean. The English, said Burke, "are generally men of untaught feelings," so that "instead of casting away all our old prejudices, we cherish them to a considerable degree, and, to take more shame to ourselves, we cherish them because they are prejudices." This was an older use of prejudice, synonymous with sentiment or passion as opposed to reason. As a motive to action, prejudice offers a surer guide than reason, said Burke.

We are afraid to put men to live and trade each on his own private stock of reason; because we suspect that this stock in each man is small, and that the individuals would be better to avail themselves of the general bank and capital of nations, and of ages. Many of our men of speculation, instead of exploding general prejudices, employ their sagacity to discover the general wisdom which prevails in them.

The appeal to prejudice was a thumb in the eye to English political rationalists such as Dr. Richard Price, the dissenting minister whose sermon in support of the French Revolution led Burke to write his *Reflections*. Burke contrasted Price's didactic sermon with the theater, which must move our emotions to succeed, and which he thought must therefore afford more reliable moral instruction. "No theatric audience in Athens would bear what has been borne" by Dr. Price's friends. In this sense, our emotions are wiser than our reason. Our sense of pity for the victims of the Revolution told us of horrors to which reason was blind.

In Goya's celebrated drawing, the sleep of reason brings forth monsters. But the sleep of passion may also be murderous. Political theorists like John Rawls who seek to explain why we should pursue justice cannot persuade us that we should first care about other people. That is left for tragedy. By awakening pity, tragedy teaches us that sympathy and love are prior to justice and desert. "O reason not the need," groans Lear, when Goneril and Regan bargain down the number of his retainers. Lacking love, they will break their promises to him, for reason can always find a justification for injustice. Goneril and Regan promised the most extravagant love for their father; Cordelia promised only to love "according to her bond." But her promise was credible, since her natural attachment was sincere. "I stumbled when I saw," said Lear, and we too see more clearly when we rely on our intuitions and emotions in addition to our unguided reason.

The very distinction between reason and passion is often suspect. Cartesian dualists identify emotions with mere feelings, like heat or cold, or with the brute physiological events to which they are correlated. Emotions are more than that, however. The distinction between feelings and calculation may be blurred and many of our judgments are as much one as the other. So thought Joseph de Maistre, who mocked philosophical deliberations about the rights of man. "I never saw a man," said Maistre. "I saw Frenchmen, Italians, Russians, but as for the creature man I never met one in my life."

Our distaste for liars is both an aversion and a sense of the harm they may impose upon us, with the aversion economizing on cost-benefit analysis. We don't have to calculate the harm they might impose—we simply know we don't like them. Similarly, feelings of boredom or disgust provide us with useful stopping rules that short-circuit wasteful mental calculation. Our natural tendency to imitate others also usefully prevents us from continuing on where others have stopped. Finally, a simple preference may take charge and tell us to stop calculating and get on with it. We might spend an endless amount of time in search of the perfect mate, but falling in love tells us to stop. As does our mate.

Once before, in the nineteenth century, we prized emotion over reason, and we are not finished with the nineteenth century. But it is different today. We are no longer encumbered with the political baggage of Romanticism, whose Blood and Earth spawned bestial political theories in the twentieth century. In addition, the idea that our emotions are an intelligent way of responding to choices dominated by desires finds a home across the academy, in disciples that did not exist in Coleridge's day. The counter-revolution in the cognitive sciences which endows our emotions and instincts with innate intelligence has created interdisciplinary alliances amongst psychologists such as Gerd Gigerenzer and Antonio Damasio, economists such as Vernon Smith and Robert Frank, philosophers such as Jon Elster and Robert Solomon, evolutionary biologists such as Robert Trivers and Steven Pinker, political theorists such as Francis Fukuyama, natural lawyers like Larry Arnhalt, and poets such as Fred Turner, all of whom recognize their common intellectual bonds as well as the chasm which separates them from the Enlightenment tradition's abstract rationalism.

This is not to attribute inerrancy to our emotions. In truth there are no infallible guides, or if they exist seldom speak *ex cathedra*. We cannot say that laughter never did betray the heart that loved her, as Wordsworth said of nature. Nothing on earth does that, and particularly not nature. The breakdown of racial prejudice in America was a positive good. It does not follow, however, that our emotions are presumptively untrustworthy, and that moral questions are always to be decided according to the dictates of pure reason unaided by emotion.

January 2004

Max Beckmann at the Guggenheim

Karen Wilkin

M Y TEENAGE YEARS can be evoked, as I think they can for a few of my former classmates at the High School of Music and Art, not by pop music, but by the street-smart dissonances and raunchy lyrics of *The Three-Penny Opera*. My closest friends and I went more than once to see the Brecht-Weill classic performed in the Village. We listened over and over to the record, held by its cynical, edgy daring and its erotic overtones — rap for would-be bohemians in the late 1950s — noting, however, that the record lyrics were less explicit than the theater version. Our parents thought it a little "adult" for fifteen-year-olds, but as old leftists, they generally approved of both the composer and the author. And since Lotte Lenya was in the cast, we were witnessing living theater history, which was educational. Later, when an amazing film of the original Berlin production with the young Lenya turned up, we rushed to see it and thrilled at its rawness, rudeness, and vitality.

As children of the 1940s, we hadn't been encouraged to be Germanophiles, but Thomas Mann fascinated us (except for my best friend's unidentical twin sister who preferred *Gone with the Wind*), and the self-conscious naughtiness of German Expressionist painting, with its frank hostility to the status quo, appealed to us as intellectually pretentious, mildly rebellious New York teenagers; that scratchy, ecstatic Kokoschka double portrait of the art historian and his wife at MOMA was a heavy favorite. But the most compelling German painting at MOMA was a strange triptych, mysterious not only because of its disturbing subject matter, but because — unlike the Kokoschka — it didn't correspond to anything we were learning about twentieth-century German art in our introductory art history class. The meaning of the picture seemed always just out of reach, but somehow, it seemed to have to do with what we liked about *The Three-*

Penny Opera. The painting was, of course, Max Beckmann's magnificent *Departure* (1932–1933).

In the intervening decades, I've lost my taste for most of the German Expressionists and learned a lot more about the period—including that Beckmann disliked much of what they were about—but *Departure*'s horrific side panels of theatrical torture and oddly comforting center panel of mythological figures in a boat have lost none of their power to make me stop and ponder.

They stopped me in the downtown Guggenheim's superlative exhibition, "Max Beckmann in Exile," ("Max Beckmann in Exile" opened at the Guggenheim Museum SoHo, New York, on October 9, 1996, and remained on view through January 5, 1997) where *Departure* more than holds its own amid a fine selection of some of this rarely celebrated modern master's most powerful works. This wonderful show is long overdue; although there have been small shows at infrequent intervals, Beckmann's last major American museum exhibition was a retrospective organized in 1964 by MOMA, the Boston Museum of Fine Arts, and the Art Institute of Chicago. The "exile" of the Guggenheim show's title is both literal and metaphorical. *Departure*, the earliest work included, was finished in 1933, when the Nazis assumed power and Beckmann, at forty-nine hailed as one the most important modern German artists, was dismissed from his teaching position in Frankfurt and forbidden to exhibit. He moved to Berlin, hoping that things would improve, but four years later, his work pilloried in the Nazi "Degenerate Art" exhibition, Beckmann and his young second wife left to spend the next decade in Amsterdam. In 1947, they left Europe definitively, to settle in the U.S. Beckmann died suddenly in New York, two months short of his sixty-eighth birthday, at the end of 1951, without ever revisiting his homeland.

The exhibition makes clear that despite the turmoil and deprivations of the war years, despite the psychological disruption of moving from the Old World to the New, Beckmann showed no slackening of productivity or invention during this period; quite the opposite, it generated some of his most ambitious and achieved work. The curator of the show, Matthew Drutt, wisely concentrated on Beckmann's "public" works—his monumental triptychs and large scale paintings—punctuating them with a few self-portraits (including one of the artist and his wife) and smaller works chosen because of their iconographic or emotional connections. As is always the case, alas, with even the best organized exhibitions, there are regrettable absences; two of Beckmann's nine completed triptychs were unavailable and a few private collectors proved unwilling to part with their pictures. Still, having seven of the thundering triptychs in one place, from the earliest,

Departure, to the last, the strangely calm *Argonauts* (1949–1950, National Gallery, Washington), is exciting and illuminating. The cumulative effect is almost overpowering: for the intensity of feeling in Beckmann's images, for their power to disturb, and for the sense of disequilibrium they provoke. It is no less dazzling for the ferocity of his color, the gorgeousness of his touch, the sensuality of his paint handling, or the assuredness of his drawing.

Beckmann's paintings are so rich, so loaded, that it is difficult to know how to begin to talk about them. They seem to operate at several speeds at once. The initial impact of their often startling subject matter is instantaneous, as is the effect of their saturated, glowing color and bottomless, velvety blacks. We are immediately struck, too, by the way Beckmann's sturdily modeled, firmly drawn figures are crammed into their spaces, straining the edges, shoving toward us as though about to burst the sacrosanct surface of the canvas. But even these observable facts, in Beckmann's hands, raise thought-provoking questions that slow us down and make us consider alternatives. Is this heated color, this aggressive pictorial structure the result of sheer force of feeling? Are they responses to chromatic and spatial possibilities suggested by Fauvism and Cubism—with which Beckmann was thoroughly familiar—or are they deliberate violations of "rules"? Are these visual equivalents of the way Brecht's characters address the audience directly, shattering theatrical illusions and calling attention to the artifice of performance?

Beckmann's unstable narratives and thrusting, confrontational compositions call up a staggering range of associations, at once precise and elusive, that can be unraveled only slowly—and then incompletely. The triptychs, for example, obviously take their format from traditional devotional images. The side panels of *Blind Man's Buff* (1944–1945, Minneapolis Institute of Arts) adhere closely to the conventions of how Renaissance donors were depicted: a kneeling woman on one side, with her blindfolded male counterpart on the other, each backed by a tightly packed phalanx of figures, like patron saints in an altarpiece. The central panel, however, is not the expected nativity or crucifixion, but a weird concert in which a splay-legged "savage" drummer seems to challenge a female harpist. They, in turn, are bracketed by a pair of reclining pipe players, male and female, like classical river gods gone awry; a suspicious woman in evening dress watches, groped by a man wearing a dinner jacket and an enormous ass's head. This unlikely assortment is knotted and twined together in a tipped architectural setting, apparently full of closed doors—a hotel room?—the whole brilliantly, pitilessly lit, like an operating room. Snatches of modern, even bourgeois, domesticity assert themselves in the alarm clock, the rug, and the spiky snake plant. The "donor panels" are similarly dislocated and dislocating. The kneeling figures, with their candles and ceremonial poses are suggestive of ritual, but the "patron saint" attendants, crushed into the background, seem to be performers, whores, musicians, partygoers, and—Beckmann's ubiquitous modern-day messenger of the gods—a diminutive bellboy. The disparate sizes of the figures push the viewer further off balance and, at the same time, sound an echo of another medieval convention, that of rendering the most important characters larger than the supporting cast.

Who are these people? What is going on? The contrast of the (almost overly literal) "primitive" drummer and the "refined" harpist (who, however, displays an indecorous amount of leg) suggests rather obvious interpretations, which puts the picture at risk. Beckmann suffers, to my eye, when his "message" is too easily read; ambiguity helps. Here, the unexpectedness of the picture as a whole and its enthralling details redeem the problematically opposed central pair. But the more we study the painting, the more it resists us, paradoxically, by triggering more and more associations at the same time that it refuses to yield a clear meaning. It's like working away at a tangled skein of yarn, teasing loose more and more promising-looking strands, but never managing to unravel the knot.

Beckmann's enigmatic allegories are enacted by a troupe of characters that gradually becomes familiar: acrobats, warriors, whores, a Fisher King, circus performers, bellboys, men in dinner jackets, women in evening clothes, even the occasional innocent—some clearly modern, others in fantastic or period dress. We recognize persistent horrors: outsized grotesque masks, monstrous birds, bound figures about to be tortured or already mutilated, giant fish that can also seem unexpectedly benign. Scale shifts. The gargantuan fruit in the left panel of *Departure*, for example, works like a zoom lens, increasing the fictive distance between the viewer and the disproportionately small figures frozen in a scene of carnage. The perfectly regular giant apple and elegantly modeled pear become monuments to aesthetic normality, to "pure" formal concerns, in the midst of the chaos of trussed, imprisoned, and maimed bodies.

Meaning is as unstable as scale and viewpoint. Beckmann seems to comment on the actual, by incorporating contemporary clothing, newspapers with recognizable, familiar names, and assorted "signs" of modern life, but at the same time, he presents them in plainly fictive groupings, like tableaux snatched from a performance whose narrative logic escapes us. We begin to question the most obvious of references. Are the heroes and soldiers what they seem to be or are they performers, dressed for a role? Are the men in black tie themselves performers or witnesses to the spectacle?

Are they comfortable bourgeois correctly dressed for evening or are they musicians or headwaiters? When Beckmann paints himself he is no more straightforward than in his most subtle allegories. The exhibition's marvelous *Self-Portrait with Horn* (1938, Dr. and Mrs. Stephan Lackner), with its lurid red-oranges and salmon pinks, is at first glance an apparently uncomplicated image of the painter in costume, holding a band instrument. The paint handling, like the color, is characteristically lush and the way the round-headed figure spreads across the square canvas, particularly harmonious. But the longer we look, the more off-kilter the picture becomes. The subject's sidelong glance sends us spiraling along the horn until we are stopped by the flat black oval of the bell, which is sliced by a roughly brushed band—the edge of a mirror? We become aware of the rectangular frame behind Beckmann's head in his painted reflection and the space of the painting suddenly collapses; only the coil of the horn, like a spring, keeps the brilliant red plane along the right edge from sliding back and obliterating the figure. The self-portrait is no less disturbing than the most brutal of the triptychs.

Beckmann's images function both as icons of a "new mythology" that he said he strove to create for his own times, and as records of that mythology's rituals—or more accurately, its performances. His figures inhabit an airless, artificially lit world of schematic interiors, a claustrophobic architecture that is at once stage set, orchestra pit, and improvised backstage space, bathed in brilliant light both theatrical and clinical, giving vivid life to the phrase "operating theater." The spaces seem ramshackle, crowded, improvised, as though the traditions of the opera house, the cabaret, the commedia dell'arte, and the sideshow had been forced unwillingly into coexistence or as though the operating theater were in a temporary field hospital. (This is not far-fetched; Beckmann served in the German medical corps during World War I, witnessing harrowing scenes that he described in a series of published letters and mined for decades afterward in his art.) The suggestion of sky or open air is rare, surprising, and exhilarating; the expanse of radiant blue in the central panel of *Departure*, for example, creates an extraordinary sense of peace and hopefulness, an almost physical relief after the closed, squeezed space of the side panels.

Often, the spaces in Beckmann's pictures seem barely large enough to contain the figures who inhabit them. There's usually considerable tension between the forward-pressing, tilted spaces of Beckmann's crowded interiors and the barely glimpsed lower levels of his jerry-built theaters (the mood darkens as you descend), just as there is often a contrast of space and emotional temperature between the center and side panels of the triptychs, with a distinct suggestion that something sinister is happening behind the scenes. "Center stage" limbs and bodies angle against one another, so that it is sometimes difficult to be sure what belongs to whom. Below, musicians seem to burst out of the pit. Men fight with knives beneath a stage where a Player King stabs himself; is it a real struggle or a rehearsal? I kept thinking of itinerant players and medieval mystery plays enacted on carts in front of the cathedrals. But that bellboy keeps bringing us back to the twentieth century, reminding us of another metaphor, beloved of 1930s moviemakers, of the hotel lobby as microcosm. The angular, prismatic structure of the picture as a whole tugs us in two directions at once, reminding us of Cubist prototypes at the same time that it returns us to the past, to El Greco, whom Beckmann admired and learned much from—and who, of course, offered the young Picasso a model for the faceting of early Cubist space.

Beckmann's titles—*Acrobats*, *Actors*, *Carnival*, etc.—reinforce the theater and circus associations, as do the curious costumes in many of his portraits and self-portraits. His writings, too, make the connections explicit. In a 1927 essay on "the social stance of the artist," he ironically referred to himself as "the black tightrope walker," an image taken from a celebrated passage in Nietzsche's *Thus Spake Zarathustra* in which actors, tightrope walkers, and "supermen" are praised as risk takers who separate themselves from the common herd. Beckmann was engaged with the book throughout his life, beginning with early diary entries that dispute many of Nietzsche's premises, and echos of it resound in Beckmann's images. The exhibition's strange *Falling Man* (1950, National Gallery, Washington), for example, with its burning buildings and "bird-boats," can be read as alluding to a fallen tightrope walker in Nietzsche, while the heroic "Aryan" nudes on the beach in the central panel of *Argonauts* seem to have as much to do with the *Übermensch* as with such obvious art-historical cognates as Picasso and classical antiquity.

What is less known is that Beckmann, like many of his artist colleagues, particularly Kokoschka, experimented with the theater himself. In the 1920s, he wrote a number of plays—three survive—heavily influenced by Wedekind, which read like descriptions of some of his most explicit images. One describes a plump bourgeois's abortive career as a bohemian free spirit among prostitutes, artists, and criminals—unlike a Nietzschean hero, however, Beckmann's protagonist goes passively back to cozy domesticity. Another, titled *The Hotel*, which incorporates varied dialects, popular songs, "fantasy and ranting," has been described by the editor and translator of a forthcoming collection of Beckmann's writings as "earthy, vulgar, and grotesque"—adjectives that would have delighted Brecht (*Self-Portrait in Words: Collected Writings and Statements, 1903–1950*; University of Chicago Press, 1997).

Beckmann's complex inventions, his elegant conflations of the art historical and the vernacular can be exhaustively "unpacked" for seemingly
endless references and meanings—sociological and political, as well as
metaphysical and aesthetic. But what gives his best paintings their unforgettable potency is their staggering material presence. That *Afternoon* (1946,
Museum am Ostwall, Dortmund), for example, is like a nightmare version
of Titian's *Danaë* is only part of what makes this smallish single-panel picture so arresting; the reclining figure, her girlish face and hair at odds with
her prostitute's "uniform" of chemise and rolled black stockings, recoils
from the threatening spiky hands of a red-brown simian figure in a vaguely
Egyptian headdress. No doubt there's a good deal to say about the role of
women in German society, the hypocrisy of the middle classes, and more,
in relation to the picture. But the urgency of the young woman's
withdrawal is signaled by the contrast of her massive legs and hands and her
small head, and the real drama of the painting comes from the way those
legs and hands are modeled with violent contrasts of brushy pigment, and
the way both figures are shoved toward the surface by the flat, densely
brushed blue-grey plane of the background.

Beckmann's heated, dissonant color, his seductively layered, masterly
paint handling, and his forthright, nuanced modeling are as crucial to the
impact of his pictures as their "encrypted" messages or their seamless fusion
of current references and time-honored structures. Part of it is simply a
combination of sensitivity to the medium of oil paint and good old-
fashioned craftsmanship. Marsden Hartley and Adolph Gottlieb shared this
ability to make the amount of paint deposited with each touch seem expressive, intuitive, and important, and I suspect Hartley, who certainly saw
Beckmann's early work in Germany, and Gottlieb, who had ample opportunity to see it during his early extended travels in Europe, of having more
than a passing interest in his paintings. (I suspect Günther Grass of having
studied Beckmann, too—think about *The Tin Drum* and *The Flounder*, for
starters.)

The emotional force of Beckmann's art is intimately bound up with its
facture. He seems to have usually worked on a dark—even black—ground,
dragging brights and lights to the surface, modulating volumes by revealing
the underlying layer of darks at the edges, and then nailing them with his
fluent, authoritative black line. But there are also numerous passages of
opaque, matte black—assertive expanses of dinner jacket, networks of im-
prisoning bars, or form-molding shadows—that are imposed on the surface
of the pictures, rather than surging from underneath, so that black seems to
eat chromatic color, rather than set it off. Subtle as it is, almost to the point
of being imperceptible, unless you look hard, this reversal helps to further

destabilize Beckmann's unquiet spaces; it makes his tightly packed figures even more uncomfortable, his assonant color chords more disturbing. It's something like the way the dense harmonies work in the most ambitious compositions of Beckmann's near-contemporary, Stefan Wolpe; individual melodic lines are lost to the ear in the layered complexities of the whole, but they remain visible on the written page and arguably make their presence felt, perhaps subliminally, when we hear the music performed, affecting our response.

"Max Beckman in Exile" is not to be missed. The wall text panels are, however, problematic; *Beginning* (1946–1949, Metropolitan Museum), Beckmann's abrasive triptych of a boyhood nursery and schoolroom just this side of Grass's *Tin Drum*, is said to "dwell upon memories of child-hood innocence," but such commentary, like the inexplicable yellow walls of the exhibition galleries, can be ignored. The catalogue can be recom-mended, with reservations. First, the plusses: surprisingly good color re-productions of everything in the show and a few things that didn't make it, including Beckmann's last, unfinished triptych; a thoughtful, felt essay by Eric Fischl about his "discovery" of *Departure* and the impact it had on his work; an intimate memoir by Beckmann's close friend Stephan Lackner; and reprints of two hard-to-find texts by Beckmann. But there is less useful back matter than we might expect and, more problematic, a couple of es-says by German scholars, full of useful facts, but poor reading, not only because the translations preserve too faithfully the cadences of German aca-demic prose, but because they are both rather supercilious and condes-cending.

The more interesting—and less aggrieved—essay, by Reinhard Spieler, identifies Beckmann's "characters" and itemizes many of the complex, varied sources of the imagery of his triptychs. That these range from classi-cal antiquity to Italian Renaissance frescoes to modern French painting, not to mention a host of German literary, mythological, and artistic antece-dents, is not surprising, given the cultivated, well-traveled Beckmann's broad firsthand experience of art. As a young painter he spent considerable time in Italy, and as a mature artist, he had maintained an apartment in Paris until the unrest of pre-World War II Europe made it impossible. Spieler is eager for Beckmann to take his place not as a "Germanic" artist, but as a universal one, a difficult distinction, no matter how much of an individual Beckmann was, or how different his art was from that of his compatriots. Far more adventurous and inventive than the inherently con-servative painters of the "New Objectivity," Beckmann nevertheless had a more sympathetic relationship with the past than the German Expres-sionists with whom he is often, misleadingly, grouped. While Beckmann certainly didn't strive to imitate the dispassionate magic realism of traditional Northern painting, neither did he reject traditional art out of hand. When he embraced modernist forms and strategies, as he did wholeheartedly, it was not—as for many of his colleagues—in a spirit of self-conscious primitivism or to suggest violence, but for their expressive possibilities.

Spieler's thesis and his evident grasp of French and Italian art notwithstanding, Beckmann's work remains, to American eyes, at any rate, stubbornly Northern, even Germanic, in its darkness, its density of form, its acerbic color, and, above all, its implicit heroic mythology. But ultimately such labeling is not very interesting. Obviously, everything that shaped Beckmann, that touched him, or that he saw in the course of his life as a painter, all of his most deeply held convictions, found their way, in some fashion, into his work. That's part of what makes it so powerful. As this exhibition shows, Beckmann is a first-rate painter whose work is vivid, original, tough, and current. That's all anyone could ask for.

December 1996

Contributors

BROOKE ALLEN has contributed to *The New Criterion* since 1991. Her most recent book is *Moral Minority: Our Skeptical Founding Fathers* (Ivan R. Dee).

STEFAN BECK writes on fiction for *The Wall Street Journal*, *The New Criterion*, and elsewhere. He is a former Associate Editor of *The New Criterion*.

ROBERT H. BORK's books include *Slouching Towards Gomorrah: Modern Liberalism and American Decline* (HarperCollins), and, most recently, *A Country I Do Not Recognize: The Legal Assault on American Values* (Hoover Institution Press).

F. H. BUCKLEY is the Director of the George Mason Law & Economics Center. His latest book is *Just Exchange: A Theory of Contract* from Routledge.

TIMOTHY CONGDON is an economist and businessman who has worked in the City of London for thirty years. He is currently writing a book on money in a modern economy.

THEODORE DALRYMPLE, a doctor, is the author of *Romancing Opiates: Pharmacological Lies and the Addiction Bureaucracy* (Encounter) and *Our Culture, What's Left of It* (Ivan R. Dee).

ANTHONY DANIELS is a doctor and writer whose most recent books are *Utopias Elsewhere* (Crown) and *Monrovia Mon Amour* (John Murray).

GUY DAVENPORT's (1927–2005) posthumous collection is *The Death of Picasso: New & Selected Writing* (Shoemaker & Hoard).

PAUL DEAN is Head of English at Dragon School, Oxford, and a Fellow of the English Association.

JOHN DERBYSHIRE, a commentator and critic, is a columnist for *National Review*. He is the winner of the Euler Book Prize for his 2003 book *Prime Obsession* (Joseph Henry Press).

BEN DOWNING is the Co-editor of *Parnassus: Poetry in Review*. The author of *The Calligraphy Shop*, a book of poems (Zoo Press), he is a frequent contributor to *The New Criterion* and other publications.

JOSEPH EPSTEIN, Editor of *The American Scholar* from 1975–1997, is the author, most recently, of *Friendship: An Exposé* (Houghton Mifflin). He is currently at work on a book about gossip.

JAMES FRANKLIN is the author of *The Science of Conjecture: Evidence and Probability Before Pascal* (Johns Hopkins).

DAVID FROMKIN is the Frederick S. Pardee Professor of History and International Relations at Boston University.

DAVID FRUM is a Resident Fellow at the American Enterprise Institute in Washington, D.C.

MARTIN GARDNER is the author of many books, including *The Night Is Large: Collected Essays 1938–1995* (St. Martin's) and *The Annotated Hunting of the Snark* (W. W. Norton), on Lewis Carroll's nonsense ballad.

JOHN GROSS, Editor of *The Times Literary Supplement* from 1974–1981, is the editor, most recently, of *The New Oxford Book of Literary Anecdotes*.

GERTRUDE HIMMELFARB's most recent books are *The Roads to Modernity: The British, French, and American Enlightenments* (Knopf) and *The Moral Imagination* (Ivan R. Dee).

LAURA JACOBS is the dance critic for *The New Criterion* and a Contributing Editor at *Vanity Fair*. Her latest book is *Landscape with Moving Figures: A Decade in Dance* (Dance and Movement Press).

ROGER KIMBALL is Co-editor and Co-publisher of *The New Criterion*, Publisher of Encounter Books, and the author, most recently, of *The Rape of the Masters* (Encounter).

ADAM KIRSCH, a book critic for *The New York Sun*, won the 2001 New Criterion Poetry Prize for his collection of poems *The Thousand Wells* (Ivan R. Dee).

HILTON KRAMER is Co-editor and Co-publisher of *The New Criterion*. His most recent book is *The Triumph of Modernism: The Art World 1985–2005* (Ivan R. Dee).

MICHAEL J. LEWIS is a professor in the art department at Williams College and the author of *American Art and Architecture* (Thames & Hudson).

WILLIAM LOGAN is the recipient of the Poetry Foundation's first Randall Jarrell Award in Poetry Criticism.

HEATHER MAC DONALD is a John M. Olin Fellow at the Manhattan Institute and a contributing editor to *City Journal*.

KENNETH MINOGUE is the author of many books, including *Alien Powers: The Pure Theory of Ideology* (Transaction) and *The Concept of a University* (Transaction).

ERIC ORMSBY is a poet and writer living in London whose new biography *Al-Ghazali* is forthcoming from OneWorld (Oxford) in 2007.

JAMES PANERO is the Managing Editor of *The New Criterion* and writes the magazine's "Gallery Chronicle" column. He is co-editor of *The Dartmouth Review Pleads Innocent* (ISI Books).

JAMES PENROSE writes about music for *The New Criterion*.

DAVID PRYCE-JONES is a Senior Editor of *National Review*. His latest book is *Betrayal: France, the Arabs, and the Jews* (Encounter).

MORDECAI RICHLER (1931–2001) was a novelist, essayist, and winner of the Canadian Governor-General's Award for literature.

ROGER SCRUTON is a British writer and philosopher, and currently Research Professor at the Institute for the Psychological Sciences, Arlington, Virginia.

JOHN SIMON is the New York theater critic for Bloomberg News. His column "Etcetera" appears on Broadway.com.

MARK STEYN's most recent book is *America Alone: The End of the World as We Know It* (Regnery).

JAMES W. TUTTLETON (1934–1998) taught at New York University for thirty years and was the author of many books, including *Vital Signs* (Ivan R. Dee) and *The Novel of Manners in America* (W. W. Norton).

KAREN WILKIN, an advisory editor at *Hudson Review*, writes regularly on art for *The New Criterion* and is an art historian at the New York Studio School.

KEITH WINDSCHUTTLE's latest book is *The White Australia Policy* (Macleay Press).

DAVID YEZZI is the Executive Editor of *The New Criterion* and the author of *The Hidden Model* (TriQuarterly), a book of poems.

Index